To Ilse Haberlandt

To Susan, Peter, and Elizabeth Haberlandt

COGNITIVE
PSYCHOLOGY

COGNITIVE PSYCHOLOGY

SECOND EDITION

KARL HABERLANDT

Trinity College

ALLYN AND BACON

Boston   London   Toronto   Sydney   Tokyo   Singapore

Vice President and Editor in Chief: Sean W. Wakely
Senior Editor: Carolyn O. Merrill
Editorial Assistant: Alyssa Dorrie
Vice President, Director of Field Marketing: Joyce Nilsen
Production Administrator: Annette Joseph
Production Coordinator: Susan Freese
Editorial-Production Service: TKM Productions
Composition Buyer: Linda Cox
Manufacturing Buyer: Megan Cochran
Cover Administrator: Linda Knowles
Cover Designer: Susan Paradise

Library of Congress Cataloging-in-Publication Data
Haberlandt, Karl.
    Cognitive psychology / Karl Haberlandt.—2nd ed.
        p. cm.
    Includes bibliographical references and indexes.
    ISBN 0-205-26416-6
    1. Cognitive psychology.   I. Title.
BF201.H33 1997
153—dc20   96-29033
                                                            CIP
Printed in the United States of America

10 9 8 7 6 5 4 3 2   02 01 00 99 98 97

See permissions credits on pages 479–482, which constitute an extension of the copyright page.

Brief Contents

CONTENTS

CHAPTER 15   APPLICATIONS OF COGNITIVE PSYCHOLOGY   409

This book is intended as a text for a basic course in cognitive psychology. Its goal is to convey fundamental information about the excitements and challenges in the study of the human mind. Learning about cognitive psychology involves gaining knowledge of the questions that researchers ask, the theories they propose, and the methods they use. In addition to introducing substantive content about the traditional areas of cognitive psychology—including attention, knowledge representation, memory, comprehension, and reasoning—this book covers significant recent advances in the field and conveys how these advances are made. The impetus for the progress comes from different sources—theory, experimentation, and application—sometimes working in tandem, sometimes not. The text reflects, within the limits of an introductory framework, the inherent appeal of the inquiry into human cognition and of doing science in this discipline.

In the last two decades, there have been fundamental changes in the study of cognition; the most visible of these include:

- The increasing influence of cognitive neuroscience
- The rediscovery of action as an important research issue
- The emergence of the neural network approach
- The renaissance of learning as a focus of research

The contributions of cognitive neurosciences to our understanding of mental processes have been fueled by the introduction of a variety of new methods and the refinement of existing paradigms. Thanks to all of these investigative tools—imaging, electrophysiological, and neuropsychological—new links have been forged between neuroscience and cognitive psychology that have benefited both disciplines. Scientists can now monitor brain events and much improved temporal and spatial precision and correlate them with behavioral measures, mostly chronometric indices, commonly used by cognitive psychologists. Parallels between neural events and cognitive phenomena are being sought in virtually every domain of cognition, from learning to problem solving.

Actions represent the physical output of the organism to the environment; this includes all uses of the skeletal muscles, from reaching for a specific target to the movements of the eyes. Traditionally, cognitive psychologists have emphasized such input processes as attention and pattern recognition more than output processes. Yet action research has served as one of the catalysts for the rise of cognitive psychology half a century ago. After all, taking account of the action side of cognition gives scientists a fuller understanding of cognition in general. Organisms act and move in order to support cognition, and a multitude of cognitive processes are used in the service of action, even if unconsciously: People adjust movements based on perceptual feedback, and they memorize and plan movements, whether in speaking, exercising, or dancing.

The now classical idea that mental processes, like computer processes, are best expressed as discrete and serial stages provided a very successful framework for cognitive research in the 1960s. However, research innovations in areas from attention to comprehension have sparked interest in parallel models of cognition, especially the neural network models. Such networks consist of many interconnected small processing units that operate in parallel, much like neurons. The neural network approach has called into question conventional mental representations as discrete and symbolic entities and contributed to a renewed interest in learning. Historically, cognitive psychology was unconcerned with learning; instead, researchers emphasized fully developed mental functions. Changes through learning, however, are at the heart of connectionist networks. Perhaps not coincidentally, information-processing theorists also have increasingly examined the development of expertise through practice and learning.

Innovations tend to engender controversy; the field of cognitive psychology is no exception to this rule. Lively debates continue among cognitive psychologists about the usefulness of the neuroscience methods, the place of action in cognition, and the validity of the neural network approach. Whatever the outcome of the debates, the new frameworks and the ensuing arguments have invigorated the field, leaving no area of cognitive psychology unaffected. Attention, knowledge representation, memory, and problem solving all have a new look as we approach the year 2000. Recent texts in cognitive psychology reflect some of these developments but not their depth and breadth. This book incorporates these formulations in a single source and integrates them with the mainstream topics in cognitive psychology while acknowledging their conceptual and empirical problems.

Cognitive psychology is a basic science; its goal is to illuminate mental representations and processes in their own right. There are, however, many applications of cognitive psychology outside the laboratory. Some of these are supported by basic research; others are not. Illustrative applications of cognitive principles are included throughout this text, such as how to remediate the effects of dyslexia and improve one's long-term retention for mathematics. One chapter of the book discusses applications from four areas in greater detail: cognitive engineering, education, law enforcement, and neuropsychological deficits. Nuts-and-bolts issues such as the design of appliances, methods of enhancing eyewitness testimony, and the rehabilitation of patients with brain damage are also described, as is the great debate on whether such applications are premature.

The 15 chapters of this book have been written independently; instructors may vary the order in which to cover the chapters, depending on student interest and the nature of the course. The chapters reflect the diverse aspects of cognitive psychology and approaches common in the discipline. Most chapters describe the interplay of theory and experimentation typical of experimental science. Other chapters cover computational issues, and still others emphasize conceptual analysis, reflecting the approaches of such related disciplines as linguistics. In several chapters, a historical approach is taken in the belief that the genesis of a framework highlights the significance of newer developments.

The study of the richness of the human mind and of mental processes is as fascinating as it is demanding. This book was written for the reader who is prepared to meet the challenge this subject offers. Doing so will open new perspectives on the rich panorama of the mind and kindle a lasting interest in the cognitive sciences.

ACKNOWLEDGMENTS

My work in cognitive psychology, including this book, is the result of years of study and research in the field. I am very fortunate for having received inspiration and support from teachers, colleagues, and students too numerous to list. I am grateful to my teachers for stirring my curiosity about the human mind, to my colleagues for sustaining that curiosity, and to my students for questioning assumptions that I held to be self-evident.

The first edition of this book benefited greatly from the suggestions of distinguished reviewers, including Robert Bjork (University of California, Los Angeles), Ira Fischler (University of Florida), Barry Hughes (University of Illinois), William Mackavey (Boston University), Michael O'Boyle (Iowa State University), Janet Proctor (Purdue University), Jeanne Scholl (Boston College), Michael Smith (Texas A&M University), and Steven Smith (Texas A&M University). My work on the second edition was greatly aided by Stephen Buggie (University of New Mexico–Gallup), Jann Cupp (Tennessee Technical University), Larry Z. Daily (George Mason

University), Paul Haerich (Loma Linda University), and Michelle Hunter (University of Connecticut).

In addition, I want to express my thanks to Lynda Griffiths for her exemplary work on copy editing and checking on every detail from references to permission; to all of the authors and publishers who permitted me to reproduce figures and tables; to the staff at Allyn and Bacon; to Trinity College; and to the federal funding agencies that have supported my work over the years.

Above all, I offer my thanks to my family—Susan, Peter, and Elizabeth—for their unfailing support and understanding as I worked on this project.

COGNITIVE PSYCHOLOGY

CHAPTER 1

INTRODUCTION

PREVIEW

Cognitive psychology involves the experimental study of human information processing in its many manifestations such as attention, recognition, action, learning, memory, language processing, problem solving, and reasoning. Information processing is based on what we know; consequently, cognitive psychology investigates knowledge structures and the processes that operate on those structures. Cognitive psychology is rooted in experimental psychology; however, its questions about knowledge are older than psychology itself and date back to philosophy: What are the sources of human knowledge? How is knowledge represented in the mind? and What are the mental processes that make use of the representations? Cognitive psychology has been influenced by several traditions in psychology, including psychophysics, structuralism, behaviorism, Gestalt psychology, and the forerunners of the information-processing approach in mental chronometry and human factors research. This introductory chapter traces these antecedents, noting the legacy of each as well as their differences from the cognitive perspective.

The chapter also describes the influence of linguistics and computer science on cognitive psychology. Linguistics has stimulated research on knowledge structures underlying language use and other cognitive skills. The computer has provided both a metaphor for theories of human information processing and a powerful tool for data collection and analysis. The chapter concludes with an examination of basic assumptions, issues, and methods in the study of cognition. Advances in cognitive psychology are characterized by debate; at issue are specific mechanisms underlying performance in cognitive tasks, the nature of mental representations and cognitive processes, the relation of the field to other disciplines, and the implication of basic research for applications in the real world.

INTRODUCTION

Your mind is constantly working even when you are unaware of it. When you remember an errand, write a message, or simply answer a question, your mind is active. Most of the time our mental processes are routine; they help us navigate through the environment, solve problems, and carry on conversations. Consider the intricate mental processes that occur in a speaker's and listener's mind during a conversation. The speaker has some thoughts she wishes to communicate; she expresses them in words and sentences. Without having to worry about it, she uses her articulatory system, facial muscles, lungs, and vocal cords to produce a comprehensible utterance. Do you know any mechanical device that works so flawlessly every time you use it? Where do thoughts come from? How do you find the words to capture thoughts? What mechanism translates a word into an utterance? What sort of knowledge must a speaker have to organize words into a comprehensible sentence?

By whatever mechanism, a speaker generates an utterance. Physically, an utterance is a pattern of sound waves that travel through the air; the sound waves enter the listener's ear, pass ossicles and membranes, and arrive at the auditory receptors in the basilar membrane. The sound energy is transformed into impulses that travel along neurons and axons into higher centers in the brain, and eventually, by some process, the listener is able to piece sounds, words, and sentences together. He knows what the words mean and what his friend is talking about. What mechanism was engaged to transform the sound waves into a neutral impulse and the latter into a recognizable

word? For that matter, how did the listener retrieve the meanings of words and understand the relation between words expressed in the sentences the speaker uttered? These are among the questions cognitive psychologists seek to answer.

Curiosity and questions are at the root of cognitive psychology, as in any other science. Cognitive psychologists wonder how the mind works in such contexts as communication, recognition, and remembering. There are also practical questions like the following: Why is math so difficult? Why do we forget names of people so quickly? How should we study a foreign language to maximize knowledge and retention? How should word-processing systems be designed to facilitate learning and use? Is speed reading efficient in terms of comprehension and retention? and Could rearranging the controls on the dashboard of cars help us avoid accidents? Cognitive psychology seeks to answer questions like these, whether they are general or specific, theoretical or practical. To develop a definition of cognitive psychology, we will consider cognitive processes in three practical contexts: eyewitness testimony, air traffic control, and composing a paper.

— The testimony of eyewitnesses who were present at the scenes of accidents and crimes is essential in our legal system. The judgment of law enforcement officers, attorneys, and juries depends on eyewitness testimony, which in turn depends on perception and memory. Often an incident, whether it is a crime or an accident, tends to be fleeting; the witness sees a suspect from the side, at a distance, or in the dark. Perceptions also depend on the witness's state of mind; frequently the witness is scared and tries to hide or get away, so impressions are formed in a hurry. When the witness later recounts the events, her memory may have dimmed or changed. In addition, the manner in which she is questioned may bias the witness to report selected or inaccurate information. Each of these aspects of eyewitness testimony—perceiving an incident, remembering it, and reporting it—involves cognitive processes (see Loftus, 1979).

— Air traffic controllers guide airplanes in landing and departure. They use a wide range of sophisticated equipment in their work, including radar, audio and video monitors, and computers. The performance of these operators is based on cognitive processes. The operator observes the displays and panels and interprets the data. Different aircraft produce different images on the radar screen. At a certain critical distance from the control station, voice contact between the tower and the aircraft is established. The controller coordinates visual input from several sources, including the radar screen and panels that show the altitude and distance of several planes relative to the tower and to each other. The operator also coordinates verbal information—for example, on the amount of fuel left in the plane, the space on the runways and in air corridors, and so on. A lapse of attention to any aspect of the operator's job can cause very serious trouble.

— Assume you are given a topic for a brief term paper, such as tuition increases at universities. Composing a paper is a cognitive activity, although quite different from giving eyewitness testimony or observing and coordinating information in a control tower. The writer must come up with ideas and organize and express them in lucid form. You, the writer, must satisfy several goals simultaneously: You must choose the correct words, form grammatically correct sentences, compose an interesting essay, and be persuasive. No wonder writing is difficult!

Performance in each of these three situations depends on the interplay between numerous mental activities, including attention, interpretation, understanding, coordination, problem solving, and decision making. These activities represent instances of information processing: We acquire information, transform it, and produce some information as output. Cognitive psychology is the field that studies these processes and the knowledge structures on which they are based. Our working definition expresses this substantive goal; it also identifies the experiment as the principal method of cognitive psychology. Though mental structures and processes are not directly observable, they manifest themselves in performance as investigated in controlled experiments. Based on performance of subjects in experiments, cognitive psychologists draw inferences about knowledge structures and mental processes. Here, then, is the definition of cognitive psychology followed by a summary of major cognitive functions.

Cognitive psychology involves the experimental study of human information processing in its many manifestations such as attention, pattern recognition, learning, memory, language processing, problem solving, and reasoning. Information processing is based on what we know; consequently, cognitive psychology investigates knowledge structures and the processes that operate on those structures.

Attention plays a role in the perception of stimuli and when we face an overload of information. *Recognition* is the process by which a person interprets a stimulus, whether simple or complex. *Learning* refers to the acquisition of knowledge, and *memory* involves its retention and use. *Language processing* includes producing and understanding language. *Problem solving* refers to the achievement of a goal with a set of constraints, and *reasoning* subsumes mental activities that result in beliefs and judgments.

Cognitive psychology developed within the tradition of experimental psychology. Its development was influenced, however, in important ways by advances in other disciplines, including neuroscience, computer science, and linguistics. Neuroscience investigates the neural bases of cognition. Computer science is concerned with information processing in computers and provides computer models used for the study of cognition. Linguistics is the study of the structure of language, which is one of the most remarkable manifestations of the human mind. This chapter will sketch the contributions of philosophy, experimental psychology, linguistics, and computer science to cognitive psychology. The final section is devoted to basic assumptions of cognitive psychology, to issues studied and to methods used in the field. Chapter 2 is devoted to neuroscience and the potential it offers for understanding cognitive processes.

PHILOSOPHY

Our interest in human knowledge—what it is, where it came from, and how it is used—is as old as humankind itself. Philosophers have pondered questions about the nature of human knowledge for centuries. Plato (427–347 B.C.) is widely credited for his inquiry into the sources of knowledge. Most of his writings are devoted to different kinds of knowledge, and the certainty and origin of knowledge. His writings are in dialogue form, with Socrates as the discussion leader. Socrates elicits knowledge from his listeners without telling them the answers explicitly. According to Socrates, having knowledge is a kind of consciousness raising; the teacher makes the student aware of what he already knows. Following Plato, there were many other thinkers who pondered the nature of knowledge and its categories. We will briefly consider the contributions of three philosophers of the seventeenth and eighteenth centuries whose impact on cognitive psychology is still felt: René Descartes, David Hume, and Immanuel Kant. Each was concerned with the nature of human knowledge but offered a different view. Descartes was a rationalist; Hume an empiricist, and Kant combined these two approaches.

René Descartes

Descartes (1596–1650) lived toward the end of the Renaissance, a period of great intellectual ferment and growth. He investigated a broad scope of subjects that included physics, geometry, physiology, and languages. After giving much thought to the sources of knowledge, he came to believe that human reason, the product of the mind, was unique. It provided insights more certain than those gained from the senses. Think, for example, of the laws of arithmetic and geometry; consider Pythagoras's theorem illustrated in Figure 1.1. The theorem states that the square of the length of the hypotenuse, h, of a right triangle equals the sum of the squares of the lengths of the other two sides, a and b. Pythagoras's theorem is true for any such triangle.

Regularities like these were thought to be pure, and not subject to the illusions and errors of the senses; they had the status of laws. Beginning with Aristotle, philosophers studied illusions, including tactile, optical, and auditory illusions. The Mueller-Lyer illusion in Figure 1.2 was widely studied. The upper line in Figure 1.2 appears longer; the two lines are, however, exactly the same length. Philosophers following Descartes

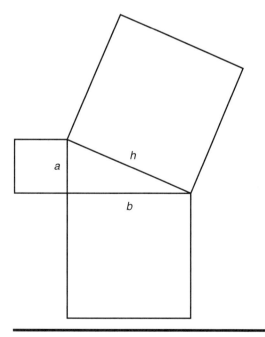

FIGURE 1.1   Right triangle with sides *a*, *b*, and *h*. Pythagoras's theorem states that $h^2 = a^2 + b^2$.

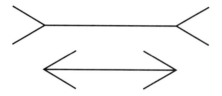

FIGURE 1.2 Mueller-Lyer illusion. The horizontal lines in the two displays are of identical length, contrary to their appearance.

generalized from such illusions to all perceptual experiences, claiming that perception is inherently uncertain. Descartes considered, for example, the fluctuations in perceiving the dot on the letter *i:* The illumination in the room differs on different occasions, the color and clarity of the print varies, as well as the distance from which one views the letter. The state of the observer also tends to vary; sometimes we are alert, at other times we are tired; and sometimes we may be sick. Each of these different states may change our perceptions. Descartes and other rationalist philosophers did not deny that we form impressions via the senses. However, he maintained that these impressions were uncertain and subject to error. According to Descartes, the only certainty was based on thought and cognition expressed in the phrase *Cogito, ergo sum—I think, therefore I am.*

Descartes also introduced the idea of mental objects or structures—something we now call **mental representations.** The mind contains thoughts, images, and models. The models represent both physical and symbolic entities. The former include a chair, a cloud, or another person, whereas the latter include abstract concepts, such as an ideal friend, teacher, or parent, or thoughts of liberty and justice. A representation is a realization of an entity in a different format. Consider different representations of the Golden Gate Bridge. Drawings, small-scale models, and photographs are physical representations, as is the image of the bridge on the retina. The thought of the bridge, however, is a mental representation. Cognitive psychologists debate the nature of such mental representations. They describe representa-

tion as symbols, which are entities other than themselves. For example, the word *cup* represents the object cup that one drinks from; a ringing bell represents the request to answer the phone; and a stop sign represents the demand to stop your car.

Mental representations make the products of thought transparent. The thinking mind manipulates these representations; thoughts can be transformed, compared, and remembered. Some representations are conscious, including our thoughts of objects; we can manipulate them by thinking of the entity. Other representations are not conscious; thus, speakers and listeners usually do not recall the definition of words. Nevertheless, they have no difficulty using and understanding them.

Descartes's views on representations exert their influence on contemporary philosophers and psychologists, whether they agree with the notion of representation or not. Behaviorists rejected mentalism and representations; cognitivists like Fodor (e.g., 1983) embraced mentalism. Fodor emphasized mental representations and innate sources of knowledge. Indeed, he proposed an abstract *language of thought,* dubbed *mentalese.* Mentalese consists of complex symbols and representations; it is necessary to understand complexities of human performance in problem solving, perception, and the comprehension of overt languages like English. Fodor stated that merely looking at the circumstances in which a person reports a mental event does not do justice to the richness of the cognitive activities that produce it, whether it is attention, pattern recognition, or language comprehension. Fodor also proposed that symbols and processes can be realized in different mediums, including organisms and machines, and that one can study mental processes without understanding their neural basis.

Descartes also inspired the **introspective method** that was to define early experimental psychology two centuries later. Being a rationalist, Descartes felt that certainty of knowledge was derived from the mind itself. He wrote that "the ultimate aim of all our studies ought to be to guide our mind so that we may pass solid and true judgments on everything that comes before us" (Beck, 1952, p. 14). He examined the contents of his mind through intuition and deduction. In systematic and careful study, he recorded the ideas emerging in his mind, from simple to complex, and from concrete to abstract.

David Hume

Hume (1711–1776) was interested in the sources of ideas, the relations among them, and their certainty. Unlike Descartes, however, Hume was an **empiricist**; he believed our ideas were based on experience with the external world and with our "internal reflection." External and internal experiences provide simple ideas like smell, color, movement, and extension in space; these are the elements of knowledge. Did reason play a role in Hume's empiricist system? Yes, it did; according to Hume, reason combines simple ideas into complex ideas or relations. For example, two events, such as two patches of red, may be identical, thus revealing the relation or complex idea of identity. On the other hand, different events, such as a red patch and a green patch, express the complex idea of difference.

Hume was not content to list ideas and establish relations among them. He wanted to know the laws by which ideas are associated. Following classical philosophers such as Aristotle, Hume proposed that ideas are associated by virtue of their similarity and *contiguity* (togetherness) in space and time. When two ideas repeatedly occur together, when they are contiguous, we tend to expect the second idea when given the first. Hume's standard example of this was the association between thunder and lightning. In our experience, lightning precedes thunder, and as a result, we come to believe that it causes thunder. Thus, Hume viewed causality as a subjective joining of two events. We call one event the cause and the other the effect, and come to believe in the necessary connection between them. Hume, however, argued that events are only linked probabilistically.

Recognizing that our perceptions, habits, and experiences must be based on operations, Hume set as an important goal of science "to know the different operations of the mind, to separate them from each other, to class them under their proper heads" (Gardner, 1985, p. 56). Hume introduced operations of the mind, including comparison and association—processes we will encounter again in this and other chapters.

Immanuel Kant

Kant (1724–1804) also sought to understand the foundations of human knowledge. In working through the many facets of this problem, Kant proposed a synthesis between the rationalist and empiricist traditions. He identified both the mind and experience as sources of knowledge; the mind provides the structure for knowledge, whereas experience with the external world provides the facts to fill the mental structures. Kant said that mind without experience is empty and experience without mind is blind. The mind with its categories provides structure and coherence to the manifold of experience.

Kant distinguished between three kinds of mental structures: dimensions, categories, and schemas.

— *Dimensions:* We experience objects as extended in space and time because our minds are innately endowed with these dimensions.

— *Categories:* Kant proposed 12 innate categories of reasoning. These categories are abstract characterizations of the relations among objects rather than categories as understood by contemporary cognitive psychologists. For example, according to Smith (1990), a cognitive psychologist, a category is a class of objects. Classes of birds, furniture, or car models represent such categories. By contrast, Kant's categories of reasoning included quality, quantity, and causality. His categories are structures that define the manner in which the human mind creates experience.

— *Schemas:* Kant wondered about the contents of knowledge and defined the *schema* as a unit of knowledge. A schema is a generic concept used to describe the general rather than the particular properties of a class of objects. Kant defined a schema as a rule used to construct a concept in a general manner. For example, the schema *dog* "signifies a rule according to which my [mind] can delineate the figure of a four-footed animal in a general manner" without limitation to an individual dog (Rumelhart & Ortony, 1977, p. 101).

As a philosopher, Kant was not interested in mental processing as cognitive psychologists are. However, his framework and the structures he proposed have shaped the thinking of cognitive psychologists. They have investigated the processing implications of each of Kant's mental structures: dimensions, categories, and schemas. We will revisit the schema when we study knowledge representations (in Chapter 5), Bartlett's research on remembering (in Chapter 7), and problem solving (in Chapter 13).

INTERIM SUMMARY

Cognitive psychology is concerned with the experimental study of knowledge structures and processes. Philosophers were the first scholars to inquire about the sources of knowledge. Plato introduced a tradition of nativism; he believed that knowledge is innate and that a person recollects knowledge when it is needed. The rationalist Descartes believed that knowledge based on reason, like mathematical laws, was more certain than the transient impressions gained through sensory experience. Descartes introduced the idea of mental representations; these are symbols of objects in the real world as well as abstract thoughts and ideas. Hume was an empiricist; he believed that knowledge was derived from our senses and that the mind is the store of these experiences. The mind is an active agent; it associates and compares sensory ideas, thus producing complex ideas. Kant falls somewhere in between the rationalist and empiricist approaches. He maintained that both sources contribute to knowledge. According to Kant, we must have mental faculties, dimensions, categories, and schemas to organize the richness of the data arriving through our senses.

The impact of Descartes, Hume, and Kant was felt throughout the nineteenth and twentieth centuries; they identified important questions that were to influence early experimental psychology as well as contemporary cognitive psychology: What is the relation of mental processes to the physical world? What are the units of the mind? What is the nature of mental processes? and How can science learn about these processes? Although they do not directly influence the research of cognitive psychologists, philosophers continue their interest in cognition. Cognitive psychology uses a large vocabulary of concepts, including *representation, symbol,* and *association.* Philosophers undertake an analysis of these concepts. They seek to clarify the theoretical issues by detecting and addressing faulty assumptions.

EXPERIMENTAL PSYCHOLOGY

The first experimental psychologists were as interested in the structures of mind as philosophers were. The psychologists broke new ground, however, by going beyond the conceptual analysis and speculation customary in philosophy. The first psychologists received their training in the sciences: Wilhelm Wundt, Johannes Mueller, and Herman von Helmholtz in physiology, and Gustav Fechner in physics. These researchers wanted to observe experience and behavior using empirical methods; they introduced the experiment to psychology. Wundt (1832–1920) founded the first psychological research laboratory in Leipzig, Germany. His experiments may seem very simple to us today, but they were radical in his time; no one had ever studied human consciousness and behavior through systematic and controlled observation. The scope of William James's (1892) *Psychology* is similar to that of a contemporary cognitive psychology text. The book includes chapters on sensation, the structure and functions of the brain, neural activity, habit, attention, conception, discrimination, and association. Wundt and James were the founders of experimental psychology, Wundt in Europe and

James in the United States. Interestingly, their personalities and approaches were very different, as Box 1.1 illustrates.

Early psychology was also shaped by an interest in applications; researchers wanted to know how to improve learning and problem-solving skills. William James gave many talks to teachers on psychological aspects of education. It was U.S. psychologist John Dewey (1859–1952) who challenged the tradition of rote learning in education and stressed creative problem solving as the goal of education. Hugo Münsterberg (1863–1916) was an applied psychologist teaching at Harvard. His research included studies on operator efficiency in the workplace and on the causes of accidents. The impetus for his studies came from outside the laboratory; managers approached him with requests and suggestions. In one study, he examined the role of human factors in streetcar accidents, which were the equivalent of car accidents today (Hilgard, 1987). Robert Woodworth (1869–1962) examined the relation between the speed of motor movements and their difficulty and initiated the time motion studies used by human factors psychologists. In such studies, workers' movements are filmed and analyzed in terms of their component movements.

From its beginning, psychology was a diverse discipline both in its research topics and methods. We will consider six approaches that reflect the different and changing interests: psychophysics, structuralism, behaviorism, Gestalt psychology, and forerunners of information processing in mental chronometry and human factors research. Each of these made its mark on cognitive psychology as we know it today. By contrasting current and historical work in the field, you will appreciate the advances cognitive psychologists have made in the last two or three decades. You will also discover that cognitive psychology is a historically grown discipline with roots in these antecedents.

Psychophysics

Psychophysicists, including Ernst Weber and Gustav Fechner, were interested in the relation of body and mind; they reasoned that physical events in the environment give rise to psychological sensations. Fechner systematically explored the relation between psychological experience and changes in a continuum of stimuli. In one type of experiment, he presented a series of stimuli and varied their intensity. For example, he presented tones ranging from soft to loud to determine the subject's **absolute threshold,** the intensity at which the person noticed the stimulus. Thus, the tick of a watch is detected at a distance of about 8 meters, and a candle 50 kilometers away is perceptible during a dark and clear night.

In another type of experiment, Fechner sought to determine **difference thresholds**; he had subjects compare different stimuli (e.g., two weights) and evaluated whether or not the subjects noticed any differences. The observer was presented with two stimuli, first the standard and then a comparison stimulus, and was asked whether or not the stimuli were different. The smallest intensity difference detectable is known as the difference threshold.

Psychophysicists found that the difference threshold was relative; a change is more easily noticed if the standard stimulus is of smaller magnitude. You can try this out with another person as an observer, using nickels as stimuli. Start out with a single nickel (the standard); place it in your friend's hand and then add another nickel. She is likely to notice the difference. When she holds 40 nickels in her hand and another is added, however, she is less likely to notice the difference. The relative nature of the difference threshold was formalized as Weber's law, named for the psychophysicist who discovered it. Weber found that the ratio of the smallest perceived difference to the standard weight was constant as shown in expression (1.1):

$$(1.1) \quad \frac{\text{Perceived difference}}{\text{Standard stimulus}} = C$$

Weber's law applies to a wide range of different stimuli, including the length of lines, luminance of light, and loudness of tones. The constant is different, however, for stimuli from different

Box 1.1_____

Wilhelm Wundt and William James:
Two Pioneers of Experimental Psychology

Wilhelm Wundt grew up as the youngest of four children of a poor but highly literate family in a small town in Germany. His childhood was marred by a series of unfortunate circumstances: Two of his siblings died; Wundt himself was frequently sick; and, finally, his remaining older brother was sent off to boarding school, leaving Wilhelm a lonely youngster. Things improved after Wundt enrolled at Heidelberg University to study medicine. Even as a student, Wundt was fascinated by research; using himself as a subject, he did research on salt metabolism. He finished his medical training with high honors and worked full time on his basic physiological research. He became an assistant to Helmholtz, a famous nineteenth-century physiologist. Helmholtz's research and the new studies published by the psychophysicists led Wundt to the conviction that consciousness lent itself to systematic empirical study. He introduced the introspective method of observation for which he became so famous. In 1879, at the University of Leipzig, he founded the first official psychology laboratory.

Wundt was a dedicated experimenter, an outstanding teacher and administrator, and a prolific writer. He published 500 research articles, book chapters, and books, totaling almost 60,000 printed pages! There were no word processors in Wundt's day; however, he was one of the first scholars to use a newfangled invention from the United States—a typewriter—presented to him by James McKeen Cattell. Wundt supervised hundreds of theses. His students represented the *Who's Who* of early psychology, including Cattell, Ralph Norman Angell, Hugo Münsterberg, Charles Judd, and Edward Scripture. These psychologists returned to the United States to found psychology departments at Cornell, University of Pennsylvania, Harvard, Wesleyan, and Yale, respectively. Wundt and his students launched experimental psychology; they introduced psychology as the independent academic discipline that we know today.

William James was the oldest of five children. His father, Henry James, Sr., was independently wealthy and devoted his life to the education of his children. He encouraged lively intellectual debates at home, engaged private tutors, and took the children to Europe, all to broaden their horizons. Whether at home in Cambridge or on their travels, he allowed his children free range. William developed an early interest in science, especially in chemistry. He enjoyed experimentation with chemicals, mixing and separating them, and delighted in the explosions and foul smells he was able to generate (see Fancher, 1979). James became a chemistry major at Harvard in 1861, but soon switched to biology and medicine. During a field trip to South America he became very ill, suffered from depression, and finally traveled to spas in Europe looking for a cure. He read widely and came across Wundt's writings on psychology. Returning to Harvard, he completed his medical degree. However, instead of practicing medicine, he became an instructor in physiology.

Like Wundt, James's interests turned to the study of consciousness and to the possibility of psychology as a science. Unlike Wundt, however, James sought to understand everyday problems, looking for answers wherever he could find them, including the arts, literature, and experimental research (Gardner, 1985). James criticized both Wundt's emphasis on laboratory experiments and his static view of mental structures. He viewed the mind as a dynamic stream of consciousness that was always changing. According to James, the introspective method was too stale and barren to capture the essence of mind and consciousness.

William James loved to teach; his lectures were lively and provocative and he regaled his students with stories and anecdotes. James was also professionally interested in the process of teaching, and he was probably the first instructor to use student course evaluations (Fancher, 1979). He published a textbook, *The Principles of Psychology* (1890), that took him 12 years to complete. Because his prose was as lively as his lecture style, the book was a great success; it makes for worthwhile reading even today. Even though he founded no psychology laboratory, James's influence on the emerging discipline of psychology was profound. He sought to take psychology out of the laboratory into the "real world." The implicit tension between basic research and psychology in the real world originated with psychology's two founders, Wundt and James, and as we shall see, it still affects contemporary cognitive psychology today (see Chapter 15).

modalities (e.g., Woodworth & Schlosberg, 1954).

Psychophysics continues today as an independent discipline; it examines sensory processes. Although psychophysicists were not concerned with mental structures, their research methods had a lasting influence on cognitive psychology. The influence of psychophysics survives in many forms, such as in research on signal detection and attention (see Chapter 3). Methods introduced by psychophysicists have also been adapted for memory research and recognition testing (Chapter 9).

Structuralism and Associationism

Wundt defined psychology as the "science of experience." He sought to break down the contents of experience into its elements and to understand the structures and qualities of consciousness. According to Wundt, the mind includes three basic states: sensations, images, and simple feelings. He explored how the elements of mental states were connected. In the tradition of the English associationists, he proposed the association as the principle of connection. Wundt investigated these issues in experiments and introduced the experiment as the essential method of psychology. Because psychology was the science of mental content, Wundt held that "psychology begins with introspection" (Boring, 1950, p. 320).

The Introspective Method. Introspection means to look inside according to principles of trained self-observation. You must train yourself to concentrate on experiences strictly related to a specific stimulus. The experimenter presents a simple stimulus and asks subjects to report their experiences as they perceive the stimulus. For example, the experimenter would strike the chord *c-e-g* and ask the person how many tones it contains. From the reports subjects gave them, psychologists distilled such dimensions of experience as clearness and quality of the stimulus, as well as affective attributes, including pleasant-unpleasant, excited-calm, and strained-relaxed.

Researchers used introspection to describe phenomena that subjects had conscious access to, such as attention and association. James and Wundt were interested in what a person experienced as she paid attention to a stimulus. James reported, for example, that focused stimuli become clearer, whereas ignored events become dimmer (see Chapter 3).

The introspective method was controversial from the beginning. Wundt used introspection in perceptual experiments when conditions could be controlled and repeated trials were possible. Wundt felt he could not apply the same standards of rigor to more complex stimuli like words. Other psychologists who used words as stimuli asked subjects how the word affected them and what they thought about when they heard the word (Titchener, 1910). The introspectionists also disagreed on how to capture the dimensions of experience the observers reported, such as whether the dimensions *excited-calm* and *strained-relaxed* were really different.

Many considered introspective observations too variable and subjective to qualify as data in a scientific experiment. Finally, the more fundamental criticism was raised that subjects' mental processes were changed by attempts to observe them. Challenges like these contributed to the rise of behaviorism. Apart from these criticisms, introspectionism became obsolete; under Sigmund Freud's influence, psychologists redefined their field to include powerful forces that guided behavior but were unconscious. Nevertheless, methods rooted in introspectionism survive to this day. For example, subjects are asked to report on their experiences in problem-solving research. Subjects' verbal reports are used in conjunction with such other measures as response times or error patterns (see Chapter 13).

Associationism. Wundt, James, and other early experimental psychologists were associationists. William James interpreted associations in neural terms. He wrote, "When two elementary brain-processes have been active together or in immediate succession, one of them, on re-occurring, tends to propagate its excitement into the other" (1892, p. 256). Looking for associations in experiments was a natural development of the associationism practiced by philosophers. Wundt was interested in connections between simple sensations and emotions. Hermann Ebbinghaus (1850–1909), who pioneered the experimental study of memory, viewed associations as the building blocks of memory (Ebbinghaus, 1885). Because he wanted to investigate memory in its pure form, without the influence of meaning, he invented the nonsense syllable. Ebbinghaus created thousands of such syllables like the following: *mev, gor, dux, bap, wab, rif*, and *tox*. He memorized many lists of nonsense syllables using the **anticipation method;** he placed the items in a stack, looked at the first item, and tried to recall it with the next item. Then he recorded the time required to learn the entire list.

After mastering a list for the first time, Ebbinghaus relearned the same list after a certain interval. Assuming he had learned four lists, A, B, C, and D, he would relearn list A after 30 minutes, list B after 24 hours, list C after one week, and list D after one month. He recorded the time it took to relearn the lists and observed that it took less time to relearn lists after shorter retention intervals.

Ebbinghaus was interested in the direction of associations—for example, between *mev* and *gor*. Association means one syllable evokes the other, so that once *mev* and *gor* are presented together, *mev* subsequently elicits *gor*. Ebbinghaus wondered if there were both **forward associations** like *mev > gor > dux > bap > wab > rif > tox,* and **backward associations** like *mev < gor < dux < bap < wab < rif < tox*. In other words, would presenting *gor* evoke *mev*? Ebbinghaus memorized an original list of 16 nonsense syllables, and sometime later memorized a derived list. This list included the same syllables as the original list, except their order was changed, as illustrated in Table 1.1. He found the greatest savings (33%) when the same list was relearned. Savings were smaller for the reversed list (12%). There was no savings for randomized lists. Ebbinghaus con-

TABLE 1.1   Methods and Stimuli Used by Associationist Psychologists

Lists to Test Forward and Backward Associations

Original List	1 2 3 4 5 6 7 8 9 10 11 12 13 14 15 16
Relearn Original List	1 2 3 4 5 6 7 8 9 10 11 12 13 14 15 16
Reversed List	16 15 14 13 12 11 10 9 8 7 6 5 4 3 2 1
Random List	14 3 11 6 8 9 5 12 2 15 1 16 4 7 10 13

Note the numbers represent nonsense syllables.

List of Paired Associates

Stimulus	Response
mev	*tox*
wab	*rif*
bap	*gor*
dux	*nal*
.	.
.	.
.	.

cluded that both forward and backward associations are formed; forward associations, however, are stronger.

Ebbinghaus also introduced the **paired associate method.** Pairs of nonsense syllables were formed, as shown in Table 1.1. The left term of each pair served as the stimulus, and the term on the right as the response. The learner studied lists like these, and then the stimulus term was presented; the learner had to reproduce the associated response term.

Unlike Wundt's introspectionist studies, Ebbinghaus's experiments have a distinctly modern flavor. His meticulous selection and construction of stimulus materials, the definition of independent variables like retention interval and direction of association, and his innovative savings measure used to assess the strength of memory traces survive in today's research laboratories. Of course, he did not solve all of the problems associated with this type of research. Indeed, the nonsense syllables he created are not totally nonsensical; it is possible to produce meaningful associations between *mev, gor,* and *dux.*

Ebbinghaus's association concept was very simple; it was a linear linking of items. Subsequent researchers were to conceive of different kinds of associations, such as remote associations. Now, over a century later, the concept of association is more complex than in Ebbinghaus's day. Cognitive psychologists use representations based on **relational** associations where the link between two concepts is defined by a relation. For example, the concept *canary* is linked to *bird* by the subset relation, and the concept *yellow* is linked to *canary* by the property relation (see Chapter 5). The association is also the key feature of **neural networks.** These include many neuron-like units that are connected via links. The units and their links collectively represent information (Chapter 6).

Behaviorism

Associationism survived the demise of structuralism and introspectionism. The associationist influence continued in behaviorism, which became the dominant force in psychology in the early part of this century. The never-ending debates and contradictions among introspectionists persuaded a new generation of psychologists such as Ivan Pavlov, Edward Thorndike, and John B. Watson to abandon introspectionism and with it the traditional subject matter of psychology—the study of the mind. According to the behaviorists, introspectionism was doomed to fail because it relied on subjective data. By studying behavior, this problem was removed. At the same time, psychology became a more global science, encompassing, at least in principle, the behavior of all organisms, from the flatworm and rat to homo sapiens.

The behaviorists were influenced by Pavlov's seminal work on conditioning. Ivan Pavlov (1849–1936) studied medicine and soon turned to basic research in physiology, like Wundt and James. His research on the digestive system was path breaking; Pavlov became widely known, and

in 1904 won the Nobel prize in medicine. He ran his laboratory with a tight reign, not permitting any absence or tardiness of his research assistants. According to one story (in Fancher, 1979), Pavlov fired a worker who showed up late for work during the Russian Revolution in 1917 because he had to find a detour around barricades and street fights. Revolution was not an excuse Pavlov would allow—science had to march on regardless!

Pavlov became one of the first researchers to study **learning,** the change in behavior resulting from practice (Pavlov, 1927). He investigated learning in the laboratory by presenting two unrelated stimuli in association. In the course of his research on the digestive system in dogs, Pavlov made an accidental discovery: He noticed that the dog he used in his research began to salivate as he led him from his cage to the laboratory where he was fed. He wondered about the salivation and assumed that the dog had formed an association between being picked up and the food he received as part of the experiments.

Studying this effect systematically, Pavlov presented the sound of a tuning fork and meat to a dog. The meat caused the dog to salivate—a reflex reaction that was involuntary or unconditioned. After a few paired presentations of sound and meat, the sound came to elicit salivation. Pavlov called the sound a **conditioned stimulus** and the response a **conditioned reaction**. They were *conditioned* because the condition necessary for the tone to trigger salivation was that the tone and meat be associated. Pavlov's contribution was the introduction of observable measures of association that did not depend on introspection or verbal reports and could therefore be studied in animals. Thorndike, Watson, Hull, and Skinner continued Pavlov's tradition in the United States.

The behaviorist model is very simple; it is the stimulus-response model graphed in Figure 1.3. The figure shows the stimulus *(S)* coming from the environment, a box depicting the organism, and a response *(R)* made by the organism. The goal of the behaviorist research model was to determine lawful relations between stimuli and responses without focusing on the organism.

Stimulus ⟶ [ ] ⟶ Response

FIGURE 1.3 The behaviorist model of performance includes the stimulus and response, but overlooks the mind mediating between them.

The contribution of behaviorism was its emphasis on learning. Learning plays a role in cognition, though cognitive psychologists have not always acknowledged it. Practice improves—indeed, automatizes—performance in many cognitive skills, such as attention, pattern recognition, and problem solving. Memory is based on learning, whether it is as explicit as in retention experiments like Ebbinghaus's or implicit as when we learn the meaning of the words of our native language. Learning is ubiquitous in cognition; it makes the organism adaptive and creative.

Behaviorists investigated many learning phenomena, including stimulus generalization, discrimination, transfer training, and educational applications (see Chapter 7). Researchers were inventive in designing experiments, building apparatus, and quantifying behavioral measures; objectivity, experimental ingenuity, and precision constitute a lasting legacy of behaviorism.

The behaviorists banned, however, the study of knowledge and thought from the laboratory and with them some of the most interesting topics, such as memory, imagery, comprehension, and problem-solving strategies. It remained for cognitive psychologists like Tulving, Shepard, Simon, and others you will encounter in later chapters in this book to develop experimental paradigms for the study of these topics.

Gestalt Psychology

Much like behaviorism, Gestalt psychology developed in response to structuralism. Gestalt psychologists wanted to understand our perception of stimulus configurations (*Gestalt* in German) rather than of elemental sensations. For example, according to Gestalt psychologists, a triangle is more than the sum of three lines, and a musical chord is more than a collection of individual tones. Gestalt researchers were contemporaries of the behaviorists but they were also their critics. Gestaltists such as Koehler (1929), Duncker (1945), and Wertheimer (1945) explored perception and thinking—two topics now investigated by cognitive psychologists. Gestalt psychologists favored an experience-based approach to research, thus ignoring the behaviorist's prohibition against the use of subjective reports. They differed from the introspectionists, however, because they used naive and untrained reports. Observers were asked to report the perceptual phenomena they experienced, thus this tradition was named the **phenomenological** approach. Gestalt psychologists sought to catalog perceptual regularities experienced by subjects. They developed the **Gestalt principles** (described in Chapter 4).

Some of the Gestalt interests continue in cognitive psychology, as we will see when we discuss perception and problem solving in Chapters 4 and 13, respectively. Gestalt psychologists, however, emphasized perceptual phenomena; they were not interested in mental processes.

Forerunners of Information Processing

The term *human information processing* was introduced in the 1960s. It captures the idea that information is transformed through a variety of mental processes. Although the term was not used then, earlier researchers investigated information processing and developed research methods still in use today. We will examine two influential traditions: the mental chronometry tradition that flourished over a century ago and the human communications research introduced 50 years ago. Mental chronometry involves measuring the time it takes to perform such mental processes as detection and comparison of stimuli. Communication researchers investigate the speed and efficiency of human operators who detect and transmit information (e.g., in spotting targets on a radar screen and sending Morse code).

Mental Chronometry. Descartes introduced the idea of the reflex arc; a stimulus impinges on the body surface and the organism makes a response. For example, when a physician taps the leg just below the patella, the patient extends her leg. Nineteenth-century physiologist Helmholtz wanted to know how fast such reflexes travel along motor pathways. He developed the **subtraction method** to determine the speed of neural transmission. Using a nerve-muscle preparation of a frog, he elicited a reaction by applying an electrical shock at two points on the frog's leg: one close to a muscle and the other more distant from a muscle. For both trials, he measured the latency for the muscle to contract—the reaction time *(RT)*—and obtained one *RT* for the close stimulus and another for the more distant stimulus. Helmholtz then subtracted the close *RT* from the distant *RT* to obtain the time the impulse needed to reach the longer distance. He divided the difference by the distance to estimate the speed of nerve conduction (see Massaro, 1988). His estimates ranged from 50 to 100 meters per second.

The Dutch physiologist Donders used the logic of Helmholtz's subtraction method to measure the duration of mental operations. Donders measured the time it took a person to make a decision between several alternatives. He had subjects press a key as quickly as possible in response to a single stimulus (e.g., a light). He defined the time between the onset of the single stimulus and the response as the detection time; on average, detection took 197 milliseconds. In the choice condition, when one of two lights was turned on, subjects had to press one of two keys. In this condition, the response time was called the choice reaction time; on average, subjects took 285 milliseconds in this condition. Donders obtained the decision time by subtracting the detection time from the choice reaction time as shown in equation (1.2):

(1.2) $RT_{\text{decision}} = RT_{\text{choice}} - RT_{\text{detection}}$
$$= 88 \text{ milliseconds}$$

Donders used the subtraction method because he believed that choice reaction time resulted from two independent mental operations—detection and decision—as shown in Figure 1.4.

Subsequently, investigators came to believe that the stages in Figure 1.4 are not independent of the nature of the task (e.g., Sternberg, 1966). By deleting the decision stage in the detection task, the overall nature of the task is changed and one really cannot compare the two conditions. Nevertheless, researchers were intrigued by Donders's method and his conclusions regarding decision processes. Donders's subtraction method has been adapted by researchers to new and different contexts. Posner and Raichle (1994) use the method to assess the activation level of specified brain regions under a load condition versus a baseline condition. These and other researchers measure the metabolic activity of specific brain regions under the load condition and the baseline condition. When a specific brain region is engaged in work, its metabolism increases. As a result, the flow of blood in the region rises. The increased blood flow is detected by a brain imaging method, the PET scan (see Chapter 2).

Using the subtraction technique, researchers compare the blood flow in, say, the vision centers of the brain when volunteers read a word (the load

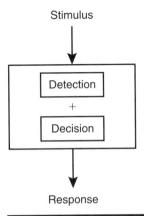

FIGURE 1.4 Donders believed that choice reaction times were based on two mental processes: detection and decision.

condition) and when they merely look at a mark on the screen (the baseline condition). Subtracting blood flow recordings of the baseline condition from the work condition provides researchers with a clue on the localization of visual processing in the brain.

By the turn of the century, it had become popular to measure reaction times as a function of the number of alternatives, stimulus intensity, and the compatibility between stimuli and response (Fitts & Seeger, 1953). Merkel (1885) found that reaction times increased proportionately as the number of alternatives increased. Merkel used digits as stimuli and key presses as responses. When the arabic digits 1 through 5 were flashed, subjects responded with the fingers of their right hand; when the roman numerals I through V were used, subjects used their left hand. The subject always knew what the assignment of digits to responses was.

Although subjects were well practiced and knew the stimulus-response assignment, reaction times increased as the number of choices increased. The extra *RT* was greatest when another alternative was added to a small set of existing alternatives. For example, when going from 2 to 3 alternatives, an additional 48 milliseconds was required by subjects, as opposed to an additional 3 milliseconds when going from 9 to 10 alternatives. Subsequent studies have shown that the *RT*s increase by a constant, by about 140 milliseconds, with each doubling of the number of alternatives, as shown in Figure 1.5.

The mental chronometry approach was important because of its research focus on cognitive operations. The chronometric method assumes that these operations take place in real time; this is plausible to us today but was not to nineteenth-century philosophers and researchers. Nevertheless, chronometric research was not cognitive research in the contemporary sense. The early researchers examined lawful relations between stimulus patterns and response times, but not the details of the mechanisms underlying performance.

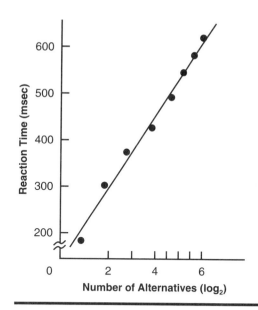

FIGURE 1.5 Choice reaction times increase linearly as the number of alternatives increases (Merkel, 1885).

Human Performance and Communications Research. The pioneers of experimental psychology were interested in improving performance in all sorts of applications, from education to motor skills. Robert Woodworth (1869–1962) explored the accuracy and speed of targeted motor movements as a function of the distance of the target. Building on that research, Paul Fitts investigated the relation between the execution speed of a movement and its difficulty. He used an apparatus in which subjects had to move a stylus between two targets whose width and distance were varied. Narrower width required more precision of the movement. Fitts found that movement time increased as a logarithmic function of distance and of precision. Subsequent researchers documented the generality of the relation Fitts had observed; so it became known as **Fitts's law** (see Chapter 4).

Communications technology advanced rapidly as our mobility by rail, car, and airplane increased. Morse code, telephone, telegraph, and visual monitoring (for example, on radar screens) became widely used. Operators had to take in information and transmit it either in original or in changed form. Communication tasks involve potential problems with noise, overload, and misinterpretation, which can lead to serious and even fatal errors. Consequently, communication research was motivated by such practical issues as: How can one reduce errors and increase efficiency of communication? and How much information can operators handle in a given unit of time?

Among the first modern communication devices was Morse code. A pattern of electrical pulses represents the letters of the alphabet; these patterns include dots, dashes, and blanks. To send a dot was fastest; dashes took longer. Morse wanted to convey messages as efficiently as possible. Consequently, he designed a coding system based on the frequency of letters. For example, he represented *e,* the most frequent letter, by a single dot; he represented the letter *x,* which is relatively infrequent, by four dots.

The applied orientation reached a high point during World War II and was known as *human factors* research. The goal of human factors research was to design equipment based on the characteristics of the human operator, including his processing limitations. Control panels in airplanes, for example, were designed to optimize readings from multiple displays. Human factors researchers also assessed performance under a wide range of stress-producing conditions, including emergencies in the cockpit and stressful monitoring tasks (see Chapter 15). A study by Sleight (1948) illustrates the human factors approach. He examined the error rates in reading different types of dials, including vertical, semicircular, round, and window-type dials, as shown in Figure 1.6. Readings were most accurate for the open-window dial and least accurate for the vertical dial. In the open-window dial, the indicator hand moves as it does in the other dials. However, here the scale itself moves too in order to highlight the current reading.

The model used by human factors workers was superficially similar to that of behaviorists; both studied inputs and outputs and the relations between them. Human factors researchers, however, were interested in the human observer. They viewed the observer as a communication channel and noted that the channel was limited in terms of its capacity to pass information. Communication theorists assumed that operators filtered relevant information, ignoring irrelevant aspects (Broadbent, 1958). Such selection prevented overloading the communication channel. The notion of **limited capacity** continues to play an important role in cognitive psychology as it seeks to understand problem solving, comprehension, and other skills. The communication model of human performance is graphed in Figure 1.7.

INTERIM SUMMARY

We have reviewed six experimental frameworks in psychology that had an impact on contemporary cognitive psychology: psychophysics, structuralism, behaviorism. Gestalt psychology, and forerunners of information processing in mental chronometry and communication research. Each of these frameworks left its mark on cognitive psychology. The measurement methods introduced by psychophysicists are used in research on attention and have been adapted for memory research. The legacy of associationism survives today in representations of semantic knowledge in memory and in neurally inspired connectionist networks. Cognitive psychologists are interested in the effects of practice on attention, pattern recognition, and cognitive skills, much like the behaviorists were interested in learning. Gestalt psychologists examined regularities in perception, a goal shared by cognitive psychologists who investigate attention and pattern recognition. Students of mental chronometry and communication were direct forerunners of cognitive psychologists; they investigated the effects of increasing the workload on the speed and accuracy of performance.

Except for Donders, however, none of the early investigators was interested in mental processes. Researchers studied the relations between inputs and outputs. Psychophysicists correlated some attributes of the stimulus—usually its intensity or distinctiveness—with psychological sensations.

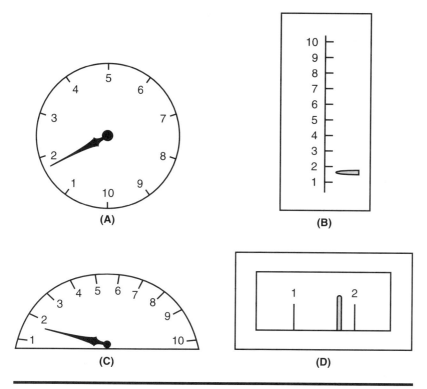

FIGURE 1.6 Different dial types used in experiment to assess error rates in dial reading. *(A)* Round, *(B)* Vertical, *(C)* Semicircular, *(D)* Open window.

Associationists and behaviorists examined the time course of learning and forgetting lists of associated items. Gestalt psychologists made an inventory of regularities in perceptual experience. Communication psychologists measured the efficiency of transmitting information. It took the recognition that mental representations and processes are needed to explain performance in attention and memory experiments, as well as developments in linguistics and computer science, to launch cognitive psychology as we know it today.

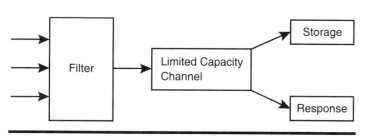

FIGURE 1.7 Human performance in a communication task is limited by the capacity of the operator. Stimuli are filtered to avoid overloading the channel (Broadbent, 1958).

LINGUISTICS

According to the great linguist Noam Chomsky, language provides a "window into the mind." Language is an expression of knowledge and therefore reflects the structure of the mind; it also has the advantage of being observable. Language researchers study a wide range of linguistic expressions, words, sounds, phrases, and sentences. When we talk and write, we produce sentences naturally, as examples (1.3) and (1.4) illustrate.

(**1.3**) Language researchers study linguistic expressions.

(**1.4**) Language provides a window into the mind.

Linguists also create special sentences like (1.5) for research purposes (see Chapter 11).

(**1.5**) The editor authors the newspaper hired liked laughed.

The study of language poses great challenges because of the mixture of regularities and exceptions found in all languages. Linguists wonder if it is possible to describe the universe of expressions of a language in terms of abstract rules or principles. Linguists and psychologists also wonder what faculties a child must have to be able to learn her native language without apparent effort. Chomsky thought that some of these faculties must be innate; for this reason, Chomsky is often considered a neo-Cartesian rationalist.

The study of linguistics has undergone great changes. At the turn of the century, linguists examined the similarities and differences between different language families and their histories. Later behaviorism was dominant in linguistics, as it was in psychology; Bloomfield, an exponent of this approach, viewed language as a physical response system. Behaviorists maintained that it was impossible to study meaning because it was not observable. They viewed meaning as a mentalistic concept and hence not legitimate for the objective study of language. Rather, linguists in the Bloomfield tradition observed and recorded language in different cultures.

The publication of Chomsky's (1957) *Syntactic Structures* and (1965) *Aspects of the Theory of Syntax* had a great impact on linguistics and psychology because of their focus on the speaker's mind. Chomsky's interest lay in the rules of language; he set out to catalog the rules of English in terms of several rule systems known as *grammars.* He maintained that a speaker must have this knowledge because he is capable of deciding whether or not sentences like (1.6–1.8) are grammatical.

(**1.6**) The boy hit the ball.

(**1.7**) Ball boy hit the the.

(**1.8**) Colorless green ideas sleep furiously.

You will have no difficulty deciding that sentences (1.6) and (1.8) are grammatical, whereas sentence (1.7) is not. Sentence (1.7) simply lists the words of sentence (1.6) in alphabetical order. It is not that there is no rule that can describe sentence (1.7); the rule is to string the words in alphabetic sequence, but that is not one of the rules to form legal English sentences. Following Chomsky, linguists tried to discover rules that speakers know and use to generate grammatical English sentences. The body of these rules was called a **grammar.** In one such grammar—phrase structure grammar—rules explain how a complex structure (on the left of an arrow) is created from smaller constituents (on the right of an arrow). One such rule is captured in (1.9).

(**1.9**) S → NP VP

This rule states that a well-formed sentence consists of a noun phrase like *the boy* and a verb phrase like *is sleeping.* There are additional rules that list the constituents of noun phrases, verb phrases, and so on. Although we do not employ these rules consciously, we know and use them. Chomsky's influence on linguistics, philosophy, and cognitive psychology was so profound that we refer to the *Chomskyan revolution* as an incisive juncture in the history of these disciplines (e.g., Lyons, 1970). By postulating mental structures and supporting them in systematic research. Chomsky turned linguistics and psychology away from their behaviorist anchor. Even though researchers may have moved beyond the particulars of Chomsky's theories, his approach still defines the questions and research issues in linguistics today.

Being a linguist, Chomsky did not conduct experiments himself; however, he had a profound impact on experimental psychology. His many followers among psychologists included George Miller. Miller wanted to find out if listeners actually used such phrase structure rules as (1.9) to produce and comprehend language. Miller's ideas inspired **psycholinguistics,** the research specialty devoted to language production and comprehension (see Chapter 10 and 11).

COMPUTER SCIENCE

Philosophers have been curious about the mind for a long time. The mind remained so elusive, however, that it was finally banned from the study of psychology, linguistics, and philosophy. Philosophers and psychologists often thought of the mind and mental processes in terms of metaphors—for example, as a *tabula rasa* (clean slate), a sieve, a clock, a telephone switchboard, and, finally, a computer. A computer processes symbols; it is the information-processing device par excellence. The first computers were serial computers; these became influential models for

cognitive psychology. Computer processing is based on systems and application programs. The computer's **architecture** features several components, such as the central processor, primary memory, secondary memory, and input and output devices, including keyboards, microphones, cameras, printers, speakers, and video terminals. Some of these components are shown in Figure 1.8 in schematic form.

The computer accepts input, transforms it according to a program, and then produces an output. The central processing unit (CPU) schedules all of these processes. The CPU also controls computer programs; the program is interpreted and its commands are executed. Memory contains the software program as well as some data. It has a small-capacity store but permits fast access and change of information. When you turn the computer off, however, the information in memory is wiped out. The computer also has a secondary store that holds a large amount of information for a relatively long time after the computer shuts down, but it takes longer to access.

The power of the computer is its ability to store and execute a multitude of different programs. Programs consist of commands; for example, a command to read a number and store it in a specific location, or a register. Simple addition is achieved by adding another number to the register and obtaining the sum, a third number. By combining simple operations like addition, one can execute

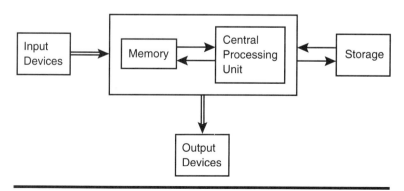

FIGURE 1.8 Computer architecture featuring the central processing unit, memory, storage, and input and output devices.

more complex tasks, both numerical and symbolic. Comparison between two symbols (for example, *a* and *b*) is an example of a symbolic operation. Examine the program segment in Table 1.2 to get a flavor of programming. These lines represent FORTRAN code, the oldest computer language available since 1958. This code calculates the average of 20 numbers stored in an array, A. Two quantities are used: SUM and AVERAGE. SUM holds the cumulative sum of the set of numbers. AVERAGE represents the average. The program segment shows that we first initialize SUM to 0.0. A loop of two lines follows: The first loop executes the command in line 100 20 times and line 100 specifies that the quantity SUM be incremented by successive numbers. In the last line, the average is computed by dividing SUM by 20.

This program can be run on any computer that supports FORTRAN, including an IBM workstation, Macintosh, a DEC-mainframe or even a Cray supercomputer. What matters, therefore, is the logic of the program, not its implementation on a particular computer that is a piece of hardware. If the programmer messes up the logic of the program, its output will be in error on any computer.

A program like the one in Table 1.2 is a set of symbols. The processor reads the symbols from memory, transforms them, and transfers the altered symbols into memory. The symbols represent certain contents, (for example, a quantity like a sum or an average) and specific operations like incrementing a sum. Figure 1.9 shows a flowchart of the program in Table 1.2. The flowchart is a visual representation of the steps of the averaging program. Flowcharts such as this illustrates the

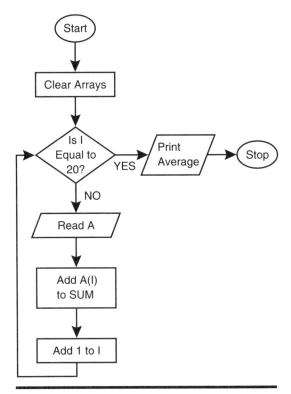

FIGURE 1.9   Flowchart of the program in Table 1.2.

information-processing approach of making symbols, processes, and their sequence explicit.

A Powerful Analogy

Information-processing researchers in the 1950s saw a similarity between the symbolic processing of the human problem solver and the new serial computer. In the tradition of Descartes, these researchers regarded thinking and problem solving as a kind of symbol manipulation. When a child first learns to add numbers (for example, 2 + 3), she increments one of the numbers one by one (see Chapter 13). Each number represents a symbol and incrementing is a symbol-processing manipulation—so are other mathematical operations, including subtraction, multiplication, and division. Observing subjects who worked on logical proofs. Newell and Simon (1972) found that

TABLE 1.2   A FORTRAN Program That Computes the Average of 20 Numbers

```
       SUM = 0.0

       DO 100    L= 1, 20
100    SUM = SUM + A (L)
       AVERAGE = SUM/20
```

subjects used strategies that could be implemented in a computer program. The rationale of the symbolic procedures in mathematics and logic remains the same, whether they are executed by a person or a computer.

It was therefore natural to view human cognition as a kind of computation, as human information processing. The physical differences between human beings and computers, though acknowledged, were not considered as important as their functional similarities. According to this **functionalist** view, we can study cognition without having to study its biological basis. Chapter 2 presents the alternative view—namely, that understanding of neural constraints is essential for the study of cognition.

Subsequent investigators were soon to follow Newell and Simon's lead. Atkinson and Shiffrin (1968) proposed an influential model of human information processing. The model includes three stores (shown in Figure 1.10): the sensory register, short-term store, and long-term store. The **sensory register** receives sensory input (visual and acoustic stimuli from the environment); the information is held for a brief period in the **short-term store,** and the **long-term store** maintains information for relatively long intervals. The Atkinson and Shiffrin model was successful in accommodating a large body of research on memory, as we will see in Chapters 7 through 9.

Information-processing models were also developed for many specific domains, including problem solving, sensory processing, and reading comprehension. These models assumed sequential stages of cognitive processing representing the stages as flowcharts. The advantage of flow-

chart models was that they spelled out the hypothetical steps involved in a cognitive process. Only later did some of the pitfalls of this approach became apparent; cognitive processes are unlikely to be serial and as orderly as portrayed in flowcharts.

Two decades later, cognitive psychologists adopted very different models of cognition. These models were based on parallel rather than serial processing and on information not stored in terms of discrete memory locations but distributed over many small interconnected units. These are the connectionist network models, also known as parallel distributed processing (PDP) models.

INTERIM SUMMARY

The introduction of computers afforded cognitive psychologists a powerful metaphor of mental structures and processes. The computer is a symbol processor of great flexibility, complexity, and adaptability. It consists of relatively fixed components, which constitute the computer architecture; these include a processor, a fast-access memory, and a long-term store with a large capacity. The software includes programs, which are lists of symbolic instructions executed by the computer. Influenced by the computer metaphor, researchers came to view perception, reasoning, and other cognitive functions as instances of symbolic computation. Borrowing from the computer architecture, Atkinson and Shiffrin proposed a model of human memory that included three components: the sensory register, short-term store, and long-term store. Psychologists also analyzed mental processes in terms of sequential stages, as in flow-

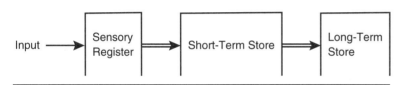

FIGURE 1.10 Model of human information processing includes a sensory register, the short-term store, and the long-term store (Atkinson & Shiffrin, 1968).

charts. As the design of computers and computer programs changed, so did the cognitive models; increasingly, parallel processing models are developed in addition to stage models of processing.

———■———

THEORIES AND METHODS IN COGNITIVE PSYCHOLOGY

This brief history of the antecedents of cognitive psychology has shown the many seeds of the study of cognition in psychology and related disciplines. The interest in knowledge and mental structures is as old as philosophy itself. Wundt and other introspectionists were the first experimental psychologists to study mental elements and their associations. Introspectionism led to an impasse and was replaced by behaviorism, which was devoted to the study of observable behavior. It was not until the pioneering work of Chomsky that psychologists became interested once again in mental structures. Theories of mental structures became more complex, however, thanks to developments in linguistics and computer science. Linguists offered a sophisticated description of the rules of language, and computer scientists provided a metaphor of the human mind as an information processor. Our views of human memory representations were directly influenced by the architecture of the computer. Similarly, processes like encoding, storing, and retrieving information were borrowed from computer science.

Cognitive psychologists benefited from methodological innovations made in several fields. The psychophysicists contributed exact quantitative methods developed to investigate the relation of mind and body experimentally. Behaviorists emphasized experimental rigor and observation and a precise definition of variables. The research of Gestalt psychologists has shown that a systematic analysis of perceptual experience reveals lawful regularities—the Gestalt principles. The introduction of mental chronometry was significant because of its emphasis on mental processes and its assumption that mental processes take time and can be measured.

Behaviorism lost its preeminence not so much because of criticisms leveled against it but rather because it excluded human knowledge from consideration and had therefore become irrelevant. Beginning in the late 1940s, there were signs of ferment in such disciplines as psychology, linguistics, computer science, and philosophy. These developments culminated in the 1960s in the emergence of cognitive psychology as a discipline with its own agenda: to advance the experimental study of mental representations and processes. Neisser published his textbook *Cognitive Psychology* in 1967 and a journal by the same name was first published in 1970. In the quarter of a century since, the field has grown steadily. Cognitive psychologists investigate human information processing—how people encode, transform, create, and output information. Unlike behaviorists who emphasized observable *outcomes,* cognitive psychologists investigate the *representations* and *processes* that produce those outcomes. Because neither representations nor processes are directly observable, researchers have had to develop methodologies to infer these constructs from performance. Next, the basic assumptions will be summarized and a general description of methods will be given.

General Assumptions and Issues in Cognitive Psychology

Two essential concepts in cognitive psychology are *representation* and *process.* You can understand their importance by trying to imagine the field without them. Research on information processing would be vastly different if it did not consider the knowledge that supports the processes as well as the change in knowledge resulting from them. Such research would be behavioristic in orientation and outlook. Investigators would present stimuli and record their behavioral consequences. However, the universe of stimuli would be limited because the most interesting stimuli—pictures, texts, and problems—require knowledge for their interpretation and use.

Representations.   Knowledge is not an amorphous substance; rather, it has some structure and format, whether it is a transient image, a memory, the meaning of a word, or a problem to be solved. Representations are not controversial among cognitive psychologists; there are, however, different views about the nature of representation. Questions frequently asked about representations reflect these differences: Does the mind represent information expressed in different modalities (e.g., spoken versus printed information) in different formats? Are representations analogous to the physical entities they capture or are they abstract? For example, does the representation of a dog reflect its physical characteristics including a head, body, four legs, and tail or is it an abstract definition expressing the idea that *A dog is an X?* If so, what is the definition: A dog is a canine, A dog is a mammal, or A dog is an animal, or a combination of these?

Because there are different types of knowledge, cognitive psychologists wonder if there are classes of different representations for them. For example, are there differences in the representations of facts like *The moon is Earth's satellite* and skills like playing chess? The manner of storing representations in memory also has given rise to many questions. The localization issue is one of these: Is there a specific storage location, as in traditional computers, or is information distributed over many locations, as in neural networks? If our memories were like a computer memory, the meaning of *dog* would be stored in a discrete memory cell. The idea of distributed representation comes from biology; many individual cells or units capture the information. Another issue concerns the overall framework of representations—the **cognitive architecture.** Is it useful to view cognition within such a framework? Is cognition best described as a dynamic and fluid process or are both metaphors useful?

Two chapters of this text are devoted to representation of knowledge (Chapters 5 and 6); representations come up in every chapter, however. They play a role in pattern recognition (Chapter 4), learning (Chapter 7), and memory (Chapter 9). We will encounter issues in the representation of meaning in the chapters dealing with language (Chapter 10), language comprehension (Chapter 11), and reading and writing (Chapter 12). Such cognitive skills as problem solving (Chapter 13) and reasoning (Chapter 14) are based on specific representations as well.

Processes.   Cognitive psychologists make assumptions about structures and mental processes that operate on those structures; they have proposed a sizable inventory of processes, including strategies, moves, operations, procedures, productions, plans, goals, actions, acts, algorithms, heuristics, and others. Processes may be characterized on several dimensions, including how global they are, how effortful they are, and what stimuli or representations they manipulate.

Processes range from small-scale operations like those that occur in letter recognition, to global procedural skills like doing math or understanding language. Global processes consist of a variety of component operations. All components work together smoothly to ensure the efficient execution of an aggregate process, whether it is reading, writing, reasoning, or speaking. Although cognitive psychologists have developed a rich inventory of processes, it is unclear what structure, if any, does the processing. Does working memory perform this function as some have argued? We will consider this topic in Chapter 8.

Another dimension of processes is the degree of effort involved. For example, perceiving requires less effort than reading, which, in turn, is less effortful than problem solving and writing. The degree to which a cognitive activity involves effort depends on the degree of practice devoted to it; we have more practice in reading than writing, reading is therefore more automatic.

As representations differ, so do the corresponding mental operations. Consider the example of receiving a phone number from an operator. You listen, write the number down or rehearse it, and try to remember it for later use. Some of the processes implicated in this sequence are encoding, recoding, storing, and retrieval. The number is first *encoded,* which means it is recognized; next, it is *recoded* in rehearsal, and, assuming you have *stored* the number in memory, it may be *retrieved* for later use.

General Issues.   We have considered the two basic assumptions that underlie cognitive psychology: representation and process. Research in cognitive psychology is based on these and other specific assumptions. Debates in the field are the result of differences in the application of those assumptions and in the interpretation of data. What makes the field so lively are the many issues with which cognitive psychologists are concerned. Three general issues are considered here; the remainder of the text will raise many specific questions. The three issues concern the relation among cognitive functions, the relation of cognition and consciousness, and the relation of cognitive to neural processes.

The first issue concerns the relation among such cognitive functions as perception, memory, language, and problem solving: Are there independent modules for each of them, governed by their own specific laws, or are there general laws of cognition? Some theorists view language processing, for example, as a highly specialized module with unique representations and processes (Fodor, 1983). Fodor also assumes independent modules for different language functions like word recognition and sentence interpretation. Others believe that different cognitive functions, including language, are based on the same general representations (e.g., Anderson, 1983).

The second problem concerns the relation between consciousness and cognition. Early psychologists, such as Wundt, equated cognition with awareness. Clarity of thinking was thought of as the highest form of consciousness, whereas the unconscious was linked to emotions.

Contemporary psychologists distinguish between conscious and unconscious cognition (Hirst, 1995; Kihlstrom, 1987). The former includes perceptions, memories, and plans of which we are aware, whereas the latter includes information and processes of which we are not aware. In speech perception, for example, we experience words but process phonemes without being aware of them. In visual recognition experiments, a word

is identified faster if it is primed by a related word flashed to viewers too quickly to reach consciousness (Chapter 3). In skill learning, we first devote much conscious effort to a task that later becomes automatic as a result of practice (Chapter 5). Consciousness continues to be a mystery for scientists as they seek to formulate tractable research questions such as (1) whether there are different brain states for conscious and unconscious cognition, (2) whether the two types of cognition occur in parallel, and (3) whether there are different representations for conscious and unconscious contents, and if so, whether conscious representations are privileged (Kinsbourne, 1995).

As for the neural basis of cognition, there is no theorist who denies it. Theorists differ on whether one can understand cognition without investigating its neural correlates. According to the functionalist view, information processing is abstract and not tied to its physical basis. We can, therefore, study cognition without concern for neural issues, much like we can understand a computer program without knowledge of its hardware. Other researchers believe that cognitive theories should be informed by the insights of neuroscience (see Chapter 2). This issue is far from resolved. Later chapters will show that the answer depends on the field of inquiry; research on attention, pattern recognition, and learning uses neural models, whereas the study of problem solving and reasoning does not.

These are issues that define the general research agenda of cognitive psychology. At least all of the players concur on the foundational assumptions of representation and processes. There are, however, prominent psychologists who do not share these assumptions. Box 1.2 samples some of these critical views. Behaviorist and ecological researchers take issue with mental representations and processes, and other critics fault the experimental method of the field.

Methods in Cognitive Psychology: The Experiment

The basic assumptions and general issues we have just discussed do not lend themselves to an empir-

Box 1.2

Fundamental Criticisms of Cognitive Psychology

■ *The Behaviorist Criticism:* Behaviorist psychologists are among the sharpest critics of cognitive psychology. B. F. Skinner himself expressed several criticisms of the field in an address to the American Psychological Association in August 1990, just two weeks before his death. According to Skinner, cognitive psychology is no more than an introspective account of the theorist's own behavior. He noted that mental representations and processes cannot be seen nor measured by cognitive psychologists because they are not accessible to consciousness. Consequently, the cognitive psychologist must speculate about these processes, much like psychoanalysts speculate about the unconscious. In the end, cognitive psychology is no more useful than folk psychology, the unscientific assumptions of the layperson. Skinner concluded his address by saying that behavioral analysis will prevail because it is committed to objectivity (Skinner, 1990).

■ *The Ecological Criticism:* According to Gibson and his students, organisms perceive and act within their environment without the intervention of mental representations and processes. These mental constructs are a "Pandora's box" invented by the theorist without regard to reality (see Reed, 1982). Furthermore, Gibson says that the concept of *memory,* though it appeals to our introspection, has no place in psychology (Gibson, 1966, 1979). The environment offers rich information about depth, texture, movement, and other features that is picked up accurately and effortlessly by the organism. Mace's (1977) recommendation, "Ask not what's inside your head but what your head is inside of," captures the essence of the ecological approach.

■ *The Fragmentation Criticism:* This criticism notes that cognitive psychologists use the divide-and-conquer approach of segmenting a problem into smaller parts and lose sight of the whole mind. According to these critics, there is no coherent science of cognitive psychology. Rather, there is a proliferation of mini-models about fragmented aspects of cognition

(e.g., Claxton, 1988; Mandler, 1985; Newell, 1973). These models are quickly invalidated as new paradigms are developed and discoveries made. Not only do cognitive psychologists study tiny facets of cognition but they are also isolated from one another like "inhabitants of thousands of little islands, all in the same part of the ocean, yet totally out of touch with each other" (Claxton, 1980).

■ *The Artificiality Criticism:* This criticism concerns the emphasis on the laboratory approach in cognitive psychology. It is captured best in a quote from Claxton (1980, p. 13) that cognitive researchers "deal with whole people but with a very special and bizarre—almost Frankensteinian—preparation, which consists of a brain attached to two eyes, two ears, and two index fingers. This preparation is only to be found inside small, gloomy cubicles, outside which red lights burn to warn ordinary people away." Claxton is referring to reaction time experiments that the mental chronometry researchers introduced and that are common in cognitive psychology today. His point is that the issues pursued by cognitive psychologists are narrow and have no bearing outside of the laboratory (see also Chapter 15).

■ *The Lack of Originality Criticism:* Asking whether the cognitive revolution was a mistake, Hintzman (1993) found that cognitive psychology had added little new knowledge to our understanding of the mind. In his view, cognitive psychology started as a justifiable reaction against extreme behaviorist positions à la Skinner. Nevertheless, the cognitive theoretical frameworks, from neural networks to production systems, are not original. They were anticipated by models of such moderate behaviorists as Neal Miller, Charles Osgood, and Clark L. Hull. Popular cognitive notions, including the schema and semantic memory, are, in Hintzman's view, either too vague or too broad to permit empirical verification. Specific phenomena like the memory span and mnemonic effects can all be accounted for by extending previously known principles.

ical test. The choices theorists make on these assumptions constitute the framework for their research. The kind of questions researchers address are like those listed at the beginning of this chapter on eyewitness testimony, attention, and composition. These are specific questions; they are, however, too complex to permit easy answers. They are as complex as problems raised in other sciences—for example, What makes the stars move? How do birds fly? and How do trees grow? Scientists approach each case as a problem to be solved; within the framework of a theory, one simplifies and divides the overall problem into smaller problems. When the problem is small enough, the scientist formulates a hypothesis and manipulates factors, often only one or two, trying to hold all other factors constant.

Experiments Are Systematic.   In an experiment, one systematically varies an independent variable and studies the resulting changes in the dependent variables. For example, in psychophysical studies of absolute thresholds, the intensity of a stimulus is changed in a certain order and the subject's response is recorded. Ebbinghaus's independent variables included list length and retention interval; his dependent variable was the savings observed in relearning the same materials. For behaviorists, independent variables included the number of times the conditioned and unconditioned stimuli were paired; and the dependent variable was the strength of the conditioned response as measured, for example, by the amount of saliva secreted.

Control of Confounding Factors.   In experiments, it is critical that researchers identify and neutralize the effects of extraneous factors on the variable of interest. Consider three of the experiments previously described: the psychophysical study of difference thresholds, Ebbinghaus's memory experiment, and Donders's simple versus choice reaction time experiment. In each of these experiments there was a confounding factor, often referred to as a **confounding.** A confounding variable covaries with the variable the experi-

menter seeks to study and thus might cause the effect of interest. It is up to the ingenuity of the researcher to eliminate such confounds, provided she discovers them in the first place.

— When investigating the difference threshold, the researcher is interested in weight differences that produce differences in sensation; the weight difference is the independent variable. In the experiment described earlier, however, the sound of dropping nickels could tip the subject off that the weight had changed. The sound made by the coin is a confounding variable. An experimenter could circumvent this problem by placing the nickels in plastic bottles, then blindfold subjects and have them judge the weight difference between bottles.

— In his studies, Ebbinghaus was interested in the pure memory trace as a function of the retention interval. However, some of his nonsense syllables may have meaning after all. It is easy to develop meaningful associations to *mev, gor,* and *dux*; for example, try *Merv, gore,* and *duct,* and the sentence *Merv gored the duck.* One cannot remove this confound; however, one can control it as subsequent researchers did. These investigators scaled nonsense syllables in terms of their meaningfulness and found that the degree of meaningfulness influenced retention.

— In his research, Donders found that reaction times were faster when subjects responded to one stimulus rather than when a choice of two stimuli was involved. He hypothesized that making a choice took additional time. The confounding might have been that the subject used his preferred hand for the simple reaction time test, but used both hands, including the less-favored hand, for the choice test. How would you remove this confound? You could use counterbalancing and have half of the subjects use their nonpreferred hand for the single-response task.

Being systematic and avoiding confounds are important considerations as cognitive psychologists conduct their research. The actual experiment, however, involves concrete logistical steps;

arrange for subjects to participate in the experiments, select or construct apparatus, develop and debug computer programs, and, of course, collect and analyze the data. Useful information on these steps can be found in books on research design and in special journals devoted to research methods such as *Behavior Research Methods, Instruments, & Computers.* You will understand the following chapters better if you know about the kinds of data cognitive psychologists collect in their experiments.

Types of Data. The data that a cognitive psychologist collects are influenced by her research perspective. There are at least three such perspectives: the phenomenological, the neurobiological, and the information processing (e.g., Posner, 1978). Proponents of the phenomenological approach have subjects describe their experience as they process a stimulus. For example, we saw that such reports yield useful information on perception; however, they are limited because subjects are usually unaware of the underlying processes. Neuroscientists take the neurobiological perspective; they examine the electrophysiological changes a stimulus produces in the sensory organs, sensory pathways and nuclei, as well as in cerebral centers. Through measurements of blood flow and electrical recordings, they study the activities in cerebral regions as the subject executes a cognitive task.

Among information-processing psychologists, the chronometric approach is very popular (see Kieras & Just, 1984; Posner, 1978). Cognitive operations, such as recognizing a shape or a word, understanding or producing a clause, or solving a problem, extend over time. Dependent variables of chronometric researchers include reaction times, decision latencies, eye fixation durations, neuroimaging, and electrophysiological measures; these variables are known as **on-line** measures because they track performance as it occurs over time, however brief the interval.

The pattern of activity spurts and pauses reflect the load on the mind. Presumably, a person engages in additional processes during pauses—

for example, planning a strategy for the next move, retrieving information from memory, or doing a particularly difficult computation. In speaking, people tend to pause longer before saying a content word than a function word. Content words include nouns, verbs, and adjectives; function words include articles and conjunctions. The pause pattern therefore indicates that the speaker faces more choices when expressing meaning than when creating the syntactic structure of the sentence (Maclay & Osgood, 1959).

In chronometric and neurophysiological experiments, there is an enormous amount of data, often collected continuously. Behaviors occur and change so rapidly that computers are required to keep track of them. Consider, for example, the pattern of eye movements as a person inspects a stimulus or reads a passage of text; tracking eye movements and fixations is an increasingly popular technique in perception, comprehension, and problem-solving research. A beam of light is projected to the eye; the light is reflected, recorded by a video-camera, and stored in a computer. The eye-tracking records reveal what a subject is looking at and for how long. In reading, for example, the eyes move very rapidly from one location to another, and there are pauses (fixations) that last 250 milliseconds on average. For each stimulus, the investigator records hundreds of such eye fixations. Research such as this became possible when computers became affordable and available. Cognitive psychologists use computers in experimentation; in a moment, we will see that computers are also employed to simulate human cognitive processes.

Here are a couple of further points about data that you might easily overlook when studying the results and figures in this text. In the typical experiment, researchers collect data from different individuals and average them both across trials and individuals. Of course, there are exceptions, such as Ebbinghaus's studies that had only a single participant (see also Chapter 8). The other aspect of data to consider is that although experimental effects may appear small to you, they are nevertheless important for the theory that is being investigated. Frequently, differences of as little as 20 to 50 milliseconds are theoretically important (one-twentieth to one-fiftieth of a second). These are time intervals of which subjects are usually unaware. Remember, however, that in other sciences even shorter time intervals are important. Physicists and astronomers measure intervals in millionths of seconds!

Computer Simulation

Executing such cognitive skills as pattern recognition, comprehension, and problem solving is a complex process that involves many components. Describing and explaining all of these is not an easy job; consequently, cognitive psychologists increasingly use computer models to do so. The theorist develops a computer model of the skill that keeps track of the component processes and their dynamic relations. Computer simulations run through the hypothetical mental operations like people are thought to do.

Computer simulations of cognition differ from programs developed by investigators of artificial intelligence (AI). The AI programs are designed to get an intelligent job done without simulating human cognitive processing.

The advantages of cognitive simulations as compared to verbal theories are that they furnish researchers with a framework to monitor mental processes and that they assist in the discovery of unexpected results and relations between processes. A potential drawback is that model builders frequently tend to be guided by programming considerations rather than by psychological theory (Lewandowsky, 1993).

One of the first computer models was developed to simulate visual letter recognition (Selfridge & Neisser, 1963). According to this model, there are several stages of analysis: encoding the visual stimulus, detecting features of the letter, describing the relations among features, and comparing this description with templates stored in memory (see also Chapter 4). Letter recognition is accomplished when the description of the stimulus matches one of the templates in memory.

Other simulation models were developed for attention (Cohen, Dunbar, & McClelland, 1990), memory (Raaijmakers & Shiffrin, 1981; McClelland & Rumelhart, 1986), word recognition (Rumelhart & McClelland, 1987), language comprehension (Thibadeau, Just, & Carpenter, 1982), and problem solving (Holyoak & Thagard, 1989). These models are usually designed to simulate the response patterns observed in experiments. When there is a discrepancy between the program output and the human data, the theorist changes specific aspects of the computer model to bring its output and the data into closer agreement. The computer simulation is a model of the skill, much like hydraulic models are used to represent the function of the heart and the circulatory system (Just & Carpenter, 1987).

CONCLUSION: WHAT TO EXPECT AS YOU STUDY COGNITIVE PSYCHOLOGY

This introductory chapter gave you a flavor of cognitive psychology; it emerged from different disciplines and is devoted to a wide range of issues. As you read the following chapters, you will discover that there is no single theory that has all the answers. The issues are too complex and therefore permit a variety of viewpoints. There is no single authority to adjudicate an issue and to settle which theory is correct. This is something you should appreciate from the outset, otherwise you will be confused and disappointed; it is rare that investigators come up with lasting conclusions. Learning about cognition involves learning the questions that investigators ask, the approach they use to address the issues, and the hypotheses they propose. You will find that the basic questions about mental representations and processes change relatively little over time. Similarly, the basic approaches and the terminology do not change all that much, at least not within a decade.

It is important to learn basic specialties of cognitive psychology, including attention, pattern recognition, working memory, and long-term memory, as well as such concepts as association, automatic processing, encoding, expertise, imagery, inference, parallel processing, proposition, schema, and working memory capacity. These constructs are implicated in many cognitive processes and recur in most of the chapters. Because the experiment is the principal research tool of cognitive psychologists, you need to understand the theoretical issues motivating an experiment—its rationale and implications. Every chapter includes experiments, some of these are explained in detail to illustrate important paradigms, such as the memory scanning task, the multiframe search task, the item-recognition task, the lexical decision, the dual-task paradigm, the protocol method, and the on-line comprehension task.

Finally, it is important to remember the names of some noted cognitive psychologists, including John R. Anderson, Alan Baddeley, Irving Biederman, Fergus Craik, Elizabeth Loftus, James McClelland, Gail McKoon, Michael Posner, Lynne Reder, Richard Shiffrin, Herbert Simon, Saul Sternberg, and Anne Treisman. These and other researchers proposed important theories and designed informative research methods; they are responsible for the advances in cognition.

PREVIEW OF CHAPTERS

This chapter began with some potential applications of cognitive psychology. The major tradition in the field, however, is that of a basic science to understand the *principles* of cognition. The chapters of this book reflect that tradition. They also reflect the diversity of approaches in cognitive psychology. Some chapters emphasize computational approaches (Chapters 6 and 10), others explain theoretical representations and concepts (Chapters 5 and 10), and two chapters include a historical perspective (Chapters 1 and 7). Most chapters reflect the interplay of theory and experimentation characteristic of cognitive psychology.

Chapter 2 describes the neurobiological foundations of cognition at the level of neurons, the brain, and the sensory systems. Chapter 3 is devoted to attention; it treats stimulus information at its early stages in the information-processing system. Chapter 4 discusses recognition and action; recognition refers to the process of identifying objects and events in the environment; action includes the planning and execution of movements. Chapters 5 and 6 are concerned with the representation of knowledge in terms of both the symbol processing and neural network approaches. Chapters 7 through 9 are devoted to learning and memory. Chapter 7 presents classical research in learning and memory from the turn of the century onward. Chapter 8 discusses theories and research of working memory, considered to be the principal processor of cognition, and Chapter 9 treats long-term memory. Chapters 10 and 11 are concerned with language and language processing. Each of the remaining chapters treats cognitive skills as well. Chapter 12 discusses reading and writing. Problem solving and reasoning are described in Chapters 13 and 14, respectively.

Ultimately, the test of success for theory and research in a field, including cognitive psychology, lies in its applications. Indeed, early cognitive researchers had an interest in applications, especially in improving education, learning, and teaching. Human factors researchers investigated human performance and perception under stress (e.g., in military applications and communication). Applications of cognitive psychology will be mentioned throughout, and Chapter 15 discusses applications in such selected areas as human factors, education, law enforcement, and medicine. There exists a tension between basic researchers and those who seek to apply cognitive psychology. The basic researchers seek to control a variety of factors that might influence performance in a task. Isolating variables in the laboratory, however, removes the phenomenon from the real world and its complexity. This is the paradox: On the one hand, the researcher can make more valid predictions in the laboratory; on the other, the scope of those predictions may be too narrow and removed from the real world.

There are different emphases within cognitive psychology; these include individual differences, cognitive development, social cognition, and human and artificial intelligence. Some of these are addressed within the context of different chapters. Developmental perspectives are included in Chapters 11 and 13, on language comprehension and problem solving, respectively. Human intelligence is discussed in Chapters 8, 13, and 14. Contributions from artificial intelligence to cognitive psychology are so pervasive that they are included in most of the chapters. Cognitive psychology has been influenced by related disciplines and a variety of research traditions. In turn, it has had an impact on other cognitive and psychological sciences, from linguistics and artificial intelligence to social and developmental psychology.

COGNITIVE NEUROSCIENCE

PREVIEW

Neuroscience has had a profound influence on our conceptions of cognitive processes. This chapter begins with a description of the imaging and electrophysiological methods that have given neuroscience its prominence. The second section of the chapter treats the neurobiological foundation of cognition from neurons and neural circuits to subcortical and cortical structures in the brain. The neuron is the building block of the nervous system; it is a communication station that transmits information along its projections and across synapses to other neurons. Communication within a neuron is recorded as the propagation of action potentials along the axon. Networks of neurons are malleable and are implicated in several types of learning, as we will see when we examine learning effects at the behavioral and neural levels.

The third section of the chapter discusses the brain, with emphasis on the cortex and the hippocampus. The cortex controls cognitive operations—our sensations, perceptions, and memories. Anatomically, it consists of two hemispheres, each composed of four lobes—the frontal, parietal, temporal, and occipital lobes. The latter three are involved in sensory processing. Though we know the frontal lobes control motor behavior and play a role in memory and language functions, details remain obscure. The left and right hemispheres of the brain duplicate some functions; however, several important functions, including language, are asymmetric. The hippocampus, located adjacent to the interior temporal lobe, is an important site for declarative memory functions. It has been implicated in the organization and consolidation of newly acquired information. This section of the chapter also discusses sensory systems focusing on the auditory and visual systems. Information is transduced by receptor neurons and sent via nuclei in the brain stem and thalamus to the sensory projection areas in the cortex. Chapter 2 concludes with a discussion of what we can and cannot learn about cognition from the insights of neuroscience.

INTRODUCTION

If you could look beneath the human skull, you would first see a light gray substance that is soft to the touch, irrigated with blood vessels, and covered with elevations and valleys. This is the brain—the organ that controls feeling, cognition, and other basic functions. The brain includes billions of nerve cells, the neurons, and supporting tissue. It has long been the object of speculation for scientists and philosophers who want to know whether the brain and mind are related and, if so, how they are related.

Although mind and body are very different entities, scholars have been convinced that the two must interact in some fashion. Descartes, for example, thought animal spirits were the communicating agents and the pineal gland in the brain stem acted as the gate between mind and brain; however, he did not offer any further details. The search for the link between mind and brain occupied physiologists and psychologists—including Mueller, Helmholtz, Cajal, Sherrington, James, Lashley, Hebb, and Eccles—for several centuries. By the time psychology emerged as an independent science in the late nineteenth century, the dependence of mental processes on brain states was taken for granted. William James expressed this view as follows: "I assume without scruple at the outset that the uniform correlation of brain states with mind states is a law of nature" (1892, p. 6). Today, nobody debates whether the brain and the mind are related; rather, scientists debate whether one can study the mind without considering neural and brain processes. Some say that information processing should be studied separately from neuroscience. Others argue that because cognition depends on the brain, cognitive research must be based on brain research.

At first glance, the neuroscientific approach to cognition seems correct; how could we study learning, memory, language, and other cognitive processes without knowing their basis in the central nervous system? In the past, cognitive psychologists used to respond to this question with a computer analogy: A computer has a hardware component—the physical machine that includes circuit boards and memory chips—and a software component—the systems and applications programs. One can understand a computer and use it well without knowing hardware particulars. Similarly, we can understand mental processes without knowing how they are implemented in the brain. Expressing the standard view of cognitive psychologists, Anderson wrote that "cognitive psychology is to physiological psychology much as computer science is to electrical engineering" (1980, p. 12). The relationship between cognition and neuroscience was acknowledged but not pursued, and barring exceptions, cognition and neuroscience remained separate fields of study throughout the 1960s and 1970s. The computer was considered the model for mental processes and the mind. The belief was that cognitive processes could be simulated by any computer and that the hardware details were unimportant (Posner, 1989).

Advances in the neurosciences have changed the functionalist approach to cognition. Even the functionalists now acknowledge the important differences between computers and brains (see Table 2.1) and agree that computer models should be consistent with our knowledge of the brain. That knowledge has been expanding rapidly, thanks to the development of new research and observational techniques.

The new research paradigms, along with traditional anatomical and behavioral methods, have been put to effective use by cognitive neuroscientists as they seek to fulfill their goal of looking for parallels between neural and cognitive phenomena. As we shall see, researchers have discovered many such parallels: Learning phenomena have been correlated with neural activity in the cerebellum and brain stem, perceptual effects can be traced to certain regions in the thalamus and cerebral cortex, and deficits in short-term memory and language have their source in the temporal lobe (Shallice & Vallar, 1990). Speculations abound concerning these relatively recent discov-

TABLE 2.1   Differences between the Brain and Today's Computers

1. The brain has 10^{12} neurons. At any instant, hundreds of thousands of neurons are communicating with each other. This vast exchange of information is more complex than that possible with even the most ambitious computers in existence today. The brain is highly interconnected, although not everything is connected to everything else.
2. Signal transmissions in the brain depend on chemical neurotransmitters. In a computer, signals are transmitted electronically through hard-wired links.
3. In a computer, information is coded through 0s and 1s, a binary code. In the brain, information is coded in terms of the frequency of spikes of neurons (see Figure 2.6).
4. Most computers have a single central processing unit (some have a few CPUs). In the brain, however, each neuron is a powerful processor. The neuron combines excitatory and inhibitory signals and when a certain threshold strength is exceeded, the neuron produces its own signal.
5. Typically, in the brain, many neurons work in parallel to complete a certain process. In a computer, work is completed sequentially, though each individual processing step is completed much more quickly. Though silicon cells work much faster than neurons, object recognition is much faster in people than computers (Feldman, 1985).
6. Computer components are discrete and separable and one can easily replace them. This is not the case with the brain (Sejnowski & Churchland, 1989).
7. The human brain has natural plasticity. Learning is its typical mode, which is not true of computers; to get computers to learn is a major effort.
8. The brain is spontaneous; a computer is not.
9. The human brain is a biological entity: It is born, grows, matures, collects information, may get sick, and eventually dies. The computer does what it is told by a brain.
10. Memories in the brain are content addressable; in computers, memories are addressed by their location.

eries, making for a rapidly changing and exciting field. The pioneers of the new cognitive neuroscience include researchers interested in attention, perception, learning, psycholinguistics, and connectionist models.

The purpose of this chapter is to share this excitement by providing you with a background on neuroscience, highlighting those cases where a parallel between mental and neural operations has been determined. There are also limits of the new approach; these will be discussed in the conclusion.

Following is a discussion of the research methods that have changed the field and an examination of neural as well as global brain processes. At the neural level, we will study neurons, synapses, networks, and communication within and between neurons. Among brain systems, we will discuss the brain stem, the hippocampus, the neocortex, and the auditory and visual systems.

RESEARCH METHODS IN NEUROSCIENCE

More than anything else, it was the development of powerful research tools—imaging, event-related potentials, and population analysis—that propelled neuroscience to its prominence in the cognitive sciences and in the public eye. The procedures underlying these tools had been known for quite some time. However, combined with the computer, a new generation of techniques has been emerging that is light years away from its ancestors. The computer enabled researchers to record and combine massive amounts of data and to obtain both spatial and temporal perspectives of the brain that previously were not attainable. Although we may be tempted to feel that we are about to unlock the final mysteries of the brain, the research pioneers themselves acknowledge the limits of the new methods and exercise caution in their interpretation of research results. Generally, scientists accord more credibility to those interpretations that are based on converging evidence from different techniques used together.

The imaging techniques and the electrical recording methods described next changed the field of neuroscience, which up to this time had relied exclusively on such classical methods as animal studies, anatomical studies, and clinical case studies. In animal studies, scientists extrapolate from processes observed in animals to the human. Anatomical studies use staining techniques to trace neural structures and pathways. In clinical case studies, inferences about function and localization are based on correlations between structural injuries and cognitive impairments. All of these methods are still in use today; however, they have been complemented with the newer techniques described next: imaging methods, recording techniques for event-related potentials, and population studies.

Imaging Methods

Imaging methods date from the early twentieth century, when German radiologist Wilhelm Roentgen (1845–1923) passed x-rays through patients' limbs and organs. In the 1970s, **computed tomography (CT) scan** was introduced. Computed tomography combines radiography and computer analysis. A person's head (or other body part) is placed in a tire-shaped ring that contains both an x-ray emitter and a detector on opposite sides of the head. X-rays are projected through several planes of the brain, the radiation passing the brain is recorded, then the ring is rotated a few degrees and the procedure is repeated. By recording x-rays of several different planes, the computer constructs a three-dimensional image of specific brain structures. CT scans are useful to analyze static brain structures; they are not

as useful, however, for the study of cognitive processes because the latter occur in real time. The positron emission tomography (PET) and functional magnetic resonance imaging (fMRI) procedures permit researchers to investigate mental operations on line (see Chapter 1). Both are based on the idea that thinking, even when it is as easy as recalling a single word, requires measurable physical energy.

Positron Emission Tomography.   The **positron emission tomography (PET) scan** detects changes in blood flow in particular brain regions. This technique is based on the discovery dating from the 1920s that mental work increases the flow of blood in specific regions of the brain. Posner and Raichle (1994) described the case of Walter K., a patient of Harvey Cushings and John Fulton, two famous Boston physicians. Walter K. had suffered terrible headaches for several years and complained of deteriorating vision. The physicians were able to treat both of these conditions to some extent. Of interest to our discussion is that in the course of examining Walter K. and using a stethoscope over the region of the visual cortex, the doctors could hear a pulsating sound, a *bruit,* whenever Walter K. opened his eyes. Stimulating other senses, such as smelling vanilla or listening to a record, did not produce the bruit. Therefore, the physicians attributed the sound to processing in the visual centers. Although the case of Walter K. was, of course, exceptional, the practice of measuring activity in the brain's regions by monitoring the blood flow continues to this day; it is, however, far more refined.

Today, cerebral blood flow is measured by injecting the patient with a nontoxic, slightly radioactive substance (e.g., glucose or oxygen-15) and monitoring the progress of the substance as it is absorbed by the blood and transported to the brain. As a specific brain region processes information and executes commands, its metabolic requirements increase relative to a resting condition. The radioactive substances in the blood are picked up by the PET scan and photographed, as shown in Figure 2.1. Investigators typically employ PET scans in conjunction with the **subtraction method;** in this paradigm, performance is compared between a baseline condition and a load condition (see Chapter 1). In the baseline condition, PET scans are taken while the subject simply rests; in various load conditions, the subject executes different cognitive and motor tasks.

The PET technique allows researchers to investigate dynamic processes as they occur. The temporal resolution of this technique, however, is insufficient. The recording time of PET images extends over minutes, whereas the cognitive phenomena (e.g., visual recognition) often take less than a second. It is for this reason that cognitive neuroscientists usually employ additional recording techniques to assess both the localization and the time course of mental activities. Good temporal resolution is achieved by magnetic resonance imaging (MRI) and recording event-related potentials (ERPs).

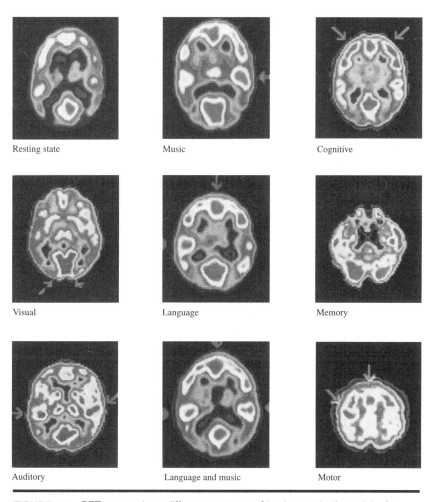

Resting state · Music · Cognitive

Visual · Language · Memory

Auditory · Language and music · Motor

FIGURE 2.1 PET scans show different patterns of brain metabolic activity for resting state and various tasks, including listening to music, solving a problem, perceiving visual and auditory stimuli, and listening to language.

Functional MRI. **Functional magnetic reso-nance imaging (fMRI)** does not require radioactive agents and is more sensitive than CT and PET scans. Yet, functional MRI can monitor changes in blood flow as brain regions plug away at a task or relax. Functional MRI is based on the properties of oxygen atoms in a magnetic field. The oxygen atoms inside and around blood vessels in the brain change according to the degree of blood flow in the vessel: When a brain region works hard, more blood and, as result, more oxygen are imported. Curiously, the oxygen is not consumed by the neurons in the brain region. This leads to a transitory surplus of oxygen in the blood vessel that is picked up by fMRI (Raichle, 1994).

Illustrative Results from Imaging Studies. Using PET and fMRI scans, scientists can watch the brain at work. They can find out the locations of specific cognitive functions in the brain; they can examine changes in brain metabolism as learners continue to practice a skill; and, using imaging methods, they can study similarities and differences in brain action between different populations (discussed later in this chapter).

Localization. Posner and colleagues (e.g., 1988) used PET scans in conjunction with the subtraction method to detect cortical centers implicated in visual and acoustic processing. In the baseline condition, the subjects were told to fixate on a cross presented on a computer screen; researchers recorded the blood flow in different cortical regions (e.g., the parietal and the occipital lobes). In the visual load condition, words were presented on a screen and subjects read the words. The PET scan established that blood flow in the occipital lobe increased relative to the baseline condition as well as relative to auditory brain centers. In the auditory load condition, the scientists presented words over headphones and recorded the brain activity in both the auditory and visual centers. When subjects listened, blood flow increased in auditory centers related to language processing but not in the visual centers (McCarthy et al., 1993).

Researchers observed differential localizations even for processes that share the same modality—namely, vision. When subjects look at words or at letterlike patterns such as an inverted *A* or a reversed *J,* for example, PET activity increases in the primary visual areas of the brain. Looking at words and pseudowords—such as *geel, reld,* and *aldober*—produces PET activity elsewhere—namely, along the inner surface of the left hemisphere. In sum, PET recordings reveal activation of different brain regions for different mental activities both across and within modalities. Because the activations are uniquely localized, they cannot be attributed to some diffuse general activation in the nervous system.

Practice Effects. PET research has shown that the level of brain activity depends on the familiarity of a task. If the task is new, the brain centers must work harder and use more blood to sustain the activity; once accustomed to a task, the blood flow diminishes. Haier and colleagues (1992) recorded PET scans from subjects at various stages of learning to play the computer game Tetris. The game involves such visuo-spatial skills as transforming squares and generating complex patterns. People participated for 30 to 60 minutes every day for one to two months. At the beginning of training, high PET activity was recorded from the spatial centers in the brain. Once the Tetris players had become experts, however, the activity in the spatial centers relaxed—playing the game had become automatic. Posner and colleagues reported a similar decrease in PET activity in the left temporal lobes and in the motor areas of volunteers who repeatedly came up with verbs for specific nouns.

Event-Related Potentials

Neurons continuously generate electrical impulses as they become more or less active in the course of fulfilling their function. The activity of a single neuron is, of course, very weak. In concert, however, the millions of neurons generate activity sufficiently strong to be detected at the surface of the skull. Researchers record this activity as brain waves, technically known as an **electroencephalogram (EEG).** EEGs are measured by placing electrodes on multiple sites on the skull. An **event-related potential (ERP)** is a pattern of brain wave activity obtained by averaging EEG patterns recorded over as many as 100 trials (e.g., Kutas & Hillyard, 1980). The ERP exhibits characteristic peaks of electrical activity that begin a few milliseconds after stimulus onset and last almost a second. This time-locked property makes the ERP useful as an index of mental processing. The peaks are either negative (N) or positive (P) at certain latencies after stimulus onset. For example, peaks are labeled N400 or P560 to indicate direction of amplitude and latency in milliseconds. Researchers have identified specific peak formations associated with cognitive operations in perception and comprehension.

ERPs have been used for chronometric analyses of cognitive processes as well as for the localization of function. Research on temporal patterns is illustrated by the work of Hillyard and colleagues on the brain's reaction to surprising events, including unusual expressions or unexpected changes in the physical shape of words. In one of their experiments, Kutas and Hillyard (1980) presented about 50 sentences like *He spread the warm bread with socks* and *The leopard is a very good napkin* interspersed among 160 normal sentences like *It was his first day at work.* There were also sentences in which the font of certain target words differed from the prior context. Presumably, subjects found the font change surprising. ERP responses to expected phrases as well as to surprising words are shown in Figure 2.2. Semantically anomalous words elicited N400 peaks, and physically surprising words resulted in P560 peaks.

Posner and Raichle (1994) used the ERP technique to find brain locations implicated in a mental activity. The two researchers recorded ERP patterns as subjects were making a quick association to a given word. They found three successive waves of increased ERP activity in the left lateral frontal cortex, the left posterior cortex, and the

right insular cortex. What is remarkable about this study is that it mirrors the PET activity recorded from the same brain regions in a companion experiment. Here, we have an instance of **convergence of evidence** that researchers are looking for when they measure mental processes (see Hillyard & Kutas, 1983). Convergence of evidence means that similar results are observed for the same task when different measures of mental activity are recorded. In Posner and Raichle's (1994) research, the two methods complement one another very nicely: ERPs offer temporal resolution on the order of milliseconds, but their spatial resolution is not very good. PET scans offer very good spatial resolution, but the temporal resolution leaves much to be desired. Used in tandem, the two methods can pinpoint both the location and the temporal pattern of brain activity.

Because the ERP patterns reflect automatic brain activity not under the control of the person, researchers have begun exploring it as a tool to detect concealed thoughts—as another "lie detector" so to speak. Bashore and Rapp (1993) showed that people have difficulty concealing the fact that they are familiar with specific target in-

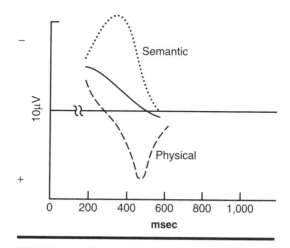

FIGURE 2.2 Event-related potentials recorded when subjects read a normal phrase (straight line), an anomalous phrase (dotted line), and a phrase in a font different from the context (dashed line) (Kutas & Hillyard, 1980).

formation. The Bashore and Rapp study included three phases: a training phase, a testing phase, and a concealment phase. During the training phase, subjects committed a list of words to memory, which they did easily enough as indicated by their success in the testing phase. In testing, the subjects were shown old and new words and they had to press a key when they recognized one of the memorized words. In the concealment phase, the learners were shown another list of words that included some of the previously learned ones. However, this time they were to conceal their knowledge of the memorized items. In other words, they were *not* to press the key when a target word appeared. Subjects succeeded in this overt task; however, their ERP patterns exhibited a P300 wave. Whenever a target word was shown, the P300 gave their knowledge away! Because subjects sought to conceal their knowledge as one does when one feels guilty, this methodology is known as the Guilty Knowledge Test.

Useful as the ERP measure is, many details of mental processing (e.g., on language processing) remain hidden. Although ERPs can pick up processing differences between content words (e.g., nouns and verbs) and function words (e.g., articles, prepositions, etc.), these are very broad categories; psycholinguists are usually interested in much finer distinctions (see Chapters 10 and 11). ERPs do not have the resolution to illuminate these distinctions (Zurif, 1990). Also, ERPs cannot detect neural activity that is not projected to the scalp or masked by other electrical activity. Scientists are on the march to refine ERP measurements and to develop new magnetic enscelephalographic measures. In fact, ERPs have already proven useful to researchers studying attention, signal detection, and visual imagery (see Chapters 3 and 15). ERPs have the advantage that they can be monitored throughout a task without interrupting or altering performance.

Magnetoencephalography (MEG) is the latest entrant in the growing field of recording tools. MEG patterns are recorded from the surface of the scalp, as are ERPs, and its recordings are based on magnetic fields generated by electrical activity in neurons. The MEG promises still finer resolution than either MRI or ERP (see Raichle, 1994).

The imagery and electrophysiological methods have enriched scientists' knowledge to a remarkable extent: Neuroscientists have made advances in localizing perceptual processes, they have identified changes in brain metabolism as a function of learning, and they have traced the time course of mental processes down to millisecond accuracy. A good question for you to consider is: Can these imaging methods be used to read a person's mind and thoughts? If your answer is affirmative, find supportive evidence; if it is negative, try to determine which improvements would be necessary to achieve the goal of mind reading.

Population Analysis and Case Studies

Cognitive psychology inherited from experimental psychology its emphasis on the idealized person, presumably represented by the average performance of subjects in an experimental condition. Differences between people were considered as a distraction, at best. Through the increasing interdisciplinary work with allied fields, especially neuropsychology, studies of individual case studies and of group differences became an important source of expanding our understanding of cognitive processes in general. Differences between individuals came to be viewed as a natural experiment on the cognitive architecture rather than as an error of observation.

Population Differences.   Population differences can be observed under a variety of conditions: in psychometric tests, in performance on a real-world task, or in controlled experiments. Consider a set of results from PET imaging studies. Such studies have revealed different patterns of brain activity in different people, even when they are executing what, on the surface, appears to be the same task. For example, in the free-recall paradigm, learners recall a list of words read to them by the experimenter. Typically, people do reasonably well recalling a fair proportion of the list. PET scans tell us that different learners favor different brain regions when they try to memorize the words (Posner & Raichle, 1994). Scientists recorded PET scans from the volunteers and found that in some subjects, the acoustic brain areas lit up, as though subjects were *rehearsing* the words; in other subjects, the visual regions were active, as though the individuals were *visualizing* the words.

Consider another study of individual differences. Scientists had a group of volunteers take the same IQ test. You already know that some people tend to do better than others in objective IQ tests. Haier (1993) found that the high-scoring volunteers exhibited less blood flow activity in several cortical regions, including the left temporal and frontal lobes, than subjects achieving average scores. This was puzzling to the researchers until they arrived at an explanation that they labeled the **efficiency hypothesis.** According to this hypothesis, highly intelligent people use their brains more efficiently and thus require less blood flow to solve problems, whereas individuals of average intelligence have to invest more effort and brain activity in solving the same problems. (Haier sees this result as parallel to the finding that experts' brains are less active in performing a task.)

In 1995, a study of group differences in brain functioning made the media. The results reportedly told a "tale of different brains" in men and women. Here is what the fuss was all about: Using fMRI, Shaywitz and an interdisciplinary team of colleagues (1995) detected sex differences in phonological processing in the brain. These researchers had a group of men and women work on four cognitive tasks while researchers recorded magnetic resonance images throughout the cortex. One of the tasks was a control task requiring the subjects to compare the length of two lines. The three experimental tasks involved linguistic comparisons—whether a pair of letters was identical, whether two words had the same meaning, and whether a pair of words was a rhyme. Needless to say, both men and women completed all four tasks successfully. The surprise comes when one compares the pattern of brain activity across the three linguistic tasks. For the letter recognition and word meaning task, both men and women activated regions in the left temporal lobe. However, for the rhyming task, the pattern differed in men and women. The inferior frontal region in the left hemisphere was active in men, but the corresponding regions of *both* hemispheres were active in women.

These results are certainly intriguing and might encourage the notion that language processing is more localized in men than in women. However, for two reasons this conclusion is not warranted. First, phonological processing is but a small component of language, and men's and women's brain activity did not differ for the two other linguistic tasks. Second, results based on another methodology, electrical stimulation mapping, suggest the opposite interpretation— namely, that language processing is less localized in men than in women. Using the mapping technique, scientists found that language-related sites are distributed over a wider brain region in men than in women (Ojemann, 1991; Chapter 11). For the moment, then, one can only conclude, as do Shaywitz and colleagues (1995, p. 609), that future research is necessary to uncover brain processes in language and any differences between the sexes.

In general, as exciting as discoveries of group differences are, caution is indicated in interpreting the findings of population studies. Such studies yield correlational data; they do not isolate the causes of the observed group differences. As for clinical populations, an additional problem exists: Averaging performance across clinical cases is problematic because each injury tends to be unique.

Case Studies. In clinical case studies, inferences about the localization of function are made by correlating a specific cognitive deficit with anatomical impairments in the brain. Here are a few illustrations of this approach.

- Paul Broca (1824–1880) discovered a lesion in the left frontal lobe of an aphasic patient and reasoned that this region is implicated in speech production.

— The role of the striate cortex in visual processing became known through an examination of soldiers who suffered injuries to the striate area and who became blind as a result.

— The memory loss of Korsakoff patients has been attributed to an organic deterioration in the hippocampus region.

These and other cases involve accidents or degenerative diseases. Neuroscientists have drawn similar inferences from patients who underwent surgery. For example, scientists advanced hypotheses about hemispheric specialization based on split-brain surgery. This procedure has been used in patients who suffer from severe epileptic seizures. Frequently, such seizures start in one hemisphere and spread to the other. Lesioning of the corpus callosum, the body of fibers communicating between the left and right hemispheres, limits the spread of the seizure much like a fire door stops a spreading fire. After the operation, patients appear normal, but careful analysis reveals characteristic deficits. The diagnosis is based on the anatomy and projections of the visual pathway. Information in the left visual field is projected to the right hemisphere, whereas information in the right visual field is sent to the left hemisphere. Usually, this is not problematic because the two hemispheres communicate. However, when the corpus callosum is severed, the two hemispheres function independently and one side no longer knows what the other is doing (Gazzaniga, LeDoux, & Wilson, 1977). Tests show dissociations between language and performance; information that does not reach the left hemisphere cannot be verbalized, but the subject can act on the information and has some knowledge of it!

Although case studies are useful tools for neuroscientists, they are not without problems. By definition, case studies involve unusual instances and a small number of typically impaired individuals. Several cognitive scientists have cautioned about generalizing from impaired to nonimpaired individuals (Sejnowski & Churchland, 1989). In addition, it is possible that any damage to an area does not remain strictly localized but, unknown to the researcher, influences other brain areas as well. Case studies are most useful when employed in conjunction with one of the other methods. For example, Broca's discovery of the laterality of language has since been corroborated by using other methods (and many other case studies). As is true in cognitive psychology in general, when case studies are used along with other methods, they can give rise to important ideas and help illuminate issues.

INTERIM SUMMARY

Neuroscience has come to occupy central stage among the cognitive sciences, in part as a result of the innovative imaging and electrophysiological techniques. Imaging techniques include the computed tomographic (CT) scan, the positron emission tomography (PET) scan, and functional magnetic resonance imaging (fMRI). Neuroscientists also use electrophysiological recordings such as event-related potentials (ERPs), population studies, and clinical case studies. Tomographic scans are based on x-ray photography or on magnetic resonance imaging; they are used to observe brain structures. PET scans and fMRI are used to detect the degree of blood flow in specific cerebral regions as the person engages in cognitive activities, such as listening and reading. ERPs are based on repeated recordings of the electrical activity of the brain during mental activity. Population studies examine to what extent various subject groups exhibit differences in neural processes in order to execute the same task. Conclusions from clinical case studies are based on correlating performance deficits with anatomical deficits. All of these methods are best used in conjunction with each other and with performance studies.

NEURONS AND NEURAL CIRCUITS

Spanish anatomist Santiago Ramon y Cajal (1852–1934) was the first researcher to show that neurons are the smallest units of the nervous system (*neuron* is the Greek word for *nerve*). He described the neuron as a communication station. Subsequent research has shown that signals travel within, as well as between, neurons. A signal passes from one neuron to the next at the synapse, the small gap between neurons (*synapse* is the Greek word for *union*).

Human neurons are similar to those in simpler organisms; they have the same basic anatomy and neurochemistry. You may wonder how a simple neuron could support such cognitive functions as attention, perception, memory, and learning, and indeed the human intellect and all its achievements. The answer lies in the fact that the human brain contains many neurons, as many as 10^{12} (Churchland & Sejnowski, 1992). Neurons are multiply connected, forming innumerable networks, each capable of learning. This section reviews the structure of neurons, communication within and between neurons, and changes in neural processes that are observed in such learning situations as habituation, conditioning, and long-term potentiation.

Neurons

A neuron is enclosed by a membrane, which includes the cell body (the soma) and projections (axons and dendrites), as shown in Figure 2.3. The **soma** contains the nucleus and tissue that supports the operation of the cell. The **axon** is a long extension, similar to a tube, that conducts electrical impulses to the terminal buttons. The terminal buttons send chemically coded information to neighboring neurons across the synapse. On the other side of the synapse, information is received by the cell body and via the **dendrites.** The dendrites are treelike projections; usually they are much shorter than the axons. Do not be misled by the simplicity of Figure 2.3. Neurons are not simple, nor are they uniform; they vary in size, shape, and function. Some have few and simple terminals, whereas others, such as the Purkinje cells in the cerebellum, sprout a veritable forest of terminals. Neurons exist in the highest density in the neocortex, where there are approximately 100,000 per cubic millimeter of cortical tissue (Sejnowski & Churchland, 1989). Neurons

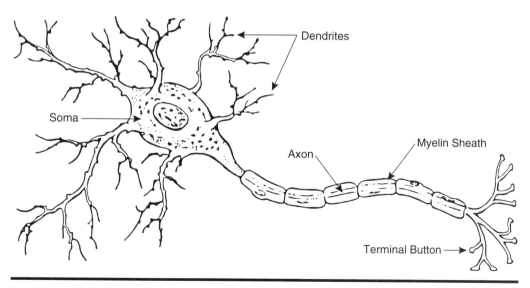

FIGURE 2.3 A neuron includes the soma, the cell body, and two types of projections: the axons and the treelike dendrites. Axons may be covered with sheaths of myelin. At their ends, axons have terminal buttons (Carlson, 1991).

are supported by the glia cells. They are easily distinguished; neurons are gray and glia cells are white. Glia cells provide an insulating envelope around neurons and axons called the *myelin sheath.*

Neurons communicate with each other, as well as with sensory organs, muscles, and other organs. Sensory neurons are located in sensory receptors. They transduce the physical energy from environmental stimuli into neural activity. Motor neurons originate in the cranial nerves (from the Latin *cranium* for *head*) and spinal cord; they control facial, head, and skeletal muscles.

A **synapse** is the junction between two neurons; here, the membranes of two neurons come into close vicinity (see Figure 2.4). The distance between neurons is about 200 angstroms. Because synapses are so small, each neuron can accommodate many of them. It is estimated that there are 6,000 synapses for each of the 50,000 neurons in a cat's visual cortex, making for a total of 300 million. There are an estimated 60 trillion (60 × 10^{12}) synapses in the human cortex (Shepard & Koch, 1990).

The structure and function of most human synapses is fairly similar. Most pass information in a one-way manner; usually, one neuron sends information and another receives it. The membrane of the sender is called the *presynaptic membrane;* it is opposite the receiving neuron, which is called the *postsynaptic membrane.*

Neuroscientists have a variety of techniques at their disposal to study the structure of neurons, including radiographic and microscopic techniques. Radiographic techniques were developed to investigate processing in neural pathways. Nontoxic radioactive substances are injected into specific structures and, using x-rays, their passage through the fibers is monitored. Slices of neural tissue as thin as 1 to 50 µm are examined microscopically (a µm, a micrometer, is 1/1,000 of a millimeter, or a millionth of a meter). Under electron microscopes, distances as small as angstroms (one ten-millionth of a meter) are discernible and synapses are visible. The microscopic images are enhanced by specialized computer programs to

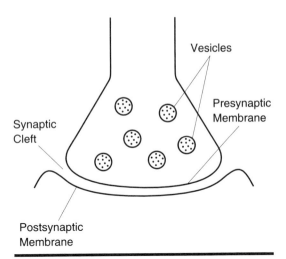

FIGURE 2.4   A synapse, formed by the terminal button of the sending neuron and the membrane of the receiving neuron. The sending neuron includes vesicles that contain neurotransmitters.

open new vistas into the inner frontier of the nervous system.

Communication within a Neuron: Action Potentials.   First and foremost, neurons are communication stations; signals travel within neurons along axons and between neurons. We will first consider communication within the axon and then transmission of neural impulses at the synapse. Neural transmission is different from electrical messages in a wire; the former is based on electrophysiological and neurochemical processes. Neurophysiologists have investigated the electrical activity in squid axons, which have a diameter of up to 1 millimeter (mm), which is about 100 times the size of human axons. Size is an advantage here! Squid axons communicate with a group of muscles that expel water from the body, thus propelling the squid through water.

In order to measure communication impulses in the squid axon, a fine microelectrode is placed inside the axon and another on the axon's membrane. At rest, the inside of the axon is slightly negative, relative to the outside, −70 millivolts, a state known as **polarization** (see Figure 2.5A). This state is the result of electrophysiological and chemical processes at the membrane. The membrane controls the flow of electrically charged particles, the ions, to and from the axon. When the axon is briefly stimulated, the balance of the ions inside and outside the axon changes. As a result, there is a momentary reversal in polarity. The inside becomes depolarized—that is, positive relative to the outside (see Figure 2.5B). The spike in activity is called the **action potential.** It lasts less than a millisecond and is followed by a negative potential that overshoots the resting potential by a small amount, known as **hyperpolarization.** If no further stimulus is applied, activity returns to its polarized resting potential, as shown in Figure 2.5C.

Stimulating the membrane at a given location is like throwing a pebble into water. The effects of the stimulus radiate from the point of impact to other points. A stimulus first changes the permeability of the membrane at one point, and then adjacent regions of the membrane change their permeability and become depolarized. In this fashion, the action potential is propagated along the axon toward the terminal buttons. Transmission speed along axons varies from 1 to 120 meters per second, depending on the diameter of the axon and the type of neuron sheathing; generally, it is faster in thicker axons and in axons sheathed with myelin.

Communication across the Synaptic Cleft. When the "wave of activity" reaches the terminal buttons of the presynaptic membrane, the terminal buttons secrete chemical substances known as **neurotransmitters.** These travel across the synaptic cleft to the postsynaptic membrane of the receiving neuron, where they are chemically bound to receptor molecules. As a result, the permeability of the postsynaptic membrane is changed in an excitatory or inhibitory manner, depending on the particular neurotransmitter and on the specific receptor where the transmitter arrives.

Excitation at the postsynaptic membrane involves a slight decrease in the negativity of the

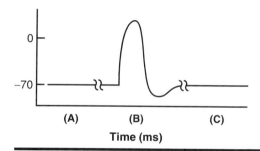

FIGURE 2.5 Electrical activity prior to stimulation (*A*), during stimulation (*B*), and after stimulation of the neuron (*C*): (*A*) Potential at rest shows polarization at –70mV. (*B*) Action potential when a stimulus is applied. (*C*) Resting level after stimulation.

resting potential, the **excitatory postsynaptic potential (EPSP).** Inhibition, on the other hand, involves a slight increase in the negativity of the resting potential, the **inhibitory postsynaptic potential (IPSP).** These postsynaptic potentials change in proportion with the intensity of the stimulating neurotransmitters; their responses are said to be **graded.**

Postsynaptic potentials at a single synapse do not have much of an effect on the rest of the neuron. However, the activity summed across thousands of synapses may trigger an electrical action in the neuron as a whole. When the aggregate stimulation is sufficient, an action potential results. Unlike postsynaptic potentials, the action potentials are formed according to the **all-or-none principle:** The neuron responds either with constant amplitude or not at all. The amplitude of the action potential does not change with the intensity of the aggregate stimulation. If the stimulation is too weak and falls below a certain **threshold,** the neuron does not respond beyond its resting activity.

The aggregate stimulation is the net result of all postsynaptic potentials of a neuron according to the summation principle captured in expression (2.1).

(2.1) Net stimulation = Sum of all postsynaptic potentials

If the stimulation is stronger than the threshold, the neuron fires a series of action potentials, as shown in Figure 2.6A. As the intensity of the stimulation increases, the neuron's firing rate increases, as illustrated in Figures 2.6B and C. When excitatory and inhibitory postsynaptic potentials cancel each other out, there is no action potential. When the excitatory potentials outweigh the inhibitory potentials, a lower firing rate results.

The neurotransmitter remains in the synaptic cleft only long enough to stimulate receptors in the postsynaptic membrane. Any excess neurotransmitter is taken up by receptacles in the terminal bulb of the presynaptic axon for later transmission.

Neurotransmitters.   There are at least 50 known neurotransmitters; they are found throughout the central nervous system, the autonomic nervous system, and the skeletal muscles. The nervous system is characterized by a great diversity of structure and function. The variety among the neurotransmitters matches that of the neural systems they serve. They differ in chemical structures, functions, and processing characteristics, and they excite, inhibit, or change the excitability of receptors, depending on the properties of the postsynaptic membrane they stimulate. Their time course varies; some are fast acting and some are slow. Because of the differences among neurotransmitters, you should not expect a global theory that explains them all; rather, researchers identify transmitters and their known functions. Box 2.1 lists some of the better-known neurotransmitters.

Neural Circuits, Neural Plasticity, and Learning

There is variety among neural circuits; some are simple microcircuits and others are complex and consist of configurations of microcircuits. One of the most important properties of neural circuits is that they are malleable; they can learn.

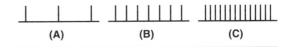

FIGURE 2.6   An increase in stimulus intensity causes a faster firing rate of the axon rather than increasing the amplitude of action potentials. Each "spike" represents an action potential such as the one in Figure 2.5B.

The capacity to learn supports an organism's adaptability to the environment. Psychologists have been intrigued by the neural basis of learning for some time. Hebb (1949) postulated the **cell assembly** as the critical building block of learning (see Figure 2.7).

According to Hebb, when two neurons are jointly activated, they become more closely linked. He imagined a biological growth process at the synapse that would increase the efficiency of transmitting impulses. Hebb's theory was debated for decades, and though some details remain unsupported, the consensus after nearly 50 years of research is that there are synaptic changes during learning (Hawkins & Bower, 1989). Hebb's contribution was significant because he was the first to develop testable hypotheses about the neurobiological basis of cognitive processes such as memory and learning. Putting it very simply, this was Hebb's hypothesis: Use of a function increases neural structure; disuse decreases it.

Changes in the Size of Neural Structure. Turner and Greenough (1985) found that in rats, both the size of synapses and their number increased as a result of learning. These researchers reared one group of rats in a stimulating environment (a cage with many toys and objects—a sort of "rat heaven") and another group in a boring environment. After training, the brains of the experimental animals, from neurons to global structures, were better developed than those of control animals. There were more capillaries and the surface area of their brains was larger. All told, the

Box 2.1

Some Important Neurotransmitters

— **Acetylcholine (ACh)** is found in nerves that serve the skeletal muscles, heart, and autonomic nervous system. It has an excitatory effect on skeletal fibers and an inhibitory effect on cardiac fibers. Acetylcholine is also found in the brain and has been implicated in memory and cognitive functions. It became well known when researchers discovered that the brains of Alzheimer's patients produce little acetylcholine; this may contribute to memory loss.

— **Dopamine** is said to contribute to attention, learning, and motor movement. It is disseminated from specific neurons in the brain and influences the activity of a large number of other neurons. It is for this reason that dopamine has been called a "neuromodulator" (Carlson, 1994). Like other transmitters, dopamine may act as an inhibitory or excitatory agent, depending on the receptor.

— **Norepinephrine (NE)** and **epinephrine** influence the degree of alertness in the brain. Norepinephrine

acts as an inhibitor in the central nervous system but has an excitatory effect in the autonomic nervous system. The action of these two neurotransmitters is influenced by drugs such as cocaine and amphetamine. Both of these drugs slow down the reuptake of norepinephrine and thereby prolong the activity of the receiver neuron, which is thought to give the person a stimulating experience.

— **Gamma-aminobutyric acid (GABA)** and **glutamic acid** are found throughout the brain; the first is inhibitory, the latter is excitatory. When GABA is applied to neural circuits and pathways, the neurons involved are inhibited.

— **Serotonin (5-HT)** has an inhibitory effect at both the synaptic and behavioral levels. Inhibition fulfills an important function in the nervous system. Without its dampening influence, excitation would travel from neuron to neuron throughout all systems and produce seizures.

---

stimulated rats thus had an advantage in processing information.

Nottebohm (1985) observed both increases and decreases in neural structure as a function of the degree of use. Investigating the song of the male canary, he found that two nuclei (HVc and

RA) in the canary's brain doubled in size as they were used during the singing season in fall and winter, yet they decreased in size during the silent season in the summer. Nottebohm believes that these nuclei support all functions related to song—namely, remembering, perceiving, and producing them. Although the type of neuronal changes that Nottebohm has documented in the canary have not been shown in primates, he believes that his discovery is nevertheless important: it demonstrates the correlation between neural change and performance.

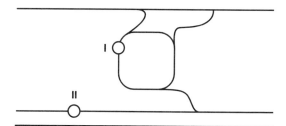

FIGURE 2.7 Simple cell assembly consisting of two neurons, I and II. Both neurons are excitable through external input. Impulses from I continue to excite the system itself and thus form a reverberating circuit.

Changes at the Synapse. Training can result in two kinds of synaptic change: the growth of more synapses or an improvement in synaptic transmission. There are several mechanisms of improving transmission at existing synapses. Some mechanisms operate at the presynaptic membrane; others operate at the postsynaptic membrane. In the presynaptic membrane, any of the following could increase: the number of vesicles that release neurotransmitters, the probability of releasing the neurotransmitter substance, and the rate of synthesizing or taking up the transmitter. At the postsynaptic membrane, the number of receptors could increase and the membrane properties could change so that the postsynaptic potential is propagated more effectively. Unfortunately, synaptic transmission can also diminish in pathological conditions—for example, in severe cases of Alzheimer's disease (Selkoe, 1991).

Improvements of synaptic transmission have been examined in such basic learning situations as habituation, sensitization, classical conditioning, and long-term potentiation. In each of these situations, as in all learning situations, performance changes as a result of experience (see Chapters 6 and 7).

Habituation refers to a decrease in the response of an organism to the repeated presentation of a stimulus, such as when you get used to the loud noise of jack hammers. Habituation is mediated by the central nervous system, unlike sensory adaptation, which is a peripheral effect at the sensory organs. **Sensitization** involves an increase in the response to a neutral stimulus if it was preceded by a painful and potentially noxious stimulus. People tend to get jumpy after hearing a gunshot, for example. **Classical conditioning** involves forming an association between a neutral stimulus (e.g., a bell) and a stimulus (e.g., food) that reflexively elicits a response. Pavlov called the latter the *unconditioned stimulus (US)* and the former the *conditioned stimulus (CS)*. Pavlov studied classical conditioning in dogs. Food causes a dog to salivate reflexively; this reflex is known as the *unconditioned response (UR)*. When a bell is sounded repeatedly as food is presented, the bell comes to elicit salivation, the *conditioned response (CR)*. (For more details, see Chapter 7.) **Long-term potentiation** is observed at hippocampal synapses in mammals. It refers to a response enhancement after rapid stimulation that may last up to several weeks.

Learning in the Sea Hare **Aplysia.**   A relatively simple mollusk, *Aplysia Californica,* the sea hare, lives in the Pacific Ocean off the California coast. It is 15 inches long and lives in sheltered mud flats below the low-tide line. *Aplysia* looks somewhat like a hare with fins. It has gills and a head with eyes and small feelerlike tentacles. Toward the back, it has a tail and a spout, called the *siphon,* for water intake and output. The siphon contracts reflexively when touched; the contraction is equivalent to withdrawal reflexes in vertebrae, except that the neural circuitry is much simpler in *Aplysia.*

Aplysia has several simple circuits, including the two circuits shown in Figure 2.8. The monosynaptic circuit involves two neurons: (1) the sensory neuron receives inputs from the siphon and (2) the motor neuron sends signals to the gill. The other circuit includes (1) the sensory neuron of the tail, (2) an interneuron, and (3) the motor neuron controlling the gill.

Habituation and Sensitization.   Kandel and colleagues (e.g., Castellucci & Kandel, 1976) studied habituation and sensitization in *Aplysia* by correlating its behavior and the rate of neurotransmitter release in the synapses. When initially touched, *Aplysia* vigorously retracted its siphon. After repeated touching, however, *Aplysia* habituated making a smaller withdrawal reflex. At the synaptic level, the behavioral habituation was correlated with reduced emission of neurotransmitter substance. Sensitization in *Aplysia* was produced by applying strong pressure to its head or tail, followed by repeated touching of the siphon. This procedure resulted in an increase of both the withdrawal reflex and neurotransmitter activity.

Classical Conditioning.   To demonstrate conditioning in *Aplysia,* Kandel and colleagues (e.g., Castellucci & Kandel, 1976) applied a gentle touch as the CS to the siphon, and an electrical shock, the US, to the tail. At the beginning of training, the touch produced no consistent siphon response. After about 10 trials of paired presenta-

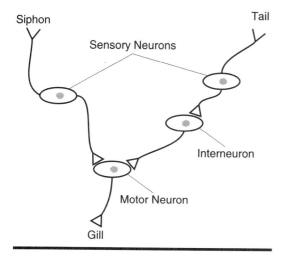

Siphon

Tail

Sensory Neurons

Interneuron

Motor Neuron

Gill

FIGURE 2.8 Two neural circuits in *Aplysia*. One circuit is monosynaptic; it includes a sensory neuron receiving input from the siphon and sending information to a motor neuron. The tail circuit involves two synapses. There is a sensory neuron, an interneuron, and the motor neuron.

tions of the two stimuli, however, there was a vigorous conditioned siphon withdrawal in response to the touch.

Aplysia is smart enough to discriminate between a CS paired with the US (the CS+) and a CS that has never been paired with the US (the CS–). The CS+ involved touching the mantle consistently in one location followed by presentation of the US. The CS– involved touching *Aplysia* in a different location without shock. After about 10 trials, *Aplysia* withdrew its siphon in response to the CS+, but did not respond to the CS–.

Conditioning was evident at the cellular level as well; the US activated the motor neuron, thus eliciting the unconditioned withdrawal. The US also caused an increase in the release of neurotransmitter substance from the sensory neurons. In discrimination learning, the CS+ produced an increase in neurotransmitter substance at the sensory neuron, but the CS– did not. Random presentation of the CS and US had no neural effect. The important factor that produces learning,

therefore, is the fact that the CS is a reliable predictor of the US.

The habituation and conditioning results in *Aplysia* are testimony to the learning at the neural level in mollusks. The following two sections will show that there is evidence of neural plasticity in mammals as well. One section treats long-term potentiation in rats; the other discusses conditioning in rabbits.

Long-Term Potentiation. Long-term potentiation has been observed at specific synapses in the hippocampus of rats (and rabbits). Experiments on long-term potentiation typically include three phases. During the first phase, the synapse is stimulated by brief individual pulses presented over several seconds. This procedure yields a baseline of response magnitude at the postsynaptic membrane. In the second phase, a rapid volley of impulses is fired at the synapse for up to five seconds at a rate of 100 impulses per second. In the third phase, individual slow test impulses are administered once again. Bliss and Lomo (1973) and subsequent researchers observed an increase in the postsynaptic response relative to the baseline; this enhancement is referred to as *long-term potentiation (LTP)*. It is long term because it may persist up to several weeks after the high-frequency stimulation is applied (Bliss & Lomo, 1973; Racine & de Jonge, 1988).

Long-term potentiation has been detected throughout the central nervous system but occurs primarily in the hippocampus, a region implicated in learning and memory. Researchers have been tempted to view LTP as support for Hebb's (1949) original learning theory of synaptic change. The relation between enhancement at the synaptic level, however, and learning at the behavioral level remains elusive, with some researchers claiming that they have found leads while others are more cautious.

One possible clue comes from a group of researchers who claim to have found a correlation between spatial learning in rats and LTP. The researchers used the drug AP5, which is known to retard long-term potentiation at the level of neurons in the hippocampus. They hoped to discover whether the drug would block the acquisition of overt spatial learning as well. They chose the water-maze paradigm, in which a rat must locate a block hidden in a small basin of muddy water. Finding the block would allow the rat to sit and rest rather than having to swim around. Learning to find the block is normally quite easy for the rats, but not when they are given AP5. This parallel between blocking of LTP at the microlevel and learning at the behavioral level was suggestive to the researchers. However, other scientists pointed out that the rats did, after all, learn the task, if at a slower rate (Churchland & Sejnowski, 1992, Chapter 5).

Conditioning in the Rabbit. Neuroscientists have uncovered correlates between synaptic and behavioral change in conditioning experiments with rabbits. Thompson (1986) investigated the neural activity in the rabbit's cerebellum and brain stem during eyelid conditioning. In eyelid conditioning, a puff of air is blown at the cornea of the eye. This is the US that causes an unconditioned eyelid closure. If you repeatedly present a tone CS together with the US (see Figure 2.9A), it will elicit a conditioned eyelid closure just prior to the US onset (shaded area in Figure 2.9D). An association is formed between the tone and eyelid closure.

Figure 2.10 shows a subset of the fibers and nuclei implicated in eyelid conditioning as described by Thompson and other researchers (e.g., Thompson, 1986; Donegan, Gluck, & Thompson, 1989). These structures are located in the cerebellum and other parts of the brain stem (see also The Brain later in this chapter). According to Thompson and colleagues (Woodruff-Pak, Logan, & Thompson, 1990), circuits in these structures provide the neural basis of an important learning rule—the delta rule—that governs the connection strength between neurons (see Chapter 6).

In the Thompson model, information about the tone CS is conveyed via the auditory nerves,

the pontine nuclei, and the granule cell, to the Purkinje neuron in the cerebellum. Information about the puff of air travels via facial nerves and the inferior olive to the Purkinje neuron. The output of the circuit, the CR, is carried from the Purkinje neuron via the interpositus nucleus to the nerves that control the eyelid. (For an expanded model, see Canli & Donegan, 1995). In order to isolate this neural circuit, researchers used lesions, electrophysiological recordings, electrical microstimulation, and anatomical staining methods.

The investigators found that conditioning was based on the joint activation of neurons, just as in *Aplysia.* The neural events during a trial are graphed in Figure 2.9. The activated structures included the interpositus nucleus (2.9B). In the Purkinje cell, on the other hand, the CS produced a decrease in the rate of firing (2.9C). Note that the neural effects began before the conditioned response started. Again, as in *Aplysia,* the critical condition for learning was that the CS predicted the US. None of these effects was observed when the CS and US were presented in a random schedule.

Researchers determined that conditioning depends on each of the structures in Figure 2.10, among several others in the hippocampus reviewed by Schmajuk and DiCarlo (1992). When a structure such as the interpositus nucleus was removed by surgery, no conditioning took place. They also found that a rabbit can be trained by using electrical stimuli administered to specific nuclei rather than external stimuli. For example, researchers electrically stimulated the inferior olive nucleus and the pontine nucleus in lieu of presenting the US and CS. The electrical stimuli were effective substitutions and eyelid conditioning occurred just as if the tone and the puff of air were presented.

These conditioning studies have demonstrated a correspondence between the behavioral and neural levels: Simple associative learning was evident in conditioned eyelid responses and in patterns of excitation and inhibition of specific cells in the brain. Additional learning phenomena—

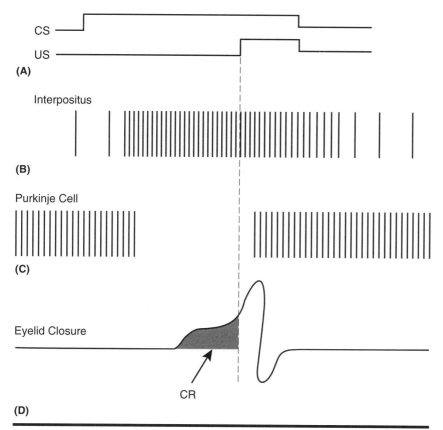

FIGURE 2.9 Correspondence between neurological activity in the interpositus and Purkinje nuclei and behavioral conditioning activity in the rabbit. (*A*) The arrangement of CS and US during a conditioning trial. The CS starts before the US and overlaps with it for a brief period. (*B*) There is excitatory activity in the interpositus nucleus. (*C*) Activity in the Purkinje cells exhibit inhibition. Note that the neurological activity in B and C becomes evident just prior to the conditioned response (shaded area in *D*). (*D*) Conditioned and unconditioned eyelid closure (Donegan, Gluck, & Thompson, 1989).

such as extinction, spontaneous recovery, and others discussed in Chapter 7—also have neural components. Indeed, they can often be detected neurally before there is behavioral evidence.

INTERIM SUMMARY

The neuron is a basic processor of the human nervous system. It includes the soma and two types of projections—the axons and the dendrites.

When stimulated by an event of sufficient intensity, an action potential is produced that is propagated along the axon to the junction with adjacent neurons—the synapse. Communication at the synapse is based on neurotransmitters; they are released from vesicles, cross the synaptic cleft, and are bound to postsynaptic receptors. Neurons are linked with each other to form neural networks. These form the basis of learning by virtue of the plasticity of synapses. Through

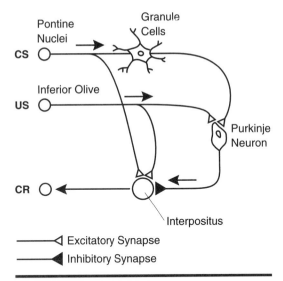

FIGURE 2.10   Subset of nuclei and fibers in the cerebellar brain stem circuit for eyelid conditioning in the rabbit. The circuit includes fibers for the US and the CS.

learning, new synapses grow and existing synapses form closer links. Correlations have been found between different types of learning and neural events: In the mollusk *Aplysia,* there is an increase in neurotransmitter activity during sensitization and conditioning, and a decrease in habituation training. In the rat hippocampus, researchers have observed an enhanced response of the postsynaptic membrane of certain nuclei after application of a series of stimulus pulses. This effect may last up to several weeks and is known as long-term potentiation. In the rabbit, during learning some nuclei exhibit an increased activity level; others show a decrease. At both the neural and behavioral levels, learning occurs only if the conditioned stimulus (CS) signals the unconditioned stimulus (US); random presentation of these stimuli has no effect.

THE BRAIN

The brain is the dominant structure of the central nervous system. During the course of evolution, it developed from a tube forming a rudimentary spinal cord, via the brain stem, into the mammalian and human brain. The brain controls cognitive activities from attention and recognition to problem solving and discovery, as well as noncognitive functions, including the digestive, cardiovascular, and reproductive systems.

For all its importance, the brain is a biological organ that requires nutrients like every other body part. Processing in the brain consumes energy, reflected by increased metabolic activity. Although it accounts for only 3% of our body mass, the brain consumes 20% of our oxygen intake. Oxygen and nutrients, including glucose, are supplied through the bloodstream. We already saw that scientists use regional blood flow and the brain's metabolism to detect sites that process information.

The brain is a multifaceted organ that includes structures at various levels of complexity from global systems down to molecules and ions. It offers a challenge to brain scientists from many disciplines, including anatomists, physiologists, neurologists, neurochemists, cognitive neuroscientists, and diverse clinical specialists who investigate various aspects of the brain and its functions. Progress in cognitive brain research has been uneven, however; more knowledge has been gathered on the brain activity underlying sensation and attention than that of such higher-level processes as problem solving, creativity, and decision making.

When anatomists in the eighteenth and nineteenth centuries mapped different anatomical structures in the brain, many of them, such as Franz Gall, thought each region was responsible for a unique function (see Figure 2.11). Based on his study of accidental injuries and his own speculation, Gall assigned faculties to a localized region (e.g., speech was thought to be localized in the frontal lobes). This view is called *localization theory.* It its extreme, the study of local function was known as *phrenology.* Phrenologists believed that bumps on the skull revealed underlying traits.

The opposing view, *distributional theory,* held

that functions were spread over different sites in the brain. Pierre Flourens favored the distributional approach. He removed certain brain areas in animals and, observing no substantial performance deficits, concluded that the remaining brain had assumed the same functions as the lesioned structures. The localists, however, came back, strengthened by Paul Broca's observation that aphasic patients had damaged left frontal lobes. (*Broca's aphasia* refers to the loss of speech in patients whose speech comprehension apparently remains intact.) Thus, Broca and other localists attributed language faculties to that lobe (see Chapter 11).

Today, neuroscientists hold an intermediate position: Localization of function in the brain is accepted, but functions are not as independent as the localists originally believed. Raichle (1994) used an orchestra analogy to describe this view: "Just as specific members of a large orchestra perform together in a precise fashion to produce a symphony, a group of localized brain areas performing elementary operations work together to exhibit an observable human behavior" (p. 58).

Major Brain Structures

The principal brain structures of interest to cognitive neuroscientists are shown in Figures 2.12 and 2.13. These include the cortex, the cerebellum, the thalamus, the limbic system, and the hippocampus. Each brain structure comes in pairs.

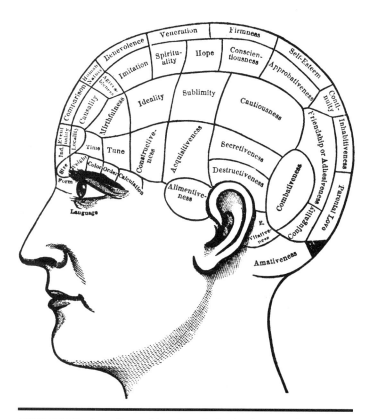

FIGURE 2.11   Locations of functions in the brain according to phrenologists (Fowler & Fowler, 1859).

There are multiple communication channels between structures and fibers within and across hemispheres. The **corpus callosum,** the best known of these channels, consists of pathways that connect the two cerebral hemispheres. If these fibers are injured or lesioned in a so called split-brain preparation, the left and right hemispheres operate independently and specific disconnections between language and performance occur (Gazzaniga, LeDoux, & Wilson, 1977).

It is one of the curiosities of the brain that fibers from one hemisphere cross over to the other side of the body. Projections from the sense organs are contralateral, although not entirely. Motor fibers also pass from the motor centers in the brain to the contralateral side of the body. For example, the movements of the right hand are governed by centers in the left hemisphere. This organization is intriguing; it poses the question of whether the left and right structures fulfill the same functions or whether there is lateral specialization as, for example, in

the processing of some language functions and spatial coordination.

The **cerebellum** is a finely fissured structure of two hemispheres. It forms part of the human motor control system. It is also implicated in neural circuits for classical conditioning (see Figure 2.10 and Donegan, Gluck, & Thompson, 1989). The **thalamus** is a major relay station for sensory pathways from sensory organs to the cortex. It is hidden under the cortex in the center of the brain (it means *hidden chamber* in Greek). The thalamus houses major relay stations for pathways from sensory organs to projection areas in the cortex. The **lateral geniculate body** is a transmission site of visual information. It receives input from the retina and passes it along to the visual cortex in the occipital lobe. The **medial geniculate body** transmits auditory information and sends it to auditory projection areas in the temporal lobes. The **basal ganglia,** located adjacent to the thalamus, are implicated in the motor system (Chapter 4).

Hippocampus. No other brain structure has attracted as much attention in the 1990s by cognitive neuroscientists as the **hippocampus.** Researchers have identified the hippocampus as a prime site for a variety of declarative learning and memory functions. **Declarative information** refers to knowledge that we can express and verbalize, such as a list of names. According to animal research and neurological case studies, the hippocampus is implicated in the consolidation of memories over time. It is believed that the hippocampus coordinates memories and confers unity on them, possibly through the process of long-term potentiation (LTP). Studies on spatial learning suggest that the hippocampus is the mind's geographer, as it monitors locations in space and the relations between them (e.g., McClelland, McNaughton, & O'Reilly; 1995; Tulving & Schacter, 1994).

The hippocampus (Latin for *sea horse*) derives its name from its sea-horse shape. It is located at the inferior edge of the cortex adjacent to the temporal lobes. Figure 2.13A shows the location of the hippocampus in a frontal section

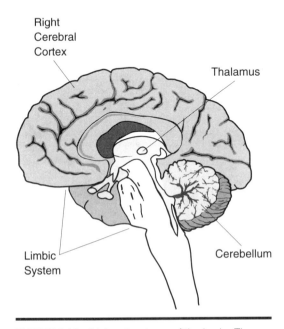

Right
Cerebral
Cortex

Thalamus

Limbic
System

Cerebellum

FIGURE 2.12 Major structures of the brain. The right cerebral cortex is shown above the limbic system, thalamus, and cerebellum.

of the cortex. Figure 2.13B, a schematic of the hippocampus in the rat, shows the principal structures of the hippocampal formation, the CA1 and CA3 regions (*CA* is the abbreviation for *cornu ammonis,* Latin for *Ammon's Horn*), the dentate gyrus, and the enthorhinal cortex. Small as it may seem, the hippocampus and such adjacent structures as the amygdala occupy a major junction for projections from the association regions in the temporal, frontal, and parietal lobes, and signals are sent back from the hippocampus to each of those regions.

The hippocampal formation came to the attention of memory researchers with Milner's report (e.g., 1966) on patient H.M., who had undergone a bilateral temporal lobe resection in an effort to curtail severe epileptic seizures. (See Hilts, 1995, for a fascinating account of H.M.) Although the surgeons were able to control H.M.'s seizures, there were two unforeseen side effects: H.M. was no longer able to remember new facts for any length of time (anterograde amnesia) nor could he remember events from the recent past (retrograde

amnesia). He was capable of short-term recall in that he remembered facts (e.g., a phone number) for a very short time, up to one minute. H.M. did remember events from the very distant past prior to his operation. Remarkably, he was able to acquire new motor skills such as mirror drawing. Because H.M. could not remember new facts for the long term, yet could retain them for a brief period of time, scientists speculated that the hippocampus contributes to the transfer of information from a relatively fragile short-term state to a more durable long-term memory.

Ever since H.M.'s case was first reported, cases similar to his became known, and animal studies pointed to the hippocampus as a critical component of the memory system. Here, we will sample the role of the hippocampus in long-term potentiation, spatial learning, and consolidation of new learning in monkeys.

Long-Term Potentiation.   There have been hundreds of studies of LTP since Bliss and Lomo (1973) first discovered LTP in the rabbit hip-

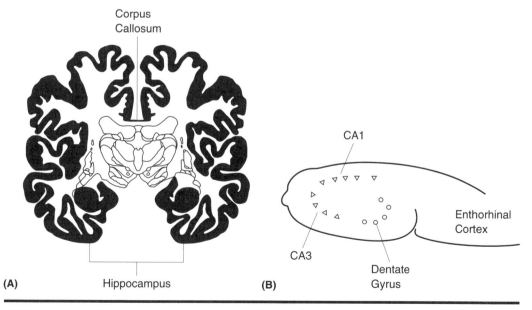

FIGURE 2.13   (A) Frontal section of the human brain shows the hippocampi adjacent to the temporal lobes (Pinel, 1993). (B) Schematic drawing of the rat hippocampus indicates the dentate gyrus, the enthorhinal cortex, and the CA1 and CA3 regions as well as pyramidal cells.

pocampus. You will recall that LTP involves a heightened response of the postsynaptic membrane after application of a volley of stimulus pulses. There are different forms of LTP in the hippocampus, including associative LTP observed in the CA1 region. Associative LTP involves joint stimulation of a weak and a strong pathway to a neuron; the result is that the weak path is potentiated for a considerable period of time. (The terms *weak* and *strong* refer to the amplitude of the reaction these pathways elicit prior to LTP training.) Associative LTP has been likened to Hebbian associative learning according to which two pathways become associated as a result of joint activation (Churchland & Sejnowski, 1992, Chapter 6).

Spatial Learning.   The contribution of the hippocampal formation to spatial learning and memory has been documented in studies involving rats and monkeys, among several other species. Olton, Collison, and Werz (1977) found that when a rat hippocampus was lesioned, the animal could not learn to navigate a radial maze that consisted of alleys radiating from a central goal box, much like spokes of a wheel. Mishkin and Appenzeller (1987) reported that monkeys with hippocampus lesions could not remember the location of hidden food (e.g., a red cup in the right hand corner of yard), whereas lesions of amygdala, another structure in the brain stem, did not impair location memory at all. O'Keefe and Dostoyevsky (1971) discovered **place cells** in the hippocampus of rats. By recording from the brains of rats exploring the radial maze, these researchers found that specific pyramidal cells are sensitive to unique locations in space; specific cells responded maximally when the rat was approaching a particular location.

Consolidation.   Squire and colleagues (1993) reviewed a study on monkey memory consolidation over a 16-week span. The monkeys underwent paired-associate training in which each learning episode involved an association of 1 of 20 different objects with food reward. Learning episodes occurred at different intervals, ranging

from 2 to 16 weeks before bilateral surgery of the hippocampus. Retention varied as the function of the interval between surgery and test: When the monkeys learned the association only 2 weeks before surgery, memory was poor; when 12 weeks elapsed between learning and surgery, retention was far better. The researchers described this retention function as evidence for a gradual process of **consolidation** in memory. They attributed the consolidation to the hippocampus and noted that "as time passes after learning, the contribution of the hippocampal formation gradually diminishes and a more permanent memory system develops, presumably in the neocortex, which is independent of the hippocampal formation" (p. 404). To date, nobody knows what the mechanisms of consolidation are and many questions remain: including the following: Are items of information reorganized after initial learning? Are irrelevant stimulus aspects forgotten? Are abstract representations developed? Is long-term potentiation one of the neuronal processes that underlies consolidation as some scientists have hypothesized (see Churchland & Sejnowski, 1992, Chapter 5)? We must await future research for answers to these questions.

What the Hippocampus Is Not *Involved In.*   The hippocampus clearly has its hand in diverse learning and memory functions. Does this mean that it participates in the learning and remembering of everything? The answer is no. You can learn certain skills without the hippocampus. Milner and other researchers had already demonstrated that H.M. was able to remember a variety of skills, although his hippocampus was lesioned. He acquired mirror drawing skills, which is a difficult task—you must draw shapes by looking in a mirror placed in front of you rather than at the sheet you are drawing on. H.M. and other amnesic patients were shown to improve their visual recognition of stimuli, whether objects or words, after prior exposure. This facilitation is known as **priming.** Amnesic patients acquire conditioned responses in classical and instrumental conditioning situations as well. Motor learning, priming, and conditioning have in common that the patient cannot verbalize what he or she has learned, nor does the patient remember that episodes (e.g., mirror drawing) ever took place. Because the patient cannot declare these memories, they are known as **nondeclarative memories.**

In sum, the hippocampus has been identified as a key structure in the acquisition of declarative memories, but it does not figure in learning of nondeclarative skills. The hippocampus does not serve as the storage site of the declarative memories. Rather, it is instrumental in the transfer of information from a fragile to a more permanent state. According to Churchland and Sejnowski's (1992) apt phrase, the hippocampus is "the teacher of the cortex" (p. 297).

The Cortex. The **cortex,** also referred to as the **cerebrum** or the **neocortex,** subserves such cognitive functions as perception, language comprehension and production, motor control, thought, and planning. Its surface is shaped to maximize area; there are elevations (gyri) and small and large valleys (sulci and fissures). The total surface is a maximum of 2,500 cm²—about the same as a newspaper page. The cortex contains most of the neurons of the human brain. Two major fissures define the structure of the hemispheres: a longitudinal fissure divides the two hemispheres into left and right hemispheres, and the central fissure divides the front and back parts of each hemisphere. Larger fissures and sulci form boundary lines between different lobes: the frontal, temporal, parietal, and occipital lobes (see Figure 2.14A). The cerebrum consists of six layers of neurons. The outer four layers receive input from other brain structures, whereas the inner two layers send output to other regions of the brain.

From the perspective of neural function, three types of cortical areas have been distinguished: projection areas, motor areas, and association areas. **Projection areas** receive input from sensory organs, including the eyes, the ears, and the body surface. **Motor areas** send fibers to the face and skeletal muscles. **Association areas** are not directly linked with the sensory organs, nor with motor activity, but with sensory projection areas and the motor areas. They are thought to play an important role in memory, problem solving, and speech. Many of the hypothetical functions of projection, motor, and association areas are shown in Figure 2.14B (Carlson, 1991). Knowledge of these areas continues to evolve and much remains unknown—that is why the brain is often referred to as the last frontier.

The cortex has four major lobes, three of which are described next—namely, the parietal, temporal, and frontal lobes. (The occipital lobes are described as visual cortex in The Visual System.)

The Parietal Lobes. The **parietal lobes** occupy the posterior top of the cortex. Their functions include somatic sensations and the integration of somatic and visual information. The sensorimotor area, located across from the motor area in the frontal lobe, receives projections from the body surface, from the toes and feet all the way to the face and head (see Chapter 4). There is no correlation between the physical size of a body part and its representation in the motor and sensory control areas. Rather, the representational space is correlated with the limb's precision of control. For example, a larger amount of sensorimotor tissue, and therefore more sensitivity, is devoted to the feet and hands than to the legs and arms.

The Temporal Lobes. Most regions of the brain fulfill many functions; the **temporal lobes** are no exception. These contain the primary auditory cortex, process visual information, and are involved in memory and attention operations. Lesions to specific temporal regions produce attention deficits. Clinical studies of patients with lesions reveal asymmetries in the temporal lobes; these cases indicate that the right temporal lobe is involved in music perception, and the left temporal lobe is crucial for speech perception.

The Frontal Lobes. The **frontal lobes** remain the most mysterious region of the cortex. The

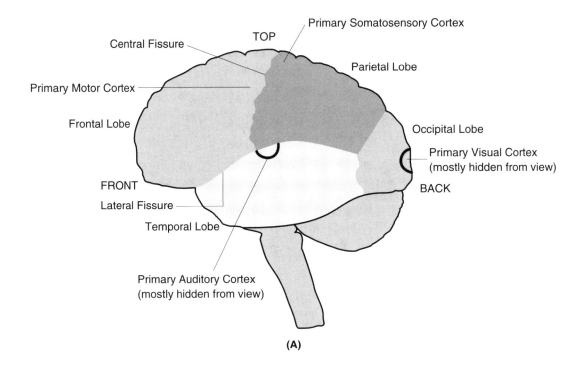

(A)

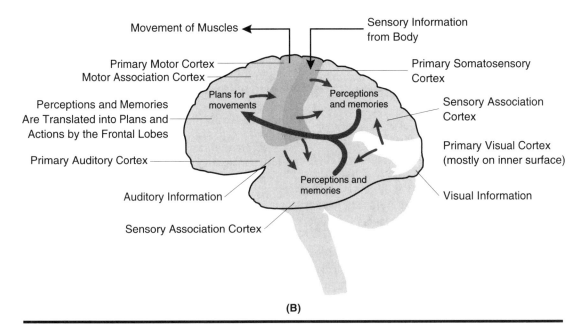

(B)

FIGURE 2.14   (*A*) Four lobes of the cortex. (*B*) Primary sensory, motor, and association areas in the cortex (Carlson, 1991).

only function that has been well documented is the motor area in front of the central fissure (see Figure 2.14B). The motor area controls voluntary movements of skeletal and facial muscles and, like the sensorimotor system, it is known that there is more sensitivity in facial and hand muscles than in leg and arm muscles. It is also known that the frontal lobes have dense lines of communications with other brain systems, unlike the specific functions served by the sensory projection areas or motor areas, for example (Baddeley, 1986). Damage to the frontal lobes leads to disruptions in a greater variety of skills than do lesions in other lobes; this has led researchers to postulate that the frontal lobes house an "executive" that schedules cognitive operations such as problem solving, speech production, and the execution of daily activities. Even if aptitude an intelligence are not impaired, planning and motivation are. Kolb and Whishaw (1990) described the case of a lawyer whose IQ and professional talent were not impaired by damage to the prefrontal region. However, he was not able to get up in the morning and go to work.

The Sensory Systems

We have at least seven sensory systems; these are listed in Table 2.2 (Carlson, 1991). Each includes sensory organs, sensory pathways, and cortical projection areas. The sensory organs receive stimuli as physical energy from the environment and transduce it into neural activity; light waves, air pressure, and chemical substances are converted into action potentials or graded potentials.

The basic functional sequence of neural events is the same for each sense, but perceptions differ for the seven senses. A **receptor** is a specialized neuron whose dendrites are sensitive to the sources of physical energy (listed in Table 2.2). Receptors translate the energy into electrical charges known as *receptor potentials,* which, in turn, trigger the release of a transmitter substance at the synapse with adjacent neurons. From there, an impulse is carried via two or three sensory neurons. Pathways then continue to projection areas in the cortex, some of them crossing to the opposite hemisphere. The cortical projection areas form six layers of neurons arranged in columns of up to 1 millimeter in width. Processing in all these structures results in several neural representations of the stimulus and ultimately in the perceiver's interpretation of the world. The next section describes the visual system and illustrates the principles of sensory processing.

The Visual System

The visual world is rich and varied. Just think of the myriad plants and animals around us, small snow crystals with their fine filaments, dark

TABLE 2.2 The Types of Transduction Accomplished by the Sense Organs

Sense Organ	Nature of the Stimulus Transduced
Eye	Light (radiant energy)
Ear (cochlea)	Rapid, periodic changes in air pressure (mechanical energy)
Vestibular system	Tilt of head; rotation of head (mechanical energy)
Tongue (taste)	Recognition of molecular shape
Nose (odor)	Recognition of molecular shape (?)
Skin, internal organs	Touch: movement of skin (mechanical energy)
	Warmth and coolness (thermal energy)
	Vibration: movement of skin (mechanical energy)
	Pain: damage to body tissue (chemical reaction)
Muscle	Stretch and change in muscle length (mechanical energy)

forests, city skylines, and the night sky that seems to envelop everything. The manifold of all of these scenes passes through visual receptors and optic nerves on its way to several cortical areas. How does the visual system accomplish this feat? First, at the visual receptors, light energy is converted into patterns of neural activation. Because of the different number of neurons at each stage of the visual system, information is recoded at various junctures, from the retina to the area striata in the occipital lobes. In the retina, there are almost 10 million rods and cones, 3.5 million bipolar cells, and 0.2 million ganglion cells. From here, information is projected to 0.03 million lateral geniculate cells in the thalamus and to 0.6 million cells in the striate cortex.

Figure 2.15 shows the major relay stations of the visual system from the eye to the visual cortex. The figure reflects the interesting property that half of the fibers from each eye are projected to the opposite hemisphere. This projection necessitates a crossing of the optic fibers; this occurs at the optic chasm. The visual tract continues to the lateral geniculate body in the thalamus and then to the hemispheres.

The Eye.   Figure 2.16 illustrates the major components of the eye through which light passes, including the cornea, lens, and retina. The retina contains light receptors and two sets of nuclei—the bipolar and ganglion cells. The light receptors are located at the back of the retina so that light must pass the ganglion and bipolar cells. This poses no problem, however, because the nuclei are translucent and light receptors are highly sensitive. Two locations on the retina are noteworthy: The **fovea** is a small region of heightened sensitivity and the optic nerves exit at the **blind spot,** a location of minimal sensitivity. The optic nerves are axons extending from the ganglion cells.

Ganglion cells are not alike; they differ, for example, in the response patterns to light stimuli projected to their receptive fields. Some ganglion cells are **on-center, off-surround cells**—a spot of light illuminating the center of the receptive field increases the firing rate of the cell, whereas a

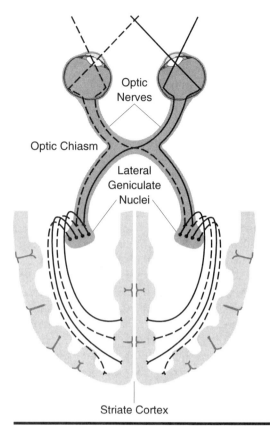

FIGURE 2.15   The visual pathway shows half-retinas projecting fibers via the lateral geniculate bodies to the visual cortex. Crossing of fibers occurs at the optic chasm.

light stimulating the periphery of the receptive field decreases the cell's firing rate (see Figure 2.17A). In **off-center, on-surround cells,** the reverse pattern occurs. Light illuminating the periphery of the receptive field increases the firing rate of the cell, and light projected to the center decreases the rate (Figure 2.17B).

Separate Channels in Vision.   Visual information is conveyed from the retinal ganglion cells via the thalamus to different cortical regions. One of the most interesting discoveries has been that different kinds of visual information travel in different major pathways. There is anatomical, ex-

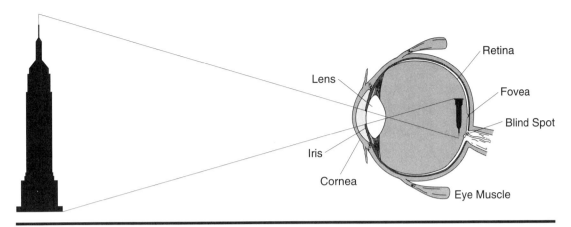

FIGURE 2.16   The eye and its primary components: the cornea, lens, retina, fovea, and the blind spot.

perimental, and clinical evidence of at least two parallel visual processing systems. One system, dubbed the **Where system,** is implicated in the perception of movement, location, and depth; the other, the **What system,** is implicated in form and color perception (see Table 2.3). Separation of the two systems is evident at all stages of the visual system, from the retina to the visual cortex. In the retina, ganglion cells differ in the size of their receptive fields. *Magno cells* have large receptive fields; they easily detect motion but not color. *Parvo cells* have smaller receptive fields; they are sensitive to color and form. These two types of cells project their axons to separate visual channels in the thalamus and cortex.

The magno cells communicate with the magnocellular system located in the **lateral geniculate body** of the thalamus. This system is phylogenetically old and present in all mammals; it processes movement and depth, but it is color blind and insensitive to spatial detail. The parvo cells communicate with the parvocellular system (*parvo* means *small*) of the lateral geniculate body. This system is phylogenetically younger

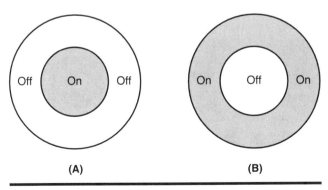

FIGURE 2.17   (*A*) Light falling in the center of the receptive field of on-center, off-surround ganglion cells activates the cell. (*B*) Light illuminating the periphery of the receptive field of an off-center, on-surround activates it.

TABLE 2.3 *Summary of Separate Pathways in Vision*

	Magnocellular System	**Parvocellular System**
Nickname	Where system	What system
Approximate location in brain	Dorsal	Ventral
Retina	Magno ganglions	Parvo ganglions
Receptive field	Large	Small
Thalamus	Large neurons in two innermost layers of the lateral geniculate body	Small neurons in the outer layers of the lateral geniculate body
Primary visual cortex	V1, V2, V3, V5	V1, V2, V3, V4
	Layers in region 4B	Nuclei in blobs and interblobs
Secondary visual cortex	Thick stripes	Thin strips
	Posterior parietal	Infero-Temporal (IT)
Function	Movement	Color
	Depth	Form
	Location	

and found only in primates; it is sensitive to color and detail.

Visual Cortex.   When we talk about *the* visual cortex, it is important to remember that there are actually some 20 cortical regions involved in vision, including regions that process the perception of color, shape, location in space, texture, and so on (Desimone & Ungerleider, 1989). The primary visual cortex occupies the occipital lobe—the **striate cortex,** so named because of its striped appearance. The magnocellular and parvocellular systems project information from the thalamus to the striate cortex; however, they do so to distinct and separate nuclei. The two systems continue separately to the secondary visual cortex; magnocellular information is transmitted to a region characterized by thick stripes, whereas parvocellular input is sent to a thin-stripe region (Kalat, 1992; Tso & Gilbert, 1988).

Livingston and Hubel (1988) demonstrated the two separate channels with the arrangement of objects in Figure 2.18. In its present form, the figure exhibits the depth dimension. However, when you make the lines red against a green background and ensure equal brightness of the two hues, all you see is a jumble of lines rather than

a pile of objects. Thus, the magno system has dropped out and so has depth perception.

In sum, there is physiological as well as perceptual evidence for separate processing channels in vision. When researchers discover separate sys-

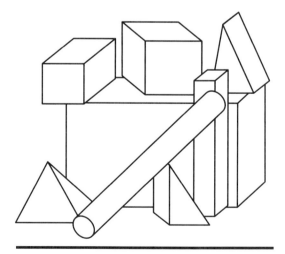

FIGURE 2.18 A black-and-white drawing shows a pile of blocks. If the lines were colored against a background of equal luminance, the viewer would see a jumble of lines (Livingston & Hubel, 1988).

tems within one modality, as they did in the case of vision, they must specify the relation between the systems, as we discussed in Chapter 1. The Where and What systems could be independent, as Fodor (1983) has argued. He postulated modular input systems for language and for each of the traditional senses. He also assumed specialized mechanisms *within* a modality. In the case of vision, Fodor wrote, there might be separate "mechanisms for color perception, for the analysis of shape, and for the analysis of three-dimensional spatial relations" (1983, p. 47). In addition, Fodor speculated about more specific systems dedicated to the visual guidance of motor movements and face recognition. Whether the visual processing channels are independent or not awaits further research. Experimental results (e.g., Livingston & Hubel, 1988) and anatomical studies suggest independence; however, there are multiple communication links between the two systems (Merigan & Maunsell, 1993).

Processing Visual Patterns. Independent from channels, there are two basic response types of neurons in the visual system: Some neurons are generalists—they are sensitive to a wide range of visual inputs; other neurons are specialists—they respond to very specific stimuli. Hubel and Wiesel (1965) discovered neurons in the striate cortex that react differentially to the orientation of lines; some neurons respond to vertical lines, others respond to oblique lines, and still others respond to horizontal lines. In addition, neurons respond differently, depending on the length of lines and whether the stimulus moves. All of these respond only to specific stimulus patterns; some researchers have even suggested that there are cells that respond only to Volkswagen "bugs," for example, or only to one's grandmother. Using monkeys as subjects, researchers discovered cells responsive to only specific stimuli, such as a hand or the front or side view of a face. Nevertheless, neurons that respond to specific *objects* are rare.

Because our perception of objects is unitary, rather than fragmented according to depth and color, there must be a locus where the different sources of information are integrated. Nobody knows for sure how this synthesis is accomplished. According to a theory by neuroscientists Mishkin and Appenzeller (1987), there are successive stages of visual information processing. At each stage, the processing becomes more inclusive. Early neurons handle elemental aspects of the stimulus, such as orientation; neurons in the thalamus process broader features such as depth; and cells in the final stage "synthesize a complete representation of the object" (p. 82).

INTERIM SUMMARY

The brain's structures have been grouped into two major divisions: the brain stem and the forebrain, including the hippocampus and the cortex with its hemispheres and lobes. The brain controls cognitive functions, as diverse as perception and decision making, and noncognitive functions. Progress on the neural basis of cognitive functions has been uneven; scientists know more about brain processes that underlie sensation and perception than creativity and decision making. Sensory functions are distributed over different sites in the thalamus and in the projection and association areas of the occipital, parietal, and temporal lobes. The frontal lobe controls motor functions and is thought to be involved in such higher-level functions as memory and planning.

Sensory systems, including the auditory and visual systems, receive, transduce, and send sensory information to cortical projection areas. Light patterns are transduced into neural activation by receptors in the retina. This activity is projected via the lateral geniculate body in the thalamus to regions in the cortex, including the primary visual cortex. The visual system is specialized both in terms of its receptors and pathways.

CONCLUSION

The relation between cognitive science and neuroscience is reciprocal. Cognitive processes depend on the brain, and they, in turn, influence brain functions. As we saw, when a person attends to a tone, reads a passage, or imagines a scene, the activity in specific brain centers changes as a result (Posner & Raichle, 1994). Research has uncovered parallels between cognitive processes and neural events in an increasing number of domains: attention, perception, imagery, learning, memory, comprehension, and even problem solving. We saw that the pattern of habituation and conditioning corresponds to changes in the rate of neural impulses, that a person's attention to specific stimuli is correlated with increased brain activity in specific regions, and that the extent of practice with a problem-solving task changes the pattern of brain activity. Such correspondences can be used to illuminate issues that are difficult to solve by performance studies alone. For example, there has been a long debate on whether visual imagery involves the visual centers in the brain. Farah (1988) found increased ERP in the visual centers when people imaged visual scenes, and she concluded that visual imagery does depend on neural activity in those centers.

The flow of ideas between the disciplines is a two-way street. Many concepts in cognitive psychology have a neural flavor. Consider the terms *excitation* and *inhibition* introduced by neuroscientists and used in influential theories of declarative and procedural knowledge (Chapter 5) and in connectionist theories (Chapter 6). Other neurally inspired concepts include *threshold, generalization, processing channels,* and, of course, *networks.* The idea of independent processing channels in the sensory system has its parallel in cognitive psychology, where some theorists speak of modular processing systems (e.g., in perception and language processing). Networks are popular among information-processing psychologists, although these networks differ from the neural networks we have discussed.

In other cases, psychological discoveries have been made well before neurophysiological methods were advanced enough to detect parallels. Many perceptual phenomena were known before their neural correlates were discovered; for example, the idea of separate perceptual channels for color and objects in perception was proposed well before Livingston and Hubel's discoveries (see Livingston & Hubel, 1988, for references).

The relationship between cognitive psychology and neuroscience can be expected to increase in the coming decades. This does not mean, however, that every cognitive phenomenon will be reduced to its neural basis and that cognitive psychology will ultimately be absorbed by neuroscience. The levels of analysis are different in the two fields.

Traditional information-processing models emphasize abstract categories and distinctions; whereas neuroscientists emphasize concrete structures and mechanisms at various levels of the nervous system. Whether people have separate memories for, say, quantitative or qualitative information, whether people scan memories serially or in parallel in order to answer a question, or whether listeners construct noun phrases one way or another may be difficult to resolve by investigating neural circuits and brain structures. It is not clear at which level one should look in the nervous system for the correspondence between a mental category and neural activity. (See Hillis & Caramazza's [1991] report on category-specific impairment.) Remember: There are 60 trillion synapses in the human nervous system; there will always be some neural activity in the nervous system that has no impact on cognition (Pylyshyn, 1984).

Where correlations between the behavioral and neural levels have been observed, such as in learning and perception, the parallels may not be the full story. Other structures may be involved and their discovery may change one's interpretation of the cognitive phenomena. Occasionally, old controversies continue on a different plane, the great advances in neuroscience notwithstanding. Consider again the localization of function in the brain. Posner's research (e.g., Posner et al., 1988) has indicated that certain cognitive operations are "strictly localized" (p. 1627), yet connectionist network models favor a distributed mode of representation (see Chapter 6). Of course, it could be that networks are localized within specific brain regions and information is distributed over the networks. Whatever the solution, neuroscience by itself has not yet found it.

The relation between neuroscience and cognitive psychology is twofold. On one hand, the great advances in neuroscience continue to inform theories of cognition, especially in attention, learning, and perception. On the other hand, much of cognitive psychology—namely, research on knowledge representation, problem solving, and decision making—continues to progress separately from neuroscience. There is no doubt that, in the future, neuroscientists will uncover parallels between these higher-level cognitive functions and neural processes.

CHAPTER 3

ATTENTION

PREVIEW

Attention plays a role in perception and performance, even though we may be unaware of it. We become aware of its role, however, when a stimulus is difficult to perceive, when we execute two tasks simultaneously, and when we face an overload of information. In this chapter we will discuss four research paradigms that demonstrate a subject's attention in a controlled laboratory environment: detection, filtering, search, and resource allocation.

Detection involves noticing the absence or presence of a stimulus or the difference between a pair of stimuli. Detection depends on the observer's sensitivity as well as the observer's response bias to be lenient or strict. *Filtering* involves the selection of one of several messages on the basis of its attributes. According to filter theories, analysis of information prior to the filter is automatic but superficial. Subsequent analyses are deeper but they require more cognitive resources and more time. There is debate whether the information is filtered before or after it is recognized, and what type of attribute forms the basis for selection.

Search refers to the identification of a target among a set of distractors. When targets and distractors differ consistently (e.g., letters versus digits), the search is automatic. When targets and distractors are mixed, however, the viewer's full attention is required. According to an integration view of attention, simple features of the stimulus such as color, size, and movement, are automatically processed without attention. Attention focuses on a subset of these features and integrates them into objects. Data supporting this two-stage theory of attention include the finding that simple features are processed in parallel, independently of how many distractors there are. If one looks for a combination of features—for instance, a white square among white circles and black squares—the search is difficult and must be done serially.

Often we execute two tasks concurrently, such as when we drive and talk. We allocate resources depending on the demands of each task and on our expertise with each. If we are highly practiced, performance on neither task will deteriorate because execution has become automatic; otherwise, there will be interference. In an effort to understand the role of attention in these diverse cases, researchers have designed a broad range of research techniques. These techniques include dual-task studies, imaging and electrophysiological methods, as well as computational approaches to attention.

INTRODUCTION

Attention makes you more alert and focuses your mind. This is true in many different situations and has important consequences. When you attend to a specific signal, everything else becomes less noticeable; you are set to respond quickly, whether it is a traffic light, the starting shot at a track meet, or the conductor's prompt in a concert about to start. You are primed for a speedy response. Attention also affects memory; when you study for an exam, you concentrate on the text in the expectation that it will help you remember information. Thus, attention (1) highlights a part of one's environment and blocks out other parts, (2) primes a person for a speedy reaction, and (3) helps the learner to retain information.

Because of its power over the mind and its importance for remembering, the first psychologists (including Wundt and James) became interested in attention. Faithful to their introspectionist heritage, they described attention in terms of one's personal experience. James (1890, 1892) made very insightful observations about attention that are still worth reading today. Box 3.1 includes a sample of quotes from his writings. James commented on the selectivity of attention, which lifts a small set of objects or thoughts and bans all others. Although we are familiar with certain aspects of attention, James acknowledged that attention nevertheless remains a mystery. It is easier to describe attention than to explain the processes that produce it. In the third quote shown in Box 3.1, James speculated on possible mechanisms of attention, including physiological ones. He noted that selective attention requires "neural machinery." This chapter will show that some of James's insights have been borne out by research one century later.

Selection is achieved at several levels of processing, including the sensory, neural, and cognitive levels. The sensory organs have limited sensitivity, and the density of receptors differs across the surface of sensory organs (e.g., across the retina). We are insensitive to many stimuli in our environment, including magnetic waves, ultraviolet light, nuclear radiation, and sound waves of very high and low pitch. We need detection devices to avoid being hurt by some of these stimuli. Neural mechanisms enhance aspects of stimuli to which we are sensitive; for example, visual receptors enhance boundaries and contrast through lateral inhibition. At the cognitive level, attention selects among stimuli that are perceptible, including light waves between 420 and 700 nanometers.

Selectivity is the result of capacity limits of the human information-processing system. These limits are relative; they depend on the type of

Box 3.1 _____

William James Studies Attention

ATTENTION PRODUCES CLARITY OF MIND

"*Attention* is the taking possession by the mind, in clear and vivid form, of one out of what seems several simultaneously possible objects or trains of thought. Focalization, concentration, of consciousness are of its essence. It implies withdrawal from some things in order to deal more effectively with others." (pp. 403–404)

THE NARROWNESS OF CONSCIOUSNESS

"One of the most extraordinary facts of our life is that, although we are besieged at every moment by impressions from our whole sensory surface, we notice so very small a part of them. The sum total of our impressions never enters into our *experience,* consciously so called, which runs through this sum total like a tiny rill through a broad flowery mead. Yet the physical impressions which do not count are *there* as much as those which do, and affect our sense-organs just as energetically. Why they fail to pierce the mind is a mystery, which is only named and not explained when we invoke the 'narrowness of consciousness,' as its ground." (p. 217)

Source: James, 1890.

PHYSIOLOGICAL CONDITIONS OF ATTENTION

- "The appropriate cortical centre must be excited before attention can take place.
- The sense-organ must then adapt itself to clearest reception of the object, by adjustment of its muscular apparatus.
- In all probability a certain afflux of blood to the cortical centre must ensue." (p. 228)

COPING WITH THE WANDERING MIND

"I can keep my wandering mind a great deal more closely upon a conversation or a lecture if I actively re-echo to myself the words than if I simply hear them." (p. 237)

ATTENTION AND EFFORT

"No object can *catch* our attention except by the neural machinery. But the *amount* of attention which an object receives after it has caught our mental eye is another question. It often takes effort to keep the mind upon it." (p. 237)

_____

activity. Well-practiced tasks are automatic and require little attention. Other activities require mental effort and engage attentive processes. Automatic and attentive processes are complementary; they play a role in each of the manifestations of attention we will study. Theories differ in terms of the respective roles attributed to attentive and to automatic processes. According to so-called bottleneck theories of attention, the two types of processes are serial: Automatic processes are followed by attentive processes. According to other theories, attentive and automatic processes occur in parallel throughout processing (e.g., Shiffrin, 1988).

Four varieties of selective attention are discussed in this chapter: detection, filtering, search, and resource allocation (see Enns, 1990).

- Detection involves the judgment as to whether a stimulus is present (e.g., Did I hear the phone ring? Was there a knock on my door? Was there a blip on the radar screen?).
- Filtering involves concentration on one of several inputs while excluding others (e.g., when you listen to one of several conversations, say at lunch in a cafeteria or at a party).
- During search, the viewer looks for a target among a set of objects. A search is automatic when the stimulus is salient or when the observer has had practice. The search requires full attention when the stimuli are difficult to discriminate or when the task is new.
- Resource allocation is necessary when one has to execute two tasks jointly. Usually, there is a trade-off between tasks. Resources devoted to

one task are not available for the other task, and as a result, performance on the less-attended task will deteriorate.

This chapter consists of four parts, one devoted to each of these aspects of selective attention. You will see that these aspects overlap; viewers filter out irrelevant attributes when searching for an object; the detection of signals requires resources; and search involves the detection of specific features.

DETECTION AND SENSORY PROCESSES

As we saw in Chapter 2, the relation between body and mind challenged philosophers and scientists who speculated about mind-body links. It was Fechner (1801–1887) who invented an *empirical* method to address the relation between mental and physical processes. Fechner, a physicist by training, founded the discipline of **psychophysics,** the study of the relationship between physical events and psychological responses. Psychophysicists explore, among other things, the **threshold** of sensitivity, the weakest stimulus intensity or smallest difference between two stimuli noticeable by an observer. Fechner presented a series of tones of varying intensity to his subjects and asked them to indicate when they heard the tone. He introduced several methods to determine the threshold, the point of a given stimulus dimension at which it is noticeable.

Psychophysical Methods

Table 3.1 illustrates the **method of limits.** In the left column are units of pitch ranging from 24 to 7 Hz. On each trial, a warning signal is given followed by an individual tone. The listener decides whether she has heard it. The entire test involves 10 series of stimuli. In the first series, the experimenter begins at the high end of the continuum and lowers the pitch until the subject

TABLE 3.1 Determination of Stimulus Threshold by the Method of Limits (Titchener, 1910)

Stimulus in Hz	Lower Limit of Audible Pitch, Alternate Descending and Ascending Series									
24	Y									
23	Y		Y							
22	Y		Y							
21	Y		Y							
20	Y		Y						Y	
19	Y		Y				Y		Y	
18	Y		Y		Y		Y		Y	
17	Y		Y		Y		Y		Y	
16	Y	Y	Y		Y		Y		Y	
15	Y	N	Y	Y	Y	Y	Y		Y	Y
14	N	N	N	N	N	N	N	Y	N	N
13		N		N		N		N		N
12		N		N		N		N		N
11		N		N		N		N		
10		N		N				N		
9				N				N		
8				N				N		
7				N				N		
T =	14.5	15.5	14.5	14.5	14.5	14.5	14.5	13.5	14.5	14.5
M =	14.5	SD = .45								

says *no.* Responses of *yes* and *no* are reported in the second column of Table 3.1. Notice that the subject said *yes* to all tones ranging from 24 to 15 Hz. The 14 Hz tone was too low to be detected on this trial. The experimenter therefore assumes that the threshold was between 14 and 15 Hz, or 14.5 Hz. On the next trial, the pitch is increased from 10 to 16 Hz. This time, the estimate of the threshold is 15.5 Hz. The experimenter continues for several more series, recording the threshold on each, and averages them to get the subject's threshold, as shown at the bottom of the Table 3.1.

Psychophysicists recorded observers' sensitivity as a function of a range of stimulus dimensions, including stimulus intensity. Typically, there is a continuous increase in the probability of *yes* responses as the stimulus is increased in intensity. This continuity is inconsistent with the notion of a specific threshold that divides the stimulus continuum into two discrete classes: stimuli above the threshold that are always perceived and stimuli that are not perceivable. The latter used to be called *subliminal* stimuli; at one time there was public concern about the potential influence of such marginal stimuli on perception and behavior. Read Box 3.2 for some reflections on this issue.

Theory of Signal Detection

According to the theory of signal detection, performance in psychophysical experiments depends on two factors: the observer's sensitivity and the observer's response bias. We will consider **sensitivity** first. Table 3.1 indicated that a person's sensitivity to stimuli that are nominally of equal intensity varies across trials. The variability results from changes in the environment and within the observer. Even in a quiet research lab there is ambient background noise; the equipment may hum or the air conditioner may turn on. The sensory system is not static either; receptors have a base-level rate of firing that fluctuates.

The observer's detection performance also depends on her **response bias.** In classical psy-

chophysical tests, there was little uncertainty; every trial was a positive trial where the observer knew that a signal was presented. Such a *signal* trial began with a warning signal to indicate that the test signal (e.g., a tone) would follow within a brief interval and the subject was then to respond. Suppose, however, that the observer was uncertain, as when one is not quite sure whether or not the phone rung (you are more likely to think that it rang if you were expecting a phone call). Your perception is influenced by your expectation; such influences are known as response bias.

Signal detection theorists not only proposed a new theory of detection performance but they also introduced an experimental paradigm designed to capture the two factors that affect performance. Their innovation was very simple: They introduced blank trials. On blank trials, a warning signal is presented but no test stimulus. The correct response on these trials is a reply of *no.* Blank trials are also called *noise trials,* thus referring to the background level of stimulation (like the humming equipment). Technically, the signal trials are *signal-plus-noise trials* because the signal occurs against the random noise level in the background.

The theory of signal detection assumes that the likelihood of a *yes* response is greater for a signal trial and the probability of a *no* response is greater on a noise trial. It is also assumed that the probability of *yes* and *no* responses is normally distributed as shown in Figure 3.1A. The abscissa reflects the stimulus continuum with an increasing intensity from left to right. Each distribution indicates the overall probability of responses. The left distribution is called the noise distribution; it represents the overall probability of *yes* responses. Finally, theorists assume that the distance between the peaks of the two distributions provides a measure of observer sensitivity.

Notice that the two distributions overlap. Thus, a stimulus of intensity *x* marked on the abscissa could produce a *no* as well as a *yes* response. This reflects the uncertainty of the observer when stimulus *x* is presented. Signal detection theory addresses the problem of the ob-

Box 3.2

Perception without Awareness

In the 1960s, many people worried that our decisions as consumers were being influenced by hidden persuasion, by subliminal messages embedded in advertisements and the news. A similar furor flared up in the 1980s when rock groups were accused of inserting satanic messages in their tapes. The claim that we perceive and act on information of which we are unaware is one that cognitive psychologists are able to evaluate experimentally. Advocates of subliminal advertising claim that inserting words with an emotional connotation makes the ads more memorable. There has been a debate among experimenters whether perception without awareness is real. Some studies dispute it, while others support such unconscious perception. Vokey and Read (1985) tested the prediction that embedding the word *sex* in small print in advertisements would increase the ads' memorability. They included the word *sex* in a set of slides and tested subjects' recognition accuracy of the slides.

A control group saw the same set of slides with random letters superimposed in place of *sex*. The subjects recognized both sets of slides equally well; the *sex*-embedded slides had no advantage. Similarly, there were no differences in experiments that used auditory presentations. Thus, subliminal messages are just that—they are not perceived nor remembered.

Several other paradigms, however, suggest that stimuli that perceivers are not aware of do, in fact, influence performance. Marcel (1983) flashed words such as *butter* on a screen followed by a visual mask. People were not aware having seen anything other than the mask; nor were they able to repeat the words when asked. The flashed words had an effect nevertheless; subsequent words were recognized more easily if they were related to the first word (e.g., *bread*). Marcel's results have been replicated many times but they are still controversial (see Holender, 1986).

Perception without consciousness has been observed in patients who have lesions in the visual center that are severe enough to render them cortically blind. Although one would not expect these individuals to identify objects placed in their visual fields, they are able to make guesses with an accuracy better than chance. Note the patients are not aware of the objects! This paradoxical capacity has been described as **blindsight** (Weiskrantz, 1986).

Remembering without awareness has been reported in research on **implicit memory.** This concept is discussed at greater length in Chapter 9. Evidence of implicit memory is observed when a person's performance in a task is improved by previous exposure to a stimulus, even though there was no instruction or intention to memorize it. Consider the word fragment completion task; the task includes an exposure phase and a performance phase. During the exposure phase, the subject is presented with a list of words that includes certain target items. In the performance phase, incomplete word frames, such as —R-EP—N- and —SA-S-N, are presented, and the subject is instructed to complete them. Subjects find this quite a challenge, unless they have been presented with the target words (*fortepiano* and *assassin*) during the exposure phase (Schacter, 1987). Note that the subjects usually do not remember the target items explicitly. The facilitation resulting from prior exposure has been observed even after intervals up to several weeks between the exposure and the performance phases. The point of Schacter's (1987) demonstration is that stimuli may influence performance in certain tasks, even though we may be unaware of having been exposed to them.

---

server's uncertainty. According to the theory, the observer chooses a response criterion—an intensity level above which she will respond *yes* and below which she responds *no*. The response criterion is represented by the vertical line in Figure 3.1.

The area of the signal distribution (shaded) on the right of the criterion represents the theoretical probability of *yes* responses *given a signal*. Similarly, the area of the noise distribution (horizontal shading) on the right of the criterion is the probability of *yes* responses *given noise*.

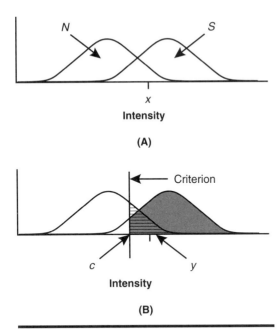

(A)

(B)

FIGURE 3.1 (*A*) Theoretical distribution of *no* and *yes* responses on noise trials (*N*) and signal-plus-noise trials (*S*), respectively. (*B*) The observer's response criterion intersects noise and signal distributions. Shaded region of the signal distribution represents the probability of hits, p(H). Hatched region of the noise distribution indicates the probability of false alarms, p(FA).

TABLE 3.2 Performance in Signal-Detection Task

| | | TRIAL | |
		Signal	Noise
RESPONSE	Yes	Hit	False Alarm
	No	Miss	Correct Rejection

Researchers estimate these response probabilities experimentally by recording the probability of *yes* responses on signal and noise trials. The correct *yes* response to a signal is known as a **hit.** The *yes* response on a noise trial is called a **false alarm,** much like the false alarm of a smoke detector when there is no fire. The shaded region of the signal distribution represents the probability of hits, p(H), whereas the hatched region of the noise distribution represents the false-alarm probability, p(FA). (Researchers often use a measure, the d′ statistic, to combine the hit and false-alarm probabilities into a single value.) Performance in the signal-detection task is captured in a 2 × 2 matrix that includes the two trial types and two types of responses as shown in Table 3.2. Together, hits

and false alarms reveal a subject's sensitivity and response bias.

Response bias is manipulated experimentally by payoff schedules. Suppose the subject is told she will receive a dime for each hit response. As a result, she is likely to be very lenient in her response criterion and move it to the left in the distribution, say to location *c* in Figure 3.1B; she will say *yes* even if she is unsure that a signal was presented. At this location, her hit probability, p(H), would be 0.90 and her false-alarm probability, p(FA), would be 0.30. Assume the experimenter payoff for a different set of trials is such that the subject receives a dime for each hit but has to pay a dime for each false alarm. This is a payoff less favorable to the subject. She is therefore likely to be strict and shift the criterion to the right, say to position *y*. She would make fewer false alarms, say p(FA) = 0.10, but also fewer hits, say p(H) = 0.70.

The ROC Curve. In the typical signal-detection experiment, an observer experiences several different payoff schedules, each involving many trials. The payoff schedules vary from very lenient to very strict. Table 3.3 shows the hit and false-alarm rates from a hypothetical experiment with five payoff levels. The payoff conditions are arranged by the experimenter through different ratios of reward and penalty. The two response rates are correlated; when the hit rate increases, so does the false-alarm rate, as the plot of the data in Figure 3.2 shows. The axes of Figure 3.2 indicate the hit rate and false-alarm rate, respectively. If a subject's hit and false-alarm responses were equal

TABLE 3.3 Hit and False-Alarm Rates in Hypothetical Experiment

Payoff Condition	p(H)	p(FA)
Very lenient	0.94	0.69
Lenient	0.88	0.47
Moderate	0.79	0.28
Strict	0.69	0.21
Very strict	0.53	0.10

under each payoff condition, the responses would fall on the diagonal in Figure 3.2; she was insensitive to the presence and absence of the signal. However, because most observers are sensitive to the stimulus, the hit rates tend to be greater than the corresponding false-alarm rates. The circles in Figure 3.2 indicate responses under the five payoff conditions. The curve is called the receiver operating characteristic curve (ROC curve). The further the ROC curve is from the diagonal, the more discriminating the observer is.

The signal-detection approach is important because the concept of a single threshold is replaced

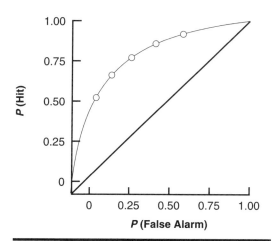

FIGURE 3.2 The receiver operating characteristic curve (ROC curve) connects detection performance in five payoff conditions. Each point indicates a pair of hit and false-alarm responses (see text for further explanation).

with a curve (the ROC curve), which gives a range of performance levels for an observer under different payoff conditions. The area under the curve represents the observer's sensitivity. The advantage of the signal-detection paradigm lies in its ability to determine observer sensitivity independently of bias.

Early Visual Processing

Every visual scene or line of print in a book contains more information than we can attend to, let alone retain. Just how much we perceive in a single glance is a difficult empirical question. Much hinges on the fate of visual input immediately after it is received. Events are fleeting; we are often bombarded by many events at any given time, and these change rapidly. Fortunately, the visual system retains visual representations for brief periods of time, up to about one second. If necessary, this interval is sufficient for visual processing *after* the stimulus has been turned off. This early sensory information is very fragile; it decays quickly and is easily interfered with by subsequent input. The typical procedure used to study early visual processing was introduced by Sperling (1960).

Sperling (1960) flashed a matrix of 12 letters, shown in Figure 3.3, for 100 milliseconds on a screen and asked subjects to report them. Subjects managed to report 4.5 letters on average, but expressed the feeling of having seen more. Sperling reasoned that the letters must have left a trace and wondered how he could tap this representation. To accomplish this, he invented the **partial reporting procedure.** Sperling showed the same letter matrix as before, but instead of asking subjects to recall all of the letters, he asked them to report only a subset. In one condition, Sperling used a locational cue; the subjects were to report one of three rows. He cued the row by presenting tones of high, medium, or low pitch. In another condition, Sperling used a color cue; letters were printed in three different colors and one of the colors could be cued.

⌐ ⌐orting cue was presented either ⌐ ⌐d off or a little ⌐⌐ ⌐sing a

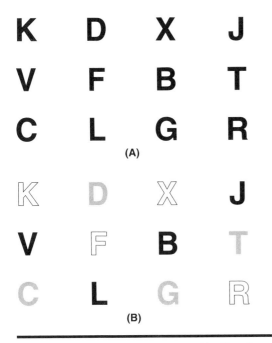

FIGURE 3.3 Matrix of 12 letters used by Sperling (1960) to investigate early visual processing. In the partial-reporting procedure, the subject is cued to report a subset of letters, either rows (A) or letters printed in a specific color (B). The person is cued after the stimulus is removed.

locational cue (for example, when the medium tone was presented), the subject had to report the middle row, V/F/B/T. If the subject reported three of the four letters, Sperling reasoned that she had seen 75% of the 12 letters. Because rows were chosen randomly, and subjects didn't know which row to report ahead of time, Sperling was able to estimate how many letters there were in the representation.

The partial-reporting technique revealed that more information was available to subjects than they could report. Neisser (1967) called this sensory trace **iconic memory;** we now call it **early visual information** or very short-term visual memory. A subject can literally read from different locations of this stored array. This read-out process is based on attention; it occurs without any eye movements because the physical stimulus is no longer there. The early visual information

store has a relatively large capacity, but information decays very rapidly and is easily interfered with by subsequent visual inputs. Partial reporting represents a kind of mental spotlight on information attended to in sensory memory.

How long does the sensory trace last? Sperling found out by presenting the reporting cue at several intervals after stimulus onset: 100 ms, 500 ms, and 1,000 ms. At intervals of 100 and 500 ms, a greater percentage of letters were reported in the partial-reporting condition than in the whole-reporting condition. But after one second there was no difference. Subjects could report about 1.5 letters per row, on average, which is equivalent to 4.5 letters for the whole slide (the same number found in the whole-reporting procedure).

The results from the whole-reporting procedure are relatively poor because the letters decay as the subject reports them. Reporting a letter takes time; you have to articulate the letter or write it down, and during this interval, the icon decays. Cognitive psychologists have discovered that there are early sensory representations for each modality, including the tactile, olfactory, and auditory modalities. These sensory representations provide the raw material for pattern recognition, the process that identifies and categorizes stimuli (see Chapter 4).

Early Auditory Processing

Early auditory processing has been studied in a procedure similar to Sperling's (1960) partial-reporting technique. The experimenter creates an acoustic experience of three channels by using a set of stereo headphones and by adjusting the perceived location of three simultaneous messages to the left, right, and center. This arrangement has been called the *three-eared-person task.* Different lists of letters are presented over the three channels. In the whole-reporting condition, the person is to recite all letters presented; in the partial condition, he reports only one of the channels, as indicated by a cue projected to a screen. As in the visual modality, subjects recall more letters in the partial-reporting condition than in the whole-reporting condition. This reflects early auditory memory, also called **echoic memory** (Neisser, 1967), which lasts up to four seconds.

INTERIM SUMMARY

Psychophysics is the study of the relationship between physical stimuli and an observer's psychological responses—the sensations. Psychophysicists use techniques such as the method of limits to determine the threshold, which is the point in the stimulus continuum at which a given stimulus is detectable. In signal-detection theory, the concept of the threshold is replaced by the receiver operating characteristic (ROC) curve, a range of hit and false-alarm probabilities at different payoff schedules. A hit response represents the correct detection of a signal; a false alarm is an erroneous detection when no signal was present.

Sensory stimuli leave a trace for a brief period—less than one second for a visual stimulus and less than four seconds for an acoustic stimulus. Early visual memory has been demonstrated by comparing reporting accuracy under the whole- and the partial-reporting techniques. In the whole-reporting technique, the observer tries to report all of the letters of a matrix briefly flashed on a screen. In the partial-reporting technique, he reports a randomly chosen subset (e.g., a row of letters). Subjects report a greater percentage of letters in the partial-reporting condition.

FILTERING

Although you may not know it, you are quite familiar with filtering situations. When you are having lunch in the dining hall, and there is the din of dishes and chairs being moved in the background, there are usually several conversations. On your left, people are talking sports; on your right, they are complaining about a quiz; and you are chatting with a friend about a recent trip she took. You are listening to her, tuning out the other conversations. This is the prototypical filter situation; you are selecting one of several simultaneous messages. Cognitive psychologists seek to understand

the mechanisms that enable us to filter a message by asking the following questions:

How is information filtered?

What aspect of information is being filtered?

Where in the stream of information processing does the filter occur?

Researchers invented the dichotic listening (Greek for *two-eared*) paradigm to answer these questions. Using two auditory channels, they conducted experiments that you can easily try with a couple of friends. Assign two people to be readers and one person as listener. Place the listener in the center, with the two readers on either side. Read one passage to one ear of the listener and have the other person read another passage to the other ear. The listener is to attend to one ear and to repeat or shadow the first passage. The shadowed channel is the attended channel; the other is the nonattended channel. Ask the volunteer what he or she heard on the nonattended channel, if anything.

Cherry (1953) conducted a dichotic listening experiment like this. He played taped messages of equal loudness via headphones to the left and right ears. Listeners reported what they had heard on the attended ear without any problems. What surprised Cherry was how little information penetrated on the unattended channel. Listeners had no knowledge of the content of the unattended message; they did not even know whether the language the message was spoken in was Czech or English. Subjects did notice whether or not somebody was speaking, when the voice changed (e.g., from a woman's to a man's voice), and when a nonverbal signal (a beep) was given. For certain stimuli, such as speech played backwards, some of Cherry's listeners detected a change. They described the irrelevant channel as sounding queer (see also Wood & Cowan, 1995). In sum, listeners fully analyzed the attended message, including its meaning. The unattended message, however, received a very superficial sensory analysis.

Researchers attributed performance in the two-channel listening task to two successive mental operations, as shown in Figure 3.4A: detection and recognition. *Detection* means the subject is

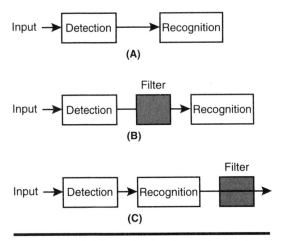

FIGURE 3.4 (*A*) Stage theory of detection and recognition. Detection of input is assumed to precede recognition. (*B*) Broadbent assumed that filtering took place after detection and prior to the recognition stage. (*C*) Filtering occurs after superficial recognition of input.

aware that there is a stimulus without being able to categorize it. *Recognition* means the subject has some degree of knowledge of the stimulus. Messages on the attended channel pass both stages. Messages on the unattended channel, however, are filtered somewhere in this chain of operations.

Broadbent (1958) postulated a filter early in the system that analyzed the input according to its physical features, including the direction of the message (left versus right ear), gender and dialect of the voice, speed of speech, and so on. The filter permitted passage of the message that had the critical feature (e.g., it came from the left). This information received further analysis and some interpretation, whereas the message sent to the right ear was ignored. Because the nonattended stimulus was not recognized, Broadbent assumed that filtering took place after detection and prior to the recognition stage, as shown in Figure 3.4B. Compared to detection, recognition is relatively complex; so, the filter limits input to this stage.

Subsequent dichotic listening studies casted doubt on Broadbent's (1958) theory of an early filter. Shadowing experiments have shown that listeners are able to detect their names, although nothing else was recognized. This indicates that the meaning of the message on the unattended channel was not totally ignored and that it received some analysis. Consequently, theorists concluded that the filter must be located later in the processing system—namely, after the recognition stage (e.g., Norman, 1968; Treisman, 1960). Each of the two messages received some rudimentary analysis, but only pertinent information—including one's own name—was noticed and remembered. This scenario is captured in Figure 3.4C.

Rather than postulating a filter, Neisser (1967) distinguished between preattentive and attentive processes, a contrast that continues to be influential. **Preattentive** or **automatic processes** take place early in the input stream; they usually analyze relatively simple features of the stimulus, including length, orientation, color for visual stimuli, and location and loudness of acoustic events. Preattentive operations are fast and operate in parallel, but spatial relations among features are not detected and the object is not recognized. **Attentive processes** occur later in processing; they operate on the output of the preattentive processes. Attentive processes register spatial relations between features and synthesize the object. They are relatively difficult and time consuming, so that the stimulus aspects are processed serially rather than in parallel.

Theorists differ in their view of the relation between automatic and attentive processes. According to filter theory and Neisser's (1967) view, automatic operations precede attentive operations; the alternative view holds that these kinds of operations may take place concurrently. Automatic and attentive processes are studied in the paradigms covered in the two remaining topics of the chapter: search tasks and dual-task situations. In search tasks, one looks for a target among distractors; in dual-task situations, one performs two concurrent tasks, allocating attention to one or both.

INTERIM SUMMARY

In filtering situations, a person selects one of several messages transmitted simultaneously. For example, in dichotic experiments, listeners receive input to their left and right ears and are asked to shadow input to one ear and ignore the other. The listener knows very little about the unattended message. Theorists attribute this attentional effect to a filter mechanism. They differ on the location of the filter in the flow of information. Broadbent (1958) postulated that a channel is selected early on the basis of its physical attributes and receives full processing, whereas nonselected channels receive no further processing. Late-selection theories (e.g., Neisser, 1967; Norman, 1968) assume that several channels receive some preattentive analysis, including some minimal semantic analysis. Then the filter selects one of the partially identified items for further processing—for example, for storage or for determining an overt response.

SEARCH—ATTRACTING ATTENTION

In detection tasks, we look for something that may or may not be there. For example, we may search for a symptom on an x-ray or a tone in a psychophysical experiment. *Search* refers to the process of locating a target among a set of other items, the distractors. You are engaged in a search when you look for a particular book on a shelf, for a sock in a drawer, or for a name in a telephone directory. The success of a search depends on many factors, including the distinctiveness of the target and the number of distractors. Search performance has been studied experimentally by using the visual search task and the memory search task. Visual search is popular among cognitive psychologists because it is easy to manipulate the simultaneous presentation of many items.

Visual and Memory Search

Look at the list of letters on the left of Figure 3.5. There are 20 rows of six letters each. The target, a *Q*, is embedded in a random location among the distractor letters. Try to find the *Q* as quickly as possible. The search time depends on the location of the letter in the display and on the similarity between the target and the distractors. The *Q* is easier to spot among the distractors in the right than in the left display.

Surprisingly the search rate does not change much when the viewer is looking for several targets, such as *K, V,* and *X,* at the same time. The set of targets is called the *memory set.* Once you have found a target, it will literally pop out at you, even

DGCGDC	XYKYVK
CDCGOC	XKKYYY
ODGCDG	YXYYXV
OCGDOD	YYVYXY
DOCOCG	XYKXVX
OGGGCG	VXVVVX
OGGGGD	VVXXXX
CDCGGD	VKYXVV
OGDCCD	KXQXXV
COOCOG	VYXVXK
OCGDCC	VVYKXV
ODOOCO	XXXKYK
GGCGGD	VXXKVX
GGQOOD	YXVYXX
DGDOGD	YXKKYY
DOCGOG	XKYVYX
CODDGD	YVYYYX
OODGDD	KXYYKX
DOOCDD	VKKKKY
GOCDCD	KVXVKY

FIGURE 3.5 Visual search task. The target in both lists is the letter *Q* (Neisser, 1967).

if the memory set contains several of them. Thus, search times as a function of memory set size are relatively flat.

In memory search, the subject first studies the memory set of up to six items, usually digits. Then one target digit is shown and the subject has to decide whether it was included in the memory set. Table 3.4 gives some examples. The subject's reaction time is measured from the time the target digit is shown to the time when she presses the *yes* or *no* key. Reaction times typically increase as the memory set size increases (e.g., Sternberg, 1966).

Results from memory search tasks and visual search tasks were different; reaction times increased as a function of the size of the memory set in memory searches but not in visual searches. Theorists proposed two search models: a serial model and a parallel model. Their predictions are illustrated in Figure 3.6.

In both types of searches, items in the memory set are assumed to be stored in memory and the test item is compared to the memory set representations. The type of comparison differs according to the serial and parallel models. In a serial search, the test item is compared with each item of the memory set one after another. This produces the positive slope indicative of a serial search shown in Figure 3.6A. In a parallel search, the target is compared to the items in the memory set in parallel, thus yielding the flat reaction time found in Figure 3.6B (see also Chapter 8).

Automatic and Controlled Processes

Schneider and Shiffrin (1977) wanted to understand the conflicting results observed during

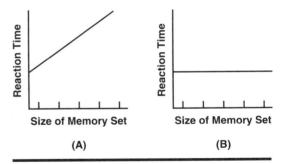

FIGURE 3.6   Models of memory search. (*A*) Serial search: Each added item of the memory set increases reaction time. (*B*) Parallel search: The target is compared in parallel to all members of the memory set so that there is no increase in reaction time as memory set size increases.

memory search and visual search tasks; they wanted to see whether each set of findings could be observed in the *same* experimental search paradigm. After all, the differences between them could stem from the different experimental paradigms: a visual search versus a memory search.

The two investigators devised a multiple-frame visual search task. On each trial, subjects saw a sequence of displays, called *frames*. They were first shown the memory set, which was then followed with 20 successive test frames, as shown in Figure 3.7. On some of the frames a target was present; other frames had no target. The subject had to make a *yes* response when he detected a target; otherwise, a *no* response was called for. The experimenters recorded reaction times.

Schneider and Shiffrin (1977) varied the relation of the targets to the distractors and the size of the memory set. There were two test conditions—the consistent and inconsistent conditions, as illustrated in Figure 3.7. In the consistent condition, targets were consistently of one stimulus type and distractors of the other type; for example, targets were digits and distractors were letters. Targets might include the digits *7 4 8 1*, as in Figure 3.7A. Any of these four digits could be a target on subsequent tests. Here, for example, *4* is the target among a set of distractor letters. In the inconsis-

TABLE 3.4   Sample Trials in Sternberg's Memory-Search Task

Memory Set	Target	Response
4 9 0 2	9	Yes
4 9 0 2	3	No
3 8 4 9	3	Yes
3 8 4 9	2	No

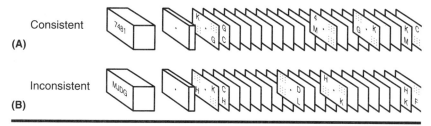

FIGURE 3.7 Sample trials in the multiple-frame visual search task. (*A*) Consistent trial. (*B*) Inconsistent trial (Shiffrin & Schneider, 1977).

tent condition, targets and distractors were mixed so that letters were used both as targets and as distractors. For example in Figure 3.7B, the letters *M J D G* were the targets among other distractor letters. The experimenters varied the size of the memory set from 1 to 4; in the former condition, subjects received only one potential target, in the latter they received four, as in Figure 3.7.

Figure 3.8 shows reaction times of hit responses as a function of the memory set size and mapping condition. In the inconsistent condition, there was a steep increase in reaction times as a function of memory set size, indicating a serial search. In the consistent condition, the reaction time function was relatively flat, suggesting a parallel search.

These results reflect subjects' experience with each type of task. After hundreds of trials, subjects gained sufficient practice even with mixed stimuli so that the slopes of reaction time functions decreased, although they did not become as flat as those in the consistent condition. Had subjects continued beyond an incredible run of 2,000 trials, search in the inconsistent condition might have come closer to that in the consistent condition. In any case, these results show that practice automatizes performance and increases a person's effective processing capacity (see also Chapters 5, 8, and 13).

Feature Integration Theory

Usually, we see an object such as a car without being aware of its basic features—its edges, texture, and shadows. Our experience suggests that we perceive whole objects rather than features and parts. According to Treisman's feature integration theory, however, object perception is not immediate; rather, it is the result of two successive visual processes: feature detection and feature integration (Treisman, 1988). Detection of such salient features as color, size, and line orientation is primary; it is relatively easy and automatic. Feature integration is a controlled process that requires the focus of attention. Treisman developed a set of clever demonstrations to separate detection and integration of features.

The contrast between detection and integration is apparent in Figures 3.9A and 3.9B. In Figure 3.9A, the white triangle is unique; it stands out because it differs from all others by one feature. Spotting a target like the triangle is easy and fast, no matter how many other items are in the display (see Figure 3.10). Next, try to find the white square in Figure 3.9B. It is defined by a **conjunction** of two features: color and shape; it is both white and square. If you want to find a conjunctive target among other items, you will need to inspect one after another. This requires integration of the two features and therefore the full attention to each of the items in the display. Integration and attention produce the steep increase in search time evident in the top function in Figure 3.10.

Treisman's Model. Summarizing her findings, Treisman proposed an attention model that included two stages: **feature detection** and **integration.** Salient features of stimuli are detected

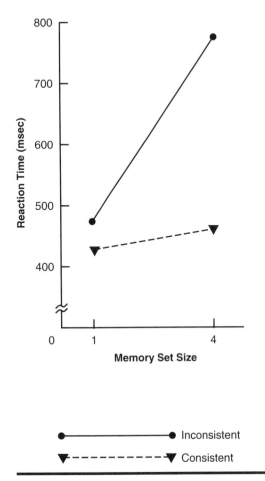

FIGURE 3.8 Search times as a function of search condition and memory set size. When the target and distractors are consistently different, search times do not increase by much, as the person is looking for more targets. An inconsistent assignment, however, leads to a steep increase in search time (see Schneider & Shiffrin, 1977).

grated, it is passed to processors involved in pattern recognition (see Chapter 4). According to Posner and Raichle, one such processor may be located in the extrastriate area of the cortex. They interpreted increased PET activity in this region during work on a feature integration task as support for Treisman's integration stage.

The independence of different feature detectors is suggested by perceptual phenomena and by an anatomical and physiological analysis of the visual system. You may be familiar with the waterfall illusion: When you look at a waterfall for a few minutes, and then shift your gaze to an adjacent scene—for example, the cliffs near the waterfall—it seems that they are flowing up. This illusion is the result of the perceptual adaptation of feature detectors that are sensitive to down-

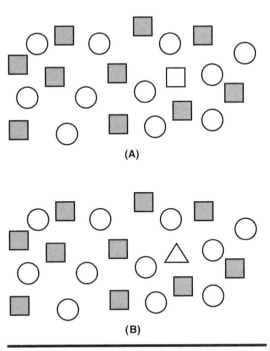

FIGURE 3.9 Displays used in feature detection and integration experiments: (A) The white triangle "pops out" against the background of distractors because it is defined by a unique feature. (B) The white square is harder to find because it involves a conjunction of features (Biederman, 1990).

automatically by independent feature modules, such as color, size, and distance. Integration is necessary when features must be integrated, such as finding the conjunction of the features white and square in Figure 3.10B. In Posner and Raichle's (1994) words, it is focal attention that provides the "glue" to integrate the features into a unitary object. When the information is inte-

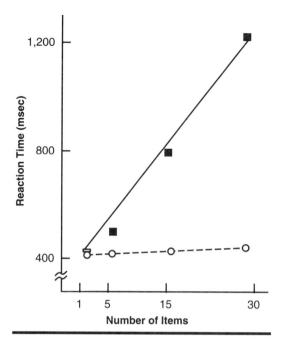

FIGURE 3.10 Search times are independent of display size when the target is defined by a single feature; they increase as a function of display size for targets defined conjunctively (Treisman & Gelade, 1980).

ward movement. The adaptation is independent of what is moving.

Neuroscientists have also concluded that neural feature processing is independent and that there are successive stages of feature detection and integration. According to anatomical analyses, there are independent channels in the visual system that process specific features of stimuli. Mishkin and Appenzeller (1987) concluded that the synthesis of more complex stimuli occurs in later stages. They wrote that "neurons have 'windows' on the visual world that become progressively broader, in both their spatial extent and the complexity of the information they admit, at successive stations. The cells respond to progressively more of an object's physical properties including its size, shape, color, and texture, until in the final stations, they synthesize a complete representation of the object" (p. 82).

Treisman's research and framework have been very influential in attention research. If you scan the titles of research journals, such as *Journal of Experimental Psychology: Human Perception and Performance,* you will get an impression of her influence. Subsequently, researchers have qualified her findings and proposed alternative views. Let us consider two of these developments.

■ Similarity theory is fundamentally different from Treisman's two-stage theory of attention (Duncan & Humphreys, 1989). Rather than assuming two stages of attention—automatic detection and attentive integration—these critics attributed the difficulty of the search to the similarity between the target and distractors, and the similarity among distractors. Search is easy when target and distractors are dissimilar, but it is difficult when they are similar (see Figure 3.5). Search is also easy when distractors are all similar to one another; but when they differ widely, the search rate slows down. According to similarity theory, these two principles guide visual processes when simple and conjoined features are involved. All that matters are these two aspects of similarity.

■ There is more preattentive processing of complex stimuli, including targets, that are defined conjunctively than Treisman had originally believed. The type of processing required depends on the features being conjoined. If color and orientation are conjoined, visual search is difficult; but if depth and color are conjoined, the search is easy (e.g., Nakayama, 1990).

According to Treisman's theory, a moving object represents a conjunction of features and therefore should be difficult to spot. Moving objects are seen very easily and detected quickly (e.g., McLeod et al., 1991). Assume you are looking at a computer screen with some stationary letters and some moving letters. Further assume that most of the time the moving letters travel in a predictable direction. When suddenly one of the moving letters travels in an unpredictable direction, it is detected quickly, regardless of how many distractors there are. According to

Treisman, the conjunction of the letter's identity and its direction of movement requires attention and thus slows down response speed. However, this was not the case.

McLeod and colleagues concluded that organisms have a special mechanism, the **movement filter,** which detects movement independent of other stimuli in the visual field. The movement filter is of ecological significance; it serves as an early warning system that helps organisms detect approaching animals, be they enemies or prey.

Neurophysiologists have reasons for assuming a movement filter; they have found visual nuclei in the medial temporal region of the cortex specialized for the detection of movement (Livingston & Hubel, 1988). These nuclei are more sensitive to moving objects than to stationary ones, whereas cells in other visual systems respond more vigorously to stationary stimuli (see Chapter 2). McLeod and associates (1991) also cited a case study in support of the idea that the movement filter is localized in the medial temporal lobe. They presented their movement-detection task to a patient, LM, who had suffered a lesion in the medial temporal region. Unlike non-patients, LM's search times increased significantly as a function of display size.

Spatial Attention

Even if you do not have the opportunity to move your eyes, knowing the spatial location of a target is advantageous: You react faster to the target. The speed-up is the result of spatial attention—the expectation that the target will be in a particular location.

The Attentional Spotlight. Posner demonstrated the advantage of knowing target locations in the spatial cuing task (Posner & Raichle, 1994). The spatial cuing task is a kind of signal-detection task in which visual cues and targets are flashed on a computer screen. Each trial starts with the cue: a cross, an arrow pointing left, or an arrow pointing right (see Figure 3.11). On about three quarters of the trials, the cue is followed by a bar

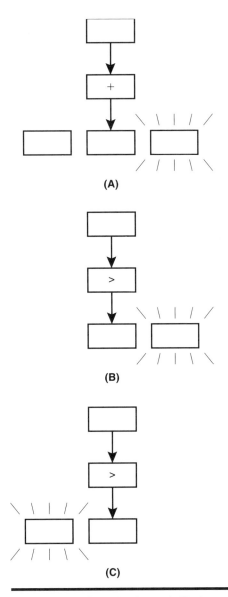

FIGURE 3.11 Spatial cuing task. Each positive trial starts with the presentation of a bar on a screen. Then a cue is shown inside the bar. Finally, another bar, the target, is shown on either the left or the right. On detecting the target bar, the subject presses a key. (*A*) The + indicates that the target has an equal probability of appearing on the left or the right of the standard bar. (*B*) Valid trial: The > indicates that the target will most likely occur on the right. (*C*) Invalid trials: the > fails to indicate that the target will appear on the left.

(the target). Sometimes the target is flashed to the left and sometimes to the right of the cue. Subjects press a key when they detect the target; they receive feedback; the stimulus is turned off and the reaction time recorded.

Posner and colleagues used the cross and arrows as cues to indicate the likely location of the target. The cross indicated that the target had an equal probability of occurring on the left or right (Figure 3.11A); these were neutral trials. On valid trials, valid location cues were presented; arrows pointed to the left or the right (< and >); this meant that the target occurred on the indicated side on 80% of the trials (Figure 3.11B). On 20% of the trials, the location cues were invalid (Figure 3.11C); for example, when the arrow pointed to the right, the target was shown on the left.

Subjects responded faster when the location cue was valid than when it was neutral or invalid. Researchers recorded subjects' eye movements as they worked through this task and found that there were hardly any eye movements during the short intervals in which the stimuli were flashed. Therefore, the advantage for known location was not a result of overt eye movements. Posner and associates concluded that an attentional spotlight, an internal eye, must be involved. They also postulated that attention is facilitated within the spotlight while it is inhibited outside.

Neural Networks in Visual Attention.   Posner's team and other research teams have proposed two primary neural networks thought to support visual attention, the **orienting network** and the **executive network** (Posner, 1995, Posner & Raichle, 1994).

The Orienting Network.   This network is implicated in overt and covert attention processes. Overt attention processes include eye movements and orienting of the head in order to get a better view of a stimulus. Covert attention refers to enhanced efficiency of processing a target stimulus even before the eyes are moved. Research indicates that such covert shifts of attention occur about 100 ms before the overt eye movement; the subject responds more quickly to the target stimulus if it is located in the attended to location (e.g., in the spatial cuing task).

The orienting network involves the following three neural structures:

- The parietal lobes
- The superior colliculus in the midbrain
- The thalamus

Each of these centers is thought to contribute a special process to spatial attention; for example, the parietal lobes are implicated in the disengagement and the thalamus is implicated in the enhancement of spatial attention.

Evidence on the contribution of the **parietal lobes** comes from single-cell studies in animals, neuropsychological case studies, and PET analyses. Researchers trained monkeys in the spatial cuing task and recorded the activity of single cells at different sites of the visual and the attentional systems. They found that the rate of firing in the parietal nuclei increased just after the occurrence of the target. At the same time, reaction time was facilitated as it is in human subjects.

Human patients whose parietal regions are lesioned in one hemisphere exhibit **visual neglect** of objects placed in the opposite side of the visual field. In the spatial cuing task, these patients perform quickly on valid and invalid trials provided that the stimuli are projected to the intact parietal lobe. However, their reaction time is slowed down disproportionally on invalid trials when the cues are projected to the impaired parietal lobe. Remember: On invalid trials, it is necessary to shift one's covert attention from the cued location to a new location. Posner and his colleagues reasoned that the parietal cortex is responsible for the **disengagement** of attention.

The **superior colliculus** is a nucleus located in the midbrain. It is implicated both in overt eye movements and in covert attention. If the superior colliculus is damaged, subjects experience some difficulty in moving their eyes and in executing covert shifts in attention in the spatial cuing task.

Eye movements and attention shifts are still possible; they are, however, much slower than in control subjects who are not impaired.

Neuroscientists have known for a long time that the **thalamus** is an essential relay station of the visual system (Chapter 2). It has been speculated that the thalamus, especially the **pulvinar region,** works like a spotlight in selecting certain information from the extrastriate areas for deeper analysis. Single-cell recordings in animals, psychopharmacological research, and PET imaging studies have lent support to the notion of the attentional spotlight in the thalamus. It has been shown that the pulvinar region in the monkey thalamus fires vigorously when the monkey shifts attention to new locations in the visual field. Similarly, using monkeys, scientists demonstrated that pharmacological substances known to block the pulvinary slows their reaction times in the spatial attention task.

In human subjects performing the letter search task, an increase of PET activity was observed in the pulvinar region. In the letter search task, the viewer sees a matrix of letters—say, an *O* among *G*s—and must focus on the target, the *O,* and ignore the distractors, the *G*s. Although this task engages visual processes, researchers were surprised to find that the primary visual cortex did not exhibit any elevated PET activity. Researchers concluded that the pulvinar serves as an amplifier of relevant information and as a filter of irrelevant information.

The Executive Network.   The executive network exercises a control function in the detection of target events, whether their source is the sensory system or the memory system. Posner and Raichle characterized this network as follows: "Once attention has shifted to a new location and the visual contents there have been transmitted forward in the brain, the executive network comes into play. . . . It has the task, sometimes called detection, of bringing an object into conscious awareness" (1994, p. 168).

Attending to the target stimulus confers a certain protection to the stimulus so that it is less interfered with by other signals. Perceivers pay a price, however, for gaining a clearer focus of the stimulus: There is a limit to the number of stimuli or aspects of a stimulus to which one can attend. It is very difficult to track two simultaneous targets, even when one of the targets is some content of memory. For example, when a person concentrates on some mental task, it may be more difficult to track an external target stimulus (Posner, 1995).

The principal brain region implicated in the executive network is the frontal lobe of the brain, especially the anterior cingulate gyrus. PET studies indicate increased metabolic activity in this gyrus in subjects performing target detection tasks. Also, when the number of targets is increased, so does the metabolic rate. Posner (1995) sees an affinity between the executive network of attention and the executive control system of working memory (Goldman-Rakic, 1990; Chapter 8).

Before concluding the section on the executive network, you should note that there are researchers who doubt the executive attention system altogether (Allport, 1993). While not denying the large body of new research data on attention, Allport has interpreted the results differently. He argued that the research indicates multiple and **parallel attention systems.** He cited the more than 20 centers in the cortex implicated in vision, and the what and where systems as well as the multiple reciprocal links between perception and action in support of his hypothesis that attentional functions are heterogeneous rather than centralized and unified.

Enhancement of Neural Activity through Attention.   Mangun and Hillyard (1990) proposed the sensory gain hypothesis, which says that visual attention increases sensory activity in the visual pathways. The enhanced activity is reflected in increased event-related potentials (ERPs) and patterns. According to Hillyard, Mangun, Woldorff, and Luck (1995), acoustic signals are similarly enhanced through attention. Hillyard and colleagues distinguished between two interpretations of the patterns of ERP activity. The enhancement hypothesis is supported if the activity shows the same qualitative pattern and location and only the amplitude differs. On the other hand, attention would be mediated by separate and independent circuits if the waveforms differed in pattern and location. Hillyard and colleagues found support for the enhancement view in several paradigms, including the dichotic listening task.

INTERIM SUMMARY

In search tasks, the viewer looks for a target among a set of distractors. In the multiple-frame task, the subject is first shown a memory set of targets and then successive test frames. On positive (but not on negative) trials, each frame contains a target among a set of distractors. Subjects are asked to make a speeded *yes/no* decision to indicate the presence or absence of a target. When targets and distractors are consistently drawn from different stimulus classes (e.g., letters versus digits), the search is automatic and search times are independent of the display size. When targets and distractors are mixed, however, the search requires attention, and search times increase as the display size increases.

According to Treisman's (1988) feature integration theory, detection of a small number of simple visual features, including color and tilt, is primary; it is automatic and preattentive. Feature integration is a controlled process that requires focused attention. Detecting a conjunctively defined target, like a white square among black squares and white circles, requires integration and focused attention. Search times for such targets increase as a function of the number of distractor items in the display. Search times for uniquely defined targets are independent of the number of distractors.

Treisman's theory of attention has been amended; for example, movement has been added to the original salient features. Competing theories have emerged as well. According to similarity theory, there are no successive preattentive and attentional stages in perception. Rather, the slope of search functions can be accounted for by the similarity between targets and distractors on the one hand, and among distractors on the other. When targets and distractors are different, and distractors are similar among themselves, search is easy; otherwise, it is difficult.

In spatial attention tasks, subjects try to detect a target in a set of possible locations. Response times are fastest when the viewer is cued about the target's likely location, thus reflecting spatial attention. Posner believed that spatial attention is like a spotlight that facilitates detection within a narrow range. Posner and Raichle (1994) proposed two principal neural networks of attention: the orienting network and the executive network. In tasks that require spatial orienting, there is increased neuronal activity in the centers of the orienting network, the parietal lobes, the superior colliculus, and the pulvinar region of the thalamus, but not in the primary visual areas of the cortex. Posner and Raichle further assumed that once attention is focused, thanks to the orienting network, the executive attention network comes into play. PET studies suggest that this network is probably located in the anterior cingulate gyrus of the frontal lobes. According to Posner, the executive attention system brings a target into conscious awareness and protects it from interference from other signals.

DOING TWO THINGS AT ONCE: THE DUAL-TASK PARADIGM

Allocation of Resources

Automatic processes are easy; they consume relatively little mental capacity, can be called on quickly, and can be carried out concurrently. For example, an experienced driver can drive and talk at the same time; an expert writer can listen to music and compose a paper, and a veteran basketball player can dribble and guard an opponent at the same time. A controlled process, however, is difficult; it consumes more capacity, has a longer latency, and is easily disrupted. For example, a beginning driver devotes attention to his driving and cannot drive and talk at the same time; a novice writer gropes for words and ideas and cannot listen to music when he is writing; and finally, a student learning basketball has difficulty dribbling, let alone watching anyone else. These intuitions have been confirmed in the dual-task paradigm. This paradigm involves two tasks—Task 1 and Task 2—and three conditions. In condition 1, a subject executes Task 1 singly; in condition 2, he performs Task 2; and in condition 3, he performs Task 1 and Task 2 concurrently. The experimenter records performance for each condition, including response accuracy and speed. Researchers are especially interested in subjects' performance in the concurrent condition and have found that performance depends on the degree of attention devoted to each task.

The results of dual-task experiments are plotted in terms of the performance operating characteristic curve, which shows the performance when the subject performs (1) Task 1 alone, (2) Task 2 alone, and (3) both Tasks 1 and 2 together. Performance levels for the single task are shown on the x- and y-axes; performance on concurrent tasks is shown in the interior of the panel (e.g., Gopher & Donchin, 1986; Schneider & Fisk, 1982). In Figure 3.12A and B, results from a hypothetical dual-task experiment are summarized. Figure 3.12A shows single-task performance for Tasks 1 and 2 as points on the two respective axes. Figure 3.12B reflects the performance on both tasks when they are executed jointly.

Gopher and Donchin (1986) used the dual-task paradigm to assess performance levels of concurrent target tracking and typing (see Chapter 15). Subjects saw a target moving across a computer screen. They were instructed to track it by controlling the joystick with their right hand. Tracking performance was assessed by an accuracy measure plotted on the x-axis in Figure 3.12C. Subjects were asked to type Hebrew letters with their left hand. Typing performance was assessed by speed, as indicated on the y-axis in Figure 3.12C. The data points in the interior of the panel reflect different priorities devoted to each of the two tasks; going from left to right, priority shifts from typing to tracking. These results reflect the trade-off as subjects shift their attention between tasks.

Summarizing several experiments like these, Shiffrin wrote that automatic processes are either

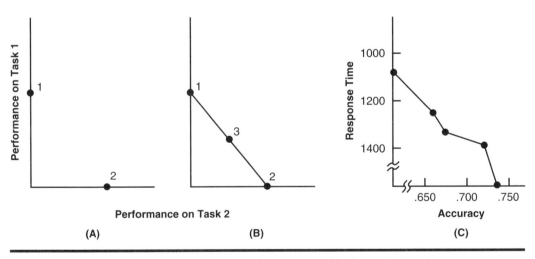

FIGURE 3.12 Performance operating characteristic as observed in dual-task experiments. Each axis represents performance on one of the two tasks. (*A*) Single-task performance on Tasks 1 and 2. (*B*) Performance decreases when two tasks are executed jointly, as indicated by point 3. (*C*) Performance in Gopher and Donchin's (1986) study.

innate or have been learned, and do not "push against capacity limitations. They can operate in parallel with certain other automatic and attentive processes without loss and without interference with those other processes. The attentive processes are limited in capacity and tend to interfere with one another, often leading them to be used successively" (1988, p. 764).

Event-Related Potentials Reveal Attention in Dual-Task Experiments.

Using the ERP, Näätänen (1990) found that listeners analyze secondary signals. He used an experimental dual-task condition and a single-task control condition. In the single-task condition, subjects listened to a long sequence of identical sounds; no other task was involved and listeners gave their full attention to the sound sequence. From time to time, the sound sequence was interrupted by a slightly different stimulus, an oddball stimulus. The subject had to detect the oddballs and press a key. Näätänen found that ERPs recorded on oddball presentations included a negative peak that he called the *mismatch negativity (MMN)*. This pattern was a telltale sign of the attention elicited by the oddball stimulus.

In the dual-task condition, subjects read a book as their primary task and detected oddball stimuli as the secondary task. Näätänen hypothesized that if a subject devoted full attention to the primary task, ERP patterns from the secondary detection task would differ from the control condition; there should be no MMNs. Results showed, however, there were MMNs even when subjects paid no attention to the sound-detection task, at least not consciously. Näätänen concluded that the secondary stimuli were analyzed in an automatic and fast process that required few cognitive resources. This preliminary analysis is the basis for switching attention should the need arise. Suppose there is a fire alarm on the secondary channel, the person would immediately attend to it. Näätänen's interpretation meshes nicely with Norman's (1968) view that stimuli from several channels receive a superficial analysis and selection is based on that analysis (see Figure 3.4C).

Divided Attention.

Wouldn't it be nice if you could do two things at once without loss of performance in either? Research by Spelke, Hirst, and Neisser (1976) has shown that you can do two things at once provided you are willing to invest the time and effort necessary. These investigators conducted a long-term study involving two subjects, John and Diane. There were over 80 one-hour training sessions during a four-month period. Subjects were engaged in two activities simultaneously. They read short stories by American and European writers and they copied down lists of words the experimenters dictated to them. During the first couple of weeks, John and Diane's reading speed and comprehension suffered, but after more practice, performance improved to preexperimental single-task levels. Recognition tests were given following specific training sessions. Lists of words were presented that included some of the items read in dictation and a set of new items. Recognition performance was initially somewhat poorer than in the single-task context but picked up after only one week of practice. Recognition was assessed by the proportion of hit and false-alarm responses (see Theory of Signal Detection).

For the initial training period, the word lists to be copied were random. Later, the experimenters manipulated the list structure; for example, they presented a block of categorized sublists, say 20 instances of furniture. At first, John and Diane remained unaware of these substructures. However, when the list included rhymes like *roll, toll, poll,* the subjects noticed it. This was associated with a temporary dip in reading speed and comprehension in the concurrent reading task. After an additional eight weeks of training, performance on both tasks continued to improve. Diane and John read at their normal rates of 325 and 450 words per minute, respectively; they comprehended the stories; they detected the structures of the word lists, and their recognition performance was also excellent.

Spelke and colleagues concluded that their subjects had achieved automaticity of simultaneous reading and copying performance. The investigators defined *automatic* as being able to extract meaning from the task without devoting attention to it. They concluded that Diane and John had "achieved a true division of attention" and that "there are no obvious, general limits to attentional skills," provided, of course, the person devotes extensive practice to the two tasks (1976, p. 229).

Tangible advantages of training involving multiple tasks were demonstrated by Gopher (1993) in pilots of the Israeli air force. He trained an experimental group of air force cadets on the computer game Space Fortress. This is a challenging arcade-type game requiring the coordination of several goals: Control the movement of the spaceship on the screen, fire missiles, defend the spaceship, and destroy an enemy fortress. All sorts of obstacles, mostly mines, seem to crop up from nowhere and must be dealt with. The students were initially overwhelmed and experienced a sense of panic. Gopher's study included a control group who received no training on the game. Remarkably, the game-trained group achieved better scores in training flights with actual aircraft than the control group!

According to Logan's (1988) instance theory of automatization, practice changes the nature of the task. Each episode of practice creates a new memory trace of the stimulus, which is a new instance. As a result, retrieval becomes easier. When a stimulus is presented, there are simply more opportunities to retrieve one of them. A good illustration of automatization of retrieval is the acquisition of arithmetic skills by children. Initially, the child uses an algorithm: She adds single digits by incrementing a counter (frequently the fingers serve as the counter). With practice, however, the child memorizes addends and the corresponding sums and simply retrieves the sum when presented with the addends (see Chapter 13). Practice increases a person's knowledge base by producing more instances of the skill to be learned. According to Logan's model, limits of performance are a result of lack of knowledge rather than of attentional resources.

Automatization has a number of consequences, including the following:

- There is a speedup of performance; the gains are relatively large early in practice, diminishing later (see Chapter 5).
- Execution of the task requires less effort because the person has more than one way of doing it—namely, by using an algorithm or memory retrieval.
- Performance becomes autonomous; it can occur without the person's intention. Merely attending to a stimulus retrieves all information associated with it, whether the person wishes it or not. (Unintended retrieval is nicely illustrated by the Stroop effect, described next.)

Interference in the Stroop Task

Two activities compete in dual-task situations. Two activities may even compete when a person executes what appears to be a single task, such as naming colors. In the Stroop task, a subject is given a list of color names. The subject must either read the words or name the color of the printed words. Reading is easy in the control condition when the color names are printed black on white, and in the congruent condition when the color name is printed in the same ink color (for example, the word *red* is printed in red). Reading is still easy in the conflict condition when the color names are printed in different colors (for example, the word *red* is printed in green). Typically, word reading times average about 470 milliseconds in each of the three reading conditions.

The conflict condition is far more difficult, however, when the subject is to name the color the words are printed in. Thus, the subject must say "green" when encountering the word *red* printed in green. In this condition, color naming takes over 800 milliseconds, because one unwittingly reads the words as one tries to name the colors. Reading is practically automatic; one does it involuntarily. Because one cannot ignore the word, it interferes with naming the color; two aspects in the stimulus compete for attention (Stroop, 1935).

The Stroop effect is very robust. Over 700 articles have been published, at least 70% of these in the last two decades (MacLeod, 1991). According to Shiffrin and Schneider's (1977) theory, automatic responses are fast and require little attention, whereas controlled processes are slow and require more attention. We have so much practice reading that it is automatic, fast, and hard to interfere with. On the other hand, color naming is controlled, slow, and more easily interfered with by other tasks, especially by reading. Interference effects similar to the Stroop effect occur in other situations—for example, when someone tries to recall her phone extension but gives her office number instead because she happens to look at it.

Navon (1977) discovered a Strooplike interference effect in a letter-naming task. Subjects saw large block letters composed of small stimuli, as illustrated in Figure 3.13. Their task was to identify either the large letter or the small letters. It was easier to identify the large letter than the small letters. When responding to the small letters, the global letter interfered.

Cognitive psychologists are interested in the Stroop effect because it provides such a handy design to induce competition between automatic and controlled processes. Theoretical accounts of the effect include associationist, information-processing, and even connectionist models (Cohen, Dunbar, & McClelland, 1990; MacLeod,

1991; MacLeod & Dunbar, 1988). Neuroimaging studies show that working on the Stroop test taxes the executive attention network. Posner and Raichle (1994) reported an increase in PET activity in the cingulate gyrus of the frontal lobe when subjects did the Stroop test.

Cognitive Skills Involve Two or More Tasks. Cognitive skill such as writing and problem solving involve different aspects, thus making them dual-task—indeed, multiple-task—situations. In executing the skill, the person performs several component activities. A writer, for example, moves the pen over the paper, chooses words, forms sentences, and expresses ideas. As the writer gains more experience during her writing career, some of these operations become automatic and demand less effort and attention. Indeed, the goal of writing instruction is to give the student sufficient practice so that the mechanics of writing become automatic and she can attend to the ideas themselves. When we solve arithmetic problems—for example, an addition problem—we also execute several tasks: We add the numbers by columns, carry when appropriate, and remember the sums of the digits themselves. It is easier to do addition if any of these components have become automatic. If a student does not know the sum of simple digits, she will need to devote attention to this component and will run into trouble with carrying as well.

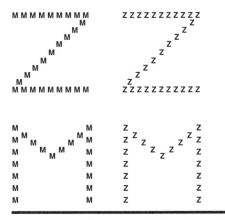

FIGURE 3.13 Letters used in letter-identification task of Navon (e.g., 1977).

INTERIM SUMMARY

In dual-task situations, one performs two tasks at the same time and allocates mental resources to each. The performance operating characteristic describes the trade-off between the two tasks: If both tasks are highly practiced, there is no performance decrement relative to single-task performance; otherwise, performance on one or both tasks suffers. There are characteristic patterns of event-related potentials in auditory dual-task experiments. These reveal that a person analyzes stimuli even if they are not overtly attended to. In the Stroop task, one sees color names printed in a different color—for example, the word *red*

Box 3.3 _____

Attention in Everyday Life

ABSENTMINDED BEHAVIOR

Who has not experienced "slips of action" like stepping into the shower with your clothes on or pouring coffee on a plate rather than in a cup? Reason (1984) studied episodes of absentmindedness by asking volunteers to keep a diary of behavioral lapses. Over a period of one week, volunteers wrote down what happened whenever their actual behavior differed from their intended action. Their reports revealed four types of slips of action:

- _Repetition:_ An action is repeated unnecessarily.
- _Wrong object:_ The person executes the intended action but applies it to the wrong object.
- _Intrusion:_ Components of some other action are unintentionally executed within a sequence of intended actions.
- _Omission:_ Components of an action were unintentionally left out of a sequence of intended actions.

Reason observed that the errors tended to occur with well-practiced skills. It is as if the action runs on automatic pilot without control from an executive. No attention is devoted to the behavior and it is triggered by some unrelated cue. The slips of action tend to occur with greater frequency in transitions between different activities, such as when a person leaves home for work. A lesson from this study is to slow down when you leave home or work and make a checklist of jobs to do.

ATTENTION AND EFFORT

There is an inverse relation between attention and interest. When an activity is exciting and novel, attention comes naturally. When we are asked to do something boring, it requires conscious effort, and attention is not easily sustained. There is no ready solution to this problem (as students know when they have to write a paper). One way to motivate yourself is to use the principle of social facilitation: Pretend that you are explaining the topic to a friend. For example, if your paper is on the economic history of the northwestern states, you would start out by making this story interesting to a listener. This approach helps you to generate ideas—a component of writing that demands great attention (see Chapter 12).

ATTENTION DEFICIT DISORDER

This is the term psychiatrists use to describe the behavior of highly distracted children (e.g., Ingersoll, 1988). The symptoms occur for an extended time, usually over six months, and include difficulty sustaining attention in tasks or play activities, frequent shifts from one activity to another, and excessive talking. There is no single source for attention deficit disorder: It has been attributed to environmental conditions, to hereditary factors, and to "minimal brain dysfunction." Even today, there are no satisfactory answers.

A suggestive study was carried out in Denmark by using brain imaging techniques (Lou, Hendricksen, & Bruhn, 1984). Researchers found a diminished blood flow in the frontal lobe of children diagnosed with attention deficit disorder. They observed that the drug Ritalin produced an increase in the frontal lobe blood flow and an improvement in concentration for about three to four hours. These results implicate the frontal lobe in attention. Data remain scarce, however, because physicians are justifiably reluctant to use radioactive agents (required for imaging techniques) with children. Also, there are side effects of the drug—for example, loss of appetite. Nevertheless, further research is necessary, because this disorder affects several million school-age children.

_____

printed in green. It is difficult to name the color that the words are printed in, because the highly practiced skill of reading interferes with the less-practiced task of naming colors.

———————

CONCLUSION

Attention was introduced as a research topic over a century ago. Today, it remains one of the most vital subjects in cognitive psychology. Many theories of attention have been proposed; sophisticated techniques have been developed and a large body of data has been amassed. There are models for selecting attended and nonattended information in filtering situations, for automatic and attentive search, and for feature detection and integration. Techniques range from speeded search tasks to concurrent task situations, and increasingly neural activity is measured as subjects execute a task.

Some of the issues that fascinated William James are still current: What are the neural structures of attentional control? What information is selected? and How can the study of attention help us in everyday situations? After a century of research there are, of course, also new research questions: What determines the effectiveness of visual search? Where in the processing system is the locus of selection? and How do we account for interference between two tasks or two aspects of the same task as observed in Stroop's color-naming test?

Because of the abundance of research on attention, no single theory can handle all of its varieties. In particular, the hope of early psychologists has not yet been fulfilled that attention research would discover ways of improving attention in everyday life. Efforts are being made, however, as the cases in Box 3.3 illustrate.

There has been progress on the research front. Although research on attention is diverse, different frameworks agree on the following:

— The human information-processing system has a limited capacity to handle all of the information arriving at the sensory organs.
— As a result of the processing limits, a person selects aspects of the task environment and devotes more resources to the attended task.
— Attention necessary for a task depends on how well practiced it is. Well-practiced skills are nearly automatic, requiring little attention; however, new skills require the full focus of attention.

RECOGNITION AND ACTION

PREVIEW

Organisms communicate with their environment through recognition and action. Recognition plays a role whenever an input from the environment is processed through learning, language comprehension, problem solving, or perception. Recognition involves two principal stages: generating a description of the input stimulus and comparing the description with a stored representation in memory.

Issues of pattern recognition will be introduced by examining David Marr's model of computer vision. A discussion of theories of human pattern recognition, applied to letter and word recognition, follows. Recognition of a stimulus depends both on features of the stimulus itself, referred to as *bottom-up information*, and on the context of the stimulus, referred to as *top-down information*. Theories of recognition include interactive and modular models. In interactive models, bottom-up and top-down information influence the recognition process jointly. In modular models, these two types of information are processed independently. The recognition of shapes and of dynamic events, including biological motion, have attracted much research interest. Biederman's recognition-by-components theory and the ecological framework offer innovative approaches to shape perception and event perception, respectively.

We are continuously engaged in motor action, whether it is walking, writing, speaking, or any other physical movement. The skeletal muscles are the effectors of movement; they are innervated by axons emanating from the spinal cord. Centers in the cerebellum, the basal ganglia, the prefrontal cortex, and the primary motor cortex control the planning and sequencing of motor behavior. Psychological research on motor behavior includes investigations of movements toward a target, the degrees-of-freedom problem, schematic structures that govern action, and the acquisition of motor skills. The study of movements toward a target led to the generalization known as Fitts's law, according to which the time to reach a target increases linearly with the difficulty of the action. Researchers have been puzzled by the degrees-of-freedom problem, which is: Although an organism has many degrees of freedom in moving toward a target, typically the optimal trajectory is chosen. We will review alternative approaches to the degrees-of-freedom problem that are based on schema theory, dynamic theory, and neural network theory.

Behaviorists considered movements as response chains that were triggered by external and proprioceptive stimuli. Since Karl Lashley's research in the 1950s, we know that movements are hierarchically structured and that their serial order is governed by abstract schemas, such as linguistic structures. The schema concept has been widely applied to the study of motor action and to the acquisition of motor skills, whether they are as trivial as tapping one's fingers in a psychological study or as important as typing on a keyboard. The chapter concludes with an in-depth examination of the patterns of typing and of a schema-based model to account for those performance patterns.

INTRODUCTION

Organisms perceive and act on their environment; using a communication metaphor, organisms accept inputs from and emit outputs to the environment. We hear sounds, observe events, and recognize objects; we also walk and run, grasp and throw things, and use tools. For each side, input and output, there are specialized organs and processes. Environmental input includes all the stimuli impinging on the sensory receptors. The inputs are transformed along the sensory pathways and the cortical and subcortical regions (see Chapter 2) through a wealth of processes psychologists describe as perception and recognition. Recognition includes processes that identify objects in the environment; in vision, for example, these processes correspond to the system that psychologists have described as the what system (see Chapter 2; Neisser, 1989). Perception, in comparison, specifies the perceiver's location in the environment, the where system.

The organism emits motor actions as output; motor action is a very broad category, including all uses of the skeletal muscles, whether it is reaching toward a target, typing, piano playing, or speaking. Although cognitive psychologists have traditionally emphasized input processes more

than output processes, recognition and action are equally important. In any case, they are intimately related. Organisms recognize their own actions and the action of other organisms, and they act and move in order to support cognition; for instance, you stretch your head to see a friend in a crowd, extend your hand to feel a contour, and move your eyes, however unconsciously, to read a text. Based on their perception of their own actions and their effects, organisms can adjust the actions if necessary. It is for these reasons that this chapter discusses action as well as recognition. Taking account of the action side of cognition is important because it will lead to a fuller understanding of cognition in general.

RECOGNITION

We recognize shapes, faces, tunes, and many other stimuli routinely without much thought. If, for some reason, your recognition system were to develop defects and you could no longer function in your environment, you would appreciate its importance. Imagine you awoke one morning and did not recognize familiar objects around you: the digits on the alarm clock, the music on the radio, and the letters in the newspaper. Case histories of such recognition failures, interesting in their own right, demonstrate the essential role of pattern recognition.

Russian neuropsychologist A. R. Luria described the case of an injured World War II veteran who suffered a specific recognition deficit. One day this patient was looking for a bathroom in the hall of his hospital. He had been told the bathroom was next door. He looked at the sign on the door but could not read a word. The patient reported that "some peculiar, foreign letters were printed there. . . . When a patient passed by, I pointed to the sign and asked him what is was. 'It's the men's room,' he replied. 'What's the matter with you, can't you read?' I stood there as though rooted to the spot, simply unable to understand *why I couldn't read that sign. After all, I could see, I wasn't blind"* (Luria, 1976, p. 62, italics added). The amazement Luria's patient experienced when he could no longer read (although he was not blind) reflects the essence of recognition: We recognize a stimulus when we know what it means. Recognition occurs, for example, when we know *A* is the first letter of the alphabet and when we associate a name with a familiar face or a title with a melody. Even though pattern recognition appears to be so easy, it presents cognitive psychologists with a daunting problem. The challenge is to illuminate the mental mechanisms that support identification of the thousands of patterns, stimuli, and events we encounter.

Pattern recognition is usually fast and cannot be slowed down or dissected for the convenience of psychologists. Therefore, researchers simplify the process by developing and testing models of recognition. Until the computer was invented, theories of pattern recognition were mainly speculative. To be sure, important and interesting questions were asked, but no one really knew how to address them within a comprehensive framework. With the advent of the computer, this changed. Suddenly, there was a proliferation of applications and theoretical models. Computerized recognition systems range from such commonplace applications as character recognition to esoteric ones that detect anomalies in specimens of blood, skin, and other tissue. Following are some illustrative applications of computer-based recognition systems:

- Computerized character recognition is used in supermarkets, libraries, banks, and postal services.
- The FBI uses computer-based data banks of fingerprints as part of its automatic identification system.
- In computerized voice recognition, a recorded voice sample is matched against stored voice templates in computer memory.
- Robot vision is widely employed in manufacturing—for example, to identify objects on assembly lines.
- Computers are used to verify the authenticity of signatures and to read checks.

These applications are based on a general model of pattern recognition that includes input devices and data banks as well as transformation and matching routines. The input devices include cameras and microphones and the data banks are repositories of stored prototypes for the set of items to be categorized. The software routines mediate between the physical stimulus and the format of the information stored in the data banks.

The theoretical models for computer and human recognition are very similar to the applied framework. In both cases, recognition is based on the matching of stimulus information with representations stored in memory. These representations have a certain format; for example, visual information is captured in terms of such features as lines, regions, sizes, and orientations. At a functional level, the general model assumes two basic steps of pattern recognition:

- *Generate a description of the object.* Stimulus properties are encoded in terms of features or some other characteristic and are transformed into the specific format of the representations in memory.
- *Compare the description with stored representations.* The comparison process produces

candidates for a match, selects the best-fitting match according to a certain criterion, and returns the label or categorization associated with the representation.

This general framework has been applied to the recognition of all sorts of patterns and shapes from different modalities. Our discussion begins with the influential model of computer vision developed by David Marr. It is a good example of how stimulus descriptions are generated.

Computer Vision

You have no difficulty recognizing Figure 4.1a as a basketball player, although physically it is nothing more than an assembly of shades of gray. How do you suppose a recognition system, whether human or computer, makes sense of these shades? Consider how Marr (1982) approached this problem. Marr's model involves matching the visual input to representations of potential stimuli in computer memory. The input is

transformed in successive stages from an array of light intensities that represent different regions of the stimulus to progressively abstract descriptions. In the first step of this process, an image is acquired. Then the image is cleaned up; edges are extracted and represented in terms of abstract descriptions.

Image Acquisition.   The eye of Marr's computer system is a camera; it records light patterns reflected from objects in the visual field in a large array of picture elements or pixels. The pixels convert the light energy into electronic signals; these, in turn, are converted into numbers, as illustrated in Figure 4.2. The result of this analog-to-digital conversion is the image array, a pattern of values for thousands of pixels. In Figure 4.2, values of 10 correspond to light regions in the display, and values of 1 correspond to dark regions.

Because the image array is often messy, there is a preprocessing stage to clean up the image and filter out smudges. A simplified image results that serves as input for higher-level processing, such

(a)

(b)

FIGURE 4.1   (*a*) Photograph of an athlete in shades of gray from dark to light (Marr, 1982). (*b*) Outline drawing, the primal sketch, of the athlete generated by difference operators. Note that edges are exaggerated.

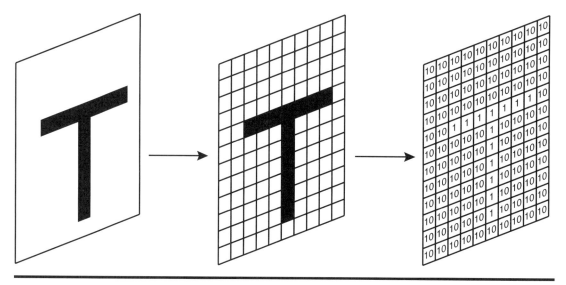

FIGURE 4.2 Transformation of light energy via electrical impulses to a digitized representation of the letter *T*.

as edge detection and analysis of regions. Deleting detail, however, is error prone; therefore, preprocessing has to be done with care.

The representations in memory are defined by lines, regions, and configurations of regions. The image array must therefore be expressed in terms of these units. The crucial step in identifying lines and regions is detecting boundaries between different shades of gray.

Edge Detection and the Line Sketch.   The detection of edges is a fundamental process in Marr's model, as it is in organisms (see Hubel & Wiesel, 1965). Edges are detected by **difference operators,** which compute the difference in brightness between regions. Their function is to enhance edges in the image. Edge detection transforms images like Figure 4.1A into a line drawing like Figure 4.1B; this is called the *primal sketch.* In developing his model, Marr took into consideration well-known visual effects in organisms, including the brightness contrast and the mechanism of edge detection in the horseshoe crab, *Limulus.* The mechanisms of edge detection are, of course, different in computers and organisms.

In *Limulus,* for example, edges are enhanced by a neural network that includes lateral inhibition. Nevertheless, the results are the same in Marr's computer system as in organisms: Boundaries, lines, and regions are recovered from shades of gray in the visual field.

Marr's algorithm produces a line sketch of shapes in the visual field. It represents an important step in transforming the sensory data into increasingly abstract representations. At its most abstract level, Marr's representation includes symbolic descriptions of stimuli. Each description identifies the stimulus and lists such predicates as length, width, and specific values. The following description illustrates this:

LINE

    (LENGTH 24)

    (WIDTH 4)

    (POSITION 12 96)

The predicates are specific attributes of elements in the line sketch. In this case, there is a line 24 pixel units long and 4 units wide, and the line stretches from some arbitrary location 12 to

96. The core of Marr's and other computer systems of visual pattern recognition is a process of signal-to-symbol conversion. This approach is captured by the title of Pentland's (1986) book *From Pixels to Predicates*. In order to get a match, the transformed visual input is compared to a set of such symbolic representations in computer memory. Identification is achieved when the best match is made according to a specific criterion.

Marr's theory has had a profound impact both on cognitive and computational approaches to vision. The theory is comprehensive in encompassing vision from the neural and sensory level to the level of object identification (Goodale, 1995; Humphreys & Bruce, 1989). As for computer vision, Marr's program handles problems that had eluded other models—for example, the perception of objects with unclear boundaries and their recognition in terms of contextual constraints (Winston, 1984).

Theories of recognition have been influenced by computer models such as Marr's. Computer models have been influential because they provide a useful framework for developing and testing hypotheses of the mechanisms of recognition. There are, however, important differences between computers and organisms. Computers have a limited set of stored representations, whereas no limit is known for humans. Computers are relatively slow and brittle, whereas human recognition is usually fast and robust. Finally, the manner in which recognition mechanisms are implemented differs between machines and organisms.

INTERIM SUMMARY

Visual pattern recognition by computer works well with a wide range of stimuli, ranging from relatively simple schematic characters used on bank checks to complex multidimensional stimuli like fingerprints. The computer first acquires an analog image of the object via its camera. Then the input is digitized for each pixel and is preprocessed. Marr's model of edge detection uses difference operators to enhance the contrast between regions of different brightness, it produces a line sketch of the regions, and develops a symbolic description of the input. It is this description that is compared to stored memory representations. Recognition is achieved when the representation is found that best matches the encoded input stimulus.

———————

**Human Pattern Recognition:
The Case of Letters**

The abstract principles by which human beings perceive patterns are similar to those governing computer vision; stimuli are acquired by sensory organs, described, and matched to stored representations in memory. In Neisser's (1967) words, the encoded stimulus contacts a "mental" representation. When this happens, the object is categorized or identified. We recognize the letter *A* when we know that the visual pattern, which includes two oblique lines meeting at the top and connected by a horizontal line, is called *A*. We recognize the outline in Figure 4.3 as a house when we identify the triangle at the top as a roof, the small squares as windows, and so on.

In this section, we will examine human pattern recognition, starting with the recognition of simple forms, including line drawings and letters, to illustrate general principles. Then we will proceed to word recognition and the perception of objects and events. Usually, letter and form perception is too quick to be accessible to introspection. Therefore, some principles of recognition will be illustrated by using a tactile pattern, a mode of recognition that is probably new to you. Try the following exercise of recognizing a tactile pattern. You will need a partner for this demonstration. Using a pencil, draw a pattern on the back of your volunteer and ask him or her to identify it. For example, draw the house in Figure 4.3 in the sequence indicated and record your partner's interpretation of this pattern.

This demonstration should help you to appreciate some important aspects of pattern

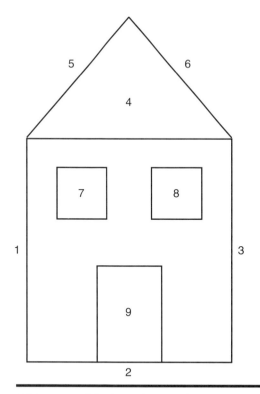

FIGURE 4.3   Stimulus to be used for tactile recognition. Draw the parts of the house on someone's back in the order shown. This demonstration illustrates that recognition proceeds by components and that the stimulus is perceived over an extended period of time rather than instantaneously.

recognition, not only for tactile patterns but for visual and auditory ones as well:

— The stimulus has components that are hierarchically grouped. For successful recognition, the perceiver must coordinate the interpretation of all the components of a pattern (e.g., windows, window rims, doors of the house in Figure 4.3).

— The presentation and reception of a pattern is not instantaneous; rather, it is extended over time. The tactile example exaggerates this aspect; it probably took several seconds to draw the house, whereas visual patterns are pro-

duced more rapidly. Acoustic stimuli, like syllables and words, however, may take up to a second to produce.

Patterns exist at various levels of complexity. Stimuli may range from very simple, one-dimensional patterns (e.g., presence versus absence of light) to multidimensional and sequential patterns (e.g., speech patterns and complex visual scenes). Instances of pattern recognition also include recognizing a goal or plot when you hear a story or spotting an attack formation in chess.

Theories of human recognition assume that pattern identification is based on the description of the stimulus and the comparison of that description with representations stored in memory, as we have seen. The theories differ when it comes to the details of the comparison stage; some assume that the input is matched to templates, whereas others assume that input is matched to a set of features. In addition, theories differ in their accounts of a range of recognition effects observed in experiments, including the word superiority effect, speech perception, and the recognition of cartoons. Do not expect to find a theory of perception and pattern recognition that encompasses all of the research results; the field is too broad for that. Rather, we will discuss general frameworks of pattern recognition, beginning with template theory.

Template Theory.   Template theory provides a simple solution to the problem of pattern recognition. It assumes that memory includes a template for each familiar object. When we encounter the object, it is recognized by matching the image to its template. There are many algorithms that calculate the correlation between the image and candidate templates. This is illustrated in Figure 4.4 by the degree of overlap between a template of the letter *A* (Figure 4.4A) and some degraded versions of the letter. The overlap, and therefore the correlation, is greater between the template and *A* in Figure 4.4B than in Figure 4.4C. Only when a satisfactory correlation is found a match is made, and a label for the input pattern is produced as

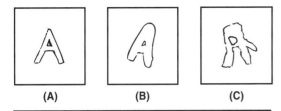

FIGURE 4.4   Matching a stimulus with a template produces correlations reflecting differing degrees of fit.

output. The template-matching principle has been used since the 1960s in the computer-based recognition tasks mentioned in the introduction of the chapter, including checking account numbers and fingerprints. None of these systems, however, has the flexibility of human pattern recognition.

There are additional problems in template matching: When the stimulus has a different position, size, orientation, or font, a mismatch results (see Figure 4.5.) Another problem with templates is that the stimulus itself is the smallest unit of recognition. Usually, however, stimuli have components, and template theory has difficulties dealing with componential stimuli.

Although template matching is feasible when the universe of characters is relatively small and well defined, it is not sufficiently flexible to handle unique stimuli and diverse sets of objects. Feature theory was developed to address some of these shortcomings. The basic principle of pattern recognition remains valid: The stimulus is com-

pared to several representations in memory and categorized according to the best fitting representation.

Feature Theory.   If the stimulus is interpreted in terms of its attributes or features rather than as one entity, many of the problems inherent in template matching are circumvented. I will illustrate feature theory for the case of letter recognition and examine the **Pandemonium** model (Selfridge & Neisser, 1963). This system assumes analyzers at four levels: the sensory, feature, cognitive, and decision analyzers. The architects of Pandemonium invented some characters to represent the four levels. The schematic in Figure 4.6 shows the four levels of analyses, including the image demons, feature demons, cognitive demons, and decision demon. In Figure 4.6. Pandemonium is looking at the letter *A*.

The **image analyzers,** or **demons,** acquire the letter, thus fulfilling the function of sensory organs and sensory memory. The **feature demons** detect unique features of the letter. There are as many feature demons as there are features in Pandemonium's repertoire; for example, a horizontal line, a vertical line, and a curve are perceived by horizontal-line demons, vertical-line demons, and curve demons, respectively. Each of them responds only to its particular feature; thus, when the letter *A* is perceived, the oblique-line demon and the horizontal-line demon are active, whereas the curved-line demons are not.

Cognitive demons look for the combinations of features that correspond to a particular letter, or the letter's structural description. The **structural description** of a letter or other object refers to the information about the configuration of the object's parts and their spatial arrangement. The structural description for the letter *A*, for example, notes that two oblique lines converge at the top and that they are linked by a horizontal line at their midsection. Structural descriptions leave out unimportant detail such as the length of lines. Feature models that include structural descriptions are very powerful models of pattern recognition. Stimuli can be recognized even when they

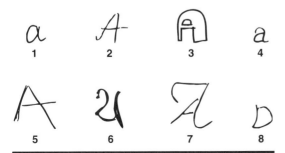

FIGURE 4.5   Variety of *A*s we are able to recognize. Do you think there is a template for each?

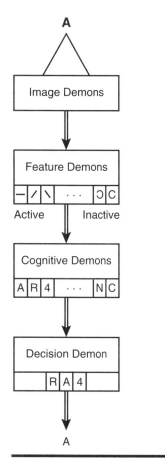

FIGURE 4.6 Pandemonium model includes four levels of analysis represented by image demons, feature demons, cognitive demons, and the decision demon.

compares the feature list of its target letter with the letter's stored feature list and its structural description. If the demon detects the corresponding configuration, recognition occurs, as illustrated in Figure 4.6. Demons for other letters will pay attention to the degree that they share some of these features. In Figure 4.6, the *R*-demon and the *4*-demon are fairly active; the *C*-demon, however, is not.

The **decision demon** is tuned to the cognitive demons and determines whose reaction is strongest, or who "yells loudest", *R, 4,* or *A,* and thus ratifies the identification of the letter.

The Pandemonium system is smart; it learns with experience! Feature demons that have successfully discriminated between patterns are given more weight for a categorization, whereas features that do not help identify a letter are given less weight. For example, the letters *B* and *E* share three horizontal lines that become less important in discriminating between them. The discontinuous curve that distinguishes the *B,* however, becomes more critical as successive recognition episodes occur.

The designers of the Pandemonium model were influenced by Hubel and Wiesel's (1965) theory of visual processing. Hubel and Wiesel (1965) discovered simple cells that are particularly sensitive to horizontal lines but not to vertical ones. Other cells respond only to vertical lines and still others only to oblique lines. The discovery of such simple cells inspired the notion of feature demons in the Pandemonium model.

The Pandemonium model exemplifies feature theories of pattern recognition. It uses a principle of recognition applicable to domains other than letter recognition: A relatively small number of features is sufficient to generate and recognize a large number of items. This is true for speech recognition, where many different speech sounds are based on a limited number of sound features. It is also true for words; 26 letters are sufficient to generate tens of thousands of words.

Pandemonium is a computer simulation program of pattern recognition. Researchers found that it nicely served as a model for human pattern

have been rotated. For example, you will always be able to recognize an *R*, whether it is upright or rotated, and to distinguish *R* from its mirror image.

The pandemonium system includes a cognitive demon, a recognition specialist, for each letter from *A* to *Z*. The cognitive demons look for the features in their target letter; the cognitive demon for *D*, for example, would respond if *D*'s features were reported by the feature demons: one vertical line, two horizontal lines, two right angles, and one discontinuous curve. A cognitive demon recognition. If human letter recognition worked like the model, we would expect that letters with more feature overlap should be more easily confused, especially when they are presented under difficult observational conditions. Flashing block letters and digits individually on a screen, Kinney, Marsetta, and Showman (1966) asked subjects to name the character. In most cases, subjects were able to identify characters correctly; a *D* was called a *D*, and so on. However, there was also confusion. Some of these errors are tabulated in the confusion matrix in Figure 4.7. The vertical dimension indicates the characters shown and the horizontal dimension indicates the characters named.

Look at letter *C* in the second row; 21 times it was erroneously called a *G*, and 6 times an *O* but never an *A* or a *D*. Just as predicted by the Pandemonium model, letters sharing more features were more easily confused.

Retrieving the Name of a Letter. Letters have both distinct features and different names; recognizing a letter includes retrieving its name. The name of each letter is presumably stored in memory along with its features and structural description. Posner and Mitchell (1967) designed a clever experiment to demonstrate the stage of name retrieval. They presented subjects with dif-

ferent letter pairs, as indicated in Table 4.1. Subjects were asked to judge letter pairs as being different or the same as quickly as possible. They were to respond with *same* when the letters were physically identical and when the capital and lowercase versions of letters shown in Table 4.1 had the same name. Otherwise, the correct response was *different.*

The conditions of interest were the same-case comparison (*AA*) and the different-case comparison (*Aa*). Subjects can complete the *AA* comparison either by a physical match, which compares the visual features, or by a name match, which retrieves the names of each letter from long-term memory. The *Aa* comparison can be achieved only through a name match. Posner and Mitchell found that same-case comparisons took 452 milliseconds, whereas different-case comparisons took 523 milliseconds. The researchers attributed the faster same-case comparisons to the physical matching process; changing the color or size of one of the letters increased the decision time for same-case comparisons, but not of different-case comparisons. Therefore, Posner and Mitchell reasoned that the added time of the different-case comparison represents the time to retrieve the names from long-term memory. Name retrieval time is one component of pattern recognition and an important indicator of individual differences in cognitive processing (Hunt, 1978; Perfetti, 1983).

INTERIM SUMMARY

Patterns to be recognized are described and matched to representations in memory. According to template theory, memory contains a template for each familiar item. Template matching works

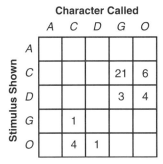

Character Called

	A	C	D	G	O
A					
C				21	6
D				3	4
G		1			
O		4	1		

Stimulus Shown

FIGURE 4.7 Confusion matrix from character naming experiment shows labeling errors when characters on the vertical dimension were presented one at a time (Kinney, Marsetta, & Showman, 1966).

TABLE 4.1 Letter Matching Task (Posner & Mitchell, 1967)

Letter Pair	Correct Response
A A	Same
A a	Same
A B	Different

well with a limited set of objects (e.g., highly uniform characters). In other cases, however, template matching is problematic because even slight deviations of a stimulus from its template will produce recognition failures.

Feature theory assumes that a pattern is analyzed in terms of its constituent features and that the pattern recognizer detects the features and compares them to a feature list stored in memory. Pandemonium, for example, scrutinizes letters for the presence of features such as straight and curved lines. If the detected features overlap with those in the stored feature list, the pattern is recognized; but confusions can result. Feature theory has been augmented by structural descriptions that make the relation of the features explicit. The advantage of feature theory is its greater flexibility. In addition, a small number of features can handle a large number of patterns. Patterns have associated names stored in memory. The time it takes to retrieve the name of a pattern (e.g., a letter) is an indication of the efficiency of pattern recognition.

Recognizing Speech Sounds

Speech consists of an ordered sequence of sounds—the phonemes. A **phoneme** is the smallest unit of sound used to differentiate words. Consider the word *Suzy*: It consists of four sounds—s, oo, z, and ee, or [s], [u], [z], and [i] in terms of the international phonetic alphabet. Speech recognition would be easy if these sounds were always produced in the same way and therefore had the same sound patterns when used in different contexts—for example [s] and [u] in *suit* and [u] and [z] in *Jacuzzi*. There is no such one-to-one correspondence between phonetic patterns and the perception of a sound, however. The patterns of physical energy that we perceive as the same sound have distinct configurations that depend on the context of the word or sentence. If we were to pronounce each consonant or vowel as a distinct sound, we might as well spell utterances to each other; this would

take a very long time and drive speakers and listeners crazy!

Things go much faster than this in normal speech; when we articulate the first syllable *Su* of *Suzy*, for example, the articulation system is already at work to produce the subsequent sounds [z] and [i]. One speaks of **coarticulation** when the articulation of each sound depends on those preceding and following it (see also the section on Action). Although not individually articulated, each speech sound exhibits common features, the **invariants,** across different contexts. Identifying such invariants has been a longstanding goal of speech perception researchers.

Features in Speech Perception. The production of speech contributes characteristic features to the speech sounds. Speech is the result of motor action produced when the air coming from the lungs is modulated in subtle ways. Muscles move the vocal cords, tongue, lips, and other structures to give different contours to the oral cavity and thereby produce different sounds (see Figure 4.8).

Sounds are produced by different components of the speech tract, different levels of air pressure, and resonance. Speech sounds differ on three dimensions: (1) voicing, (2) place of articulation, and (3) manner of articulation.

1. **Voicing** indicates whether the vocal cords vibrate as the stream of air passes them. When the vocal cords vibrate, voiced phonemes such as [b] are produced; otherwise, the sounds are voiceless, as in [p].
2. **Place of articulation** refers to the structure of the vocal tract that blocks the air stream. A sound has the alveolar feature when the alveolar ridge, the upper gum, is involved. The upper gum links the teeth and the hard palate; you touch it with your tongue when you produce a [d] or [t].
3. **Manner of articulation** refers to the way a stream of air is modulated as it passes through the vocal tract. A stop is produced by placing the tongue on the alveolar ridge and releasing

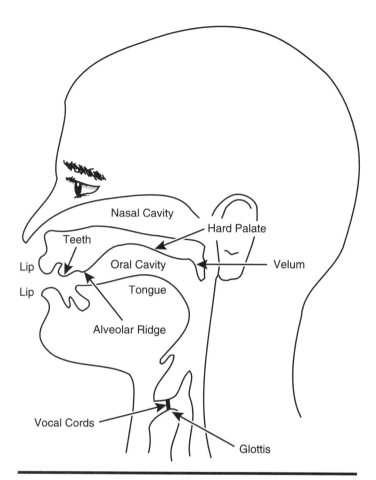

FIGURE 4.8   Major features in the vocal tract (Matlin, 1988).

it, for example, [d] and [t]. A fricative sound occurs when you restrict the passage of air in the vocal tract, as you do when you pronounce [f] and [v]. Table 4.2 includes six phonemes and their distinct phonetic features.

Speech Sounds and the Sound Spectrogram. Speech sounds differ in the patterns of air flow; when a speaker utters different sounds for a brief duration, he transmits air pressure in certain frequency bands. Researchers have devised techniques to photograph patterns of energy associated with speech sounds; such a record is called a *sound spectrogram* (see Figure 10.6, p

286). The abscissa of the spectrogram represents time, and the ordinate represents frequency. The dark regions in the graph are known as **formants;** these represent energy levels at a certain frequency that extend over a brief period of time. The contours of spectrograms of real speech usually show overlapping formants with unclear contours. Spectrograms are noteworthy for what they do *not* show: There are no discernible boundaries between words.

Like phonographic devices, spectrograms can be played back to produce sound. When you feed the spectrogram in Figure 10.6, for example, into the appropriate apparatus, you will hear *Jc*

TABLE 4.2   Phonetic Features of Six Phonemes

	d	t	m	w	f	v
Place						
Alveolar	x	x				
Bilabial			x	x		
Labiodental					x	x
Manner						
Stop	x	x				
Fricative					x	x
Nasal			x			
Semivowel				x		
Voicing						
Voiced	x		x	x		x
Unvoiced		x			x	

Note: Bilabial refers to the upper and lower lips; *labiodental* refers to the lower lip and upper teeth.

father's shoe bench out. Researchers who study speech perception synthesize schematic spectrograms by computer. These are used to simulate human speech sounds. Researchers use these synthetic sounds to find the relation between patterns of acoustic energy and different speech sounds. Figure 4.9 shows synthetic spectrograms composed of two formants, one at a low frequency and one at a higher frequency. The formants in Figure 4.9 represent the phonemes /di/ as in *dim* and /da/ as in *dam*, respectively.

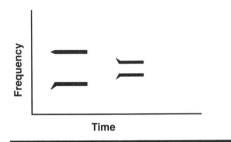

FIGURE 4.9   Spectrograms for sounds. The dark bands, known as formants, represent energy levels at certain frequencies. The relation between the formants produce different vowels.

Formants differ in their position relative to each other as well in the formant transitions. **Formant transition** refers to rapid frequency change in the initial segment of the formant. Researchers have determined that the perception of vowels depends on the relative position of formants (Liberman et al., 1957). Holding the relation between formants constant, it is the change in transitions that determines the perception of consonants.

Theories of Speech Perception.   Speech perception presents a real puzzle to researchers. There are, however, speculations on how it occurs. Massaro (1988) assumed that memory contains prototypes of speech sounds. The prototype specifies the acoustic features of the sound. When a sound first arrives, it is maintained for a brief period as an early auditory memory (see Chapter 2). According to Massaro, "The recognition process operates to find the prototype in long-term memory which best describes the acoustic features" (p. 413) in the early auditory representation.

A different approach was taken by Liberman and colleagues (1967), who proposed the motor theory of speech perception. According to motor theory, speech as a sound and its perception are unique to the human species. Hearing speech sounds elicits a kind of resonance in the speech production center in the brain. As a result, the motor command that produces the sound is triggered without actually uttering the sound and this, in turn, leads to recognizing the sound. In short, human beings recognize a sound by implicitly producing it.

These and other theories have been debated without a firm resolution (e.g., Remez, 1994). Nevertheless, the advancement of theories of speech perception remains an important goal for cognitive psychology. Fundamental questions about speech perception, such as the following, await an answer: What are the invariants of speech sounds and how do listeners process them? What are the mechanisms of speech perception in infants? and How do listeners identify discrete words although there are no apparent boundaries in the stream of speech? Developing responses to these problems will eventually tell us whether speech is a unique stimulus with a special recognition mechanism or whether it is like other stimuli served by general mechanisms of pattern recognition. Whatever theory turns out to be correct, the mechanism of speech perception must accommodate rapid processes because speech perception is usually very fast. The mechanisms are also flexible because speakers and listeners readily acquire the sounds of one or more languages.

Learning a new language involves, among other things, learning new sounds. Initially it is difficult to understand a new language because listeners have not fully developed representations of unfamiliar sounds and the skill of matching sounds with their meaning. As a speaker becomes more fluent with practice, recognizing speech sounds in a second language becomes as easy as it is in the speaker's native language.

INTERIM SUMMARY

Because sounds are produced in the context of other sounds, there is no exact correspondence between the patterns of acoustic energy and the sounds we perceive. Sounds exhibit sets of features based on voicing and the place and manner of articulation. As a result of different articulations, different sounds have characteristic patterns of acoustic energy. In a spectrogram, the frequency composition of a sound is made visible; it consists of formants or frequency bands that last for only a brief period. Perception of vowels is based on the frequency relation between formants. Perception of consonants is based on formant transitions: the rapid change of frequency in the initial segment of a formant. Despite great advances in understanding the speech signal, theories of speech perception, including prototype and motor theory, remain speculative.

Word Recognition

Communication depends on word recognition; we must recognize words in order to understand a message. Fortunately, word recognition is easy in everyday life; we can identify words quickly regardless of dialect or writing style. Word recognition, however, is a difficult challenge to researchers of several disciplines, including linguistics, computer science, and cognitive psychology. Linguists are concerned with the structure of the lexicon, the body of knowledge about words that speakers and listeners are assumed to have. Computer scientists investigate word recognition in order to program computers to understand language. Cognitive psychologists seek to uncover the mental processes that make word recognition possible. These researchers have amassed a body of experimental results—for example, characteristic context effects that have become test cases for every theory of word recognition. Context effects are observed when an item is recognized more quickly and accurately within the context of a global stimulus, whether it is a word or sentence.

The Word Superiority Effect. The word superiority effect refers to the apparently paradoxical observation that letters are recognized better when they appear in the context of a word rather than when presented individually. For example, *K* is recognized better in *WORK* than when it is presented alone or when it occurs as part of a letter string like *ONFK*. Researchers have puzzled for a long time why it is easier to recognize a letter in a word than a letter presented alone.

In an effort to find an answer, Reicher (1969) presented stimuli like the three samples in Figure 4.10A. Each stimulus was presented for a very brief exposure in a tachistoscope (from the Greek term *tachos skopein*, which means *brief viewing*). After the stimulus had disappeared, some dashes and an arrow were shown. The subject had to indicate the identity of the letter in the position prompted by the arrow. Each type of stimulus (word, letter alone, and string) was presented on one-third of the trials. The letter *K* was recognized best in the word condition. Reicher reasoned that this result stemmed from a guessing advantage subjects had in the word condition. Assume that

(A)

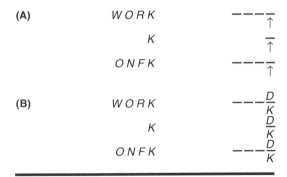

FIGURE 4.10   Word, letter, and string conditions to illustrate the word superiority effect. (*A*) Subjects have a guessing advantage in the word condition as explained in the text. (*B*) By using a two-choice test, the guessing advantage is equal in all three testing conditions.

the subject recognized the letters *W O R* but not the last letter. Knowing that words are presented on one-third of the trials, the subject may simply guess a likely word candidate starting with the three letters he recognized. Rather than going through all 26 letters to make *W O R?* into a word (from *WORA* to *WORZ*), the perceiver can confine his search to the five candidates he knows to be words, including *WORK*, and then guess at one of the letters (e.g, *K*), giving him a relatively good chance of identifying the fourth letter correctly. On nonword and letter-alone trials, however, the subject's chance of guessing correctly is much less (3.85%.)

Reicher figured out a way to equate the three trial types in terms of guessing. He removed the guessing advantage of the word trials by giving subjects a choice between two letters during testing. The subject had to choose between two letters, including the correct one, *K*. If we want to equalize the guessing opportunity across the three types of trials, the other letter should be one that, when combined with *W O R*, would also form a word—for example, *D* (see Figure 4.10B.) In each of the conditions, the probability of being correct by guessing alone was now at $p = 0.50$. Reicher found the word superiority

effect in this condition as well, and ruled out guessing as the reason for the word advantage. Therefore, we must look for another interpretation for the word superiority effect. (For an acoustic superiority effect, see Rubin, Turvey, & Van Gelder, 1976.)

Interactive Network Model of Letter and Word Recognition.   The word superiority effect and other context effects illustrate **constraint satisfaction,** a common phenomenon in recognition. Several sources of information simultaneously suggest one interpretation of a target while excluding other interpretations. Consider the ambiguous phrase in Figure 4.11. There are two words whose center letters are identical; however, in one case, we interpret the letter as *H*, in the second as *A*. We do so because the context *T_E C_T* suggests a likely interpretation for the middle letter in each case. We know that *THE CAT* makes sense, but *TAE CAT* and *THE CHT* does not. Recognition of the display seems paradoxical: We cannot identify the individual letters without recognizing the word, and we cannot identify the word without knowing the letters. How is this possible? According to the influential network model introduced by McClelland and Rumelhart (1981), our recognition system entertains several hypotheses about each letter

FIGURE 4.11   Ambiguous stimuli illustrate recognition by constraint satisfaction. In each case, interpretation of letters and words must be consistent (McClelland & Rumelhart, 1981).

and the word; it examines these hypotheses and finally settles on the interpretation that best satisfies the constraints. The network model is a computer simulation that combines bottom-up and top-down influences on recognition. **Bottom-up** information refers to the perceptual features of individual stimulus components, such as letters. **Top-down** information provided by the context is acquired knowledge about the normal configuration of a pattern of stimuli, such as a word.

The network model makes the following assumptions:

— There are three levels of analysis.
— Neighboring levels of analyses interact.
— Units of the stimulus are represented by nodes in the network.
— There are connections between the nodes.
— Each node or analyzer has a certain level of activation.

Figure 4.12 gives a global view of the three levels of analysis in the network, one each for features, letters, and words. Analysis at each level is carried out by nodes. Working like the demons in Pandemonium, the nodes embody information about each of the components, including features, letters, and words that the system knows about. Altogether, the network model includes 16 features, 26 letters, and 1,179 words. Figures 4.13A and 4.13B show the features and the letters used in the model. The model's lexicon, its set of words, includes items of relatively high frequency in English—for example, *WORK, ABLE, TAKE,* and *CART.*

The flow of information in the network is based on the connections between the levels, as illustrated in Figure 4.14. Letter nodes communicate with feature nodes and word nodes in terms of excitation and inhibition, as described in the next section. The three levels of the network operate in parallel; they influence each other and know of each other's work, hence the term *interactive network.*

The model naturally accommodates bottom-up and top-down information. When a feature

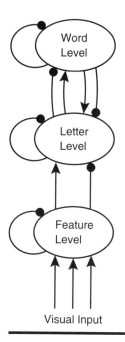

FIGURE 4.12 Three levels of analysis in network model. Excitatory connections between levels are shown. Connections within a level are inhibitory (McClelland & Rumelhart, 1981).

becomes active, it passes activation from the bottom up to all of the letters containing that feature. Activated letters propagate activation to the words of which they are part. In each of these cases, information from the constituent stimulus suggests the more complex stimulus; features suggest letters, and letters suggest words. Information flows from the top down when the more global stimulus suggests the presence of a specific component. For example, when a word becomes active, its letters are activated from the top.

Excitation and Inhibition in the Network. Each node has a certain level of activation expressing the confidence that a specific hypothesis is true. When two interpretations are consistent (e.g., when you see the slash in a *Q,* its presence and *Q* are consistent), your confidence increases (the letter you see is a *Q* rather than an *O*). As a result, the activation level of *Q* is greater than that of *O.*

(A)

(B)

FIGURE 4.13 Set of 16 features (A) and 26 letters (B) used for the network simulation (McClelland & Rumelhart, 1981).

The activation level of a node is influenced by the input from other nodes via two types of connections: excitatory and inhibitory. **Excitatory** links increase the node's level of activation, whereas **inhibitory** links decrease it. Excitatory

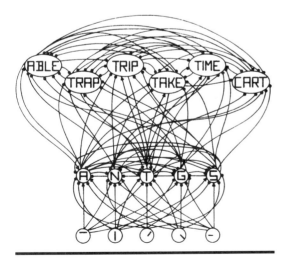

FIGURE 4.14 Network including six nodes at feature, letter, and word levels is still a simplification (McClelland & Rumelhart, 1981).

and inhibitory inputs to a node are combined so that the net level of activation is the total amount of excitatory information less the total amount of inhibitory information (see Chapter 6). In general, a connection between two units is excitatory when they are consistent with one another, such as the letter A in the first position and the word *ABLE*. On the other hand, if two nodes are inconsistent, their relationship is inhibitory.

Recognizing Partial Stimuli. Let us examine how the network model accounts for both the recognition of partially visible words and for the word superiority effect. Consider the display at the bottom of Figure 4.11. The letters W, O, and R are clearly visible, but the last letter is not. The visible letters suggest the four-letter words beginning with W, O, R, including *word, wore, work, worm,* and *worn.* Any of the letters D, E, K, M, and N could occupy the fourth position and complete the word. The visible features of the degraded fourth letter suggest R and K as candidates.

According to the network model, in the word condition there are five letters that receive an increase in activation levels from the top down: D, E, K, M, and N. Because features of the letters K and R are present in the display, their units are excited from the bottom up. The only letter that receives excitatory activation from *both* directions is K. As a result, K will become more active than the other letters, and the recognizer is likely to identify the word as *WORK.* A letter presented by itself has only one source of feedback—namely, the letter features. It will thus collect less activation and be recognized less well than in the word condition.

The Modular Approach: Search Theory. The network model is an interactive model; there is communication and influence among all analyzers that travel via the multiple connections within a level and between adjacent levels. Importantly, the recognition of words and letters is influenced by contextual information. The search model differs from the network model in several respects:

Information flows only from the bottom up, there is no top-down activation, and there is no interaction among the two stages of the model—letter recognition and word recognition.

Once letters are recognized and a string of letters is produced, the string is entered into the lexicon and compared to each lexical entry in a serial search. Entries are stored in the lexicon according to their occurrence frequency in English; thus, a word such as *work* is found more quickly than a word such as *wart*. This explains the **word frequency effect:** the finding that frequent words are recognized more rapidly than rare words of equal length. According to search theory, there are no top-down influences and word recognition depends entirely on component letters; it is therefore independent of sentence context. Because letter recognition and word recognition are executed by separate modules, search theory is known as a *modular* recognition theory.

Recognizing Spoken Words: The Cohort Model.

Like recognizing printed words, the recognition of spoken words is a fast process that usually escapes our awareness. Sounds pass by quickly and listeners find word meanings rapidly, although, unlike in reading, there is no opportunity for looking back. The cohort model captures the process of on-line interpretation in word recognition. According to the model, as soon as two phonemes are completed, listeners develop a set of likely word candidates, the cohort. As successive phonemes are perceived, the cohort becomes smaller and smaller. Take the word *elephant* (Massaro, 1989). For the first few milliseconds, the listener only has heard the phoneme /e/, which leaves the field wide open to include hundreds of word candidates, from *aesthetic* and *any* to *elephant* and *entry*. As the sound segments become longer /el/, /ele/, /elef/, and /elefa/, fewer words in the lexicon remain consistent with the target word. Finally, when all but one candidate have been eliminated, the target word is identified. In real speech, of course, this process occurs too quickly to be noticed by perceivers.

Imaging and Electrophysiological Methods Help Pinpoint Brain Centers of Recognition.

Psychologists have studied pattern recognition and perception by presenting stimuli under all sorts of conditions—speeded, changed context, degraded—and having the perceiver report the stimulus. Based on these reports, researchers made inferences about the mechanisms of recognition. With the emergence of the new imaging and electrophysiological methods—PET, ERP, and fMRI (see Chapter 2)—all that has changed. Now, scientists can probe the brain centers that are activated as the perceiver interprets stimuli. Studies by Posner and McCandliss (1993) illustrate this approach.

Using positron emission tomography (PET) and event-related potential (ERP), Posner and McCandliss (1993) sought to identify the brain centers involved in letter and word recognition. They found increased activity in the prestriate region in the right hemisphere when letter features and words were presented visually. Converging evidence from ERP recordings and PET scans suggests to researchers an interesting interpretation of the word superiority effect. Posner and McCandliss reported that the lower side of the left occipital lobe was activated when subjects recognized words such as *work* and pseudowords such as *korw*, but not when consonant strings like *brkw* are presented. Words and pseudowords correspond to the orthographic rules of the language and, according to Posner and McCandliss, such knowledge is represented in terms of abstract visual word forms. The two scientists speculated that it is these word forms that enhance the recognition of letters when they are embedded in words, thus producing the word superiority effect. Auditory word perception has been tracked by PET imaging techniques as well. When words are presented via head phones and repeated by the subjects, regions in the auditory cortex and the left temporoparietal cortex exhibited elevated PET activity. To date, these results help scientists to localize recognition centers in the brain. As the imaging methods are refined in the future, it may be possible to discover the neural correlates of the encoding and pattern matching stages that underlie recognition.

INTERIM SUMMARY

Word and letter recognition is one of the liveliest research areas in cognitive psychology. We reviewed two classes of recognition theories: interactive and modular approaches. According to interactive recognition models, several sources of information communicate during the recognition process. In the case of letter recognition, this includes bottom-up information from the letter features and top-down information from the word context. The connectionist network model we reviewed is an exemplar of interactive theories. The model includes three levels of analysis: features, letters, and words. Communication flows up and down between and within levels, and levels collaborate to arrive at an interpretation of the stimulus consistent with all constraints.

Modular recognition theories include separate processing modules, each of which undertake component jobs independently—for example, feature analysis, letter recognition, and a search for the word in the lexicon. Both interactive and modular models can account for important research results, including context effects. Like written word recognition, recognition of spoken words proceeds on-line. The cohort model assumes that listeners start out with a large candidate set of possible words upon hearing the first two phonemes of a word. The large set is narrowed down as additional phonemes are added. The word is recognized when only one candidate remains in the cohort.

Imagery and electrophysiological methods have been used to identify locations of visual and auditory recognition in the brain. In the future, these methods may assist scientists in uncovering the processing stages of recognition and perception.

Shape Recognition

Take a look at your surroundings; there are books, magazines, paper clips, a chair, a lamp, and other objects. Regardless of their color and context, you have no difficulty recognizing them. The best minds in philosophy have wondered how we manage to identify so many objects without apparent effort. It remained for psychologists to analyze shape recognition in terms of stimulus properties and cognitive processes. Early psychologists viewed stimuli in terms of elements. The Gestalt psychologists and their successors examined how elements are grouped into objects and how lines combine into regions. After the introduction of the computer, theories of shape recognition were influenced by the computer metaphor. Marr's theory of computer vision, including his algorithm of edge detection, is an example of this approach.

This section describes Biederman's recognition-by-components (RBC) theory and a set of experimental findings in support of the RBC theory. According to Biederman's theory of object recognition, we recognize shapes in two stages: (1) we identify edges and boundaries and (2) we see a small set of basic shapes, called *geons*, that include spheres, cones, cylinders, blocks, and wedges (Biederman, 1990). The recognition-by-components theory reflects the influence of Marr's work on computer vision as well as the Gestalt principles of perception. In the tradition of the Gestaltists, Biederman formulated a set of properties that define regions.

Regions. The Gestalt psychologists have made an inventory of perceptual organizations known as **Gestalts** (German for *configurations*). Our experience suggests that such stimulus configurations are immediately perceived. Figure 4.15A–D shows four rows of dots; three of these illustrate a Gestalt principle. The first row exhibits no organization, the second row illustrates the principle of **proximity,** and the third row illustrates the principle of **similarity.** We group stimuli that are close or similar to each other. The fourth row of dots demonstrates a Gestalt principle introduced as recently as 1992, the principle of **common region.** When stimuli are surrounded by a common contour, perceivers join them in to a group (Palmer, 1992). Figure 4.15E demonstrates the

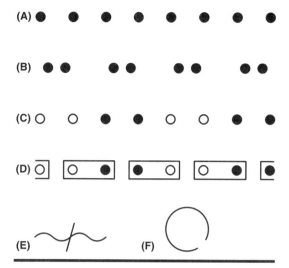

FIGURE 4.15 Four Gestalt principles.
(*A*) Equidistance between dots. (*B*) Proximity.
(*C*) Similarity. (*D*) Common region. (*E*) Continuation.
(See text for explanation.)

principle of **continuation:** If uninterrupted, straight lines and curved lines are seen as continuous lines. Figure 4.15F illustrates the principle of **closure:** perceivers tend to fill in gaps.

Gestalt psychologists described another basic perceptual phenomenon, the **figure-ground effect,** illustrated in Figure 4.16. The white vase appears as a figure against a dark background. Or do you see two faces looking at each other?

FIGURE 4.16 The figure-ground effect (Papalia & Olds, 1985).

Guided by the computer metaphor, Biederman (e.g., 1990) extended the Gestalt work on regions. He proposed four invariant properties of boundaries that define regions; they are illustrated in Figure 4.17 (Biederman, 1990). The properties represent four pairs of contrasts:

1. *Smooth Continuation*: Straight versus curved lines.
2. *Cotermination*: Two or more edges may or may not terminate in a common junction.
3. *Parallelism*: Edges may or may not be parallel.
4. *Symmetry*: Edges may or may not be symmetrical.

These properties are simple and image invariant. They describe kinds of edges and define the components of objects we encounter in the visual world.

Recognition-by-Components Theory.   Biederman's recognition-by-components (RBC) theory assumes that the two-dimensional view of an object consists of simple volumes, called **geons** (from *geometrical ion*). A geon is created by combining edges, as illustrated in Figure 4.18. Biederman's model includes 24 distinct geons that make up a sort of visual alphabet. For each object, the relations between different geons are specified; the same geons, when combined differently, produce different objects, much like the same set of letters produces different words. The set of *geons* produces different *objects* in Figure 4.18—for example, cylinder (geon 3) and arch (geon 5) combine to produce a coffee cup and a pail.

The relations among geons are specified in structural descriptions that are represented in an object dictionary. Biederman's model specifies over 100 different relations—for example, top-of, side-connected, and larger-than. Combining three geons and all possible relations between them yields a total of 1.4 billion possible three-geon objects, but we use only about 30,000 of those and have names for a mere 3,000 (Biederman, 1990).

According to RBC theory, objects are recognized by identifying their constituent geons and the relations among them. Once the geons are

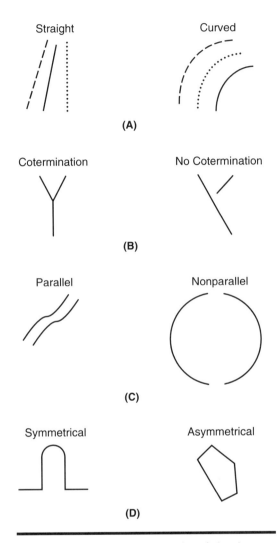

FIGURE 4.17   Four basic properties of visual shapes are independent from an observer's viewpoint (Biederman, 1990).

Experimental Support for the Recognition-by-Components Theory.   It is a straightforward matter to evaluate the recognition-by-components theory in experiments. The theory states that a shape is recognized by identifying the object's geons. It is not necessary that all of them are present; the system tolerates the deletion of as many as half of an object's geons. Geons specify a shape uniquely. Color, shading, and texture are not necessary for object identification, unless you wish to discriminate between different similarly shaped objects (e.g., plums and peaches).

Biederman and colleagues used an object-naming task to test the predictions of the RBC theory. A line drawing was presented for 100 milliseconds on a screen while a subject was to name it as quickly as possible. Here are some of Biederman's research results on the recognition of objects differing in completeness, complexity, and quality:

— *Completeness:* Objects were recognized with equal facility, whether all of its geons or only a subset was used.
— *Complexity:* Defining complexity as the number of constituent geons of an object, researchers found that more complex objects were identified more quickly. The reason is that any combination of geons suffices to recognize the object, and since more combinations are possible in complex objects, their recognition is faster.
— *Quality:* When objects were degraded by deleting joints, subjects experienced difficulty identifying the stimuli even when they had previously seen the full line drawings. This result indicates that, as in computer vision, it is the joints that form the most informative part of an object's contour.

Biederman's research indicates that the recognition-by-components theory accounts well for shape recognition data and is consistent with insights from computer vision. It also extends to more complex stimuli than the ones shown in Figure 4.18. However, as we will see in the next

parsed, they are matched against representations in long-term memory. (*Parse* means to identify the parts of a unit.) Matching components with representations is a parallel and automatic process executed at great speed. The process is robust, ensuring recognition even under nonoptimal conditions.

Geons   **Objects**

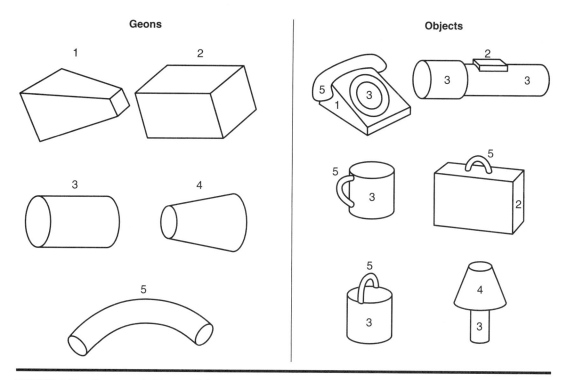

FIGURE 4.18 Geons and objects. Objects are represented as configurations of geons, which are simple visual volumes (Biederman, 1990).

section, there are special cases that are difficult for RBC theory to explain.

The Special Case of Face Recognition. There are objects far more complex than line drawings of flashlights and telephones. Consider the many shapes of animals and the changes in shape when they move. These are hundreds of different kinds of mammals alone, each with a characteristic shape and gait. One of the most varied of living shapes is the human face; we can distinguish thousands of faces, recognize facial expressions, and judge age and gender based on facial features. Recognition of such dynamic stimuli is not readily captured by a set of 24 geons. Here are few highlights of face recognition:

— Subjects are surprisingly good at guessing a person's gender and age (e.g., Pittenger & Shaw, 1975).

— One- to three-month old infants recognize faces, particularly the faces of their mother and father. If given a choice, three-month-old infants prefer to look at faces rather than at some other display (Siegler, 1991).

— Changing such features as hairstyle or hair color, or adding a moustache or shaving it, reduces face recognition. Putting a stocking mask over the face is a very effective disguise, as burglars have long known (Bruce, 1988).

— A face presented upside down is recognized less well than other stimuli (e.g., a house shown upside down). This finding also suggests that the face is special.

— When put to a test, subjects recognize a caricature of a person better than his or her line drawing (Rhodes, Brennan, & Carey, 1987). Caricatures are recognized better because they exaggerate the features that distinguish the caricatured person relative to the norm; they are superportraits (Mauro & Kubovy, 1992).

— People tend to recognize faces of their own race more accurately than faces of other races (e.g., O'Toole et al., 1994).

Face recognition remains an enigma. In some respects, it is similar to recognition of other stimuli; in others, it is very different. We see thousands of different faces, yet we recognize the uniqueness of each and we can attribute emotional qualities to it. Face recognition is very good, in general, and does not often fail us. There are, however, rare cases of prosopagnosia, the failure to recognize familiar faces. Read Box 4.1 for one case history and ponder the implications it has for theories of pattern recognition (Damasio, Tranel, & Damasio, 1990).

INTERIM SUMMARY

According to the recognition-by-components theory, shape recognition proceeds by detection of edges and identification of prototypical shapes, the geons. There are four basic properties of edges: smooth continuation, cotermination, parallelism, and symmetry. Shapes are characterized by a small number of constituent elements, the geons. The RBC model includes 24 geons. Geons are visual elements that can be placed in a large number of configurations, thus defining many objects, just as a few letters may be combined into many words. Objects are recognized when their geons and the relations between them are identified. Recognition of objects is fast, even when the object is highly complex, degraded, and presented without much detail. Face recognition, however, constitutes a special case: Face recognition depends on features. On the other hand, faces pro-

---

Box 4.1

Prosopagnosia: When You Do Not Recognize Your Own Face

Antonio Damasio and his colleagues at the University of Iowa School of Medicine have worked on *prosopagnosia*, the failure to recognize faces, and other instances of recognition failure (*prosopon* is Greek for *face* and *agnosia* means *failure of knowing*). The following case history illustrates this disability:

> A 65-year-old woman suddenly developed an inability to recognize the faces of her husband and daughter. She could not even recognize her own face in the mirror—although she knew the face she was observing must belong to her, she did not experience a sense of familiarity when viewing it. The faces of other relatives and friends became equally meaningless. Yet she remained fully capable of identifying all those persons from voice. (Damasio, Tranel, & Damasio, 1990, pp. 89–90)

This patient's visual system remained intact: Her visual acuity was perfect in both eyes; she completed a variety of visuospatial tests successfully;

and she was able to read and write normally. She did have some difficulty in distinguishing colors. However, according to Damasio, this deficit by itself was not responsible for the patient's prosopagnosia. Rather, her symptoms were attributed to a rare neurological deficit, a bilateral infarction in the ventral visual association cortexes. From a cognitive perspective, the important issue concerns the mental mechanisms that these cortical centers support. Revealing those mechanisms remains a mystery and a challenge for future research.

There are variations of prosopagnosia and combinations with other agnosias. Interestingly, in most of these patients, category recognition remains intact. The patients are able to discriminate between classes of objects and they know faces from cars and houses; their difficulty lies in identifying *particular* faces, houses, and cars. One patient could not identify her car by any other means than by reading the license plate.

vide more information than a collection of features would suggest; a face usually reveals a person's age, gender, and his or her emotions and mood.

Perceiving Events

Visual objects are not stationary; indeed, a stationary image is an exception. Either the perceiver moves or the object moves; nevertheless, we recognize both the object and the nature of the movement without a problem. Using stationary stimuli would not tell us much about movement, the dynamic aspect of the stimulus. For example, we would not learn about moving stimuli by looking at a successive series of still frames. We would not see what happens until we ran the film to see motion. This insight inspired ecological psychologists to study event perception. Following Gibson's (1979) lead, the ecological approach defines **events** as follows: "The common insight behind an 'event' approach is that, unlike most perceptual psychologists' stimulus displays, the natural world doesn't usually sit still for a perceiver, nor does a perceiver typically sit still when exploring his or her surroundings. Our perceptual encounters with the world are dominated by events, or changes in structure over time" (Warren & Shaw, 1985, p. xiii).

A good demonstration of event perception comes from Johansson's (1985) research on biological motion. He asked subjects to observe a moving pattern of lights in the dark. Johansson placed lights on a person (see Figure 4.19), much as the suit of lights worn in the movie *Electric Cowboy*. Johansson had the person stand still or move and had observers interpret the light patterns under both conditions. When the person stood still, the observers saw a random pattern of dots. However, as soon as she began to walk, subjects recognized the movement as walking. This was true even though each individual light simply made a line in the dark, as shown in Figure 4.20.

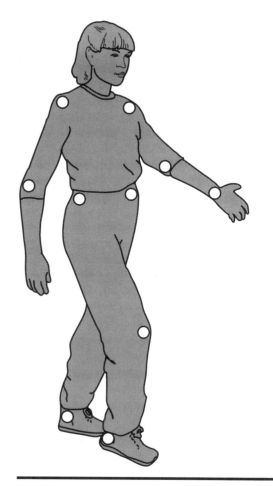

FIGURE 4.19 A person wearing lights is getting ready for a light-movement experiment. The person will move in a totally dark room (Goldstein, 1989).

Subjects are unaware of movements of individual lights, yet they recognize the movement of the entire configuration. Different experimenters have shown that observers are able to recognize a number of different light-pattern events, including the following:

Whether a man or a woman is walking
A dancing couple
A person doing pushups
Weight of objects lifted
Distance of trajectiles thrown

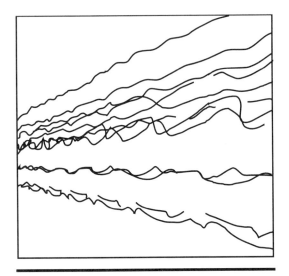

FIGURE 4.20 Tracers made by lights attached to a person's head and joints as she walks in darkness (Johansson et al., 1980).

Light dots on faces of actors playing out emotions

Often only 100 milliseconds are required to identify an event accurately. It is clear that people perceive dynamic events; however, research has not uncovered the mental processes underlying event perception. At this stage, researchers have made an inventory of the empirical effects and the stimulus parameters, but have no knowledge of the neural mechanisms that support event perception (Lappin, 1985).

Event perception illustrates the interdependence between cognition and action: Essentially, events are perceived actions. We have seen other links between perception and action as well, such as, in speech production and perception and in person perception. Cognitive processes, in turn, support actions in multiple ways—you need to memorize and plan actions, as any figure skater, pianist, or surgeon knows. The figure skater studies and tries each element of a jump and turn and then combines the components and practices the triple axel as a whole. The pianist has learned and practiced a piece hundreds of times.

Beginning with plastic tubing, the surgeon must do hundreds of practice sutures on plastic tubing before being allowed to suture a blood vessel. Movements reflect cognitive processes; they provide cognitive psychologists with the dependent variables in their research, whether they are key presses, vocal responses, choice responses, or eye movements.

ACTION

Although cognition and action are intimately linked, action research has not been as prominent as many other areas of cognition. Neither Neisser's (1967) influential text *Cognitive Psychology*, nor its many successors, nor such important treatments as the *Handbook of Cognition* (Estes, 1975) included chapters on action and movement. To his credit, however, Bower (1975) wrote that the study of cognition should cover input systems such as perception as well as output systems such as movements (see Rosenbaum, 1984, pg. 220). George Mandler also noted the gap of knowledge on action. According to Gallistel (1980, p. xii) Mandler said that "what cognitive psychology lacks most is any sort of theory of action." Fortunately, there have been significant advances in the field; many of these anticipated the advent of cognitive psychology by several decades.

Historically, the study of motor movements was among the first topics of the fledgling field of experimental psychology at the turn of the twentieth century. Robert Woodworth (1869–1962) examined the relation between the speed and accuracy of targeted movements. Karl Lashley (1890–1985) was puzzled by the problem of serial order (Lashley, 1951). Paul Fitts resumed Woodworth's study on the trade-off between speed and accuracy and proposed his theory of skill acquisition that is still influential today. Cognitive psychologists study movement in its own right, but movement research advances our understanding of cognitive processes as well (Keele, 1973; Rosenbaum, 1984). Indeed, Lashley's and Fitts's research contributed to the emergence of cognitive psychology in the 1960s.

Following a review of the physiological basis of movements, this part of the chapter treats such advances of movement research as discoveries about movements toward a target, the degrees-of-freedom problem, the serial order of movements, and the acquisition of motor skills. The chapter concludes with an examination of typing, a familiar and important motor skill that has been widely investigated.

Physiology of Movement

In this section, we will treat the components of the movement system from the bottom up, from the muscles to the cortex. The muscles represent the effector organs of the motor system. The cortex is the site of the primary control centers of movement. Other neural systems implicated in movement are the spinal cord, the cerebellum, and the basal ganglia. Highlights of the review include an account of simple spinal reflexes, of the control function exercised by the prefrontal and premotor cortexes, and of specific place cells in the primary motor cortex. Figure 4.21A includes a schematic overview of some of these systems.

Muscles.   There are almost 800 muscles in the human body. Some of them are well known, such as the *biceps brachii* (better known as *biceps*) and the *triceps lateralis* (*triceps*) in the arm. Other muscles are less well known, such as the *procerus nasi,* a nose muscle, or the *extensor hallucis longus* in the lower leg. These four muscles are among the striped or **skeletal muscles.** Skeletal muscles have bundles of many fibers demarcated by stripes. These muscles produce the movements that act on the environment; it is these movements that are investigated by motor researchers. Skeletal muscles are monitored via sensory receptors sensitive to the position and movement of the muscle. The kind of information picked up by these receptors is known as **proprioception. Smooth muscles** are the other major kind of muscles. Consisting of

thin long fibers, these muscles control the movement of the body's internal organs, such as the intestine. A third kind of muscle is the cardiac muscle, which controls the heartbeat; it is only found in the heart.

Muscles are innervated to varying degrees by the axons of motor neurons. The precision of movement depends on the density of the axons; the more axons there are in a muscle, the finer is the movement. The muscles that control our eye movements, for example, are densely innervated, whereas the muscles in our thighs and shins have far fewer axons.

It may surprise you to learn that muscles can only contract. Stretching is the result of the contraction of antagonistic muscles. Thus, the triceps, for example, is stretched when the biceps is contracted. A contraction is the result of the release of the neurotransmitter acetylcholine. The contraction, in turn, produces kinetic energy.

Reflexes Under the Control of the Spinal Cord. From medical examinations, almost everyone is familiar with the knee jerk reflex, the automatic stretch of the quadriceps muscle in response to a tap below the knee. This reflex is controlled entirely by a spinal motor circuit rather than the brain. The speed of the knee jerk reflex—the leg kicks within 50 milliseconds—is a telltale sign of spinal cord control. Any brain involvement would take longer. The knee jerk is the best known reflex under the control of the spinal cord; however, there are others, including the stretch reflex of the biceps when a weight is placed in one's hand.

Cerebellum.   The word *cerebellum* means *small brain* in Latin. Its role in cognition and movement, however, is far from small. The cerebellum is known to

— Coordinate motor movements (e.g., in aiming toward a target)
— Control the muscle tone, the base level of tension in a muscle
— Prime the motor system just prior to the onset of a movement

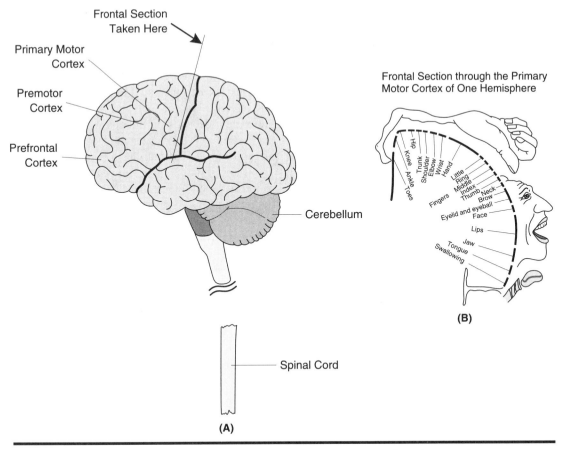

FIGURE 4.21 (*A*) Neural control centers of motor action are found in the prefrontal cortex, the premotor cortex, the primary motor cortex, the cerebellum, and the spinal cord. (*B*) The motor homunculus. The correspondence between regions in the primary motor cortex (see frontal section) and movement in specific body parts was discovered by electrical stimulation studies (Pinel, 1993).

— Contribute to motor learning (e.g., in classical conditioning)

Basal Ganglia. The basal ganglia are a set of nuclei (caudate nucleus, putamen, and globus pallidus) located in the cortex. These nuclei communicate with the primary motor cortex and the substantia nigra and other structures involved in motor control. Scientists infer the function of the basal ganglia from patients who suffered injuries to these structures and the concomitant loss of

specific aspects of motor function. Based on such case studies, it is thought that the basal ganglia are involved in directing the movement of limbs and in coordinating programs for automatic action (Fuster, 1995). When the basal ganglia are impaired, dysfunction of motor control results as in Parkinson's disease, for example. **Parkinson's disease** is a condition afflicting elderly patients. Its symptoms include tremor of the hands at rest, rigidity of the limbs, and spontaneous motor actions apparently not under the control of the patient. This disease has been linked, among other things, to a loss of the neurotransmitter dopamine generated in the substantia nigra region.

Cortex. The involvement of the cerebral cortex in motor control is all too familiar to physicians who treated patients suffering from brain injuries. Lesions of motor regions in the cortex are known to result in motor deficiencies on the contralateral side. For example, damage to the right motor hemisphere affects movement in the limbs on the left side. Experimental work on the role of the cortex in motor behavior was pioneered in 1870 by two German physicians, Gustav Fritsch and Eduard Hitzig, working with dogs. They administered mild electrical stimuli to one side of the dog's cortex and found that the stimulation resulted in movements on the opposite side of the body. Investigations by subsequent researchers, using dogs as well as other animals, replicated these results and the correlation between overt movements and brain regions was mapped for the different species. The mapping for humans, known as the *motor homunculus* is shown in Figure 4.21B.

Exciting as the discovery of these mappings was, they posed a puzzle to scientists because there are no direct links between the cortex and the muscles, which are the effectors of movement. The muscles are innervated by axons coming from the spinal cord and other lower centers, but not the cortex. What, then, is the role of the cortex in motor behavior? The answer is that the cortex is responsible for planning movements rather than their execution. The cortical areas implicated in motor control are the prefrontal cortex, the premotor cortex, and the primary motor cortex.

Prefrontal Cortex and Premotor Cortex. The prefrontal cortex and the premotor cortex are believed to govern the temporal sequencing of motor acts, including speech production. Interestingly, the prefrontal cortex is thought to serve as planning center of cognitive processes as well (see Chapter 8). Support for the temporal control function of the prefrontal and premotor areas comes from clinical case studies, brain imaging studies, and single-unit research: Prefrontal patients confuse the order of the constituent components of a motor act. Lesions in the premotor area affect both learning and execution of motor sequences (e.g., in limb movements). PET studies show elevated cerebral blood flow in the prefrontal and premotor regions as a person speaks or plans a motor movement.

Single-unit studies revealed that neurons in the premotor area do not control individual muscles or muscle groups. Rather, these neurons appear to govern global movements toward a target. The neurons are activated prior to movements relative to a specific location in space, even if different effectors (hand, foot, mouth) are involved to reach the target (Fuster, 1995, p. 184).

Primary Motor Cortex. The primary motor cortex is located anterior to the central sulcus, one of the major sulci of the neocortex. The frontal neighbors of the motor cortex include the prefrontal and the premotor cortexes; its posterior neighbor, across the central sulcus, is the primary somatosensory cortex. The motor cortex is connected to these neighboring areas. All of these send output via multiple axons to the spinal cord. Direct electrical stimulation of specific regions of the motor cortex produces movements in specific body parts. For example, stimulation at dorsal sections of the motor complex produces toe and leg movements, and stimulation at the ventral region elicits movements of tongue and lips; these mappings have been captured in the motor homunculus in Figure 4.21B. Research by a team of neuroscientists working at the Johns Hopkins School of Medicine under the direction of Apostolos Georgopoulos and colleagues provides a compelling illustration for the control function of the primary motor cortex.

"Reaching" Neurons in the Primary Motor Cortex. Using single-cell recording electrodes, Georgopoulos and colleagues (1989) identified specific populations of neurons in the motor cor-

tex that are selectively sensitive to certain directions of reaching. For example, cells fired preferentially when a monkey made a movement in a specific direction, say toward 45 degrees from the starting position. These cells would respond less when the monkey moved toward 90 and 0 degrees, and barely at all when the movement was directed toward 135 or 315 degrees. In general, different cell groups were maximally responsive for movements in specific directions while participating in lesser degrees in controlling the movement in neighboring directions.

This activation pattern of reaching neurons led researchers to formulate the concept of **population coding.** Georgopoulos described population coding as the involvement of a given cell in movements of various directions and, conversely, a movement in a particular direction is associated with the activation of a population of cells. Such distributed coding protects the motor system better against injury. If some cells should be lesioned, there are others to take up the slack. Distributed representations have been observed for other cognitive functions, including vision. Not coincidentally, findings like these have encouraged theories of distributed parallel processing in the brain (see Chapter 6).

Disorders of Motor System.   The motor system includes many components, ranging from muscle fibers and motor neurons to command centers of movement in the cortex. Deficiencies in any of these components, neurotransmitters, innervation, muscles, basal ganglia, and higher command centers may result in motor disorders, as the following common disabilities illustrate: myasthenia gravis, multiple sclerosis, cerebral palsy, and apraxia (also see Parkinson's disease, discussed earlier).

Myasthenia gravis is a muscle weakness associated with malfunction of the transmission of acetylcholine at the neuromuscular junctions. **Multiple sclerosis** is a loss of movement typically in the lower torso and limbs due to a loss of myelin sheathing in the motor and sensory tracts. The term **cerebral palsy** describes a set of dis-

abilities encompassing the failure of muscle coordination and an increase in muscle tone leading to muscle rigidity in the limbs. Cerebral palsy has been attributed to a variety of causes, including trauma to the brain's motor centers prior or during birth.

In addition to these and other disorders resulting from deficiencies in the primary motor organs—whether muscles, nerves, or basal ganglia—there is a group of motor disabilities known as apraxias. This set of disorders has been attributed to lesions in cortical centers that control motor actions, presumably through representations of motor programs. Using CAT scans, researchers have identified characteristic lesions in the left hemisphere of apraxic patients, including the left motor cortex and the parietal lobe. **Apraxia** is the inability to execute an intended action even when the motor system is intact otherwise. Apraxias are assessed by different gesture imitation tests. For example, an examiner might ask a patient to mimic the use of a tool (hammer, screwdriver, saw) just by using the hands; or to imitate an arm movement the examiner demonstrates, such as touching the right ear with the right arm; or to copy a facial expression, such as blinking with the left eye. Patients have difficulty performing these actions.

INTERIM SUMMARY

Motor movements result from an intricate interplay of muscles whose actions are controlled by neural systems from the spinal cord, the cerebellum, and the basal ganglia to the cortex. Such cortical regions as the prefrontal cortex, the premotor area, and the primary motor cortex are implicated in the planning of movements rather than their execution. Based on lesion studies and electrophysiological stimulation, scientists have mapped the relation between regions in the motor cortex and specific body parts. Nuclei in the prefrontal and premotor cortex are thought to be responsible for the temporal sequencing of movements. Dysfunction in any component of the motor system may lead to disorders of the motor system, such as multiple sclerosis, Parkinson's disease, and apraxia.

———

Psychological Control of Motor Behavior

Psychologists have investigated functional aspects of movements and sought to discover principles to account for the systematic patterns of motor action. This section reviews four research topics that have occupied scientists' attention: (1) the lawfulness of movements directed toward a target; (2) the problem of choosing a trajectory, known as the degrees-of-freedom problem; (3) the problem of serial order of action; and (4) the patterns of motor behavior thought to reflect the hierarchical structure of movements.

Moving toward a Target. Suppose you are trying to hammer nails into a board as quickly and accurately as you can. Skilled carpenters do this automatically, but you, as a novice, will find hammering more difficult, especially as you speed up. The proverb Haste makes waste captures the inverse relation between speed and accuracy well. The psychological study of movement began about a century ago when Woodworth happened to watch a crew of construction workers hammering. In a systematic study, he found the **speed-accuracy trade-off** that was subsequently documented in time motion studies done in industry for many other motor skills.

Woodworth and his students examined the effects of other factors on movement time, as well, including the distance between the starting point of a movement and its target. They established that movement time, *MT*, increases as a function of the logarithm of distance, *D*, as seen in expression (4.1). This means, for example, that movement time increases more as one increases the distance from 1 to 2 inches than when distance is increased from 10 to 11 inches.

(4.1) $MT = fn \log (D)$

Fitts's Law. University of Michigan psychologist Paul Fitts (1912–1966) augmented the func-

tion Woodworth had discovered. Fitts found that movement time varies as the requirements for precision, *P,* are varied: As precision is increased movement time is increased. Compare a calligrapher writing a fancy invitation and a student taking notes in class, for example. The calligrapher aims at the greatest precision of letters, whereas the student is satisfied with handwriting that is barely readable.

Fitts and Peterson (1964) sought to express movement time as a function of both factors, distance and precision. Using the apparatus in Figure 4.22, he had the person move a stylus between two targets whose width and distance were varied. Width of the target, *W*, represents the precision factor: The narrower the target, the more precise the pointing movement must be. Fitts found that movement time increased as the distance between the targets increased and as their width decreased. Equation (4.2) best captures Fitts's data:

(4.2) $MT = a + b \times \log (2D/W)$

Terms *a* and *b* represent the intercept and the slope of the function.

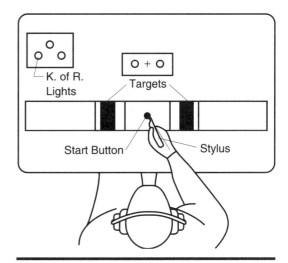

FIGURE 4.22 Fitts developed the stylus-tapping task in which operators tried to touch rapidly moving targets of varying width (Fitts & Peterson, 1964).

Subsequent research (see Keele, 1986) confirmed the generality of expression (4.2) for a wide range of movements and targets, including the following:

— Directing a rotary handle toward a target
— Pulling a joystick in a required direction
— Moving wrist and fingers in assembling instruments under the microscope
— Throwing darts at a target
— Moving a cursor on a computer screen
— Directing feet toward a target

Because of its generality, expression (4.2) has become known as **Fitts's law.** The only quantities that differed for the various actions were the slopes and intercepts of the MT function; the logarithmic relation held constant across movements.

Meyer and colleagues (1988) refined Fitts's law and discovered that the law represented but one case of a more general expression. Unlike Fitts, who focused on global movements, Meyer and associates analyzed such movements in terms of their component movements. They noted that each of the components requires adjustments in order to achieve the target. The greater the distance toward the target, the greater the number of component movements and adjustments necessary. Adding the number of components as a parameter to Fitts's original factors of distance and width culminated in the family of functions in Figure 4.23.

The parameter of the functions is the number of component movements, n. If there is only one component movement ($n = 1$), MT increases linearly as a function of difficulty, $2D/W$. As the number of submovements increases, MT increases in terms of a power function. As n becomes very large and approaches infinity ($n = \infty$), Fitts's logarithmic function is observed.

Meyer and associates viewed the family of curves in Figure 4.23 as an expression of a highly adaptive neuromotor system. Unlike Fitts, who focused only on how long it took to get from a home position to a target, Meyer and colleagues analyzed the components of the aiming movements themselves. According to their model, the

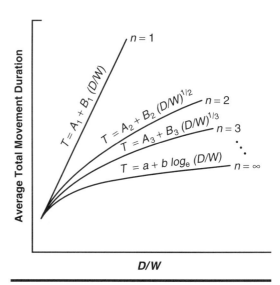

FIGURE 4.23   Movement time as a function of difficulty and of the number of constituent submovements (n) of the global movement. Fitts discovered the logarithmic function (at bottom) in the stylus-tapping task (Meyer, Smith, Kornblum, Abrams, & Wright, 1988).

component movements are subject to noise in the neuromotor system. Fitts had already observed that repeated movements never duplicate one another; rather, distances and movement times vary relative to their target. If a submovement misses a target either by overshooting or undershooting, secondary submovements correct the error. Collectively, the submovements are assumed to optimize motor performance, much as problem-solving activities are optimized given one's limits in memory and information-processing capacity (see Chapters 8 and 14).

Degrees of Freedom in Movements.   However natural and easy movements may seem to us, their study poses many challenges for researchers; one of these is the degrees-of-freedom problem. The problem is that in making a movement, the organism has great latitude in combining component movements in order to reach a goal. When the movement is actually executed, however, only very few of the movements possible are used. The **degrees of freedom of a movement** refers to the number of distinct ways the movement can be performed. A movement can vary in many ways, including its angular direction, extent of muscle contraction, and motor neuron discharge.

Consider, for example, the arm and its three joints, the shoulder, the elbow, and the wrist. The shoulder can move sideways, up and down, and it can rotate. The elbow can move forward and backward and it can twist. The wrist can move sideways and up and down. Not even counting the fingers, there are seven degrees of freedom in moving the arm. By varying the force of each movement, the number of degrees of freedom can be expanded even further. Clearly, there are multiple ways in aiming the arm (and finger) toward a target. The task of scientists is to identify the mechanisms by which organisms move toward targets so routinely and simply. Rosenbaum (1991) identified three factors that affect the selection of a movement: efficiency, interactions, and mechanics.

— *Efficiency:* Usually, people aim straight toward a target rather than making convoluted movements. As the action is completed, the person then adopts a neutral base from which any new movement can be launched. Consider a tennis player, who, after running toward the net or the sides of the court, positions herself in the center of the court so as to be prepared for the next play. Efficiency also means avoiding extremes in those movement parameters that are hardly apparent to casual observation but nevertheless measurable by researchers. These include rate changes in the velocity of movement, in muscle torque (the force to produce rotational motion) and in jerk (the time rate of change of acceleration).

— *Interactions between Limbs:* The movements of our limbs and their joints tend to be coupled so that the movement of one limb or joint limits the movements of the other. For example, shoulder and elbow movements are coupled, as are movements of the arms. You can demonstrate the cou-

pling of your arms easily: Try to draw a circle with one hand and a square with the other at the same time. You will find that this is very difficult; people tend to draw the same figure with both hands or they draw intermittently rather than simultaneously. These and other interdependencies between the limbs reduce the number of independent choices the motor system must make in executing movements; thus, they reduce the degrees of freedom of movement.

— *Mechanics:* Mechanical properties of the organism and of the environment aid in selecting movements without having to plan and coordinate. For example, when you swing your leg, even in walking and running, gravity takes over and no motor commands are needed.

The degrees-of-freedom problem has fascinated theorists of different theoretical persuasions. This section discusses three of these: Turvey (1990), who favored the ecological perspective; Jordan (1988), who advocated a neural network approach; and Rosenbaum and colleagues (1995), who proposed a knowledge-based model.

Working in the tradition of James Gibson (1904–1980), Turvey (1990) reasoned that organisms coordinate movements in terms of the constraints of their perceptual field. The components of the motor system collaborate dynamically in meeting the objective without external control, representations, or an executive system. Turvey used the marionettes in Figure 4.24 to illustrate the contrast between external and dynamic control. The marionette at the top is controlled externally by an operator. The figure at the bottom moves without external instructions according to "some kind of mutual understanding of achieving a common goal" (p. 939). Turvey's theory of motor coordination is akin to theories in thermodynamics and biology. He and his colleagues have used the dynamic approach to investigate rhythmic movements of the limbs, juggling, and different types of walking.

Jordan (1988) approached the degrees-of-freedom puzzle as a learning problem. Learning is

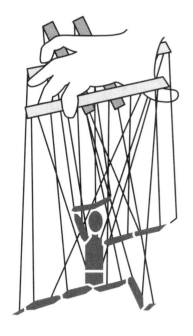

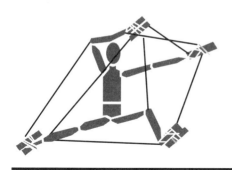

FIGURE 4.24 Marionettes to illustrate external control (*top*) and a self-organizing system (*bottom*) of coordinating targeted movements (Turvey, 1990).

learns to adjust its weights to reduce the error of the motor responses. Jordan has successfully implemented his network in teaching simple robots with two fingers to reach for one of four targets in two-dimensional spaces.

Rosenbaum and colleagues (1995) proposed a knowledge-based model as an approach to the degree-of-freedom problem. According to their model, postures are the key ingredients to the planning of movements. The organism is assumed to have a repertoire of stored postures for reaching particular targets. The choice of a posture depends on evaluating all of the postures that potentially could achieve the target. Each of the postures receives a weight that is based on the likelihood of the success of the posture. There is a weight for each degree of freedom, for each joint of the robotlike stick figures the researchers use in their simulations. The weights capture the costs of the posture, both in terms of accuracy and execution effort. Once a posture has been selected, a trajectory is chosen based on the laws of physics. Rosenbaum and associates validated their model in a variety of situations, including aimed single movements, continuous movements (as in writing), and rhythmic movements.

Serial Order of Action. In the heyday of behaviorism, motor behavior was *the* research subject of psychology. Behavior was observable, regular, and could readily be brought under experimenter control. It is no wonder that scientists called their approach behaviorism. The behaviorists appealed to the concept of reflex chaining to account for behavioral patterns and their serial order. According to this account, each component movement is elicited by sensory feedback of the immediately preceding movement. For example, in speech, the kinesthetic feedback of pronouncing a phoneme serves as the trigger for the next phoneme in the series. Although response chaining did appear too simplistic to some behavioristic writers, it was not until Lashley's (1951) influential article on the serial order of actions that a new theoretical approach was adopted.

implemented in a neural network consisting of several layers of simulated neurons (see Chapter 6). The neurons are connected via weighted links, where the weights express the strength of the connection. The network learns a mapping between the states of the environment—for example, the coordinates of the target and the output of the motor program, including the coordinates of a limb as it aims toward the target. The network also

Lashley criticized the chaining theory for its failure to account for the timing of responses, for coarticulation, and for the hierarchical structure of responses. He argued that in response chaining, the time to wait for feedback of the next response is simply too long to account for the fast occurrence of movements. For example, in typing and in piano playing, certain movements are initiated well before the previous movement is completed. Thus, in typing the word *epic*, the *i* is launched well before the letters *e* and *p* are typed (see Figure 4.25) At the same time, this example illustrates **coarticulation**, the preparation of a set of movements in its entirety.

Using the pronunciation of linguistic utterances as an example, Lashley criticized the chaining theory for failing to acknowledge structural units higher than elementary motor actions. He compared the articulation of the words *right* and *tire* and noted that both of them involved the same motor elements, except in reverse order. In pronouncing *right*, the speaker must first retract and elevate the tongue, exhale air, activate the vocal cords, and so on. These elemental movements could be permutated in any number of ways. So where does the particular organization used for the words come from? Lashley said that it was the linguistic structure of the words that controls the serial order of movements in pronunciation.

Speech errors had been a curiosity for many scholars before Lashley put his keen intellect to this interesting topic. He believed that speech errors were neither random nor the result of errors in chaining. Rather, Lashley discerned a pattern in many speech errors such that phonemes (or other units of speech) are introduced that should occur later in an utterance. Consider the speaker who utters *Our queer old dean* instead of the intended phrase *Our dear old queen*. According to Lashley, this particular spoonerism indicates that the speaker had more information available than merely the next word.

Lashley noted that all skilled movements are structured, citing, as further examples, the gaits of the horse (trotting, pacing, and single footing) and piano playing (the placement of fingers on the keyboard). In each case, the same pattern of muscular actions can be realized in a different tempo or on a different scale. In other words, there is a higher order of movements that subsumes the component actions.

Hierarchical Structure of Actions.   Each of the cases of serial motor order reflects a hierarchical organization rather than a chain of actions. Hierarchical structures are common in cognition; they are found in learning, memory, problem solving, and decision making. It is easier to memorize information that is arranged hierarchically rather than scrambled. Problem solving is easiest when the problem is structured in terms of a hierarchy of goals and subgoals (see Chapter 13). Decisions are most effectively arrived at when they are organized in hierarchical structures (see Chapter 14). It is not surprising, then, that hierarchies have been invoked to capture motor actions as well.

In an early seminal study, Bryan and Harter (1899) found that students learning to receive and interpret Morse code improved their performance in terms of plateaus. Bryan and Harter believed that a new plateau was achieved whenever a student mastered a new hierarchy, first recognizing the Morse code for individual letters, then for words, and finally for entire phrases.

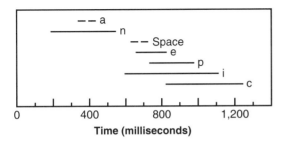

FIGURE 4.25 In typing the phrase *an epic*, movements to initiate key strokes do not necessarily correspond to the sequential order of the letters; the *i* stroke is initiated well before the *e* and *p* strokes (Gentner, Grudin, & Conway, 1980).

There are several models of hierarchical organization of movements (e.g., see Gallistel, 1980; Keele, 1986; Rosenbaum, 1991). Hierarchical programs are assumed to control motor behavior of animals, from primates down to insects. Gallistel (1980) reported research on the coordination of leg movements in cockroaches. According to Gallistel, phase relations between leg movements are governed by a movement hierarchy. Reviewing instances of other movement hierarchies, Gallistel (1980) described hierarchy as one of the core ideas of action.

Rosenbaum, Kenny, and Derr (1983) conducted an informative study that revealed the hierarchical organization in a simple keyboard task. Subjects were asked to memorize motor sequences and to press corresponding buttons as quickly as possible. Consider the sequence *MmMmIiIi*, where the *m*s represent the middle finger and the *i*s represent the index finger, and capital letters denote the right hand and lowercase letters the left hand, respectively. Thus, *M* denotes a key press by the right middle finger. Average response times were recorded from six successive trials. Response times as a function of the serial position of responses are shown in Figure 4.26.

The figure exhibits a jagged pattern of ups and downs in response speed. Rosenbaum, Kenny, and Derr (1983) were not satisfied with this pattern and so they sought a more parsimonious way of representing the data, as all good scientists would do. They expressed the series *MmMmIiIi* as a hierarchy—namely, the structure of three levels in Figure 4.27 The top level subsumes the entire response sequence; the second level includes the two *Mm* and *Ii* units, respectively; and the third level represents each individual motor response.

The researchers assumed that the motor output occurred according to the structure in Figure

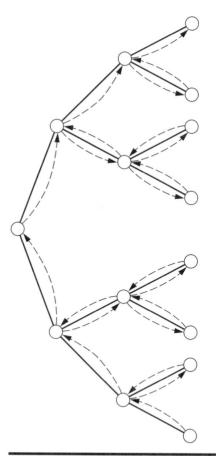

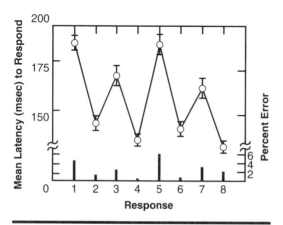

FIGURE 4.26 Irregular pattern of response latencies in finger-tapping task when responses are plotted in the sequence of their occurrence (Rosenbaum, Kenny, & Derr, 1983).

FIGURE 4.27 Hierarchical structure of motor responses in tapping task (Rosenbaum, Kenny, & Derr, 1983).

4.27. In responding, the subject decodes the levels of the hierarchy and arrives at each motor response by traversing the paths of the tree, one by one. The longer the traversal from one terminal unit at the bottom of the hierarchy to the next, the longer the response time should be. Here are some illustrations: Moving from *M* to *m* for response 2 takes two arcs, moving from *m* to *M* for response 3 involves four arcs, and moving from *m* to *I*, for response 5 involves six arcs When Rosenbaum replotted the same data of Figure 4.26 as a function of the nodes traversed, he found a very orderly relationship, as Figure 4.28 indicates.

Qualitative response patterns can be accounted for by hierarchical motor programs, too. Consider a study in which subjects were required to write a string of words on a sheet of paper (see Keele, 1986). This sounds easy enough, except that subjects were asked to use different body parts to produce the strings. They had to write the strings using the right hand, right arm, left hand, mouth,

and foot, respectively. Although the quality of the writing samples decreased as people used the unusual response systems, the writing patterns of the individual letters were remarkably similar. To Keele (1986), these data "suggest that the program that guides movement is abstract in the sense of independence from the articulators that execute it" (pp. 30–44).

INTERIM SUMMARY

Turning away from behaviorism, psychologists came to view motor movements as structured acts, much like mental acts rather than as linear response sequences. According to the structural view, movements are best characterized as nested hierarchies of acts of varying complexity, from relatively global acts to fine muscular responses. It is these hierarchies that determine the serial order of motor actions, not response chaining.

Psychological research on motor control has focused on parametric aspects of targeted movements and on the degrees-of-freedom problem. Research on movements toward a target has yielded a lawful relationship between the difficulty of a movement and its speed. This relation, known as Fitts's law, states that the time to execute a movement increases as a logarithmic function of the difficulty of the movement. The degrees-of-freedom problem is that, although one has many choices in making a targeted movement, one chooses only one of them, typically the optimal movement. Researchers seek to explain how organisms make this choice; three theories of the degrees-of-freedom problem were given: Turvey's notion of self-organization, Jordan's neural network approach, and the posture selection model proposed by Rosenbaum and colleagues.

Jordan's neural network was designed to address the degrees-of-freedom problem. At the same time, the model serves as a good example of an approach to motor acquisition. We saw that the network learns the association between target locations and specific movement trajectories. The network does so by adjusting its connection

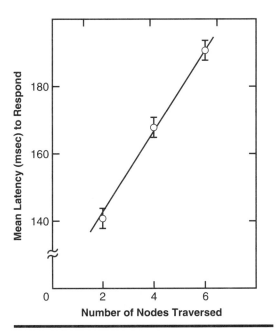

FIGURE 4.28 Response latencies replotted from Figure 4.26 according to the tree-traversal model in Figure 4.27 (Rosenbaum, Kenny, & Derr, 1983).

weights to minimize the discrepancy between actual and intended targets. This is, of course, the goal of acquiring motor skills in general.

———————

Acquiring Motor Skills

In the behaviorist era, motor learning was considered the result of forming chains of stimulus-response sequences. Thanks to Lashley's criticisms, however, the chaining theory of motor learning was no longer tenable. It was replaced with new approaches: the schema theory of motor learning and the stage model of the acquisition of motor skills.

Schema Theory.   The schema concept has wide currency in the study of cognition. A **schema** is a structure of abstract knowledge with variable parameters for filling in more detailed information. Schemas include knowledge structures for objects, events, and movements (see Hintzman, 1993, for criticisms of the schema approach). Examples for movement schemas are hitting a tennis ball, writing a word, playing a chord of notes on the piano, and tapping the fingers in sequence. The overall organization of the movement is the schema; the use of particular muscles (left hand, right hand, mouth), the speed of the movement, and the direction of the movement represent parameters.

Schemas typically subsume other schemas to produce the hierarchical structure of movements considered in the previous section. Further examples of such hierarchies are sentences, musical chords, and keystrokes. A sentence consists of phrases, phrases consist of words, and words consist of letters. A musical chord consists of a combination of several tones that sound harmonious when played together. Keystrokes, whether on the keyboard or the piano, include several levels of motor action, from global movements of the hands down to movements of the smallest finger muscles. The same applies to other motor skills as diverse as entering Morse code, horseback riding, cigar rolling, and swimming.

Hierarchies of movements are acquired as a result of practice. Individual movements may, at first, be unrelated, then they get chunked or grouped into a unit, and become a hierarchy. The better organized the hierarchy, the faster the response will be executed. Rosenbaum, Inhoff, and Gordon (1984) offered finger tapping as an example of schema acquisition and transfer. The researchers showed that there were considerable savings in the speed of finger tapping when subjects were asked to tap mirror rather than nonmirror patterns with the left and right hands. An example of a mirror pattern is *left index, left middle, left middle—right index, right middle, right middle*, whereas *left index, left index, left middle—right index, right middle, right middle* illustrates a nonmirror pattern (Rosenbaum, 1991). The mirror pattern was easier to learn because it preserved the same schema of finger movements across hands.

Stage Theory.   Following Fitts's lead, Anderson (1980) viewed the acquisition of motor skills, along with other cognitive skills, in terms of three successive stages: the cognitive stage, the associative stage, and the autonomous stage. In the **cognitive stage,** the learner acquires the skill by following verbal instructions. A tennis instructor will remind the student time and again to keep his eyes on the ball, hold the racket back, and bend the knees. In the **associative stage,** the learner tries to gain control over his skills by consciously noting the success and failure of individual movements. Only the successful ones are kept. The advice tennis coach Al Secunda (1984) gave to beginning players in his book *Ultimate Tennis* illustrates the cognitive stage: "When practicing, concentrate on consciously performing only one action at a time. While your body will unconsciously be performing many actions, your mind should focus and concentrate on only one. Don't think about the results of your stroke; just execute the specific action" (p. 200). During the **autonomous stage,** both speed and accuracy of the movement improve (see also Chapter 5). The learner executes movements almost automatically and appears to devote little effort to them. Tennis seems to come easy to a seasoned player—she serves effectively, moves gracefully, rarely misses a ball, and can even talk as she plays a volley.

An example of the speedup in movement, even after it was executed for as many as a million times, is Crossman's (1959) study of cigar rolling. Crossman measured the time it took factory workers to roll cigars. The study extended over a seven-year period. Plotting performance time and number of practice opportunities on logarithmic scales yields the linear decrease in time plotted in Figure 4.29.

Newell and Rosenbloom (1981) reviewed many other instances of learning motor skills and cognitive skills and found that the relation in Figure 4.29 held for many of them. They formulated the power law of practice in expression (4.3) to describe these functions. The symbol T refers execution time, P to the amount of practice, and a and b are constants, where $a > 0$ and $b \geq 1$.

(4.3) $T = aP^{-b}$

Read Box 4.2 for an example of speeding up execution of a rather different motor skill—making surgical sutures under a microscope.

The speedup and improved accuracy of responses are the visible effects of practicing a mo-

tor skill. There may be dramatic changes to the neural, muscular, and circulatory systems as well. Researchers at the National Institutes of Health have found changes in brain activity as a result of a four-week long practice period of finger-tapping sequences (Karni et al., 1995). A greater region of the primary motor cortex was activated when subjects tapped a highly practiced sequence compared to an unpracticed sequence. Research on championship athletes has revealed that the extended training required by star athletes results in significant differences in the size, structure, the distribution of fast-twitch to slow-twitch muscles, the capillary support of the muscles, in addition to changes in bone structure, heart size, and lung capacity. Contrary to earlier beliefs that these structures are genetically determined, investigations have shown that such morphological changes in the body are reversible. The body structures that support elite performance grow during extended practice and they diminish when the athlete no longer practices for competition (Ericsson, Krampe, & Tesch-Roemer, 1993). Indeed, research indicates that a few weeks of intensive training can lead to palpable changes in the athlete's musculature.

A Case Study: Typing

The keyboard is one of the most widely used machines by human operators, and typing and other keyboarding tasks are of great practical significance (see Chapter 15). At the same time, typing provides the researcher with a great opportunity for systematic and controlled investigation: Thanks to computerized recording and control methods, typing can be assessed with great precision. A rich body of empirical studies of typing documents several attributes of motor behavior, including the speed of responding, the coordination of different limbs, and parallel processing.

The typing speeds of expert typists are legendary. According to the *1986 Guinness Book of World Records*, the typing record for a five-minute stretch is held by Carole W. Bechen of

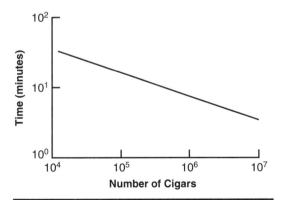

FIGURE 4.29 Schematic function indicates continuous speedup in rolling cigars, even after extended practice. This type of function holds for a wide variety of motor and cognitive skills.

Box 4.2

Training a Microsurgeon

Microsurgery is used in various surgical specialties, from eye surgery to neurosurgery. It involves surgery under the microscope using miniature tools on very small tissue structures. The microsurgeon must learn to focus the microscope, to adjust to the forty-fold magnification, and to handle the new tools. Microscopic adjustments are done by continuously using foot pedals. Nothing in a surgeon's training would have prepared him or her for handling the microscopic tools. The surgeon must inhibit wrist movements and the slight tremor of the fingers of which most people are normally unaware. Movements that appear gentle to regular visual inspection are huge and jerky under fortyfold microscopic magnification.

Janet Starkes, a researcher of motor control, observed an accomplished surgeon (M) as he learned suturing tiny blood vessels under the microscope. On the first day, it took M more than two hours to complete 3 sutures. After five days of training, he could do 10 sutures in less than an hour. An expert microsurgeon would require only 5 to 7 minutes for the same task! Remarkably, microsurgery involves movements that are not visible to the naked eye. Allard and Starkes (1991) concluded that the motor system can use "sensory information that falls outside the range of normal self-produced movement, speaking against any innate sensorimotor integration and for the power of strategy in motor-skill learning" (1991, p. 146).

Dixon, Illinois. During her test in 1959, Bechen typed at a rate of 176 words per minute. Albert Tangora still holds the record for a one-hour stretch of typing. On October 22, 1923, he achieved a rate of 147 words per minute using an Underwood Standard typewriter.

One does not have to be a world champion to type this fast; cognitive psychologist David Rumelhart submitted to a test typing a manuscript of 90,000 characters. For certain letter sequences—for example, *th*—his interstroke interval was about 60 milliseconds. Physiologists have determined that at high speeds such as this, sensory feedback from successive keystrokes is impossible. Sensory feedback usually takes about 200 msec. It was for this reason that Lashley (1951) argued that typing and piano playing necessitate motor control by abstract schemas or plans.

Not only is typing very fast but there is also a characteristic pattern of typing speed as a function of the combination of hands and fingers in typing successive letters.

— Intervals between cross-hand keystrokes are shorter than those for the same hand. For example, typists type the letter *y* in about 90 milliseconds in the word *by*. When the *y* appears in *my*, however, it takes over 200 milliseconds. Look at the keys for these three letters: *b* and *y* are typed by different hands; *m* and *y* are typed by the right hand.

— Keystrokes within one hand are a function of the number of fingers involved and the distance between keys. Figure 4.30A illustrates the effects of distance when the same finger is used; it takes 215 milliseconds to type an *e* after a *c*, 201 milliseconds to type a *d* after an *e*, and only 165 milliseconds to repeat an *e*. Here, the same finger, the left middle finger, usually taps these three keys. In Figure 4.30B, you see a similar pattern, except two different fingers are involved. By comparing Figures 4.30A and B, you will see that the intervals between keys are generally shorter when three fingers type them than when one finger does.

— About 80% of all typing errors in skilled typists are transposition errors and most of these are cross-hand transpositions. Examples of these are

because → becuase

which → whihc

There are also within-hand errors; the majority of these involve adjacent keys (such as *e* and *r*, and *o*

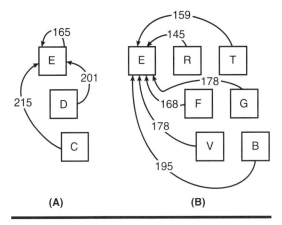

FIGURE 4.30   (*A*) Interstroke intervals in milliseconds to type a key when the preceding letter was typed with the same hand and the same finger: *e* to *e*, *d* to *e*, and *c* to *e*. (*B*) Intervals between letters typed with the left index finger followed by the letter *e* (Rumelhart & Norman, 1982).

and *p*). An example of a within-hand transposition is

supremely → supermely

When a word contains a double letter, a different letter is frequently repeated, such as

school → scholl

▬ Typists tend to copy a manuscript word by word; they tend to look ahead one word and to encode letters in terms of words (Inhoff, 1991). Consider sentences (4.1) and (4.2).

(4.1) His painful accident caused him trouble.

(4.2) His painful fracture caused him trouble.

The sentences differ in one word, *accident* versus *fracture*. The first is a high-frequency word, the other a low-frequency word. Inhoff (1991) found that interkey press times were 10 milliseconds faster for high-frequency than low-frequency words. He concluded that lexical information about a word is used in planning of a key-press sequence.

The great speeds in typing are, to some extent, due to preparing and executing keystrokes in parallel. Analyses of finger movements in typing using high-speed films revealed two basic components: the launch or initiation and the completion of keystrokes. Recording the response times for stroke initiation and completion, Gentner and colleagues (1980) found that typists often initiate keystrokes for subsequent characters sooner than those for early characters of a word. Figure 4.25 shows such a coarticulation pattern for typing the phrase *an epic*.

A Network Simulation of Typing.   Rumelhart and Norman (1982) developed a computer simulation of typing that accounts for the major empirical results, the high speed of typing, the response patterns, and the coarticulation effects. The simulation includes a recognition schema or node for each word. Each word node communicates with a set of nodes for the corresponding keystrokes. For example, typing of the word *very* is based on the word node *VERY* and keystroke nodes for each of the characters, *V, E, R,* and *Y,* as illustrated by the network in Figure 4.31.

The model includes the two types of movements that researchers recorded in making films of finger movements of typing: initiation and completion of a keystroke. The association between keypress nodes and keys in the model reflects the conventional assignments of fingers to keys—for example, the left index finger presses the *v* key, the left middle finger presses the *e* and *r* keys, and so on. These conventions are built into the simulation so that the V node, for example, controls the left index finger, and the E node controls the left middle finger.

The nodes of the network are connected via excitatory and inhibitory links, as shown in Figure 4.31. The links between the word nodes and the keypress nodes and between the keypress nodes and the response system are excitatory. Connections between the keypress nodes are inhibitory. According to the principle of distributed representation, the same keystroke nodes are used by other words, as well (see Chapter 6). The key-

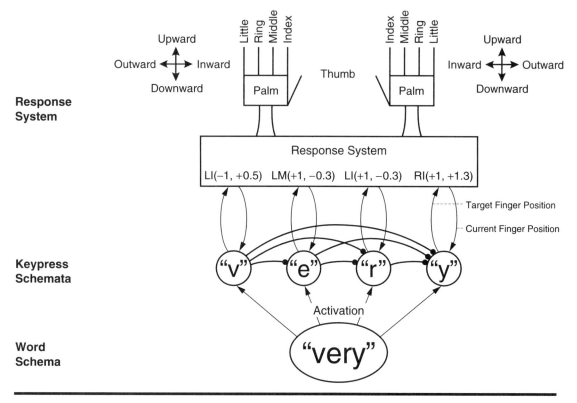

FIGURE 4.31 Rumelhart and Norman's model of typing includes a word schema, keypress schemas, and a response system (Rumelhart & Norman, 1982). (See text for explanation.)

press and word nodes control the response output system, which, in turn, controls the two mechanical hands shown in schematic form in Figure 4.31.

The performance of the simulation is achieved through a balance of excitation and inhibition passed along the links between nodes. Each node has a net activation value assumed to be zero at rest. Excitation increases the activation value, while inhibition decreases it. When the activation of a node exceeds a certain threshold, the node is triggered into action. Usually, this occurs in the appropriate word and letter context. However, because there is a background level of noise in the network, a node may be triggered in a wrong context, resulting in a typing error.

Hitting a key is based on activation at the word node and the set of corresponding keypress nodes. The most active keypress node elicits the initial

finger and hand movement toward the appropriate key and triggers the keystroke. In preparation of typing *very*, for example, the word node VERY becomes active. At this point, several things happen simultaneously: The V node is activated as the first keypress node, movements of left index finger and the hand are initiated, and *v* key is tapped. Because links between keystroke nodes are inhibitory, the keypress nodes linked to V— namely, E, R, and Y—are inhibited.

As soon as a keystroke is executed, the current keypress node becomes inactive and inhibition is lifted from the subsequent node. For example, after the *v* has been tapped, the activation of V node decays and the E node is no longer inhibited. The sequence of letters making up a word is thus generated by a sequence of changing activation and inhibition values of a set of keypress nodes. No additional assumptions about serial order are necessary in the simulation.

Here is how Rumelhart and Norman's (1982) model simulates important patterns of typing:

— *Speed of interkey stroke intervals:* According to the model, these short intervals do not reflect complete responses from initiation to pressing. Because keystrokes are made in parallel, they may succeed each other by as little as 60 msec. The complete responses themselves usually consume more time. The model can handle the parallel occurrence of keystrokes by (1) assuming separate initiation and completion phases of keystrokes and (2) assuming that, while excitation and inhibition change quickly, they do so in terms of a gradient. This explains why a typist can press a key with one finger while launching another finger toward a different key at the same time.

— *Between-hand versus within-hand interkey strokes:* Between-hand interkey strokes are faster than within-hand interkey strokes. The model has several mechanisms, including an inhibition mechanism, to account for the between-hand advantage. Initiating a keystroke inhibits subsequent keystrokes of the same hand, but not of the other hand. As a result, the typist can launch keystrokes between hands more readily than within hands.

— *Error patterns:* Rumelhart and Norman's model assumes that errors stem from noise in the network. The most frequently occurring errors are transposition errors, such as *which → whihc*. The model mimics such an error by positioning the wrong finger over its key—for example, *h*—and by temporarily activating its node prior to the appropriate time. Because the fingers of the other hand are less constrained than fingers of the same hand, such errors more frequently involve cross-hand errors.

Rumelhart and Norman's (1982) network model of typing can handle additional data and simulate very specific aspects of continuous typing. Nevertheless, the authors themselves acknowledge certain problems with their model. For example, there are certain typing patterns the model does not predict (e.g., the letter pair *er* is typed faster than *re*), and the pattern of interstroke intervals produced by the model does not fully agree with the data from human typists who pace their typing rates according to instructions to slow down or speed up. Although the Rumelhart and Norman model does not handle every detail of the patterns of typing, it does account for the temporal aspects, interactions of components, and constraints of typing. The model serves as an illustration of the neural network approach to motor behavior and to cognition in general.

CONCLUSION

This chapter has covered recognition and action, both of which are means of communication between the organism and its environment. Recognition entails the identification of objects in the environment; action represents the physical output of the organism to the environment. Recognition involves the description of the input stimulus and a match of the encoded stimulus to abstract representations in memory, the structural descriptions. Although scientists understand pattern recognition in its broad outlines, intriguing theoretical questions remain—for example, on the manner in which the components of the recognition process communicate, on the mechanisms that support the recognition of specific stimuli from letter features to faces, and on the mental operations needed to interpret dynamic and novel stimuli. As subsequent chapters will show, pattern recognition is an integral part of almost all cognitive operations, including learning, concept formation, developing expertise, language comprehension, and memory retrieval.

Actions result from movements of the skeletal muscles. Relatively simple reflex movements are controlled by the spinal cord, whereas complex motor action is governed by nuclei in the cerebellum, the basal ganglia, and such motor centers as the premotor area and primary motor area in the cortex. Psychological investigations of the patterns of movements have yielded important successes, such as on movements directed toward a target and on the schematic structure of movements, but they have also left crucial questions unanswered, such as on the mechanism that selects the optimal trajectory of a movement when many are available. The acquisition of motor skills has been described in terms of neural networks, schema theory, and stage theory—approaches that have been useful in capturing the acquisition of such other cognitive skills as reading, arithmetic, and problem solving.

Recognition and action are reciprocal in many different ways. Several of these were mentioned in the chapter: Perceivers perform movements from large to small in order to focus on a stimulus; objects tend to move rather than remain stationary; and we observe our own movements in order to adjust them to environmental requirements. In Chapter 5, we shall see that even production rules, the basic units of knowledge of skills, embody the linkage between recognition and action in terms of the recognize-act cycle. The *recognize* component of the cycle identifies conditions in the environment that trigger a set of actions specified in the *act* component. Although recognition and action are interdependent, there are crucial differences between them, nevertheless. Recognition and action involve different forms of energy, different directions in the flow of information, and different bodily organs—from the periphery to the cortex—to process the information.

CHAPTER 5

REPRESENTATION OF KNOWLEDGE: DECLARATIVE AND PROCEDURAL KNOWLEDGE

PREVIEW

A broad distinction is made between declarative knowledge (the knowledge of facts) and procedural knowledge (the knowledge underlying our actions). Declarative knowledge is easily expressed; we can define familiar concepts, describe typical events, and call up images. The first part of the chapter describes such explicit knowledge and how it is represented, whether in networks, propositions, scripts, frames, or mental models. There are interesting controversies about these representations, especially about visual imagery, with new twists added from computer simulation models and neuropsychological studies. Procedural knowledge embodies the implicit knowledge of how to perform a cognitive skill, such as numerical, language, and problem-solving skills. Procedures are represented in terms of production rules that include a set of conditions and a set of actions to be executed. Productions are acquired and automatized through practice. The chapter concludes with a description of three frameworks of knowledge and mental processes—symbolic architectures of cognition.

INTRODUCTION

Cognitive psychology is the science of the mind. It is therefore natural for students of cognition to ask: What makes up the mind? If you answer that knowledge is the stuff of the mind, you are cor- rect. We need to inquire further, however, as to how knowledge is represented in the mind. Our current understanding of mental representations has been shaped by various disciplines, including philosophy, linguistics, psychology, and computer science. Each discipline tends to focus on a different aspect of knowledge; and because our knowledge is so vast, a great variety of mental representations have been proposed. These include concepts, features, propositions, scripts, schemas, images, mental models, productions, conditions, actions, and symbols.

Cognitive psychologists have organized the multitude of representations by following the lead of philosophers who distinguish explicit from tacit knowledge. Computer scientists adopted this distinction as well, using the terms *declarative* and *procedural knowledge*. Declarative knowledge is easily made explicit; we can access it and talk about it. For example, we define a bird as an animal that flies; we know that George Washington was the first President of the United States and that one plus two equals three. On the other hand, procedural knowledge includes motor and cognitive skills—such as comprehending language, problem solving, and numerical skills—that are not easily described, though we have great expertise in executing them. We know how to tie a shoelace, how to ride a bicycle, and how to add three-digit numbers, but we find it difficult to explain this knowledge to a novice.

The representations of declarative and procedural knowledge covered in this chapter are symbolic representations. The theories that postulate and describe such representations are known as *symbolic-processing theories*. **Symbols** stand for entities other than themselves; for example, a stop sign signifies the command to stop a vehicle; a fire alarm means a fire is out of control; and a country has national symbols such as an anthem and a flag to represent its history and traditions. Notes on a sheet of music symbolize certain sounds. Even dreams are believed to symbolize subconscious thoughts and desires. Symbols may also refer to other symbols, for example, X is the roman numeral representing the number *10*, which is itself an abstract symbol denoting a specific quantity. Similarly, words are symbols for underlying concepts that signify objects or relations. For instance, the word *bird* denotes the con-

cept BIRD, which refers to winged animals that lay eggs and usually fly.[1] Different languages have different words for the same concept. Thus, BIRD is referred to as *ptiza* and *uccello* in Russian and Italian, respectively.

DECLARATIVE KNOWLEDGE

Concepts

Concepts are fundamental units of thought. Philosophers from pre-Socratic times to the present have been intrigued by the nature and meaning of concepts. Concepts help us organize the multitude of objects, events, and relations in our physical and mental worlds. Concepts reduce that multitude to a smaller number; if we had no concepts, we would have to refer to all individual instances one by one. Just imagine the world without the concept BALL and the different instances of ball. It would not only be difficult to distinguish between different kinds of balls, such as tennis balls, volleyballs, footballs, golf balls, and squash balls, but there would be a distinct name for each individual tennis ball as well. Concepts also embody knowledge about objects that is not perceptually apparent. For example, even if you have never seen a snake in the wild, you know that snakes can bite and that you should take the necessary precautions to avoid them. Finally, concepts have meanings that cognitive psychologists have long sought to represent. We will discuss two major approaches to the representation of concept meanings: the semantic network and prototype models.

Semantic Networks. One of the first influential theories of representation was Collins and Quillian's (1969) semantic network model that was developed to achieve efficient retrieval of information from a computer memory. At the time, computer memories were still rather limited and storage was very expensive. As part of the program's knowledge, Collins and Quillian included an information network about a set of concepts—for example, about animals and plants. They took advantage of the fact that these concepts were related to one another. We can detect these relations for ourselves simply by posing questions about the meaning of a concept and noting the nature of the correct answer. Suppose I asked you: What is a canary? Your likely answer would be: A bird (or more completely: A canary is a bird). You answer by referring to other concepts, much as is done in a dictionary (see Lindsay & Norman, 1972). Now, what is a bird? A bird is an animal. What is an animal? An animal is a thing. Let us stop here.

Collins and Quillian represented class, or subset membership, in terms of a hierarchical network. In addition, they included property relations describing the features of the classes and instances. The network in Figure 5.1 depicts a subset of the animal kingdom in a three-level hierarchy, including the category ANIMAL, two classes (e.g., BIRD, FISH), and several subclasses (e.g., CANARY, SALMON). The top

level, ANIMAL, is designated as 2; the classes represent level 1 of the hierarchy, and the subclasses represent level 0.

Each concept forms a configuration of links pointing to other words. This configuration captures the meaning of the concept. Concepts are represented economically without redundancies; for example, CANARY does not contain general information about breathing and flying that could be inferred from superordinate categories. Exceptions like OSTRICH, however, have special tags to indicate that the superordinate property does not apply.

Collins and Quillian's (1969) model was, at the time, something new in computer science. The idea of conceptual hierarchies, however, was not. It had been advanced by Aristotle long ago. Collins and Quillian's model, however, represents a great advance compared to Aristotle's work, because they formulated a processing model in addition to the structural assumptions

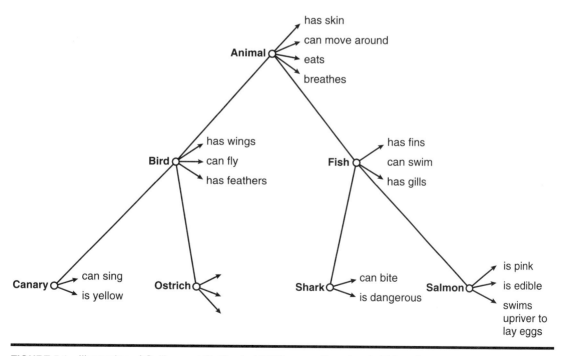

FIGURE 5.1 Illustration of Collins and Quillian's (1969) semantic network. This subnetwork shows the hypothetical memory structure for a three-level hierarchy.

graphed in Figure 5.1. The processing model tells us how the knowledge is used, such as when you want to retrieve facts.

Processing Assumptions about Fact Retrieval. According to Collins and Quillian (1969), when a person reads and encodes a statement, the corresponding concepts become active and the activation spreads along the links in the semantic network. If you read the statement *A canary is a bird,* activation spreads from CANARY and BIRD along the links like water through an irrigation ditch. When the two sources of activation intersect, the statement is found to be true. *A canary is a bird* is verified when the activation spreading from CANARY reaches the activated node BIRD.

Collins and Quillian (1969) tested their network model using a sentence verification paradigm in which people were asked to verify statements of the form *A subject is a predicate.* Their hypothesis was that verification would take longer the more distant the subject and predicate nodes are in the network. According to this distance or category size effect, *A canary is a bird* would be verified faster than a *A canary is an animal.* Collins and Quillian's experiment was ingenious in terms of both its theoretical assumptions and its method. It was a **semantic memory** experiment in that the subjects did not have to memorize the information about which they were queried. In episodic memory research, retention of items is investigated that subjects acquired in an identifiable episode—for example, in a specific experimental context (see Chapter 7). It was also one of the first of many experiments run on a computer, a PDP-1. The test statements were shown on a computer screen and response times were automatically recorded. By pressing one of two buttons, the subject indicated whether the statement was true or false. Test sentences included the following: *Baseball has innings, An oak has acorns*, and *Coca-cola is blue.*

Collins and Quillian's data graphed in Figure 5.2 reflected the distance effect implied by their network model. This model had a profound in-

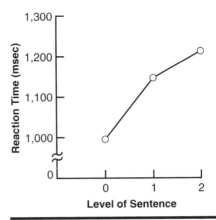

FIGURE 5.2 Average reaction times for different types of sentences in Collins and Quillian's (1969) sentence verification experiment. The abscissa represents the level in the network hierarchy and the ordinate indicates the response latency in milliseconds.

fluence on cognitive psychology; it spawned research on semantic memory, or declarative knowledge, as it is called today. Despite its successes, however, the model failed to account for two critical results, among others. First, the model was strictly taxonomic, arranging the representation of animal species as a zoologist would. The predictions of the model did not always hold true. Statements like *A dog is an animal* are verified faster than *A dog is a mammal,* though the order should be reversed according to the category size prediction. Second, statements that should take the same time to verify do not; the statements *A robin is a bird* and *A chicken is a bird* have the same relation to their superordinate term BIRD but they differ in their **typicality.** Most people consider a robin a more typical bird than a chicken (see Table 5.1). As a result, people verify the first statement faster than the second. Collins and Quillian's original model made no provision for such typicality effects. The prototype model that we consider in the next section was constructed to account for typicality.

TABLE 5.1   Similarity between Instances and the Prototype BIRD

Properties	Robin	Bluebird	Swallow	Starling	Vulture
Flies	+	+	+	+	+
Sings	+	+	+	+	−
Lays eggs	+	+	+	−	−
Is small	+	+	+	+	−
Nests in trees	+	+	+	+	+
Eats insects	+	+	+	+	−
Similarity to bird	$6 - 0 = 6$	$6 - 0 = 6$	$6 - 0 = 6$	$5 - 1 = 4$	$2 - 4 = -2$
Properties	**Sandpiper**	**Chicken**	**Flamingo**	**Penguin**	**Bird**
Flies	+	−	−	−	+
Sings	+	−	−	−	+
Lays eggs	+	+	−	+	+
Is small	+	−	−	−	+
Nests in trees	−	−	−	−	+
Eats insects	+	−	−	−	+
Similarity to bird	$5 - 1 = 4$	$1 - 5 = -4$	$0 - 6 = -6$	$1 - 5 = -4$	

Prototype Models.   The network model represents the meaning of a concept through its associations with neighboring concepts and properties. In contrast, in prototype models, the meaning of a concept is defined in terms of its similarity with a prototype; there are no hierarchical relations. Similarity is expressed empirically by the overlap between the features of the concepts. Malt and Smith (1984) had subjects report typical features of concepts, for example, BIRD, ROBIN, PENGUIN, and others. Experimenters then subtracted the number of dissimilar features from the number of overlapping features to get a similarity score as follows:

Similarity = number of common features
– number of unique features

This is illustrated in Table 5.1. The experimenters simply asked subjects to list all the properties they could think of in 90 seconds. Properties mentioned by 2 or more of the 30 subjects are indicated by a + sign. Features not mentioned are indicated by a – sign.

Table 5.1 shows the similarity of each of the concepts with the prototype bird. ROBIN, BLUE-BIRD, and SWALLOW are most similar to BIRD, whereas CHICKEN, FLAMINGO, and PENGUIN are most dissimilar. Sentence verification and categorization experiments have shown that decision times correlate with these similarity measures. In the categorization paradigm, the subject sees the name of a category (for example, *bird*) and then a concept that either belongs to the category or not (such as *robin* or *shark*). Decision times are faster for typical instances of concepts (e.g., *robin*) than for atypical ones (e.g., *chicken*).

The properties in Table 5.1 are listed in order of their typicality. Malt and Smith (1984) found that more typical properties tend to be mentioned first and verified fastest by subjects. People will mention that a bird flies before they mention that a bird nests in trees. Incidentally, children tend to acquire typical properties before less typical ones (Smith, 1988).

So far, we have been using natural concepts from the animal kingdom. People represent and process artificial concepts like FURNITURE and CLOTHING in a similar manner. Thus, SHIRT and SLACKS are typical instances of clothing, whereas WATCH and BELT are less typical.

Note that subjects produced WATCH and BELT as instances of clothing, though you may disagree with this classification. A belt is worn like other clothing, but it does not have buttons and keep you warm, which are two typical properties of clothing. Thus, the prototype view naturally allows for flexible and imprecise definitions—those that the philosopher Zadeh called *fuzzy concepts*.

Prototype analysis also lends itself to composite concepts (for example, RED JUICY FRUIT), to abstract concepts including numbers, and to social concepts. Try to think of the typical odd number. If you came up with 3, you were right. However, 15 is an atypical odd number. When subjects had to verify sentences like *Is N an odd number?* they responded faster for typical than atypical numbers. Social concepts represent a person's stereotypical knowledge. For example, we have stereotypes about groups of people, including jocks, nerds, yuppies, lawyers, senior citizens, WASPs, and so on.

Neuropsychological Perspectives.   The semantic network model and the prototype model were developed within the context of classical cognitive science, with computer simulation and experimentation serving as the research methods. Neuropsychological case studies have provided us with a different perspective on the representation of concepts. Based on case studies of patients, neuropsychologists have come to consider the possibility that information of different types of concepts—for example, animate versus inanimate concepts—may be subserved by different memory systems.

Hillis and Caramazza (1991), for example, studied two patients, J.J. and P.S., who exhibited remarkable performance deficits in a category naming task. J.J. was a stroke victim with injuries to the temporal lobe and the basal ganglia, among other structures. P.S., the owner of a construction company, suffered injury to his temporal lobes from a severe blow to his head. In the naming task, the subject was shown line drawings of objects from different categories and asked to name

them. The categories included land animals, water animals, birds, vegetables, fruit, body parts, transportation, and furniture.

Patient J.J. exhibited an advantage of animal identification over such categories as foods, furniture, and body parts. P.S., on the other hand, did much better on the latter categories than on the former. Hillis and Caramazza (1991) discussed two hypotheses in accounting for their results, both assuming that different semantic information is represented by different neural structures. According to the holistic hypothesis, word meanings are based on holistic representations. Instances of a category are assumed to be represented in adjacent neural regions so that damage to the region will have an effect on other members of the same category. According to the common features hypothesis, an object's physical features are represented neurally. If the neural structures are damaged, the feature representation would be affected and thus identification of the corresponding categories would be impaired. As interesting as this research is, it is problematic nevertheless: There are too few cases to evaluate the proposed memory models and there is a potential proliferation of memory systems with each new case of impairment reported (Roediger, 1993).

I N T E R I M   S U M M A R Y

In semantic network models (Collins & Quillian, 1969), concepts are defined by their associations with related concepts. The network is hierarchical and exhibits an economy of storage so that information stored within superordinate categories can be inferred. Facts are retrieved through a process of spreading activation. A sentence verification study supported the prediction that fact retrieval takes longer the greater the distance between two concepts. Network models do not capture the typicality of concepts. Prototype models do; researchers use empirical ratings to determine the typical properties of concepts. They determine the similarity of concepts by subtracting the number of dissimilar features from the number of similar features. This similarity measure accounts for the decision times in verification and categorization experiments. Neuropsychological case studies suggest the possibility that information of different semantic categories is represented in different regions of the brain. In a few clinical cases, categorization performance of specific categories was impaired depending on the patients' brain injury. Future research on a wider set of cases must determine the generality of these findings.

Events

Our interaction with the environment and with other people consists of sequences of events. Usually, we have no difficulty understanding and participating in events, and we know the likely consequences of actions. We are also familiar with the objects and the roles of participants in typical events—for example, when we go shopping, attend a lecture, or go to a restaurant. Cognitive psychologists have developed several theoretical structures to represent our knowledge of events, including propositions, causal links, and schemas. You will see that these representations do not replace concepts; rather, concepts form part of these representations.

Simple Actions and Propositions.   The following sentences express simple actions of the type *actor-action-object:*

Albert threw the book.

Cynthia bought the ticket.

Mother is sending a package to Mary.

In each of these sentences, agents and objects are linked by a verb (see also Chapter 10). Lindsay and Norman (1972) represented such actions in terms of propositional networks, as in Figure 5.3. The figure shows the networks for the sentences *Albert threw the book* and *Mother is sending a package to Mary.* The oval represents a predicate, usually a verb, and the arrows indicate classes of concepts we expect based on the verb. These include the agent (the person who performs the action), a direct object, and a recipient (for other cases, see Chapter 10). Verbs differ in terms of their conceptual frame; all verbs require an agent, and many verbs require an object and/or a recipient.

The network in Figure 5.3 is a graphical rendition of a proposition. A **proposition** represents a simple idea that is either true or false; you can apply this test only to propositions, not to concepts. A proposition is an ordered list of concepts.

(Predicate: x, Agent: y, Object: z . . .,)

For example, the proposition in 5.3A may be represented as follows:

(Predicate: THROW, Agent: ALBERT, Object: BOOK)

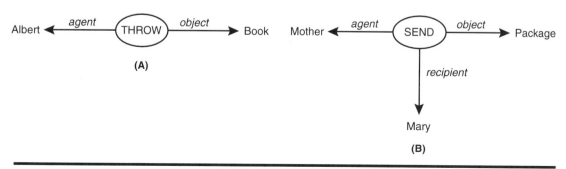

FIGURE 5.3   Network representations for the sentences (*A*) *Albert threw the book* and (*B*) *Mother is sending a package to Mary.*

(Predicate: SEND, Agent: MOTHER, Object: PACKAGE, Recipient: MARY)

As you consider the details of propositional representations, you may wonder whether or not the propositional theory is valid: People are certainly not aware of propositions. There are data, however, that suggest propositional representations. In an item-recognition study, Ratcliff and McKoon (1978) showed that subjects appear to remember facts in terms of propositions. The subjects established closer links between two concepts that belonged to the same rather than to different propositions. The experiment consisted of several alternating study and testing phases. During the study phase, subjects memorized sentences like (5.1) displayed on a computer screen. Sentence (5.1) contains the two propositions shown in (5.1a).

(5.1)   The bandit who stole the passport faked the signature.

(5.1a) (STEAL, BANDIT, PASSPORT)
        (FAKE, BANDIT, SIGNATURE)

During testing, a list of words was presented on the screen one word at a time for a speeded recognition test. Subjects had to decide as quickly as possible whether or not the word had appeared in one of the sentences just read. For example, the test list for one person might include the set of words shown in list (5.2).

(5.2) . . .

clouds	*no*
colonel	*no*
signature	*yes*
passport	*yes*

. . .

Another person might receive test list (5.3):

(5.3) . . .

clouds	*no*
colonel	*no*
bandit	*yes*
passport	*yes*

. . .

The correct response for each word is printed in italics on the right.

McKoon and Ratcliff found that subjects responded more quickly to targets that were preceded by a concept from the same proposition; they responded to words like *passport* after *bandit* in 560 milliseconds, whereas they took 584 milliseconds to respond to *passport* after *signature*. Based on these results, McKoon and Ratcliff reasoned that the subjects represented sentences in terms of propositions. Data from other studies also made a similar point. For example, when subjects read sentences, their comprehension time was related to the number of propositions in the sentence rather than to the number of words (see also Chapter 10).

You may feel that a proposition is too sparse and does not include images you might have of a bandit stealing a passport. Cognitive psychologists note, however, that a mental representation does not need to include every aspect of a stimulus, only a subset of the relations and objects. The goal of a theoretical representation is to predict task performance—for example, in recognition and reading experiments (Rumelhart & Norman, 1988).

Causal Relations.   Usually an event forms part of a sequence of other events and one action leads to another. Thus, Albert may have thrown the book in frustration when writing a paper on a very difficult topic. He may have studied articles for many days, taken notes, tried some drafts, and, seeing no progress, threw the book on his sofa. One could choose to represent this sequence of events as a list of propositions as in (5.4).

(5.4) 1 (STUDY, ALBERT, ARTICLES)
        2 (TAKE, ALBERT, NOTES)
        3 (WRITE, ALBERT, DRAFTS)

and so on. This list is superficial and does not reveal the underlying causal dependencies between the events, let alone the emotional drama. Propositions alone do not capture information in situations. Other structures are needed to support inferences of listeners; causal links and chains, schemas and scripts, for example.

Schank's (1973) conceptual dependency theory captures the underlying causal links between events. In his analysis, Schank showed that each individual action is actually composed of a sequence of events. Consider his example *John grew the plants with fertilizer*. This statement embodies much more information than is at first apparent. Growing plants means that the plants' size change from small to large as a result of some actions John took: He watered them, removed weeds, and applied fertilizer. Each of these actions involves supporting activities, and these in turn depend on specific prior events. There is no evidence that listeners and readers elaborate a message this fully. It has been shown, however, that they tend to remember causally connected events better than isolated statements. Read the story about Peter in Table 5.2 and consider the relation of each sentence to later sentences. The sentences differ in the extent to which they lead to subsequent events. Sentence 2 states Peter's goal and thus motivates the entire story; it is linked to many other sentences, including sentences 3, 4, 8, and so on. Sentences 6 and 7, however, are not related. Sentences like 2 are said to form part of the causal chain of the story, whereas sentences 6 and 7 are isolated dead ends (see also Chapter 12).

Schemas and Scripts.   A **schema** is a configuration of knowledge about objects and events, including general information. A typical office, for example, contains a desk, a lamp, a telephone, and filing cabinets. Other information is peripheral, such as how many windows there are in the office, the color of the telephone, the number of chairs, and the size of the filing cabinets. The schema expresses typical information, not the unique features of a specific office. A schema usually includes subschemas; each of the objects in the office may be viewed as a schema, from desks to computers, and in turn each of these include subschemas. Thus, a desk includes a desk top with a calender, writing utensils, and different

TABLE 5.2   Sample Text for Illustrating Causal Structure (van den Broek, 1990)

1. There once was a boy named Peter
2. who wanted to buy a bike.
3. He called a bike store to ask for prices.
4. He counted his money.
5. The money was not enough for a bike.
6. He put his piggy bank back on the top shelf of his closet
7. and covered it with clothes.
8. Peter wanted to get some money
9. so he asked his mother for some.
10. His mother said "No, you should earn your own."
11. Peter decided to get a paper route.
12. He called the newspaper agency
13. and asked about a route.
14. The secretary told him to come in.
15. Peter talked to the manager
16. and got his job.
17. He worked very hard on his job
18. and earned a lot of tips.
19. Pretty soon he had earned $200.
20. He went to a bike store
21. and bought a beautiful bike.
22. He was the happiest kid in town.

types of drawers. Schemas for physical objects like room, desk, and house are known as **frames.** Schemas for events are known as **scripts.** There are also **problem schemas** that depict the typical structure of problems in a variety of contexts from games and computer programs to arithmetic problems. You may remember different types of problem schemas from junior high school, such as River-Current, Interest-Rate, and Amount-Rate-type problems (see Chapter 13).

Rumelhart and Ortony (1977) list four basic features of schemas.

— A schema has variables. A typical house, for example, includes such variables as ROOF, WALLS, and DOORS. Particular features of each of these differ for different houses.

— Schemas can include other schemas. The schema of going to college includes schemas about typical examinations, lectures, labs, and dorms.

– Schemas vary in their abstractness. A computer program, for example, may include a loop; at the most abstract level, loop refers to some repeated operation. At a less abstract level, one would specify the function of the loop—for example, adding numbers (see Chapter 1).

– Schemas are flexible. Certain aspects may be missing—for instance, the typical theater has a stage, seats, and a curtain, but there are theaters without stages, seats, or curtains.

Cognitive psychologists have invoked schemas in many different contexts: in memory studies (Chapter 7), reading comprehension (Chapter 12), and problem solving (Chapter 13). We will discuss scripts here and problem schemas in Chapter 13. Frames play an important role in computer simulation models (see, for example, the section on Visual Imagery in this chapter). Although schemas have found wide use in cognitive psychology, they have also been criticized precisely because they are so flexible and useful in so many different contexts; according to critics, the schema concept is too broad to permit empirical testing (Hintzman, 1993).

Schank developed scripts for his research, which involved getting computers to read texts and answer questions about them. As mentioned, a script is a schema that describes a typical sequence of events, such as attending a lecture, going shopping, seeing a health professional, or going to a restaurant. The restaurant script represents the knowledge we have of eating in a restaurant. Table 5.3 illustrates one type of restaurant script: the coffee shop track. There are props, roles, and four scenes: entering, ordering, eating, and exiting. Scripts, like schemas, are generic; they describe typical events and allow for some variability. In some coffee shops, for example, the menu may be printed above the counter or drawn on a blackboard; in others, customers select the food at the counter; in still others, customers stand at tables to have their meal; and so on.

TABLE 5.3 The Restaurant Script

Title:	RESTAURANT
Track:	Coffee Shop

Props:	Tables	*Roles:*	Customer
	Menu		Waiter
	Food		Cashier
	Check		Owner

Scene 1: Entering
  Customer enters the restaurant
  Looks for a table
  Goes to table and sits down

Scene 2: Ordering
  Waiter brings the menu
  Customer studies the menu
  Customer signals to the waiter
  Waiter takes the order

Scene 3: Eating
  Waiter brings the meal
  Customer eats the meal

Scene 4: Exiting
  Waiter writes the check
  Customer takes check to cashier and pays
  Customer leaves the restaurant

Implied Script Concepts. Based on script knowledge, we are able to infer actions not explicitly stated in a text or conversation. We have no difficulty understanding text (5.5).

(5.5a) John went to a restaurant.
       He ordered a chicken.
       He left a large tip.

According to Schank and Abelson (1977), reading the first sentence of (5.5) activates the restaurant script with its underlying knowledge, so that the reader's understanding may look something like the passage in (5.5b).

(5.5b) John went to a restaurant.
       He sat down.
       He looked at the menu.
       He ordered chicken.
       He ate the chicken.
       He left a large tip.

He paid the check.
He left the restaurant.

The statements in italics are easily inferred; in recall and recognition experiments, subjects believe that they actually read such implied statements (Bower, Black, & Turner, 1979; Graesser, Gordon, & Sawyer, 1979). These results indicate that scripts function the way they are supposed to; they add information not stated in the story. It is not clear, however, whether the subjects make the inferences as they read the stories or during the retention test.

Researchers agree that the script concept is useful to account for recall of familiar stories. They note, however, that there are many other type of texts that are less familiar than restaurant stories, and listeners usually understand them without much trouble. Apparently they call on additional sources of knowledge not fully captured by schemas and scripts.

INTERIM SUMMARY

Cognitive psychologists represent simple actions in terms of propositions. A proposition links such concepts as agent, object, and recipients via a predicate, usually a verb. A variety of studies indicate that subjects process information in terms of propositions; for example, information is more quickly recognized when it is primed by concepts from the same proposition. Sequences of events tend to be causally linked, forming causal chains. Events are remembered better to the extent that they influence subsequent actions. Schemas are generic knowledge structures that express the basic properties of objects and sequences of events. Schemas for physical objects are known as frames, and schemas for events are called scripts. Schemas are flexible and abstract; they enable people to infer implied information and are useful in problem solving.

Visual Imagery

It is easy to generate visual images. Try to answer the following questions: *Which is the shortest way to the library? Where did I leave my keys?* and *Which is greener—a fresh pea or a pine needle?* Undoubtedly you will use visual images to answer several if not all of these questions. Moreover, you will have little difficulty conjuring up images of real and fictitious objects; it is not hard to imagine a dinosaur walking in the woods or a unicorn running down a street. Although no one disputes that images are real, they have always been a topic of heated debate in psychology.

The introspectionists of the late nineteenth century who examined ideas and thoughts were divided on the question of images. One camp maintained that ideas are accompanied by images, whereas the opposing camp held that thought could be imageless or abstract. Researchers performed experiment after experiment without ever agreeing about the results. It was the controversy about images that contributed to the demise of the introspectionist school, which was replaced by behaviorism. One cannot measure or verify an image. As a result, psychologist John Watson and his followers suspended all study of imagery and the mind. Practically no experimental or theoretical effort was devoted to imagery until the 1970s when a Stanford University researcher, Roger Shepard, and his students discovered a way to make images measurable. They succeeded where the introspectionist psychologists had failed. As we shall see, however, the topic of images remains controversial.

Shepard's Rotation Experiments.   Roger Shepard was interested in imagery throughout his life. His father was a professor of engineering at Stanford University and had a vivid imagination that helped him in his design work. Shepard's curiosity was stimulated by his father's work, and he began investigating the role of imagery in creative thinking. He and his students (e.g., Metzler & Shepard, 1974) developed an innovative rotation technique to make the effects of visual imagery observable. Metzler and Shepard (1974) used pictures of pairs of three-dimensional objects like those in Figure 5.4. In some cases, the paired objects were identical except they were rotated in the picture plane, as in Figure 5.4A. In other

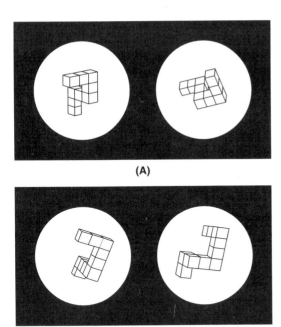

(A)

(B)

FIGURE 5.4 Comparison stimuli used by Metzler and Shepard (1974) in their study on mental rotation (1971). (*A*) The objects differ by an 80-degree rotation in the picture plane. (*B*) The objects are not congruent (Shepard & Metzler, 1971).

cases, the two objects were incongruent (5.4B). Subjects were shown one pair of objects at a time and asked to judge whether or not the two were the same. Metzler and Shepard found that people's decision times for yes responses increased linearly with the degree of separation between the two objects. The greater the difference, the longer it took to make the yes response. These results are graphed in Figure 5.5.

These results suggested to Metzler and Shepard that subjects form a visual image of an object and rotate the image until it is congruent with the comparison object. Mental rotation is analog to physical rotation. Images are, therefore, called **analog** representations, unlike propositions that are abstract and symbolic. Analog means the mental representation maintains some of the same physical features of the original. The contrast be-

tween a watch with hands and a digital watch is an illustration of the distinction between analog and symbolic. The movement of the watch hands is analog to the passage of time, but the change of digits is symbolic. Theorists who subscribe to the analog theory include Paivio and Shephard. On the other hand, Pylyshyn (1981), resurrecting the imageless thought theory of a century ago, opposes the analog view and argues that images are based on abstract thought processes that simulate physical events. According to Pylyshyn, Shepard's rotation effect occurs because people know that it takes time for objects to move in space, and that the greater the distance traversed, the more time movement takes.

Kosslyn's Theory: Images and Computers.
Like other cognitive scientists, Kosslyn (1983) used a computer metaphor of the mind (see Chapter 1). A computer includes a central processor, a long-term store, input devices, and output devices, including a video terminal. A video terminal is a cathode-ray tube (CRT) with a buffer that holds the information for the screen image.

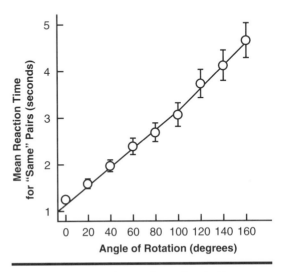

FIGURE 5.5 Mean time to determine that two objects are congruent as a function of the angular rotation in the picture plane (Shepard & Metzler, 1971).

Kosslyn called this theory the CRT theory of visual imagery. According to this theory, images have a limited capacity, much like CRT screens are limited in size. The theory includes two levels of imagery: the **buffer level** and the **long-term level.**

The buffer corresponds to the image that we experience—the surface image. It receives input from either the visual system or the long-term store. The buffer has cells, each with a certain level of activation. Collectively, the cells form an array that functions like a space. Information in the visual buffer is analogous to the imaged object; it has spatial properties, a certain resolution or grain size, and a rate of decay. The surface image is of relatively short duration and is not always present, just as people do not experience images all the time. Having spatial properties means that the image is extended in space like a physical object and when it is too large, it will not fit on the screen. Due to the capacity limitations of the buffer, images may compete with one another. Images also fade and need to be refreshed.

The long-term store includes frames of the image; frames carry information about the size of the image, the relations among components, and the relation to other images. The frame acts like a blueprint for the generation of the image; it is not something we experience as the image. The description includes a list of coordinates to indicate the spatial extension of the object. The coordinates are used to place the image in the visual buffer. In addition to the buffer and the long-term store, Kosslyn's CRT model includes a list of procedures that generate and manipulate images. Images are rotated and zoomed, and parts of the image are found and put in a specific location. Kosslyn's theory combines the analog and symbolic views of imagery; the image in the CRT buffer is analog, its blueprint in long-term memory is symbolic. According to Kosslyn, both aspects are needed to support images.

Evidence from the Laboratory. Kosslyn (1983) performed many imagery experiments. He had subjects generate, manipulate, and scan a great variety of images on a computer screen. In one of Kosslyn's more startling experiments, he found that small images are tougher to "read" than large ones. In this experiment, he asked subjects to generate mental images of two animals—a target and a context animal. One of the context animals was large, the other small. When subjects were asked to imagine an horse alongside a cat, the cat was relatively small. On the other hand, when they imagined a beetle next to the cat, the cat's image was relatively large. The target animal, cat, was small in one condition and large in the other, as shown in Figure 5.6. According to Kosslyn's theory, size manipulation is based on the limited screen size; the horse takes up more space on the screen than the cat, and therefore leaves less space for the latter, whereas the beetle takes less space than the horse. Subjects had no trouble generating images like these.

Next, the experimenter asked subjects to focus on a specific part of the target animal (for example, the cat's ears) and press a response key when they saw the part. It turned out that the ears were seen more quickly in the cat-beetle image, where the cat was large, than in the cat-horse image, where it was small. Kosslyn argued that the resolution was better in the large cat image, and thus speeded up the response time. The faster readout from the larger image supported the idea that the image was analog.

Metzler and Shepard (1974) and Kosslyn (1983) investigated visual images, demonstrating that people generate such images and that images are subject to experimental control. People have no difficulty forming images in other modalities as well, whether it is the sound of someone's voice, the taste of a favorite dish, or the weight of a heavy load. Here is an interesting study that involves kinesthetic and motor images.

Imagine carrying a cannonball for 100 feet. Then imagine carrying a balloon for the same distance. Which would take longer, the mental walk with the imagined cannonball or balloon? Intons-Peterson asked subjects to take a mental walk across campus with either a cannonball or balloon. Whenever they arrived at a landmark

FIGURE 5.6   Images such as these were used in Kosslyn's (1983) imagery size study: a cat and a horse versus a cat and a beetle.

location—for example, the student union or the library—they were to press a button (Intons-Peterson & Roskos-Ewoldsen, 1989). The subjects imagined walking faster when they carried the imaginary balloon than when they lugged the hypothetical cannonball.

This result indicates that images are linked to our knowledge about the typical properties of objects; the knowledge that cannonballs are heavy slowed the imagined walk. It appears, then, that images are not isolated representations but that they depend on other types of declarative information.

The Imagery Debate Continues. Despite Shepard and Kosslyn's impressive results, the debate about the sensory nature of images continues. Critics do not question the research results themselves, but their interpretation. They attribute the results to artifactual aspects of the experiments (such as experimenter bias or subject expectancy) or to confounds with some variable. There is Pylyshyn's argument that subjects have tacit knowledge about images and how visual processes ought to behave. Pylyshyn argued that people implicitly compute rotations, transformations, and image manipulations symbolically or numerically rather than in the analog fashion claimed by Shepard and Kosslyn. In the cannonball study, subjects might have guessed the experimenter's hypothesis and adjusted their responses accordingly; cognitive psychologists call this a *demand characteristic*. Such demand characteristics are a potential factor in imagery research that is difficult to account for. Indeed, it has been shown that subjects are more likely to show the imagery size effects that Kosslyn discovered when the experimenter expects them to occur! Thus, imagery effects are, at least to some extent, the result of experimenter expectation.

Finally, there is evidence on images involving people who are born blind. Using Kosslyn's imagery size task, Kerr (1983) found that congenitally blind subjects responded faster to images of larger than smaller objects, much like sighted subjects. Kerr concluded, therefore, that images do have spatial properties but need not be visual.

Perspectives from Cognitive Neuroscience. Some of the alternative interpretations of imagery have been eliminated through subtle and complex experimental control procedures, but the question remains whether or not visual imagery involves the visual centers and pathways in the brain. As Farah (1988) argued, there are some direct and indirect indications that visual imagery does involve the visual system. For example, specific deficits in the ability to form visual images are found in patients with lesions in the primary visual cortex in the occipital area of the brain. Consider also results from ERP and PET studies on visual image formation.

Farah (1988) measured event-related potentials during periods when people were processing visual images in a reading and imagery experiment (see Chapter 2). The experiment included two experimental conditions. In one condition, readers simply read words (for example, *cat*). In the other condition, they read words *and* imagined the objects. Each word was presented for 200 milliseconds and ERPs were recorded from 16 different sites on the scalp, including occipital and temporal locations. The ERPs were similar for the first 450 milliseconds, but differed thereafter: In the imagery condition, the ERPs recorded at the occipital sites were highly positive relative to those in the reading condition. According to Farah (1988), these results suggest neural activity in the occipital lobe as the person generates visual images.

Kosslyn and his colleagues (1993) found that PET activity was evident in the same brain regions, whether subjects engaged in visual perception or in visual imaging. The study included three conditions: a visual imagery condition, a perceptual condition, and a control condition. In each condition, subjects were looking at a computer screen displaying a grid with a cross in one of the cells. Subjects had to make a judgment about the cross relative to the location of a block letter, such as the letter *F*. In the imagery condition, the volunteers were asked to imagine the *F* superimposed on the grid. In the perceptual condition, the *F* was physically displayed; it occupied some of the cells of the grid. In both conditions, volunteers had to indicate whether the cross occurred within the *F*. In the control task, subjects simply saw the cross on the grid without having to imagine or perceive any letters. PET recordings showed increased metabolic activity in the parietal and temporal lobes for both the imagery and perceptual conditions, thus demonstrating that visual perception and imagery

are subserved by similar brain regions. Although recording the blood flow in these regions is important, you should remember that the recordings by themselves do not reveal the mechanisms of creating images (nor percepts). The discovery of such mechanisms remains a task for future research.

INTERIM SUMMARY

Images continue to be controversial among psychologists. They were taboo for much of this century, until Shepard and his students devised a way to make images accessible in experiments. In Metzler and Shepard's mental rotation experiment, subjects took longer to rotate geometrical shapes when they were separated by a wide angle. In Kosslyn's imagery experiments, subjects took longer to inspect a small image. These experiments suggest that visual images are analog representations that include objects' spatial features. According to Kosslyn's CRT model, images are created from an abstract representation in long-term memory. These results and others support the reality of images and the fact that images can be studied experimentally. Nevertheless, these experiments raise new issues about imagery; one of these concerns the extent to which visual images involve the visual centers in the cortex.

Mental Models

Each of the representations we have considered thus far, from concepts to images, was relatively constrained by referring to individual entities. Even the schema, although it may involve subschemas, is relatively simple compared to the mental model. Mental models are global representations of one's environment, a visual scene, or a story.

Mental models are structural analogues of the environment (Johnson-Laird, 1983). They may encompass several concepts, schemas, or images, as well as the relations between them. A study by Glenberg and colleagues illustrates that mental models capture the spatial relations between objects. These investigators asked subjects to read short paragraphs like those in Table 5.4 (Glenberg, Meyer, & Lindem, 1987). Two story versions reflected the relation of an item—for example, a sweatshirt—to the character described in the story. In the close version, John wore the sweatshirt; so it remains part of the picture, or, in terms of the theory, it remains part of the mental model. In the distant version, however, John took the sweatshirt off, it therefore dropped out from the mental model. Glenberg and his colleagues took care to construct the two versions of the passage so as to keep their propositional structures nearly identical.

After reading a study paragraph like the John story, a recognition test followed. A test word was presented on the computer screen and subjects indicated whether or not they had seen the word in the passage. The measure of interest were the decision times for *yes* responses; these were 200 milliseconds faster for target words in the close than in the distant story versions. Close concepts apparently remain part of the reader's mental model, whereas distant concepts drop out. The mental processor operates according to the strategy "out of sight, out of mind." This is what the mental model captures but a propositional representation does not.

TABLE 5.4   Passage Versions in Glenberg Experiment

Close Version
John was preparing for a marathon in August. After doing a few warm-up exercises, he put on his sweatshirt and went jogging. He jogged halfway around the lake without too much difficulty.
Target: *sweatshirt*

Distant Version
John was preparing for a marathon in August. After doing a few warm-up exercises, he took off his sweatshirt and went jogging. He jogged halfway around the lake without too much difficulty.
Target: *sweatshirt*

According to Johnson-Laird's theory, we use mental models when we solve problems, read a novel, and perceive a visual scene. A simple illustration from perception is Marr's primal sketch of a visual scene used in computer vision (see Chapter 4). For a mobile robot, the mere transformation of individual objects into a symbolic representation is insufficient; if the robot is to move through a room full of objects, it must have a global model that includes both the objects and their relation to one another. It must know when it is about to bump into an object and anticipate the behavior of other objects. So, the representation includes the robot's entire dynamic environment. A mental model in problem solving includes a goal and many of the steps required to reach it. A successful computer programmer, for example, organizes the components of a program in terms of its overall goal. Similarly, when a reader reads a novel, he keeps track of the fate of the most important characters, their interaction, and the background. Thus, the reader's mental model may include several individual representations. Of course, neither the programmer nor the reader is fully aware of mental models.

PROCEDURAL KNOWLEDGE

Procedural knowledge is the knowledge that underlies motor and cognitive skills, including arithmetic, computer programming, playing chess, and recognizing letters. (For motor skills, see Chapter 4.) The knowledge that affords us such skills differs from declarative knowledge. You can express declarative knowledge with relative ease, provided you know the facts required. On the other hand, even if you know how to decode print and recognize letters, you are unlikely to express that knowledge explicitly. In fact, the reader may have intuitions about decoding that are quite inaccurate. In other cases, it is possible to express procedural knowledge, but it is surprisingly difficult. For example, try to write down the rules you use when adding two-digit numbers. Although you cannot easily articulate it, you can use procedural knowledge accurately.

Another difference between procedural and declarative knowledge is the speed with which you use each. The use of procedures is relatively fast and automatic. It takes no longer than 1/10 of a second to recognize a letter, for example. It takes much longer to access declarative knowledge, even when the facts are relatively well known. In sentence verification experiments, subjects take over one second to retrieve such information as *A canary is a bird*. If you play the game Trivial Pursuit, you know how much longer it takes to come up with facts you know but do not use very often.

Declarative and procedural knowledge also differ in the ease with which they are acquired by patients suffering from amnesia. Such patients frequently exhibit rapid forgetting of new declarative knowledge but are quite capable of learning new skills like the Tower of Hanoi puzzle (see Chapters 8 and 13). Theorists represent the two types of knowledge differently. Declarative knowledge is represented as propositions, scripts, and images, whereas procedural knowledge is represented in terms of rules. The rules connect declarative knowledge to the real world.

Although the two types of knowledge are different, both are necessary in problem solving, including arithmetic, computer programming, language understanding, and other skills. When we learn a new skill, say another language or a complex game like chess, we first acquire declarative knowledge that describes the domain. After extended practice, often hundreds and thousands of hours of it, the knowledge becomes procedural and automatic. Becoming an expert at something is based on the transition from using slow declarative knowledge to fast procedural knowledge.

Representation of Procedural Knowledge

Cognitive scientists have sought to make procedural knowledge transparent by representing it in terms of rules. Computer scientists have been in the forefront of this effort; they simulate cognitive skills by using if-then rules (Newell & Simon, 1972). Because a skill has many components, many rules are needed to describe it adequately. Arithmetic, for example, requires operations like addition, subtraction, and multiplication, each requiring numerous subskills. Thus, one of the components of adding numbers involves adding digits, and one of the addition rules is the following:

> If you have added the digits in one column, then continue adding the digits in the column to the left.

These if-then rules are known as production rules; they have the general form:

> IF this is the situation, THEN do that.

Production rules are assumed to be stored in long-term memory (see also the section on Symbolic Architectures of Cognition). A set of rules designed to execute a specific skill is also referred to as a production system. Each production rule may be thought of as a little demon. Usually the demon rests; however, when its conditions are met, it awakens (is activated) and screams out the command on its action side: "Do this" (see Morelli & Brown, 1992; Pandemonium model in Chapter 4).

Formally, a **production rule** consists of an IF clause and a THEN clause. The IF clause includes a set of conditions that must be met in order to execute the actions specified in the THEN clause. For example, the recognition of geometrical shapes may be expressed as a production rule (see Gagne, 1985).

(R1) IF a FIGURE is two dimensional
and the SIDES are all equal
and number of SIDES is less
than eight
THEN classify the FIGURE as a polygon
and write the word *polygon*.

Production rule (R1) has a list of three conditions and two actions. The conditions specify that the geometrical figure must be two dimensional, that it must have less than eight sides, and that the sides should be of equal length. If these conditions are met, the figure is recognized as a polygon and the word *polygon* is written out.

Two of the words (besides IF and THEN) in R1 are capitalized: FIGURE and SIDES. These concepts represent variables and they make the productions general. Different shapes (e.g., pentagons, squares, and hexagons) will fit the general category FIGURE, and the number of SIDES and will differ from one case to the next.

Here are some production rules from different domains, including driving, language skills, and arithmetic.

(**R2**) IF you are driving a car with a manual transmission
>   and you come to a stop sign
> THEN press down the clutch
>   shift into neutral
>   and apply the brakes.

(**R3**) IF the goal is to add two NUMBERS
>   and the FIRST NUMBER ends with a DIGIT
>   and the SECOND NUMBER ends with a DIGIT
> THEN the subgoal is to add the two DIGITS.

In (R3), one condition specifies an abstract goal, which is a cognitive entity rather than a physical fact. Rule (R3) is identical to the first of seven rules shown in Table 5.5 (from Anderson, 1980). In addition to the overall goal of adding two numbers, (R3) contains two conditions that specify facts that may appear obvious to us but that must be made explicit to a novice or for a computer simulation.

According to Anderson (1983), every skill is represented as a production, and people use thousands of productions unwittingly. Production rules used in a particular instance may not be the most efficient ones. Indeed, productions may be incorrect and contain "bugs" (VanLehn, 1990), as illustrated in Box 5.1. The next section illustrates a familiar domain of procedural knowledge: adding two numbers. Although addition is well known, you may be surprised how complex this apparently simple skill is. We will consider addition in three steps: We list informal rules used in

addition, study a production system of seven rules, and apply this system to the addition of the numbers 32 and 18. The goal of this exercise is to illustrate mental processes. Remember that the caveat still holds—these processes are tacit; it is not claimed that people are aware of them.

An Example: Adding Numbers

Try to express your knowledge of addition in English. Although an addition problem is simple, the task of explaining how to do it is difficult. It becomes a little easier when you imagine that you must teach addition to an otherwise intelligent person. Assume that the person already knows how to add single digits, for example, 1 + 1 = 2, 1 + 2 = 3, 1 + 3 = 4, . . . and so on. After some thought, you may come up with addition rules like the following:

1. Perform the addition by columns.
2. Begin by adding the digits in the right-most column.
3. Add all of the digits of a column; do not leave any out.
4. If the sum of digits in a column is 10 or greater, then set a carry.
5. If there is a carry, then add a 1 to the sum of the digits in the next column.
6. If you have the sum "in your head," write it out.
7. If all of the digits in a column have been added, and there is another column on the left, then repeat the process.

Next, we will express these informal addition rules and others in terms of a small production system we will dub PLUS (Anderson, 1980).

PLUS contains the seven production rules in Table 5.5; they are similar to the preceding informal rules. Each production represents a small component of the overall skill of addition. One crucial difference between the informal rules and PLUS's more formal productions is the inclusion of a goal and subgoals. The overall goal is to add two numbers. There are several subgoals; adding digits, writing out a number, and processing digits in the next column. These goals ensure that the

TABLE 5.5   PLUS: A Set of Production Rules for Adding Two Numbers (Anderson, 1980)

	Production Rules	Explanations
(P1)	IF the goal is to add two numbers and the first number ends with a digit and the second number ends with a digit THEN the subgoal is to add the two digits.	This production responds to the main goal of adding two numbers. It sets as the subgoal to add the digits in the first column.
(P2)	IF the subgoal is to add two digits and a number is the sum of the two digits THEN the subgoal is to write the number.	This production finds the sum of two digits and sets the subgoal to put out this sum.
(P3)	IF the subgoal is to write a number and there is a carry flag and a second number is the sum of the first number plus 1 THEN the subgoal is to write the second number and remove the carry flag.	When there is a carry, this production adds 1 to the number to be put out and removes the carry flag.
(P4)	IF the subgoal is to put out a number and there is no carry flag and the number is less than 10 THEN write the number and the subgoal is to process the two digits in the next column.	When there is no carry and the number is less than 10, this production writes the number out.
(P5)	IF the subgoal is to put out a number and there is no carry flag and the number is the sum of 10 plus a digit THEN write the digit and set the carry flag and the subgoal is to process the digits in the next column.	When there is no carry and the number is 10 or greater, this production writes out the difference between the number and 10 and sets the carry flag.
(P6)	IF the subgoal is to process the digits in the next column and the first number contains a digit in that column and the second number contains a digit in that column THEN the goal is to add the two digits.	This production shifts attention to the digits in the next column.
(P7)	IF the subgoal is to process the digits in the next column and there are no digits in that column THEN the problem is finished.	This production recognizes when the last column of digits has been processed and the problem is at an end.

adding procedure does not stop when a specific production is fulfilled. There are four subsets among the seven productions of PLUS:

- Productions (P1) and (P2) set up the goal structure of the problem.

- Productions (P3), (P4), and (P5) are necessary to calculate the sum of a column.
- Production (P6) shifts attention to the next column on the left.
- Production (P7) states the terminating condition. This is the rule that tells you to stop

Box 5.1

Buggy Procedures

There is no guarantee that people acquire productions that work correctly. VanLehn (1990) found about 100 systematic errors, or bugs, that students commonly make in arithmetic problems. Many of these bugs are observed in subtraction problems, in particular when borrowing is required. Here is a sample of problems reflecting the use of buggy procedures:

234	387	462	615	723	493
−153	−124	−234	−351	−258	−289
121	263	232	344	535	216

See if you can identify the bug in the problems above. You have probably noticed that the student subtracted the smaller from the larger digit no matter whether it was in the top or bottom row.

---

adding numbers; without it, you would try to keep adding.

Processing in production systems such as PLUS is based on the **recognize-act cycle.** During the recognize stage, a production is activated if specific conditions are met. A condition is satisfied if it matches information currently in working memory, which is the workhorse of the production system (see Figure 5.8B later in the chapter). In the act stage, the production's actions are executed. Actions include external responses such as writing a number or adding new information to working memory (e.g., a new subgoal or an interim result). Each cycle of running production system changes the content of working memory. Thus, execution of production rules is dynamic rather than sequential; a rule is triggered when its conditions are met.

Acquisition of Procedural Knowledge

We have assumed, thus far, that the system had the knowledge necessary for addition. This section describes how procedural skills are acquired. We are competent at a skill when our performance at the task has become fast and error free. According to cognitive psychologists, the transition from slow and error-prone performance to skilled performance proceeds in three stages: the cognitive stage, the associative stage, and the autonomous stage (Anderson, 1980; Fitts, 1964).

During the **cognitive stage,** a teacher tells the student the rules underlying the skill. In the case of addition, for example, the teacher shows the student simple addition problems and tells her that one first adds the digits in the right-most column. In the **associative stage,** the student practices the rule as she does many addition problems. She begins using the rule almost without being aware of it. Finally, in the **autonomous stage,** rules are used automatically and their application is well coordinated. As a result, addition problems are solved faster and with fewer errors.

Research has shown that the improved performance of experts is supported by changes in physiological processes and anatomical structures. Raichle and colleagues (1994) found that blood flow activity decreased even after relatively brief practice periods (of a verbal association task). They argued that specific brain circuits are formed that facilitate performance. Ericsson and Charness (1994) reported that extended periods of practice on athletic and motor skills result in anatomical changes of the blood vessels, bones, and muscles that are exercised by the activity.

Figure 5.7 shows the speedup in performance typically observed in the acquisition of a skill, whether it is a cognitive or motor skill. In these experiments, performance is observed for thousands of trials, sometimes for as many as 100,000! It takes a very determined and patient person to do this. There is a continuous speedup in performance, as Figure 5.7 indicates. The or-

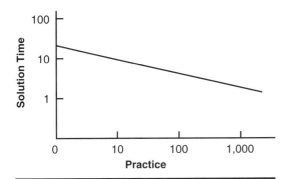

FIGURE 5.7   The speedup of performance with added practice reflects the power law of practice.

dinate indicates the time spent executing the task and the abscissa indicates the amount of practice measured as the number of trials or problems finished. Usually, time and amount of practice are plotted on a logarithmic scale. Each panel reflects the **power law of practice.** There is a linear relationship between solution time, T, and the amount of practice, P, which is expressed in equation (5.6).

(5.6) $\log(T) = A - b \log(P)$

The coefficient A is the intercept and the coefficient b reflects the slope of the function. These two differ for different skills, but the linear relation holds for many skills studied by cognitive psychologists.

According to Anderson's theory of skill acquisition, there are two processes underlying skill acquisition: proceduralization and composition. **Proceduralization** refers to the transformation of slow declarative knowledge into fast-access procedural knowledge. Take the fact that 4 plus 3 equals 7. Initially, this knowledge is represented as a proposition in declarative memory. With added practice, the same information becomes part of procedural knowledge as a production rule. The difference is that the person automatically recognizes 7 as the answer when given 4 and 3. It has become an instance of pattern recognition (see Chapter 4) rather than fact retrieval, as described in the first section of this chapter.

Composition involves combining two production rules into one, thus saving time as the rule is executed. Composition occurs when two rules are, in part, redundant, as illustrated with two rules a child might use to recognize a cat, rules (R4) and (R5). Production rule (R6) represents the new rule that results from the combination of rules (R4) and (R5). In short, composition streamlines existing production rules.

(R4) IF you see a thing that moves
and the thing says "meow"
and the thing is furry
THEN classify the thing as a cat.

(R5) IF you see a thing that is furry
and the thing says "meow"
THEN say *cat*.

(R6) IF you see a thing that moves
and the thing says "meow"
and the thing is furry
THEN classify the thing as a cat and say
cat.

There are two additional processes by which existing production rules are refined: generalization and discrimination.

Generalization occurs when a rule is applied to new examples. Suppose a child, familiar with the concept CAR, sees a new car. Identifying the new car as a car is an instance of generalization. Similarly, the geometry student who successfully classifies a figure with five sides as a polygon generalizes when he extends this knowledge to figures with seven sides. In terms of production rules, generalization produces a new production that applies to more instances.

Discrimination is the mechanism that enables the learner to distinguish between members and nonmembers of a category. In terms of production rules, it involves adding a new, more specific condition to an existing production rule. For example, a production rule to identify geometric figures as polygons might include as initial conditions the stipulations (1) that the figure is two dimensional and (2) that its sides are of equal length. However, open figures whose sides are not connected would be subsumed under these two conditions. By adding a third condition—namely (3) that the figure is closed—only those figures are identified as polygons whose sides are connected throughout.

Polygons are, of course, patterns. The identification of polygons through production rules illustrates pattern recognition. According to influential symbolic-processing theories, pattern recognition is generally based on production rules, whether it involves recognition of words, chess patterns, or problem types in algebra (Anderson, 1983; Just & Carpenter, 1992; Newell, Rosenbloom, & Laird, 1989). We have acquired expertise in a domain when we have honed the skill so that it has become a pattern recognition routine (see Chapter 13).

INTERIM SUMMARY

Procedural knowledge, the knowledge of how to do things, is represented in terms of production rules in long-term memory. Production rules are IF-THEN expressions; the IF clause specifies conditions that must be satisfied for the rule to fire, and the THEN clause includes actions executed by the rule. Execution of the rules in a production system is dynamic, with a rule being triggered when its conditions are met. After extended practice, procedural knowledge is accessed quickly, as in pattern recognition. Practice allows us to combine several productions into a single production and to learn to make critical discriminations. As a result of practice, declarative knowledge is transformed into procedural knowledge and performance becomes faster and less error prone.

SYMBOLIC ARCHITECTURES OF COGNITION

Thus far, we have considered the contents of the mind, including declarative and procedural knowledge. Cognitive scientists are also con-

cerned with the relation between these kinds of knowledge within the structure of the mind. The relatively permanent framework of the mind is referred to as the architecture of cognition. This expression is borrowed directly from computer science, where the term *architecture* refers to the relatively permanent design features of the computer (see Chapter 1). Figure 5.8 includes three models of cognitive architecture, the classical information-processing model of Atkinson and Shiffrin (1968), the Act* model (pronounced *act-star*) of Anderson (1983), and Newell's Soar (e.g., Newell, Rosenbloom, & Laird, 1989).

The architecture a theorist adopts provides an overall context for his or her research. Cognitive psychologists use an architecture to organize the information accumulated in cognition research. Choosing an architecture also compels an investigator to address the relation among different cognitive processors and between the cognitive system and the environment.

Atkinson and Shiffrin's **three-store model** reflects the influence of the computer metaphor on model building in cognitive psychology popular in the 1960s. The system accepts stimuli as input and produces an output. Three intervening processors are assumed: the sensory register, short-term store, and long-term store. The sensory register stores early visual and auditory information, presumably before they are recognized. The short-term store has a limited capacity, maintaining information for up to a minute, and long-term memory is a large-capacity store that holds information for relatively long time intervals. This three-store model has provided the impetus for a large body of research on short- and long-term memory (see Chapter 7).

The **Act*** architecture includes three components: declarative memory, production memory, and working memory. Production memory includes all of the system's production rules. Declarative memory contains the declarative knowledge we discussed in the first part of this chapter. In Act*, declarative information is represented in terms of propositions. Each proposition

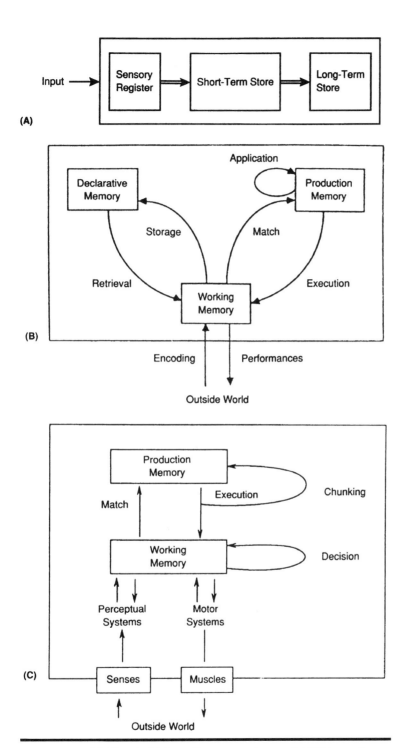

FIGURE 5.8 (*A*) Classical information-processing model (Atkinson & Shiffrin, 1968). (*B*) The Act* model (from Anderson, 1983). (*C*) The Soar model (from Newell et al., 1989).

has a certain baseline of activation, which can range from an extremely low to a very high activity level. Working memory contains the most active propositions of declarative memory.

The contents of working memory change continuously as a result of environmental and cognitive influences (see also Chapter 8). Working memory not only includes the most active propositions but it is also the processor of Act*. When a specific event is encoded—for example, you encounter a stop sign while driving—it is represented as a set of propositions in working memory: (DRIVE, I) and (COME-TO, I, STOP-SIGN). As a result of these propositions in working memory, the conditions of production rule (R2) are satisfied; the rule fires and its actions are carried out. You press down the clutch, shift into neutral, and apply the brakes. Thus, in working memory there is a continuous and automatic matching of productions with environmental or cognitive conditions. Cognitive conditions include goals like the ones in the adding productions in Table 5.5. Working memory is said to be a dynamic processor because of the continuous change of its contents.

According to Newell's **Soar** theory, cognition is best understood in terms of problem solving. (The acronym *Soar* stands for Start, Operator, And Result.) In solving a problem, one faces an initial problem state and transforms it via specific operators to the final state, the result. For example, the initial state of our addition problem is given in expression (5.6), its result is 50, and the intermediate states and operators are described above. The Soar system includes a long-term production memory that serves the function of both declarative and procedural memory. The working memory is the repository for goals and subgoals like the ones in PLUS. The match process refers to matching production rules to conditions currently active in working memory. As production rules are executed, they become more efficient in a process called *chunking*—the Soar system's learning process. The system interacts with the environment via senses and muscles, as indicated in Figure 5.8C.

Act* and Soar have relatively fixed components, although processing is thought to be dynamic. Just and Carpenter (1992) emphasized the dynamic nature of cognition. In their view, the interaction among subsystems of the cognitive architecture is not fixed, but depends on the overall processing capacity. They note that the term *architecture* reminds us of the fixed structure of a house with separate rooms, each serving well-defined functions. According to Just and Carpenter's analysis, a river may provide a more adequate metaphor for the mind. Rivers may be partitioned but they are best characterized by the dynamic principles of flow and hydraulic pressures.

Act* and Soar are symbolic architectures; they assume explicit and symbolic representation of factual and procedural knowledge. There are also nonsymbolic architectures in which information is distributed over a network of small processors connected to each other. These are known as neural networks, connectionist models, or Parallel Distributed Processing (PDP) systems (see Chapter 6).

CONCLUSION

Human knowledge is vast; we have knowledge of objects and events, and their contexts and relationships. We are also competent in numerous skills and have acquired many different talents. This chapter covered symbolic representations thought to underlie these diverse sources of knowledge. Cognitive psychologists have broadly grouped these different sources into declarative and procedural knowledge. Declarative knowledge includes concepts, propositions, schemas, and images. Concepts represent knowledge of physical objects and abstract entities. Propositions express the relations among a set of concepts. Schemas capture the components of complex objects and the typical sequence of actions in a general and flexible manner. This chapter emphasized visual images and the lively debate over the extent to which they involve the visual system. Because neuropsychological research has revealed increased activity in certain visual centers of the brain, some cognitive neuroscientists believe these centers are implicated in visual imagery. Mental models include concepts, schemas, and images to represent the global environment of a visual scene, problem states, or the context of a story.

Cognitive skills such as language, problem solving, and reasoning constitute procedural knowledge. Such knowledge is represented in terms of production rules, or IF-THEN rules. They are triggered if specific conditions exist in working memory. Production rules underlie our ability to solve problems, recognize patterns, and execute routine everyday skills.

We have seen that theories of knowledge representation have benefited from insights of computer scientists. Collins and Quillian's network model, Kosslyn's CRT model of visual imagery, and Anderson's Act* theory of procedural knowledge have all been implemented as computer simulation programs. Each of these models includes a structural component that describes relatively static features of the theory, and a processing component that describes mental operations.

Although the coverage of knowledge representation has been broad, its treatment in this chapter has not been exhaustive. Chapter 6 offers a different perspective of knowledge representation: the connectionist framework. Several chapters introduce additional representations of knowledge; for example, Chapter 10 discusses language knowledge. Other chapters will show how knowledge representations are used in specific domains (e.g., Chapters 11 through 14).

ENDNOTES

1. Capital letters will be used to indicate concepts and italicized print will represent technical terms.
2. Note that there are two types of associative links in semantic network models: *isa* and *has-property*. Now we are adding such argument relations as *agent, recipient*, and *object* to the list of associative links.

CHAPTER 6

REPRESENTATION OF KNOWLEDGE: NEURAL NETWORKS

PREVIEW

Neural networks consist of a set of small processing units that operate in parallel. They include input units, output units, and connections between them. Environmental events are presented to a network as associations of input and output patterns of activation. Activation is entered at the input units and travels via connections to the output units. Each connection has a weight that reflects the strength of the connection. The weights influence the level of activation passing the connection. In connectionist networks, information is distributed across sets of units and their connections.

We will study how new associations are learned by changing the connection weights. Three learning procedures will be examined: the Hebb rule, the delta rule, and learning by backpropagation. According to the Hebb rule, a connection is strengthened when two neurons are active at the same time. In delta and backpropagation learning, weights are modified whenever the network makes an error. Learning results in reducing the error by improving the match between the actual and the target performance. Neural networks have found wide application in cognitive science and in other fields. Because of their ability to simulate both rulelike behavior and exceptions, they have been used to mimic pattern recognition, category learning, and language acquisition. The chapter concludes with a discussion of the appeal of the connectionist approach and some of its problems. Connectionist models can account for a wide range of empirical effects in recognition, learning, and memory. However, some of the assumptions in the models are arbitrary.

INTRODUCTION

No scientist would doubt that cognition is based on the millions of neurons in the brain. The information-processing approach of the 1950s and 60s, however, developed independently of neural considerations. Rather, cognitive psychologists made use of the ascendant technology of its day, the serial computer, and of the symbolic architectures inspired by the computer metaphor (see Chapter 5). There were speculations about the neural basis of cognition and neural models from time to time in the literature, but they did not become part of mainstream research in cognitive psychology. Early neural models included McCulloch and Pitts's model of the neuron (1943), Hebb's theory of neural circuits (1949), and Selfridge and Neisser's Pandemonium model (1963). In the 1960s and 70s, neural modeling gathered steam (for a summary, see Hinton & Anderson, 1981). Subsequently, a great variety of neural network models emerged.

Neural network models differ from symbolic approaches to cognition in important ways. Taking advantage of their large number of elementary units, neural networks process information in parallel, much like living organisms. Parallel processing enables neural networks to consider many pieces of information simultaneously, however ambiguous or ill defined they may be (see Chapter 4). It is for this reason that neural networks are more powerful than the symbolic approaches when it comes to simulating the recognition of complex stimuli, the great achievement of organisms.

It is a curious paradox that computer chips process information much faster than neurons, yet organisms recognize objects in the environment much faster. Examples of fast recognition abound, both in the animal kingdom and in human perception. The impala usually recognizes a predator within a fraction of a second and escapes; a hawk also recognizes its prey in less than a second and goes after it in another second. People recognize faces, spoken and written words, objects, scenes, and dangerous situations

in about 250 to 350 milliseconds. Fast recognition is necessary for survival. Suppose the impala needed several seconds to recognize a predator, or imagine a driver with recognition like that of a computer. The driver would need a complex algorithm to determine that he is about to collide with another car. Both the impala and the driver would be hurt or dead.

Recognition has been a challenge to model builders because many, often conflicting, conditions must be met at the same time. Other than recognition, numerous everyday situations require that several constraints be satisfied at the same time. When you assemble anything— whether it is an outdoor grill, a kickstand, a toy railroad, or a jigsaw puzzle—different pieces have to fit together. For example, when you build a grill, the left and right shelf boards, the cart handle, and the lower shelf all must fit. Of course, the components of each of these parts must have been joined together first—hex bolts, lock washers, hex nuts, hooks, and supports. Satisfaction of multiple constraints is no less a requirement for mental activities, whether in games, puzzles, or problem solving, or such language skills as speaking, reading, and writing. Symbolic-processing models have had some success modeling performance under multiple constraints but these models are cumbersome and brittle; they tend to break down when the stimulus conditions are poorly specified. Connectionist models are well suited for just such situations.

Perception and action occur under constraints that must be satisfied in parallel in order to assure smooth performance. When you recognize an object, there are several conditions—distance, illumination, motion, and context—that influence the act of recognition concurrently. Successful communication between two people requires that certain conditions are met at the same time. These include a common language, a topic of conversation, cohesion among phrases, and coherence between discourse and context. In executing motor responses—for example, a jump shot in basketball—the player must speed to the net, jump high, propel the ball into the net, all while she watches out for the players from the other team. It is a remarkable accomplishment that we perform many of these acts quickly and usually without fail. What enables us to do so? In the final analysis, our brains do. The brain consists of a vast number of neurons—some 10^{12} of them (that is a 10 with 12 zeros!). Each of these neurons is alive and engaged in neural activity. Neurons are connected forming networks, small and large. Neurons achieve their power by acting in concert and are thus equipped to respond to multiple constraints in parallel.

Neural network theorists have claimed many successes for their models. Not only can the networks act quickly but they are also robust vis-à-vis noise, distraction, and even insult. They are capable of acquiring and retrieving information without programmer intervention. It is no surprise, then, that the connectionist approach has had a great influence on research in cognitive psychology. Of course, there has also been opposition to neural network models of cognition. They have been criticized for being too arbitrary and too flexible to permit an adequate empirical test, and, perhaps inevitably, as the network models have been tested against empirical data, they have become more complex than their advocates initially claimed. We will review the criticisms in the conclusion.

Neural Net Components

A *neural net* is a computer simulation of a circuit of neurons that accepts input from the environment, passes the information through its units, and produces an output. In organisms, inputs and outputs are measured in terms of physical energy; patterns of light emit energy in the form of waves, as do sound patterns, although at a different range of the wave length continuum. The responses of organisms are forms of mechanical energy expressed in all kinds of bodily actions, from moving the entire body to subtle changes of the vocal cords (see Chapter 4). In network simulations, such levels of energy are expressed as levels of activation, both excitatory and inhibitory.

Neural networks consist of simple processing units, the cells or neurons. The neurons are connected through links that carry excitatory and inhibitory information, much like in the nervous system. Networks vary in complexity from two units to thousands of units. Figure 6.1 shows typical kinds of networks.

The role of the units varies. Input units shown at the bottom of a network in Figure 6.1 receive stimuli from the environment; output units shown at the top produce responses. Hidden units are intermediary between input units and output units; they do not communicate with the environment. In general terms, a unit transforms input signals in terms of an activation function and passes them along links to other units. The links between units function like axons in biological nervous systems. Activation levels as well as the strength of links vary from weak to strong. Activation levels depend on the characteristics of the input signal, as illustrated in the next section. The strength of links depends on the network's learning history, as explained in the section on learning. In simple models, the output of a neuron is based on the input activations, as illustrated in Figure 6.2.

Networks vary in the number of layers, their pattern of connectivity, and the flow of information. Figure 6.1A shows networks consisting of one layer in addition to the input units. Figures 6.1B and 6.1C show two-layer networks and Figure 6.1D shows a multiple-layer network. Units are connected via links that are assigned different weights. A weight is like a gain setting in an audio system. Weights may be excitatory or inhibitory. An excitatory weight increases the activation of the target neuron; an inhibitory connection decreases that activation. A network may conduct information only one way, also known as *feedforward mode*, from the input units to the output units. Figure 6.1C shows a recurrent network where activation is passed symmetrically between units, including self-excitement.

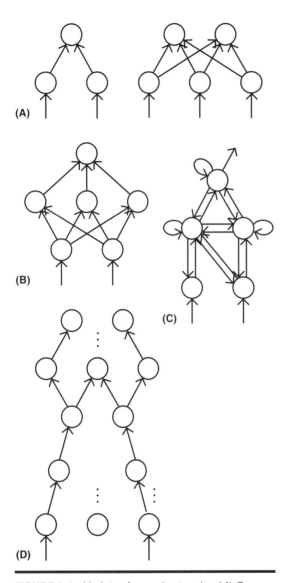

FIGURE 6.1   Variety of neural networks. (*A*) One-layer networks with feedforward connections. (*B*) Two layers of units connected via feedforward links. (*C*) Two-layer network with recurrent links. (*D*) Multiple-layer network.

In sum, neural networks consist of:

- Small units known as neurons
- Connections between the neurons

- Weights that determine the strength of the connection

The pattern of units as well as their connections and weights represent the knowledge of the network at a particular time, t_0. The output of a neural net is based both on the input activation and the pattern of weights of the network. An important property of neural networks is that they are adaptable; they can learn.

Crucial issues faced by connectionist theorists include the following:

- How are activation values represented and determined in the network?
- What does distributed representation mean?
- How is information retrieved from a neural network?
- Where do the weights come from?

These questions are the topics for the four principal sections of the chapter: the activation rule, distributional representation, retrieval, and learning. The learning section is the longest of these; this is because the knowledge of networks depends on learning.

DETERMINING ACTIVATION: THE ACTIVATION RULE

Scientists have found it convenient to express activation levels in terms of numbers, both positive

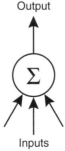

FIGURE 6.2   Neuron represented as a summing unit. The sum of the inputs represents the output of the neuron. In backpropagation learning, the aggregated inputs are scaled to produce outputs within the range of 0 and 1.

and negative. Because there are usually several input units, there is a set of activation numbers. These sets are known as **vectors**—for example, [0 1 0 0 1] and [–2 .5 –3 4] are vectors. (A *vector* is an set of numbers arranged in a specific order.) These activation levels may reflect an external stimulus, such as, light energy stimulating a specific set of light receptors in the retina, or activation levels propagated to hidden units in the network (see Figure 6.1B). The simulated neuron has a resting level, like its biological counterpart. In both cases, excitation and inhibition are expressed relative to the resting potential and are given positive and negative signs respectively.

As in biological neurons, the output activation of a given unit is the sum of activations arriving at the unit. You will recall from Chapter 2 that a biological neuron integrates all of the synaptic inputs received at the postsynaptic membrane and that the activation traveling between neurons is modulated at the synapse. In neural network models, such modulation is expressed by multiplication of an activation level and a **weight.** For a network of two input units, one output unit, two connections, and two weights (as in Figure 6.3A and B), one multiplies the first activation by the first weight and the second activation by the second weight. The sum of these represents the output activation of the unit. This is why the output unit is also referred to as a *summing unit* (See Figure 6.2). The summing of input activations to yield an output activation, output$_r$, is captured in expression (6.1).

(6.1) Output activation = sum of (input activation$_s$ × weight$_{rs}$)

The subscripts $_r$ and $_s$ in expression (6.1) refer to receiving and sending units, respectively. In this case, the receiving unit is an output unit and the sending unit is an input unit. (Appendix A, found the end of this chapter, lists expressions and subscripts presented in Chapter 6 for easy reference.)

Presenting the output activation as the simple sum of products is a simplification that serves us well for now. In the section entitled Learning in Neural Networks, we shall see that in backpropagation learning, the summed output activation is

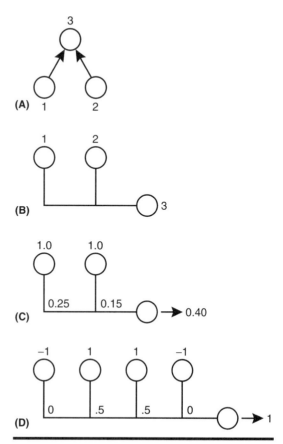

FIGURE 6.3 Simple neural networks. (*A and B*) Network with two input units (1 and 2) and one output unit (3). (*C*) Illustrative connection weights of 0.25 and 0.15 for the two links in the network. Input activations are 1 and 1, and the output activation is 0.40. (*D*) Five-unit network used in examples of Hebbian and delta learning. (See text for explanation.)

pushed through a transformation function, a logistic function. The technical literature describes further activation functions (e.g., see McClelland & Rumelhart, 1988).

Putting the Activation Rule to Work: Examples

With the activation rule in hand, we can consider a couple of relatively simple neural networks to illustrate how activation levels are determined. The first network, shown in Figure 6.3, has two input units (numbered 1 and 2) and one output unit (numbered unit 3). As in Figure 6.1, the input units are located at the bottom of the net and the output unit is at the top. Figure 6.3B is the preferred rendition of the three-unit network in Figure 6.3A. Here, the input units are located at the top and the output unit is on the right. Figure 6.3C shows the network with illustrative input activations and weights. There are input activations of 1.0 at each of the two input units and the weights are 0.25 and 0.15 between the respective input units and the output unit.[1] According to expression (6.1), the output activation is 0.40. The calculation is as follows:

Output = $1.0 \times 0.25 + 1.0 \times 0.15 = 0.40$

Table 6.1A shows these vectors as well as three additional examples of input and weight vectors and the respective output activations.

Figure 6.3D shows a network of four input units and one output unit with illustrative input activations and weights. Figure 6.4 shows a network of two input units and two output units with two sets of input units and weights. The activation for each output unit is calculated according to the activation rule in expression (6.1). The information in Figure 6.4 is represented in Table 6.1B in terms of a matrix. Each section of Table 6.1B represents a set of different input vectors and weight matrices. Each matrix consists of two rows of weights, one for each output unit. The output activations at the two output units differ accordingly.

The examples in Figures 6.3 and 6.4 permit us to arrive at some important generalizations about neural networks:

— Activation spreads in parallel from the input units to the output unit(s).

— Neurons accept input regardless of modality and source. Every input is quantified in terms of activation levels and the activations are integrated according to the activation rule in expression (6.1).

TABLE 6.1 Illustrative Activations and Weights in Neural Networks

A. Three-Unit Network

Inputs		Weights		Output
il	i2	w13	w23	
1.0	1.0	0.25	0.15	0.40
1.0	1.0	0.25	0	0.25
1.0	0	−.25	0.25	−.25
1.0	1.0	−.25	0.25	0

B. Four-Unit Network

il	i2	
1.0	1.0	
0.25	0.15	0.40
0.10	0.50	0.60

il	i2	
1.0	−1.0	
0.25	0.15	0.10
0.10	0.50	−0.40

il	i2	
1.0	0	
0.25	0.15	0.25
0.10	0.50	0.10

— After the aggregate output activation is determined, the details of the input signals are lost. In other words, from the result of expression (6.1), it is no longer possible to recover individual input activations.

— Every unit in the system calculates an output except for the input neurons. These merely transmit the input activation.

Here are two points concerning the output of neural networks:

— In the examples thus far, the output was simply based on the sum of the products of activations and weights. The sums were unconstrained so that they could assume positive or negative values of any size—for example, −3.67, 6.07, 1.12, or even 3,000. In the section entitled Backpropagation Learning, a logistic function

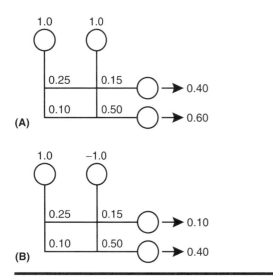

FIGURE 6.4   (*A and B*) Four-unit networks with illustrative activations and weights.

will be introduced. It transforms or squashes output values so as to fit them within the range between 0 and 1.

— Network output may be viewed from several perspectives. Psychologically, it may be regarded as the level of confidence the system has in its decision. For example, classification systems seek to identify input patterns, as illustrated by the following queries: *Is this an A? Is this an insect?* or *Do these symptoms represent pneumonic plague?* The greater the values, the greater is the confidence of the system in its judgment. Another perspective views the output function in expression (6.1) in terms of a governmental analogy. According to this analogy, the output of a cell represents the polling of all of the inputs in a sort of democratic process.

DISTRIBUTED REPRESENTATIONS

Distributed representations are best understood when contrasted with localized representations. In localized representations, items of information are stored in discrete and separate units so that each of the units holds a unique item. In Collins

and Quillian's (1969) semantic network, for example, each node stores only one concept; there is one node for CANARY, another for ROBIN, another for BIRD, and so on. In distributed representations, concepts are presented across different units and each unit contributes to the representation of several items. No single unit represents a concept all by itself.

Example 1: Representation of Animals

Figure 5.1 in Chapter 5 shows the prototypical localized network, Collins and Quillian's (1969) semantic net. Here, each individual node is dedicated to an individual concept. A distributed system of animal concepts, however, represents an individual animal across multiple units. For the moment, visualize the units as features and assume that there are binary values for each feature, as in Table 6.2. In Table 6.2, several animals are represented by five features, each of which may assume a value of +1 or –1. Note that each concept is represented by a unique vector of values.

One could expand this small universe easily, by adding creatures, for example, SHARK and GOLDFISH shown at the bottom of Table 6.1. One can add more concepts to the network without having to add more features, at least up to a limit. An advantage, then, of distributed representations is that more items can be stored relative to the number of units than in a localized storage system.

One may visualize each of the features as meaningful. For example, the features in Table

TABLE 6.2   Distributed Representation of Animals

dog	+1	−1	+1	−1	−1
elephant	+1	+1	+1	−1	−1
eagle	−1	+1	−1	+1	−1
robin	−1	−1	−1	+1	−1
shark	−1	+1	−1	−1	+1
goldfish	−1	−1	−1	−1	+1

6.2 can be taken as representing four-leggedness, large size, mammal, flies, and lives in water, respectively. Accordingly, a dog has four legs, is relatively small, is a mammal, does not fly, and does not live in water, whereas a goldfish does not have four legs, is small, is not a mammal, does not fly, and lives in water.

Example 2: Representation of Letters

In a local representation of letters, each letter from *A* through *Z* is stored at a unique node, while distributed representations involve multiple units or features, as in example 1. Theoretically, many distributional schemes are feasible, depending on the features chosen to represent the letters and on the number of units in the neural network. Consider the scheme in Figure 6.5A used by McClelland and Rumelhart (1981). In Figure 6.5, there are 16 features to represent the set of 26 letters. Each feature is a line defined by its orientation and location in the grid. Thus, feature 1 is a horizontal line in the upper left quadrant of the grid and feature 11 is an oblique line in the lower left quadrant. For the purpose of our example, let us make the simplifying assumption that there is an input unit or receptor unit for each of the 16 features. Furthermore, when a letter is presented, the corresponding features, but no others, are activated, as illustrated in Figure 6.5B. (This figure shows the grid and features corresponding to an *H* in block form.)

An illustrative network that accepts visual letter symbols as input and pronounces the letters is shown in Figure 6.6. The inputs are captured by the 16 units in Figure 6.5A. We will assume for simplicity that there are also 16 output units to represent vocal output in terms of sound features (that are not detailed here). This network of 16 input units, 16 output units, and 256 connections is designed to process all input strings whose letters conform to the font of Figure 6.5. If we present the word HORSE to the network, for example, we would activate the units according to the vectors in Table 6.3.

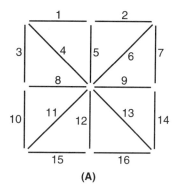

(A)

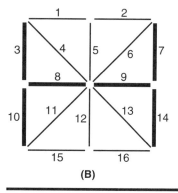

(B)

FIGURE 6.5 (*A*) Sixteen features to represent the 26 letters of the alphabet (McClelland & Rumelhart, 1981). (*B*) Capital *H* uses features 3, 7, 8, 9, 10, and 14 from the feature set in (*A*).

Example 3: Input-Output Mapping in a Robot

Clark and Thornton (in press) described a mobile robot located in a small space (see Figure 6.7). The robot has some limited sensors and effectors that enable it to perceive specific events and to make very simple responses to specific constellations of objects in its environment. If there is no object in the robot's sensory field, it swivels by 10 degrees to the right. If the object is distant, then the robot approaches it. If the object is large and is close, then the robot stands still. The robot has seven sensors spaced at 10-degree intervals. Each sensor emits probe rays that the objects project back to the robot. If an object is detected, the sensor's energy level is set to 1; otherwise, it remains

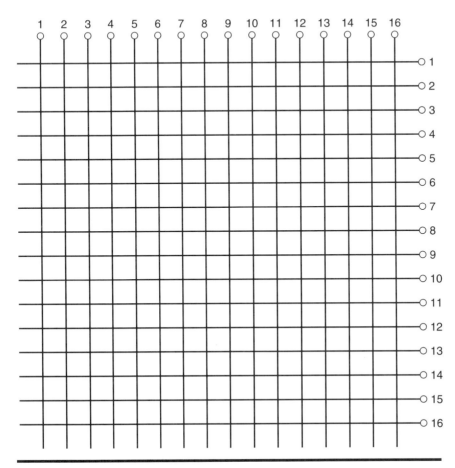

FIGURE 6.6 Network to represent 26 capital letters via 16 input units (at the top) and 16 output units (on the right). Assume that the input is visual and the output is vocal.

inactive at 0. The activation values of the seven sensors constitute the input vector and reflect the presence of objects in the robot's environment. For example, the vector [0 0 1 1 0 0 0] indicates an object located center left ahead of the robot, as in Figure 6.7, while a vector of [0 0 0 0 0 0 0] indicates empty surroundings. The robot has a left and a right wheel. Specific activation patterns

TABLE 6.3 Distributed Representation for the Letters of the Word *HORSE*

	1	2	3	4	5	6	7	8	9	10	11	12	13	14	15	16
H	0	0	1	0	0	0	1	1	1	1	0	0	0	1	0	0
O	1	1	1	0	0	0	1	0	0	1	0	0	0	1	1	1
R	1	1	1	0	0	0	1	1	1	1	0	0	1	0	0	0
S	1	1	1	0	0	0	0	1	1	0	0	0	0	1	1	1
E	1	1	1	0	0	0	0	1	0	1	0	0	0	0	1	1

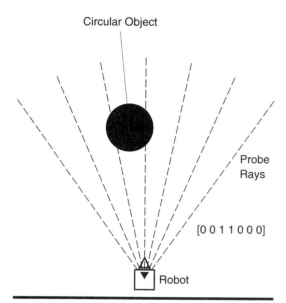

Circular Object

Probe Rays

[0 0 1 1 0 0 0]

Robot

FIGURE 6.7 Schematic of mobile robot and its environment. In this example, a large object is located north of the robot. The robot detects the object via its set of seven sensors. Activation of the sensors is captured in terms of the vector [0 0 1 1 0 0 0] (Clark & Thornton, in press).

sent to the wheels causes the robot to move by a certain amount toward a specific target.

In each of the three examples, information is represented across several units of the network, whether we are dealing with abstract concepts or visual features. We could have equally chosen other domains, such as digits, phonetic attributes, economic patterns, or olfactory features. In the examples, the features may be interpreted meaningfully: In the animal network, features correspond to identifiable properties of the animals; in the letter scheme, features correspond to specific lines in the input letters; and in the robot example, features correspond to the shadow projected by an obstacle in the robot's visual field. It is not necessary, however, to render the vectors "meaningful" by using semantic primitives such as size, species, and other biologically defined values. One may use arbitrary units decoupled from the input. Thus, unlike in Figure 6.6, there would be no re-

lation between an identifiable stimulus feature and the input units. Mathematically, the system works as long as the vector representations discriminate between the items.

We have discussed distributed representations of inputs. The next section will show that distributed storage of information follows the same principles. A **distributed** storage system has overlapping or superimposed memories. This means that (1) a memory is represented across a number of storage elements and (2) the set of elements holds several memories simultaneously.

RETRIEVAL FROM NEURAL NETS

The best knowledge representation is useless if there is no retrieval. Information retrieval is a key attribute of natural and humanmade storage systems. Human memory provides a multitude of instances for retrieval, whether they come from episodic memory experiments in the laboratory or real-life situations. One of the most widely used memory paradigms is the paired-associate task. In training, pairs of stimulus and response terms are presented together—for example, pairs of nonsense syllables (*XRM-BLC*), pairs of numbers and words (*26-lamp*), or pairs of objects and corresponding labels. The person commits both members of each pair to memory and retrieves the response term when presented with the stimulus term in testing.

Retrieval in everyday contexts is so common that one may overlook it altogether. Every act of word recognition and word use constitutes a retrieval. For example, in reading aloud, the reader sees a visual symbol and retrieves the associated sound. Retrieval occurs as well when one uses words and their inflected forms, whether it is the plural of nouns or the past tense of verbs. One presumably forms the past tense of a verb based on the association between the infinitive and the past-tense forms of the verb. The challenge of retrieval is more noticeable to novices than to experts. Any student of foreign languages experiences retrieval difficulties when she tries to memorize the vocabulary of the language, such as the French word *cheval* for the English word *horse*.

Any representational system developed by cognitive psychologists must address the issue of retrieval. In the case of neural networks, retrieval is a natural by-product of the system's assumptions on activation. In fact, we discussed retrieval earlier in the guise of determining output activations of networks consisting of three and four units in Figures 6.3 and 6.4. Next, we will examine retrieval in a network of four input units and four output units. Such networks still appear simple relative to the 16 × 16 network representing letters in Figure 6.6, let alone compared to networks used in commercial applications. Fortunately, the simplification of the 4 × 4 network does not affect the logic of retrieval processes in any way.

In the 4 × 4 network in Figure 6.8, each of the input units is connected to each of the output units, yielding a total of 16 connections (see McClelland, Rumelhart, & Hinton, 1986). We shall examine the association of input and output patterns of activation and see how one pattern can be reconstructed when the corresponding pattern is presented to the network as input. This arrangement produces the retrieval of a pattern. The input-output associations may represent the association between the visual pattern of a letter and its name, or between two paired associates such as *horse-cheval*.

Processing in the eight-unit network in Figure 6.8 proceeds according to the same principles as in the smaller networks that we have studied earlier. Assume the network in Figure 6.8 has learned the word pair *horse-cheval*. Let us represent the input *horse* by the following pattern of activations: 1 −1 −1 1. We represent the output *cheval* by this pattern of activations: −1 −1 1 1. Finally, we assume that the four sets of connection weights are, respectively, −.25 +.25 +.25 −.25, −.25 +.25 +.25 −.25, +.25 −.25 −.25 +.25, and +.25 −.25 −.25 +.25. This information is summarized in matrix (M1), which captures the essential information in Figure 6.8. The input values are represented in the row at the top (Input *Horse*). The output activations are shown in the right-most column (Output *Cheval*). The connection strengths between the input and output units are expressed in the cells of the matrix. Representing networks in terms of matrices facilitates the calculation of output activations according to equation (6.1) and is easier to generalize to larger networks.

(M1)	Input "Horse"				Output
	+1	−1	−1	+1	"Cheval"
	−.25	+.25	+.25	−.25	−1
	−.25	+.25	+.25	−.25	−1
	+.25	−.25	−.25	+.25	+1
	+.25	−.25	−.25	+.25	+1

For each output unit, we multiply the activation of the connected input units with the relevant weight and add all of products according to equation (6.1). For the first output unit, this calculation is as follows:

$$(+1)(−.25) + (−1)(+.25) + (−1)(+.25) + (+1)(−.25)$$
$$= (−.25) + (−.25) + (−.25) + (−.25) = −1$$

Applying expression (6.1) to the inputs and the weights of the remaining rows of matrix (M1), the output pattern of −1 −1 1 1 is produced. It represents the word *cheval*.

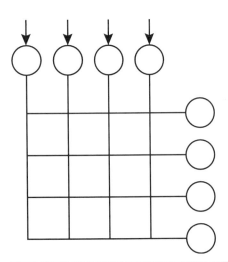

FIGURE 6.8 Eight-unit network of four input units and four output units.

In sum, retrieval of information is accomplished by presenting a connectionist network with a pattern of input activations and then regenerating the output based on the input and the connection weights, according to expression (6.1). Retrieval assumes that the association between input and output was previously established. Information about the horse, for example, is not stored locally in one cell or unit. Rather, it is represented in terms of connection strengths distributed over the entire network. Processing in the network is parallel in that activation spreads simultaneously from the input units to the output units.

Frequently, recognition and perception involve unclear stimuli. Using the horse example again, we represent degraded input by blurring the values of input activation as in pattern 1 −1 0 1 in matrix (M2) rather than 1 −1 −1 1. The connection weights remain the same as in matrix (M1).

(M2)	Input "Horse"			Output
+1	−1	0	+1	"Cheval"
−.25	+.25	+.25	−.25	?
−.25	+.25	+.25	−.25	?
+.25	−.25	−.25	+.25	?
+.25	−.25	−.25	+.25	?

Activation levels for the output units are computed as before. The products and the output activation for the first output unit is as follows:

	Input "Horse"				Output
	+1	−1	0	+1	"Cheval"
Weights	−.25	+.25	+.25	−.25	
Products	−.25	−.25	0	−.25	−.75

The activation levels for the remaining output units reveal a pattern similar to that computed in matrix (M1). The signs of the activation levels of each output unit are the same as in M1, only the absolute values are a little smaller. This illustrates that a person is somewhat less certain about the identity of a blurred pattern than a clear one.

The network we have discussed held just one memory—namely, the association between words

of two different languages. Natural memories hold more information than just one association, as the section entitled Learning in Neural Networks will show.

Now that we have an understanding of retrieval from neural networks, we can consider the advantages of distributed representations compared to localized ones.

Content-Addressable Memory

Distributed representations are **content addressable.** In a localized storage system, the address of an item must be known in order to retrieve it. In a content-addressable system, an item is accessed and retrieved by using a prompt that consists of a subset of the item's features. The subset initiates a search of representations that fit the probe set best. Finally, the best fitting representation in memory is returned.

Degraded Inputs

Because retrieval from neural networks is based on partial as well as full input, degraded inputs may serve as retrieval probes. According to this view, degraded input is a kind of partial input, even if there are some infelicities (as in matrix [M2]). This capability of networks reflects the remarkable flexibility of human memory: We can retrieve the same memories through different prompts. We can recall the target DOG, for example, from different partial descriptions such as "it is one of the oldest domesticated animals," "it is man's best friend," "it wags its tail," or "it barks." A localized storage scheme would require additional assumptions to explain recall from a partial description.

Generalization and Discrimination

Distributed representations make it easy to determine the similarity and distinctions between items. Consider a 20-unit network to represent animals rather than the 5-unit network in Table 6.2. Further, suppose the network knows the following pattern as the concept of IRISH SETTER:
IRISH SETTER +1 −1 +1 −1 −1 +1 +1 −1 −1 −1

−1 +1. . . . Now, assume the system encounters a Golden Retriever, an animal it has never seen before, and that the pattern for the unknown beast is −1 −1 +1 −1 −1 +1 +1 −1 −1 −1 −1 +1 . . . , which is almost identical to the previous pattern. What does the network retrieve in response to this prompt? From what we have learned thus far, the network will produces the best fitting response—namely, *Irish Setter*. The network classifies the animal as a kind of dog, much like a 2-year-old would label any small four-legged creature *dog*, including a cat. The network has generalized past knowledge to new stimuli. It is up to further training to get the system to discriminate between different breeds of dogs such as Irish Setters and Golden Retrievers.

Given the dynamics of retrieval, it is easy to see why scientists consider distributed representations as knowledge. In a neural network, output patterns are produced by the interaction of input activation and weights stored in the network. The next section will show that the pattern of weights in a network is the product of training. As a result of experiencing different pairs of input and output patterns, the weights come to accumulate and preserve the contribution of each pairing so that the original input, together with the set of weights, will regenerate the matching output. In Churchland and Sejnowski's (1992) words, a set of different input vectors becomes associated with a set of corresponding output vectors via a single weight configuration: "In this sense the configuration of weights embodies the knowledge. It is not as though little pictures are stored, one on top of the other. Storage in a weight configuration is a very different, if essentially simple idea. A matrix is an array of values and the elements of an incoming vector can be operated on by some function to produce an output vector. It means, therefore, that different vectors, pushed through one and the same matrix, will give different outputs." Applying the matrix and weight notion to the nervous system, the authors continue as follows: "Were we to extend this idea to nervous systems, the weight configuration of synapses is

a kind of living matrix, through which vectors can be pushed to give appropriate outputs" (pp. 167–168).

Now it is also easy to see that neural nets have no knowledge other than what they gained through experience. The question How does experience lead to knowledge in neural networks? must be rephrased as follows: Where do the weights of neural networks come from? The next section will show that weights are changed through experience with the environment, through learning.

LEARNING IN NEURAL NETWORKS

Every theory of knowledge representation faces the problem of learning: How does the representation acquire its knowledge in the first place? Symbolic models have difficulties with this challenge, although some of them have been augmented to handle learning (e.g., Anderson, 1983; Langley, 1990). Neural networks not only handle retrieval easily but learning is a natural feature as well. Learning means that the connection weights in the neural network are changed either because of a series of pairings of input and output patterns or because the network is capable of modifying itself without feedback (see page 185). As a result of learning, the current weights are changed by a certain change factor, C. In order to get the new weight, one simply adds the change in weights, C_{weight}, to the current weight, as expressed in (6.2).

(6.2) New weight = current weight + C_{weight}

We consider three learning procedures in neural networks: the Hebb procedure, the delta procedure, and learning by backpropagation. In each of these, the network is presented with a series of pairs of input and output patterns and learning is a matter of adjusting weights over successive learning episodes. The procedures differ in terms of how the change in weights takes place. In the Hebb procedure, joint activation produces learning; in the delta procedure, error adjustment produces learning. Learning by backpropagation generalizes the delta procedure to a greater variety of input and output patterns than can be handled by delta learning.

Hebbian Learning

Joint Activation Produces Learning. Donald Hebb's (1949) research was influenced by the discoveries of neurophysiologists who investigated neurons, synapses, and neural circuits, then known as neuron loops. During Hebb's times, our knowledge of neurons was still rudimentary. In the decades since, much information has been added about changes in synaptic strength, especially long-term potentiation in the hippocampus (see Chapter 2; Brown, Kairiss, & Keenan, 1990). According to Hebb, each memory, thought, and sensation was based on the activity pattern in a neural circuit. He postulated that two neurons in a neural circuit, A and B, become associated when some activity flows through them at the same time, whether it is a memory, feeling, sensation, or some other psychological event. Hebb reasoned that the two neurons become more closely linked through the actual growth of buttons (knobs) at the synaptic junction between them. This, then, is the Hebb rule of learning:

When unit A and unit B are simultaneously active, increase the strength of the connection between them in proportion with their joint activation.

Figure 6.9A shows the connection between two neurons in the nervous system that are simultaneously active (see synapse surrounded by circle), while the third neuron is not active. Figure 6.9B shows a schematic 4 × 4 unit network with one active input unit and one active output unit. The arrows converging toward the weight on the connection between the two active units point to the weight that is changed, according to the Hebb rule.

Theorists assume that the increase in the connection strength depends on the energy or activation levels of the two neurons. When the neurons are highly energized, their link will be substantially strengthened. When their activation levels are low, their link will increase but not by much. According to Hebb's rule, one multiplies the activation levels of A and B. If the activation are weak, say each is 0.1, the increment is quite small—namely, 0.01. When the activations are relatively high, such as 0.5, there is a greater increment of 0.25. Formally, the change in weights, Cw_{io}, is the product of the activation

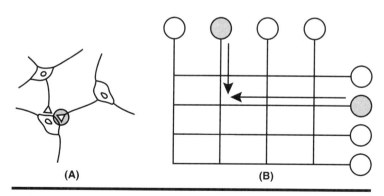

FIGURE 6.9 (*A*) Connection between two active neurons. The joint activation is highlighted by the circle around the synapse. Note that the third neuron is resting. (*B*) One input unit and one output unit are active in 4 × 4 network. The arrows point to the link whose weight is changed according to the Hebbian learning rule.

levels of the two neurons as expressed in equation (6.3).

(6.3) $Cw_{io} = a_i \times a_t$

The weight w_{io} refers to the connection between an input unit and an output unit. The a terms refer to activation levels presented to the input and output units, respectively. The a_i term refers to the input activation; a_t is the target activation, the output the network is supposed to produce. The target activation is governed by the teaching signal presented to the output units while the input pattern is presented to the input units. The target activation must be distinguished from the actual output activation, as calculated by expression (6.1).

In order to complete equation (6.3), we must add a value to express the learning rate, which may vary from rapid to very slow. In the extreme case, learning would occur in one trial; the learning rate would be 1.0. At the other extreme, no learning takes place at all and the learning rate would be 0.0. A learning rate of 0.5 indicates an intermediate pace of learning. Values such as the learning rate are known as **parameters.** A parameter is a quantity that remains constant over some test conditions. Researchers usually set parameters based on certain assumptions. In the case of the network in Figure 6.9, we assume that the learning rate depends on the number of input units, specifically, that it is equal to 1 divided by the number of input units ($r = 0.25$.) Including the learning parameter, lr, in the product in (6.3), we obtain equation (6.4):

(6.4) $Cw_{io} = lr \times a_i \times a_t$

An Example of Hebbian Learning. Next, the Hebb rule will be illustrated for a network of five units (adapted from McClelland & Rumelhart, 1988; see Chapter 4). There are four input units and one output unit, as well as four connections. Figure 6.10A shows the network with its initial weight values of 0. Four patterns will be presented to this network (see Table 6.4). Each pattern consists of a set of input activations and a target output. Each row of Table 6.4 contains a

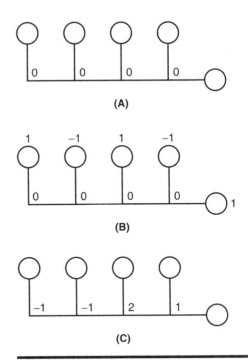

FIGURE 6.10 (*A*) Five-unit network. (*B*) Network prior to first learning trial with pattern p1 as input pattern. Note that the intended output is 1 and the initial connection weights have been set to 0. (*C*) Weights after 20 cycles of delta learning with four patterns.

different pattern. The first pattern, p1, involves activation levels of 1 –1 1 and –1 to the four respective input units, labeled i1 through i4. The activation required from the output unit is 1.

Figure 6.10B represents the five-unit network with pattern p1 as input pattern at the beginning of the first learning trial—that is, prior to learning.

TABLE 6.4 Input and Output Patterns in Hebbian Learning Trials

Input	i1	i2	i3	i4	Output
p1	1	−1	1	−1	1
p2	1	1	1	1	1
p3	−1	1	1	−1	0
p4	−1	−1	1	1	0

Figure 6.10B depicts the target output, 1, associated with the input pattern of p1. We use equation (6.1) to compute the actual output at this early stage. With initial weights of 0 for each of the four connections, all of the cross products and their sum are 0. Thus, the actual output for pattern p1 on its first trial is 0.

In the next step, we compute the change for each of the four weights. Using equation (6.4), the resulting changes are 0.25, –0.25, 0.25, and –0.25, respectively. As shown next, for each connection, one multiplies the input activation, a_i, the target activation, a_t, and the learning parameter, lr. The first subscript of each weight (1–4) refers to the respective input unit and the second to the output unit (5).

Change of Weight$_{15}$ = 0.25 × 1 × 1 = 0.25
Change of Weight$_{25}$ = 0.25 × 1 × –1 = –0.25
Change of Weight$_{35}$ = 0.25 × 1 × 1 = 0.25
Change of Weight$_{45}$ = 0.25 × 1 × –1 = –0.25

Table 6.5A shows the changes in the weights as a result of encountering all four patterns. Each row represents a learning episode where an input pattern and the desired output are presented to the network. The left-most column indicates the learning rate, lr, of 0.25. Then the input activations and the target output follow. The right section of the table shows the change-of-weight factors resulting from the learning experience on this trial. The table assumes that the network starts out with 0 weights in each case. The bottom row of Table 6.5A shows the final weights of 0.5, 0, 0.5, and 0 for the four respective connections. These weights produce the correct target output for each of the four input patterns as shown in Table 6.5B. This is an instance of superposition, the distributed property of neural networks.

Next, consider learning in the 4 × 4 network that we have used to learn associations between French and English words. It is assumed that all of the initial weights are 0, as indicated in matrix (M0).

(M0)	Input "Horse"				Output
	+1	−1	−1	+1	"Cheval"
	0	0	0	0	?
	0	0	0	0	?
	0	0	0	0	?
	0	0	0	0	?

TABLE 6.5   Learning of Four Patterns Under the Hebb Rule

A. Training

Pattern	lr	Input Activations				Output	Change-of-Weight Values			
p1	.25	1	−1	1	−1	1	.25	−.25	.25	−.25
p2	.25	1	1	1	1	1	.25	.25	.25	.25
p3	.25	−1	1	1	−1	0	0	0	0	0
p4	.25	−1	−1	1	1	0	0	0	0	0
Sum							.5	0	.5	0

B. Testing

Pattern	Inputs				Output	
					Target	Actual
p1	1	−1	1	−1	1	1
p2	1	1	1	1	1	1
p3	−1	1	1	−1	0	0
p4	−1	−1	1	1	0	0
p5	1	1	1	−1	0	1

According to Hebb's rule, presentation of the *horse-cheval* pair yields the following changes of weight.

(M C$_w$)	Input "Horse"				Output "Cheval"
	+1	−1	−1	+1	
	−.25	+.25	+.25	−.25	−1
	−.25	+.25	+.25	−.25	−1
	+.25	−.25	−.25	+.25	+1
	+.25	−.25	−.25	+.25	+1

According to expression (6.2), the weights in the change-of-weight values are added to the initial weights. Therefore, we add the change-of-weight matrix to matrix (M0) to get matrix (M1). One does so by adding corresponding elements of each matrix. For example, adding the top left weight of (M0), 0, to the corresponding change of weight in (M C$_w$, −.25, yields 0 + (−.25) = −.25.

(M1)	Input "Horse"				Output "Cheval"
	+1	−1	−1	+1	
	−.25	+.25	+.25	−.25	−1
	−.25	+.25	+.25	−.25	−1
	+.25	−.25	−.25	+.25	+1
	+.25	−.25	−.25	+.25	+1

Now present the network with the *two-deux* pattern and you get the following change-of-weight matrix.

(M3)	Input "Two"				Output "Deux"
	+1	−1	−1	+1	
	+.25	−.25	+.25	−.25	−1
	−.25	+.25	−.25	+.25	+1
	−.25	+.25	−.25	+.25	+1
	+.25	−.25	+.25	−.25	−1

The network learns according to expression (6.2), which states that the new weight equals the current weight plus the change of weight factor *C*. Adding the corresponding weights for *horse* (M1) and *two* (M3), we obtain matrix (M4).

(M4)			
0	0	+.5	−.5
−.5	+.5	0	0
0	0	−.5	+.5
+.5	−.5	0	0

Matrix (M4) is a composite matrix that contains the information for both the *horse* and *two* patterns. This is demonstrated by presenting the *horse* and *two* inputs to the network on successive trials. We should get the *horse* and *two* outputs, respectively. First, we present the *horse* input to the composite matrix and compute the output for each output unit according to equation (6.1).

(M5)	Input "Horse"				Output "Cheval"
	+1	−1	−1	+1	
	0	0	+.5	−.5	−1
	−.5	+.5	0	0	−1
	0	0	−.5	+.5	+1
	+.5	−.5	0	0	+1

The experiment succeeds: The matrix does indeed produce the correct output for *horse*. In other words, the network remembered *cheval* when given *horse*. For the second test, we present the input values for *two* to the same network.

(M6)	Input "Two"				Output "Deux"
	−1	+1	−1	+1	
	0	0	+.5	−.5	−1
	−.5	+.5	0	0	+1
	0	0	−.5	+.5	+1
	+.5	−.5	0	0	−1

Once again, the correct output is obtained. In sum, the network with its composite weights regenerates the correct output for each of the two input stimuli; it exhibits memory for both associations. The same set of weights (in matrix [M4]) handles both kinds of input equally. This illustrates Hebbian learning in an eight-unit neural net and the principle of distributed representation.

Learning in networks is achieved through a change in connection weights. A new connection weight is equal to the previous weight plus the change-of-weight factor. According to the Hebb rule, a weight is strengthened when two connected neurons are active at the same time. The increase depends on the degree of activation of the two neurons. High activation levels produce a greater increase in the connection strength than low levels of activation.

Matrix (M4) illustrates the principle of distributed memory representation through superposition. The same network retains information on several inputs. Items are not stored in veridical form. Retrieval is the result of joint processing of the input stimulus AND the set of weights that the network has acquired over an accumulated practice period.

Limits to Hebbian Learning. If we had to represent each input-output association or each memory in a different network, our long-term memory would have to hold an enormous number of different and unrelated networks. Fortunately, networks have the capacity of storing **superimposed** patterns so that one network accommodates several input-output associations. Could we continue and add more and more patterns to a matrix like (M6)? The answer depends on the size of the network and the types of patterns presented to it. Larger networks have a greater capacity. They can store more patterns than the small networks we have been using. There is, however, a limitation to the kinds of patterns that can be represented in a Hebbian matrix.

The patterns that can be acquired in Hebbian learning must be independent or uncorrelated; otherwise, there will be cross-talk between them, producing inaccurate retrieval. To illustrate this limit, we present the network of Figure 6.10 with a fifth pattern, p5. A trial involving this pattern is shown in Table 6.5B. The input activations of pattern p5 are 1, 1, 1, and –1, respectively. The target

output is 0. Using the current weights of 0.5, 0, 0.5, and 0, we obtain an actual output of 1 for p5.

Next, we calculate the changes in the weights for pattern p5. Because the target is 0, the change factors, C, for each of the weights is 0 as well. The current weights are not changed at all, and the pattern is not acquired on trial 5. If you run each of the patterns through additional trials, you will find that pattern p5 will not be learned by this network. It will be confused with the other patterns. If you were to reverse the sequence of trials, pattern p5 would be learned but one or more other patterns would not have been remembered.

Why can't the network remember all five patterns? What distinguishes pattern p5 from the set of the previous four patterns? The answer is that patterns p1 through p4 are uncorrelated, whereas p5 is correlated with the other patterns. When patterns are uncorrelated, they are dissimilar and no pattern can be predicted from the others. The patterns provide independent information. Two correlated patterns are similar and one pattern can be used to predict the other, at least to some extent. Pattern p5, for example, can be partially predicted from pattern p1.

Mathematically, two patterns are uncorrelated when the sums of cross-products are 0. This is illustrated in Table 6.6. For two pairs of patterns—p1 and p2, and p3 and p4—the table shows the input activations of a pair of patterns, their cross-products, and the sum of cross products. The two pairs on the left are uncorrelated patterns, whereas pattern p1 and pattern p5 on the right are positively correlated. Similarly, p5 is correlated with the other patterns.

I will conclude this section with another example involving correlated patterns. They are shown in Table 6.7 (McClelland & Rumelhart, 1988). In Table 6.8, the change-of-weight factors from two learning cycles with four trials each are shown, one for each pattern from Table 6.7.

The change-of-weight terms for a given pattern do not change from the first to the second cycle. One could continue the experiment for another 10 or 20 trials and the change-of-weight quantities would remain exactly the same. If you

TABLE 6.6   Independence and Correlation between Pairs of Patterns

Patterns			Patterns			Patterns		
p1	p2	Cross-Products	p3	p4	Cross-Products	p1	p5	Cross-Products
1	1	1	−1	−1	1	1	1	1
−1	1	−1	1	−1	−1	−1	1	−1
1	1	1	1	1	1	1	1	1
−1	1	−1	−1	1	−1	−1	−1	1
Sums of products		0			0			2

examine expression (6.4) one more time, you will see why this has to be so. According to (6.4), the change of weights depends on the input activation and the target activation of a given pattern. Because those activations remain the same, the change-of-weight terms should also remain constant.

You may wonder why neural network models have become so popular in light of the fact that they cannot acquire correlated information, at least not with the Hebb rule. Remember, however, that the small networks we have used here are simplifications. If you use thousands of units, it is much easier to find independent sets of patterns. More input and output units are required by the kinds of stimuli we have been discussing. One could store thousands of uncorrelated memories in such 1,000 × 1,000 matrices. This thought is not too farfetched if you consider that there are millions of neurons in the brain. In addition, there are more powerful learning procedures, including the delta learning procedure. The delta procedure

overcomes the limits of Hebbian learning and supports acquisition of such patterns as pattern p5. The delta learning procedure is described next.

The Delta Procedure: Learning through Error Correction

Delta Learning Uses Feedback.   One of the reasons why Hebbian learning does not work with correlated input patterns (see Table 6.7) is that there is no direct relationship between the actual output and the intended target output. In Hebbian learning, the weights are simply the product of the input and target activation. The connection weights are not influenced by any feedback. The system is given feedback via the target activations but it does not register any discrepancies between the actual output and the target output. Just think of a student repeating the same mistake over again, the person taking tennis lessons who is told to hold her racket back but does not do so, and the novice studying the French word for *pen* who keeps saying incorrectly *le plume* (masculine) instead of the correct *la plume* (feminine). Such errors should be the trigger for learning, but this is not the case in Hebbian learning (nor is it true for all human learning situations).

Delta learning takes advantage of feedback. The system adjusts its response to the expected target. It does so by recording the error and correcting it, bit by bit, on every trial. Let us see how errors are corrected and how learning is

TABLE 6.7   Patterns for Learning Using the Hebb and Delta Rules

Input	i1	i2	i3	i4	Target Output
p1	1	−1	1	−1	1
p2	1	1	1	1	1
p3	1	1	1	−1	−1
p4	1	−1	−1	1	−1

TABLE 6.8   In Hebbian Learning, Change-of-Weight Factors Remain the Same across Trials

	Cycle 1				Cycle 2			
	i1	*i2*	*i3*	*i4*	*i1*	*i2*	*i3*	*i4*
p1	0.25	−0.25	0.25	−0.25	0.25	−0.25	0.25	−0.25
p2	0.25	0.25	0.25	0.25	0.25	0.25	0.25	0.25
p3	−0.25	−0.25	−0.25	0.25	−0.25	−0.25	−0.25	0.25
p4	−0.25	0.25	0.25	−0.25	−0.25	0.25	0.25	0.25

achieved under the regimen of the delta rule. If the output unit is off but should be on according to the pattern to be learned, adjustments are made in the weights to turn the output unit on. If the output unit is on but should be off, adjustments are made to turn the output unit off. When the output unit produces the correct output, no adjustments are made at all. The rule-of-weight adjustment known as the delta rule is expressed in (6.5). The term *delta* comes from the Greek symbol Δ representing change. Equation (6.5) is similar to expression (6.4); it includes the learning parameter, *lr*, and the activation of the input unit as before. What differs is the presence of the error term.

(6.5) $Cw_{io} = lr \times a_i \times error_o$

The error term is the error of a given output unit on a specific learning trial. It represents the difference between the target activation, a_t, and the actual activation of the output unit, a_o, as shown in expression (6.6).

(6.6) $error_o = a_t - a_o$

Let us ponder expression (6.5) for a moment to see how this expression captures the idea of learning by error reduction. If the response of the output unit is correct, the error term is zero. As a result, the product on the right of (6.5), $lr \times a_i \times error_o$, is zero and there is no change in the connection weight. If, however, the response deviates considerably from the target, the error is large and contributes to the product, $lr \times a_i \times error_o$, thus causing a relatively large change in the weight.

An Example of Delta Learning.   Success with the delta procedure where Hebbian learning failed is demonstrated by using the same patterns as before (see Table 6.7). They are presented to the network in Figure 6.10. We will see that the errors decrease with learning, unlike in the Hebbian procedure. The first pattern to be learned involves input activations of 1 −1 1 −1 and a target output of 1. Initially, the connection weights between each input unit and the output unit are set to zero. The output activation is computed according to expression (6.1). The learning parameter is $lr = 0.25$. Given the input activations and the initial weights, we can now calculate the actual output on the first learning trial. Because all the connection weights are zero, the cross-products are zero. As a result, the actual output prior to learning is zero as well. We compute the error, the difference between target and actual output activation, according to expression (6.6). With a target of 1 and an output of 0, the error is 1 − 0 = 1. Next, using expression (6.5), the delta rule is applied to calculate changes for each of the four weights as follows:

Change of Weight$_{ij}$ = learning parameter $\times$ error $\times$ input activation

Change of Weight$_{15}$ = 0.25 × 1 × 1 = 0.25

Change of Weight$_{25}$ = 0.25 × 1 × −1 = −0.25

Change of Weight$_{35}$ = 0.25 × 1 × 1 = 0.25

Change of Weight$_{45}$ = 0.25 × 1 × −1 = −0.25

Table 6.9 shows these calculations for all four patterns. Each row indicates a learning episode with one pattern. The left-most section includes

TABLE 6.9   A Cycle of Delta Learning

	Current Weight			i1	i2	i3	i4	Target	Actual	Error	lr	cw1	cw2	cw3	cw4
0	0	0	0	1	−1	1	−1	1	0	1	0.25	0.25	−0.25	0.25	−0.25
0.25	−0.25	0.25	−0.25	1	1	1	1	1	0	1	0.25	0.25	0.25	0.25	0.25
0.5	0	0.5	0	1	1	1	−1	−1	1	−2	0.25	−0.5	−0.5	−0.5	0.5
0	−0.5	0	0.5	1	−1	−1	1	−1	1	−2	0.25	−0.5	0.5	0.5	−0.5

the four weights at the beginning of a learning episode, the next section shows the input activations, then the target output, the actual output, and the error term for each episode are shown. Next, the learning rate, $lr = 0.25$, is tabulated. The rightmost section includes the change-of-weight values resulting from the current learning episode.

Note that the current weights reflect the cumulative learning experience up to that learning episode. For the second trial, the current weights are .25, −.25, .25, and −.25. These weights were computed according to expression (6.2). In pattern p2, all input units are fully activated at 1, and the output activation is also 1. Given the input activations and the current weights, we calculate the output for trial 2 as 0. It should have been 1. Therefore, the error is 1. The changes in the weights are shown in the right section of the second row of Table 6.9.

Table 6.9 summarizes the results for patterns p1 through p4 during the first learning cycle. In subsequent cycles, the four patterns are presented in the same order again. The errors are reduced on trial 2 and on the subsequent trials. After 20 cycles of learning, the weights are −1 −1 2 1 for the four weights, respectively. You can verify that these weights produce the correct output for each of the four patterns shown in Table 6.7. The five-unit network is shown in Figure 6.10C after successful learning.

In general, delta learning finds the weights for a given set of paired input-output patterns. One can add weights from learning trials involving different pairs of patterns and obtain a composite set of weights that represents many such paired associations.

As a result of training, the composite set of weights minimizes the error for **all** pairs of patterns. The search for the minimum error through learning may be presented graphically. To do so, we use the simple network in Figure 6.11A. It has two input units, one output unit, and two weights, w_{13} and w_{23}.

Figure 6.11B shows the coordinates for the weights w_{13} and w_{23} in the horizontal plane and the error on the vertical axis. The figure captures the error occurring in the three-unit network, given a certain set of weights. Initially, the error is large. In Figure 6.11B, it would be plotted high above the plane formed by w_{13} and w_{23}. Training moves the error down toward the lowest plane. This gradient descent is captured by the paraboloid in Figure 6.11C. The bottom of the paraboloid represents the combination of weights under which the error is minimal.

Applications of Delta Learning.   Delta learning detects the average tendency in a set of input patterns through error reduction. Because of this property, it has been used to mimic a number of important learning and classification effects in psychology and such other disciplines as signal processing, weather forecasting, financial and economic analysis, and computer-based pattern recognition.

Rules and Exceptions in Language.   One of the most interesting applications of delta learning in cognitive psychology has been the simulation of acquiring linguistic regularities and exceptions. The simulation of past-tense learning of English verbs is a case in point. Research has shown that

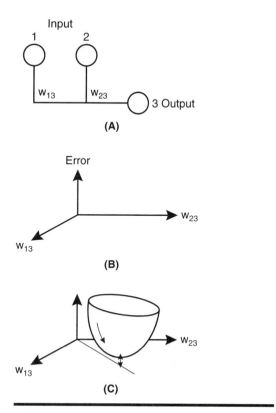

FIGURE 6.11 (*A*) Search of weights to minimize error in three-unit network. (*B*) Coordinates for the two weights and for the error in the three-unit network. (*C*) Three-dimensional schematic of gradient descent toward minimum error.

children acquire both the regular pattern of generating the past tense of English verbs and a large number of irregular verbs. In English, the past tense is usually formed by adding the suffix -*ed* to the stem of the infinitive, as in *walk–walk-ed* and *climb–climb-ed.* Irregular verbs, although they occur quite frequently, have idiosyncratic forms of the past tense, as in *run–ran, write–wrote, think–thought,* and *eat–ate.* Children acquire the past-tense in three stages in a combination of rote learning and rule learning. First, they learn to use a small number of frequently occurring irregular verbs. As the child encounters more and more regular verbs, he learns to form the past tense by adding -*ed* to the verb's stem. He learns this rule

so well that he applies it incorrectly to irregular verbs as, for example, in saying *sleeped* instead of *slept.* Eventually, by adolescence most children have mastered both regular and irregular verbs.

Rumelhart and McClelland (1987) constructed a connectionist network of 460 input units and 460 output units to learn a corpus of about 500 English verbs and their past tenses. They first presented a small corpus of irregular verbs, then a mixture of regular and irregular verbs, and finally the whole set of verbs. The infinitives of verbs and their past-tense forms were presented to the input and output units, respectively. Outputs were produced according to expression (6.1) and errors were adjusted according to the delta rule in expression (6.5). There were 190 learning episodes, each involving the entire training set of verbs. The network not only mimicked the three stages of children's past-tense learning successfully but it simulated some subtle empirical effects as well. For example, researchers had found that children more easily learn those irregular verbs that use the stem for the past tense, as in *hit.* Children also use alternate past-tense expressions of a verb during the second stage, for example *go+ed* and *went+ed.* The network produced these patterns as well as some formulations that researchers had not yet tested. One of these was that children would produce double inflection responses for verbs whose stem ends on *p* or *k* so that they will say *dripted* instead of *dripped.*[2]

Models of cognition are judged by the economy of their assumptions, as is the case of models in other domains: The fewer the assumptions and the simpler, the better. According to this measure of parsimony, it is a strength of the neural network approach that it can accommodate the learning of regular forms and exceptions within a common framework rather than having to assume different mechanisms. There are other formulations of rules and exceptions that call for different mechanisms for each; for example, the learner acquires a set of rules by one procedure and memorizes exceptions by another procedure (see Pinker & Mehler, 1988). Seidenberg (1992) cited other cases of rules-plus-exceptions in the

English language that are readily handled by connectionist networks, such as pronunciation patterns in English. The correspondence between spelling and pronunciation may be considered rulelike for such words as *mint, lint*, and *splint*. Pronouncing each of these words is rulelike, as researchers discovered when they asked people to pronounce pseudowords such as *bint*. Subjects typically pronounce this string to rhyme with *lint*. So far, so good; there is, however, the exception—namely *pint*. Speakers of English acquire exceptions like these easily without giving them a thought.

Classification Learning.   Successful learning of the past tense is possible because the delta rule detects regularities contained in a set of related patterns. The rule picks up the prototype among related patterns and notes exceptions, if necessary. The delta rule is an excellent vehicle for many other instances of such concept learning. In concept learning, exemplars that are similar are subsumed under a specific category, whereas other items are sorted with other categories. Concept learning is more fully treated in Chapter 14; that discussion includes discussion of an example of the acquisition of diagnostic categories in medicine according to the delta rule.

Classification learning is also easily achieved by machine. In each case, the goal is to discern—and to predict—a pattern from a jumble of data. Engineers have used delta learning in signal processing where the input consists of a signal and random noise. As a result of training, the system comes to isolate the signal from the noise (Widrow & Hoff, 1960). Using the delta rule, meteorologists can predict the weather on the basis of a variety of data, including the air pressure at various altitudes, wind direction and speed, humidity, temperature in many different locations, and so on. Economists and financial analysts use data patterns from one time period to predict performance in subsequent time periods, $t + 1$, $t + 2$. For example, using delta learning, mortgage bankers have assessed the credit worthiness of borrowers, and investors have used economic data in trying to predict the stock market, albeit with limited success.

The Delta Rule in Animal and Human Learning.   Delta learning expresses the associative strength of pairs of events in both human and animal learning. Working independently from neural network researchers, two learning theorists, Robert Rescorla and Allan Wagner, discovered the delta rule in the context of animal learning (Rescorla & Wagner, 1972). They developed a rule of learning, the Rescorla-Wagner rule, that predicts a wide range of phenomena in animal learning (see Chapters 1 and 7). This rule describes the changes in the associative strength, *V,* of a conditioned stimulus to elicit a response. According to the rule, the change in strength, *ΔV,* is a function of the difference between the maximum strength, *lambda,* and the current strength of the stimulus. As a stimulus component gains more associative strength on a given trial, the weaker it is relative to the maximum strength attainable. The Rescorla-Wagner rule is shown in expression (6.7) and the delta rule from expression (6.5) is printed immediately below. Note the parallels between Cw and ΔV, and the target output and lambda, respectively.

(6.7) $\Delta V = lr \times (\text{lambda} - V)$

(6.5) $Cw_{io} = lr \times a_i \times (\text{target} - \text{actual})_o$

According to the Rescorla-Wagner rule, an initially weak stimulus, however unexpected, will get a big boost in strength if it is paired with reinforcement. The rule explains the phenomena of surprise very well—animals learn to pay attention to unexpected events precisely because their initial associative strength, *V,* is so weak.

I N T E R I M   S U M M A R Y

Delta learning is based on changing connection weights when there is a difference between the actual and the target output of the network. As a result of training, this difference continuously decreases. Unlike in Hebbian learning, even correlated patterns can be learned in delta learning. Because delta learning can determine the central tendency in an input, it has found use in simulations of diverse learning and classification phenomena, including verb-tense learning, concept learning, and associative learning in animals.

So far, we have learned three important attributes of connectionist networks: (1) the parallel propagation of activation through the network, (2) the distributed representation of information across sets of weights, and (3) the learning of new patterns by changing weights according to the Hebb and delta rules.

———

Backpropagation Learning

As powerful as delta learning is, it cannot acquire patterns that are **not linearly separable.** The XOR pattern in Table 6.10 is a prime example for such patterns. The pattern produces an output of 0 when both input values are identical; otherwise, it produces an output of 1. For comparison, the Table also includes AND and OR patterns, which are **linearly separable.** As Box 6.1 explains, these three patterns are equivalent to the logical connectives of the same name.

Figure 6.12 clarifies the difference between the AND and OR patterns on the one hand and the XOR pattern on the other. The x-axes of Figure 6.12 represent the activations of input 1; the y-axes represent input 2. The solid circles represent an output activation of 1; the hollow circles indicate an output activation of 0. When the 0 output space and the 1 output space can be separated by a single line, as with AND and OR patterns, the patterns are linearly separable. For the XOR pattern, there exists no single line to divide the output space.

Rumelhart, Hinton, and Williams (1986) discovered that patterns like XOR can be learned by (1) constructing a three-layer network that includes a layer of hidden units and (2) generalizing the delta rule to this three-layer network. The new units are called **hidden units** because they are located between the input and output layers and, as a result, they neither receive external inputs nor produce an external output.

Changing weights is more complex in three-layered networks than in two-layered networks; the familiar delta rule no longer works, at least not without some revision. Rumelhart and colleagues came up with a revision: the backpropagation algorithm, or the generalized delta rule. In addition to hidden units, backpropagation learning requires a nonlinear activation function, a **logistic function.** The calculation of the change-of-weight terms and error terms is more complex, as well.

The logistic function adjusts the output of units to fit within a range of 0 and 1. By contrast, in a linear function, such as that used in delta learning, the output changes in equal proportions (straight line) as a function of the input. For example, the logistic function converts a unit output of –5.0 to 0.007, and output of 2.0 to 0.881.

The researchers successfully used three-layered networks and the backpropagation algorithm for a wide range of patterns. One of them, the XOR pattern, was successfully learned after 289 learning epochs by the five-unit network illustrated in Figure 6.13. The network includes two input units, two hidden units, and an output unit, with connections between, but not within, layers.

Lloyd (1989) explained the rationale of backpropagation learning well: In the learning cycle, the network runs backward, adjusting the weights from top (output) to bottom (input). First, the target output is compared with the actual output in order to determine how far off the network's last effort was. Then all the weights feeding into the output unit are nudged in the direction that reduces their contribution to the error. This nudging

TABLE 6.10 The AND, OR, and XOR Patterns

AND		OR		XOR	
Input	*Output*	*Input*	*Output*	*Input*	*Output*
00	0	00	0	00	0
01	0	01	1	01	1
10	0	10	1	10	1
11	1	11	1	11	0

Box 6.1

The Logical Connectives AND, OR, and XOR

The terms *AND, OR*, and *XOR* used in neural network models are based on the logical connectives, AND, OR, and XOR. Each of these has well-defined truth values. The logical term *AND* corresponds to the meaning of the English word *and*. However, because of the ambiguity of the English word *or*, logicians required two terms for the word *or*. The logical connectives OR and XOR differ in subtle ways reflecting the two different senses of the English word *or*. The logician Copi (1982) illustrated these two senses, the inclusive and the exclusive sense, with a couple of sample statements. The following statement from an insurance policy illustrates the inclusive sense of *or:*

Premiums will be waived in the event of sickness or unemployment.

This statement means that premiums will be waived for people who are sick, who are unemployed, *and* who are *both* sick and unemployed. In general, the inclusive meaning of *or* is "either, possibly both." The meaning of the statement is captured in the following:

Sick	Unemployed	Premium Waiver
no	no	no
no	yes	yes
yes	no	yes
yes	yes	yes

When used in the exclusive sense, the word *or* has the meaning "at least one and at most one." This meaning is illustrated by the menu entry soup or salad often found in restaurants. In this context, or means that the customer may choose one or the other item but not both. This meaning is captured here:

Soup	Salad	Customer Choice
no	no	no
no	yes	yes
yes	no	yes
yes	yes	no

The following table shows the definitions of the connectives AND, OR, and XOR as formulated by logicians. Statements are represented by abstract variables, p and q, each of which has a truth value T or F. The definition of each connective is given by the four combinations of the two variables and their possible truth values and the corresponding compound statement. Table 6.10 is based on these definitions.

DEFINING THE LOGICAL CONNECTIVES AND, OR, AND XOR

AND		OR		XOR	
$p\ q$	p AND q	$p\ q$	p OR q	$p\ q$	p XOR q
F F	F	F F	F	F F	F
F T	F	F T	T	F T	T
T F	F	T F	T	T F	T
T T	T	T T	T	T T	F

---

is backpropagated from layer to layer, adjusting the whole in the right direction, thus slightly improving performance on every trial.

Applications of Learning by Backpropagation. Backpropagation is useful in situations in which physically different stimuli must be transformed to produce functionally similar responses, as in the XOR problem. In the case of learning the

XOR pattern, the trick for the network is to acquire the weights and biases to accomplish the goal of delivering the same response (of 0) when very different input patterns are presented. This mirrors the accomplishment of organisms: Sometimes it is necessary to respond with similar responses to different situations. For example, teachers award an A to different types of performance, whether it is an excellent term paper, a

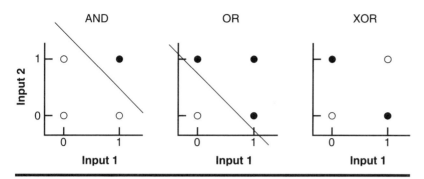

FIGURE 6.12 Linear separability illustrated by AND and OR patterns. XOR pattern is not linearly separable.

high score on an objective test, or a creative analysis of a set of complex lab data. Consider another example, this one is from ice hockey: Players receive a penalty for diverse derelictions, including tripping another player, hitting someone with the hockey stick, and lifting the stick too high.

Rumelhart and Todd (1993) illustrated physical similarity among inputs (e.g., *r* and *n*) and contrasted it with functional similarity (e.g., *a* and *A*). The *a-A* pair is physically less similar than *r* and *n*. The *a-A* similarity must be captured by some mechanism other than relations among input units. Networks with a layer of hidden units furnish that mechanism. The layered

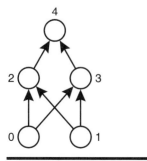

FIGURE 6.13 Backpropagation learning. Five-unit network capable of learning the XOR pattern includes two hidden units.

network translates the input stimuli into a new similarity space, using different relations than their physical similarity. The trick for the network is to learn this transformation—and backpropagation is the mechanism to do just that. In general, learning by backpropagation is useful for a large variety of transformations between input and outputs. Here we consider two such transformations, recoding of capital letters into (1) simple visual codes and into (2) acoustic output as occurs in reading.

Recognizing Visual Patterns. Chapter 4 describes the principles of visual pattern recognition: A stimulus—for example, the letter A—is shown to a person and she responds by giving the appropriate vocal response, in this case /a/. According to the general recognition model, the person encodes the stimulus, transforms it into a format compatible with the memory representation, and retrieves the associated auditory response. Multilayered neural networks are designed to code and transform stimuli, whether the transformation is of the visual-to-auditory form, as in reading out loud; the visual-to-visual variety, as in recoding letters into Morse code; or transcribing handwritten Zip codes into codes readable by automatic scanners.

Table 6.11 represents the input and output units of a network that transforms nearly veridical letters into a shorthand like a Morse code (Caudill

TABLE 6.11 Recoding of the Letter *A*

Input

0.0	0.0	1.0	0.0	0.0
0.0	1.0	0.0	1.0	0.0
1.0	0.0	0.0	0.0	1.0
1.0	0.0	0.0	0.0	1.0
1.0	0.0	0.0	0.0	1.0
1.0	1.0	1.0	1.0	1.0
1.0	0.0	0.0	0.0	1.0

Output

0.0	1.0	0.0	0.0	0.0	0.0	0.0	1.0

& Butler, 1992). The input units form a 5×7 matrix of receptors to encode capital letters—for example, *A*. The network has eight output units represented by the vector at the bottom of Table 6.11. The network also includes 2×5 hidden units not shown in the table. Networks like these can easily be trained to learn the transformation. In fact, you can buy them for less than $40.

Although transformation of handwritten symbols—for example, Zip codes—is more complex than the letter transformation in Table 6.11, the principles are the same: one visual symbol is transformed into another. Gallant (1993) reviewed successful backpropagation learning of such transformations in a five-layer network. The network has 10 output units, three layers of hidden units totaling about 900 units, 250 input units, and over 60,000 weights. After 170,000 trials involving over 7,000 different handwritten digits, the network had a recognition accuracy of close to 100% for previously presented digits. Importantly, the system was able to recognize digits it had not seen before with an accuracy of 95%. Systems like these will go a long way in solving the problem of deciphering the handwriting of postal patrons.

Reading Text. NETtalk, one of the most famous neural networks, learns to read aloud. The network accepts English text as input and learns to pronounce the words correctly, even if it sounds a bit metallic. The network's architecture includes three layers of units (see Figure 6.14). There are seven sets of 29 input units corresponding roughly to the English alphabet, 80 hidden units, and 26 output units to capture articulatory features of over 50 English phonemes. All of these units are widely interconnected, requiring 18,629 weighted links. Sejnowski and Rosenberg, the creators of NETtalk, started their mechanical reader on a set of 1,000 words selected from informal speech of a child. Subsequently, the researchers added a corpus of common words selected from a dictionary. The target output was the correct pronunciation of the text read by a human reader. NETtalk learned to read the sample text after thousands of learning cycles. Of course, this does not mean that NETtalk understands the text. Its accomplishment is that it has learned the letter-to-sound correspondence in English, which is no small feat—just ask anyone who is learning English as a second language.

In general, backpropagation learning is useful whenever an input must be transformed into an output that includes both regularities and exceptions. There are many such applications, as the following short list illustrates:

- Control of a simulated car driving on a highway
- Visual quality control of items transported at high speed (1,000 per minute) on a conveyor belt (e.g., parts of car engines or canned goods)
- Interpret x-rays to detect symptoms of diseases
- Simulate the actions of a fighter pilot
- Control of robot movements

Other Types of Networks

Recurrent Networks. Recurrent networks are an offshoot of backpropagation networks except they are designed to capture relations between *successive* outputs of the network. This is accomplished by having hidden units that feed their output back to themselves. As a result, the network has available the current inputs and outputs as well as the previous inputs and outputs. This facility is advantageous for learning contextual relations, including those found in syn-

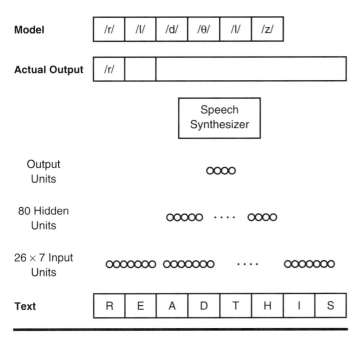

FIGURE 6.14 Schematic drawing of NETtalk. Text at bottom is processed through input units, hidden units, and output units. The output is fed through a speech synthesizer whose output is compared to the model output at top.

tax. Elman (1993) trained a recurrent network to learn syntactic structures such as relative clauses. He found that the network's ability to learn syntax depends on the order in which sentences are presented to the network. If the entire population of sentences, including relative clause sentences, is presented at the outset, the network will not learn. However, learning does occur if the network is started out with simple sentences, presented next with more complex sentences, and, finally, trained with the most complex sentences. This is what happens in human language development as well; we start out with simple sentences and gradually proceed to more complex ones. Indeed, according to Elman (1993), it is the limitations in the child's working memory that protects her from the exposure to syntactic structures too complex to handle.

Unsupervised Learning. In the delta and back-propagation procedures, learning involves supervision by a teacher who provides feedback to the network. The network is presented with pairs of input and output patterns and the output is compared with the target pattern and adjusted accordingly. In unsupervised training schedules, the network encounters only input patterns but no feedback. Training consists of self-organization so that the network comes to mimic the input. Unsupervised learning is of interest to theorists because it is ubiquitous in the real world from the acquisition of motor skills to diverse cognitive skills.

CONCLUSION

Neural networks are enjoying such a popularity in applied disciplines such as engineering, signal analysis, financial analysis, and weather forecasting that some people have claimed that neural networks will soon be as commonplace as spreadsheets are today. In applications of neural networks, the yardstick of success is simple: Does the application do the job required? In cognitive psychology, the yardstick is a different one. Here, researchers ask: Do the neural networks explain cognitive phenomena and do they do so parsimoniously? Let us consider the promises and problems of the neural network approach in cognition.

Neural networks are based on a set of relatively simple assumptions. There are primitive processing units, the neurons, that are connected via multiple links. The strength of the connections depends on past experience, the result of which is a set of weights that embodies the knowledge of the network. Events from the environment are registered by the network as patterns of input activation. This activation is passed through the network to produce an output that depends on the current configuration of the weights and pathways in the network.

Given this simple set of assumptions, the connectionist approach has been able to account for a wide array of empirical results in word recognition, categorization, and concept learning. As an added advantage, connectionist networks can learn both regularities and exceptions in a domain, as well as a number of subtle effects that theorists had not known about, such as learning the past tense in English.

One of the appeals of neural networks is that they acquire their knowledge without programmer intervention. This is a bonus, in light of the expense researchers have had to invest for expert systems in the symbolic processing framework. It frequently takes years to program an expert system to represent all of the knowledge that experts possess in a domain.

There are also problems inherent in neural networks. Although they have been used successfully to simulate diverse data in cognition, there have been both failures of prediction and too powerful predictions. Consider the latter point first. Massaro (1988) developed a neural network simulation of speech recognition. He found that the network was able to predict the results typically found in speech recognition experiments.

However, the network also predicted many results that have not been and are not likely to be observed in experiments.

There have been failures of prediction as well. In a study of retroactive interference, one of the best documented instances of forgetting in the laboratory, McCloskey and Cohen (1989) found that the network broke down when it was given successive sets of arithmetic problems. The network suffered total amnesia rather than exhibiting forgetting as human learners do. It is true that neural network theorists have rescued the network approach vis-à-vis this challenge (Chappell & Humphreys, 1994). However, the theorists had to pay a price: Their system had none of the simplicity of the original neural networks. Instead, it included a variety of subnetworks each with different learning algorithms of greater complexity than the connectionist pioneers had first envisioned.

In addition, there are criticisms of specific models and learning algorithms, including the backpropagation procedure, the most widely used algorithm. The drawback is that learning is too slow and that it is not clear that there are backpropagation pathways in the brain (although some theorists claim that there are). The averaging capability of networks has also been a topic for criticism—specifically, that new learning is averaged with prior learning and that it is therefore hard to explain that people manage to retain memory for specific exemplars.

Finally, whereas neural networks acquire their knowledge without programmer intervention, the programmer has great latitude in shaping the architecture and processing assumptions of the simulation. The theorist can determine all sorts of attributes of the model: the number of layers of the network, of input units, of hidden units, if any, and of output units; the pattern of connections between units; the learning algorithms and parameters; the output function; and on and on. Whatever one may say about the neural network approach, it has become a part of the landscape in cognitive science and in cognitive psychology, and will continue to be a significant player in the field.

ENDNOTES

1. Assume, for the present, that activation levels reflect the clarity of a signal. Thus, an input pattern of [1.0 1.0] represents a clearer signal than a [0.75 0.75] pattern. The value of weights reflects the degree to which the connection modulates the activation passed along it; the greater the number, the greater the modulation. The meaning of activation patterns is more fully explained in the section on distributed representations. Where weights come from is explained in the sections on learning.

2. Pinker (1990) examined Rumelhart and McClelland's (1987) research on past-tense learning in a highly critical light (see also Bechtel & Abrahamsen,

1991; Lachter & Bever. 1988). He argued that Rumelhart and McClelland's model is arbitrary, and that it is based on erroneous empirical assumptions. Pinker also criticized that the model's shift from correct to overgeneralized verb forms between stages is too abrupt. The simulation started out with 80% irregular verbs and then suddenly switched to 80% regular verbs. However, these distributions do not agree with the distributions of verbs in children's vocabularies. An empirical analysis of the verbs children actually encounter shows that there is a 50-50 distribution of regular and irregular verbs during the period simulated by Rumelhart and McClelland's past-tense model.

APPENDIX: EXPRESSIONS AND SUBSCRIPTS PRESENTED IN CHAPTER 6

Expressions

(6.1) Output activation$_r$ = Sum of (input activation$_s$ × weight$_{rs}$)   Linear activation function

(6.2) New weight = current weight + C$_{weight}$ New-weight rule

(6.3) $Cw_{io} = a_i \times a_t$ Change of weight (Hebb)

(6.4) $Cw_{io} = lr \times a_i \times a_t$ Change of weight including learning rate (Hebb)

(6.5) $Cw_{io} = lr \times a_i \times \text{error}_o$ Change of weight (Delta)

(6.6) $\text{error}_o = a_o - a_t$ Error term (Delta)

(6.7) $\Delta V = lr \times (\text{lambda} - V)$ Rescorla-Wagner rule

Subscripts

r = receiving unit
s = sending unit
o = output unit
i = input unit
t = target output

CHAPTER 7

LEARNING AND MEMORY

PREVIEW

This chapter presents classical research in learning and memory, spanning the period between 1900 and the early 1970s. The chapter consists of two major parts: The first part is devoted to associative learning in animals and the second part discusses human memory. The two major paradigms of animal learning are presented—classical and instrumental conditioning—and basic learning phenomena are discussed, including the time course of learning and discrimination learning. The conditions necessary to produce learning are explored and we note that the critical condition is the contingency between two events rather than their contiguity. The attributes of reinforcers, both stimuli and responses, are also characterized. The contribution of associationism to learning and memory research is summarized, and attention is drawn to the important changes in associationist theories brought about by several developments.

The second part of the chapter is devoted to human memory research from Ebbinghaus to the information-processing period. Two paradigms designed to induce forgetting are discussed—the retroactive and the proactive interference conditions—and empirical factors that produce interference between memory traces are described. A different view of memory emerged with the development of the information-processing framework: the computer metaphor. Two memory stores are distinguished: the short-term store and the long-term store. Information decays from the short-term store unless it is rehearsed. Rehearsal also results in the transfer of the information to the long-term store. Evidence for and against this two-store model is considered. The chapter concludes with a description of how the two-store model evolved into the levels-of-processing approach.

INTRODUCTION

Learning and remembering are fundamental to human cognition. **Learning** refers to changes in behavior and knowledge through experience. Almost everything we know is learned, whether it is bike riding, algebraic skills, piano playing, or one's native language. Much of the information in the knowledge representations discussed in Chapters 5 and 6 is learned, and in order to use our vast knowledge successfully, we must remember what we learn. The ability to learn is an expression of our adaptiveness to a continuously changing environment. Psychologists, and philosophers before them, made learning a central concern of their investigations.

According to early views, learning is based on associations between ideas. When two events occur at the same time, we tend to connect them in our mind, so that when one occurs, the other is evoked as well. Hume's example of thunder and lightening illustrates associations; when we see lightning, we expect the sound of thunder because these two events have occurred together in the past. We encounter instances of associative learning all the time, although we are not usually aware of it. You salivate when you enter a deli, hear the sizzle of pastrami on the griddle, smell its aroma, and see it placed on toasted rye. You are reminded of the winter fun you had as a child when the snowflakes fell outside your window; you may remember school closing at noon or the sled rides you took down the hill in the park or the snowman you built with friends.

Advertisers pair positive images with the product they want to sell, whether it is an insurance policy, a can of soda, a car, or a bar of soap. A typ-ical ad shows a cool mountain brook against the spectacular background of the Rockies to entice you into liking cola X. Association sometimes works against someone, as captured in the phrase *guilt by association*. For example, Japanese Americans living in California were detained during World War II for no other reason than their Japanese ancestry. Associationism influenced the work of psychologists at the turn of the century; the experimental investigations of memory by Ebbinghaus (1885) and of conditioning by Pavlov (1927) were shaped by associationism. It has dominated the study of learning despite some limitations we will explore.

Learning has been investigated in both humans and animals. First, let us consider to what extent the study of animal learning informs human learning research.

Does the Study of Animal Learning Teach Us Anything about Human Learning?

This chapter describes, among other topics, research on animal learning. Why do researchers use animal subjects? They do so because, as human beings, we are members of the larger universe of animals and share much in common with creatures that are our biological relatives. Although organisms are very diverse, their basic design includes similar functions, such as the intake of food and the output of waste products, their responsiveness to stimulation, their mobility, and their drive to reproduce. Reflex actions and the change of behavior as a result of experience is observed in all species. Because of these behavioral similarities, many early researchers believed that the basic laws of learning in the different species were similar, too. Thorndike expressed this philosophy when he wrote in 1911 that all organisms are "systems of connections subject to change by the law of exercise and effect, and they differ only in the particular connections formed as well as in the efficiency of the connections" (p. 280). Nevertheless, there are differences between human beings and animals. Without prejudice, animals are simpler than humans and animal learning is therefore simpler than human learning.

The comparative simplicity of animal systems was another reason why early researchers studied animal learning. They believed that complex learning processes were based on simple associations and that simple associations were governed by the same laws in all mammals. Consequently, investigators believed insights gained about learning in animals could be extended to human beings. Today, neuroscientists study neurons in the horseshoe crab and physiologists investigate hemoglobin in rabbits for the same reason: They study animal systems in order to gain a better understanding of more complex human systems.

Finally, researchers study animals because they are better able to control animal learning environments. Investigators can identify and control stimulus events and observe animals for long periods of time and they can regulate and monitor food intake and the resulting drive level. It is clear that learning theorists believe the study of animal learning informs the study of human learning. Nevertheless, traditions in animal and human learning research differ, as we will discuss next.

Relation between Animal and Human Learning Research

Although an understanding of animal learning was considered by many to be foundational for an understanding of human learning, the two research traditions developed different experimental paradigms and terminologies. First, their basic emphases were different; animal learning researchers focused on the acquisition of responses, whereas human learning researchers emphasized the retention of responses over time. Even when the issues were similar, different terminologies were used. No reference was made to interference in animal learning; indeed, the term *memory* was not used by classical theorists of animal learning.

Finally, the types of stimuli used in research were different; memory researchers used verbal materials, even though many of these were nonsense syllables. The bond between classical learning theorists and memory researchers was their behaviorist view. Both were interested in the functional relations between stimuli and responses, not in the mental apparatus that mediates between observable events. And both groups of researchers were associationist in orientation, calling themselves stimulus-response psychologists.

Learning and Information Processing

When memory researchers in the 1960s adopted the information-processing approach to cognition, the link with animal learning research was severed and the animal model was replaced by the computer model. Unlike stimulus-response psychologists, information-processing psychologists emphasized the important and fundamental differences between human beings and animals. Chomsky (e.g., 1959) made this point when he demonstrated that the principles of animal learning could not account for our knowledge of language. In addition, many of our cognitive skills, although they may not involve language, are nevertheless symbolic. The classical animal learning theories, however, did not address issues of symbolic processing. Symbolic and linguistic processing is very complex—so complex that Chomsky and his students thought our linguistic competence may well be innate.

The development of the connectionist approach and the interest of symbol-processing theorists in procedural knowledge led to a reemergence of learning as a topic of interest. According to connectionist theories, complex knowledge and performance is the result of elementary associations between simple units. The connections between units are acquired and changed through learning. The interest of symbol-processing theorists in learning stems from their quest to explain the acquisition of procedural knowledge. Such rule-based knowledge must be acquired by the person; rules must be practiced, corrected, and refined. In short, rules must be learned (see Anderson, 1983).

LEARNING

Two Paradigms of Animal Learning

Classical Conditioning. Ivan Pavlov, a physiologist by training, devoted his life to the study of conditioning. Using dogs as subjects in his research, he investigated the nerves supporting the heart and the stomach. He also became interested in digestive physiology and, in the course of this research, found that secretions in the stomach and pancreas, as well as salivation in the mouth, were involved in digestion. Pavlov observed that dogs salivated before they received food, much like you salivate when you smell food. Pavlov and colleagues puzzled for several years over this phenomenon and wondered if they could reproduce it experimentally. What evolved from Pavlov's curiosity was the classical or Pavlovian conditioning paradigm. Consider the case of Pavlov's famous dogs in detail.

When we give meat to a dog, the dog salivates while eating the meat. This is a natural reflex occurring without prior conditioning. Hence, Pavlov chose the term **unconditioned stimulus (US)** for the meat and **unconditioned response (UR)** for the flow of saliva triggered by the meat. The saliva serves to lubricate the food. Incidental events associated with the meat do not at first produce salivation. However, if the event—say, the sounding of a bell—occurs each time the dog is fed, the bell soon comes to elicit salivation. An association is established between the bell and the food; and as a result, the dog salivates when the

bell rings. Pavlov called incidental stimuli like the bell **conditioned stimuli (CS)** and the responses elicited by the Conditioned Stimuli **conditioned responses (CR)**.

The arrangement of CS and US in Pavlov's conditioning trials is shown in Figure 7.1A. The panel shows time lines for the CS and the US, respectively. The CS starts well *before* the US; both are turned off at the same time. Figure 7.1B shows the cumulative amount of saliva on one of the first conditioning trials; it is a response to the US. In Figure 7.1C, however, the CS elicits saliva prior to the presentation of the US. This response is anticipatory; it is therefore a conditioned response. Conditioning may be viewed as an adaptive phenomenon; the CR prepares the organism for the US. Thus, the saliva helps to dissolve the food.

Pavlov found that at least 10 trials are required to produce conditioned salivation in dogs. In

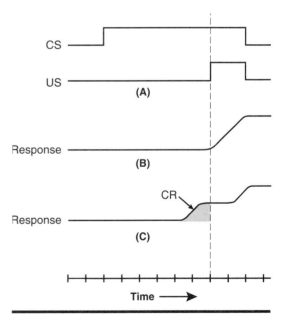

FIGURE 7.1 Classical conditioning in dogs. (*A*) shows temporal pattern of CS and US presentations. (*B*) and (*C*) show cumulative amount of salivation on trials early and late in training, respectively. The shaded region in (*C*) indicates the CR.

other classical conditioning situations, as many as 100 trials are required to produce learning. When it comes to learning events that signal danger, however, one trial is sufficient.

Conditioning in One Trial.   If a hungry rat eats some poison for the first time and gets sick after a few hours, it will learn never to eat the poison again. This assumes that the poison has a characteristic taste, say, it is sweet. Such conditioned taste aversion has also been studied in the laboratory. Rats are usually fed with flavored water and then injected with a harmless drug like lithium chloride that makes them feel sick. In this situation, the flavored water is the CS and the drug represents the US. As a result of pairing the flavored water and the subsequent sickness, the rats learn to avoid the water. Interestingly, unlike in Figure 7.1, the US need not immediately follow the receipt of the CS. Acquired taste aversion is adaptive in some situations and maladaptive in others. It helps organisms to avoid toxins that are frequently found in the environment. On the other hand, taste aversion is maladaptive in cancer patients who become nauseous as a result of chemotherapy and develop aversions to harmless foods eaten prior to therapy sessions. In some cases, food aversions are so general that patients have no appetite for any type of food and suffer serious weight loss (Bernstein & Webster, 1980). In order to ameliorate this problem, patients are instructed not to eat prior to chemotherapy.

Constraints of Conditioning.   Not all events lend themselves to become conditioned stimuli. For example, taste aversion learning depends on the taste of the food; other stimuli will not do. Suppose a rat is given normal water and the imminence of sickness is signaled by a loud noise. This arrangement is called the *noisy-water condition.* When the noisy water is presented again, the rats drink it although it had previously been associated with sickness (see Bolles, 1979). The rat learns a wide range of associations, but not that noise signals subsequent sickness. The point of the noisy-water demonstration is that not everything is learnable by every organism; what an or-

ganism can learn is constrained by the disposition of that organism. Thus, the laws of learning are not as general as theorists like Thorndike believed.

Instrumental Conditioning.   Suppose you want to train your dog to lift her front paw. How would you do this? You could move the dog's front paw, but then how would you get the dog to do it herself? Fortunately, teaching a dog is not as difficult as it sounds. Dogs are very playful and in the course of her play your dog will lift her upper body quite naturally. If you give her a little piece of hamburger when she stands up, she is likely to do so again. After she continues standing up for you, you should change the criterion by rewarding her only after she lifts a paw. Your dog will learn this trick quickly. Lifting the paw is the instrumental response that brings about the reinforcing stimulus—the piece of hamburger. Instrumental responses become more frequent when they repeatedly produce a reinforcement. This observation led Thorndike to formulate the **Law of Effect:** The probability of a response increases if it is repeatedly followed by reinforcement.

Psychologists have devised many situations for instrumental learning; the standard is the Skinner box in which hungry rats press a bar or hungry pigeons peck a key for reinforcement. There are also mazes, shuttle-boxes, discrimination chambers, and other types of equipment. In addition to diverse experimental apparatus, there are different types of reinforcers, positive as well as negative. In all cases, however, the reinforcement (the US) is contingent on the organism's behavior. In each case, the experimenter motivates the animal (for example, by restricting access to food) and then shapes the animal's response through successive approximations, as we illustrated with the dog. Initially during shaping, the animal is reinforced for a wide range of behaviors, including the target response. As the target response becomes more frequent, only the behaviors similar to the target response are reinforced. If necessary, organisms learn not to make a response or to suppress an ongoing activity, as in the CER paradigm (see next section).

Finally, only the target response itself is reinforced. Once again, however, you should note that there are constraints. Clearly, not every response can be learned by every organism. Bar pressing is relatively easy for rats and dogs, for example, but not for cats. Pulling on a string, however, is easy for cats but not for rats and dogs.

Next, we will discuss a paradigm that combines components of both classical conditioning and instrumental learning: the CER paradigm. (CER is an acronym for Conditioned Emotional Responses.) In the CER paradigm, the subject learns to be fearful and the reinforcing is the removal of fear.

Conditioned Emotional Response Learning. CER training involves two stages of training. First, the animals, usually rats, are trained to press a bar in a Skinner box in order to receive food reward. After the rats have learned to press the bar continuously, the classical conditioning stage is introduced. The CS is usually a three-minute tone and the US is a 0.5-second electrical shock delivered through a grid. When the rat is shocked, it immediately stops pressing the bar. During the first few trials, the rats still continue to press during the first 2.5 minutes the CS is presented. However, after a few additional trials of CS-US pairing, the number of bar presses decreases as the CS is turned on. The CS has acquired some of the response-suppressing properties of the shock; the rat is afraid of the tone. When the tone is turned off, the bar pressing resumes. The performance measure in the CER situation is the suppression ratio, which is defined as the ratio of the number of responses during the CS to the total number of responses. The latter includes the responses during the CS and during the time period immediately preceding it.

INTERIM SUMMARY

In classical conditioning, an initially neutral stimulus, the conditioned stimulus (CS), and the un-

conditioned stimulus (US) are paired independently of what the organism does. As a result of these CS-US pairings, the organism learns to respond to the CS by making a conditioned response (CR). The acquisition of the CR usually takes several trials, except in taste aversion training where one trial suffices. In instrumental conditioning, reinforcement is contingent on the organism's response; the organism's response produces the reinforcement. In the CER paradigm, subjects acquire fear as a result of pairing a CS with an electric shock. The fear suppresses an instrumental response (for example, bar presses) previously acquired.

Though the contingency of stimuli and learned responses are different in classical and instrumental conditioning, the course of learning is basically the same. The time course of learning and some other basic aspects of learning are described next.

Basic Learning Phenomena

Acquisition and Extinction. Usually conditioning, whether classical or instrumental, begins with strengthening the response through repeated reinforcements. This phase is known as the **acquisition** phase; the probability and the amplitude of the response increase. In the **extinction** phase, no reinforcement is given when the organism makes a response and the probability of the response diminishes. In Pavlov's experiment, for example, after the acquisition phase, the experimenter would present the CS (bell) without feeding the dog. Initially, the CS would still elicit the CR, but after several trials it no longer would. Figure 7.2A shows response patterns in acquisition and extinction phases of a typical learning experiment. If a rest period intervenes between two phases of extinction training, during which the animal is removed from the experimental apparatus, the CR is made again, an apparent case of **spontaneous recovery**. As the extinction schedule continues, the CR continues to diminish further, as shown on the right of Figure 7.2A.

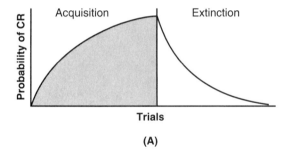

(A)

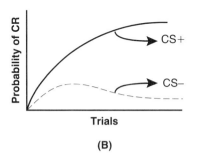

(B)

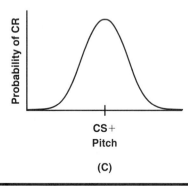

CS+
Pitch

(C)

FIGURE 7.2 Basic phenomena in associative learning. (*A*) shows aquisition and extinction of conditioned responses. (*B*) reflects responding to a reinforced CS+ and an unreinforced CS– in a discrimination schedule. (*C*) exhibits a stimulus generalization gradient. Subjects are trained to respond to a CS+, say a 400 Hz tone. Testing with new higher and lower pitch tones follows. The probability of conditioned responses is proportional to the similarity of the test and training stimuli.

Discrimination Learning and Stimulus Control. A discriminative training schedule involves the presentation of two distinct CSs to the organism during acquisition: the CS+, which is reinforced, and the CS–, which is not. Using Pavlov's experiment once more, assume that the dog hears an 800 Hz tone followed by food and a 1,000 Hz tone not followed by food, as illustrated in Table 7.1. In this case, the dog will come to make the CR to the 800 Hz tone but not to the 1,000 Hz tone. This pattern of responses is shown in Figure 7.2B. There is the usual increase in response probability to the CS+. The response pattern to the CS– is unexpected in that there is an initial increase in response.

Why would the dog respond initially to the nonreinforced CS–? The reason is that the dog at first confuses the two stimuli. The tendency to respond to similar stimuli is referred to as **stimulus generalization.** The CS+ and CS– are both auditory stimuli and the capacity of the CS+ to elicit the CR extends to some degree to the CS–, at least during the early phases of discrimination training. At first, the dog confuses the reinforced and the nonreinforced tones; later

TABLE 7.1 Schedule of Discrimination Training

Trial	Types of CS	Tone (cps)	Presence/ Absence of US
1	CS+	800	yes
2	CS–	1,000	no
3	CS–	1,000	no
4	CS+	800	yes
5	CS+	800	yes
6	CS+	800	yes
7	CS–	1,000	no
8	CS–	1,000	no
9	CS–	1,000	no
10	CS+	800	yes
11	CS+	800	yes
12	CS–	1,000	no
.	.	.	.
.	.	.	.
.	.	.	.

the dog discriminates between them. According to Pavlov, the CS+ acquires excitatory strength, which generalizes to the CS–. After additional exposures to both the CS+ and CS–, the dog's response to the CS– diminishes. Pavlov attributed this response decline to inhibition acquired by the CS–.

Stimulus generalization is illustrated in Figure 7.2C. The abscissa indicates the stimulus dimension—for example, the pitch of tones. The CS+ is located at the center. Similarity decreases with increasing distance from the CS+. The ordinate indicates response probability. The gradient in Figure 7.2C reflects the decrease in response with a decrease in stimulus similarity.

Schedules of discrimination learning are used in other learning paradigms as well. In instrumental learning, a CS+ and a CS– are presented to the subject and a response is reinforced when made in the presence of the CS+, but not in the presence of the CS–. In concept learning, the subject learns that a certain set of stimuli are subsumed by one concept, whereas other stimuli belong to another concept. For example, all square objects represent concept A, whereas all red objects represent category B (see Chapter 14). Similarly, in everyday life we continuously learn to discriminate between situations that call for different responses.

Issues in Learning Theories

What Causes Learning? According to influential learning theories by Estes (1950), Guthrie (1935), Hebb (1949), Pavlov (1927), and others, the association of the CS with the US is sufficient to produce learning. When the two stimuli and the CR occur at the same time, the CR is strengthened. The Hebb rule is representative of such **contiguity** theories of learning (from the *Latin contiguus* meaning *near in time or sequence*). According to the Hebb rule, the association between two neurons is strengthened when both of them are activated at the same time; the CS triggers one neuron as the US triggers another neuron. Contiguity, between CS and

US, however, is not sufficient for learning. Rather, the CS should be informative, as the next study illustrates.

Researchers compared the rate of learning under two training schedules: the free-US condition and the contingent condition.

— In the free-US condition, CS and US were paired for a certain number of trials—for example, 100. In addition, there were 100 free-US trials on which only the US was presented without being signaled by the CS.
— In the contingent condition, CS and US were paired 100 times. There were no trials on which the US occurred without the CS.

According to the contiguity theory, the rate of learning should be equal in both groups because the number of CS-US pairings was equal. However, this was not the case; the rate of learning was better in the contingent condition. Only in this condition was the CS a reliable predictor of the US. If the CS predicts the occurrence of the US reliably, it is informative and it has a high signal value. On the other hand, if the CS predicts the US only half of the time, as it does in the free-US group, it is not as valuable a signal.

The poor rate of learning in the free-US group lent support to the cue value theory formulated by Rescorla and Wagner (1972): The effectiveness of a CS depends on its value as a signal or predictor. In the free-US condition, the CS did not predict the US as well as in the contingent condition, because the US was frequently presented without warning. Rescorla and Wagner (1972) quantified the change in strength the CS, ΔV, in Expression 7.2 (see expression 6.7).

(7.2) $\Delta V = lr \times (\text{lambda} - V)$

The symbol *lambda* represents the greatest association strength the CS can acquire theoretically, its asymptote. *V* is the strength of the CS at the beginning of the current trial. The symbol *lr* is the learning rate.

Despite its apparent simplicity, expression 7.2 accounts for a wide range of conditioning phenomena, including the following:

— The greatest increases in learning occur during initial learning trials when the CS and US are least expected. It is during the initial trials that V_n is far lower than lambda. Inspect the typical learning curve plotted in Figure 7.2A: The increase in CS strength is greater early in the first block of acquisition trials than in subsequent trial blocks.

— The signal value, V, applies to individual CSs as well as to compound CSs, say a light and a tone presented together. The strength of the compound CS is given by the compound strength rule: $V_{ab} = V_a + V_b$. If an experimenter initially trains the animal on each stimulus separately and then combines them, their individual strengths are added; their joint presentation suggests the occurrence of the US even more strongly.

— Kamin's Blocking Effect is readily explained by the Rescorla-Wagner rule. The effect occurs in compound conditioning situations where two stimuli, say a tone and a light, are introduced successively. Blocking occurs when the light stimulus is introduced *after* the tone has been has been trained to full effectiveness. The light stimulus gains no additional associative strength; it is being blocked by the tone. Blocking of the light by the tone follows from the CER situation where a second CS, added after extensive training with the first CS, did not acquire any predictive strength of its own.

Learning theorists have shown that expression 7.2 is mathematically equivalent to the delta learning rule used in neural network models (see Chapter 6). This is a powerful illustration of converging evidence from different research domains. However, even a powerful theoretical model like the Rescorla-Wagner theory is not without problems. For example, organisms readily learn configural aspects of stimuli as in the XOR-problem (see Chapter 6), but such learning is difficult to handle in terms of expression 7.2 (see also DeVito & Fowler, 1986; Sutton & Barto, 1981).

Which Events Are Reinforcing?   According to the Law of Effect, any event that increases the likelihood of a response is a reinforcer. In other words, any event the organism is willing to work for is a reinforcer. Learning theorists have sought to identify such events. The classic view has been that there are only a few specific stimuli, such as food and drink, for which animals are willing to work. These were called primary reinforcers. However, research has shown that animals will acquire an instrumental response just to be able to perform a consummatory response like eating and drinking. Thus, certain responses may serve as reinforcers for other responses.

Premack formulated the **probability-difference** principle that "for any pair of responses, the more probable one will reinforce the less probable one" (Premack, 1965, p. 132). In one of his experiments, Premack showed that children exhibited an activity that was initially infrequent when they were rewarded for it by being allowed to engage in their favorite activity. First, Premack established the baseline rate of the children's behavior. The children were observed in a room that contained a candy dispenser and a pinball machine. Some children were players; they tended to play more on the machines than to eat candy. Other children were eaters, they spent more time eating candy than playing.

The second phase of Premack's study was the reinforcement phase; here, the children's activities were restricted in two ways. In the eat-if-play condition, the children received candy only if they played. In this condition, the eaters increased their amount of playing; they played more in order to be able to eat. Players, however, who did not care to eat anyhow, did not increase their amount of playing. The second condition was the play-if-eat condition; here, the children were allowed to play only if they ate some candy. In this case, the players increased eating, but the eaters did not. Thus, under each condition, the activity that initially was more likely served as reinforcer for the activity that was initially less likely. This reflects the probability-difference principle that responses serve as reinforcers and that the reinforcement value of a response is relative; under different conditions and for different individuals, different activities will serve as reinforcers.

Staddon and Ettinger (1989) pointed out that the probability-difference principle cannot be the whole story, because there are certain low-probability responses that do serve as reinforcers. According to Staddon, activities have a certain baseline rate of occurrence **equilibrium** that is frequently disturbed. Restoring an activity to its optimal baseline is a reinforcing event.

Applications of Associative Learning

The shaping method of increasing the occurrence of responses is known as **behavior modification** when it is used with human patients in the context of clinical applications. Behavior modification has been used to improve dental flossing in children, to reduce the number of cigarettes people smoke, and so on. Other associative techniques have been used in weight-loss programs, in the treatment of enuresis (bed wetting), and in educational settings. Sometimes these methods are successful, but not always. One of the limitations is that people quickly learn to discriminate between the settings where the reinforcement schedule is valid (for example, a weight-loss clinic) and all those settings where it is not (including cafeterias and restaurants). Therefore, much depends on cognitive factors.

Shaping methods are generally more successful with animals, whether they are pets at home or inhabitants of zoos or aquariums. One interesting application involves training monkeys to harvest coconuts in Malaysia. The coconut crop in Malaysia represents more than half of the economic income of rural Malaysian regions. Years ago, people had to climb trees to harvest the crop, but the labor was hard and slow. Today, macaque monkeys are trained to pick coconuts from 100-foot palm trees. The macaques are fast and seemingly tireless; after all, palm trees are their natural habitat. Monkeys can learn the skill of picking in several days. On the first day, the trainer holds the monkey on a short leash and demonstrates with his own hands how to twist off a coconut. Then he places the monkey's hands on the coconut showing him that turning the coconut will remove it from the tree. Finally, he opens a coconut and feeds the monkey as a reward. On the second day, the trainer coaxes the monkey to climb a small palm tree and twist off coconuts. On successive days, they attempt larger trees. At the end of each training session, the monkey is rewarded with a coconut. After about three weeks, the monkey has become an expert and is capable of working up to six hours per day harvesting 500 coconuts (Pfeffer, 1989).

Learning in Natural Environments

A dog does not require a reinforcement schedule to learn its way around the neighborhood. A rat does not need an experimental procedure to avoid poisons, nor does the humpback whale to find its mate. A wide range of behaviors are learned and shaped through the organism's exposure to his natural habitat. Consider how the white-crowned sparrow learns to sing (Keele, 1973; Marler, 1970). There are different dialects of the song of these birds in different regions. These dialects are easily learned by the white-crown males. The adult song emerges about eight months after a bird has hatched. The bird will not learn the dialect properly, however, if it has not been exposed to the dialect during a critical period about one month after hatching. It is during this period that the white-crown picks up the unique features of the local dialect, which constitutes a kind of template. If the white-crown is not exposed to the template in this critical period, later on it will not sing the local dialect but the generic white-crown song. The case of song learning in the white-crown is one of many to illustrate the importance of learning by imitation and of a critical period necessary for learning.

Nonassociative Learning

Habituation. Whenever you get used to an environment, you habituate to it. Consider a couple of examples:

- When traveling long distances, drivers tend to "tune out," which can lead to fatigue. When they encounter anything unusual (such as the scene of an accident), however, they notice it.
- A two-month old infant will look intently at a new object in its environment, such as a mobile suspended over the crib. As the hours pass by, the mobile evokes less and less attention. The infant has gotten used to it.

Habituation has been observed in many different species—from *Aplysia* to human beings—and for a wide range of responses—from the evoked potential response to the startle response. The startle response in rats has been well investigated. It is elicited by exposing the rat to moderately loud tones (60 dB). Using this technique, Marlin and Miller (1981) observed two groups of rats over two phases interrupted by a one-hour break. The experimental group received habituation training during both phases. During the first phase, the control group was placed in the experimental chamber but no sounds were presented. In the second phase, both groups received habituation training. Figure 7.3 shows the results of this experiment. The experimental group shows a continued habituation during the first phase; after the break, the startle response is stronger than before—it dishabituates—but then it decreases rapidly once again. Hearing no noise during the first phase, the control group exhibits a much lower level of activity than the experimental group. After the break when the sound started for them, the control subjects became as active as the experimental animals had been when they first heard the sound. Then the control subjects habituated as well.

Sensitization. **Sensitization** refers to increases in responsiveness as a result of repeated application of the eliciting stimulus. Sensitization is of-

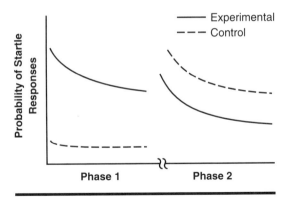

FIGURE 7.3   Habituation of rats' startle responses to a loud tone. The experimental group received two phases of habituation training interrupted by a break of one hour. The control group was placed in the experimental chamber during phase 1 without any tone presentations. During phase 2, the control group was exposed to the tone for the first time (Marlin & Miller, 1981).

ten observed in the same context as habituation. Suppose you present a 90 dB tone to rats rather than the moderate 60 dB tone. When the tones are this loud, the magnitude of the startle response increases. The animal gets more jumpy with additional presentations.

Neuroscientists have identified some of the neural circuits involved in habituation and sensitization in *Aplysia*, the California sea hare (Chapter 2). They found that habituation was associated with a reduced emission of neurotransmitters, whereas sensitization was correlated with an increase in neurotransmitter activity (Castellucci & Kandel, 1976).

Priming.   When a stimulus—for example, a word, a line drawing, or a photograph—is presented to people several times, the time to recognize the stimulus decreases with each repetition. Also, recognition is improved when the person is given a degraded copy of the stimulus, such as a fragment of the word or line drawing. Usually the person is not aware of this facilitation, referred to as **implicit memory.** Remarkably, amnesic patients whose explicit memory is impaired exhibit evidence of implicit memory (Tulving & Schacter, 1990; see Chapter 9).

INTERIM SUMMARY

Animals form associations between environmental events. In classical conditioning, initially neutral events come to predict events that are rewarding or threatening to the organism. In instrumental conditioning, an association is formed between a response and a reinforcement.

Habituation, priming, and sensitization involve the repeated presentation of a particular stimulus. When the intensity of the repeated stimulus is relatively moderate, the response diminishes over time, producing habituation. Priming is observed when the recognition of a stimulus is facilitated with repeated presentation. When the stimulus has a relatively high intensity, its repeated presentation produces an increase in response magnitude.

There can be no learning without memory. Pavlov's dog, Skinner's pigeon, and Marler's sparrow must remember what they learn. Animal learning researchers such as Pavlov and Thorndike knew that memory was important but, curiously, they did not examine it. Their interest lay in learning. The learning researcher emphasizes performance as a function of the number of reinforcements. By contrast, the memory researcher emphasizes performance as a function of time. The second part of this chapter treats memory, covering the period from Ebbinghaus's (1885) seminal work to early information-processing models (Atkinson & Shiffrin, 1968), to the level-of-processing framework.

MEMORY

Hermann Ebbinghaus

Hermann Ebbinghaus, a contemporary of Wilheim Wundt and Ivan Pavlov, began his training as a philosopher interested in mental processes. He was keenly interested in measuring mental events and was inspired by the psy-chophysical methods introduced in the 1860s (see Chapter 3). After much research, Ebbinghaus (1885) published *Über das Gedächtnis (On Memory)*, a volume describing his pioneering work on memory. Ebbinghaus had the idea to investigate memory experimentally, and he formulated the important questions that were to guide memory research for the next century. It was Ebbinghaus who asked under what conditions a memory trace is acquired, how long a memory trace lasts, and what causes forgetting. He was aware that memories and meanings are confounded; something that is meaningful is remembered better. Seeking to study the pure memory trace without the contribution of meaning, Ebbinghaus invented the nonsense syllable as his stimulus material. Here are some examples of nonsense syllables: *qif, bpd, ngy, xcl, hfm, ckj, fon, cum, qap, hos, leq, kof,* and *mec.* Ebbinghaus came up with over 2,000 of these syllables, which is not an easy feat.

For his research, Ebbinghaus needed extremely motivated subjects who would be available at specific retention intervals. The subjects had to be willing to learn these monotonous lists as well as possible. I am sure you would not want to learn a lot of nonsense syllables. Well, Ebbinghaus did not have much luck with subjects either; there were no departmental subject pools in his day, and so he decided to run his research with only one subject—himself.

Ebbinghaus's experiments consisted of two phases: original learning and relearning. For original learning, he formed lists of syllables ranging from 7 to 36 and tried to memorize them. He recorded the number of trials and the amount of time necessary for one perfect recitation. He found that the amount of time required to learn one syllable increased with the length of the list. To learn one syllable from a 7-item list required 0.4 second. To learn one syllable from the 36-item list required 22 seconds!

The Forgetting Curve. Ebbinghaus assessed his memory by using the **savings method.** He learned sets of lists in an original learning phase and then relearned the same lists after varying retention intervals. He compared the study time required for original learning and relearning of each list. Assume he conducted an experiment involving two retention intervals: half an hour and 48 hours with different lists, A and B, for each interval. Further assume that he required 4 seconds to learn list A on the first trial and that he took 2 seconds to relearn it after a 30-minute rest. List B also took 4 seconds to learn at first; relearning B after a 48-hour interval took 3 seconds. Using equation (7.3), Ebbinghaus calculated the amount of savings for each interval.

$$\textbf{(7.3)}\quad \text{Savings} = \frac{\begin{array}{c}\text{Time for original learning}\\ -\text{ Time for relearning}\end{array}}{\text{Time for original learning}}$$

Accordingly, the savings after 30 minutes were 50%; savings after 48 hours were 25%. The savings method provided a measure of the durability of the memory traces he had learned originally. The result was Ebbinghaus's famous forgetting curve, shown in Figure 7.4.

The savings method continued to be popular for years after Ebbinghaus introduced it. A good illustration of its use is Burtt's research with memory for stanzas from the classical Greek described in Box 7.1.

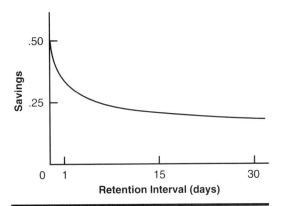

FIGURE 7.4 Ebbinghaus's (1885) forgetting curve. Note that the ordinate indicates amount of savings observed by Ebbinghaus when he used his savings method. Forgetting is most rapid immediately after learning.

Box 7.1 _____

It Is All Greek to Me!

A DRAMATIC CASE OF SAVINGS OBSERVED BY BURTT

Burtt (1941) read daily a passage from Sophocles *Oedipus Tyrannus* in the original Greek to a boy beginning shortly after his first birthday. Each section consisted of approximately 240 syllables of verse. Each of 12 selections was repeated about 90 times over a span of three years. The boy relearned some of the old passages when he was 8, 14, and 18 years old, respectively. He also was given new control passages to recite. Burtt found that at ages 8 and 14, the boy required significantly fewer trials to learn selections that had been read to him years ago than the new selections. At age 18, the advantage of prior learning was gone; either the trace of the earlier learning was no longer accessible or, after so much learning, the student had simply become proficient at reciting Sophocles that it made no difference whether the selection was new or old. The interesting point is that at ages 8 and 14, savings was observed for what were initially nonsense materials.

Stimulus-Response Learning in Memory Research. Ebbinghaus and his followers, including Hull, Irwin, McGeoch, Martin, Osgood, Postman, and Underwood, adhered to the same associationist tradition as the animal learning theorists. McGeoch (1942) described stimulus-response associations as follows: "Two or more psychological events [are] associated when, as a function of prior experience, one elicits or stands for the other" (p. 25). Not surprisingly, the favored learning paradigm of this era was the *paired-associate* method. The person is presented with a stimulus term, A, and a response term, B, and is asked to respond with B when A is presented again. Stimulus materials were drawn from a wide variety of sources. The nonsense syllables continued to be popular. Foreign-language words are frequently learned by paired-associate learning. Table 7.2 shows a list of English and French words a student of beginning French will learn.

TABLE 7.2 Learning Foreign Words through Paired Associates

English	French
room	la chambre
taxi	le taxi
traveler	le voyageur
to come	venir
bank	la banque
to discuss	discuter

Much as in animal learning, human memory research emphasized the functional relations governing retention, not mental structures and processes. This reflected the behaviorist tradition common in several fields, including psychology, linguistics, and sociology. Researchers examined the relation between time and retention, and they graphed forgetting curves for all kinds of materials. As we will discuss in a moment, their main interest was the cause of forgetting. To some extent, they also studied acquisition and, like the animal learning theorists, they believed that the strength of the S-R connection grew gradually as a function of the number of pairings. Researchers found that the largest increases in response occur early in training with smaller increments later on, as is the case in many animal learning situations (see expression 7.2).

The major concern of the verbal learning researchers was forgetting. What was the course of forgetting over time? Why does it occur? How can forgetting be overcome if at all?

Causes of Forgetting: Disuse versus Interference

By the turn of the century, every psychologist was familiar with Ebbinghaus's forgetting curve. For very practical reasons, psychologists sought to determine the causes of forgetting. There were two major accounts of forgetting—one was the Law of Disuse and the other the interference theory. Thorndike (1911) was the learning theorist who developed the operant conditioning procedure known as *Thorndikian learning*. He believed that practice or use strengthens an association, whereas disuse weakens the association. According to this law, we forget information because we do not use it over time. The memory trace becomes automatically weaker; it decays with time.

This view was challenged by psychologists who noted that forgetting results from the activities the person engages in during the intervening interval. McGeoch (1942) made the case most strongly when he wrote: "Forgetting could not be accounted for by disuse, if disuse means only passage of time, for time, in and of itself, is not a determining condition of events in nature. It is a conceptual framework in which activities go their ways and in terms of which events are plotted. In time, iron may rust and men grow old, but the rusting and the aging are understood in terms of the chemical and other events which occur in time, not in terms of time itself" (p. 455).

McGeoch distinguished two different types of interference: retroactive and proactive interference. Retroactive interference refers to the inhibiting effects of later learning on earlier learning, whereas proactive interference refers to the competition of earlier learning with later learning.

Retroactive Interference. *Retroactive interference* means that new information blocks out some prior information. Say you wanted to mail a letter and you receive a phone call telling you that you just won a million dollars in the lottery. You forget mailing the letter. The news that you struck it rich retroactively interfered with mailing the letter.

Memory researchers introduced the A-B, A-C paradigm to study retroactive interference. In original learning, experimental subjects receive paired-associate training trials on a list of stimulus items denoted A, paired with a list of responses denoted B. Then, after an interval, experimental subjects receive training with the original list of stimuli paired with a new list of responses, denoted C, whereas control subjects rest.

Interference is reflected by the result on the subsequent A-B test list. Recall is poorer for the experimental group than the control group.

Experimental Group: A-B, A-C, A-B
Control Group: A-B, Rest, A-B

Table 7.3 contains sample lists of paired-associates for the experimental and control groups of the A-B, A-C design used to study retroactive interference. Note that the experimental group sees the same stimulus terms in the A-B and A-C phases of training. What differs is the response term. Thus, the first stimulus term, *xej*, must be memorized together with *fon* during original learning and then with *sec* during interpolated learning. In testing, *fon* is the correct response. In the control group, *xej-fon* is the only combination learned and tested. This group rests while the experimental group must learn the A-C list in their interpolated learning phase. You will not be surprised to learn that the control group performed better on the final A-B test than the experimental group. The deficit of the experimental group versus the control group is defined as **retroactive interference.**

Researchers identified the amount of learning during the interpolated learning phase as a major cause of forgetting. According to the unlearning hypothesis, the original A-B associations were extinguished during interpolated learning. When the subject responded with *fon* to *xej* in interpolated learning, the *xej-fon* association was not reinforced (see Table 7.3). Supporting this extinction view, researchers found that intrusion errors like *fon* from the original A-B list diminished as the number of interpolated learning trials increased (Melton & Irwin, 1940).

The Melton and Irwin (1940) study used the typical paired-associate procedure in which a subject is given the opportunity to make only one response—either *fon* or *sec*. It should not be surprising that learners come to respond with *sec* during interpolated learning. Does this mean, however, the *fon* response has been forgotten? If given a chance, the subject might produce it as well. Barnes and Underwood (1959) modified the paired-associate procedure by asking subjects to recall both the B terms and the C terms, rather than only the C terms. Using the associations in Table 7.3 as an illustration, the subject was given *xej* as a stimulus and was asked to respond with *fon* and *sec* if she could. Figure 7.5 shows that recall of the B terms decreased, whereas recall of the C terms increased as a function of interpolated learning. The Barnes and Underwood (1959) study therefore strengthened the notion that items acquired in original learning are unlearned during interpolated learning. At the same time, these data demonstrate the contribution of retroactive interference to forgetting.

TABLE 7.3   A-B, A-C Design for the Study of Retroactive Interference

Experimental Group		
Original Learning A-B List	*Interpolated Learning* A-C List	*Test* A-B List
xej-fon	xej-sec	xej-fon
tel-cum	tel-qih	tel-cum
cij-dul	cij-pac	cij-dul
hod-bof	hod-jek	hod-bof
bip-qes	bip-loj	bip-qes

Control Group		
Original Learning A-B List	*Rest* Rest	*Test* A-B List
xej-fon		xej-fon
tel-cum		tel-cum
cij-dul		cij-dul
hod-bof		hod-bof
bip-qes		bip-qes

Proactive Interference. **Proactive interference** refers to the interfering effects of prior learning on later learning. It is as if the prior learning absorbs some of the capacity available for later learning. Assume you are studying Italian and French vocabulary lists; first you study the Italian words, then the French words. Proactive interference means that learning the

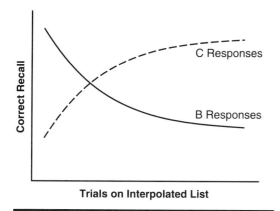

FIGURE 7.5 Retroactive interference. Original B responses are unlearned. C responses increase as subjects receive added trials on the interpolated list.

Italian words first may slow down the rate of learning the French words. Thus, remembering an association may be inhibited by *prior* associations. In one study of proactive interference by Greenberg and Underwood (see Underwood, 1983) subjects learned four lists of 10 adjective pairs on four successive days. Two days later, they had to recall each list. Underwood found that recall decreased substantially with the number of prior lists. This is evidence of proactive interference.

Limits of Interference Theory. In 1961, a memory theorist wrote that "interference theory occupies an unchallenged position as the major significant analysis of forgetting" (Postman, 1961, p. 152). The theory was indeed able to account for a broad array of experimental results, but limits of interference theory were ultimately discovered. For example, researchers found that the occurrence of interference depends on the type of stimulus material. When meaningful passages are used rather than nonsense syllables and lists of words, no interference effects are found. Furthermore, according to interference theory, there have to be multiple learning phases of prior, original, and interpolated learning to produce interference. Yet forgetting occurs even when sub-

jects have to learn single lists or even only single items. In these cases, one must identify sources of interference outside the laboratory. Even Underwood, who devoted his entire career to advancing interference theory, concluded that there must be causes of forgetting other than interference. In Chapter 9, we shall learn that forgetting also results from retrieval failure, which is the failure to access the correct memory trace.

Associationism: Review and Outlook

Our discussion of animal learning noted the changing face of associationism. We said that not all events become associated and not all responses can be learned. Furthermore, the mere contiguity of events is not sufficient for an association. The signal must be significant. Similarly, association theory is undergoing change in the field of human learning. McGeoch's (1942) basic view still stands that two events are associated when, as a function of prior experience, one comes to elicit the other. What has changed is a definition of the events that participate in an association, the interpretation of the concept *association* itself, and the view of prior experience. For McGeoch and his contemporaries, prior experience meant a long sequence of trials during which events were paired. However, as we saw, associations can be learned in as little as one trial in animal learning and in human learning as well.

Early theorists conceived of events as very simple stimuli and responses—for example, the sound of a bell or a nonsense syllable. During the 1960s, events came to be seen as complex configurations of component stimuli. It was also recognized that events are not isolated but are part of a context that includes other items on the list and the experimental environment. Indeed, stimuli should be considered as compounds of more elemental dimensions. A typical nonsense syllable like *xcl* has visual, phonetic, semantic, and other features. The visual features of *xcl* refer simply to the pattern of printed lines formed by *x, c,* and *l.* Because of its phonetic features, *xcl* can be pronounced by producing a sound similar to *excl.*

This sound may remind you of the word *excel*, thus illustrating a semantic feature of *xcl*. The syllable includes serial order information—namely, *x* in position 1, *c* in position 2, and *l* in position 3.

Traditionally, associations were simply regarded as a link between two events without further specification of the link. However, research by linguists, computer scientists, and cognitive psychologists with meaningful stimuli, including words and sentences, led to a specification of different types of links, including labeled associations. Semantic memory researchers postulated that concepts are associated with other concepts via subset relations. For example, in *A canary is a bird*, the concepts CANARY and BIRD are linked via a relation known as an *isa* relation (see Chapter 5).

The early learning and memory theorists investigated the effects of number of trials on learning and the effects of retention intervals on forgetting. They emphasized functional relations between overt factors rather than mental structures, processes, and mechanisms underlying performance. Today, associationism is embedded within theories that emphasize mental structures and processes rather than functional relations.

With all these changes, associationism remains alive. It survives in the symbol-processing approach (see Chapter 5) and in the connectionist approach (see Chapter 6). The semantic representations of concepts and their relations sketched above are part of many cognitive theories. Connectionist theories are based on connections—associations—between very simple processing elements. It is the pattern of many such associations that constitutes knowledge, according to the connectionist approach. The retrieval models of memory that emerged in the 1980s are associationist as well (see Chapter 9).

Constructive Memory

The typical S-R learning experiment did not provide much opportunity to observe the constructive and active participation of the learner. However, there was another research tradition

founded by the English psychologist, Sir Frederic Bartlett, who published his influential book *Remembering* in 1932. His approach differed in several respects from the associationist school. He used different types of stimulus materials, had a different view of the learner, and speculated about mental structures of the learner.

Sir Frederic Bartlett.   Unlike Ebbinghaus and his students who sought to investigate so-called pure memory (uncontaminated by meaningful materials), Bartlett devoted his energies precisely to people's memory of meaningful materials. Rather than having his subjects memorize nonsense syllables or even individual words, Bartlett presented real texts to his subjects and asked them to retell the stories they had read. One of the stories was a tale that had originated in the oral tradition of American Indians of the Northwest. It contained references to ghosts unfamiliar to Western readers.

Bartlett's subjects were British college students. They read the story twice in succession and recalled the passage after varying intervals. Bartlett found that his subjects recalled this passage quite well. However, they reproduced the original passage in a more concise and coherent form. They adapted unfamiliar material to what they knew. For example, one person omitted reference to the ghosts and another interpreted *ghosts* as the name of another tribe rather than as ghosts. In short, the subjects reconstructed the information to fit their own schematic view of the world. Bartlett assumed that people have acquired certain knowledge structures, which he called *schemas*. According to Bartlett, a **schema** is a configuration of prototypical knowledge we have of familiar situations (see also Chapters 1 and 5).

The Ebbinghaus and Bartlett traditions, however different, had one concern in common. They were interested in memory over the long term. Accordingly, they studied retention over long intervals, up to 20 years—what we now call long-term memory. In the next section, we will learn that in the 1950s, researchers began to examine memory for information just presented. The research on such short-term memories became part of a new approach to memory—the information-processing approach.

Early Information-Processing Theories and the Two-Store Model of Memory

The *information-processing* approach emerged quite independently of the increasing criticisms of associationism and behaviorism. You may remember from Chapter 1 that the information-processing framework was inspired by several influences, among them research on human factors, on communication during World War II, and the computer metaphor introduced in the 1960s (Miller, Galanter, & Pribram, 1960). Communications researchers were interested in the transmission of signals by radar and telephone operators. The abstract laws governing signal transmission in communication channels were well understood and some of these were extended to human communication (Broadbent, 1958). An important characteristic of communication channels is their capacity limit; only a certain amount of information can be passed in a unit of time (for example, a minute). Miller (1956) was one of the researchers to investigate the limited channel capacity of humans. It was in this context that he advanced the notion of the short-term memory as a limited-capacity buffer.

At about the same time, the influence of the computer metaphor began to be felt in psychology. The computer is a device that accepts input information, transforms it based on stored programs, and produces a symbolic output (see also Chapters 1 and 5). Information processing in humans is quite similar to that of computers, at least at an abstract level. A person registers information, recodes the information in terms of her knowledge, makes decisions, and produces a response as output. As the computer metaphor gained ground among psychologists, rule-based systems and symbol-processing approaches became the focus of study. Interest diminished in associations of elemental units and in the laws of learning.

It was against this background that theories of memory changed substantially. The view surfaced that there are distinct memory traces—indeed, two different memory stores: a *short-term store* and a *long-term store*. The two stores differ in several respects: in the types of codes stored, in the causes of forgetting, in the state of awareness, and in several other ways. Psychologists discovered the distinction William James (1890) had made long ago between primary and secondary memory. **Primary memory** refers to knowledge we are currently aware of, whereas **secondary memory** includes the wealth of information we are not aware of. We will discuss several differences between short-term and long-term memory: differences in capacity and in the rate of forgetting of the two stores, and different contributions to the shape of the free-recall curve. In addition, we will discuss a clinical case frequently cited in support of the two-store memory model.

Capacity. Miller (1956) used the immediate memory span test to assess one's capacity to remember information from one presentation. You are familiar with the digit span test. It was introduced as part of intelligence tests over a century ago. Sets of digits are read to a person (for example, 5 4 3), and the person must repeat the digits. Then the series of digits is increased by one until the person can no longer repeat the series. Thus, the next series might be 8 2 1 4, 3 9 7 2 5, 5 2 8 4 9 3, and so on until the person gives up. Miller found that whatever stimulus materials experimenters used—binary digits, decimal digits, letters of the alphabet, or English words—subjects were able to repeat no more than five to nine items. He concluded that there was a specific limit to immediate memory. He went on to speculate that there is a specific internal structure—namely, immediate memory—that has a certain limited storage capacity. Fortunately, people can circumvent this limit to some extent by **recoding** and **chunking** of information (see Chapter 9). Long-term memory, of course, has no such limit.

Ebbinghaus found that he could remember lists of 40—indeed, 100—nonsense syllables over long periods of time given that he had memorized them well enough.

Rate of Forgetting.   A study, innovative for its time, was performed by Peterson and Peterson (1959). They used retention intervals of less than 30 seconds in order to study the fate of the memory trace very early in the retention interval, much earlier than Ebbinghaus had tested. Peterson and Peterson presented to their subjects nonsense syllables like *wrm, hfz,* and *qns,* and asked them to recall the strings after intervals of 3, 6, 12, 15, and 18 seconds, respectively. Immediately after a letter string was presented, the person was also given a number—for example, 88—and asked to count backwards by threes until the recall signal was given. Thus, the person had to say 85 . . . 82 . . . 79 . . . until the experimenter gave the signal. Peterson and Peterson made the startling discovery that a string of only three letters was lost very rapidly—more rapidly than had been thought. After only 18 seconds, the subjects' correct recall was only about 20%!

Keppel and Underwood (1962) showed that proactive interference contributed to this dramatic loss of information. They analyzed the retention data in the Peterson and Peterson task for each trial separately rather than averaging them across trials. Keppel and Underwood found that on the first trial, there was no forgetting during the 18-second interval. On subsequent trials, as proactive interference built up, there was more forgetting. Their results, averaged across trials, reflected the steep loss of information over 18 seconds that the Petersons had found.

The forgetting results from the short-term memory task were quite different from Ebbinghaus's results. The Peterson and Peterson task used different methods from the familiar memory experiment, but the difference in results was too large to be attributed to details of procedure alone. Theorists concluded, therefore, that the usual memory experiment and the Petersons had in fact studied different memory traces:

Ebbinghaus had investigated the long-term trace and the Petersons had studied a short-term trace. The short-term trace is fragile and subject to rapid decay, unless the person maintains the information through rehearsal. As a result of those rehearsals, the long-term trace is more durable over time. It has a greater memory strength. Therefore, a key difference between long-term store and short-term store was that information in the short-term store decays rapidly unless it is rehearsed. A by-product of the rehearsal is transfer of the information to the long-term store. The more rehearsals accorded an item, the better its long-term retention.

According to early researchers, the nature of the codes was different in the two stores. Because rehearsal involves an acoustic process, it was thought that the short-term trace was acoustic. Indeed, the errors made in short-term memory experiments were due to acoustic confusions: People tended to confuse letters on the basis of their acoustic rather than their visual similarity.

Evidence for Two Stores from the Free-Recall Paradigm.   Results from the free-recall paradigm were also interpreted in terms of the two-store model of memory. In free-recall studies, the person is read a list of words and asked to recall them in any order. For example, the subject might listen to the following list: *roof latch hot shirt clog mare court slot hand dirt.* When asked to recall the list immediately, the subject usually recalls the most recent and the very first items best. This recall pattern is captured in the characteristic U-shaped serial position effect shown in Figure 7.6.

The abscissa in Figure 7.6 expresses the serial position of the words in the list. The ordinate indicates the probability of recall. Recall is best for early and late items, known as primacy and recency effects, respectively. According to an influential theory (Glanzer & Cunitz, 1966), the subjects maintained the most recent items through rehearsal in a short-term store. When hearing the recall prompt, a subject would simply "dump" the content of this rehearsal buffer. Recall of the first items of a list was good because they had been

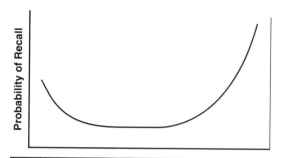

FIGURE 7.6 Recall level as a function of serial position of items in list in free recall.

transferred more successfully to long-term memory. The first few items formed a short list, affording a good opportunity to rehearse each word thoroughly. Recall of the intermediate items was relatively low because they benefited neither from the rehearsals given the first items nor from being in short-term memory.

Glanzer and Cunitz wanted to evaluate the two-store model experimentally, so they developed a critical test. They had two groups of subjects who learned a list of words in the free-recall paradigm. One group was given the recall prompt immediately after learning the list, whereas the other group received the prompt after a delay of 30 seconds. During the delay, these subjects were given some arithmetic problems in order to pre-

vent rehearsal. The prediction of the two-store hypothesis is that the delay should diminish recall of only the most recent items—those items that are in the short-term store—but it should have no effect on the early and intermediate items that had already been transferred to the long-term store. The view that memory is unitary would predict an equal drop in performance for all the serial positions. The two predictions are shown graphically in Figure 7.7.

Glanzer and Cunitz found the pattern in Figure 7.7A, thus supporting the two-store hypothesis. The Glanzer and Cunitz interpretation rests on the transfer notion: For information to be remembered, it has to be transferred from the short-term to the long-term store. The transfer notion is supported as well by specific memory deficits in amnesic patients, as described in the next section.

Clinical Perspectives.   Milner (1966) described a patient HM, an epileptic, who, at age 27, underwent hippocampal surgery in order to contain the frequent and severe seizures he suffered. The surgery was successful in reducing the patient's seizures, but it also had an extremely deleterious effect on his memory. He was no longer able to learn new information; he recalled no events that took place after his operation. His life literally stood still sometime in 1953 when the operation

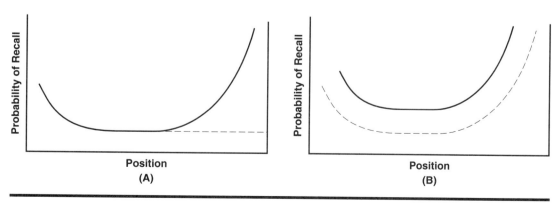

FIGURE 7.7   Effect of delaying recall prompt in free-recall experiment as predicted by (*A*) the two-store model and (*B*) the unitary theory of memory.

was performed. Years later, HM still gave his age as 27; he had not learned his new address, yet he knew the old one perfectly well. He would also read and reread newspapers without noticing that he had read them before. Milner concluded that HM's memory deficit did not affect long-term memory because he correctly remembered information from long ago. Neither was his short-term memory affected because he could be made to retain information by constantly rehearsing it, at least for a limited time span. Milner attributed HM's amnesia to a faulty transfer mechanism from the short-term store to the long-term store.

The principal site for the transfer of information to long-term memory is thought to be the hippocampus. Neural circuits in the hippocampus have been implicated in the consolidation of recently acquired declarative memories. Implicit memory is largely spared when the hippocampus is lesioned (Chapter 2).

The Atkinson and Shiffrin Theory of Memory

The Atkinson and Shiffrin (1968) model is the culmination of a decade's work on two memory stores. It also influenced research during the next decade. The model summarized the structural assumptions put forth by Sperling's (1960) research on the iconic trace, Peterson and Peterson's (1959) research on the short-term store, and traditional long-term memory work. The model is captured by the flowchart in Figure 7.8. The left-most box represents the sensory register, the center box represents the short-term store, and on the right is the long-term store. Atkinson and Shiffrin (1968) listed the visual icon investigated by Sperling (1960) as the primary example of information in the sensory register (see Chapter 3). The information is sensory because it has not yet been recognized. It is also extremely fragile, as you may recall. Once the information is recognized, the person can verbalize and rehearse it in the short-term store. According to the model in Figure 7.8, the short-term store includes a rehearsal buffer. It serves as a transfer device, moving information to long-term memory.

In addition to their structural assumptions, Atkinson and Shiffrin (1968) proposed **control processes** to describe the subject's mental activities. Introducing mental processes was an important step. It breaks with the views of the stimulus-response approach; the person was no longer viewed as a passive receiver of information but an active participant of remembering. The subject's mental activities became an important focus of research. Atkinson and Shiffrin and their students were most interested in rehearsal processes that resulted in the transfer of information from the short-term to the long-term store. We will next discuss rehearsal and its role as a transfer process. (Other examples of control processes include attentive, strategic, and search

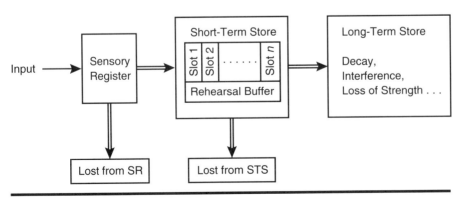

FIGURE 7.8 Architecture of Atkinson and Shiffrin model (Atkinson & Shiffrin, 1968).

processes described in Chapters 3, 4, and 8, respectively.)

Rehearsal Processes. You practice rehearsal whenever you talk to yourself in order to remember telephone numbers, names, appointments, and so on. Even children know that rehearsing information helps them remember it. Experiencing rehearsal and quantifying it are quite different matters, however. How could a researcher assess a subject's rehearsal? Rundus (1971), a student of Atkinson's, thought of a way to make rehearsal visible: the overt rehearsal technique. He implemented that technique in a free-recall study. Rundus's subjects saw a list of words, projected one word at a time for five seconds on a screen. Rundus asked his subjects to say each word they thought of aloud as the words were presented. He recorded the subjects' utterances on a tape recorder. Every five seconds, the carousel projector would emit a click, which was also recorded on the tape. At the end of the list of words, a recall prompt was given and subjects recalled the words in any order. Rundus therefore had two related sets of data: the usual recall probabilities of words and the rehearsal protocol. The latter was divided into rehearsal sets of five seconds' duration corresponding to the exposure duration of each word. Rehearsal sets are illustrated in Table 7.4.

Rundus correlated the rehearsal frequency and recall probability of the words in the list, and he

TABLE 7.4 Rehearsal Sets Observed in Free Recall Experiment (adapted from Rundus, 1971)

Item	Words Rehearsed
1. reaction	*reaction, reaction, reaction, reaction*
2. hoof	*hoof, reaction, hoof, reaction*
3. blessing	*blessing, hoof, reaction, reaction*
4. research	*research, hoof, reaction*
.	
.	
.	
20. cellar	*cellar, . . .*

was able to observe two important relationships that earlier researchers had not detected. First, the recall probability of words was positively correlated with their frequency of rehearsal. The more a word was rehearsed by a subject, the more likely it was recalled. This included the initial words in the list—those words that contributed to the primacy effect. Second, Rundus found that items in the last rehearsal set were the ones recalled first. These are the most recent items of the list accounting for the recency effect.

With studies like Glanzer and Cunitz's (1966) and Rundus's (1971) experiments, the two-store model of memory had achieved its high point. Subsequent researchers discovered important problems for the model. There had been critics all along who argued that it was not efficient to assume two, three, or even more different memory traces. However, experimental evidence calling into question the rehearsal and the buffer notion was more damaging. The two-store model had become popular because of two successes: it predicted the positive correlation between frequency of rehearsal and recall, and it could handle the recency effect. Next, I will describe two sets of results that cast doubt on these two achievements.

Critics of the Two-Store Model

Glanzer and Cunitz (1966) had observed that the recency effect was wiped out when recall was delayed by 30 seconds. They attributed this to loss of the information from the short-term store. Eight years later, however, two researchers demonstrated that the recency effect does survive a delay! Bjork and Whitten (1974) had subjects learn a word list in a free-recall experiment. Their recall experiment differed in one respect from the usual procedure: After each item, the person was given a number and had to count backwards for a 12-second interval. Then, after the last item of the list, there followed the 30-second interval of mental arithmetic that Glanzer and Cunitz had used. Unlike Glanzer and Cunitz, however, Bjork and Whitten did observe a recency effect. According to the two-store theory, the 30-second interval of backward counting should have resulted in a loss of the most recent items from the short-term store, but it did not.

The repetition view of association was soon challenged by a wide range of studies showing little or no effect of mere repetition on memorability. A remarkable set of results was reported by Bekerian and Baddeley (1980), who assessed the effectiveness of saturation advertising. The British Broadcasting Corporation (BBC) was to change some wavelengths for its broadcasts and advertised the new wavelengths for several weeks 10 times per hour. Even casual BBC listeners must have heard the information at least 1,000 times. Bekerian and Baddeley found that people simply did not remember what had been presented to them so many times. They concluded that mere repetition does not ensure good retention.

Challenges to the rehearsal theory and therefore to the two-store theory of memory were raised by additional studies. Studies by Craik and colleagues demonstrated that rehearsal as such was not as important as had been believed; what mattered most was the type of processing accorded the words to be studied. Craik and Watkins (1973) presented a list of words to their subjects, such as *daughter, oil, rifle, garden, grain, table, football, anchor, giraffe*. The person's task was to keep certain words in mind, which should produce implicit rehearsal of the words. For example, in the preceding list, the subject was asked to think of each word beginning with a *g* until the next word with a *g* would appear in the list. The experimenters carefully generated the lists so as to vary the amount of rehearsal devoted to a target word. The more items that intervened, the more a person would think of the target word and, theoretically, it should be rehearsed more often. Thus, the word *grain* should receive more rehearsals and be better recalled then the word *garden*. However, this was not the case. There was no difference in the recall level of words as a function of the rehearsal interval after a target word. The crucial point is that rehearsal does not automatically lead to better transfer of information to the long-term store. The retention of a word was not related to the number of repetitions but to the **level of processing,** accorded the word.

A study by Craik and Tulving (1975) demonstrated the effect of levels of processing on retention. These investigators presented nouns one at a time to the subjects—for example, *horse, potato,* and *orange*. For each noun, the person had to answer a question. There were three types of questions intended to manipulate the degree to which the person had to think about the noun. Questions and examples are listed in Table 7.5.

The first type of question called for a superficial and easy analysis of the target word. All the person had to do was to indicate the physical shape of the word. Phonemic analysis, as required by the second type of question, requires somewhat more thought and hence more processing. Still more processing was required by the third type of question. According to Craik and Tulving, memory strength and performance should increase with the depth of processing elicited by the question—that is, in the order 3, 2, and 1. That is what they found. They concluded that it is not the mere number of repeated rehearsals, **maintenance rehearsal,** that determines memory strength, but the degree of elaboration, **elaborative rehearsal,** that the item receives.

TABLE 7.5   Sample Questions and Responses Used by Craik and Tulving (1975)

	Yes	No
1. Feature analysis: Is the word in capital letters?	*TABLE*	*table*
2. Analysis of sounds: Does the word rhyme with *weight?*	*crate*	*market*
3. Semantic analysis: Does the word fit in the sentence *The man peeled the . . . ?*	*orange*	*roof*

INTERIM SUMMARY

Early information-processing theorists distinguished between two memory stores: short-term and long-term memory. After some early success, the two-store model of memory was called into question. Short-term memory was viewed as a relatively passive storage medium with a limited capacity. Its primary function was as a transfer station of information to the more permanent long-term store. Transfer and recall were presumably improved by the number of rehearsals accorded an item. We saw, however, that the number of rehearsals did not produce an increase in the ability to recall items. Rather, it is the type of processing that determines the recall strength of items. Semantic elaboration helps recall more than mechanical repetition.

CONCLUSION

Reviewing the two-store model of memory, Kintsch (1977) concluded that it began with two types of memory stores—short-term store and long-term store—and ended with two types of rehearsal—maintenance and elaborative rehearsal. He stated that "many psychologists today are no longer satisfied with the box metaphor that underlies the earlier models of short-term memory.

Instead, a more dynamic conception of the memory system is evolving, with an emphasis on differential processes rather than on separate boxes for the short-term store and long-term store" (p. 225). Indeed, after 1977, the term *short-term store* has been largely replaced by the term *working memory*. The notion of working memory emerged when the activation concept became popular. *Activation* refers to the momentary excitation of information. The memory traces that are currently the most active constitute working memory. Less active traces constitute long-term memory. As the ongoing processing demands change, there is a continuous shift of active and less active traces.

The working memory is viewed as the most active part of memory. It is the principal cognitive processor where mental operations such as rehearsal, elaboration, search, comparison, recoding, and others are assumed to take place. Chapter 8 is devoted to the working memory and its processes. You can see, then, that although Atkinson and Shiffrin's structural model no longer survives, their idea of control processes does. Cognitive psychologists continue to be interested in retention over long time intervals. After all, long-term memory is important in real-life situations. However, as we shall see in Chapter 9, the theoretical framework is broader than it was in the first half of this century.

WORKING MEMORY

PREVIEW

Working memory is the hub of cognition. Its functions include both the storage and the manipulation of information. According to an influential theory, working memory consists of three components, the visuo-spatial sketch pad, the phonological loop, and the central executive (Baddeley, 1990). The working memory processes we will discuss include search and comparison, numerical transformation, language comprehension, and problem solving. Working memory supports these operations by holding intermediate results and scheduling the coordination of component processes. Working memory is an efficient processor that allows rapid access to information necessary for executing cognitive skills. However, working memory has a limited capacity that necessitates trade-offs between storage and computational processes. Fortunately, capacity limits are not absolute; they can be expanded by practicing memorization of digits, chess positions, and other specific content.

The contents of working memory change dynamically according to the demands of ongoing cognitive processes. We will discuss how cognitive operations are recorded on-line through neurophysiological and behavioral measures. In addition, individual differences in working memory and cases of impaired working memory will be discussed. We shall see throughout the chapter that working memory is implicated in a wide range of cognitive operations; it represents the most active portion of our knowledge.

INTRODUCTION

Working memory is where the cognitive action is; therefore, it is fortuitous that this chapter should occupy the center of this book. The study of working memory is a microcosm of the field of cognition. It includes pattern recognition, knowledge representation, long-term memory, language comprehension, cognitive skills, problem solving, and creativity. However different these processes may be, they share important properties; mental processes are extended over time and they consist of component operations, each of which produces temporary results needed by other subprocesses. A good illustration of this principle comes from syllogistic reasoning. In order to solve a syllogism, a person must remember each premise of the problem. This is relatively easy when the number of premises is small. Compare problems (8.1) and (8.2) (Raphael, 1976, p. 116):

(8.1) If I read an interesting book, I am happy. This book is interesting. Therefore, I am happy.

(8.2) The maid said that she saw the butler in the living room. The living room adjoins the kitchen. The shot was fired, and could be heard in all nearby rooms. The butler, who has good hearing, said he did not hear the shot. Therefore, if the maid told the truth, the butler lied.

You will find problem (8.1) much easier to understand than problem (8.2). There are fewer facts to remember and fewer comparisons to make. In order to solve problems like these, interim results must be available to you.

An illustration from arithmetic reinforces the idea of available interim results. It is much easier to solve 3×15 without pencil and paper than 234×15, let alone $1,234 \times 153$. In order to solve the latter two problems, you must keep all intermediary terms (for example, 4×15, 3×15, and 2×15), in mind.

Finally, consider sentence comprehension. In order to understand long sentences, you must remember the antecedents of pronouns. Consider sentence (8.3) (Carpenter & Just, 1989):

(8.3) A familiar example used to illustrate the function of working memory is the storage of a telephone number between the time when it is looked up in a phone directory and the time when it is dialed.

The word *it* in the last clause refers to an antecedent, *telephone number*, which was mentioned 17 words earlier. In order to understand the pronoun, the listener must remember the noun it refers to.

Working memory is the processor that holds the premises, numbers, and referents in these examples. Holding information for a short period of time is one of the functions of this processor. The other is to execute the processes themselves: encoding numbers, adding and carrying comparing premises, and applying rules. The processes must be scheduled so that they occur in the appropriate sequence. In a multiplication problem, for example, one cannot add any products unless they have first been computed. The product of 4×15 must be computed before it is added to the overall result. Executing and scheduling all of these processes makes working memory a highly active component of the cognitive system. Working memory is active in two senses; it supports cognitive processes and it maintains the activation of information needed by those processes. Active information can be accessed rapidly by mental processes; it is available for ready use.

Ponder for a moment what is difficult about syllogistic reasoning, mental arithmetic, and sentence comprehension. Are the words used in syllogisms difficult to understand? Are addition and multiplication inherently difficult? Or is logic an esoteric and artificial system? None of these explanations is true; the difficulty in solving these types of problems lies in the limited capacity of working memory. The number of processes that can be executed is limited, and so is the amount of information active in a given unit of time.

Theories of working memory have benefited from research in cognitive psychology and computer science. In Chapter 7, we saw that the two-store model of memory was inspired by the computer metaphor. We also learned how the concept of working memory developed from the notion of short-term memory. Short-term memory was viewed as a relatively passive storage medium with a limited capacity. The short-term store functioned as a transfer station for information on its way to the more permanent long-term store. A great deal of research was devoted to justifying the existence of the short-term store and explaining how information was maintained in it. Atkinson and Shiffrin (1968) introduced control processes in the short-term store and emphasized rehearsal—a process based on the phonological system.

Cognitive psychologists whose theories reflected aspects of computer architecture viewed working memory as a central processor. In production system models, like Anderson's (1983) Act* theory, working memory is the processor in which productions are matched against facts and goals. In these models the most active part of our cognitive system is the working memory. Similarly, in Kosslyn's (1983) model of imagery, the CRT model, the buffer represents the working memory. Kosslyn and other researchers examined a variety of processes that control images in working memory, including zooming, panning, rotation, and other transformations.

The wide range of processes—including phonological, imagery, and control operations—attributed to working memory gave rise to Baddeley's (1990) multicomponent model. Baddeley built on theories of short-term memory; however, his model advances beyond the traditional view of short-term memory as a store because it emphasizes mental processes as well.

MULTIPLE-COMPONENT MODEL

Baddeley's multiple-component model includes three parts: a phonological loop, a visuo-spatial sketch pad, and a central executive. The phono-

logical loop and the visuo-spatial sketch pad accommodate auditory and visual processes, two modalities that cognitive psychologists have examined extensively.

In addition to these three components, researchers have identified information in working memory from other sources, including procedural knowledge and semantic-abstract information (e.g., Anderson, 1983; Potter & Lombardi, 1990). These sources of information in working memory and the central executive are shown in Figure 8.1. The empty circle indicates potential other sources that have not been as widely investigated—for example, tactile and motor memory. Although not shown, there are presumably communication links between the working memory sources in Figure 8.1. This section emphasizes the three components that Baddeley included in his model: the phonological loop, the visuospatial sketchpad, and the mystery component, the central executive.

Phonological Loop

We encounter phonological processes in two broad contexts: in verbal communication and in memorizing information. We learn to listen and

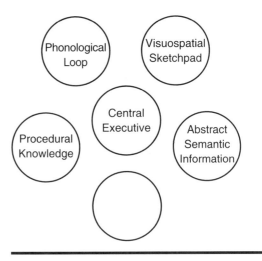

FIGURE 8.1 Multiple-component model of working memory.

talk long before we learn to read and write, and even after we become literate, it is usually easier to talk and listen than it is to compose a written message or to read one. Preliterate societies depend entirely on the phonological system for transmitting facts and ideas. Auditory and speech systems are our primary means of communication, and we have special cognitive processors to support verbal communication. Speech is not a discrete event; rather, it is extended over time. A spoken sentence extends over several seconds, and a listener must remember how a speaker started out in order to guarantee successful communication of the entire message. Memory researchers have known for some time that the phonological system plays an important role in memorization and they advise using our "inner voice" when learning new materials.

When you try to remember new information, you repeat it to yourself. When a reader works through a difficult technical text, she silently talks to herself. These are instances of rehearsal, a phonological process that involves the auditory or articulatory system. Although a learner can control rehearsal processes, they usually occur automatically, even in children. It is therefore not surprising that rehearsal was the first mental process to receive recognition by cognitive psychologists, including Atkinson and Shiffrin (1968), Rundus (1971), and Craik and Tulving (1975).

The phonological nature of working memory is reflected by at least four additional findings:

— *Phonological Suppression Effect.* If you interfere with rehearsal by having a person repeat an otherwise easy word, such as *the,* retention of target materials is suppressed, even if the information is presented visually.

— *Phonological Confusion Effect.* There is greater memory interference for letters that sound similar. People often confuse letters that sound alike, for example *P G T V C D,* but do not confuse dissimilar letters, like *R H X K W Y.*

— *Word Length Effect.* The span of working memory is related to the length of the words to be memorized. For example, it is easier for people to remember one-syllable words such as *wit* and *mate* than multisyllabic words such as *university* and *opportunity.* An interesting difference in the digit span[1] of speakers of different languages is attributed to the length effect. The digit span depends on the time it takes to pronounce digits in a particular language. The span is greater in languages such as Chinese, in which digits are spoken quickly. Hoosain and Salili (1988) found a negative correlation between articulation length and digit span for three languages: Chinese, English, and Welsh. Their results are shown in Table 8.1.

The phonological loop is assumed to serve in language processing, but few details are known. Research with 4-year-olds indicates that the ability to repeat nonsense words predicts the child's vocabulary at a later date (reviewed in Baddeley & Hitch, 1994). Other than that, there is little evidence that deficits in the phonological loop interfere with the comprehension or learning of one's native language. However, tasks that tax the phonological loop impair vocabulary learning in a second language. The apparent contrast between learning a second language and the native language is puzzling and remains an issue for future studies.

Visuo-Spatial Sketch Pad

The second major component of Baddeley's theory of working memory is the visuo-spatial sketch pad. This processing component is dedicated to visual imagery and spatial processing (e.g., Metzler & Shepard's [1974] rotation and

TABLE 8.1 Relation between Articulation Length and Digit Span in Three Languages

Language	Length (in ms)	Mean Digit Span
Chinese	265	9.9
English	321	6.6
Welsh	385	5.8

Kosslyn's [1983] scanning). The sketch pad accepts input from visual perception as well as from visual memory.

A classic study by Brooks (1968) demonstrates that visual perception and imagery share many processing resources and interfere with each other. Brooks had subjects trace block letters from memory, such as the one in Figure 8.2. The block letter has ten corners at which the direction of the outline changes. Four of these corners are located on the top or bottom outline (points 1, 2, 3, and 10 in Figure 8.2B) and the remaining corners are not. Suppose a subject inspects a block letter for a period of time. After removing the letter from view, he is asked to categorize from memory each corner of the block letter as located on the top or bottom outline versus in between. If the subject starts at point 1 (asterisk in Figure 8.2C) and classifies all corners in turn, the correct sequence of responses would be *yes, yes, yes, no, no, no, no, no, no, yes*.

Brooks used the time it took subjects to categorize the corners of diagrams as the dependent variable in his experiment. He assumed that subjects would rely on visual imagery in this task; they would visualize the block letter and imagine the asterisk traveling the outline of the block letter while responding with *yes* and *no*. Another visual activity would interfere with the subject's visual tracking of the block letter and the reporting of *yes* and *no* responses. In a visual interference condition, Brooks asked the subjects to make their responses on a visual display by pointing to *Y*s and *N*s printed in an irregular ar-

ray. The subject had to point to a *Y* when the corner of the block letter was on an upper or lower outline and point to a *N* for the remaining corners of the block letter.

On the other hand, Brooks believed verbal *yes* and *no* responses should not interfere with the visual image. Indeed, response times were more than twice as long for pointing as for speaking. It took subjects an average of 28.2 seconds to point to the *Y*s and *N*s, as opposed to 11.3 seconds to utter their responses vocally. Subjects said they could easily picture the block letters while saying *yes* and *no*, but picturing the block letter was not possible while they were trying to point.

In a phonological control condition, Brooks read sentences to subjects and asked them to remember the sentences while making certain statements about the sentences. One of the sentences was *A bird in the hand is not in the bush*. After hearing and repeating the sentence, the subject had to categorize each word as a noun or a non-noun by saying *yes* or *no*. In this case, the correct response sequence was *no, yes, no, no, yes, no, no, no, no, yes*. Brooks assumed that people stored sentences phonologically. There were two modes of output: (1) saying *yes* and *no* (interference condition), and (2) pointing to *Y*s and *N*s on an output sheet (noninterference condition). In this condition, speaking took 13.8 seconds on average, while pointing took only 9.8 seconds. In the phonological condition, the subjects reported they could say the sentences to themselves while pointing but not while saying *yes* and *no*.

Baddeley's model emphasizes visual and auditory codes in working memory. Models authored by other theorists make provision for other types of information, including semantic information (e.g., Anderson, 1983; Clark & Chase, 1972; Potter & Lombardi, 1990). In addition, there are alternative views of the function and role of working memory. Some of these critical views are summarized in Box 8.1.

According to symbolic-processing theories, we represent semantic information in terms of propositions (see Chapter 5).

Abstract propositional representations may

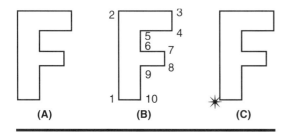

FIGURE 8.2 Block letter used in Brooks's (1968) mental scanning experiment.

Box 8.1

Alternative Views of Working Memory

The standard view of working memory is that it is a cognitive processor of limited capacity in which resources must be shared among competing processes. It is separate from long-term memory; the information is highly active, and phonological and visuo-spatial codes predominate. There have been alternative views of working memory right from its inception in the early 1960s.

■ Some psychologists criticize the view that short-term memory involves working memory (Klapp, Marshburn, & Lester, 1983; La Pointe & Engle, 1990). According to these investigators, remembering digits in the digit span task is independent of the mental operations assumed to occur in working memory. The serial recall of digits does not compete with such mental operations. Indeed, it has been known for a long time that simple span measures are not related to such complex processes as reading comprehension (Daneman & Carpenter, 1980).

■ Scientists have debated whether there is or is not a general working memory capacity. Kyllonen and Christal (1990) and Cantor and Engle (1993) have taken the former view, whereas Carpenter and colleagues (1995) support the latter. Ericsson and Kintsch (1995) proposed two types of working memory: LT-WM as a domain-specific processor and ST-WM as a general processor for familiar as well as unfamiliar information.

■ There may be no central executive and no scheduling of processes at all. Rather, according to a dynamic view of working memory, the coordination of processes might emerge from the interaction among several processors, whether they are production rules in a production system (Just & Carpenter, 1992) or nodes in a connectionist network (Chapter 6).

■ Prominent psychologists have disputed the usefulness of the working memory concept altogether (e.g., Melton, 1963; Wickelgren, 1973). According to these critics, nothing is gained by assuming the existence of a separate working memory store. The strength of the memory trace diminishes with time—first at a faster rate, then at a slower rate. It is not necessary to postulate discrete stores for two aspects of the same trace.

---

enter working memory in several ways. They may be activated from semantic memory; for example, when you retrieve the fact that a robin is a bird, presumably the proposition (IS A, ROBIN, BIRD) becomes active. Similarly, environmental information, linguistic information (Potter & Lombardi, 1990), and the interim results of problems are represented in terms of propositions.

Central Executive

As its name indicates, the central executive is the processor that controls the operations of working memory. Although the central executive is very important, researchers do not know much about it. There are, however, many promising speculations that serve as an invitation to aspiring cognitive psychologists who wish to expand the frontiers of knowledge into this terra incognita. Baddeley defined the central executive by what it does *not* do: It is not a store nor is it a processor of modality-specific operations. Rather, the central executive is the processor that allocates resources to the two subsidiary systems; it governs attentional and automatic processes (see Chapter 3) and it schedules the onset and offset of mental processes. For example, how does a learner know when to rehearse, when to imagine, when to retrieve information, when to integrate information, or when to stop a process and do something else? Later in this chapter and in other chapters (e.g., Chapters 11–14), we will see the careful choreography between the components of a cognitive skill, such as addition. The central executive is the director of these activities. (See Box 8.1 for an alternative view.) Some of the processes under the control of the central executive include the following:

- Problem solving
- Storage versus computation
- Comprehension
- Search and comparison

Less is known about the central executive than about the other components of working memory. However, new discoveries continue to be made, thanks to the dual-task strategy and neuropsychological case studies among other research strategies.

In the dual-task situation, subjects work simultaneously on a target task in a certain modality and on a secondary task in the same or different modality. Brooks's research, for example, has shown that memory for visual information was diminished by visual responses but not by verbal responses. Such interference constitutes evidence for the visual component of working memory, according to the dual-task paradigm.

Researchers have used the same logic to identify processes that place processing demands on the central executive. Assuming that the central executive coordinates reasoning activity and using the dual-task test with some syllogisms as the primary task, Gilhooly and colleagues (1993) found that of several possible secondary tasks, it was the random generation task that produced the greatest amount of decrement in the primary task. In this task, the subject is asked to produce a novel sequence from the elements of a well-known set, such as, the alphabet or the digits from 0 to 9. Novel sequences exclude such familiar runs as 1 2 3 or A B C. In order to perform the random generation task, the person must suppress the output of these easy runs and continuously keep track of the responses she is producing so as not to repeat them. The central executive controls both of these activities, keeping track and suppressing irrelevant information as well as the primary task of problem solving. Handling both tasks simultaneously is too much of a load for the central executive and performance suffers.

Neuropsychological research has also added to the ferment of speculation on the central executive. Linking the central executive to the frontal lobes, neuropsychologists have argued that damage to the frontal lobes produces a performance decrement that may reflect impairment of the central executive. Baddeley and Hitch (1994) called such performance decrements **dysexecutive syndrome.** These authors reported a study that examined the dysexecutive syndrome in Alzheimer's patients. The study used a dual-task paradigm involving a tracking task and each of three concurrent tasks—for example, the auditory digit span. For comparison purposes, the experimenters matched each of the Alzheimer's patients by a person of equal age who was not afflicted with the disease. When each task was executed individually, there were no large differences between patients and controls. There was, however, a substantial decrement in the Alzheimer's patients when they worked on both tasks simultaneously.

The hypothesis that the frontal lobe is implicated in scheduling activity was strengthened by investigations with patients who suffered frontal-lobe lesions. Posner and Raichle (1994, p. 121) reported that such patients have great difficulty in performing the card-sorting test. This task involves sorting of cards (for example, playing cards) according to one of the card's attributes that is not revealed to the person, such as color or number. From time to time, the experimenter shifts the criterion without telling the subject. Normal subjects sort and shift with ease, whereas patients with frontal lesions do not. Their deficit is attributed to an inability to control and shift their performance criterion.

INTERIM SUMMARY

According to Baddeley's theory, working memory consists of three processing components: the phonological loop, the visuo-spatial sketch pad, and the central executive. The phonological component is implicated in remembering information and in language processing. There are several sources of evidence for this processor: verbal suppression, phonological confusion, the verbal loop, and word length effects. The visuo-spatial sketch pad processes visual and spatial information from both the environment and the long-term store. The rotation and tracing of mental images is attributed to the visuo-spatial sketch pad. Brooks's tracing study demonstrated that visual imaging and making visual responses involve the visual system. The central executive is assumed to integrate, plan, and organize the component processes of cognitive activities. Researchers make inferences about these processes from people's performances in dual-task situations and from neuropsychological case studies. The random-generation task is thought to be an effective technique to interfere with executive processes in working memory.

―――――■―――――

MENTAL PROCESSES IN WORKING MEMORY

Problem Solving

The term **working memory** was first used in the context of problem solving. According to Greeno (1973), working memory contains the plan used to solve the problem; the problem solver represents the structure of the problem (its initial, intermediate, and goal states), much like a list of words in a recall experiment. Transformations and intermediary results are also held in working memory for easy access. Difficulties in problem solving arise when the plan does not fit into working memory, either because it is too complex or because working memory is limited or impaired. A common problem used by cognitive psychologists is the Tower of Hanoi puzzle. It involves the movement of a set of disks from one location to another—for example, from peg 1 to peg 3 in Figure 8.3. The problem is difficult because of specific constraints. There are only three pegs, only one disk may be moved at a time, and smaller disks must always be placed on larger disks.

Consider Simon's (1975) pyramid subgoal strategy for solving the Tower of Hanoi puzzle in Figure 8.3. This strategy involves three stages:

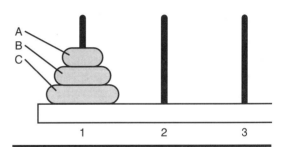

FIGURE 8.3 The Tower of Hanoi puzzle. Disks must be moved from peg 1 to peg 3 under specific constraints explained in the text.

1. Move the pyramid of all disks but the largest from peg 1 to peg 2.
2. Move the largest disk from peg 1 to peg 3.
3. Move the pyramid on peg 2 to peg 3 (see also Chapter 13).

The idea of moving a pyramid specified in stage 1 is a conceptual plan; it is not an executable move according to the constraints of the problem.

Given three disks, A, B, and C, the problem is solved by satisfying three goals: (i) moving AB from peg 1 to peg 2, (2) moving C to peg 3, and (3) moving AB from peg 2 to peg 3. The first goal requires that disk A be moved individually to peg 3. It cannot be placed on peg 2 because it is the destination for the larger B disk, which must be at the bottom. Disk B, however, can be moved to peg 2, once disk A is on peg 3. Then disk A is moved to peg 2. Thus, the first goal has been fulfilled in three moves. Now the second goal can be attacked and so on. The problem solver must keep each goal, the sequence of subgoals, and the moves to be made in working memory. As the number of disks is increased, the number of subgoals and moves also increases, thus pushing the load of working memory to its limit and beyond (Simon, 1975).

Research in problem solving convinced theorists that working memory is a computational processor in addition to being a store. The next section shows that the storage and computational functions compete if the load resulting from either function is too great.

Storage versus Computation

Posner and Rossman (1965) demonstrated in a dual-task experiment that the workload in working memory competes with the storage capacity in a direct way. Subjects tried to memorize a set of digits as well as perform different numerical transformations on the digits. In four different conditions, subjects heard eight digits on each trial—for example, 8 3 4 4 2 5 9 1. In each of the conditions, one of four types of transformations were performed on the final two digits: recording, addition, backward counting, and classification, respectively. Subjects in the recording condition wrote down the last two digits that were presented—for example, 9 1. Subjects in the addition task had to add two adjacent digits and report the result—for example, 10. In the backward counting condition, subjects counted backwards by threes from the last two numbers of each trial— for example, 91 88 85 and so on. Subjects in the classification task had to identify each pair of digits as *high* (50 and above) or *low* (below 50). In this case, 91 would be classified as high. After reporting the results of the transformation, subjects had to recall the first three digits of the series— namely, 8 3 4. Posner and Rossman's study involved four retention intervals: 5, 10, 20, and 30 seconds. The results are presented in Figure 8.4.

The figure shows that the more difficult the transformation, the more recall errors subjects make. After 5 seconds, there were only about 3% errors in the recording condition, but 12% errors for the classification condition. As the retention interval increased, so did the difference between the four conditions. At the 30-second interval, there were about 10% errors in the recording condition and 30% errors in the classification condition. This response pattern reflects a trade-off between transformation and storage; the more work the subject expends on the transformation task, the less capacity remains for storage.

Language Comprehension

Working memory plays a key role in sentence comprehension as it does in problem solving. We

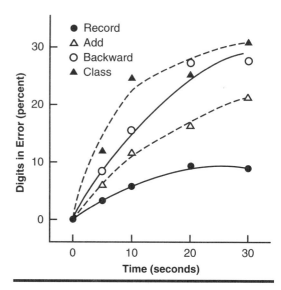

FIGURE 8.4 Correct recall of digits as a function of the difficulty of numerical transformation (Posner & Rossman, 1965).

could not understand a full sentence if we did not remember words from its initial phrases. Consider the word *it* in the last clause of sentence (8.3) on page 213. The pronoun *it* refers to *telephone number*. About 16 words intervened between the referent and its pronoun. In order to understand the pronoun, the referent must be active in the reader's working memory, either through continued activation or by reinstating the activation. This example illustrates that reading and listening taxes the storage capacity of working memory. In Chapter 11, we will learn more about other processes, such as lexical access, syntactic parsing, and semantic interpretation. For now, we will note that a reader must recognize the word *it*, search working memory for an antecedent, and relate the components *telephone* and *number,* realizing they represent one concept. To some extent, these operations are all concurrent, thus illustrating again the function of working memory as both a processor and a store.

Daneman developed a span test expanding on the familiar digit span test (see Carpenter & Just,

1989; Just & Carpenter, 1992). This span test evaluates both processing and storage capabilities. The subject reads a list of unrelated sentences aloud and recalls the final word of each sentence. The reader must store several unrelated words—namely, the final words of the sentences—while comprehending sets of sentences. This is a kind of stress test of the memory span. When comprehending a sentence such as (8.3), the reader decodes the words, accesses their meanings, processes the sentence structure, and keeps long-distance dependencies in mind; the span test requires that the subject maintain an extraneous load. Consider the following list of two sentences:

(8.4) When at last his eyes opened, there was no gleam of triumph, no shade of anger.

(8.5) The taxi turned up Michigan Avenue where they had a clear view of the lake.

After reading these two sentences the subject was to recall the words *anger* and *lake*. If the subject is able to do so, three sentences are presented and three final words must be recalled, and so on, up to seven sentences. The reading span is the largest number of sentence-final words recalled.

Daneman and Carpenter (1980) reasoned that remembering referents like *telephone number* in (8.3) should be easy for a person with a high reading span. They tested their hypothesis in a reading experiment. The experiment consisted of two phases: In the first phase, the reading span was measured for each of the subjects using test sentences like (8.4) and (8.5); in the second phase, the subjects read passages like (8.6) and later answered questions about each passage.

(8.6) Sitting with Richie, Archie, Walter, and the rest of my gang in the Grill yesterday, I began to feel uneasy. Robbie had put a dime in the jukebox. It was blaring one of the latest rock and roll favorites. I was studying, in horror, the reactions of my friends to the music. I was especially perturbed by the expression on my best friend's face.

Wayne looked intense and was pounding the table furiously to the beat. Now, I like most of the things other teenage boys like. I like girls, I like milkshakes, football games, and beach parties. I like denim jeans, fancy T-shirts, and sneakers. It is not that I dislike rock music, but I think it is supposed to be fun and not taken too seriously. And here he was, "all shook up" and serious over the crazy music.

Readers had to answer questions like (8.7) immediately after reading the passage.

(8.7) Who was "all shook up" and serious over the music?

Question (8.7) asks the person to retrieve a referent several sentences back. Without looking at the passage, can you identify the correct referent the question is looking for? Daneman and Carpenter found that subjects' ability to identify the correct referent increased with their reading span. The difference between high-span and low-span individuals increased as the number of intervening sentences between the question and the referent increased. These results are graphed in Figure 8.5.

Search in Working Memory

We have seen that working memory provides the resources for such processes as rehearsal, computation, coordination, and the interpretation of referents. One of the best investigated operations in working memory is search; searching involves looking for a target among a set of items. For example, when you search for a sock in a drawer, you have an image of the sock and you compare the socks in the drawer, one after another, to the image. You have found your sock when the image and one of the socks match. In general, in a search, one forms a mental representation of the target and compares the target to items in a search set. Sternberg (1966) introduced the short-term memory scanning task, a memory search paradigm (Chapter 3). Subjects were first shown a

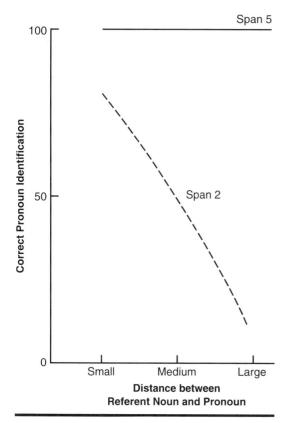

FIGURE 8.5 Readers with higher reading spans identify the referents of pronouns more correctly. Their advantage increases as the distance between the pronoun and its referent increases (Daneman & Carpenter, 1980).

memory set of one to six digits, well below the digit span, and then a single target digit. They had to decide whether or not the target digit was a member of the memory set. Assume the memory set consists of the digits 4, 9, 0, and 2, and the target digit is 9. In this case, the correct response is *yes*. If the target is a 3, the correct response is *no*.

Sternberg recorded reaction times as a function of the size of the memory set. He found that reaction times increased linearly with the number of digits in the memory set. Sternberg reasoned that the person represents the memory set in working memory, encodes the test digit, and searches the memory set for a match. The search could be either parallel or serial.

In a parallel search, the target digit is compared simultaneously to each of the digits in the memory set; in a serial search, it is compared sequentially. The two search models predict different reaction time functions. According to the parallel model, reaction times do not increase with the size of the memory set; the function is flat. The serial model assumes that each comparison takes a discrete amount of time, however short, and therefore each added digit increases the reaction time.

Sternberg distinguished further between two types of serial searches: self-terminating search and exhaustive search. Consider the trial with a negative outcome given a study set of 4, 8, 0, 9 and a test digit of 3. The 3 is compared to each of the four digits from the memory set in what is known as an **exhaustive search.** If each comparison takes k units of time, the comparison takes $4 \times k$ units of time. This is shown in the second column of Table 8.2.

Next, consider the **self-terminating search** using the same memory set with 8 as the test digit. The target is first compared to the 4, and then to the 8; because there is a match, the search is terminated. Assuming that the test digit is drawn randomly from the memory set of 4, the average number of comparisons is 2.5, yielding $2.5 \times k$ time units. The third column of Table 8.2 lists the average number of comparisons and the comparison time for the four set sizes in the

TABLE 8.2 Number of Comparisons in Exhaustive and Self-Terminating Search of Sternberg Task

Set Size	Exhaustive Search	Self-Terminating Search
1	1	1
2	2	1.5
3	3	2
4	4	2.5

self-terminating search. According to the self-terminating model, therefore, the slope of *yes* times should be less than that of *no* times. These functions are plotted in Figure 8.6A. If *yes* responses were based on an exhaustive search, the slopes of reaction times for *yes* and *no* responses should be the same. The slope represents the mean increase in search time with each added digit in the memory set; the lower the slope, the greater the scanning rate and the efficiency of working memory.

Now compare the prediction in Figure 8.6A to Sternberg's (1966) actual results in Figure 8.6B Sternberg found parallel functions for *no* and *yes* responses; this result supports the exhaustive search hypothesis, however counterintuitive this might seem.

In general terms, Sternberg's scanning results fit well with the capacity view of working memory. According to this view, working memory ca-

pacity is limited and as workload increases, the time it takes to execute a task increases as well. Thus, adding digits to the memory set taxes the capacity and slows down processing.

INTERIM SUMMARY

Working memory fulfills both storage and computational functions. In problem solving, the subjects must develop a set of goals and remember them. In comprehending sentences, listeners execute several concurrent processes as they store information about referents mentioned earlier in a sentence. In dual-task experiments involving memorization and transformation of items, there is competition between these operations. In Sternberg's memory scanning task, an increase in work-load increases the processing time. In sum, competing operations in working memory involve a trade-off: As computational demands in-

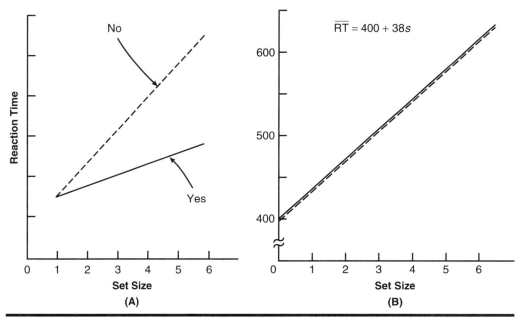

FIGURE 8.6   Pattern of reaction times predicted on the basis of a self-terminating search (*A*) in Sternberg's item-recognition task. (*B*) Pattern of mean reaction times actually observed by Sternberg. Open circles represent *no* responses and filled circles indicate *yes* responses. The best fitting line reflects a scan rate of about 38 ms per digit (Sternberg, 1966).

crease, performance decreases, whether it is measured in terms of accuracy or speed.

———■———

EXPANDING YOUR WORKING MEMORY: LONG-TERM WORKING MEMORY

The storage and processing capacity of working memory is limited; fortunately, however, there are strategies to use these resources to their fullest extent. This section describes how working memory can be stretched by practice that creates retrieval structures in *long-term working memory*. We study such memory skills in three different domains: the digit span, remembering restaurant orders, and chess positions. In each case, the working memory load depends on the manner in which the information is chunked or packaged. Chunking is a process that expands the capacity of working memory (Miller, 1956) by accessing and retrieving more information from long-term memory (see Chase & Ericcson, 1981).

According to Ericsson and Kintsch (1995), long-term working memory (LT-WM) is not a general-purpose processor with equal capacity for all possible skills and contents. Rather, LT-WM is specific to a particular domain and skill acquired through extensive practice, such as, in memorizing digits, chess playing, reading comprehension, and problem solving. LT-WM differs from short-term working memory (ST-WM) in the duration of the memory trace. Traces in ST-WM are transient; they are lost when the person momentarily shifts attention from one activity to another activity. LT-WM traces, on the other hand, are readily reinstated after an interruption. When you interrupt a person reading a text by asking them to do some mental calculations, they easily pick up where they left off. In experiments, interrupted readers do as well as normal readers in terms of accuracy and speed of responding to questions that assess their comprehension of the text. The only price they pay is that the interruption slows their reading speed immediately after being interrupted (Glanzer, Fischer, & Dorfman, 1984). In sum, LT-WM has a larger capacity than ST-WM, has more resistant traces, and allows ready access to information. Unlike ST-WM, however, LT-WM is reserved for highly practiced skills.

Digit Span

In the digit span test, increasingly longer lists of digits are presented to a subject for immediate recall. The person is first given three digits, then four, and so on until he can no longer recall the entire sequence correctly. The average digit span is seven. Chase and Ericsson (1981) developed an effective mnemonic technique to increase the digit span dramatically (see also Chapter 9). They trained a person to expand his digit span tenfold over a 40-week period.

Their subject, SF, was an undergraduate of average intelligence (SAT = 990) at Carnegie-Mellon University. His digit span was also average (eight) when the study began. Over a two-year time period, SF participated in the experiment for about 250 sessions, being paid each time. During the course of those sessions, his digit span increased tenfold!

During and after each session, the researchers recorded experimental protocols. A **protocol** is a list of comments and remarks subjects make as they perform a task. For example, SF rehearsed numbers and talked about the mnemonic aids he used. During the first few sessions, SF's protocol showed no difference from other subjects. On the fifth day, however, SF started using a new coding scheme and his recall exceeded his previous day's recall by four standard deviations. Being a runner, he coded some of the digits as running times. (SF was a member of the cross-country team and several other running clubs. He also participated regularly in races in the East. His best events were the three-mile, five-mile, and marathon. His best times in these events were 14:39, 25:40, and 2:39:36, respectively.) Over subsequent sessions of memory training, SF continued to use the running-time coding scheme and refined it over the two-year period. For example, given the sequence (4 1 3 1 7 7 8 4 0 6 0 3 4 9 4 8 7 0 9 4 6 2) he coded the last four digits by saying, "I ran it in nine forty-six point two." He had 11 categories of running times, ranging from a short distance of half-mile to marathon length. Thus, he memorized the 9:46.2 as running time for a distance of two miles. Beginning with the shortest distance, SF used these categories to code the digits for each session. At recall, he used the different race categories as a retrieval system.

Remembering 20 Restaurant Orders

JC is a waiter who can remember orders from up to 20 different customers without writing them down (Ericsson & Polson, 1988). Though the restaurant has a relatively simple menu, JC's accomplishment is still impressive. There are seven types of entree (steak oscar, sirloin brochette, filet mignon, rib eye, barbecue, Boulder steak, and teriyaki) that can be served at five different temperatures (well done, medium well, medium, medium rare, and rare). The restaurant serves three starches (fries, baked potato, rice) and five kinds of salad dressing (blue cheese, creamy Italian, French, oil and vinegar, thousand island). Customers would order various combinations of these—for example, "ribeye, medium well, thousand island dressing, and potato," "sirloin brochette, rare, French dressing, and fries," and so on. JC correctly remembers who ordered what and he does so for up to 20 customers.

How did JC become so talented at remembering orders? Ericsson and Polson (1988) found out that he used essentially the same technique SF did—a retrieval structure. JC encoded the orders in terms of the four categories—entrees, temperature, salad dressing, and starch—and instances in terms of letters. For example, blue cheese was encoded as B, oil and vinegar as O, and thousand island dressing as T. Next, JC would form words and sentences of those initials, for example, B-O-O-T. He used the food categories, letters, and words as retrieval cues when reporting the orders to the kitchen staff.

Ericsson and Polson (1988) invited JC to their laboratory and examined whether his memory was as good for other kinds of information. They found that initially he did not remember animal names as well as restaurant orders, but he could train himself to do so, much like SF trained himself to memorize digits. Ericsson and Polson also had control subjects of comparable intelligence; these individuals took much longer studying restaurant orders and committed far more recall errors.

The point of the studies with SF and JC is this: You can strengthen retention by mapping the to-be-remembered information in terms of something that is familiar and sensible to you. This is the principle that the inventors of mnemonic techniques have unwittingly used since ancient times (see Chapter 9). It makes no difference what the content is—whether it is computer programming, typing, arithmetic, interpreting x-rays, reading architectural plans, or chess strategies—all that is required is that the learner devote extensive practice to it.

Both memory experts, SF and JC, had practiced their memorization skills. When presented with a list of digits or orders from a menu, they could repeat it. Experts in other domains also exhibit superior recall of information specific to their area of expertise. Consider next Chase and Simon's (1973) study on memory for chess.

Memory for Chess

Chase and Simon have shown that chess masters have excellent memory for chess positions on a chess board even though their memory capacity for digits is no greater than that of novices. With extended chess training, players learn to chunk chess positions and are able to fit more into working memory. This is analogous to learning a retrieval structure in Chase and Ericsson's research (1981). The expert's advantage includes his richer knowledge structure in long-term memory, and a better retrieval system for pulling that information into working memory.

Chase and Simon (1973) presented chess boards to three people: a master player, an intermediate player, and a beginner. The subjects inspected the chess positions for five seconds and recreated the positions from memory. There were two conditions in the experiment: a chess and a control condition. In the chess condition, real chess games copied from chess books were presented to the subjects. In the control condition, randomized games with an equal number of pieces as in the chess condition were shown. Naturally, the chess master recalled more chess positions in the chess condition than the other players. Surprisingly, however, the master did no better in the randomized control condition. The master's better retention of the chess positions was not due to any differences in working memory. Rather, his knowledge of chess made the difference.

In order to appreciate that difference, consider the following statistics. The master player was one of the top 25 players in the country at the time of the study; he had played or studied chess for an estimated 25,000 hours. The intermediate player was ranked at the 85th percentile of players by the Chess Federation; his estimated playing time was 3,000 hours of chess. The beginner had played no more than 100 hours. To give you an idea of just how much time the master spent on chess, imagine that you work at chess for 40 hours of each week of the year, thus totaling 2,080 hours per year. You would have to work at chess full time for about 12 years to approximate the time the Chase and Simon's master spent on it. Of course, as a result of such extended training, you would learn anywhere from 10,000 to 100,000 different chess configurations. This number is comparable to the number of words in a reader's vocabulary. In other words, masters have learned to "speak" chess.

INTERIM SUMMARY

We can expand the capacity of working memory through training in a particular domain, whether it is remembering digits, restaurant orders, or chess positions. Such domain-specific memory has been referred to as long-term working memory. New information is encoded in long-term work-

ing memory in terms of knowledge with which the learner is already familiar. Familiar information forms a structure used at retrieval to reproduce the to-be-remembered material. With hundreds and thousands of hours of dedicated practice in a specific domain, the speed and accuracy of performance increases to resemble pattern recognition.

DYNAMIC PROCESSING IN WORKING MEMORY

Working memory is the hub of cognition; its content fluctuates as one's goals, thoughts, and environment change. We are unaware of much of these fleeting contents and therefore unable to track them. But cognitive psychologists have intuitions that capture the dynamics of working memory. The psychological theories are based on the concept of activation and the activation is tracked by neurophysiological and behavioral methods.

Activation in Working Memory

When we say that some material in working memory is highly active, what do we mean? One interpretation is that active information is available for immediate use. Does this mean the individual is aware of the information? That is what William James (1890) and many other psychologists thought when they used the term *primary memory* to refer to conscious information and the term *secondary memory* to refer to information of which we are unaware. Working memory, however, is not like James's primary memory; rather, it contains both conscious and unconscious information. When you concentrate on a certain task, you may become so absorbed that you are unaware of what you are doing and your surroundings. For instance, when you watch a basketball game, read a thriller, or listen to a CD, you are often "dead to the world," yet your working memory is busily executing complex mental operations. We are unaware of much active information, including the features we use in object recognition, the components of procedural skills, and the goal structure in problem solving. Many of these processes are thought to occur in parallel; in any case, these processes are too fast for introspection. For example, each comparison in Sternberg's memory scanning task takes less than 40 milliseconds, one-twenty-fifth of a second.

In propositional and procedural theories, working memory represents the most active part of declarative memory (Anderson, 1983). Active information in working memory includes abstract conceptual and procedural knowledge, as well as phonological and visuo-spatial information (see also Box 8.1). In some cases, learners can control the activation process—for example, by rehearsing facts to be memorized. In most cases, however, information is activated automatically. I will illustrate automatic activation of declarative knowledge with the **priming** effect as it is observed in lexical decision studies. Subjects are shown strings of letters on a computer screen (e.g., *plame*) and must decide whether or not the string represents an English word. Findings reveal that if two strings shown in succession are related English words, such as *doctor* and *nurse*, the second word is recognized faster than if it were preceded by an unrelated word (e.g., *bread*). According to several theories, including Collins and Quillian's (1969) and Anderson's (e.g., 1983), when the first word is presented, it becomes active and the activation spreads to words linked with it in declarative memory. By definition, activated words form part of working memory.

Tracking Mental Work On-Line

Working memory is the workhorse of the mind. How can we document the work that takes place there? Both experiments and everyday applications show the results of mental work, such as numbers added, problems solved, skills practiced, and conversations carried out. The real challenge for the researcher is to track an operation as it un-

folds on-line. The term *on-line* refers to the process as it extends over several seconds. During this period, an individual's mental load usually changes. Frequently, these changes are reflected by overt activity; for example, readers move their larynx in silent speech when grappling with difficult passages; as people commit digits to memory their pupils dilate; in visual problem solving, people fixate their eyes on critical aspects of the stimulus; and even sleepers exhibit rapid eye movements when dreaming. There are changes in the electrophysiological activity of the brain, and, of course, subjects can tell an experimenter what they are thinking about and provide a record of their thoughts, a think-aloud protocol. While no single measure is perfect, the use of several measures allows researchers to track the activities of working memory and provide a window into the mind. Following is a description of neurophysiological and behavioral techniques to assess mental operations on-line.

Neurophysiological Measures of Increased Activation. Hebb (1949) was among the first theorists to speculate that immediate memory involves increased activity in neurons. He proposed the idea of reverberatory circuits; these are neuron loops activated by electrical activity over a short period of time, as illustrated in Figure 8.7. Hebb's proposal inspired a search for reverberatory circuits in the brain; these were difficult to isolate until reliable single-cell recordings could be made.

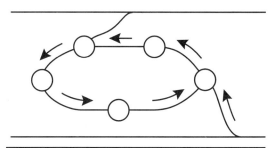

FIGURE 8.7 Reverberatory circuit of neurons maintains relatively high level of transitory activation.

Recording Single-Cell Activity. Using monkeys in a visual discrimination task, Fuster and Jervey (1981) found increased electrical activity in specific neurons implicated in visual processing. Fuster and Jervey implanted monkeys with electrodes that recorded activity in single nuclei in the inferior temporal cortex. The researchers used the delayed matching-to-sample task (see Figure 8.8).

On each experimental trial, a monkey was shown a sample color projected to a button; the colored light was turned off when the monkey pressed the button. After a delay of up to 32 seconds, four buttons were simultaneously illuminated, one of them identical with the sample. If the monkey pressed the button matching the sample, she received fruit juice as reinforcement. The investigators found that, after extended training on the task, specific neurons exhibited increased spike activity when the sample was lit. These results are shown in Figure 8.9.

The neuron activity increased only during the delay and only when the sample was red, as indicated in Figure 8.9B. As soon as the match was made at the end of the delay, the neuron's activity returned to its baseline level. Fuster and Jervey interpreted the increased activity as a reflection of mental work necessary to retain the information of the sample stimulus, a kind of rehearsal. Using the 2-deoxyglucose method (see Chapter 2), Goldman-Rakic (1990) demonstrated an increase in the metabolic activity of specific neurons during the delay in the matching task. Goldman-Rakic (1990) interpreted this transitory activation as an expression of the kind of work that gives working memory its name.

Using the delayed-response paradigm, Funashi, Bruce, and Goldman-Rakic (1989) were able to show that the single-cell activity in the brain was apparently necessary for correct retention. These researchers trained monkeys to gaze continuously at a centrally located fixation point while a 40 ms light flashed in one of several locations in the periphery. After an interval of up to six seconds, the monkey had to shift its gaze to the location of the flash for a reward. The researchers monitored the activity of almost 300

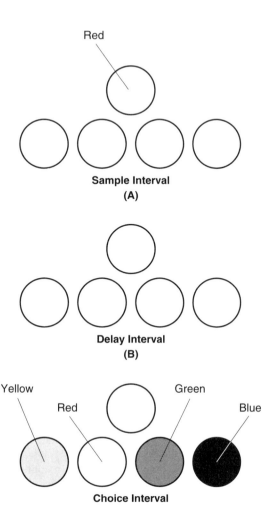

FIGURE 8.8 Delayed matching-to-sample task. Each panel includes five lights—a sample and four choice lights. The top panel (*A*) indicates the sample for this trial—a red light. The middle panel (*B*) shows sample and choice lights during the delay. After the delay, the monkey faces lights, as shown in the bottom panel (*C*) (Carlson, 1991).

single cells in the principal sulcus. They found that certain neurons became active during the delay right after the light flash. The researchers took this activity as evidence of maintaining the location of the cue in working memory. If the neuronal activity continued for the full length of the

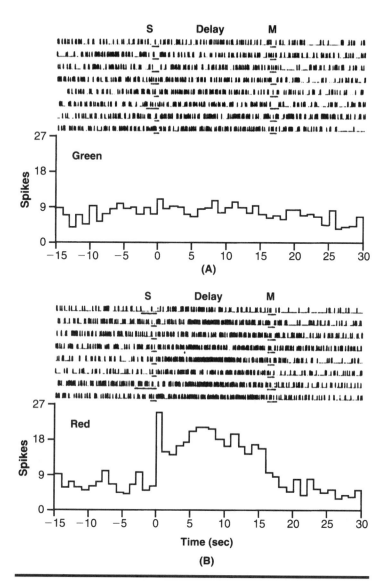

FIGURE 8.9 During the delay in the matching-to-sample task, cell activity increases only for red but not for green sample (Fuster & Jervey, 1981). Spike activity recorded on individual trials is shown in samples at the top of each panel. The histograms show the average spike activity across trials.

delay, the monkey was more likely to make a correct response than when the activity ceased.

Fuster (1995) reported of a surprisingly simple experimental procedure to interfere with working memory activity: Researchers literally cool down the brain's activity by placing a cooling device over the cortical region that sustains the activity. The cortical region is cooled to 20°C (from

36°C). For example, the retention of colors in the delayed-response task has been experimentally reduced when a cooling probe is applied to the inferotemporal (IT) cortex, which is the region implicated in color retention.

Activity Revealed by PET Scan. Posner, Petersen, Fox, and Raichle (1988) used another technique to measure mental activity in human subjects: the PET scan (see Chapter 2). The PET scan detects changes in the flow of blood in cerebral regions. Posner and colleagues compared PET activity during rest and during one of two mental tasks—reading or listening. Any increase in PET activity relative to rest was attributed to mental work. In Posner's reading task, a subject read a list of nouns; during the rest period, he fixated on a dot on a screen. Posner found that during reading periods, but not during rest, blood flow increased in specific regions of the occipital lobe, one of the visual processing areas. When the same nouns were presented to subjects on audiotape, there was increased activity in the auditory regions but not in the visual regions. Like the single-cell recordings, these results reflect the transitory activity associated with cognitive processes. They also show that the activity is localized to neural structures specific to the modality of the task, reading or listening.

Revealing as the neurophysiological measures of brain activity are, researchers have used noninvasive behavioral measures to track the activity of working memory quite successfully. The next section describes the use of eye fixation patterns in inferring mental processes in working memory.

Eye Fixations Reveal Image Transformations. Metzler and Shepard (1974) studied the transformation of images, one of the cognitive processes that presumably takes place in working memory. These researchers presented pictures of three-dimensional objects to their subjects. The objects were rotated in the picture plane as shown in Figure 5.4. Some of the objects could be rotated into congruence, but others could not. Subjects had to indicate whether the objects were the same

or not. Metzler and Shepard (1974) found a linear increase in the response times as the angular separation of the figures increased. According to Shepard, subjects formed an image of the object and rotated the image until it was congruent with the target object (see Chapter 5).

Is it possible to track the mental rotation process even though it can neither be made directly visible nor experienced by the subject? Just and Carpenter (1976) thought of a way to detect the processes underlying mental rotation; they recorded a subject's eye movements while she compared two stimuli such as the, pairs of the three-dimensional objects shown in Figure 5.4. Each figure consisted of a center piece and two end or arm pieces pointing in different directions.

Just and Carpenter assumed that the eyes reflect the mind's current work; that is, a person looks at the part of the stimulus currently being processed in working memory. Just and Carpenter called this hypothesis the *eye-mind assumption*.

The investigators used an eye-tracking technique to monitor the subject's eye movements. They projected a small beam of light onto the cornea of one eye while recording the reflection of the light with a television camera. Through careful calibration of the recording equipment, the fixations and the movements of the eye were correlated with specific coordinates in the stimulus display. Using this methodology, researchers have discovered that eye movements are not smooth and continuous. Rather, we fixate on specific segments of a stimulus for durations of 100 to 500 milliseconds. Rapid sweeps, called *saccades,* of less than 15 milliseconds result in new fixations.

Just and Carpenter (1976) recorded the eye movement patterns of subjects as they compared the Metzler and Shepard objects. Eye fixation records indicated that subjects switched their focus rapidly from one stimulus to another. The researchers distinguished three discrete movement patterns of the eyes: the search phase, the comparison phase, and the confirmation phase.

During the search phase, subjects scanned the two comparison objects unsystematically. During the comparison phase, they looked back and forth between corresponding parts of the figures. During the confirmation phase, eye fixations started at the center of each figure and went out toward the ends, or the arms.

Similar to Metzler and Shepard's (1974) findings, Just and Carpenter (1976) found that the length of each of these phases increased as a function of the angular separation between the two objects. This analysis of eye movements yielded a reliable signal of cognitive operations. Eye fixations have proven to be good indicators of mental processes—for example, in problem solving and language comprehension (e.g., Just & Carpenter, 1987).

INTERIM SUMMARY

Neurophysiological and behavioral techniques enable researchers to track changes in mental load as experimental subjects perform cognitive tasks. Using single-cell recordings and PET-scans, mental activity is detected in different neural sites depending on the nature of the task. Based on the eye-mind assumption, eye fixations are monitored to discover the current focus of the mind, such as when a person compares pictures of two three-dimensional shapes. The sequence and duration of eye fixations has revealed the presence of discrete mental operations in working memory.

INDIVIDUAL DIFFERENCES IN WORKING MEMORY

We have seen that working memory is the critical processor of mental operations. When processing demands are within its capacity, several operations are executed simultaneously. However, when the load increases beyond capacity, performance deteriorates and working memory becomes a bottleneck. Does this limit differ for different individuals, and is the working memory span correlated with intelligence? Designers of the first intelligence tests, the Stanford-Binet and

Wechsler tests, thought so; they included the digit span as one of their measures of intelligence. This reflected the common view that the ability to remember information from a brief exposure is a sign of intelligence. Haven't you been impressed by individuals who remember the names of people presented to them in a reception line, or by the debater who remembered the arguments of several of his opponents flawlessly? Scientists debate whether there is a relation between working memory and intelligence. Kyllonen and Christal (1990) reported a correlation between working memory capacity and reasoning ability, whereas Daneman and Carpenter (1980) found only a weak correlation between memory span and intelligence.

According to research by Hunt (1978), intelligence depends more on efficient processing of working memory than on the number of items a person can recall. The search rate, the slope, in Sternberg's memory scanning task, represents the speed of accessing information in working memory. In fact, Hunt reported that search rates differ for different subject populations; mental retardates and Parkinson patients have relatively slow search rates (90 ms per item), whereas people who train their memories, like SF, have fast search rates (10 ms per item). If item-recognition tasks involve mental computation in addition to the search, slope is a good predictor of intelligence. This is related to Hunt's finding that intelligence and the speed of pattern recognition are correlated (see Chapter 4). Intelligent individuals have faster access to name codes in semantic memory.

While examining verbal intelligence, Gathercole and Baddeley (1990) found that children with low verbal scores had deficient phonological memory skills, but a comparable level of nonverbal intelligence as a control group. The phonological skill these investigators tested was the ability of children to repeat nonwords like *defnonlel*. Subjects were asked to repeat nonwords as in the usual memory span test. Children with lower vocabulary scores committed more errors than high-vocabulary children when they tried to mimic the nonwords. This result is quite understandable; when a child encounters a new word, it is at first a nonword. In order to learn it, the child must encode the word in working memory and ultimately in semantic long-term memory. It is an important educational challenge to design techniques to help children overcome, or at least to compensate for, their deficiency in phonological memory.

Reading comprehension depends on the capacity of readers' working memory. We saw that individuals with a high reading span remember the appropriate referent of a pronoun over larger distances than low-span readers (see Figure 8.5). High-span readers also have an advantage when it comes to understanding ambiguous sentences such as *The defendant examined by the lawyer shocked the jury.* Just and Carpenter (1992) argued that these readers have sufficient memory capacity to maintain multiple interpretations of such ambiguous phrases as *the defendant examined* in the sentence above. Because of their larger processing capacity, high-span readers comprehend these sentences faster and are not thrown off course when they encounter the disambiguating information. In our example, the phrase *by the lawyer* clarifies the sentence.

Individuals with smaller capacity must devote more effort to a given task, as reflected by observable measures of mental energy. These include changes in a person's pupil size and glucose metabolism as detected by PET scans (Haier, 1993). As you interpret this evidence, remember that capacity and skill are not immutable faculties; both can be expanded with practice.

INTERIM SUMMARY

There are individual differences in working memory capacity; these are captured best by measures of information processing rather than the traditional digit span. Intelligence, for example, is correlated with the speed of working memory processes, including access to complex information. Verbal intelligence is related to phonological access skills in working memory. Reading com-

prehension depends on readers' memory capacity as measured by the reading span; high-span readers remember referents better and read ambiguous sentences more quickly.

———

Impaired Processing in Working Memory. Working memory impairments have been studied in individual patients who suffered brain damage in accidents or who underwent neurosurgery to ameliorate severe illness. Baddeley (1990) examined several clinical cases in relation to the multiple-component theory of working memory. He found that impairments are often selective; they affect one component of working memory but not others. Thus, a person may have difficulty with the visual aspects of imagery but not spatial features. Another patient may suffer deficits in phonological but not visual processing. Still others whose phonological and visual processes are intact may be impaired by difficulties in planning and executing mental processes.

Vallar and Baddeley (1984) worked with a 30-year-old Italian woman, PV, who had suffered from a stroke. Computerized tomography revealed lesions in the left hemisphere of PV's brain, the primary language area. Neurologists determined a number of language deficiencies, which Vallar and Baddeley attributed to problems in the phonological loop. The researchers found that PV had a poorer memory for auditory than for visual materials. In addition, compared with 10 normal subjects matched in terms of age and intelligence, PV exhibited none of the typical phonological effects: She did not confuse acoustically similar letters, articulating an extraneous word did not suppress memory for other items, and there was no evidence of the word length effect. This pattern of results indicates that PV stored information visually. She did so very effectively, as her recall did not differ from that of control subjects.

Farah and colleagues (1988) investigated a 36-year-old minister, LH, who had suffered an injury to the occipital lobe in a car accident when he was 18 years old. He made a remarkable recovery after the accident, successfully completing his undergraduate education. Unfortunately, some deficits of visual imagery processing remained; LH had difficulty comparing animals in terms of color, shape, and size. On the other hand, he performed no differently from control subjects in tasks involving the spatial rotations of three-dimensional shapes (see Metzler & Shepard, 1974) and letters, and in mental scanning tasks. Farah and colleagues argued that this patient's injury had selectively impaired the visual but not the spatial component of the visuo-spatial sketch pad, thus arguing for independent visual and spatial processors in working memory.

Frontal lobe syndrome is a condition involving disjointed and disorganized behavior patterns. It is observed in patients who suffer injuries to the brain's frontal lobes as a result of organic disease or accident. According to Baddeley (1990), damage to the frontal lobes interferes with the planning and organization of mental activity, presumably controlled by the central executive of working memory (Chapter 2). Such patients have no access to the mental representation of goal structures; they are highly distracted, attending to extraneous environmental stimuli. Shallice (1982) described patients who were unable to perform the Tower of Hanoi problem with only three disks; these patients also had difficulty solving jigsaw puzzles. Shallice attributed these difficulties to patients' inability to plan and organize otherwise simple moves.

Frontal lobe syndrome is also known as the environmental dependency syndrome. In the words of Goldman-Rakic (1990), in the absence of representational knowledge, an organism is forced to rely on external stimuli present at the time of response; it is at the "mercy of the environment." Patients with this condition tend to be easily distracted by stimuli even when performing routine tasks. For example, when pouring coffee for several people, a patient with environmental dependency syndrome may suddenly run to a window to watch traffic on the street, then turn on the TV or make a phone call, never returning to the previous activity.

Paradoxically, on other occasions, while performing a card-sorting task, for example, the same patient may persevere in one strategy, failing to switch to another when it is necessary. In card sorting, the patient is given a deck of playing cards on successive trials and asked to pick out cards of one suit (for example, hearts). Patients can do this on the first trial but not on subsequent trials; they keep selecting cards relevant to the first task. There are many hypotheses to account for this paradox, but none is quite satisfactory. The central executive is not operating properly in either case. In the first instance, too many goals are executed within a given time; in the later, too few are executed.

CONCLUSION

Working memory is the cognitive center responsible for problem solving, retrieval of information, language comprehension, and many other cognitive operations. Depending on task demands, information is maintained in a phonological loop, a visuo-spatial sketch pad, or an abstract conceptual form. Working memory also schedules the component processes involved in each skill and makes intermediate results available for other component processes. Working memory's storage and processing functions compete for limited resources that can be expanded through practice. Working memory differs from long-term memory; long-term memory is the store of our knowledge, whereas working memory provides a means for using that knowledge.

Working memory is like a stage with rapidly changing scenery. Its content shifts according to the demands of the situation and changing goals of the person; information is activated and processes take place in real time. Research into on-line processes has benefited from the development of sensitive new methodologies. In addition to using traditional measures like the probability of a correct response or a latency, researchers use the slope of latencies, the sequence and patterns of eye fixations, and neurophysiological measures to reveal mental processes.

This chapter has given you a glimpse of working memory and its panoply of mental operations. Much about this processor and its processes remains unknown. We do not know how these processes are organized or scheduled. We do not know how information leaves working memory—does it drop out because of decay, interference, or active suppression? Finally, we do not know to what extent these processes are automatic or under our deliberate control.

ENDNOTE

1. In the digit span test, a subject memorizes lists of digits of increasing length. The subject's digit span is the largest number of digits he can correctly repeat, usually 7 ± 2 (see also Chapter 7).

LONG-TERM MEMORY

PREVIEW

Successful performance in a wide range of experimental and everyday occasions depends on long-term memory. This chapter covers important manifestations of long-term memory, beginning with memory for lists of words in episodic memory experiments. The first section of the chapter describes factors that influence list learning, and a framework of associative memory (SAM) in which the memory strength of items determines their retention in recognition and recall tests. The memory strength or familiarity of an item depends on the item's association with other items in the list and with the learning context, and how often it has been rehearsed.

The chapter also discusses the relation between meaning and memory, including how people make lists meaningful and how they remember meaningful materials such as sentences and brief passages. We will see that memory is highly flexible; depending on the circumstances, we remember typical or atypical events, verbatim or approximate information. Real-life episodes are best remembered when they are distinctive and unique. Frequently, we remember only partial information, which is usually not a problem except for eyewitness testimony in court. Encoding information sufficiently and making it meaningful through elaboration is one of the surest ways to increase the chances of remembering. Mnemonic techniques are based on this principle: One links to-be-learned materials with familiar knowledge in long-term memory. In implicit memory situations, the learner's perceptual and problem-solving performance is improved through repeated exposure to the learning stimuli; no explicit recall or recognition is required. We will see that there are interesting differences between implicit and explicit memory.

The chapter concludes with a section on the pathological aspects of memory. Throughout the chapter are discussions about the many discoveries that memory researchers have made that help us remember information. Some of these are listed in Box 9.2. They are practical hints on how you can improve your retention.

INTRODUCTION

On Tuesday, October 17, 1989, 62,000 baseball fans had come to Candlestick Park in San Francisco to see the Oakland Athletics battle the San Francisco Giants in the third game of the 1989 World Series. Suddenly, at 5:04 P.M., a series of tremors, each no longer than 15 seconds, shook the stadium. My son and I had just started watching the game on TV. We saw players run from the dugouts and heard the announcer wonder if this was a quake. It was an earthquake all right, killing hundreds of people. Years later, people will remember that day—the day of the California Earthquake of 1989. For those who experienced it, the earthquake is a flashbulb memory—a memory of unusual vividness. Ask your teachers and parents where they were and what they did when they learned of the assassination of an important person, such as John F. Kennedy or Martin Luther King. They will give you an account similar to Kulik's when he heard that President Kennedy had been shot:

> *I was seated in a sixth-grade music class, and over the intercom I was told that the president had been shot. At first, everyone just looked at each other. Then the class started yelling, and the music teacher tried to calm everyone down. About ten minutes later I heard over the intercom that Kennedy had died and that everyone should return to their homeroom. I remember that when I got to my homeroom my teacher was crying and everyone was standing in a state of shock. They told us to go home. (Brown & Kulik, 1982 pp. 41–42)*

Similarly, you will have vivid memories of episodes of personal significance to you—your first bicycle, your bar mitzvah, your first big trip away from home, or your first date.

Of course, your memory includes much more than significant episodes. You remember the house you lived in as a child, your best friend's telephone number, and a few of your coaches and teachers. You retain facts and skills acquired in school, as well as much trivia. There is no known limit to long-term memory as far as the amount of information, its complexity, and its duration are concerned. Unfortunately, you also forget much information, and memories may be inaccurate even if they are as vivid as flashbulb memories (see Neisser, 1982).

The scientific study of memory simplifies the complexities of memory in natural contexts by controlling the many variables that influence memory. This chapter is devoted to the experimental investigation of memory, and is divided into five sections: (1) list learning, (2) memory for meaningful materials, (3) failure to remember and what to do about it, (4) implicit memory, and (5) clinical studies of memory.

Dimensions of Memory

Memory has many facets. We remember many different things, under various circumstances and over different time intervals. In addition, memory researchers have identified several types of memory representations and different stages in the life of a memory representation. At the beginning of our discussion of long-term memory, we consider three of the dimensions of memory: stages in the life of a representation, attributes of the representation, and the different kinds of information remembered.

Stages of Representation.

Cognitive psychologists distinguish between three stages in the life of a representation: **encoding, storage,** and **retrieval** (see Chapter 7). Encoding refers to the acquisition of information. Encoding occurs under diverse circumstances: when a person is told some facts, reads a story, sees an event, or memorizes information explicitly in the study phase of an experiment. Encoded information persists over time; it is stored in a representation of a certain strength and activation state. At any given time, most of our stored representations are inactive. Retrieving information involves bringing it back from the recesses of long-term memory into a more active state.

Attributes of Representations: Strength and Activation.

Remembered information has two distinct attributes: its **memory strength** and **state of activation** (e.g., Wickelgren, Corbett, & Dosher, 1980). Memory strength refers to the durability of the representation over time. Information that is firmly encoded and stored has great strength. This includes the names of your parents and friends, your telephone number, and your address. You may not think of these items at every moment of the day, but they are nevertheless very persistent in long-term memory. On the other hand, facts that you learned a long time ago and have not revisited since have a low memory strength. For example, try to remember a quadratic equation you learned in the ninth grade or the name of the sixth president of the United States.

The activation state is temporary, unlike memory strength. When you are told the name of a person at a party, the information is momentarily active. You may forget it rather quickly, however, and it may never acquire a high level of memory strength. The level of activation refers to the availability or energization of an item. Relatively few items can be active at any one time. The most active information is said to constitute the working memory.

Types of Information.

Information and knowledge exist in many forms. Cognitive psychologists distinguish between procedural and declarative knowledge and between semantic and episodic memories, among others. Procedural knowledge includes our motor and cognitive skills that we cannot easily verbalize. Declarative knowledge contains information about the physical, social, and linguistic environment, including semantic memory and our knowledge of word meanings. We remember semantic information over long periods of time, although we may no longer remember the particular episodes in which we acquired specific knowledge. Episodic memory differs from semantic memory in that we remember both particular facts and the episode when we learned the information. Episodic memory is memory of "personally experienced events" (Tulving & Schacter, 1990).

There is a debate among cognitive psychologists whether the different types of information are processed by different memory systems. Roediger (1990) took the unitary view of memory arguing that the same fundamental memory processes apply to all kinds of information. On the other hand, cognitive neuroscientists have postulated that there are multiple memory systems subserved by different structures in the brain (Schacter, 1996; Schacter & Tulving, 1994). Tulving and colleagues (1994), for example, have argued on the basis of PET findings that the encoding and retrieval of episodic memories is supported by the right prefrontal lobe, whereas the retrieval from semantic memory is mediated by the left prefrontal lobe.

The first part of this chapter emphasizes episodic memory manifested when people memorize lists in laboratory experiments. List learning has attracted much attention because insights gained from this research help us understand the retention of meaningful materials; the study of list learning offers many practical clues about improving one's memory as well. Though list learning is important, this chapter will also show that long-term memory research should not be understood in terms of list learning alone.

LIST LEARNING

We will begin by considering memory for single items and their strength without initial concern for the relationship between items. As our discussion progresses, however, we shall see that understanding the relation between items themselves and their context is crucial to understanding retention. List learning is studied using two major methods: recall and recognition.

Recall.   In recall tasks, a person is given a list of items followed by a prompt to recall the items. Unlike the recognition paradigm, the person actually has to reproduce the stimulus items. For example, on a given trial, the person might be given a list like (9.1).

(9.1) roof latch hot shirt clog mare court slot hand dirt

In free recall, the order does not matter. On such a trial, a person might recall the following words:

(9.1a) dirt hand latch slot shirt roof

You see that the person first recalled relatively recent words from the list. Generally, recall is better for recent and for initial words. These are known as the recency and primacy effects, respectively.

Recognition.   The recognition paradigm includes two phases: a study phase and a testing phase. During the study phase, the experimenter presents a list of items to the subject such as the one in Table 9.1. Then retention is assessed by presenting a test list consisting of a subset of studied items, the "old" items (italicized in Table 9.1), and a subset of items not studied, the "new" items. New items are also called *foils* or *distractors*. They are included in order to prompt subjects to discriminate rather than respond with *old* indiscriminately. During testing, new and old items are randomly mixed in the list. The test list is presented one item at a time, and the subject has to decide whether each test item is new or old.

TABLE 9.1   A Recognition Trial: Study Phase and Testing

Study List	
CATTLE	FORM
TRIBUTE	STYLE
HINT	ANSWER
GOLF	PUDDING
MAIDEN	RADIO

Test List	
TRIBUTE	*PUDDING*
COTTON	ATTIC
SEA	*ANSWER*
RADIO	*STYLE*
FACILITY	MADNESS
STAR	*HINT*
GOLF	OPINION
CATTLE	*FORM*
POLICEMAN	ELBOW
PENCIL	*MAIDEN*

Protocol of Subject's Response			
TRIBUTE	o	*PUDDING*	o
COTTON	n	ATTIC	o
SEA	n	*ANSWER*	o
RADIO	o	*STYLE*	n
FACILITY	n	MADNESS	n
STAR	n	*HINT*	o
GOLF	o	OPINION	o
CATTLE	n	*FORM*	o
POLICEMAN	n	ELBOW	n
PENCIL	n	*MAIDEN*	n

Note: Old items are italicized only for purposes of illustration. Participants do not receive such visual aids!

The list of responses a person made, her response protocol, is shown at the bottom of Table 9.1. Each test word is shown with the person's response: old (o) or new (n). Both stimuli and responses may be classified in terms of old and new, yielding four categories, as shown in Table 9.2. Table 9.2 also classifies the response protocol from Table 9.1 in terms of the four categories. A hit results when the person correctly identifies an old item as old. A false alarm is made when the person mistakenly classifies a new item as old. A

TABLE 9.2   Categories of Responses in Recognition Testing

		Stimulus	
		Old	New
Response	Old	Hit	False Alarms
	New	Miss	Correct Rejection

Responses from Table 9.1 Classified in Terms of Categories

Response "OLD"

Correct Hits: TRIBUTE, RADIO, GOLF, PUDDING, ANSWER, HINT, FORM

False Alarms: ATTIC, OPINION

Response "NO"

Correct Rejections: COTTON, SEA, FACILITY, STAR, MADNESS, POLICEMAN, PENCIL, ELBOW

Misses: CATTLE, STYLE, MAIDEN

miss means the person missed an old stimulus by calling it new. Finally, a correct rejection is a new response correctly made to a new stimulus.

In addition to these basic recall and recognition paradigms, there are variations of these paradigms as well as other methods to study memory—for example, Ebbinghaus's savings method (see Chapter 7) and the production technique where a person draws a stimulus from memory.

Basic Retention Results

Retention depends on many factors; some of these are already familiar to you, and others will be new. We have already discussed the effects of the retention interval, the list length, the position of the item in the list, and the depth of processing in Chapter 7. To recap briefly:

— *Retention Interval:* Retention decreases with an increase in the retention interval.

— *List Length:* Holding other factors equal, retention performance decreases as list length increases.

— *Serial Position:* In free recall, the first and last items of a list are more likely to be recalled than items in the middle of the list. This pattern of recall is known as the serial position effect.

— *Depth of Processing:* Retention is improved when learners process items semantically rather than in terms of the physical features of the stimulus.

Retention depends on a wide range of additional factors that often, but not always, work in concert. We will explore four of these: study time, the encoding context, the distinctiveness of cues, and the testing method. First, I will summarize each of these factors and then describe a representative study to illustrate each.

— *Study Time:* In general, retention improves as the study time the learner devotes to the material increases.

— *Encoding Specificity:* Retention improves when the testing environment is similar to the learning environment.

— *Distinctiveness of Cues:* Information is remembered better when it is distinctive.

— *Testing Method:* It is usually easier to recognize an item than to recall it. A number of variables affect retention differently in recognition and recall tests.

Study Time.   Usually, the longer you study the same material, the better you remember it. A problem of practical interest is how one should use a given amount of study time. Based on research, we can conclude that it is better to distribute practice over several sessions rather than cram it into a single session. Baddeley (1990) described a study with postal workers who took a course in typing that lasted several weeks. Of interest to us are two groups of workers who received different daily practice schedules. The distributed group practiced typing for one hour per day. The massed group practiced twice each day for a total of four hours per day. The results are shown in Figure 9.1. The abscissa shows the number of hours of practice and the ordinate indicates correct key strokes

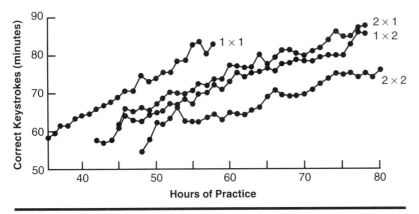

FIGURE 9.1   The effects of massed versus distributed practice in learning to type. The distributed group practiced typing for one hour per day (1 × 1), whereas the massed group practiced twice each day for two hours (2 × 2) (Baddeley, 1990).

per minute. It is clear that for a constant amount of time, distributed practice produced better results.

Encoding Specificity.   We have already seen that encoding refers to the first stage of a memory representation—namely, to its acquisition when one perceives or studies an item. Memory researchers have discovered that the encoding stage is critical for the subsequent access of a memory trace. It is easier to access the trace when the context at retrieval is similar to the encoding context. When the context is changed, retrieval becomes more difficult. This generalization is known as the **encoding specificity effect.** It was discovered by Tulving and his colleagues. The literature contains many demonstrations of this effect; we will discuss a classic study by Tulving and Osler (1968).

Tulving and Osler had subjects learn and recall lists of 24 words. In the learning phase, the to-be-recalled words were typed in capital letters. They were presented in two encoding conditions, either alone or together with another word (a cue). Thus, in the alone condition, subjects would see *HEALTH* and in the cue condition, they saw *soar-EAGLE*. The subjects were told that they did not have to memorize the cue but that it might help them remember the target word.

Two testing conditions were combined factorially with the two encoding conditions: cued and noncued testing. Subjects were given the cue (for example, *soar*) in cued testing but not in noncued testing. Recall was better in the two conditions in which the encoding and testing environments were the same. A change, either dropping or adding the cue between learning and testing, resulted in poorer recall.

Context-Dependent Retrieval.   Retrieval of a memory trace depends on the environment in which the trace was first formed. In a remarkable study, Godden and Baddeley (1975) trained deep-sea divers to memorize a list of words in two training environments, either on land or in an underwater tank. The divers were tested in the same or in a different context. Figure 9.2 shows the findings. The divers' recall was better when they were tested in the same rather than in a different environment.

Context-dependent recall is not a trivial matter; it can prove critical to a diver's safety. The initial training of divers takes place in a classroom. It could be dangerous, indeed, if the divers did not remember routines and drills under water, such as a slow ascent to prevent the bends.

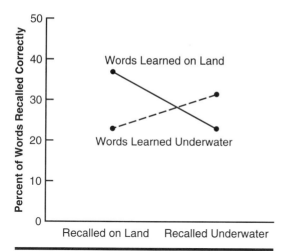

FIGURE 9.2 Context-dependent retrieval. Divers retain more information when tested in the same environment in which they studied the materials (Godden & Baddeley, 1975).

Retrieval is also a function of the learner's inner environment during learning and testing. Eich (1980) reviewed over 50 experiments of such state-dependent retention. Subjects were in one of two pharmacological states, intoxicated or sober, during learning. For testing, they were in the same state as in learning or they were shifted to the other state. Retrieval was better when the subject was in the same state during learning and testing; however, overall retention was better in the sober conditions. Findings such as this demonstrate the two conditions of remembering embodied in the encoding specificity principle: the existence of a trace or representation *and* a context to remind us of it (Tulving, 1974).

In Chapter 7, we viewed forgetting in terms of the memory trace alone. Forgetting was attributed to a weakening in the memory trace due to either decay or interference from other traces. The encoding specificity principle provides an additional interpretation of forgetting—namely, that forgetting is to some extent a retrieval failure. Even if a memory trace is fully intact, it may be inaccessible to the learner. There had long been speculation that memory representa-

tions may be permanent. These hopes were fueled by a discovery made by the neurosurgeon Penfield while performing surgery on epileptic patients. Using local anesthesia, Penfield stimulated specific brain sites and elicited very vivid acoustic memories in some of his patients. One person said she heard a piano recital given a long time ago, and another heard a conversation from his childhood days. Penfield interpreted these experiences as evidence for permanent memory traces (Penfield & Milner, 1958). However, he lacked a means of verifying that these experiences were based on events that had actually taken place in the past.

Distinctiveness of Cues. Flashbulb memories are highly memorable because they capture unique events. In general, we tend to remember anything that is distinctive, even when the number of items is large. A study by Mäntylä (1986) demonstrated that learners can retain over 500 items provided they make the items distinctive. Mäntylä presented lists of 600 words to eight subjects. Under the usual free-recall conditions, people would recall 30, perhaps 40, of the 600 words. In Mäntylä's study, however, the usual free-recall procedure was changed and subjects were asked to generate one or three associations for each word shown to them. For the target table, the following associations illustrate the one- and three-association conditions, respectively: table—chair, and table—dinner, chair, cloth. The subjects were asked to write their associations in a booklet; they were not told there would be a subsequent recall test. After the association phase, the surprise recall test was given. People were shown the associations they had generated and asked to recall the corresponding target words. The results are shown in Table 9.3 (Mäntylä, 1986).

Table 9.3 shows a spectacular result. When they developed three associates to each of 600 target words, subjects remembered 90% of the targets. This is about 550 words instead of the 40 words one would remember typically. Subjects remembered 60% of the words (360 words) with

TABLE 9.3 Probability of Recall as a Function of Number of Associations

Condition	Subject				
	1	*2*	*3*	*4*	*M*
3 associations	.932	.872	.900	.915	.905
1 association	.635	.692	.623	.515	.616

only one associate. There are two reasons for the impressive level of retention. The retrieval cues were highly distinctive for each person and, as predicted by the levels-of-processing view (Craik & Tulving, 1975), subjects processed items more thoroughly and recalled them better than in the usual recall experiment.

Testing Method: Recognition versus Recall. It is usually easier to recognize an item than to recall it. If you are given a long list of words and you are asked to recall half of them and recognize the other half, the number of correctly recognized words will be greater than the number of recalled words (but note Watkins & Tulving, 1975). Interestingly, there are some variables that influence recognition and recall performance in the same way, while other variables have opposite effects. For instance, opposite effects are produced by the occurrence frequency of the word in the English language and by the organization of the test list.

Words with a high occurrence frequency in English such as *table, dog*, and *door* are better recalled than low-frequency words such as *invidious, sir*, and *brogue*. On the other hand, recognition performance is better for low-frequency than for high-frequency words (Glanzer & Adams, 1990; Mandler, Goodman, & Wilkes-Gibbs, 1982).

Organization refers to the presentation of nouns in conceptual categories (e.g., names, cities, fruit) rather than presenting them in a mixed list. The grouping of words has no effect on recognition but increases recall, presumably because it provides a retrieval path (Kintsch, 1977).

INTERIM SUMMARY

Retention of information is improved by an increase in study time, by increasing the similarity of learning and testing environments, and by making items highly distinctive. Item recall is also improved when subjects are tested after a relatively short retention interval, when items belong to a short list, and when they appear at either the beginning or the end of a list. It is easier to retrieve an item in a recognition test than in a recall test. Converse conditions lead to forgetting. If study time is too short, if learning and testing situations are dissimilar, if retrieval cues are confusing, or if the learner processes the items superficially, then retention is poor. Likewise, retention declines after long delays, when the list of items is too long, and when items appear in the center of the list.

SAM: A Framework of Retention

Memory researchers have been looking for models and theories to account for the wide range of memory effects, many of them apparently contradictory. Many models, theories, and hypotheses have been proposed. Most of these attempted to account for one individual effect or set of effects. Rundus (1971) applied the two-store notion of memory to the serial position effect in free recall. Baddeley and Longman (1978) proposed a theory of study time effects. Kintsch (1977) theorized about the effects of organization in recall and recognition. Glanzer and Bowles (1976) developed a very persuasive model of the different effects of word frequency on recall and recognition performance (see also Glanzer & Adams, 1990; Mandler, Goodman, & Wilkes-Gibbs, 1982). The list of different models for specific effects could easily be continued. Most of these models accounted for the particular findings for which they were designed, but they were not meant to be general.

Theorists have also developed more comprehensive frameworks of memory. These include Anderson's Act* theory (Anderson, 1983), a major effort addressing list learning, sentence learning, and the learning and memory of procedural skills. Additional frameworks include those of Raaijmaker and Shiffrin (1981), Hintzman (1984), Metcalfe (1991), Murdock (1982), and Ratcliff and McKoon (1988). All of these approaches are broadly based and seek to account for results from many paradigms using a common set of assumptions. Although there are important differences between these models, they all share two major assumptions:

1. Target items are viewed in relation to the memory representations of all other items learned. For example, the items in Table 9.1 are related to each other, to items not presented in the list, and to the experimental context in which the person learns the list. Presumably the learner establishes some link between *cattle* and *answer, cattle* and *radio, cattle* and *form,* and so on.

2. To-be-learned materials are associated with context during learning and retrieval. Retrieval is facilitated if the context that exists during encoding is reinstated during retrieval.

Here I have chosen one of the general theories—Raaijmakers and Shiffrin's (1981) retrieval model. The model is known as SAM, the acronym for Search of Associative Memory. The model is representative of the other approaches, and more accessible than Hintzman's (1984) Minerva model, Metcalfe's (1991) CHARM model, and Murdock's (1982) convolution theory. In the next section, I will describe the fundamental assumptions of the Raaijmakers and Shiffrin theory, then I describe its retrieval structure and explain the role of the experimental context at retrieval. Finally, we will examine how retrieval works in recognition and recall experiments and interpret some classical list-learning results in terms of Raaijmakers and Shiffrin's theory.

Fundamental Assumptions of the SAM Model. Words such as those in Table 9.1 are assumed to have a certain memory strength or familiarity value. (I will use these terms interchangeably.) When a word is presented during the study phase, you think about it and rehearse it, which increases its memory strength. Because distractors are not presented during the study phase, there is no change in their memory strength.

In recognition testing, a person bases her decision about whether an item is old or new on the familiarity of the item. If the item is familiar (in the sense of having recently been seen), the person will say *old*; otherwise, she will say *new*. It is assumed that the person adopts an implicit **criterion** of familiarity on which she bases her old/new decision. If the familiarity value of the stimulus is greater than the criterion, the person judges it as *old*; otherwise, she says *new*. Note the word *implicit*. This means that the person is not aware of her criterion, nor of any of the decision processes involved.

Let me illustrate the use of a criterion for a subset of the items from Table 9.1. Table 9.4 lists four old words (*cattle, answer, radio,* and *form*) and two distractors (*madness* and *pencil*) and their memory strengths. Assume the person's response criterion was $c = 0.40$. If the familiarity of a word is greater than 0.40, the response will be *old;* if it is less than 0.40, the response will be *new*. Given this criterion, the words *cattle, radio, form,* and *pencil* would be judged as old. The response *pencil* is a false alarm, and *answer* is a miss.

We assume that the memory representation of each item incorporates information about the context in which the item was learned, about other items in the list, and about the item itself (for example, its name). In simplified terms, a representation will be retrieved to the extent that it is cued by any of these.

TABLE 9.4 Illustrative Strength Values of Four Old Items and Two Distractors

cattle	0.60
answer	0.39
radio	0.94
form	0.40
madness	0.185
pencil	0.41

Memory Strength.   We begin our examination of memory strength by inquiring where the strength values in Table 9.4 come from. The short answer is that the memory strength depends on the three cues we have just named context cues, associative cues, and item cues.

The item cues and associative cues depend on the number of rehearsals an item together with other items receives during encoding; items rehearsed frequently have greater item strength than those rehearsed less often, and distractor items are, of course, not rehearsed and therefore not strengthened. However, distractor items have a certain preexperimental strength called *distractor strength.*

The strength of the item cue expresses the degree of association between the item and its memory representation. It reflects the similarity between the item and its representations. The item is the physical manifestation of a word on a page or computer screen, or the sound of the word if the experiment involves auditory stimulus presentation. The representation refers to the stored image or proposition of the word in memory; it is abstract. Strength of item cues and associative cues varies. It may range from very high, as expressed by coefficients close to 1.0, to very low, as expressed by coefficients close to 0.0.

A list of items does not exist in isolation; it occurs in a particular context, and as Tulving and Osler's (1968) and many other studies have demonstrated, the study context has a large effect on memory strength. The context cues include the trial number, the list number, and retrieval cues, as well as more general attributes such as the date, time of day, and location where the experiment took place.

The subject retrieves an item's memory trace by using a prompt given by the experimenter—for example, "Please recall the items on the third list you studied today." This prompt is a context cue in that it enters working memory. Activation passes from the probe cue in working memory to associated information in long-term memory. Retrieval is based on a **retrieval structure** that reflects the interrelatedness among the factors that govern the memory strength of items and retention performance: context cues, associative cues, and item cues. In the next section, I use numerical examples to illustrate how they jointly bring about the retrieval of memory traces.

Retrieval Structure.   The retrieval structure of the SAM model reflects the three factors affecting retention identified by memory researchers.

1. In list learning, learners remember information about each **individual item**—its sound, its spelling, and its meaning.
2. In addition, as subjects rehearse the list, they establish **associative relations** among the items of the list—for example, *cattle, answer, radio*, and *form.*
3. Memory research has revealed **context** as another source supporting retrieval; the encoding specificity effect illustrates the influence of context on retention.

Expression (9.2) summarizes these three retrieval sources

(9.2) Retrieval = function (item information, associative relations, context)

Figure 9.3 captures the three information sources of the retrieval structure. There is a representation of each memorized item in the structure called *image* by Raaijmakers and Shiffrin (1981). In Figure 9.3, individual images are represented as double circles with arcs pointing back to each circle. The arcs reflect the rehearsal of each item—for example, the person might say *cattle, cattle, cattle*. Arcs connecting double circles represent the associative relations the learner forms among list items during rehearsal, such as between *answer* and *radio*. The experimental context and its links with representations are represented on the right of the figure. The circles on the left of the figure represent the probe cues; they are widely connected to the list items. For simplicity, only a subset of the contextual connections is shown.

Figure 9.3 helps us visualize the information sources supporting retrieval according to the SAM model; however, it does not generate quantitative predictions of the contributions of each

Cue   Representation   Context

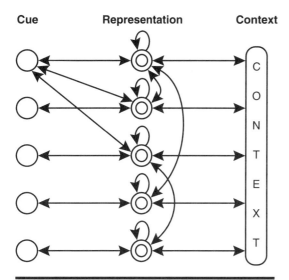

FIGURE 9.3 Three information sources of retrieval structure of the SAM model. Individual images are shown as double circles in the center of the figure. The experimental context is represented on the right of the figure. Circles on the left represent the probe cues.

type of information to retrieval. Raaijmakers and Shiffrin (1981) proposed a numerical scheme to calculate the retrieval strength of each probe cue. Consider the illustration in Table 9.5. The table has two dimensions: probe cues on the left and representations at the top. There are four columns, one for each representation. Table entries reflect the information sources for each probe cue. The

TABLE 9.5 Retrieval Structure of Inter-Item Associations

	Memory Representation			
	Cattle	Answer	Radio	Form
Context	.5	.3	.8	.4
cattle	**.3**	.3	.4	.1
answer	.3	**.4**	.1	.1
radio	.4	.2	**.7**	.3
form	.1	.1	.2	**.4**
madness	.1	.05	.1	.1
pencil	.2	.1	.3	.1

first row indicates the context strength of each representation. This value reflects the degree of activation of the specific representation by the experimental context. The six remaining rows indicate item strengths and associative strengths. The diagonal, represents the links of each probe cue to its own representation; the other values represent the associative strength of a probe cue with other list items. In general, item information has greater strength than associative relations.

Some probe cues are similar to the representations of other cues—for example, the association of 0.40 between *cattle* and *radio*. This correlation depends on how often *cattle* and *radio* were rehearsed together as the subject was memorizing the list.

Generally, the distractor items have a lower similarity to the list items than the latter have among themselves. As mentioned earlier, the strength values depend on the number of rehearsals and on the depth of processing of the items during the study phase of the experiment; on the familiarity the person had with the items prior to the experiment; and on the similarity between the context cues during study and during testing.

Our next goal is to calculate the memory strength of each probe cue. Table 9.5 contains all the information required. All we need to do is to aggregate the appropriate strength values of each cue. Raaijmakers and Shiffrin (1981) did so in two steps.

1. *Combine the context with associative or item information for each representation.* We multiply the context strength by the item or associative strength. The cells of Table 9.6 represent these products. Consider *radio*. Its item strength is 0.7 and its context strength is 0.8. Multiplying these two values, we get a trace strength of 0.56 to the probe cue. This value is shown in Table 9.6.

2. *Sum the products for each probe cue to get the aggregate memory strength of each cue.* Illustrating this step for *radio*, we add .20 + .06 + .56 + .12 to obtain a memory strength of .94. This value is listed in the right column of Table 9.6. This column represents the familiarity values we have worked with in Table 9.4. We have now an-

TABLE 9.6 Strengths to Probe Set

	cattle	*answer*	*radio*	*form*	**Memory Strength**
Context	.5	.3	.8	.4	—
Context × *cattle*	.15	.09	.32	.04	.60
Context × *answer*	.15	.12	.08	.04	.39
Context × *radio*	.20	.06	.56	.12	.94
Context × *form*	.05	.03	.16	.16	.40
Context × *madness*	.05	.015	.08	.04	.185
Context × *pencil*	.10	.03	.24	.04	.41

swered the question where the values in Table 9.4 come from. The activation of an item's representation in response to a probe cue depends on the joint contribution of the experimental context, of other items in the study list, and on the strength of the item itself.

In SAM, the manner of arriving at the memory strength of items is unique. Memory strength for each probe set is global; it does not only depend on the memory strength of an individual representation but also on the strengths of *all other representations in memory*.

INTERIM SUMMARY

The effective strength of a cue at retrieval is based on the preexperimental familiarity of the item and on experimental factors, including the self-strength of the item and the strength of its association with the experimental context as well as with other items on the list. In order to obtain the effective retrieval strength of a cue, its activation level, one multiplies the strength of the item with its association to the context and adds these products across all the item strength and associative strength values. The sum expresses the global memory strength of a retrieval cue.

Retrieval in List Learning. Using the retrieval structure just discussed, this section describes retrieval in recognition and recall situations. The two tasks differ in the manner of identifying the target item in long-term memory. For recognition,

a direct familiarity check of the target item compared to other items in long-term memory takes place. For recall, a search is necessary for each individual item.

Recognition. The familiarity check in recognition tests is fast and automatic. It is global because the familiarity value of an item is based on the extent to which all items in long-term memory are activated by a retrieval cue, as we saw above. The probe cue and the context form a compound that elicits a representation in memory; its familiarity is compared to a criterion value (e.g., $c = .40$ in Table 9.4). If it is greater than the criterion, the person responds *old;* otherwise, a *new* response is made. This strength theory of recognition memory is illustrated in Figure 9.4.

The abscissa represents the net familiarity level, increasing from left to right. Familiarity corresponds to the global memory strength to the probe item; the values in the right-hand column of Table 9.6 are an example. The ordinate represents the frequency of items at given levels of familiarity. Presenting a word during the study trial raises its familiarity value, as captured by the distribution on the right of Figure 9.4A. The familiarity of the distractors is less because they were not presented and rehearsed; they are shown in the left distribution.

The vertical line in Figure 9.4B represents the criterion. It intersects both the new and old distributions. The old distribution has a relatively large region to the right of the criterion; this area repre-

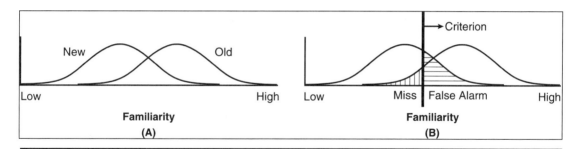

FIGURE 9.4 Strength theory of recognition memory. (*A*) reflects the effect of boosting the familiarity values of old items. (*B*) includes the decision criterion selected by the subject. The criterion intersects the old and new distributions.

sents the probability of making an *old* response given that the stimulus is old (a *hit*) (see Table 9.2). The area of the old distribution located on the left of the criterion represents the probability of *miss* responses (vertical shading). Note that the probabilities of *hit* and *miss* responses total 1.0.

The distribution of distractor items is also intersected by the criterion. In our example, the area to the right of the criterion is relatively small (horizontal shading). It represents the probability of making an *old* response to a new stimulus (a false alarm). The larger area of the new distribution to the left of the criterion represents the probability of a correct rejection (see Chapter 3). In Figure 9.4B, the criterion is shown in a fixed location. This is true for any given trial. Across trials, however, the response criterion may vary depending on the payoff the subject receives for making *hit* and *false alarm* responses.

Retrieval in Recall. For recall, the person searches the long-term structure. The search process is more complex than the familiarity check in recognition; it involves checking and selection of a starter word and then of additional words. All along, the person checks if selected words fit the correct context. The subject uses a context cue as the starting point—for example, the name of the experimenter and the trial number, say, John's third list. The context cue triggers several search cycles until a word is recalled—for

example, *dirt* from list (9.1). Usually, the most active word in the retrieval structure is recovered first. Then another search process starts, based on the context cue and the word just recalled—for example, *John's third list—dirt*. This process is repeated several times. As a result, list (9.1a) is produced: *dirt hand latch slot shirt roof.* For each of the words, at least one search cycle was required. In immediate free recall, the items with the greatest activation levels are the most recent items on the list and they are recalled first. If the activation levels are relatively low, no item can be retrieved and the search is stopped after a certain number of failed attempts.

Application of SAM to Important Memory Experiments. I introduced the SAM model with the claim that it could account for a large set of results. Let me show you next a sample of the retention results SAM can handle, the effects of presentation time, retention interval, and so on. These illustrations are representative of many other findings: paired associate learning, the effects of spacing trials, interference, priming effects, cued recall, sentence learning, semantic memory, discourse memory, and implicit memory.

- *Presentation Time:* An increase in presentation time improves both recall and recognition performance because item strength and associative strength increase, whereas the distractor familiarity remains unchanged. Thus, the associative strength increases for rows 2 through 5, but not for the distractors in rows 6 and 7 of Table 9.5.

— *Retention Interval:* We all know that we retain less when more time has lapsed since study. According to SAM, this occurs because the context cues have changed more as the retention interval increases. New and different contexts emerge during the interval, thus reducing the similarity with the item cues.

— *Serial Position Effects in Free Recall:* Retention in immediate free recall is especially good for items early and late in the list. The curve exhibits primacy and recency effects. The recency effect occurs because the recent items are the most active ones and, therefore, recovered first, unless an arithmetic task or other task intervenes. The primacy items, on the other hand, receive relatively more rehearsals and, therefore, greater item strength than items in the middle of the list. (This account is similar to that given by the classical two-store model of memory. This should not surprise you, as Shiffrin was an author of both models.)

— *Recognition Superiority:* Usually, it is easier to recognize information than to recall it. According to the retrieval framework, in a given time interval more information can be retrieved in a recognition test than in a recall test. This is because the recognition test involves a global familiarity check of the target item, whereas the recall test involves successive search cycles, at least one cycle for each item. As a result, more retrieval time is required for an item recalled than for each item recognized. During the increased time interval, the context cues change and performance decreases in recall.

— *Encoding Specificity:* In the retrieval framework, the encoding specificity effect is explained naturally through the context cues in Tables 9.5 and 9.6. Any changes in the context between study and test lower the product of context and item cues in Table 9.6, the level of

familiarity, and thus reduce retention performance.

— *Part-List Cuing Effect:* This effect refers to a paradoxical finding frequently observed in free-recall experiments. The basic finding is that providing the learner with a subset of words from the original learning list does not aid in recalling the remaining words of the target list; if anything, there may even be a slight advantage of *not* providing any items of the original list. For example, researchers had two groups of subjects learn a list of 30 common English words. At test, members of the control group were given a blank sheet of paper and asked to write down as many words as they could remember. The experimental group was given a sheet that contained 15 words of the original list and was asked to fill in the remaining 15 words—the critical items. The expectation based on every association model was better recall of the 15 critical items in the experimental group. Presenting some of the words during testing should give experimental subjects some additional retrieval paths yielding better recall. But this is not what happened. The experimental group recalled about the same amount of the critical items as the control group.

The SAM model accounts for this null effect in terms of the quality or prompting effectiveness of the cues a subject uses for retrieval. Raaijmakers (1993) distinguished between experimenter-generated and subject-generated cues, noting that the former are "inferior to self-generated cues, because experimenter-provided cues slightly bias the sampling process in favor of cue items" (p. 476). The bias is that any cue given to the learner involves self-sampling of that cue to the exclusion of other cues. It is a kind of inbred process that reduces the yield of critical items.

Raaijmaker and Shiffrin's (1981) SAM model successfully met its original objective of handling a wide range of empirical memory findings, including such unexpected ones as the null effect in partial cueing (Raaijmakers, 1993). SAM's power was achieved on the basis of relatively simple assumptions. However, according to Roediger (1993), the very power of the SAM model entails a weakness as well: The model has too many parameters, not all of which may have counterparts in performance and mental processing. Roediger cited 10 parameters from the SAM model, including such measures as "context-cue-to-image strength, word-cue-to-image strength, context-to-image increment, and word-cue-to-image increment." The power of the SAM model reflects a problem of quantitative models, in general: Once the model is sufficiently broad, the danger looms that the model includes too many parameters to permit empirical testing (see Chapter 6). Fortunately, researchers have a remedy for this problem, at least in principle: Introduce parameters only to the extent that they are warranted by aspects of performance or mental processes.

INTERIM SUMMARY

Raaijmakers and Shiffrin's SAM model is based on a retrieval structure that includes both old and new items of the study and test lists, as well as context cues. The memory strength of an item in response to a probe cue depends on the context cues, item strength and associative strength, and the item's representation relative to the memory strengths of all other items. Highly familiar items are more likely to be recognized and recalled. Changing the context, whether through experimental manipulation or the passage of time, reduces the global memory strength of items, and therefore, their probability of retention. Raaijmakers and Shiffrin's view of familiarity is different from that of other frameworks; they assume that it depends on the sum of familiarity values across all representations in memory.

MEMORY FOR MEANINGFUL MATERIALS

Memory and Meaning

In the first part of this chapter, we covered retention of individual stimulus items. We also made the simplifying assumption that the learner en-

codes, stores, and retrieves items without an effort to elaborate the materials. This section explores memory for meaningful materials and discusses efforts of the learner to add meaning to the information to be remembered. In list-learning studies, the learner is given a list of individual syllables or words to memorize. It is rare that a learner would merely rehearse the items just as they are presented to her. Even Ebbinghaus knew that one thinks of related items, of words that sound similar, and of anything meaningful that helps to memorize them. Often, learners will make up a little story to connect the words; in short, learners project meaning into the materials (see Bartlett, 1932). These embellishments and elaborations enrich the memory representation by adding information from the learners' long-term memory.

We will start this section with a sentence-recognition experiment by Anderson (1974). We continue with several experiments that illustrate the beneficial effects of elaboration on retrieval and memory performance. We will then see how our knowledge of familiar situations influences retention performance. In some situations, this knowledge may help retention; in others, it may hinder it. The section concludes with a review of memory for verbatim information and for more global information, as is required when we answer questions.

Retrieval through Spreading Activation. We have already seen that remembering items requires that they be activated. Anderson's sentence-recognition experiment (1974) is based on the retrieval-by-activation principle as well. This experiment consisted of two phases: learning and testing. During the learning phase, subjects received approximately two dozen sentences such as (9.3) through (9.6). Each sentence conformed to the template *A person "P" is in location "L."*

(**9.3**) The sailor is in the bank.   (1–1)

(**9.4**) The hippie is in the park.   (1–2)

(**9.5**) The doctor is in the church.   (2–1)

(**9.6**) The doctor is in the park.   (2–2)

The sentences differed in the number of times specific agents and locations were mentioned in a set of sentences. For example, *sailor* appears in only one sentence, whereas *doctor* and *park* each appear in two sentences. The frequency of each person and each location occurring in the set of sentences is shown in parentheses. Thus, sentence (9.3) is a 1–1-type sentence because its agent and location are unique for this set.

In the learning phase of the experiment, Anderson had his learners study the list of sentences thoroughly. In the recognition test, he presented old sentences such as (9.3) through (9.6) mixed with distractor sentences such as *The sailor is in the park*. In the distractor sentences, old persons were paired with old locations in new combinations. The subjects had to make a recognition decision for each test sentence. Thus, for any sentence taken from the list (9.3) through (9.6), the correct response would be *old*. Distractor sentences such as *The sailor is in the park*, however, should be judged *new*. Anderson measured people's recognition speed and found that response times were fastest for 1–1-type sentences and slowest for 2–2-type sentences. In Figure 9.5 these sentences are shown in terms of a propositional network (see Chapter 5). Each concept, agent, and location is shown with its connection to its associated concepts. Figure 9.5 illustrates that sentence (9.3) is not connected to any other.

According to Anderson, retrieval works as follows: On seeing a test sentence, the person acti-

vates its underlying concepts in long-term memory. For example, when reading *The hippie is in the park*, the person would activate HIPPIE and PARK. Activation spreads from these concepts as in a semantic memory network (see Chapter 5). When the paths of activation intersect, an *old* response is made; otherwise, a *new* response is made. Anderson assumed that there is a constant amount of activation available for a given retrieval episode. When more links fan out from a concept, activation is dispersed and its spread through the network is slowed down. This causes longer decision latencies and produces the **fan effect**; the more information that is stated about a given concept, the longer it takes to verify it.[1]

Assimilation—Adding Knowledge. In the Anderson (1974) experiment, the sentences were unrelated. Anderson, however, was fully aware that subjects elaborated the isolated sentences the experimenter gave them. Indeed, an imaginative person would create a scenario involving the people in one or more of the target sentences. Consider the following elaboration thought up by one subject:

> *In the middle of the night, the sailor broke into the small bank near the town green to get some money. He owed the money to the hippie who was waiting for him in the park. The hippie commanded a gang of tough guys who would go after the sailor if he didn't pay up. The hippie had been hurt. . . .*

Adding knowledge helps to assimilate the to-be-remembered facts in memory. Next, we will look at three studies that illustrate such assimilation. The first study demonstrates that people remember facts better if they are given relevant rather than irrelevant information (Bradshaw & Anderson, 1982). The second investigation shows that recognition memory improves to the extent that the target information is associated with individuals the learner is familiar with (Keenan & Baillet, 1980). In the third study, memory for apparently jumbled facts is greatly improved when they are tied to a meaningful scenario (Bransford & Johnson, 1973).

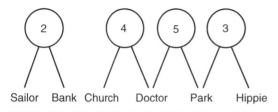

FIGURE 9.5 Network representing sentences in Anderson's recognition experiment. Nodes indicate propositions and arcs indicate arguments. The nodes are numbered for sentences (9.3) through (9.6). Note differences in overlap between 1–1, 1–2, 2–1, and 2–2-type propositions, and the isolation of the 1–1-type proposition.

Relevant versus Irrelevant Elaboration. Bradshaw and Anderson (1982) manipulated the relatedness of elaborations to the targets and compared their effectiveness in three conditions, as illustrated in Table 9.7. In the single-fact condition, a group of subjects was presented with individual facts about 28 well-known historical figures such as Mozart, Newton, and Locke. In the effect condition, the single fact was presented with two additional statements describing effects of the information given in the target sentence. In the irrelevant fact condition, a different group of people received two true but unrelated facts about the famous person.

In the study phase, the subjects read the facts on a computer screen and committed them to memory. One week later, in testing they were given the name of each historical figure and asked to write out what they knew. The students recalled 61% of the target facts in the effect condition, 38% in the single-fact condition, and 32% in the irrelevant-fact condition. Irrelevant facts do not

TABLE 9.7 Three Types of Elaborations in Bradshaw and Anderson (1982) Study

Single-Fact Condition
  Newton became emotionally unstable and
    insecure as a child.

Effect Condition
  Newton became emotionally unstable and
    insecure as a child.
Two consequences of this fact are:
  Newton became irrationally paranoid when
    challenged by colleagues.
  Newton had a nervous breakdown when his
    mother died.

Irrelevant-Fact Condition
  Newton became emotionally unstable and
    insecure as a child.
Two unrelated facts about Newton are:
  Newton was appointed Warden of the London
    mint.
  Newton went to Trinity College in Cambridge.

aid retention; if anything, they interfere with it. Facts related to the target information improved retention by adding new retrieval paths and by helping the learners draw inferences and reconstruct target facts.

Familiarity. The next two studies illustrate the beneficial effects of familiarity on retention. The first study was done by Keenan and Baillet (1980). These investigators conducted a recognition experiment where subjects elaborated target information in terms of people more or less familiar to them. During the study phase, each subject was presented with different encoding conditions. The subject was instructed to think about a person, ranging from yourself to the president, of the United States. Then a question of the form *Person X is ⟨adjective⟩?* was presented, and the subject had to decide whether or not the adjective described the person. In each case, the adjective slot was filled with an adjective such as *kind, rude, or curious.* For example, a question might read "Your best friend is curious?" In testing, old adjectives were mixed with distractor adjectives for old/new recognition decisions. The experimenters recorded the recognition performance and how long it took people to answer the encoding questions. After testing was completed, the subjects were asked to rank the persons in the encoding questions in terms of how much they knew about each person.

Keenan and Baillet found that retention was best when subjects encoded the information in terms of knowledge they were highly familiar with—namely, themselves. Not only did they remember the information better that described themselves, but they required less time to encode it.

The point of the Keenan and Baillet study is that when you encode information in terms of a familiar schema, retention is improved. Note the similarity of this interpretation to Brown's and Kulik's concept of flashbulb memories. People tend to remember circumstances of those events that pertain to them in a personal way. Therefore, African Americans had more elaborate recollections of where they were when they learned of

Martin Luther King's assassination than white Americans (Brown & Kulik, 1982).

A dramatic effect of familiarity was discovered by Bransford and Johnson (1973). They used passage (9.7) in their experiment.

(9.7) If the balloons popped the sound wouldn't be able to carry since everything would be too far away from the correct floor. A closed window would also prevent the sound from carrying, since most buildings tend to be well insulated. Since the whole operation depends on a steady flow of electricity, a break in the middle of the wire would also cause problems. Of course, the fellow could shout, but the human voice is not loud enough to carry that far. An additional problem is that a string could break on the instrument. Then there could be no accompaniment to the message. It is clear that the best situation would involve less distance. Then there would be fewer potential problems. With face to face contact, the least number of things could go wrong.

People were asked to read passage (9.7), judge it for its comprehensibility, and recall it. I am sure you will not be surprised that the subjects did not think much of this passage, nor did they recall very much. They recalled about 26% of the ideas from the text. Another group of subjects were given some background for this passage. They were shown a picture providing the context for the events described in the story (see Figure 9.6). Their recall was 57%, and not surprisingly, they judged the story as quite comprehensible. The point of the Bransford study is that we remember more of a passage if we have background knowledge to integrate the information with. Otherwise, the many facts remain disjointed and difficult to recall.

Distinctiveness of Events. Learning something familiar helps memory but not always. Research has shown that people tend to confuse typical and familiar events, whereas they may remember very unusual events. Two studies make this point.

Confusing Typical Events. We saw that familiarity helped retention but, depending on the circumstances, it may also interfere with correct retention. It may lead to intrusion errors and false alarms, as Bartlett already had found. This effect has been replicated many times. In a recognition experiment, Bower, Black, and Turner (1979) found that what we know can lead to false alarms. They presented several brief passages such as story (9.8) during the study phase of the experiment.

(9.8) Bill had a bad toothache. It seemed like forever before he finally arrived at the dentist's office. Bill looked around at the various dental posters on the wall. Finally the dental hygienist examined and x-rayed his teeth. He wondered what the dentist was doing. The dentist said that Bill had a lot of cavities. As soon as he'd made another appointment, he left the dentist's office.

In testing, Bower and his colleagues presented three types of sentences: old sentences that had been studied by the subjects, new sentences that had not been presented but could have been part of the passages, and unrelated new sentences. Examples follow:

> *Old sentence:* The dentist said that Bill had a lot of cavities.
> *New sentences (related):* Bill checked in with the dentist's receptionist.
> *New sentence (unrelated):* The receptionist took out the coffee pot and filled it with water.

The researchers found that people mistakenly judged the new related sentences as old, thus illustrating that familiar background information may actually contribute to inaccurate recognition performance.

Recognizing Unusual Events. Many studies show that we generally remember familiar materials better than unfamiliar ones. There are, however, exceptions to this generalization. Graesser (1981) found that people remember unusual

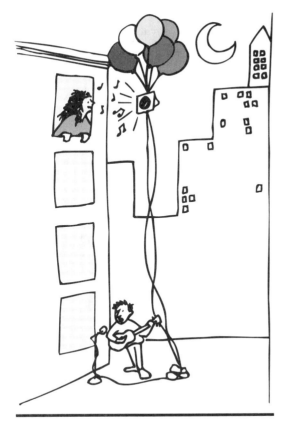

FIGURE 9.6 Meaningful context for the *Balloon* passage shows a serenade (Bransford & Johnson, 1973).

events from an otherwise typical and familiar narrative. He had subjects listen to a story about eating at a restaurant. The story contained both typical statements such as *Jack confirmed his reservation with the hostess* and statements unrelated to the restaurant visit such as *Jack cleaned his glasses*. Recognition performance for the unrelated statements was better than for the typical ones. This effect illustrates the principle of distinctiveness; the more distinctive the target information, the better it is retained. Graesser (1981) cited the von Restorff effect that had been observed long ago in list learning. An atypical item in a list of homogeneous items stands out and tends to be better recalled. Consider the following

list: *ford, chevy, mazda, pineapple, toyota, cadillac, chrysler.*

In the section on list learning, we saw that distinctiveness of cues improves retention (Mäntylä, 1986). The Graesser study, among others, shows that the distinctiveness of an event increases the chances of remembering it.

INTERIM SUMMARY

Good retention depends on several factors, including the type of elaboration, the familiarity, and the distinctiveness of information. Elaborations help only when they are causally related to the to-be-remembered materials. Memory is improved when the target information is linked with a familiar context. If you read an account of a familiar scene, you may later confuse sentences that have and have not been mentioned in the account. Finally, we tend to remember distinctive events even if they do not fit with familiar patterns.

Endpoints on a Continuum—Verbatim Memory and Giving Plausible Answers.   Take a moment to think of your favorite comedy show on TV. The show is a success because of its funny dialogue and natural give-and-take between the actors in the show. Have you ever wondered how the actors, both on the screen and on stage, manage to perform as well as they do? One very important part of an actor's job is to memorize the script, and, believe it or not, actors must memorize their scripts verbatim. Consider the lengthy response the Devil gives Don Juan in the third act of Shaw's *Man and Superman*. They had been discussing the nature of man and the nature of man's achievements throughout history. The Devil gives a 1,000-word speech that the actor playing this part must remember verbatim. Here is the beginning of the speech:

And is Man any the less destroying himself for all this boasted brain of his? Have you walked up and down upon the earth lately? I have; and I have examined Man's wonderful inventions. And I tell you that in the arts of life Man invents nothing; but in the arts of death he outdoes Nature herself, and produces by chemistry and machinery all the slaughter of plague, pestilence, and famine. (G. B. Shaw, Man and Superman, *Copyright by GBS, 1932, Penguin Books, 1962, p. 145)*

Try to memorize this piece plus 900 additional words spoken by the Devil to Don Juan in just one of several exchanges during the entire dialogue. This will give you a feeling for how many words an actor must memorize.

Intons-Peterson and Smyth (1987) are two cognitive psychologists who were interested in such repertory memory. They compared verbatim recall by actors and novices; they recruited theater students and psychology majors of comparable age and intelligence. The drama students had at least four years' experience in theater and repertory groups and therefore were relative experts. Subjects were asked to memorize two 200-word passages, rehearsing the passages aloud. In recall testing, verbatim recall was very good for the experts. It was also surprisingly good for most of the novices, even after a three-day interval. The experts, however, had an important advantage over the novices; they managed to retrieve the words faster than the novices. On the first recital, an expert took 0.8 second to retrieve a word, whereas a novice required 1.1 seconds. The faster retrieval of experts stems from the extended practice they have in their drama and repertory experience. The point of this study is that even novices can memorize information verbatim, but experts retrieve the information more quickly.

The Intons-Peterson and Smyth experiment involved relatively short passages. Even a 1,000-word passage is not long compared to an entire chapter or book. How do you retrieve facts you have acquired from an article or book, for example, when asked in an essay exam? Do you search your memory for the verbatim information? Do you make an inference to produce a response, or do you use some combination of these techniques? Research by Reder (1987) indicates that people use one of two basic strategies to answer questions, depending on circumstances. When a

question is posed immediately after we have read a passage, we are likely to search memory for the stored information. On the other hand, when a longer interval has passed, we first decide how plausible the question is. We may actually ignore specific facts we know. This is demonstrated by peoples' responses to questions such as "How many animals did Moses take on the ark?" We tend to respond "two," although we know that it was Noah, not Moses, who sheltered the animals on the ark.

These studies show once again how adaptive our memory is. When necessary, we can remember verbatim information, but for all other purposes, whether quizzes in school or use in everyday situations, we only need to know the gist of a sentence or passage. When asked about a passage, we are unlikely to retrieve facts verbatim; rather, we give an answer we consider plausible.

FAILING TO REMEMBER AND WHAT TO DO ABOUT IT

Some Cases of Forgetting

When we remember well, we usually do not worry much about memory. It is forgetting that prompts our curiosity about memory. We probably forget more than we remember. We forget last week's baseball scores, our Social Security number, locker combinations, and friends' telephone numbers. We forget that there was a downpour the last Sunday in August. We forget most of the names of our classmates in first grade. Thirty years from now, you will have forgotten most of the names of your college friends and acquaintances. We forgot what we had for lunch a week ago and possibly even yesterday. We forget many of these items because they are unimportant; forgetting helps to clean clutter from our memories and thereby increases the chance of recalling important information.

Forgetting can be painful if the information is important. To improve your chances for a good grade in this course, you better remember the correct answers to the multiple-choice questions in Table 9.8. Similarly, you do not want to forget to

TABLE 9.8 Sample Questions from a Cognitive Psychology Quiz

Proactive interference is frequently observed in list learning studies. It refers to
  (1) the temporary forgetting of information when two response lists are similar
  (2) the interfering effects of earlier learning on later learning
  (3) the interfering effects of later learning on earlier learning
  (4) the permanent forgetting of information when two response lists are dissimilar

The researcher who investigated serial and exhaustive search in working memory was
  (1) G. A. Miller
  (2) A. Baddeley
  (3) S. Sternberg
  (4) M. Daneman

---

call your mother on her birthday, nor an appointment with your advisor or a job interview. These are cases of prospective memory—of remembering to do something in the future (Neisser, 1982). Retrospective memory, in contrast, refers to memory for past events. Other cases of prospective memory include returning books to the library, mailing a letter, submitting a paper, paying your telephone bill, buying party supplies, and so on. We remember such everyday chores better by using external memory aids, like a calendar marked with birthdays and deadlines, or by doing chores at regular intervals, such as paying bills on the first day of each month. Sometimes people tie knots or write notes to remind themselves that a job needs to be done.

Forgetting Everyday Episodes.   Consider the following:

What did you do on your vacation a year ago, two years ago, six years ago?

What was the first name of your homeroom teacher in tenth grade?

Quickly, which courses did you take in your second semester freshman year?

These are the sort of facts and events people often try to remember. Just how much do we retain of regular everyday events? First of all, we have to agree on the definition of an event. Consider these three items and decide whether or not you would judge them events:

(**9.9**) John took a shower.
(**9.10**) Helen beat Lew at tennis.
(**9.11**) Lillian got salmonella after dinner at the student union.

Probably we would not characterize John's taking a shower as an event (unless it happens only once a year!). Similarly, if Helen usually beats Lew at tennis, it is not much of an event. On the other hand, if she beat Lew for the first time, that is an event. Having food poisoning clearly qualifies as an event. An event, therefore, is relatively unique and distinctive. Linton (1982) studied her own memory for events like (9.10) and (9.11) over a six-year period. Every day she would record several items on index cards and date them on the back. For 1972, she recorded 1,345 items, for example. At certain time intervals—weeks, months, or years—she would pick a sample of cards at random and try to remember the date of each selected event. Linton's memory was surprisingly good. On average, she forgot only 5% of the events per year, thus beating Ebbinghaus's memory by a good margin. Of course, she had the advantage of trying to remember meaningful events rather than nonsense syllables.

When Linton originally recorded an event, she also rated it for distinctiveness, importance, and emotional value. Surprisingly, she found that neither rated importance nor rated emotionality had much of an impact on the memorability of an event. Distinctiveness, however, did influence remembering so that "failure to recall" results in part from a "failure to distinguish."

In a study of his autobiographical memory, Wagenaar (1986) replicated and expanded Linton's findings. Wagenaar recorded 2,400 events over a five-year span in terms of *who, what, where,* and *when.* For example, one of the events was a visit to see a painting by Leonardo da Vinci in Milano, Italy. Wagenaar gave the event an arbitrary number and recorded the following attributes:

Who: Leonardo da Vinci
What: I went to see his *Last Supper*
Where: In a church in Milano
When: Saturday, September 10, 1983

At recall, Wagenaar used one, two, or three of these pieces of information to retrieve the full set of facts. Thus, given *Leonardo da Vinci* he would try to recall the remaining three state-ments. Wagenaar found recall of these events torturous; he had to limit his retrieval attempts to five per day. As a result, the retrieval period took him a full year. Recall decreased as a func-tion of the retention interval and as a function of the number of prompts used. He found three of the prompts—*who, what,* and *where*—to be equally effective as retrieval cues, whereas *when* was a less effective cue. Wagenaar attributed the difficulty of retrieving *when* to the possibility that dates of events are stored in a very rough form, if at all.

Linton's (1982) and Wagenaar's (1986) stud-ies demonstrate that event recall tends to be frag-mentary; we retain a portion of the event. The next section describes partial memory for word meanings and names. Technically, memory for words represents semantic memory rather than episodic memory. Nevertheless, we discuss such partial forgetting here because it characterizes both semantic and episodic memory.

Remembering Words: Tip of the Tongue Phenomenon.

The Tip of the Tongue phenom-enon occurs when you know the name of a con-cept but you fail to recall it. It is a tantalizing experience. You may remember one syllable or even half of the word, and you feel on the verge of generating it but you just can't spit it out. You can induce this phenomenon in your friends by select-ing a set of rare words from a dictionary. Read the definition of each word and ask a friend if she can produce the name that fits the definition. Here are a couple of examples:

> What do you call the following? *A waxy sub-stance found floating in or on the shores of tropical waters, believed to originate in the in-testines of the sperm whale, and used in per-fumery as a fixative.*

> What do you call the following? *A naviga-tional instrument used in measuring angular distances, especially the altitude of the sun, moon, and stars at sea.*[2]

You will find yourself producing strings that contain significant features of the word you are seeking, but not the word itself. The number of syllables may agree; the stress pattern of the word may be right; some of the syllables may overlap; or you may come up with a synonym. For the sec-ond of the two targets above, Brown and McNeill (1966) observed semantically related words such as *astrolabe* and *compass,* as well as words that sounded similar such as *secand* and *sexton.* The Tip of the Tongue phenomenon results from the fact that memory representations are rarely uni-tary. Rather, each representation contains several features, some of which may not be accessible when needed.

Memory Illusions.

We are all familiar with the feeling that our memory frequently seems to be playing tricks on us and we often wonder: Did I mail that letter? Did I lock my room? Did I re-ally say such and such? There are also instances when we believe having seen or heard something that, in fact, did not occur. Remembering an event that did not take place is referred to as a **memory illusion.** Such illusions have been stud-ied in research laboratories using traditional list-learning methods. Payne and colleagues (1996) assessed false memories through recall and recognition tests. In one of their studies, the re-searchers presented a list of 60 words consisting of six sublists. Each sublist included 10 items typically associated with a given concept or cat-egory—for example, a funeral. The sublists ex-pressly omitted specific target terms that were highly typical of the category such as the category name itself.

The point of the study was to see to what extent subjects would recall and recognize the non-presented items as if they had been presented. Here is a sample list. Nonpresented words are shown in parentheses:

(Secret) private, hidden, tell, admirer, gossip, confidential, code, personal, trust, unknown, (Test), exam, quiz, grade, study, school, question, score, answer, fail, pass, (Drunk) alcohol, beer, drive, sober, liquor, bar, intoxicate, booze, wine, inebriated, (Sick) ill, cold, vomit, doctor, flue, bed, fever, hurt, medicine, nausea, (Funeral) dead, sad, procession, black, home, parlor, wake, burial, service, casket.

There were two different recall conditions: free recall and forced recall. In the free-recall condition, subjects were asked to recall any number of items in any order. In the forced-recall procedure, they were encouraged to recall at least 60 words. There were three successive recall tests. Following the recall phase, there was a recognition phase during which subjects saw old items and distractor items, including nonpresented targets such as *funeral.*

The memory illusion was observed in all testing conditions—free recall, forced recall, and recognition. In free recall, subjects falsely recalled almost the same proportion of nonpresented items as presented items. In forced recall, they tended to recall a slightly greater proportion of the nonpresented items. The tendency for false recall increased as a function of successive test trials. In recognition testing, subjects falsely judged nonpresented items as old items. When asked about the certainty they had about having heard the nonpresented items, subjects expressed high degrees of certainty of having heard them.

Payne and colleagues (1996) interpreted the memory illusion in terms of fuzzy trace theory (Reyna & Titcomb, in press). According to this theory, people form at least two representations of a series of events: a verbatim representation and a gist representation. The verbatim representation includes the veridical sequence of events or items. The gist representation includes the theme or general topic of the items. The two representations differ in their durability. The verbatim representation lasts for a relatively short time, whereas the gist representation is more durable. Payne and colleagues believe that memory illusions are based on the theme a person forms of events experienced. The theme captures important aspects of the events although not veridically. (Similar representations are formed in discourse comprehension. See Chapter 12.)

Research on memory illusions has an important implication for the use of memory in everyday settings. False memories are more likely when a person is repeatedly prodded to recall as much as she can. This tends to occur in legal proceedings when witnesses are questioned repeatedly by different officials. Witnesses' "recollections," however, may include false memories. The next section describes the role of memory distortions in legal settings.

Memory and the Law: Eyewitness Testimony. Partial recall can be a nuisance; it may even lead to memory distortions. A person's retention may be distorted by events he expected to happen (Bartlett, 1932; Bower et al., 1979). Memory distortions can be problematic when a person is asked to give eyewitness testimony in a court of law. It has been shown that witnesses' recollections can be shaped by the type of questions asked of them (see Loftus, 1979). Indeed, sometimes people tend to "recall" events that never happened (Schooler, Gerhard, & Loftus, 1986). None of this should be surprising; we are rarely tested for exact retention in everyday situations, and approximate recall is usually sufficient. In trial situations, however, the fate of a defendant often depends on the recollection of witnesses.

Whether faulty or not, eyewitness memory will continue to be a vital source of evidence in the legal system. Cognitive psychologists can assist in improving the use of this important source of evidence. (See also Chapter 15 for enhancement of eyewitness memory.)

Coping with Poor Memory

People have invented mnemonic techniques to overcome memory failures and inaccuracies. Building on the close relation between working memory and long-term memory, these techniques have proven helpful to remember information of all kinds. They work because they create an effective retrieval system in long-term memory. A dramatic demonstration of such retrieval paths was given by Chase and Ericsson (1981). They trained a person to expand his digit span tenfold over a 40-week period.

Skilled Memory.   Chase and Ericsson reported the experience of one person, SF, who was an undergraduate of average intelligence (SAT = 990) at Carnegie-Mellon University. His digit span was also average (8) when the study began. Over a two-year span, SF participated in the experiment for about 250 sessions. As described in Chapter 8, SF, a long-distance runner, developed a scheme to recode a list of numbers to be learned in terms of running times for various distances. Toward the end of the study, SF's digit span measured as many as 80 digits!

SF's digit span clearly increased, but did he improve his short-term memory? According to Chase and Ericsson, he did not. SF's coded groups rarely exceeded three or four digits, thus remaining well within the usual digit span. Rather, SF developed a retrieval structure in long-term memory and a facility to use this structure for digit recall. The point of the Chase study is similar to that of the Bradshaw and Keenan studies: You strengthen retention by mapping the to-be-remembered information in terms of something that is familiar and sensible to you. This is the principle that the inventors of mnemonic techniques have used unwittingly since ancient times.

Mnemonic Techniques.   Before inexpensive external memory aids like paper became widely available, there was a great need for mnemonic techniques. Cicero, a famous orator in Roman times, was one of the first authors to describe mnemonic techniques. Expressed in our terminol-ogy, the learner elaborates to-be-learned information in terms of something he already knows. At the time of recall, the familiar information and the associated new information is accessed at the same time. Suppose you have to memorize a list of names. One way of doing this is to make a story about each of them and then remember the story titles and the newly learned names. Another method is to associate the new names with TV shows familiar to the learner. Each name is linked with a show, and at recall the show titles and the associated names are retrieved. A time-honored mnemonic technique is the method of loci reportedly invented in antiquity by the poet Simonides.

According to legend, the poet Simonides was invited in to a banquet in a big hall. While he stepped outside for a moment, an earthquake struck and destroyed the building, killing all the guests and obliterating their identities. By remembering the places where the guests had been seated in the hall, Simonides was able to recall each identity and help ensure that each victim received a proper burial. From a cognitive perspective, Simonides recalled the information by mentally passing through each location and by retrieving the name stored there. The peg method works similarly. One forms a rhyme of a number and a noun (for example, one is a bun, two is a shoe, and three is a tree) and associates the to-be-remembered items with the nouns.

Mnemonic techniques of great sophistication are used by preliterate societies to remember the fables and tales of the culture. Neisser's (1982) volume contains several accounts of story memory in the oral traditions of different cultures; the Tswana in South Africa, the Iatmul in New Guinea, and Serbocroatians in the Balkans. Common to most of these is the use of stereotypic formulas, certain recurrent themes, rhymes, and melodies. It is through their stories and ballads that these cultures carry on their cultural tradition.

Exceptional Memories

Popular and professional journals report from time to time about individuals with an apparently special aptitude for memory. Rajan Srinivasan Mahadevan is such a person. He made the *Guiness Book of World Records* by recalling the first 31,811 digits of π from memory. He did this in two and one-half hours, excluding breaks reciting 3.5 digits per second! Thompson and colleagues (1991) investigated Rajan's retention performance in several standard tasks, including the digit span, letter span, list recall, and prose recall. Except for the recall of prose materials, Rajan's recall was superior to that of four control subjects in all of the memory tasks. Rajan started out at a higher initial level of recall and proceeded to improve his recall in subsequent training sessions. Thompson and colleagues concluded that Rajan's superb recall, although aided by practice, was due to an exceptional ability. They noted that even as a five-year-old, Rajan exhibited an excellent memory. This was recounted by his father in a letter to Professor Thompson:

My wife and I first became aware of Rajan's phenomenal memory in March 1963, when we had a small party at home to celebrate our daughter's first birthday. Rajan was about 5 years and 9 months old at that time. I do not remember the exact number of vehicles at the party but I should think there were about 20 or so. Rajan did surprise us all by reciting correctly the license numbers of all the vehicles and the corresponding owners. He could also easily recall many telephone numbers and railway time-tables.

Could you become another Rajan? Answers to this question depend on one's theoretical bent. If you believe, as Ericsson and Charness (1994) do, that memory is a skill like any other, you could train yourself to replicate Rajan's feat. As predicted by the memory skill theory, Rajan benefited from practice and there was a speedup in his performance with practice. On the other hand, if you agree with Thompson and colleagues (1991) that a particular memory ability is required to support practice in the first place, it is unlikely that you could duplicate Rajan's performance. Defending the notion of an innate

mnemonic capacity, Thompson and associates pointed out that Rajan exhibited an unusual memory capacity at an early age; that unlike SF's memory capacity, Rajan's was general; and that he did not use meaningful materials as an encoding strategy.

Other dramatic instances of exceptional memory were reported by Luria (1976) and Hunt and Love (1972). Luria's *The Mind of a Mnemonist* describes the life, achievements, and problems of S, who remembered everything and forgot nothing. The subtitle, *A Little Book about a Vast Memory,* is an apt summary of S's performance as a newspaper reporter who didn't need to take notes and who exhibited astounding memory feats both on stage and in research laboratories. S remembered information by associating it with a richly developed subjective panorama of colors and moods. Hunt and Love's subject, VP, excelled in long- and short-term memory, including scanning of short-term memory. His scanning rate in the Sternberg task was about 20 milliseconds compared to 40 milliseconds for other subjects.

Improving One's Memory—
Lessons from Cognitive Psychology

Even if your memory is not exceptional, there are ways you can improve it. We have had several opportunities throughout this chapter to discuss ways of improving one's memory. I have put them together in Box 9.1. Remember that we have been discussing declarative memory in this chapter. For good performance in procedural skills, practice is the best insurance against forgetting (see Chapter 13).

INTERIM SUMMARY

A mnemonic device includes an encoding component and an associated retrieval plan. During encoding, the person associates the new information with a body of familiar knowledge. When the new information is needed, it is retrieved by using the familiar information as an intermediary retrieval path.

Box 9.1

What Can You Do?

— The first lesson for good retention is to pay attention to the materials you wish to memorize. Remember that encoding information is the first stage in the life of a representation.

— If the amount of information is not too much and you have only a little time for study, it is best to memorize it right before you need it.

— If the information is really important to you, then overcome the limits of memory by overlearning the materials. This means you should repeat it frequently and in different contexts. You want to ensure that the information remains of sufficient memory strength, even after forgetting takes its course.

— Two lessons from the encoding specificity principle:

Lesson 1: You can improve retention when you memorize the necessary information in a context that is as similar as possible to the test situation. If you want to improve your chances of getting an A on a chemistry test to be given at 8:30 A.M. in Hillary Hall Room 4201, then you had better study several times in Hillary Hall in the morning and memorize compounds, formulas, and equations.

Lesson 2: Realize that the encoding specificity principle reveals a limit of your performance. Because your retention depends on the context, it is also limited by the context. Knowing this principle suggests a way to overcome its limitations: You should study the information several times under different occasions so that it is associated with different contexts rather than to one specific context. This is the better lesson to learn from the encoding specificity principle. There is also experimental evidence to support this view (see Madigan, 1969).

— Process information deeply by assimilating it to your own knowledge through mnemonics, elaboration, or organizational schemes. Think of facts that are causally related to the target information to be learned. Get knowledge from additional sources; in a history, chemistry, cognitive psychology, or other class, find materials that are related to the assignments given by the teacher. In sum, read up on a subject to be tested in a variety of sources.

IMPLICIT MEMORY

Given the emphasis of education and of the information-processing approach on explicit learning and memory, it is easy to overlook that we acquire much of our knowledge implicitly. Memory researchers, however, know of many everyday and experimental contexts where memories are established implicitly. In this section, we will distinguish between two broad categories of implicit memory: facilitation and rule learning. *Facilitation of identification* refers to improved performance on the repeated occurrence of a stimulus, even when the perceiver does not remember having seen the stimulus. *Rule learning* refers to the implicit acquisition of a rule system from an encounter with a set of stimuli generated according to those rules (Reber, 1993).

Facilitation

Improved performance has been found in priming, social facilitation, and fragment completion. Each of these tasks consists of (1) an implicit study phase during which the person encounters the stimuli and (2) a performance phase where the person has to identify or use the stimuli in some manner. In the fragment completion phase, for example, the person is exposed to rare words such as *trombone, ratification,* and *crankshaft.* During the performance phase, the person is given a word fragment such as __O_BO__ and C__NK___FT and asked to complete it. Usually, subjects identify words they had seen during the study phase faster than new control words. Previous presentation of a word **primes** the subsequent completion of the word fragment.

Priming effects are observed after days, weeks, and even months (Schacter, 1987). This kind of performance represents implicit memory: The person is not explicitly tested for the target information but there is evidence of learning and memory nevertheless. Implicit memory has been observed for a range of visual stimuli: words, faces, geometric shapes, and object drawings (Tulving & Schacter, 1990).

Implicit and explicit memory performance differs on several dimensions. Such differences are known as **dissociation effects.** Time delay produces dissociation. When presented with both implicit and explicit memory tests, subjects show continued evidence of implicit memory, whereas their explicit memory decreases with time. Tulving, Schacter, and Stark (1982) presented their subjects with a set of 96 words. The subjects were subsequently tested using a recognition and fragment completion task. There were two retention intervals for both tasks: one hour and seven days. Tulving and colleagues found that explicit recognition accuracy decreased after seven days, whereas performance on the fragment completion task did not (for typical dissociation results, see Figure 9.7.)

The data in Figure 9.7 reflect dissociation because the performance differs for the explicit recognition task and the implicit fragment completion task. Researchers have discovered additional dissociations:

- *Developmental Dissociation:* Explicit memory performance increases with age in children, whereas implicit memory is as good in three-year-olds as in college students.
- *Drug-Related Dissociation:* People's explicit memory performance is reduced when they are under the influence of drugs such as alcohol and scopolamine (an amnesia-inducing drug). Their implicit memory, however, is not impaired.
- *Clinical Dissociation:* Patients suffering from amnesia have no recollection of explicit memory episodes (see also next section), yet their

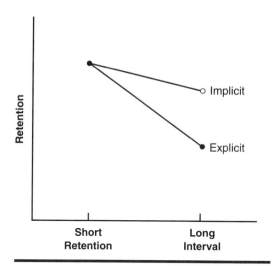

FIGURE 9.7 Typical dissociation between implicit and explicit memory. Explicit memory performance declines as a function of the retention interval, whereas implicit memory is maintained better.

implicit memory performance is no different from that of normal subjects.

Of course, there are also similarities between implicit and explicit memory, otherwise we would not use the term *memory* to capture performance in the two situations. Both kinds of memory benefit from additional exposure to the stimuli during the study period, and both exhibit forgetting over a period of time. Because implicit and explicit memory share some attributes and differ on others, there is a debate among theorists whether to view both kinds of memory as one or two systems. Roediger (1990) maintained that performance in both tasks may be understood in terms of general principles. Schacter (1996), however, advocated two different memory systems for explicit and implicit memory tasks. The explicit memory system includes episodic and semantic memory. Implicit memory is closely linked with the perceptual system. In support for his hypothesis, Schacter cited many dissociation phenomena, including the preceding ones, and the fact that implicit memory does not involve consciousness, unlike episodic and semantic memories.

According to researchers at Washington University, patterns of cerebral blood flow suggest that two different memory systems support performance in explicit and implicit memory tasks. Squire and colleagues assessed explicit memory in a recall task and implicit memory in a priming task. In both tasks, subjects first studied a list of about 30 words—for example, *motel*. In testing, word fragments were shown—for example, MOT__. The recall subjects had to recall the words, whereas the priming subjects were asked to complete the word fragments. The researchers found that the recall task produced increased activity in the right hippocampus. The priming task, however, resulted in a *reduction* of blood flow in the right posterior cortex. In sum, both the pattern of activity and the locus of activity change differed in the recall and priming tasks (Squire et al., 1991). A number of researchers have entertained the hypothesis that different brain systems mediate implicit and conscious memories; specifically, implicit memories are thought to be supported by neocortical association regions of the brain, whereas explicit memories are processed via the hippocampus (Schacter & Tulving, 1994; see also Chapter 2).

Rule Learning

Native speakers typically learn the rules of their language without explicit instruction (see Chapter 10). Unless one believes that people have innate knowledge of the rules of language, the assumption most scientists make is that people induce language rules implicitly from an encounter with the utterances of the language. Reber (1993) developed a laboratory equivalent to study such implicit rule learning. He used an **artificial miniature grammar,** with letters as primitives, and letter strings to mimic the sentences of natural languages.

Reber formulated a grammar including *n* states and any number of transitions between them. Figure 9.8 illustrates one such grammar, where

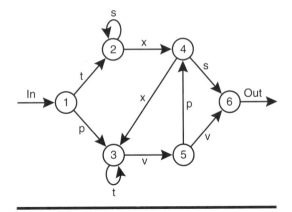

FIGURE 9.8 Artificial grammar used by Reber (1965) to investigate implicit rule learning.

circles indicate states and arrows reflect transitions. The vocabulary of the grammar consists of the letters *P, S, T, V,* and *X*. The sequence of grammatical letter strings is dictated by the transitions provided in the grammar. Any string is grammatical that follows the sequence of states and transitions in Figure 9.8; for example, *PVV* is a simple string based on the transitions between states 1, 3, 5, and 6. Strings *PTVV* and *TSXXTVPS* are also grammatical according to the grammar, just more complex. Ungrammatical strings violate either the sequence of transitions or the permissible vocabulary. For example, *TVV* and *BVV* are ungrammatical according to the grammar in Figure 9.8.

Miniature grammars of the kind in Figure 9.8 are well suited to study implicit learning. Experimenters can generate a relatively complex set of sentences. Although small, the grammar is too complex to be abstracted by conscious reflection, thus enhancing the likelihood of implicit learning. Also, it is unlikely that subjects have encountered such grammars before, so there is little likelihood of preexperimental transfer or interference.

Reber (1993) had subjects memorize grammatical and ungrammatical strings (defined above) and found better retention for grammatical than for ungrammatical letter strings, although subjects were not aware of the difference. In another study, Reber sought to isolate the structures that subjects abstracted during learning. He compared performance in two transfer conditions: the syntax-change condition and the vocabulary-change condition. There were two phases in each condition. In the syntax-change condition, Reber changed the grammar used to generate the letter strings between phases but kept the set of letters, the vocabulary, constant. In the second condition, he changed the set of letters but kept the same grammar to generate the stimulus sentences. Reber found a greater drop in performance in the syntax-change condition than in the vocabulary-change condition. He concluded that subjects had acquired the abstract **rule** from which the stimuli were generated rather than individual stimulus **exemplars.** Researchers have determined that implicit grammar learning is relatively immune from impairment, much as priming. For example, amnesic patients are able to learn to classify new instances of a grammatical category as defined by an artificial grammar as well as normal control subjects.

Reber concluded that subjects learned the rules of the grammar implicitly without conscious awareness; the result of such learning is abstract knowledge that cannot be verbalized. Hence, Reber speculated on evolutionary aspects of implicit learning, viewing it as phylogenetically prior to and therefore more robust than explicit learning. It is for this reason that implicit learning and memory persist better in impaired populations than explicit and conscious learning. The latter is like a superstructure that is more complex and more easily disrupted.

CLINICAL STUDY OF MEMORY

Outside the mainstream of business, government, and schools, there is a large population of individuals with organic and emotional memory dysfunctions. It is estimated that about 5% of the population of industrialized nations suffers from some kind of amnesia, caused by accidents, the use of drugs, or sickness, including Alzheimer's disease.

Amnesia

Amnesia describes a collection of memory deficits resulting from organic or emotional dysfunction. We have encountered one dramatic case of amnesia—Milner's (1966) HM—when we considered the two-store model of memory and the transfer of new learning from short-term to long-term memory (see Chapter 7). **Anterograde amnesia** involves the difficulty or inability to acquire new episodic information despite an intact working memory and adequate recall of old long-term memories. Wilson (1987) described the case of a patient, CM, who was an assistant bank manager. In his early forties, he suffered from a malignant tumor in his left temporal lobe. The tumor was treated with radiotherapy; however, severe memory deficits persisted, making it impossible for CM to return to work. Though he remembered the names of his wife and children, he could not learn new names. He did not remember errands or TV shows shortly after they began. He continuously worried about forgetting something important.

Anterograde amnesia is associated with deficient anatomical structures in the brain, including the hippocampus, mammilary bodies, and the limbic system. Brain damage may be caused by accidents, surgery, or deficient nutrition. Nutritional problems may also occur in extreme cases of alcoholism, as first described by Korsakoff. The alcoholic patient consumes so much alcohol that an important vitamin, thiamine, is no longer absorbed by the digestive system. **Retrograde amnesia** also occurs after traumatic head injuries received in traffic accidents. Patients cannot recall events prior to the accident but have good memory for old events and can acquire new information. In many cases, the amnesia is reversible and the person begins to remember some of the events leading up to the accident. Usually, the older memories tend to return first, while more recent ones return later or not at all.

Do amnesic patients remember anything at all? The answer is yes, as we saw in the section on **implicit memory.** Consider two particularly informative cases. One is a classic observation made by Claparede (see Schacter, 1987) and the other was described by Tulving and Schacter (1990). Claparede, a Swiss neurologist, had an amnesic patient who did not remember meeting him or any other member of the hospital staff. Nevertheless, Claparede believed that the woman was capable of learning. One day, when he greeted her with a handshake, he had a small needle hidden in his hand and gave the woman a gentle pinprick. Later, the woman hesitated shaking hands with Claparede, although she had no conscious memory of ever having met him before.

Tulving and Schacter (1990) reported the case of a patient, KC, who did not remember a single event from his past. When given three-word phrases such as *strongman started dynasty* and later asked to complete word fragments such as D_N_S__, he was able to do so, although he did not remember ever having seen the phrases. Schacter (1983) observed the dissociation between episodic and procedural memory in a golfer, MT, who suffered from amnesia. Schacter and MT played golf together on several occasions; MT remembered his golf skills very well, hitting, putting, and choosing the correct golf club, but one minute after teeing off, he had forgotten the location of his golf ball. Schacter's (1983) observations of MT mirror the dissociation effects observed with amnesic patients in the laboratory: Patients can acquire and remember procedural skills and they exhibit implicit memory. Their principal difficulty concerns explicit memory, such as acquiring new memories or in accessing previous memories.

These deficits have been attributed to each of the stages of learning—encoding, storage, and retrieval. Some investigators attribute amnesia to the patient's inability to process to-be-remembered information deeply enough; other researchers suggest that there is greater interference among stored representations. Still others say that amnesic patients fail to use contextual cues for retrieval. None of these explanations is sufficient to account for severe memory deficits, however. We can only hope that neurophysiological research will provide new perspectives on amnesia and its rehabilitation.

In the absence of an overall theory of amnesia, therapists use techniques that work for individual patients. Wilson (1987), a clinical psychologist, had notable success with individual amnesic patients. She used imagery-based mnemonic techniques to help patients remember the name of staff members in a hospital. For example, patients eventually learned the name Stephanie by associating Stephanie, a physiotherapist, with a picture showing a step and a knee. Wilson had four patients, each of whom began to recall names as soon as this mnemonic technique was introduced, as shown in Figure 9.9. Prior to imagery training, no names were recalled at all. Imagery training, however, resulted in good to moderate learning independently of when it was introduced.

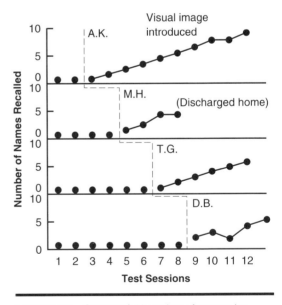

FIGURE 9.9 Successful learning of names by amnesic patients as a result of using an imagery-based mnemonic technique (Baddeley, 1990).

Alzheimer's Disease

Alzheimer's disease is associated with severe memory disabilities that increase over time. Initially, the patient may not remember names, errands, or items on shopping lists. Later, the person may become disoriented and loose his way around town and around the neighborhood. Eventually, the patient no longer even recognizes family members. Alzheimer's disease is particularly pernicious because it is difficult to diagnose in the early stages. Researchers have, however, isolated specific anatomical and neurophysiological abnormalities in patients with severe cases of the disease. Alzheimer's patients exhibit both atrophy of normal neural structures and the growth of abnormal structures. Their brain processes, as revealed by PET imaging and ERP methodology, differ from that of normal populations. Even DNA mutations have been discovered in some patients. There are also neurochemical changes, including a reduced level of choline, an enzyme needed for the production of the neurotransmitter acetylcholine, ACh.

Periodically, there are optimistic reports of a cure for Alzheimer's, of a "nerve growth factor" or of "fountain-of-youth proteins" that would rehabilitate brain function and fading memories. Unfortunately, to date, no satisfactory treatment has been found to restore the memory deficits in Alzheimer's patients. Many drugs such as choline and lecithin have been tried to stimulate ACh production, but they did not help patients. Because of the great cost to society, increasing research efforts are undertaken to understand Alzheimer's disease; after all, four million Americans are estimated to suffer from the disease. Neuropsychologists, medical researchers, and cognitive psychologists contribute to these efforts.

We have reviewed two major categories of clinical memory deficits and noted that these deficits may result from a variety of causes: organic deficiencies, emotional trauma, malnutrition, or age-related diseases such as Alzheimer's. It is a common characteristic of clinical memory deficits that they affect episodic memory to a greater extent than implicit memory or procedural skills. To date, there is no theoretical framework that can account for clinical memory deficits. Major interdisciplinary research programs have been launched to gain a better understanding of these disabilities and to treat them in individual patients (see also Chapter 15).

CONCLUSION

Memory is not a unitary system; the wealth of materials presented in this chapter should therefore not be surprising. Memory fulfills many functions and holds diverse kinds of information, ranging from lists of words to plausible facts, from errands to telephone numbers, and from sports trivia to information quizzed in a multiple-choice test. We have mentioned various types of memory, including explicit and implicit memory, semantic and episodic memory, long-term and working memory, and retrospective and prospective memory. We have seen that cognitive psychologists have devised many techniques to gain an understanding of the structures and processes underlying these memory systems: the savings method, various kinds of recall and recognition tests, and the fragment completion task.

Cognitive psychologists have also proposed a variety of models and theories to account for broad sets of results. We studied the theory of Raaijmakers and Shiffrin (1981), a framework of list learning. According to this theory, the context and the memory strength of a representation jointly determine its activation level and likelihood of retrieval. Retrieval is also facilitated when the learner generates additional retrieval paths through elaboration and assimilation with familiar knowledge. We discussed forgetting and memory distortions, as well as pathological memory deficits. In spite of these problems, we can conclude, however, that our memory is very adaptive, serving us successfully in most situations.

ENDNOTES

1. Immediately after Anderson's fan effect was published, cognitive psychologists began to discuss the Paradox of the Expert, referring to the idea that the more we know about something, the longer it takes to retrieve the information. However, subsequent research showed that there was no such paradox. The fan effect occurs only when the information to be learned is unrelated to each other and to what people already know. Thus, be warned not to use the Paradox of the Expert as an excuse in preparing for a test in cognitive psychology!

2. The respective words are *ambergris* and *sextant*.

LANGUAGE: STRUCTURE AND MEANING

PREVIEW

This chapter deals with the structure and meaning of language from a linguistic perspective. The chapter has three parts, one for each of the three basic linguistic units: sentences, words, and sounds. Following Noam Chomsky's view of grammar, it will be shown that sentences are best represented as a hierarchical structure rather than as a string of words. Chomsky distinguished between two types of syntactic rules—phrase structure rules and transformational rules. Phrase structure rules are used to generate simple active sentences that reflect underlying meaning relations; transformational rules generate the surface form of a sentence. In addition to rules, linguists use principles to account for the syntactic structure of sentences. The theta principle, for example, addresses the relation between verbs and nouns in sentences. Sentence meaning has been represented in terms of propositions, which include the predicate of the sentence, usually the verb, and its arguments.

Next, we will see that lexical knowledge comprises the information that speakers have of words. The internal structure of words, the syntactic role they fulfill, and the meaning of words will be discussed. Finally, under the heading of phonology, we will see how sounds are produced in the vocal tract, illustrate how they are classified into groups of phonemes, and sketch some patterns of English phonemes. The regularities of language have been described in terms of rules and principles. They are not meant to give an account of cognitive processes in language use. These will be discussed in Chapter 11.

INTRODUCTION

We usually talk so effortlessly and understand speakers of our native language so easily that we are unaware of how vast the knowledge is that underlies our use of language. We know the meaning of words, their sounds, and their appropriate uses, and we know how to combine words into comprehensible sentences. Consider the word *dog.* Even before a child knows how to read, she understands the word *dog.* She knows the sound of *dog,* the animal that it refers to, the role it plays in sentences, and that one can speak about a singular dog or about several dogs. The word *dog* is simple and occurs frequently in English; it is one of the first words an English speaker learns. Then there are other words you may or may not know: *table, thaumaturgy, somatic, headset,* and *claymore.* It is estimated that a U.S. high school student recognizes about 40,000 words (Miller, 1988). For almost every one of these words, you can say whether or not you have heard it before. You cannot do this for the sentences you encounter. This comparison suggests that knowledge about sentences is represented differently from knowledge about words. Our knowledge of sentences and words and their representation is the focus of this chapter.

A speaker may not remember sentences he has heard before, but he does know what constitutes an acceptable sentence and what does not. Strings (10.1) through (10.3) are grammatical sentences, but (10.4) through (10.6), marked with asterisks, are not.

(10.1) The boy hit the ball.

(10.2) The boy greeted the girl who called the man.

(10.3) The woman thinks the girl slept.

(10.4) *The the hit boy ball.

(10.5) *The boy greeted the girl the girl called the man.

(10.6) *The woman thinks the girl.

Usually a person's intuitions about the acceptability of a sentence are quite accurate, even when the sentence is very complex. People can judge the grammaticality of entirely novel sentences. Indeed, except for frequently used clichés such as *Nice meeting you,* one rarely encounters the same sentence twice. Speakers also know that there are many constraints on sentences that permit some interpretations and exclude others. For example, English speakers know that the pronoun *he* may refer to John in sentence (10.7) but not in sentence (10.8).

(10.7) John thinks he won.

(10.8) He thinks John won.

In (10.7), John thinks of himself as the winner, whereas sentence (10.8) indicates that another person thinks John has won. That *he* may refer to John in (10.7) but not in (10.8) is very intriguing; for what is the principle governing the relationship between pronouns and their referents? Furthermore, how is this knowledge acquired by speakers of a language? Neither our teachers nor our parents taught us this principle. The same is true for many other constructions that speakers use and listeners interpret all the time.

Linguistics is the scientific study of the structure of sentences, words, and sounds and the knowledge necessary to interpret them. The preceding examples illustrate the many facets of linguistic knowledge, including knowledge of the sound and meaning of words, as well as their grammatical combination and interpretation in sentences. Linguists study our knowledge of language at an abstract level by cataloging the rules and principles used to describe the regularities of language; they do not claim that people actually use these rules and principles as they produce and comprehend language. Psycholinguists are interested in language production and comprehension and the mental processes that underlie the use of language. Chapters 10 and 11 are devoted to language and language use. In this chapter, the perspective of a linguist is taken in an examination of three components of linguistic knowledge: knowledge of sentences, words, and sounds.

Linguists refer to these knowledge sources as syntactic, lexical, and phonological knowledge, respectively. In Chapter 11, we will consider language performance within the framework of human information processing and offer neuropsychological perspectives as well. Of course, one cannot strictly separate our abstract knowledge of language and its use. Therefore, I will mention processing issues in Chapter 10 and structural issues in Chapter 11.

Before we proceed with our study of linguistic knowledge, let me alert you to two particular features of this chapter. The first point is that learning about a new discipline involves some exposure to the technical terms of the field. You will see that linguistics, like every other discipline, has its own vocabulary. In describing the regularities of language, linguists have invented many terms that you will encounter: *phrase structures, phrase markers, transformational rules, principles, deep structures,* and so on. These will be defined when first introduced and you would do well to memorize them. You will also see less reference to experiments in this chapter. The data used by linguists are sentences, words, and sounds, rather than reaction times, correct responses, and electro-physiological recordings. Therefore, be prepared for a fair number of sample sentences that will be used to illustrate the phenomena investigated by language researchers.

The second point to bear in mind is the following: Because English is the language you are likely to understand best, reference is made to examples in English and to the regularities of the English language. Linguists, however, strive to describe language universally so that the regularities of all languages are expressed. This is called the **universality principle.**

We will begin our study of linguistics with the sentence. The sentence is the principal source for linguistic research and theory. After all, a *language* is defined as the set of all the sentences that it generates (Lyons, 1970). We will examine a body of rules and principles that produces sentences in their great variety. Then we will study what linguists have learned about words, one of

the constituents of sentences. We will conclude this chapter with sounds, which form one of the elements of both sentences and words.

SENTENCES

Let us examine some simple English sentences as they occur in a wide range of sources, whether it is a first-grade reader, some other type of book, a magazine, a newspaper, or a conversation. The sentences are grouped into three sets.

Set 1: *Jane likes Peter. Peter likes Jane. Peter and Jane like the big dog. The dog chases the cat. The boy throws the ball.*

Set 2: *Peter throws the ball to the girl. Researchers are collecting bone marrow cells from patients' bloodstreams.*

Set 3: *Peter was bitten by the dog. The ball was kicked by the boy. The patient was treated by the emergency room doctor.*

Study the sentences in groups 1, 2, and 3 and, before you read on, see if you can identify features common to sentences both within and across sets.

Some of the attributes these sentences share are readily apparent, whereas others are more subtle. Sentences in all three sets consist of groups of words that intuitively belong together. For example, the phrase *the boy* sounds more natural than the phrase *throws the* or *ball to.* Such word groups have been called parts of speech, phrases, categories, or constituents. The phrase *the boy,* for instance, is a noun phrase, abbreviated NP. One could substitute a pronoun, in this case *he,* for the noun phrase but not for the words *throws the.* Examples of verb phrases (VPs) are *likes, are creating,* and *was bitten.* Table 10.1 lists several syntactic categories introduced in Chapters 10 and 11.

It is also easy to detect some commonalities within sets. The sentences in set 1 have the format: NP, V, NP. This is a format frequently found in so-called subject-verb-object (SVO) languages

TABLE 10.1   Syntactic Categories

Symbol	Interpretation
S	Sentence
NP	Noun phrase
VP	Verb phrase
PP	Prepositional phrase
N	Noun
V	Verb
ART	Article
ADJ	Adjective
AUX	Auxiliary verb
PRTCL	Particle

such as English. The sentences in set 2 are very similar to those in set 1, except they have one additional phrase beginning with a preposition, for example, *to the girl,* and *from patients' bloodstreams.* Such phrases are known as prepositional phrases (PPs). Sentences in set 3 are also of the form NP, V, NP, except the logical relation is different from that in sets 1 and 2. The sentences in set 3 are passive sentences, whereas the two prior sets contain active sentences. An active sentence describes events in the order of agent, verb, object. In passive sentences, the object is stated before the verb, and the agent after. Sentences in all three sets are declarative sentences because they declare specific facts. This is to distinguish them from sentences that express questions and commands. It is regularities like these that led linguists to develop taxonomies of sentences and sets of rules to generate them.

Syntactic Rules and Principles

Phrase Structure Rules.   Syntax is the body of abstract knowledge that determines grammatical word orders, as seen, for example, in sentences (10.1) through (10.8). Native speakers of a language can make the distinction between grammatically correct and incorrect sequences of words because they possess intuitive syntactic knowledge. According to influential theories, including Chomsky's early work, syntactic knowl-

edge is best described in terms of **phrase structure** rules such as rules 1 through 6 in Table 10.2. We will see that theorists have also characterized syntactic knowledge in terms of principles in addition to rules (Berwick, 1991).

The six rules in Table 10.2 are called **rewrite rules** because the symbol on the left side of the arrow is rewritten or defined in terms of the symbols on the right side. The left side expresses a syntactic category, and the right side lists the constituent categories of the category on the left, in their grammatical order. Rule 1, for example, specifies that a sentence, S, consists of a noun phrase, NP, and a verb phrase, VP. These rules are used to generate grammatical English sentences, although no theorist suggests that speakers actually use them. Remember that we are concerned here with abstract formalisms rather than the manner in which people produce language.

At the abstract level, the rules in Table 10.2 are applied cyclically. For example, in cycle 1, we start with the first rule in the list by writing out S → NP +. . . . The name NP is a request for the rule that rewrites NP, namely rule 2. In plain English, we are looking for the definition of the noun phrase. This request initiates cycle 2 and we get NP → ART +. . . . The symbol ART on the right side of rule 2 invokes rule 4 in cycle 3, and so on. Rules are called until we encounter an English word, as specified in rules 4 through 6. A word is formally known as a terminal constituent because the application of rules is terminated when a word is encountered. A terminal element does not issue a request for another constituent, unlike the nonterminal constituents, S, NP, VP, and so on. The

TABLE 10.2   A Grammar of Six Phrase Structure Rules

1. S → NP + VP
2. NP → ART + N
3. VP → V + NP
4. ART → the, a, . . .
5. N → boy, man, girl, ball, . . .
6. V → hit, . . .

latter define the hierarchical structure of the sentence and do not appear in the actual sentence. (The nonterminal constituents are real, nevertheless, as we will see when we discuss sentence (10.36).)

Phrase Structure Trees. The term **phrase marker** is used for the hierarchical structure of sentences. When a phrase marker is diagrammed as in Figure 10.1, it is known as a **phrase structure tree.** The grammatical sequence of words in a sentence is referred to as the **surface form** of the sentence. This is distinguished from the **deep structure** of the sentence. Simplifying matters, we can say that the deep structure expresses the underlying meaning relationship of the sentence: Who did what to whom? The deep structure is an abstract entity rather than a English sentence. However, we may think of the deep structure as an active declarative sentence (e.g., sentences in

sets 1 and 2). Later in this chapter, I will represent deep structure in terms of propositions. Figure 10.1A shows the phrase structure tree, the surface form, and the deep structure of sentence (10.1), *The boy hit the ball.*

You will notice that phrase structure trees appear upside down, with the root S at the top. The terminal elements, or words, are located at the bottom of the tree with nonterminal categories in between. The S category is said to dominate the NP and VP categories, conforming to rule 1. In Figure 10.1, the symbol NP dominates two categories, ART and N, conforming to rule 2, and so on.

Do not be misled by the apparent simplicity of rules 1 through 6. This set of rules has considerable generative power. Using only the six rules in Table 10.2, including the single verb *hit* in rule 6 and the four nouns of rule 5, many additional sentences can be generated. By adding more verbs

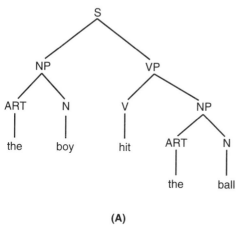

(A)

Surface Sentence: The boy hit the ball.

Deep Structure: Predicate   HIT
 Logical Subject BOY
 Logical Object BALL

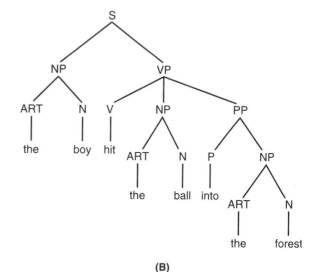

(B)

FIGURE 10.1 (*A*) Representation of a simple active declarative sentence in terms of its phrase structure. The same phrase structure governs all sentences of this type subject-verb-object—for example. *The dog bit the boy* and *The girl read the book.* (*B*) Phrase structure including a prepositional phrase.

and nouns, the number of possible sentences increases dramatically. The power of phrase structure rules 1 through 6 may be further increased by adding optional nonterminal elements to our existing rules, as we will see next.

Optional Categories.   Consider sentence (10.9), which is grammatically incorrect according to the set of rules 1–6, because there is no rule among them capable of generating a noun phrase without an article, such as *John.*

(10.9) John hit the ball.

This illustrates that rule 2 must be augmented to permit noun phrases without articles. The fact that the article is optional is shown in rule 7, where ART is enclosed in parentheses.

7. NP → (ART) + N

The noun category, N, is obligatory. It may be filled by a noun, as in sentences (10.1) and (10.9), or a pronoun. Rule 7 is more powerful than rule 2 because it can generate more noun phrases. Rule 8 includes ADJ as an optional element and is thus even more powerful than rule 7.

8. NP → (ART) + (ADJ) + N

Rule 9 is still more powerful because it incorporates the fact that a noun may be modified by any number of adjectives. The asterisk indicates the repeated application.

9. NP → (ART) + (ADJ)* + N

Rule 9 is capable of generating phrases such as *the big red ball, the old big red ball, the expensive big red ball,* and *the cheap old big red ball.* Note that rule 9 does not restrict the order of the adjectives. Thus, *the cheap old big red ball* and *the red old cheap big ball* and other permutations are equally acceptable as far as rule 9 is concerned. Does this accord with your intuitions? If not, how would you change rule 9 so that it satisfies your own feeling of the proper order of adjectives in English noun phrases?

We have increased the generative power of our original rules in several ways—namely, by (1)

adding terminal elements, (2) allowing optional categories, and (3) recognizing that some categories may be repeated. Additional categories such as prepositions (PREP) and prepositional phrases (PP) (see rules 10 and 11), must be included to handle the second set of sentences presented on page 269.

10. PP → PREP + NP
11. PREP → into

We must also augment rule 3 to reflect the fact that prepositional phrases are dominated by verbs. Rule 12 indicates this by listing prepositional phrases as optional elements of verb phrases. Noun phrases are optional, not obligatory.

12. VP → V + (NP) + (PP).

Using rule 12, in addition to the other rules, enables us to generate sentence (10.10). The corresponding phrase structure tree is shown in Figure 10.1B.

(10.10) The boy hit the ball into the forest.

Table 10.3 lists the set of rules we have introduced so far.

Linguists call a set of rules that generates grammatical sentences a **grammar.** Of course, there are many more phrase structure rules than those shown in Table 10.3. For example, one rule that we will encounter in Chapter 11 is the rule

TABLE 10.3   A Grammar of Twelve Phrase Structure Rules

1. S → NP + VP
2. NP → ART + N
3. VP → V + NP
4. ART → the, a, . . .
5. N → boy, man, girl, ball, . . .
6. V → hit, . . .
7. NP → (ART) + N
8. NP → (ART) + (ADJ) + N
9. NP → (ART) + (ADJ)* + N
10. PP → PREP + NP
11. PREP → into
12. VP → V + (NP) + (PP)

that defines a noun phrase in terms of a noun phrase and a prepositional phrase as follows: NP → NP + PP. This rule generates such constructions as *the girl with freckles*.

Next, we will increase the power of phrase structure rules considerably, by giving the rules in Table 10.3 the power of recursion.

Complex Sentences and Recursion. Consider the following sentences:

(10.11) The boy hit the ball.

(10.12) The boy greeted the girl.

(10.13) The girl called the man.

(10.14) The boy greeted the girl who called the man.

Sentences (10.11) through (10.13) are called simple sentences; they each have one subject and one predicate. Sentence (10.14), however, is a complex sentence containing two subjects and two respective predicates. The sentences are linked by

the noun phrase *the girl* that forms the object of a simple sentence (10.12) and the subject of another simple sentence (10.13). Sentences like (10.14) are generated by an augmented version of rule 9. The new rule, 13, rewrites noun phrases in terms of several constituents as before, yet it is fundamentally different from rule 9.

13. NP → (ART) + (ADJ)* + N + (S)

Rule 13 is different because it includes the symbol for sentence, S, on the right side. As a result, one can place a sentence inside another sentence. In theory, this gives us the power to form an infinite number of sentences, as well as sentences of infinite length. Rule 13, in conjunction with the other rules, exhibits the power of *recursion*. A rule is defined as a recursive rule if it calls itself. In Box 10.1, a mathematical example of recursion is explained.

Sentence fragment (10.15) illustrates the power of rule 13.

Box 10.1

An Example of Recursion

Do you remember the meaning of factorial multiplication? The example 4!, read as four factorial, tells us to form the product of all integers up to n, which in our example is 4. A recursive definition of the factorial rule is shown in rule (1).

(1) $n! = n * (n - 1)!$
(2) $0! = 1$

This rule is called recursive because the factorial (!) on the left side is defined in terms of the factorial expression on the right side. The definitions (1) and (2) provide a description of how to calculate the factorial of any integer n. One unravels n in successive steps, as indicated by (1) until 0 is reached. Then the solution $0! = 1$ is supplied and the result is computed in successive steps of multiplication. Let's apply this to the example 4!

$4! = * 3!$
$= 4 * 3 * 2!$
$= 4 * 3 * 2 * 1!$
$= 4 * 3 * 2 * 1 * 0!$

When we reach 0!, we have reached a terminal condition, one whose answer is known, $0! = 1$. At this point, we complete the calculation upwards as shown next:

$$1 * 1 = 1$$
$$2 * 1 * 1 = 2$$
$$3 * 2 * 1 * 1 = 6$$
$$4 * 3 * 2 * 1 * 1 = 24$$

So the factorial of 4 is 24. We calculated this using the recursive definition of the factorial function as "n factorial equals n times $n - 1$ factorial, and zero factorial equals 1."

(10.15) The boy greeted the girl
        who called the man
        who admired the artist
        who listened to the violinist
        who . . .

Of course, we do not encounter sentences like (10.15) in everyday English. Sentences like (10.14), however, are very common.

INTERIM SUMMARY

We have introduced a grammar, a set of phrase structure rules that generates grammatical English sentences. Each rule lists a single syntactic category on the left side, which is defined in terms of its constituent(s) on the right side. The grammar is recursive in that the category S may appear on the right side as well as on the left. The rules are powerful enough to generate an infinite number of sentences.

Transformational Rules.   Chomsky developed transformational rules because he discovered important weaknesses in the phrase structure grammar. We will consider two of these weaknesses here. First, although powerful, phrase structure grammars have difficulty generating the great variety of sentence patterns found in English, including questions, negative sentences, passive sentences, relative clauses, and so on. If a phrase structure grammar could be found to generate all of these sentences, it would be very cumbersome.

Second, phrase structure rules do not assign any functional or thematic roles to the constituents. As a result, they are insufficient to express alternative meanings of ambiguous sentences. Consider sentence (10.16) and, before continuing to read, identify its two different interpretations.

(10.16) They are cooking apples.

A little thought will reveal the two readings of sentence (10.16). The two readings differ in their interpretation of *they*. According to the first interpretation, *they* refers to a type of apples used for cooking. The other interpretation of *they* refers to some unspecified people who are cooking apples. These two meanings are captured in the two phrase structure trees in Figure 10.2. For sentences like (10.16) it is difficult to decide which

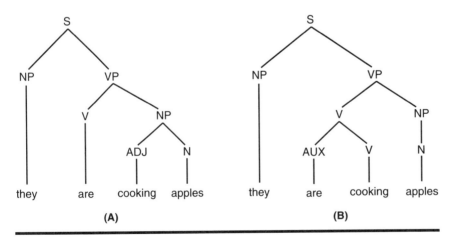

FIGURE 10.2   Two different phrase structure trees reflect the two readings of the ambiguous surface sentence *They are cooking apples.* (*A*) The word *they* refers to *cooking apples.* (*B*) The word *they* refers to some unspecified *people who are cooking apples.*

phrase marker to use. Should it be the one in Figure 10.2A or 10.2B? Chomsky demonstrated that ambiguities such as these can be resolved within the framework of transformational grammar.

According to Chomsky's (1965) theory, both phrase structure rules and transformational rules are required to generate surface sentences. Phrase structure rules are used to generate active declarative sentences, and these are then transformed into different surface forms according to transformational rules. An *active declarative* sentence is a sentence that states a certain content in the active voice. Declarative sentences differ from questions and commands such as *Did the boy hit the ball?* and *Hit the ball!* According to transformational theory, an entity like an active declarative sentence underlies each surface sentence. This is the *deep structure* referred to earlier, which expresses who did what to whom.

Let us use the passive transformation in Table 10.4 as an illustration of transformational rules. Consider sentences (10.17) and (10.18)

(10.17) Marty sent the parcel to John.

(10.18) The parcel was sent by Marty to John.

Both sentences convey the same meaning of Marty sending John a parcel. According to Chomsky, passive sentences such as (10.18) are

TABLE 10.4 Transformational Rules

Passive-transformation: Active declarative sentence ⇒ Passive
The dog chased the cat ⇒ The cat was chased by the dog
NP1 V + ed NP2 ⇒ NP2 AUX V + ed by NP1

Question: Active declarative sentence ⇒ Question
The boy will greet the girl ⇒ Will the boy greet the girl?
NP1 AUX V NP2 ⇒ AUX NP1 V NP2?

Particle-movement transformation:
John called up his wife ⇒ John called his wife up
NP1 V PRTCL NP2 ⇒ NP1 V NP2 PRTCL

---

formed via the following transformation of phrases.

NP1 V NP2 ⇒ NP2 AUX V +ed by NP1

(10.17) ⇒ (10.18)

In general, as shown in Figure 10.3, a transformation rule takes a phrase marker generated by phrase structure rules and produces a grammatical phrase marker as output. Table 10.4 lists two additional transformations.

The second transformation in Table 10.4 is the *question transformation,* which transforms an active declarative sentence into one type of question. This type of question may be answered with *yes* or *no.* There are other types of questions, the *wh-* questions, that inquire about agents (who), location (where), time (when), and so on. More complex rules are used to generate such *wh-* questions than the type of question shown in Table 10.4.

The third transformation, the *particle-movement transformation,* moves the particle from the position right after the verb to immediately after the object.

Beyond Transformational Grammar. Transformational grammar can account for more regularities among English sentences than phrase structure grammar could alone. It can successfully generate passive sentences, negative sentences, questions, and other types of sentences, without the need to explain away exceptions. It can give an account of surface ambiguities in sentences such as (10.16). It can also handle the dependencies between nonadjacent words and other more subtle phenomena of English. Nevertheless, Chomsky (1981) began to think beyond transformational grammar. This section discusses some of the reasons why new directions were needed.

— Transformational grammar is too powerful because it can be used to generate word orders that are not found in English at all. Consider the passive transformation in Table 10.4. The reversals and insertions of the passive transformation are fairly complex. In theory at least, a simple

FIGURE 10.3   A schematic view of how transformational rules operate.

reversal transformation would be as legitimate as the passive transformation, but of course it does not exist. Such a reversal transformation would generate the string seen in (10.20) (Anderson & Bower, 1973).

(10.19) The dog chased the cat. ⇒
The cat was chased by the dog.

(10.20) The dog chased the cat. ⇒
*Cat the chased dog the.

The point of this illustration is that transformational grammar remains incomplete without principles that explain why certain transformations exist and others like the reversal transformation in (10.20) do not. Many linguists have sought solutions to this vexing problem, but have been unsuccessful.

▬ Transformational rules do not illuminate the structure of the human mind. One of the reasons Chomsky wanted to study language was because he was interested in the human mind. He believed that research on linguistic structures would deepen our understanding of mental processes. Although the linguistic structures and rules he proposed were abstract, according to Chomsky, they still should have implications for language use by people. To be sure, there was evidence for the abstract deep structures that Chomsky proposed. But a test of a comprehension model based on transformational grammar failed, as we will see in a moment.

According to transformational theory, each sentence has an abstract meaning structure in addition to its surface structure. It was not difficult to find support for this hypothesis. Several re-

searchers found that people remembered the meaning of sentences much better than the surface features, including the sequence of the words and the voice of the sentence (Sachs, 1967; Wanner, 1974; see also Chapter 11). Indeed, people combined the underlying meaning of different sentences into one composite structure rather than remembering the surface sentences individually (Bransford & Franks, 1971). Though there is support for deep structures, then, this does not imply support for transformational rules. The fate of a sentence comprehension hypothesis, the derivational theory of complexity, illustrates this. Note that we discuss sentence comprehension rather than sentence generation in this section.

Chomsky and colleagues formulated the complexity theory of comprehension (Miller & Chomsky, 1963). According to this theory, the comprehension of a sentence should be the mirror image of generating the sentence via transformational rules. The more transformations used in deriving the sentence, the more complex it should be; and, as a result, it should be more difficult to comprehend. In other words, comprehension consists of extracting the sentence's deep structure. Presumably this is accomplished by reversing the transformations used to generate the surface sentence, word by word. Undoing each transformation would take one extra unit of time. For example, because passive sentences are generated via the passive transformation (see Table 10.4), they should be more difficult and take longer to comprehend than active sentences.

This prediction was supported only in reversible sentences, as illustrated by sentences (10.21) and (10.22), but not in nonreversible sentences such as (10.23) and (10.24). These results were contrary to the derivational complexity hypothesis that transformational rules are used in language processing (Slobin, 1966).

(10.21)   The dog is chasing the cat.

(10.22)   The cat is chasing the dog.

(10.21a) The cat is being chased by the dog.

(10.22a) The dog is being chased by the cat.

(10.23)   The girl is watering the flowers.

(10.24)   The flowers are being watered by the girl.

(10.23a) *The flowers are watering the girl.

(10.24a) *The girl is being watered by the flowers.

According to Pinker (1994, p. 219), the negative verdict on the psychological validity of transformations was premature. He argued that the early investigators had failed to use research methods that were sufficiently sensitive. Electrophysiological methods such as the ERP track the mind's processing load more effectively than reading times do (see Chapter 2). Pinker cited a study in which ERP patterns were used to track mental processes in sentence understanding. Researchers found an additional processing load in readers when they encounter a transformational trace in a sentence. A *trace* is a place holder of a phrase that has been moved and remains empty, as illustrated in sentence (10.26).

(10.26)   The police officer saw the boy that the crowd at the party accused (trace) of the crime.

Readers expect a noun phrase, in this case the object *the boy,* after *accuse.* However, the object has been moved via a transformation to the position of *that* at the beginning of the relative clause, thus leaving the slot after *accuse* empty. ERP patterns indicate that understanders experience a transient difficulty at this position in the sentence.

▬ Some theoretical developments did not necessarily contradict transformational grammar as such, but simply shifted the research emphasis. Such developments took place not only in linguistics itself but also in computational linguistics,

psycholinguistics, and discourse analysis. These new approaches generated new questions and theories that made transformational grammar less central. For example, computational linguists could not find ways to implement transformational grammars efficiently on the computer. One critic wrote about transformational grammars that they "include types of representations and processes which are highly implausible, and which may be totally inapplicable in complex situations because their very nature implies astronomically large amounts of processing for certain kinds of computations" (Winograd, 1973).

From discourse analysis came another perspective that weakened the appeal of transformational grammars (van Dijk, 1972). One of the strengths of transformational grammar was that it could account for ambiguities in interpreting sentences such as sentence (10.16). According to discourse analysis, however, sentence (10.16) is ambiguous only because it occurs in isolation rather than in a broader context such as in sentence (10.25). Here, the initial clause makes the interpretation in Figure 10.3A more likely than the interpretation in Figure 10.3B.

(10.25)   As he looked at the pile of bruised apples, Enrico asked the grocer, "Who do you think will buy those apples?" The grocer replied, *"They are cooking apples.* They are a bargain; a quarter a pound."

INTERIM SUMMARY

In this section, we learned both the strengths and weaknesses of transformational grammar. We saw that transformational grammar was more powerful than phrase structure grammar alone because it could account for a greater variety of the surface forms of English sentences. On the other hand, the successes of the transformational approach were qualified by several problems. One problem is that no principle has been discovered that would allow some transformations (e.g., the ones in Table 10.4) and disallow others. Another weakness is that, while a sentence's deep structures may be valid, its transformational rules are not. According to the complexity theory, the comprehension difficulty of a sentence should depend on the number of transformational rules used to generate it. However, this is not always the case. Finally, the transformational theory was superseded by other approaches in computational linguistics, discourse analysis, and linguistics itself.

The next section introduces linguistic approaches that complemented transformational theory and rule-based approaches in general (Berwick, 1991; McCloskey, 1988).

From Rules to Principles. Beginning with Chomsky, linguists started to introduce principles in addition to rules. Principles account for simple language constructions that are difficult to capture within a rule-based framework. The principle-based approach will be illustrated using the **argument structure** of verbs and the **theta criterion.** A verb's argument structure refers to the set of noun phrases that the verb requires, to its complement structure. Pinker (1994) described the verb as a little despot that dictates who its neighbors should be and where they should be located. Consider the distinction between transitive and intransitive verbs. Transitive verbs such as *hit* require a direct object, whereas intransitive verbs do not. Linguists have adopted finer distinctions among verbs to reflect the verbs' complement structure (Lasnik, 1990). For example, the arguments for the verbs *sleep, hit,* and *think* are expressed in (10.27). This representation shows that each verb has at least one argument, the subject. The verb *sleep* has no additional arguments, not even optionally. The verb *hit* has one obligatory argument, a direct object, in addition to the subject role. The verb *think* has an argument to be filled with a sentence, S.

(10.27) sleep: SLEEP <SUBJ>
        hit: HIT <SUBJ><OBJ>
        think: THINK <SUBJ><S>

According to argument structure of the verbs listed in expression (10.27), sentences (10.28

through 10.30) are grammatical because they satisfy each verb's case requirements. Expressions (10.31 through 10.33), on the other hand, do not.

(10.28) The girl slept.

(10.29) The boy hit the ball.

(10.30) The woman thinks the girl slept.

(10.31) *The girl slept the bed.

(10.32) *The boy hit.

(10.33) *The woman thinks the girl.

Linguists have formulated a principle, the theta criterion, that expresses the relation between verbs and noun phrases. The term *theta* comes from the term *thematic* role. The theta-criterion is captured in (10.34).

(10.34) Every NP must be an argument of a verb, and every argument must be assigned to a verb.

Expression (10.34) stipulates that every noun phrase must fulfill a certain thematic role as governed by the meaning of the verb. All of the verb's required arguments must be filled with noun phrases and there must be no free-floating noun phrase.

The theta criterion is one of several principles recently invoked by linguists to describe a large body of linguistic phenomena such as *wh-* movements, pronoun distribution, coordinate structures, and case markings. Illustrations of some of these constructions are shown in Table 10.5. It is not necessary for us to examine these phenomena; this is best left to linguists. We need to remember, however, that the rule-based approach has difficulties in accounting for these cases. As a result, many linguists use principles, in addition to rules, to account for certain sentence constructions.

One of the fundamental differences between rules and principles is that rules are specific for particular constructions in particular languages. For example, there are different rules for generating relative clauses in English, Japanese, and Warlpiri (a language of native Australians). Similarly, the rules for constructing passive sentences are different for different languages.

TABLE 10.5   Illustration of Three Linguistic
Principles

Pronoun distribution (Lasnik, 1990)
John thinks he won. *He* may refer to John.
*He thinks John won. Ungrammatical if *he* refers to
John.

Wn-movement (Riemsdijk & Williams, 1986)
In which book did you say that you found that
quote?
Which book did you say *in* that you found that
quote?

Case assignment under government
I believe she is a spy.
*I believe her is a spy.

Unlike rules, principles are neither language nor construction specific. Thus, the theta criterion is valid for all languages; verbs command certain thematic roles in all languages. What differs are certain parameters such as the location of the verb in a sentence. In subject-verb-object (SVO) languages such as English, the verb is placed before the object. In SOV languages, the verb is placed after the object. Constraints on verb placement are represented with each verb, as in (10.27). We will see in a later section that this information is stored with the verb in the lexicon.

Because of their flexibility, principle-based grammars can also handle languages that exhibit freer word order than English does, such as Finnish, Japanese, and Warlpiri. Warlpiri has no fixed word order at all and words may appear in any order. For example, in Warlpiri, the sentence *I am taking the boomerang from John* can be expressed as *Taking I am from John the boomerang* or *The boomerang from John I am taking* and still be perfectly grammatical. It would be very cumbersome to develop a rule-based grammar for Warlpiri and other free-order languages, let alone one that could be implemented on a computer.

Not surprisingly, their flexibility makes it easier to use principles in computerized translation systems. Rule-based translation systems require two sets of rules, one set for each language. In principle-based systems, however, only one set of principles is required because they are general across languages, as we saw earlier. All that differs are specific parameters for each of the two languages (Berwick, 1991).

I have described the specificity of rules as their disadvantage. At the same time, however, the specificity of rules is also their strength. Because a rule is construction specific, only a few steps are required to generate a surface sentence. This is not the case with principles because all principles are involved in generating a sentence. With both systems, however, the same sentence and the same sentence structure is generated.

Connectionist theorists see great advantages in principle-based grammars compared to rule-based grammar. The former includes several modules, each of which contributes independently to the construction of well-formed sentences. Seidenberg (1992) characterized the principle-based grammar as follows: "Well-formedness is treated as a constraint satisfaction problem, which is certainly congenial to the connectionist approach."

Do We Need Syntax at All?   As we conclude this section on syntax, we must face an issue raised by some theorists: Do we need syntax at all? There have been linguists, especially computational linguists, who are unconcerned with whether syntactic knowledge consists of rules or principles. Indeed, several have questioned the need for a syntactic analysis (Schank & Abelson, 1977). Schank and Abelson defended this position by referring to sentences where meaning is carried by content words, as, for example, in telegraphic messages such as *Chief arrives Tuesday Kennedy* and to children's utterances that are not grammatical. Phrases such as *Me eat now* are understood, although they are not correct according to the rules of syntax. Such cases suggest that a semantic analysis is sufficient, and a syntactic analysis is secondary if it is undertaken at all.

Also, according to Schank and Abelson (1977), the syntactic phrase marker NP VP NP S reveals nothing about the meaning of the sentence. The syntactic structure only describes formal attributes of the sentence and, by itself, conveys no semantic content. Finally, it has been argued that much of the semantic content is implied, as in sentence (10.35), for example. One could represent (10.35) formally as NP1 V1 NP2 V2 NP3, indicating that the sentence has three noun phrases and two verbs. Understanding, however, is not based on such analyses and representations. A person understands easily that it was a driver who stopped the car by stepping on the brake.

(**10.35**)   The police officer held up his hand and stopped the car.

The driver did so in response to seeing the policeman's hand. Neither driver nor brake are mentioned in the sentence. It is not necessary to mention these concepts because the speaker assumes, with justification, that the listener fills in or infers that information. We can infer the requisite information because we are familiar with the job of a traffic cop (see Chapter 5).

Linguists do not deny that sentences imply semantic information. They maintain, however, that the syntactic structure of a sentence helps us recover semantic information. Indeed, Frazier (1983) stated that, in many cases, the syntactic structure plays a critical role in conveying meaning unambiguously. Consider sentence (10.36). The meaning of this sentence remains ambiguous until the surface structure is clarified, as in (10.36a) and (10.36b).

(**10.36**)   He showed her baby pictures.

(**10.36a**)   He showed her baby the pictures.

(**10.36b**)   He showed her the baby pictures.

Sentences (10.36a) and (10.36b) consist of the same words but their order differs in a crucial respect and so do their meanings. The point is that the syntactic structure of a sentence is important in conveying its meaning.

In sum, most linguists attribute an important role to syntax and believe that people use their knowledge of syntax to understand sentences. Not only are there examples like sentence (10.36) to demonstrate the essential role of syntax, but native speakers of English also generate and interpret the sentences in Table 10.5 correctly. This demonstrates our competence with highly technical aspects of grammar that we are never taught. Though we may be unaware of them, syntactic rules and principles are something we know. If nothing else, the linguists' discovery of principles and rules helps us catalog our knowledge.

Representing the Meaning of Sentences

Propositional Representation.   Linguists assume that surface sentences have an underlying meaning known as the deep or propositional structure. In this section, we will discuss the representation of sentence meaning in terms of propositions as well as some empirical evidence for such representations (Chapter 5). A proposition preserves the essential information of a sentence while disregarding such details as word order, voice, and tense. There are several propositional notations. We will use a notation suggested by Fillmore (1968) and developed by Kintsch (1972). According to Kintsch's (1972) notation, the format of a proposition is as follows:

(Predicate, Argument$_1$, . . . , Argument$_n$)

The predicate of a proposition expresses a property or the relation between arguments. On the surface, sentence properties are captured by adjectives such as *sad, beautiful,* and *lovely.* Relations are expressed by verbs such as *hit, cook,* and *plant.* Arguments are capitalized in propositions to distinguish them from surface words and verbs are shown in infinitive form. This format is illustrated for two of the sentences studied previously, sentences (10.1) and (10.36).

(**10.1**)   The boy hit the ball.

(**10.1a**)   (Predicate: HIT, Agent: BOY, Object: BALL)

(**10.36**)   He showed her baby pictures.

(**10.36a**)   (Predicate: SHOW, Agent: HE, Object: PICTURES, Recipient: HER BABY)

(10.36b) (Predicate: SHOW, Agent: HE, Predicate: SHE, Object: BABY PICTURES)

The propositional representation makes explicit the meaning relations. Note that the indirect object is called recipient. It is one of six thematic roles or arguments typically in use. A list of these cases include:

agent (A): The instigator of an action

experiencer (E): The person who experiences a psychological event

instrument (I): The psychological stimulus of an experience or action elicitor

object (O): The object of an action that undergoes change

source (S): The source of an action in time or space

goal (G): The goal or result of an action

recipient (R): The person receiving an object

I illustrate arguments for sentences (10.37) and (10.38) (e.g., Kintsch, 1974).

(10.37) Mary opened the door with a key.

In sentence (10.37), the action is *open,* performed by the agent *Mary.* The object of the opening is *door* and the instrument of the action is *key.*

(10.38) Mary cried from morning to night.

In (10.38), *Mary* is the agent and *morning* and *night* are source and goal, respectively. In (10.39), *John* is the experiencer.

(10.39) John was sad.

Arguments are optional, as illustrated with sentences (10.40) and (10.41). In sentence (10.40), the verb *cook* has three arguments, as shown in (10.40a) (Kintsch, 1974).

(10.40) The butler is cooking supper for Mary.

(10.40a) (Predicate: COOK, Agent: BUTLER, Object: SUPPER, Recipient: MARY)

One could also add another argument—for example, the argument representing an instrument, (1), as in sentence (10.41).

(10.41) The butler is cooking supper for the girl with a spoon.

In addition to the full propositional version exemplified by (10.40a), we will use a shorthand version where the argument slots are indicated by their positions rather than their names. Thus, proposition (10.40b) is equivalent to (10.40a).

(10.40b) (COOK, BUTLER, SUPPER, MARY)

In (10.40b), it is simply assumed that the slots are occupied by the predicate, agent, object, and recipient respectively.

Another way to represent propositions is in terms of networks, as shown for sentence (10.40) in Figure 10.4. Here, the node represents the sentence predicate, in most cases its verb, and the arcs indicate the predicate's arguments. You can see that propositions are abstract in both the list notation illustrated in (10.40a) and the network notation used in Figure 10.4. Word order, tense, modularity, and the voice of the sentence are ignored. For example, proposition (10.40a) and Figure 10.4 represent the passive sentence (10.42), as well as its active version (10.40)

(10.42) The supper for Mary is being cooked by the butler.

Propositions may also be used to represent nonlinguistic information—for example, information conveyed in a visual scene (Carpenter & Just, 1975; Clark & Chase, 1972). Here is a

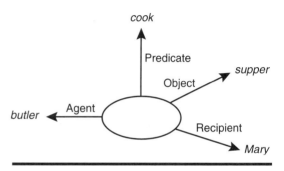

FIGURE 10.4 Representing a proposition in terms of a node and arcs.

representation of a simple visual scene consisting of two objects and their relationship:

*

+

We see an asterisk above a plus sign. The shorthand propositional representation of this arrangement is given in (10.43).

(10.43) (ABOVE, ASTERISK, PLUS)

Carpenter and Just (1975) chose a propositional representation because people are able to compare visual and linguistic inputs and state whether or not the two inputs convey the same scene. The representation serves as a common medium for expressing information from different modalities.

So far, we have restricted our attention to representing individual sentences in terms of propositions. Another advantage of this type of representation is that it is easily extended to entire texts, as illustrated in Table 10.6 for a text consisting of two sentences (see Kintsch et al., 1975).

Because texts elaborate on a topic, their constituent sentences repeatedly refer to the same entities, known as *referents*. The underlying propositions reflect the referential coherence by the repetition of arguments such as BABYLONIAN and GARDEN in Table 10.6.

TABLE 10.6   The Babylonian Passage as Represented by Propositions (Kintsch et al., 1975)

1 (BUILD, BABYLONIAN, GARDEN)
2 (BEAUTIFUL, GARDEN)
3 (LOCATION: ON, GARDEN, HILL)
4 (PLANT, BABYLONIAN, FLOWER)
5 (LOVELY, FLOWER)
6 (CONSTRUCT, BABYLONIAN, FOUNTAIN)
7 (DESIGN, BABYLONIAN, PAVILION, 8)
8 (HAS, QUEEN, PLEASURE)

Text: The Babylonians built a beautiful garden on a hill. They planted lovely flowers, constructed fountains, and designed a pavilion for the queen's pleasure.

Note: Location in proposition 3 serves as predicate. It sets its argument into a spatial relation.

According to many psycholinguists and cognitive psychologists, propositions are used by listeners and readers as psychological processing units (e.g., Anderson, 1983; van Dijk & Kintsch, 1983; Just & Carpenter, 1987; Ratcliff & McKoon, 1978). In cued recall studies, words from the same proposition are better recall prompts than words from different propositions, although they are all part of the same sentence. For example, the word *faked* in sentence (10.44) cues *bandit* more effectively than *signature,* although it is physically closer to *signature.*

(10.44) The bandit who stole the passport faked the signature.

In recognition experiments, there is priming for words from the same proposition (see Chapter 5). In reading experiments, comprehension times of sentences were better predicted by the number of propositions than by the number of words in the sentence (Kintsch & Keenan, 1973).

INTERIM SUMMARY

In the first part of this chapter, you were introduced to the structure of sentences. You learned that there are two abstract structures that underlie a sentence. There is the meaning structure known as the deep or propositional structure that expresses who did what to whom. The other structure is the hierarchical phrase marker comprising the parts of speech of the sentence, its constituents. Phrase markers may be generated by both rule- and principle-based grammars. There is also the surface form of the sentence that we encounter in discourses, whether in speech or in print. Finally, much of the information conveyed by sentences is inferred by the listener or reader. To what extent listeners actually do so will be considered in the coming two chapters.

———■———

WORDS

There was good reason to begin our study of linguistics with sentences; sentences are the means of expressing ideas, and they are the chief concern of linguists. The great variety of sentence structures has given rise to numerous grammars and will continue to do so. Sentences consist of words, however, and we must therefore turn to words and what we know about them. Words have an internal structure; they fulfill certain syntactic roles, as indicated earlier, and they convey specific meanings. The knowledge we have of words is called *lexical knowledge* (derived from the Greek term *lexis,* meaning *word*). Linguists and psycholinguists assume that lexical information is represented in the **lexicon,** a kind of mental dictionary.

This section discusses three components of lexical knowledge: the morphology of words, their syntactic role, and their meaning. Like other mental structures, the lexicon is a functional, not an anatomical, term. No theorist assumes that there is a discrete brain structure called the lexicon, although neuropsychological studies have implicated several brain structures in lexical processing (see also Chapter 11).

Morphology

Morphology is the study of the structure of words in terms of **morphemes.** A morpheme is a word component that has a unique sound and also bears meaning. Morphemes include both word stems and affixes: prefixes and suffixes. Thus, the word *dogs* consists of two morphemes, *dog-* and *-s*. The morpheme *dog-* is the word stem. It is associated with the meaning, a four-legged canine, man's best friend, that barks. The suffix *-s* reflects the plural to indicate that reference is made to two or more of the entity represented by the word stem.

Word stems such as *dog-*, suffixes such as *-s,* and prefixes such as *in-* and *re-* are morphemes that express a specific meaning. The prefix *in-* modifies the subsequent word stem to express negativity—for example, *inability, inadequate,* and *incomplete*. The prefix *re-* expresses repetition of an action, as shown in the following examples: *rework the problem, rewrite the draft, restate the conclusion, rejuvenate one's spirits,*

and *reconstruct the accident.* You can see that morphemes and their combinations enrich the vocabulary of a language considerably. Just think of such words as *thermoluminescence, cineangiocardiography,* and *antidisestablishmentarianism.* To be sure, these are technical terms. They are, however, English words that can be found in the dictionary.

Even if a speaker never heard the term *morpheme,* he has knowledge of morphemes and can easily distinguish among them. One interesting demonstration of peoples' implicit knowledge of morphemes comes from an analysis of speech errors. One investigation shows that word stems are often involved in errors of exchange, whereas prefixes and suffixes are not. For example, Emmorey and Fromkin (1988) reported the following case. The person they observed said *We have a lot of churches in our minister,* intending to say *We have a lot of ministers in our church.* The speaker erroneously exchanged the word stems *minister-* and *church-*, but correctly expressed the suffix *-s*.

Syntactic Information

We already examined how words fit into syntactic structures. When we discussed the theta criterion, we saw that verbs require certain arguments and thus give shape to the propositional content of a sentence. You will remember sentence (10.40) and its propositional structure, both of which are reprinted here.

(10.40)   The butler is cooking supper for Mary.

(10.40a) (Predicate: COOK, Agent: BUTLER, Object: SUPPER, Recipient: MARY)

The syntactic information for *cook* might be represented in its lexical entry as follows:

(10.40b) cook: COOK <SUBJ> <OBJECT> <RECIPIENT>

Let's change the propositional notation in (10.40a) to give it the means of representing variables. Variables are added to make the representation applicable to any context rather than a particular one. The representation in (10.40b) does not provide explicit slots to be filled by specific nouns. When we replace the specific terms in (10.40a), the instances, with general terms, we get expression (10.40c).

(10.40c) (Predicate: COOK, Agent: someone, Object: something, Recipient: someone else)

It is an easy step from the terms *someone, something,* and *someone else* to the symbolic variables *x, y,* and *z.* Both notations indicate variables that may be filled by specific nouns. Substituting *x* for *someone, y* for *something,* and *z* for *someone else* in expression (10.40c), we get (10.40d) and its short form (10.40e).

(10.40d) (Predicate: COOK, Agent: *x,* Object: *y,* Recipient: *z*)

(10.40e) cook (*x,y,z*)

Expression (10.40e) is applicable to a wide range of cases, each with different instances. We may imagine that the lexicon captures the syntactic roles of the verb in such a general format. In order to complete the picture introduced by (10.40e), specific people and entities must exist to fill those roles. This is done in representation (10.40f). Here, the existence of a *butler, x,* of some *supper, y,* and of a *Mary, z,* are postulated.

(10.40f) butler (*x*)
supper (*y*)
Mary (*z*)
cook (*x,y,z*)

The theta criterion implies that verbs have one role and nouns have another: Verbs organize the sentence framework by providing argument slots, whereas nouns fill those slots. Interestingly, even when a speaker gets confused, she respects the distinction of the syntactic roles of nouns and verbs: These word classes do not get mixed up in speech errors. For example, nouns are misplaced from one noun phrase to another, as in (10.45) and (10.46) (Garrett, 1990). The first sentence of each pair was the one expressed by the speaker; the second was the one intended.

(10.45) We'll sit around the *song* and sing *fires.*
We'll sit around the *fire* and sing *songs.*

(10.46) That *kid's toy* makes a great *mouse.*
That *mouse* makes a great *kid's toy.*

Note that the nouns are exchanged between two noun phrases. A construction like (10.45a) in which an exchange is made between a noun and a verb is rarely, if ever, found.

(10.45a) We'll *fire* around the *sit* and sing songs.

The Meaning of Words

The representation of the meaning of a word is closely tied to the sentence in which it is embedded and to its syntactic role. In representing the meaning of verbs, we can take advantage of the propositional representation illustrated for *cook* in (10.40e). By listing the verb's arguments, this expression reflects the meaning of *cooking* to some extent, although not fully. Verbs frequently imply a change of state and a causal chain of events. If we want to express change and causation, we need to spell out the meaning of the verb, as illustrated with sentences (10.47) and (10.48). The representation in (10.47a) does not fully express the meaning of kill as *becoming not alive,* but expression (10.47b) does.

(10.47) Mary killed the mosquito.

(10.47a) Mary (*x*)
mosquito (*y*)
kill (*x,y*)

(10.47b) kill(*x,y*) = cause (*x,* become (not-alive (*y*)))

Expression (10.47) reveals implicit meaning. One can go further than (10.47), however, and represent both implied causation and implied arguments (see (10.48)):

(10.48) The butler is cooking supper.

Cooking involves, among other things, a change in the temperature of food. This process is enabled by some instrument, a stove, a range, or a grill. Whatever the butler used, it resulted in changing the temperature of the food from temperature $= m$ to temperature $= m + n$. Unless one reheats last night's meal, *cooking* supper usually involves more than merely changing its temperature. It means that one adds ingredients in certain proportions and at certain points as specified by a recipe. Indeed, some recipes like bouillabaisse and chili con carne may include several processes and take hours to complete (see Chapter 5).

Consider next the meaning of nouns. Some linguists have defined nouns as a bundle of primitive semantic features (Katz, 1972). Each of the features may be represented as a proposition, much like a sentence. Take the meaning of *boy,* for example. A boy is a male human being who is not an adult. The three features—male, human, nonadult—and the fact that they must occur jointly to define *boy* is represented in terms of the three propositions joined in (10.49a), where *x* could be any boy—Pedro, Bill, or Vladimir. The propositions express the features of boyhood: It is male as opposed to female, it is nonadult as opposed to adult, and it is human as opposed to animal.

(10.49a) Boy(x) = Male(x) and Nonadult(x) and Human(x)

The definitions of terms such as *boy, girl, woman,* and *man* are relatively straightforward because they involve few features and these are binary. Unfortunately, most nouns are not so easily analyzed. Features are frequently fuzzy and indiscernible, especially when one considers abstract words such as *liberty, justice, law, feature, principle,* and so on. Many nouns imply relations. The relation specified by those nouns can be expressed as a proposition. For example, the term *father* implies the concept *FATHER OF* represented as *father (x,y), "x is the father of y."* Other nouns describe entire scenarios, such as *operation, composition, race, banquet,* and *funeral.* Another issue complicating the representation of a noun's meaning is the ambiguity of many nouns. Their meaning frequently depends on the context. Consider the meaning of *container* in sentences (10.50) and (10.51) (McClelland, 1992).

(10.50) The apples were in a container.

(10.51) The cola was in the container.

In each case, the container contains a certain quantity, but there the commonality ends. An apple container is typically much larger than a cola container. The former has holes to permit the apples to breathe, whereas a cola container cannot have holes. Experiments by Anderson (1990) have shown that when people memorize sentences such as (10.50) and (10.51), retrieval is improved by different cues. For example, the word *basket* is a better cue for (10.50) than the word *container,* although the latter appeared verbatim in the sentence. You can see that much research remains to be done on the meaning of nouns and verbs as well.

We have discussed the meaning of two kinds of words: verbs and nouns. These are known as **content words,** along with adverbs and adjectives. These words convey the semantic content of a message. They are also called **open-class words** because over time we continue to add new nouns, verbs, adjectives, and adverbs to the language. Think of *nuke, disco, modem, debug,* and so on—these words were not known even in 1950. By contrast, the corpus of **closed-class words** or *function words* does not change appreciably over time. If you read the Bill of Rights or a novel by Charles Dickens, you will find the same set of function words still used today. Function words signal the syntactic role of the subsequent content words—for example, whether reference is indefinite or definite, as in *a house* and *the house,* respectively. The article indicates whether an argument is new or repeated. In addition to such determiners, function words include conjunctions, quantifiers, prepositions, and so on.

We have discussed some of the information in the lexicon, the knowledge of words shared by speakers of a language. The lexicon includes a word's morphological structure, its syntactic roles, and information about its meaning. Researchers continue to forge ahead, illuminating each of these components. Additional research on lexical knowledge, not treated here, has been guided by these general questions:

What is the relation between the lexical components: Are they modular and independent or do they interact?

What is the relation between the lexicon and other components of memory; in particular, what is its relation to general world knowledge, the kind of knowledge that is used to support inferences?

How is lexical information represented and accessed?

What are the neural correlates of lexical processing?

Lexical access is mainly a processing issue and will be covered in Chapter 11. Lexical information is related to the sound of words—a topic that we now investigate.

PHONOLOGY: THE SOUND OF LANGUAGE

As speakers of a language, we know how to pronounce and perceive words; we know the word's sound. We have acquired this phonological knowledge without explicit teaching and appar-

ently without much effort. It is remarkable that we perceive individual words at all. Spectrographic studies have revealed that the sound signals associated with words do not signal the boundaries between them. A *spectrogram* is a photographic record of the sound pattern produced by speech. A sound consists of energy bands at specific frequencies that extend over a brief period of time. The technical term for these energy bands is **formant.** Figure 10.5 shows the spectrogram, the formants, recorded when a speaker said *Joe took Father's shoe bench out.* The horizontal axis represents time, and the vertical axis represents frequency. Figure 10.5 illustrates that pauses in the air flow do not necessarily coincide with word boundaries.

Our knowledge of words enables us to isolate them as individual entities. Linguists have wondered for some time how we accomplish this. It is clear that our ability to segment the speech stream into words depends on our familiarity with the language. Try to see if you can identify any segments in this excerpt in a foreign language, *heuteabendseheihcdichzumabendbrot* (German for *I'll see you at dinner tonight*). Although the phenomenon of segmentation of speech is very pervasive, researchers have had difficulty accounting for it. Fortunately, however, advances

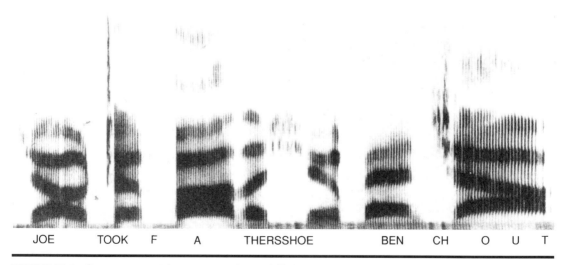

FIGURE 10.5   Spectrogram of the sentence *Joe took Father's shoe bench out* (Tartter, 1986).

have been made in understanding speech production, pronunciation, and the classification of phonemes, the units of sound.

Phonological Rules

Our ability to pronounce words correctly has been expressed in terms of rules. Consider the morpheme signaling the plural -*s* as in *dogs* and *cats.* Even casual listening indicates that the -*s* sound in these two words is different: It sounds like /z/ in *dogs* and like /s/ in *cats.* The use of /s/ and /z/ (and /iz/) in forming the English plural is not random, but exhibits the regularities stated in (10.52a) through (10.52c) (see Halle, 1990).

(10.52a) If the word stem of the noun ends in /s z č ǰ š ž/, then use /iz/

(10.52b) If the noun ends in /p t k f θ/, then use /s/

(10.52c) Else use /z/

Examples of these respective cases are shown in (10.53a) through (10.53c).

(10.53a) /z/ *places, adzes, porches, cabbages, ambushes, camouflages*

(10.53b) /s/ *cats, lips, lists, maniacs, telegraphs, hundredths*

(10.53c) /z/ *dogs, clubs, herds, phonemes, cellos, colleagues*

Native speakers of English have implicit knowledge of these regularities. If you present a native speaker with the singular form of a novel or nonsense word and ask the person to pronounce the string, he is able to do so. Try to pronounce *blorbs* and *bachs* (Halle, 1990). Although these are not English words, speakers tend to pronounce them according to rules (10.52a) through (10.52c) as *blorb*/z/ and *bach*/s/.

Not every sound pattern is regular. Consider the case of the long /a/ sound in words ending in *ave,* such as *save, gave, brave, wave,* and so on (Sejnowski & Rosenberg, 1986). An exception to the long /a/ in -*ave*-type words is the pronunciation of /a/ in *have.* This /a/ sound is short rather than long. Other idiosyncrasies a speaker

must know concern words that are pronounced differently when they fulfill the role of verbs versus nouns. You can convince yourself of this by thinking of the following words as nouns and then as verbs: *survey, permit,* and *record.* In rule-based systems, such exceptions are stored in the lexicon. On the other hand, Sejnowski and Rosenberg developed a connectionist representation of word sounds based on a distributed representation rather than on rules and exceptions (see Chapter 6).

Phonemes

A **phoneme** is the smallest unit of speech used to differentiate words. The distinction between /s/ and /z/ in *cats* and *dogs* is referred to as a phonemic distinction. The two phonemes /s/ and /z/ are distinct in terms of voicing but they also have common features. Both are *alveolar* and *fricative.* The terms *voiced, alveolar,* and *fricative* refer to features that result from subtle differences in producing sounds in the vocal tract. The vocal tract modulates the stream of air coming from the lungs. The components of the vocal tract—palate, teeth, tongue, nasal passage, vocal cords, lips, and other structures—are shown in Figure 4.8. These structures cooperate in intricate ways to produce the range of phonemes we continuously use.

A phoneme is categorized in terms of three dimensions: voicing, place of articulation, and the manner of articulation. Voiced phonemes such as /b d g v z/ are produced when the vocal cords vibrate as the air passes them. Otherwise, the phoneme is voiceless, as in /p t k f s/. Place of articulation refers to the part of the vocal tract that blocks the air stream from the lungs. Alveolar sounds, for example, are produced through blocking by the alveolar ridge, the structure linking the teeth and the hard palate (see Figure 4.8). Manner of articulation refers to the way the stream of air is changed as it passes through the vocal tract. If the passage of air is restricted, fricative sounds such as /sh s f v th/ are produced. If the air is completely stopped, a stop such as /p t k b d g/ is produced. Each of these anatomical components and types of air modulation gives rise to specific sound features. A phoneme may be characterized by the presence, (+), or absence, (–), of a specific feature—for example, voiced (+ voiced) or (– voiced), and fricative (+ fricative) or (–fricative) (see also Chapter 4).

The sketch on phonology demonstrates the complexity of language at the level of sounds and complements the linguistic analyses of sentences and words.

CONCLUSION

We have discussed the structure and meaning of three components of language: sentences, words, and sounds. We have done so from the perspective of a linguist who seeks to document the regularities of language without primary concern for processing issues. Perhaps the most fitting description of language is that it is so rich and multifaceted. The heterogeneous nature of language has given rise to a diversity in approaches and to many debates. In documenting the lawfulness of language, linguists have addressed many fundamental questions like these: Which of the linguistic components is primary, if any, syntax, semantics, phonology, or something else? What is the relation between the components? What is the best formalism to express the regularities of language principles or rules? and If the choice is rules, are phrase structure rules sufficient or should transformational rules be postulated? Even the definition of language remains to some extent controversial. Some argue it is a communication system, like many others in the animal kingdom; others maintain that language is a faculty unique to the human species (Pinker, 1990). Box 10.2 reflects some of these issues.

In light of the complexity of language, linguists had to face at least one processing issue after all—namely, how linguistic knowledge is acquired. Read Box 10.3 for some thoughts on this question. According to some reviewers of the field (Lasnik, 1990), there is actually more agreement among linguists of different persuasions than the "linguistic wars" (Tanenhaus, 1988)

Box 10.2_____

Communication in Dolphins

Researchers at the University of Hawaii have trained dolphins to perform truly astounding feats. The dolphins live in huge tanks at the Marine Mammal Laboratory of the university. According to Susan Chollar (1989), the dolphins, who have been dubbed our "cognitive cousins," understand the meaning of symbols as well as sentences. One of the dolphins, Ako, understands four hand signals given by the trainer to communicate the command "get the frisbee on your right and take it to the basket." The four hand signals represent *get, frisbee, right,* and *basket.* After additional training, Ako and other dolphins have come to understand prepositions such as *in* and *under,* a variety of objects, such as bucket and fish, and the words *yes* and *no.* Indeed, Ako and his friends can understand novel combinations of these symbols. Their achievements remind us of similar accomplishments by such famous chimpanzees as Washoe and Sarah (see also Savage-Rumbaugh, Sevcik, Brakke, & Rumbaugh, 1991).

The question is whether or not these achievements represent language. Following the lead of Chomsky, most linguists think that they do not. They cite the fact that human languages are far more complex than any other means of communication, in terms of both vocabulary and utterances. In addition, children learn their language naturally, without reward systems, reinforcement schedules, and training. Finally, the use of language is spontaneous only in humans, and not in any other species studied. These arguments do not preclude the fact that other species have unique communication systems that fulfill the needs of their respective species (Pinker, 1990).

Box 10.3

Language Acquisition

In discussing the rules and principles that form our knowledge of language, we have assumed the linguistic knowledge of an adult speaker of the language. This was a simplifying assumption. Each child must acquire her native language, but how a child masters it is a puzzle in itself. Undoubtedly, imitation plays an important role, as any parent or older sibling knows. Do the parents, however, reinforce the child for acceptable utterances and correct her for unacceptable ones? This was implied by the reinforcement theory of learning, which was the predominate theory during much of the first half of this century. This view lost ground when the complexity of a person's linguistic knowledge was recognized. Study again the sentences in Table 10.5 and consider if any parent or teacher would give you feedback on those sentences. Remember that Table 10.5 lists only a rather small set of the myriad of constructions that we use everyday.

Another reason for doubting the reinforcement theory of language learning is the result of empirical studies of the language interaction between parents and children. Such studies have shown that parents do not correct the incorrect phrases produced by a child. The sheer complexity of the constructions found in language and our ability to use them has persuaded linguists that the principles underlying language use are not learned; rather, they are innate. What a child learns are the parameters, specific sounds, and the vocabulary of a language. Halle (1990) expressed a similar view of phonological knowledge. According to Halle, this "highly recondite knowledge" is part of the human genetic endowment, similar to our genetic predisposition to walk upright (see also Pinker, 1990).

---

would suggest. Both rules and principles are useful in capturing the structure of language. We saw that each of these formulations has specific strengths and weaknesses. Ever since Chomsky, there has also been wide agreement on the centrality of language for the study of cognition in general.

It is no wonder, then, that disciplines other than linguistics and cognitive psychology are concerned with language. Philosophers have pondered the relation between thought and language: Do we think in terms of language or some other medium? Is the manner in which we think influenced by the language we speak or not? and Does linguistic competence form a part of a more general cognitive capacity or is it an independent faculty? Computer scientists have worked on programs intended to process language and speech. Neurolinguists investigate structures in the central nervous system implicated in language comprehension. Among other things, they have studied linguistic specialization, language deficits, and electrophysiological brain activity during language comprehension and production. Sociolinguists have explored different expressions of the diverse groups that together constitute a linguistic community. In Chapter 11, we will study processing issues of language as they are examined in psycholinguistics, a subdiscipline of cognitive psychology.

In addition to these issues of basic language research, language has been a practical as well as social concern throughout history. Consider the problem of learning a second language. This affects millions of immigrants all over the world, whether they are Chinese workers in Australia, Algerian immigrants in France, or people of Hispanic descent in the United States. As a college student, you may also be concerned with second language learning. Perhaps you have just taken or are preparing for a test in Spanish, French, Japanese, or another language. People of a tribe or nation are proud of their language; the Quebecois in Canada, the Walloons in Belgium, the Basques in Spain, and many other ethnic groups have fought battles for the right to speak their language in schools and in the workplace. On the other hand, there are groups in these countries defending the primacy of the language spoken by the major linguistic group. In France, the French language is periodically purged of anglicisms. In the United States, "English First" groups have made appeals for English. In Israel, an ancient language, Hebrew, has been modernized to forge cohesion within the modern nation. In short, language is not just of concern to scientists, it is a social concern as well. Language is everyone's business.

LANGUAGE COMPREHENSION

PREVIEW

This chapter is an introduction to psycholinguistics, the branch of cognitive psychology that investigates the mental processes involved in language understanding and their relation to one another. This perspective differs from that of linguistics, which seeks to describe the structure of language, apart from issues of comprehension. One of the issues of concern to psycholinguists is whether comprehension processes operate independently or whether they interact. Other issues concern the manner in which people process language at various levels of structure: words, clauses, sentences, and discourses.

In this chapter, we will learn how people encode words and retrieve their meanings from memory. Then we will examine how people interpret sentences. We shall see that listeners segment sentences into phrases and clauses using syntactic strategies. They also construct representations of sentences in working memory. A sentence representation captures phrases and the meaning relations between them. Because the capacity of working memory is limited, we chunk information at clause boundaries and transfer it to long-term memory. For the same reason, we economize when generating sentence representations by using the minimal attachment strategy. This strategy sometimes leads to an initial interpretation of a sentence that must later be changed.

Neurolinguistic and computational approaches to language are also discussed in this chapter. Our knowledge of the relation between the brain and language has come mainly from clinical case studies. According to the Geschwind-Wernicke model, Broca's and Wernicke's area in the left hemisphere of the brain are implicated in language processing. This model has been modified as a result of electrical stimulation mapping and studies of regional cerebral blood flow, however. These investigations indicate that other brain regions play a direct role in language processing. Although research of brain functions and language has yielded the locations of language processing, it has not yet illuminated how the processes operate.

In the last part of this chapter, we will sketch two computer models designed to understand language. One of these, the Augmented Transition Network (ATN), uses a syntactic rule-based approach to comprehension. The other simulation is a connectionist model that does not involve explicit rules but learns to behave in a rulelike manner. Computational models advance research on language understanding because they generate specific predictions that can be tested experimentally.

INTRODUCTION

Understanding language is perhaps the most varied, flexible, and subtle of all our cognitive skills. We understand our native tongue regardless of context or speaker. We read and comprehend notices, letters, recipes, good literature, comics, and many other types of texts. We also know how to keep track of a conversation and how to interpret questions, commands, jokes, puns, metaphors, and other subtle aspects of language. Consider sentences (11.1) through (11.3):

(11.1) The waiter gave Lynn the menu.

(11.2) Can you close the window?

(11.3) Bill kicked the bucket.

A native speaker of English comprehends these sentences without any hesitation, although a little thought shows that each of them is quite complex. Sentence (11.2), for example, is a request to close the window, not a question about your ability to do so. Sentence (11.3) actually means that Bill died; it is concerned with neither kicking nor a bucket. Even when a speaker utters single words, incomplete sentences, or several sentences during a conversation, we usually understand what is meant. When a child finishes drinking her milk and says, "More," her parents know that she would like to have more milk. As for conversations, see if you understand the dialogue in (11.4) (from G. B. Shaw's "The Man of Destiny").

(11.4) *Napoleon:*   What shall we do with this soldier, Guiseppe? Everything he says is wrong.
Guiseppe: Make him a general, Excellency, and then everything he says will be right.

Our understanding of this dialogue depends, among other things, on knowledge of stereotypical roles in the army.

Comprehension almost always works flawlessly, unless we encounter topics with which we are less familiar. Consider paragraphs (11.5) and (11.6):

(11.5) In a car race, a Jaguar starts the course at noon and averages 80 miles per hour. A Stingray starts at 12:05 and averages 90 miles per hour. If a lap is 15 miles, on which lap will the Jaguar be passed?

(11.6) If you acquired stock in a mutual fund by gift and its fair market value at the time of the gift was less than the adjusted basis to the donor at the time of the gift, your basis for gain on its sale or other disposition is the same as the donor's adjusted basis. Your basis for loss is its fair market value at the time of the gift. In this situation, it is possible to sell the stock at neither a gain nor a loss because of the basis you have to use.

We may find the algebra word problem in (11.5) relatively difficult because we may not have done such problems in quite some time or not remember that it is one of the distance-rate-time type. Paragraph (11.6) is incomprehensible to all but a tax accountant. This paragraph was copied from Publication 564 of the Internal Revenue Service, the tax collection agency of the government. Both cases, (11.5) and (11.6), illustrate that specific background knowledge is necessary for comprehension. Indeed, this is true for sentences (11.1) through (11.3) as well. Sentence (11.1) is easy because we have knowledge of restaurants and their typical routine. We would, however, hesitate a moment when reading a sentence such as (11.7).

(11.7) The waiter gave Lynn the tent.

Clearly, comprehension requires knowledge of the topical background (e.g., (11.5) and (11.6)) and of the prior context (e.g., (11.4) and (11.7)) of a sentence. We need to know the meaning of the words, the syntactic rules, principles of combining words, pragmatic conventions (e.g., (11.2)), and idiomatic usage (e.g., (11.3)). We must also understand the basic sounds, phonemes, and letters of a language.

Chapter 10 gave an overview of several of these linguistic knowledge sources. Language understanding, however, is not merely a matter of having linguistic knowledge. The listener also needs to have some knowledge of the world and its physical regularities—for example, that objects fall to the ground, that day and night alternate, and that burning things usually hurt us. Finally, the listener needs to know the general background of the discourse, whether it is algebra, law, or baseball. To treat all of these aspects of language understanding would exceed the scope of this chapter. Rather, this chapter describes some selected aspects of language understanding; how we access word meanings, interpret sentences, and construct sentence representations. Our working definition of *understanding* will be the following:

> Understanding a sentence is to extract meaning from it, to represent the meaning, and to use it for some purpose.

Understanding a sentence means that the person knows who did what to whom. Consider sentence (11.8) and what a reader knows about it. The reader knows that the butler is the person who does something, that the action is cooking, that the object is supper, and that the person who is to receive the supper is Mary.

(11.8) The butler is cooking supper for Mary.

This knowledge may be represented in a proposition of the form, (11.8a), familiar from Chapters 5 and 10.

(11.8a) (Predicate: COOK, Agent: BUTLER, Object: SUPPER, Recipient: MARY)

Psycholinguists seek to determine the processes used to generate such a meaning representation from a sentence such as (11.8). These processes—including word level, sentence level, and discourse level—operate under the constraints of a limited working memory (WM), our principal language processor (see Chapter 8). In their quest to understand understanding, psycholinguistic researchers face broad theoretical and empirical questions. One of the basic theoretical issues is to identify the relation between the different subprocesses of comprehension. Do the component processes do their job independently in a **modular** fashion? Or do they influence each other in an **interactive** fashion? This contrast between the modular and interactive view is illustrated graphically in Figure 11.1.

The basic empirical problem in psycholinguistics is how to find out what processes a person uses in comprehension. Could we ask people to introspect and report their experiences in comprehending sentences? Although this may be an interesting exercise, it would not yield much information about actual comprehension processes. By the time a person introspects on these short-lived operations and formulates a response, they are likely to have been completed and simply escape her attention. Furthermore, if you were to force yourself to attend to comprehension, you might run the risk of altering the very process you want to observe. As a result, researchers

FIGURE 11.1 Illustration of the modular and interactive approaches to language understanding.

generally do not use self-reporting methods in their efforts to uncover comprehension processes. Rather, they record certain measures of performance while a person listens to a sentence or reads a passage. For example, researchers record the pattern and duration of a reader's eye fixations, or simply the time it takes to read a word, sentence, or paragraph. In addition, decision latencies in recognition experiments (tachistoscopic and lexical decision studies) are used. These measures are online because it is assumed that they measure the duration of mental operations as they occur in real time.[1] Experimenters also study the products of comprehension; they ask subjects to paraphrase a text, recall it, or answer questions about it.

We will discuss a number of experiments that have used comprehension times as their dependent variable. One method of recording comprehension times, the eye-tracking method, produced the data in Figure 11.2. This figure shows a passage fragment and the eye fixation times of individual words. In the eye-tracking method, the subject reads the text word by word from a computer screen. As the subject looks at the text, the researcher projects a beam of light on one of her eyes. When she moves the eye in reading, the reflection moves as well; these movements are recorded with a video camera and analyzed relative to specific locations in the text.

The average eye fixation duration takes about 250 milliseconds; fixations, however, vary widely, as Figure 11.2 shows. Figure 11.2 contains the opening segment of a description of flywheels. Usually readers read left to right. Sometimes, however, the eyes regress to an earlier word, and occasionally words are skipped altogether.

Psycholinguists use eye-tracking and such other methods as ERP measurements (see chapter 2) and interpret their data in light of comprehension theories. This chapter describes theories and research of word-level and sentence-level processes, including neurolinguistic and computational perspectives. Most researchers share

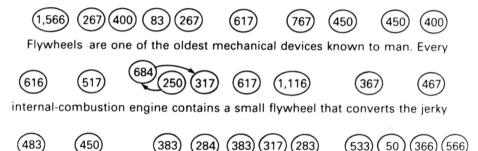

FIGURE 11.2 Reading times observed in an eye-tracking experiment (Just & Carpenter, 1987).

some general convictions about the mental operations that underlie comprehension. A basic assumption is that the reader creates a mental representation of the sentence. Starting from a foundation, this representation develops with each subsequent word. Nobody knows exactly what a sentence representation is like. In Chapter 10, we assumed that it consists of propositions. In this chapter, the propositional assumption is maintained, except in the section on connectionist processing. The connectionist approach proposes that the content of sentences and discourses is represented in distributed networks, rather than in lists of discrete propositions.

WORD-LEVEL PROCESSES

Discourse does not usually consist of single words, except for unusual circumstances as when someone calls "Help!" or "Fire!" Nevertheless, a listener or reader must process discourse in terms of words. The person must isolate a word, whether on the page or in a stream of sounds, and identify its meaning. Theories of word recognition have a time-honored tradition in psychology dating back to the turn of this century. As we saw in Chapter 4, the physical word stimulus must be transformed into a format that is compatible with the way in which the word's meaning is represented in the mental lexicon.

This transformation is called **encoding.** Retrieving the word's meaning from the lexicon is known as **lexical access.** Both encoding and lexical access are usually automatic and not subject to our introspection nor to our conscious control (Marslen-Wilson & Tyler, 1981). In other words, a listener cannot tell us how he decodes the phonemes of a word or how he accesses the word's meaning. Indeed, once hearing a familiar word, the listener has no other choice than to retrieve the word's meaning—the process is obligatory. In this section, we will discuss theories of encoding and lexical access, describe three empirical effects, and interpret them in terms of these theories: the length effect, the frequency effect, and the context effect (see also Chapter 4).

Take a moment to inspect the comprehension times in Figure 11.2. You will notice that these times depend, in part, on the word's length: The more characters the word has, the longer it takes to read, unless it is located at the beginning or end of a sentence. This is called the **length effect.** Compare, for example, the reading times of *devices* and of the last occurrence of *the* in the bottom row in Figure 11.2; the word *devices* took 767 milliseconds to process, whereas *the* took only 50 milliseconds.

Next, consider a problem in attributing the differences in comprehension times exclusively to the length of the words. The words *devices* and *the* not only differ in length but also in their familiarity. We can obtain a measure of familiarity by the occurrence frequency of the word in the English language. Box 11.1 describes how Kučera and Francis (1967) counted the occurrence frequency of different words in English texts. The word *devices* appears only 37 times in Kučera and Francis's corpus of one million English words, whereas *the* appears 69,971 times. It turns out that *the* is the most frequently used word in English. *Of* is the runner-up, appearing 36,411 times.

Word length and word occurrence frequency are therefore confounded. In other words, both of these variables influence comprehension time:

A word will take more time to read when it is longer or when it occurs less frequently in English. How do researchers handle this confounding? They separate length and frequency by studying the effects of one variable while keeping the other variable constant (Just & Carpenter, 1987).

The effect of occurrence frequency on processing time is known as the **frequency effect.** The frequency effect is observed in other experimental situations as well—for example, in word recognition studies, lexical decision tasks, and reading experiments that used neuropsychological methods (see Chapter 2). In word recognition studies, more frequent words are recognized more rapidly (see Chapter 4). In lexical decision stud-

---

Box 11.1

What Is the Most Frequent English Word?

On a beautiful day in February 1963, six scholars gathered for a meeting at Brown University in Providence, Rhode Island. They had been discussing a very ambitious project for several months. They planned to count all of the words in American English and the occurrence frequency of each of those words. After much deliberation they finally decided on a sampling method to accomplish this gargantuan task. Some 500 samples of text were selected, each containing approximately 2,000 words. The total number of words in these passages, known as the Kučera-Francis Corpus, came to 1,014,232 words. The passages were randomly selected from sets of editorials, reports, reviews, religious writings, popular lore, biographies, scientific journals, mystery novels, adventure and western stories, classical literature, love stories, humorous passages, and others. The restriction was that the texts were first printed in 1961 and located in the Brown University Library, the Providence Athenaeum, the New York Public Library, and some other institutions (for example, the largest secondhand magazine store in New York City).

The texts were keypunched (remember, it was 1963) and transferred to tape. An individual word (token) was defined as a continuous string of let-

ters. There were 50,406 unique words, called types, in the Corpus. The frequency of each of these words in the Corpus was determined by a computer program. The results are available on tape as well as in a 424-page book (Kučera & Francis, 1967). A subset of the results, the occurrence frequency of 13 of about 1 million words, appears below.

SELECTED WORDS AND THEIR OCCURRENCE FREQUENCY IN ENGLISH

Word Frequency	Word
69,971	*the*
36,411	*of*
542	*small*
351	*best*
246	*study*
162	*medical*
96	*books*
58	*smile*
37	*devices*
34	*pencil*
1	*cache*
1	*aura*
1	*modality*

ies, they are responded to more quickly (see Chapter 5). Finally, under certain circumstances, electrophysiological processing as measured by event-related brain potentials (see Chapter 2) is more pronounced for rare words such as *cache* than for more frequent words such as *small* (Kutas & Van Petten, 1994). It is as if the brain must work harder to recognize less familiar words. We will learn shortly that the frequency effect also has theoretical consequences for the representation of words in human memory.

We saw that word reading times of words are influenced by attributes of the words themselves, like their length and familiarity. Word reading times also depend on sentence context; sometimes a word is understood more quickly when the reader expects it. This **context effect** has attracted considerable attention because it fits in well with the theory that initial information in a sentence (or discourse) to some extent predicts subsequent information. In short, the earlier text generates an expectation for subsequent information. Zola (1984), among others, tested this expectancy theory and his results offer some support for it. He presented sentence pairs such as (11.9a) and (11.9b) to readers and measured the time the readers' eyes fixated on each word, in particular the target word *popcorn.*

(11.9a) Movie theaters must have buttered popcorn to serve their patrons.

(11.9b) Movie theaters must have adequate popcorn to serve their patrons.

In sentence (11.9a), *popcorn* is more likely because the adjective *buttered* limits the choice of subsequent words. The modifier *adequate* in sentence (11.9b) is more general, thus permitting a broader range of subsequent nouns, including *seats, air conditioning, lighting,* and several others. Zola observed a small context effect in his experiment: Readers fixated on *popcorn* 15 milliseconds less in (11.9a) than in (11.9b). Because the context *buttered* narrows the number of possible choices, readers expected the target word *popcorn* to some extent and required somewhat less time to recognize it.

Encoding and Lexical Access

Encoding.   According to an early theory by Gough (1972), readers identify individual letters of a word serially left to right. Assuming that identifying each letter takes a certain unit of time, *k,* the encoding of a hypothetical six-letter word would take $6k$ units of time. Gough's serial theory was controversial, however, because in some cases the perception of whole words was shown to be faster than Gough's model predicted. For example, the word *Philadelphia* is recognized faster than one would expect on the basis of its length and word frequency. Clearly, other attributes, such as letter groupings, the characteristic shape of the word, and context of the word, play a role in word recognition. Nevertheless, barring these exceptions, Gough's serial encoding hypothesis is now widely accepted.

If reading is a visual analog of listening, as many believe, word encoding should be a serial process. In speech, the phonemes of a word are created and transmitted serially; listeners receive phonemes serially. Using the initial information of the word, listeners often recognize a word as soon as the first syllables are complete and usually before the full word is heard (Marslen-Wilson & Tyler, 1981; see Chapter 4). Another reason to accept the serial encoding hypothesis is that, in tachistoscopic recognition and lexical decision studies, word recognition times depend on word length as well. It would be inefficient, therefore, to postulate a serial encoding process in these experiments and some other process in reading comprehension. In any case, the result of encoding is the transformation of a letter string into a form that can be read by the mental lexicon.

Lexical Access.   Psycolinguists and linguists generally agree that our knowledge of words is represented in a mental lexicon, a kind of dictionary that contains information about words: their sound, spelling, meaning, relation to other words, and the syntactic role they typically occupy in sentences (see Chapter 10). There is also general agreement on the role of the lexicon in language comprehension; listeners and readers access the lexicon in order to retrieve the meaning of a word they encounter in a conversation or text. There are questions, however, about the details of lexical access: Does the listener search the lexicon or not? Is lexical access independent of other comprehension processes? What is the structure of the lexicon and type of meaning representation of the word entries? Theorists differ in their answers to these questions. There are a great variety of theoretical models of lexical access. We will consider two classes of models: search models and direct-access models. Search models tend to be modular; lexical access is thought to be independent of other comprehension processes (Forster, 1990). Direct-access models, however, are usually interactive; lexical access is continuously influenced by parsing and interpretation processes at the sentence level.

Search Models.   According to search models, the listener compares a letter string with entries stored in the lexicon until a match occurs. It is assumed that this search process is independent of the sentence context. Let us illustrate the search model using the string W-O-R-K as an example. Assume that lexical entries are arranged as in Figure 11.3. The string, WORK, is compared to *time, man, way,* and so on. As soon as a match occurs between the string and an item stored in the lexicon, the word is recognized.

To explain the frequency effect, search theorists assume that entries in the lexicon are arranged by their occurrence frequency in English, rather than alphabetically or in some other order (Forster, 1976). Words with a higher occurrence frequency, such as *small,* are listed earlier in the lexicon than infrequent words, such as *cache.*

Direct-Access Models.   Direct-access theorists assume that the lexicon contains a unique detector for each word. Each detector is particularly tuned to the attributes of that word. If the word is presented, its features activate its corresponding word detector. Thus, there is a detector for the word *cat* that is triggered by the letters *c, a,* and *t*

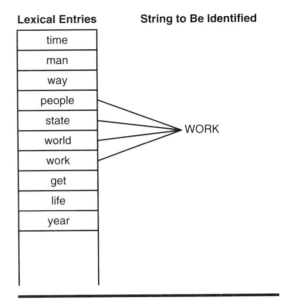

Lexical Entries   **String to Be Identified**

time
man
way
people
state
world
work
get
life
year

WORK

FIGURE 11.3   Search model of lexical access. The string to be identified, *work,* is compared with lexical entries, one at a time.

in that order. When the activation level of the detector exceeds a specific threshold, the string of letters or phonemes is recognized as that word. This model is described as a direct-access model because the presence of the word's features leads to the immediate activation of the detector without any serial search. This detector theory is similar to the template theories discussed in Chapter 4. Different theorists have assumed such detectors but labeled them differently—for example, *logogens* (Morton, 1979) and *word units* (McClelland & Rumelhart, 1981).

Like the search model, the direct-access model easily explains the frequency effect. Direct-access theory assumes that a detector's activation threshold is lower for more frequent words. The detector for a frequent word such as *small* is more sensitive than the detector for *cache;* less input activation is required to trigger it. Because of their interactive nature, direct-access models easily explain context effects such as Zola's (1984). It is thought that a word's detector is receptive to any sort of input, including orthographic, phonemic, syntactic, and contextual information. The target word *popcorn* used in Zola's (1984) experiment takes less time to recognize because its detector is boosted by the prior context of the word as well as by its letters, P-O-P-C-O-R-N. In short, the word *buttered* serves as a prime for *popcorn*.

The modular search theory can also account for the context effect, it does so by postulating a *post-access check* of recognized words. The reader accesses each word meaning independently of the word's prior context. After the word's meaning has been recovered (that is, *post access*), the reader checks whether that meaning fits in with the prior context. Thus, when reading *popcorn* in sentence (11.9a), the reader first accesses its meaning and then checks how well it fits in with the prior context. Because *buttered* and *popcorn* are typically associated, the post-access check is completed quickly and the reader proceeds to read the next word. On the other hand, in sentence (11.9b), *popcorn* does not fit quite as well with *adequate,* and as a result, the post-access check takes somewhat longer. As you can see, the interactive and modular explanations differ in their interpretation of the role of context. Interactive theorists believe that context influences the recovery of the word's meaning *prior* to lexical access, whereas modular theorists think its influence occurs *after* access, and hence separate from it.

A Test of the Interactive versus Modular Approaches to Lexical Access. One's preference for either the interactive or modular framework depends to some extent on the experimental paradigm chosen to test them. Consider two different paradigms: the study of neighborhood effects and the bimodal lexical decision technique. The former supports the interactive theory, whereas the latter is handled more readily by the modular approach.

Neighborhood effects refer to the effects of the size of the set of the orthographic neighbors of a word on the time it takes to recognize the word. By convention, one changes one letter of a given word at a time and counts the number of English words that are produced by substituting the letter. For example, the word *game* has many neighbors, including *came, dame, fame, lame, name, same, tame, gale, gape, gate,* and *gave,* whereas *film* has relatively few (*firm, fill*). Search models predict that the larger the neighborhood, the greater the search time because more lexical entries must be searched. Interactive models, however, predict that the mutual activation, and, hence, facilitation between words, increases as a function of their similarity; the more similar the words are, the greater will be the facilitation. This is analogous to the mutual support between words and their constituent letters in neural network models of the word superiority effect (see Chapter 4). Supporting the interactive view, researchers have found faster recognition times for words with large neighborhoods (see review by Balota, 1994).

Support for the modular nature of lexical access comes from the **bimodal lexical decision paradigm,** however. In this paradigm, the person receives linguistic input from two modalities, acoustic and visual, hence the description *bimodal.* The paradigm involves a lexical decision task: The subject is presented with a string of letters like BURN or BIRN and has to decide whether or not the string is an English word (see Chapter 5).

Swinney (1979) used this method to assess the independence of lexical access from context. As illustrated in Figure 11.4, Swinney's subjects listened to a context sentence presented over headphones and were then tested with a target string shown on a screen (visual modality). The subject had to decide whether the visual target was a word or not. Swinney chose context sentences that biased one of the meanings of an ambiguous word, as illustrated by *bugs* in sentence (11.10).

(11.10) Because he was afraid of electronic surveillance, the burglar carefully searched the room for bugs.

Immediately after the person heard the word *bugs,* a string was flashed on the screen for the lexical decision test. Consider three different

FIGURE 11.4   The bimodal lexical decision task.

target cases: ANT, SPY, and SEW. The word *ant* is related to *bugs,* but it does not fit with the meaning of the context sentence; *spy,* however, fits the context. *Sew* is a neutral word used to establish a base line for lexical decision. Balancing target and control words for occurrence frequency and word length, Swinney found that both *spy* and *ant* were facilitated relative to the neutral word *sew.* The priming of *ant* was unexpected because it was not implied by the context sentence. It is this finding that supports the claim of an independent lexical module.

INTERIM SUMMARY

Lexical access involves the recovery of the meaning of a word from the mental lexicon. We have sketched two models of lexical access: the direct-access theory and the search theory. We also learned of two major approaches to language processing, the interactive and the modular framework. Because of its openness to inputs from different sources—including phonemes, letters,

and context—the direct-access model is characterized as an interactive-processing model; information from several levels of structure are continuously available for interpretation and can influence each other immediately.

The opposing view is the modular theory, which holds that the different subprocesses of comprehension act independently, at least up to a point. According to the modular view, the recovery of a word's meaning is independent of the prior context. Both interactive and modular theories can explain the word frequency effect. The context effect can also be handled by both, but the interactive theory does so more easily. The modular theory must postulate an additional mechanism, post-access check, in order to explain context effects. Bimodal priming studies show that two word senses are activated simultaneously and independently of context; this result is better explained by the modular theory. For the moment, we conclude that the neighborhood size effect fits better with the interactive approach, whereas the priming results fit better with the modular approach.

SENTENCE-LEVEL PROCESSES

Sentence comprehension involves both analysis and synthesis. The listener analyzes the sentence in terms of smaller units, clauses, and builds a larger, more abstract unit, a sentence representation. This representation expresses the meaning relations between clauses and their underlying propositions. In this section, we will consider both analysis and synthesis at the sentence level; we discuss some strategies comprehenders use to group words into phrases, segment sentences into clauses, and generate a sentence structure. These strategies are called **parsing** strategies. The verb *parse* is derived from the Latin expression *pars orationis* which means part of speech. Different theoretical models describe the outcome of the parsing process in different terms. Syntactic models emphasize the treelike nature of the parsing process (e.g., Frazier, 1987), whereas semantic approaches assume that the outcome of parsing is a thematic assignment, for example, of arguments to verbs (reviewed by Mitchell, 1994).

Parsing Strategies

If listeners and readers represent sentences as propositions (van Dijk & Kintsch, 1983; Just & Carpenter, 1987), we need to explore how they extract these propositions from the sentence. To simplify matters, assume that listeners and readers group words into constituents and then assign thematic roles to each constituent. Because language is so rich in its expressive forms, there are no fixed parsing rules; rather, readers and listeners use flexible parsing strategies in order to transform phrases into propositions (Bever, 1970; Clark & Clark, 1977; Kimball, 1973). People use these strategies automatically and without awareness or deliberate effort. Clark and Clark (1977) formulated six major syntactic strategies, including the constituent strategy and the content-word strategy. We'll consider these two complementary strategies and Bever's (1970) noun-verb-noun strategy next.

Constituent Strategy. According to the constituent strategy, listeners use function words to start a new constituent. The strategy works as follows:

Whenever you find a function word, begin a new constituent.

Different types of function words signal specific constituents: determiners signal noun phrases, prepositions indicate prepositional phrases, and auxiliary verbs indicate a new verb phrase. For example, in sentence (11.11), the determiner *the* signals the beginning of the noun phrase *the butler*. In sentence (11.11), the preposition *for* indicates the beginning of a prepositional phrase. Note that the prepositional phrase includes the noun phrase *the girl* signaled by *the*. Determiners tend to be followed by content words, specifically

nouns or adjectives, never by verbs. This and other similar strategies have been included in Clark and Clark's content-word strategy.

(11.11) The butler is cooking supper for the girl with a spoon.

Content-Word Strategy. According to the content-word strategy, after a perceiver has started a constituent, he looks for an appropriate content word for that constituent. The strategy may be stated as follows:

After identifying the beginning of a constituent, look for content words appropriate to that type of constituent.

For example, after detecting a determiner, expect a noun that terminates the noun phrase. Thus, in sentence (11.11), the word *butler* concludes the initial noun phrase of the sentence.

Another strategy related to the content-word strategy is the following: *After locating a preposition, expect a noun phrase to close out the prepositional phrase.* An example of this is the phrase *a spoon* in sentence (11.11). An additional related strategy processes verb phrases. This strategy directs the listener or reader to look for a main verb after she encounters an auxiliary verb.

Noun-Verb-Noun Strategy (NVN). Bever (1970) proposed the NVN strategy to generate a meaning representation for the simple subject-verb-object (SVO) clauses of SVO languages (see also Chapter 10). The NVN strategy creates a proposition by assigning constituents to thematic roles:

If the first constituent of an utterance is a noun phrase, assign it the role of agent.

If the second constituent of the utterance is a verb, interpret it as the action.

If the third constituent is a noun phrase, interpret it as the object of the action.

The NVN strategy is specific to SVO languages, which account for about a third of all languages. Analogous strategies exist for SOV and

VSO languages that together constitute almost two-thirds of the remaining languages. The noun-verb-noun strategy fits a large number of English sentences (e.g., (11.12) through (11.14)), although certainly not for all of them (e.g., (11.15a)). But even for sentence (11.15a), the NVN strategy is invoked at first.

(11.12)   John wrote the letter.

(11.13)   The boy hit the ball.

(11.14)   The driver finished the steak.

(11.15a)   The boat floated down the river sank.

(11.15b)   The boat that floated down the river sank.

In sentence (11.15a), we initially interpret the first six words, *The boat floated down the river* as a single clause. We stop and reinterpret the entire sentence, however, when we encounter *sank* (see Kaplan, 1975). Sentence (11.15a) contains an implicit relative clause; sentence (11.15b) contains the same relative clause. Here, however, the clause is signaled by the relative pronoun *that*. Sentences (11.15a) and (11.15b) are relatively simple, containing only two clauses. Our next example is more complex. Consider sentence (11.16a):

(11.16a)   The editor authors the newspaper hired liked laughed.

(11.16b)   The editor the authors the newspaper hired liked laughed.

Bever found that his subjects used the NVN strategy and interpreted the word *authors* in (11.16a) as a verb to arrive at the meaning *An editor authors a newspaper*. Proposition (11.16c) captures that interpretation.

(11.16c)   (Predicate: AUTHORS, Agent: EDITOR, Object: NEWSPAPER)

The three verbs following the noun phrase *the newspaper* quickly reveal that this interpretation is inaccurate. In (11.16b), the definite article *the* makes understanding easier. The article indicates that *authors* must be a noun. Although sentence (11.16b) is still difficult, listeners can manage to interpret it.[2]

The result of the constituent, content-word, NVN, and other parsing strategies is a set of clauses and propositions in the listener's mind. These are briefly held in working memory, along with the products of other comprehension processes such as encoding and lexical access. Comprehenders not only extract phrases and propositions from sentences but they also detect the semantic relations between them, as we will see in the following two sections.

Clausal Processing.   Parsing strategies can handle phrases and single-clause sentences but not complex sentences. Consider sentence (11.17):

(11.17)   The late Italian film director Luchino Visconti having been acknowledged by those who study the cinema to be a very great filmmaker, and a Visconti Film Retrospective having been scheduled at the Library and Museum of the Performing Arts, at Lincoln Center, and a preview screening of Visconti's latest film, "The Innocent," having been set up in the Bruno Walter Auditorium at the Library on a recent Monday night, and the Italian Cultural Institute, which takes an interest in affairs of this sort, having arranged a special opening-night party afterward in its building at 686 Park Avenue, ... (*New Yorker,* October 29, 1979)

The sample in (11.17) is actually a fragment of a sentence that spans over one page of the *New Yorker*. Such super-sentences are unusual; the average sentence length in natural texts is certainly shorter. It would be easy for listeners to understand sentences of any word length, if working memory were not limited to only a few chunks. If we assume for the moment that a word represents a chunk and that working memory can hold up to seven words (Miller, 1956), working memory would be filled to capacity well before an average sentence is complete. But what if the surface information in a clause could be recorded and then transferred to a more permanent memory? According to the clausal chunking hypothesis, this is exactly what happens (Fodor, Bever, & Garrett, 1974; Jarvella, 1979). The listener takes advantage of the clausal structure of sentences and compacts the surface sentence into a more abstract proposition, such as (11.8a) (Bever, 1970; Clark & Clark, 1977; Kimball, 1973). Certain details of the information are lost (for example, the precise word order and the voice of the input string) but what remains is the semantic gist (Sachs, 1967).

Sachs (1967) conducted a classic study that made this point. The study involved a recognition experiment in which subjects listened to passages and then to individual test sentences. Each passage contained a target sentence, such as sentence (11.18).

(11.18) He sent a letter about it to Galileo, the great Italian scientist.

Some of the test sentences were identical to sentences that appeared originally in the passage (11.18); other sentences were changed in voice (11.19a)—for example from the passive to the active—but the meaning remained the same. In another set of test sentences, the meaning was changed (11.19b). Finally, some of the test sentences were entirely new; they had not been part of the passages.

(11.19a) A letter about it was sent to Galileo, the great Italian scientist.

(11.19b) Galileo, the great Italian scientist, sent him a letter about it.

Subjects tended to confuse test sentences with the voice-changed sentence (11.19a) to a greater extent than sentences with changed meaning (11.19b). However, when the sentence voice and other so-called surface features are important, subjects remember them (see Craik, 1979).

Item-recognition studies have also shown that sentence information becomes less accessible after a clause boundary unless it is foundational for the sentence representation. We will consider studies by Chang (1980) and by Gernsbacher and Hargreaves (1988) to illustrate the fate of information after clause boundaries. Chang (1980)

used a self-paced reading task. He presented such sentence pairs as (11.20a) and (11.20b).

(11.20a) Now that artists are working in *oil*/prints are rare.

(11.20b) Now that artists are working fewer hours/*oil* prints are rare.

The slash, /, indicates a clause boundary. The slash is shown here for purposes of illustration only; it was not shown to the subjects in these experiments. The word *oil* was the target word. Highlighted here, it was shown in regular font in Chang's experiment. Relative to the end of the sentence, the target word occupied the same position in each of the test sentences. Each member of a pair was presented to different subjects, followed immediately by the target word. People had to decide whether or not the target word had occurred in the sentence. Correct *yes* decisions took 794 milliseconds when the target word was in the final clause, as opposed to 863 milliseconds when it was in the initial clause. The point of Chang's finding is that information from earlier clauses becomes less available as it is transformed into a more abstract proposition.

The study by Gernsbacher and Hargreaves (1988) illustrated the importance of foundational information. According to them, foundational information is used as the basis for the mental representation of the whole sentence. Usually it is the person mentioned first in a sentence. Consider the word *Tina* is sentences (11.21a) and (11.21b). *Tina* is mentioned first in (11.21a) and second in (11.21b).

(11.21a) Because of Tina, Lisa was evicted from the apartment.

(11.21b) Because of Lisa, Tina was evicted from the apartment.

Gernsbacher and Hargreaves presented sentences such as these in the study phase of a recognition experiment. They flashed target words such as *Tina* for the recognition test. They found that the response times were 94 milliseconds faster when the target *Tina* was mentioned first, as in (11.21a).

Because the first-mentioned information is foundational in (11.21a), it has a special status and is therefore more accessible, even though a clausal boundary has intervened.

INTERIM SUMMARY

People are sensitive to major clause boundaries in reading. They segment sentences into clauses and exhibit brief reading pauses at clause boundaries. According to experimental evidence, people use the boundaries to transfer information in the previous clause from working memory to a more permanent representation. As a result, the earlier information becomes less available, unless it is used as a foundation for the sentence representation itself.

Generating Sentence Structure.   In the previous section, we learned that readers use a clausal strategy to process sentences. They chunk clauses in terms of more abstract units, which are probably propositions. Next, we examine how people attach clauses to one another. The reader or listener could simply form a long chain of the clauses he has encountered. Alternatively, comprehenders could recreate the hierarchical structure of a sentence, as captured in its phrase marker (see Chapter 10). The phrase marker reflects the semantic relations between the phrases of the sentence. It is assumed that listeners generate phrase markers in working memory to express the relations between constituents. We represent phrase markers just as we did in Chapter 10; you will recall that phrase structure trees are usually graphed in terms of nodes and arcs. The nodes represent the constituents of the sentence and the arcs reflect relations between constituents and point to terminal elements. Consider sentence (11.22a) and the two phrase markers in Figure 11.5.

(11.22a) John hit the girl *with a book.*

According to the phrase marker in Figure 11.5A, the prepositional phrase (PP) *with a book* is an instrument of hitting; John used a book to hit the girl. This is indicated by attaching the PP node directly to the VP node (see double link). Proposition (11.22b) captures this interpretation.

(11.22b) (Predicate: HIT, Agent: JOHN, Object: GIRL, Instrument: BOOK)

The phrase marker in Figure 11.5B expresses another interpretation. Here, the girl has a book, and John hit the girl who possesses the book. The PP

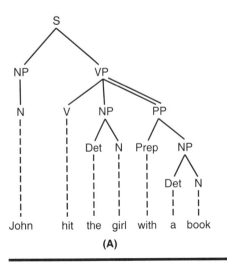

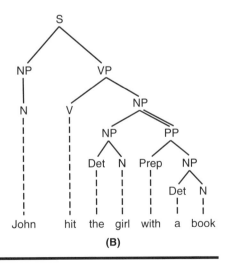

FIGURE 11.5   Alternative phrase markers for the sentence *John hit the girl with a book.*

with a book is attached to the NP node that represents the girl (see double link). Two propositions are necessary to express this reading of sentence (11.22a).

(11.22c) 1 (Predicate: HIT, Agent: JOHN, Object: GIRL)
2 (Predicate: POSSES, Agent: GIRL, Object: BOOK)

Figure 11.5 shows two alternative interpretations of sentence (11.22a). We constructed them deliberately after viewing the sentence as a whole. Readers and listeners, however, process each word left to right and are thought to determine a word's syntactic role immediately (Frazier, 1987; Just & Carpenter, 1987).

According to Frazier's (1987) theory, listeners and readers generate a syntactic sentence representation; they do so automatically and independently of other comprehension processes. The growth of the phrase marker for sentence (11.22a) with each additional word is shown in Figure 11.6. First, the reader assigns the word *John* to the category NP. In Frazier's words, the reader "opens a node NP." Next, the word *hit* is identified as a verb and a VP node is generated and so on. The process runs smoothly until we come to the prepositional phrase (PP) *with a book.*

At which point in the phrase structure tree is the phrase *with a book* attached? It could be attached to the verb phrase *hit,* thus representing an instrument of hitting (as in Figure 11.5A), or it could be attached to *girl,* thus indicating that the girl was the possessor of a book (as in Figure 11.5B). In sentence (11.22d), on the other hand, the phrase *with a book* clearly expresses an object in the possession of the girl (Frazier, 1987).

(11.22d) John hit the girl *with a book* with a bat.

Frazier formulated the principle of minimal attachment to explain the linking of prepositional phrases such as *with a book*. According to this principle, readers and listeners initially interpret *book* as an instrument, as in Figure 11.5A. In structural terms, perceivers attach the ambiguous propositional phrase to the verb phrase. The **min-imal attachment principle** states that listeners attach incoming words to the most recently generated node, rather than to open a new one. Of course, when subsequent information overrules the attachment, it must be revised, as in (11.22d). Here, the second prepositional phrase disambiguates the sentence by indicating that the bat was the instrument of hitting rather than the book. A similar relation is shown in sentence pairs (11.23) and (11.24) (Foss, 1988; Taraban & McClelland, 1988).

(11.23a) Susan ate the cereal with the spoon.

(11.23b) Susan ate the cereal with the raisins.

(11.24a) The spy saw the cop with binoculars.

(11.24b) The spy saw the cop with a revolver.

The minimal attachment principle derives its name from the assumption that perceivers generate a phrase structure with the minimal number of new nodes. In Figure 11.5A, the prepositional phrase is attached to the verb phrase. The structures represent verb-phrase attachment. In Figure 11.5B, it is attached to the second noun phrase representing noun-phrase attachment. Figure 11.5B has one additional node, as compared to Figure 11.5A. The minimal attachment principle implies economy on the part of the listener; no extra node is generated unless dictated by subsequent input material. Research by Rayner, Carlson, and Frazier (1983) has shown that people process sentences in accordance with Frazier's principle. Rayner and colleagues found that reading times were longer in sentences that contained an extra node, such as in (11.23b).

The minimal attachment principle may well agree with our intuitions, but it is still controversial. Several researchers, including Taraban and McClelland (1988), have argued that the principle does not always apply. The differences in the processing of (a)- and (b)-type sentences may be based on differences in the reader's expectations about the likelihood of the semantic content. Taraban and McClelland (1988) performed a rating study in which subjects were given (a)- and (b)-type sentences and asked to

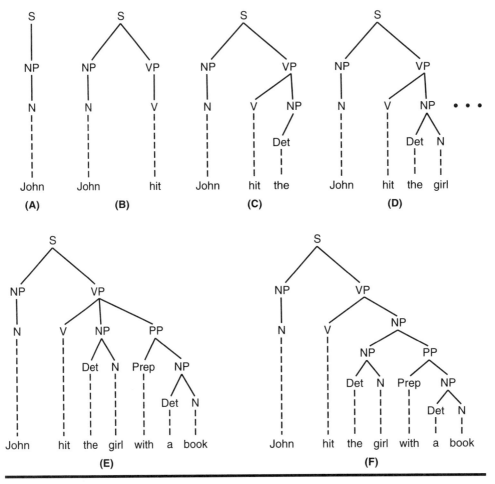

FIGURE 11.6 (*A*) through (*D*): Growing phrase marker for the sentence *John hit the girl with a book* and two interpretations for the complete sentence. Phrase marker (*E*) represents the minimally attached interpretation. Phrase marker (*F*) represents noun-phrase attachment indicating the girl as the possessor of the book.

judge how well the sentences met with their expectations. Subjects said that among Rayner's set, the verb-phrase attachment sentences were more sensible than the noun-phrase attachment sentences. On the other hand, Taraban and McClelland composed sentence pairs in which the reverse held: Noun-phrase attachment sentences agreed better with readers' expectations than their counterparts with verb-phrase attachments. Consider sentence pairs (11.25a) (11.25b) and (11.26a) (11.26b):

(**11.25a**) The thieves stole all the paintings in the night.

(**11.25b**) The thieves stole all the paintings in the museum.

(**11.26a**) I read the article in the bathtub.

(**11.26b**) I read the article in the magazine.

In these pairs, readers judged the (b) versions as more likely and, not surprisingly, an independent group of readers read the (b) versions faster than the (a) versions. Using these results, Taraban and McClelland questioned the syntactic minimal attachment principle. According to them, the increase in processing time occurred because the reader's expectations were not confirmed and had little to do with syntax.

And where do readers' expectations come from? Perhaps they are based on the frequency with which one has encountered certain concepts and syntactic structures. It has been argued that listeners accumulate information about the occurrence frequency of structures in an "actuarial" manner and when an ambiguous phrase is encountered, the more frequent one will be chosen. For example, both the verbs *remember* and *suspect* may introduce either a simple noun phrase, as in *The doctor remembered the idea* or a sentence complement, as in *The doctor remembered the idea was bad.* Actuarial analysis of English sentences reveals that *remembered* is followed more frequently by a noun phrase, whereas *suspected* is followed more frequently by a sentence complement. Results from several different paradigms indicate that readers use such statistical knowledge, tacit as it is, to process ambiguous regions of sentences (Carpenter, Miyake, & Just, 1995; Mitchell, 1994).

The disagreement between the minimal attachment position and its critics is not mere quibbling over details. Rather, it concerns the modular versus interactive issue we encountered before. In this case the question is over the role of the syntactic component in language processing. Rayner and colleagues (1983) maintained that the syntactic processing component is modular and largely independent of semantic processes. They constructed a corpus of sentences and demonstrated that readers analyzed those sentences in accordance with their modular theory. In contrast, Taraban and McClelland (1988) asserted that syntactic and semantic processes interact. The truth probably lies somewhere in between these two positions: In general, the minimal attachment principle holds, but it may be overruled by the semantic interpretation of the sentence (but see Frazier, 1990).

INTERIM SUMMARY

People use flexible parsing strategies to group words into constituents and to represent the relations among those constituents. The minimal attachment principle asserts that we use the minimum number of nodes to link an ambiguous phrase to a sentence. Some theorists question this principle, but not the idea that the relation between phrases is captured in the sentence representation. Readers and listeners are likely to use both syntactic information and semantic expectations. The result of all these processes is a person's understanding a sentence, which enables one to recall the sentence, paraphrase it, and answer questions about it.

NEUROLINGUISTICS: LANGUAGE AND THE BRAIN

Our first insights into the role of the brain in language functions were based on clinical case studies. Based on autopsies, physicians discovered that strokes in the brain's left hemisphere interfered with language comprehension and speech. In the nineteenth century, medical knowledge about the role of the left hemisphere was advanced by the two neurologists, Broca and Wernicke. They are credited with having isolated specific language regions in the temporal and frontal lobes. Most of what we know today about the brain and language is still based on clinical research. This research has yielded consensus on the following findings (Caramazza, 1988):

— In most individuals, major language processing takes place in the brain's left hemisphere.

— Different linguistic components—including syntactic, lexical, and phonological processing—are located in the perisylvan region of the left hemisphere (shaded region in Figure 11.7A).

— The right hemisphere contributes to an individual's appreciation of irony and humor, as well as to speech patterns.

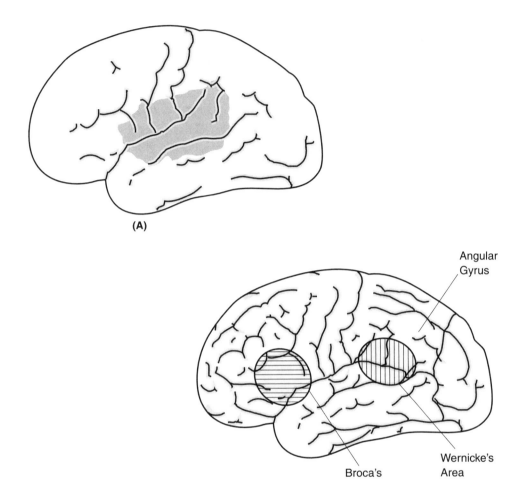

(A)

(B)

Angular
Gyrus

Broca's
Area

Wernicke's
Area

FIGURE 11.7 (*A*) The perisylvan region (shaded) includes principal sites of language processing. (*B*) According to the Geschwind-Wernicke model, Broca's area (horizontal shading) is thought to be the motor-speech area and Wernicke's are (vertical shading) is considered the comprehension center. The angular gyrus mediates between auditory and visual information. (*C*) Electrical stimulation mapping revealed great variability in the localization of sites implicated in naming. The upper number in each zone indicates the number of subjects in whom the site was tested; the circled number indicates the percentage of subjects who exhibited naming errors when stimulated at that site (Ojemann, 1991). (*D*) PET scans reveal sites activated in visual reading (triangles), and in the naming-a-use-task (squares). The view is lateral (Posner et al., 1988).
Source: Figure 11.7A is reproduced, with permission, from the *Annual Review of Neuroscience,* Vol. 11, © 1988 by Annual Reviews Inc.

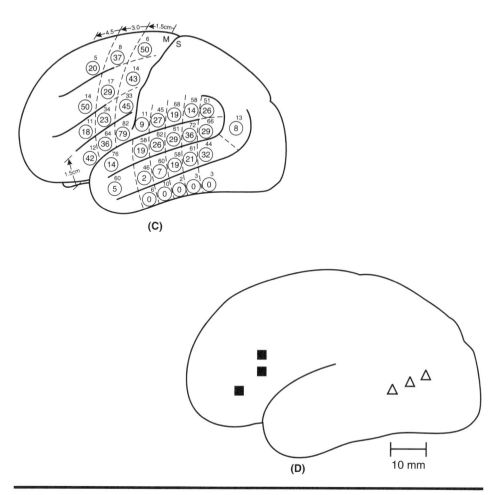

FIGURE 11.7 (*continued*)

During the last decade, clinical research has made further advances and there are new research efforts in other disciplines as well. Cognitive neuropsychologists have begun to investigate the neural basis of language. These researchers seek to illuminate details of language processing in addition to identifying language sites in the brain. New research avenues suggest that language is processed in areas beyond the perisylvan region and that there are greater individual differences in the distribution of language centers than neurologists first assumed.

The Geschwind-Wernicke Model

In the nineteenth century, Broca performed an autopsy on a patient who had been mute for over 20 years. He found that this patient had sustained severe damage in left frontal lobe, in the region labeled Broca's area in Figure 11.7B. Broca subsequently studied other patients, including some who could talk. In almost all of these patients, sites in the left frontal and temporal lobes had incurred some injury. The speech of these patients was "agrammatical," with confusions of function words. As the utterances in (11.27) indicate, the patient cannot think of the word he is seeking and often repeats himself. This lack of fluency in speech is known as **afluent aphasia** or **Broca's aphasia.**

(11.27) Well I had trouble with . . . oh, almost everything that happened from the . . . eh, eh . . . golly . . ., the word I can remember, you know, is ah . . . when I had the . . . ah biggest . . . a . . . that I had the trouble with, you know . . . that I had the trouble with, . . . (Tartter, 1986, p. 454).

Because there was no apparent loss of comprehension, Broca's area was at first implicated in the *production* of speech.

Some years after Broca's discovery, the neurologist Wernicke examined patients who had comprehension problems. Their speech appeared to be fluent, although it was not very sensible as sample (11.28) indicates.

(11.28) Boy, I'm sweating, I'm awful nervous, you know, once in a while I get caught up, I can't mention the tarripoi, a month ago, quite a little, I've done a lot well, I impose a lot, while, on the other hand, you know what I mean, I have to run around, look it over, trebbin and all that sort of stuff (Tartter, 1986, p. 455).

Wernicke found that patients exhibiting **fluent aphasia** or **Wernicke's aphasia** had suffered lesions in a region in the left temporal lobe, known as Wernicke's area (see Figure 11.7B). Broca's and Wernicke's original findings were supported by subsequent clinical and anatomical studies. The neuroscientist Geschwind (1970) summarized the evidence accumulated over a century and proposed the Geschwind-Wernicke model of language. He noted that speech signals travel from the inner ear via the auditory nerve to the primary auditory cortex in the temporal lobe. From there, the information continues to the angular gyrus (see Figure 11.7B), an association area located at the juncture of the parietal, tempo-ral, and occipital lobes. Geschwind viewed this association area as the *concept center,* the processor responsible for computing word meanings and for naming objects. Next, the information is projected to Wernicke's area and from there to Broca's area. Wernicke's area was thought to be involved in hearing and comprehension, whereas Broca's area was thought to be the locus of speech production and to control the movement of the lips, tongue, and other speech organs.

Revising the Geschwind-Wernicke Model

Initial case studies and anatomical analyses supported the Geschwind-Wernicke model that language comprehension is primarily localized in Wernicke's area and language production is localized in Broca's area. This view proved to be an oversimplification, however, as researchers amassed more case studies and as linguists provided a richer set of distinctions in syntactic structure. It was found that Broca's aphasics also had comprehension problems, and Wernicke's aphasics had speech problems. Patients with Broca's aphasia had particular difficulty understanding articles, conjunctions, and other function words (Zurif, 1990); in many cases, these patients did not seem to notice function words. Try to understand passage (11.29) to get an idea of the difficulties a person with Broca's aphasia experiences.

(11.29) --lived-old man--old woman---son.-old man-poor;-wanted-place-boy--apprentice,---rejoice-parents--youth, help---old age,-pray--souls--death.---do,-no wealth?-led-son-many cities, hoping---take---apprentice;--

Some patients suffering from Wernicke's aphasia have difficulty retrieving word meanings, as the dialog in (11.30) between a therapist and patient indicates (Kalat, 1992, p. 179).

(11.30) *Therapist:* (holding picture of an apron) Can you name that one?
Patient: Um . . . you see I can't, I can I can barely do; he would give me sort of umm . . .

T: A clue?

P: That's right . . . just a like, just a . . .

T: You mean, like, "You wear that when you wash dishes or when you cook a meal . . ."?

P: Yeah, something like that.

T: Okay, and what is it? You wear it around your waist, and you cook . . .

P: Cook. Umm, umm, see I can't remember.

T: It's an apron.

P: Apron, apron, that's it, apron.

The emergence of linguistic and psycholinguistic theories has added a new dimension to the neurological approach to language. Psycho-linguists explore specific linguistic skills (including naming, phoneme comparison, and sentence completion) rather than the global issues (including comprehension and production of speech). These researchers were aided by newly developed research methods, imaging techniques, and electrical stimulation mapping. PET scans studied by Posner and colleagues indicate that brain regions other than the perisylvan region are involved in language processes. Using electrical simulation mapping, Ojemann came to a similar conclusion. Ojemann's studies also suggest more distribution of function than was assumed originally.

Electrical Stimulation Mapping

The neurosurgeon Ojemann (1991) has examined over 100 epileptic patients who underwent brain surgery. The patients suffered from severe seizures that were triggered in small regions of the cortex called epileptic foci. Neurosurgeons demonstrated that it was safe to remove these small foci to contain epileptic seizures when medication no longer helped. In this procedure the surgeon opens a segment of the skull gaining access to the surface of the cortex. The open area is anesthetized locally so patients do not experience discomfort, though they are fully conscious as the surgeon probes different brain nuclei.

The surgeon does everything to spare important brain functions. If the left hemisphere is in-volved, she tries to minimize damage to regions implicated in language comprehension and production. She does so by assessing the functions of nuclei in the perisylvan region. Electrical impulses are administered to one nucleus at a time, using delicate electrodes. Because the patient is awake during this procedure, he can talk with the surgeon and participate in the tests.

Ojemann uses several tasks in his research, including a naming and a reading task. In the naming task, the patient is shown pictures of objects and is asked to name the object. In the reading task, he sees a sentence fragment of 8 to 10 words and is asked to complete it, as sample (11.31) illustrates.

(11.31) The driver will turn at the intersection and then . . .

Performance with and without stimulation is compared on these tasks. In the naming task, stimulation at certain sites produced a temporary inability to name the object, although the patient could still carry on a conversation. In the reading task, the person had difficulty reading the sentence; certain words were skipped or reading stopped altogether. In general, stimulation in very specific nuclei produced these disruptions. If the electrode was placed a few millimeters away from a given nucleus, there was no interference. Ojemann concluded that language functions such as naming were strictly localized; however, the location of nuclei involved in naming was highly variable among patients. Figure 11.7C shows the distribution of sites involved in the naming task. These locations extend well beyond the Broca and Wernicke areas and beyond the perisylvan region.

Ojemann and colleagues also found that the area containing language-related sites tends to be larger in males than in females. This means that the locations at which language functions could be disrupted were spread over a larger region in males. It would be inaccurate, however, to conclude from these results that all language functions are more distributed in males. Using functional magnetic resonance imaging, Shaywitz and colleagues (1995) found more localized processing in males than in females (see also Chapter 2).

In bilingual individuals, the weaker of the two languages was disruptible over a larger region. Apparently, the stronger of the two languages was localized more tightly in the brain.

Although the stimulus-mapping results are based on a population of patients who had severe brain dysfunctions, they are important nevertheless, especially when considered in the light of the PET studies considered next. These studies also led to the conclusion that language functions are more distributed than originally assumed. The advantage of PET scans is that they can be administered to nonpatient as well as patient populations. In the PET scan, blood flow in specific brain regions is measured. The subject consumes a benign radioactive agent, which is absorbed by the blood and detected by scanners. When a brain region is especially active, more blood circulates there as reflected by the radioactive agent. It is as if the active brain region becomes hot.

Cerebral Blood Flow in Comprehension

Using PET scans and the subtraction paradigm, Posner and colleagues found that language processing is modality specific; processing of visually presented words occurs in the occipital lobe, while spoken words are processed in the temporoparietal cortex (see Posner et al., 1988; Chapter 2). Researchers established a baseline of activity by having subjects do nothing except look at a fixation point on the screen. In the visual condition, nouns were presented on a screen. Subjects were merely asked to study the nouns silently without reading them aloud. Compared to the baseline condition, this task resulted in an increase in blood flow in the occipital region only (see triangles in Figure 11.7D).

Semantic operations were tested by asking subjects to name the use of a noun such as *hammer* (to pound). This task produced activation in the anterior left frontal lobe (see squares in Figure 11.7D). Activation in this area is not tied to either modality. It is triggered by abstract conceptual processes. Posner and Raichle (1994) even speculated that we "approach the occurrence of conscious thought in our brains, because much of our conscious thinking consists of concepts" (p. 120). In the auditory condition, words such as *pint* and *lint,* and *row* and *though* were flashed to the screen. Readers had to judge if these words formed rhymes. In order to do this, subjects had to perform a phonological task on words presented visually. In this task, increased blood flow was recorded in the left temporal lobe, the region implicated in auditory processing.

Event-Related Potentials Reveal Syntactic Processing.   Event-related potentials (ERPs) are patterns of brain activity linked to environmental events, including acoustic and visual stimuli and linguistic input. The ERP consists of negative (N) or positive (P) peaks in electrical activity relative to a baseline. The N or P peaks occur within a few hundreds of milliseconds from the onset of the stimulus and are labeled accordingly to reflect the direction of the peak and its latency in milliseconds (see Chapter 2).

In Chapter 2, we saw that lexical anomalies are easily detected by a characteristic pattern in readers' ERP responses. When an anomalous word occurs in a sentence or the font is suddenly changed, the reader's surprise is reflected in a N400 response. This measure indicates a deflection toward negativity 400 ms after the unexpected word was presented to the reader. In a review article appropriately entitled "Psycholinguistics Electrified," Kutas and Van Patten (1994) reported that ERP responses reflect syntactic processes in addition to lexical processes. Scientists varied the acceptability of a set of sentences as illustrated by the following set:

(11.32a)   *Pure intransitive:* The doctor hoped the patient was lying.

(11.32b)   *Biased intransitive:* The doctor believed the patient was lying.

(11.32c)   *Biased transitive:* The doctor charged the patient was lying.

(11.32d)   *Pure transitive:* The doctor forced the patient was lying.

As you can imagine, subjects rated sentences less acceptable in the order from (11.32a) to (11.32d). Interestingly, the ERP patterns recorded from subjects' scalps correlated with these judgments. Recording ERPs at the word *was,* researchers found the greatest deviation in pure transitive sentences, yet there was little deviation in the first two sentence types. In this study, the ERP response was positive rather than negative—the syntactic anomaly produced a P600 response.

Imaging techniques such as PET and on-line records like the event-related potential are still in their infancy. However, you may expect that they will be used increasingly as another research tool in the effort to unravel the secrets of language comprehension.

INTERIM SUMMARY

Brain-mapping techniques, including the electrical stimulation method and the PET scan, have shown that a wider range of brain regions are involved in language processing than had been assumed by the Geschwind-Wernicke model. According to this model, language comprehension was localized in Wernicke's area and articulation in Broca's area. Electrode mapping revealed that (1) additional regions of the parietal and temporal lobe are involved in linguistic operations and (2) there is great variability between individuals. The PET scan suggests that language processing is modality specific with separate pathways for visual and auditory information. These studies are important for clinical purposes; however, they do not illuminate the details of linguistic processing. They have shown where language is processed but not how it is processed. ERP recordings can detect additional mental processes when the person encounters a lexical or syntactic anomaly.

COMPUTATIONAL APPROACHES

For almost four decades, computer scientists have tried to develop computer programs that understand language. They strove to write programs that could paraphrase and translate inputs and answer questions. Initially, these efforts were applications oriented, as exemplified by query and translation systems. Query systems include rudimentary syntactic parsers and a data base about a certain domain, such as about baseball or lunar rocks. Early translation programs used dictionaries to translate one language into another on a word-for-word basis; these efforts failed, however, because they did not consider syntactic rules.

Weizenbaum (1966) created a whimsical simulation that mimicked the conversation between a psychiatrist and a patient (see Box 11.2). In the wake of Chomsky's work on syntax, there were several efforts to implement a grammar in a computer program. Popular among them was the Augmented Transition Network (ATN) model. In the 1970s, semantic programs emerged; Schank was one of the pioneers of this tradition. The 1980s saw the development of more parsing programs, systems devoted to limited domains (e.g., money transfers between banks) and psychological simulation models—for example, CAPS (Collaborative Activation-based Production System). More recently, connectionist parsing solutions were offered (St. John & McClelland, 1988; McClelland, 1992). In the next section, two models are described: the ATN model and a connectionist model.

Augmented Transition Networks (ATNs)

The ATN approach embodies the perspective of syntactic parsing strategies formulated by Bever (1970) and Clark and Clark (1977), as we have discussed. In ATNs, parsing strategies are captured in flowcharts that represent possible word orders in English. An input string of words is fed into a chart and each word is assigned a specific thematic role (see Chapter 10). Kaplan (1975) illustrated the ATN approach with Bever's (1970) NVN strategy. The NVN strategy assumes three constituents in a sentence and assigns them to the roles of actor, action, and object, in that order.

Box 11.2 _____

Does ELIZA Understand You?

One of the earliest attempts to mimic language understanding by a computer was undertaken by Joseph Weizenbaum at the Massachusetts Institute of Technology (Weizenbaum, 1966). Weizenbaum wrote a program that simulated the dialogue between a nondirective psychotherapist and a patient. The following excerpt illustrates the operation of Weizenbaum's program ELIZA, named after Professor Higgins's student, Eliza Doolittle. The user input is printed in lowercase letters, whereas ELIZA's output is shown in capitals.

Men are all alike.
IN WHAT WAY?

They're always bugging us about something or other.
CAN YOU THINK OF A SPECIFIC EXAMPLE?

Well, my boyfriend made me come here.
YOUR BOYFRIEND MADE YOU COME HERE.

He says I'm depressed much of the time.
I AM SORRY TO HEAR THAT YOU ARE DEPRESSED.

It's true. I am unhappy.
DO YOU THINK COMING HERE WILL HELP YOU NOT TO BE UNHAPPY?

I need some help, that much seems certain.
WHAT WOULD IT MEAN TO YOU IF YOU GOT SOME HELP?

Perhaps I could learn to get along with my mother.
TELL ME MORE ABOUT YOUR FAMILY. (Boden, 1977)

Do you think, after reading this dialogue, that ELIZA has understood the patient? Some researchers thought so; others, including Weizenbaum, did not. Rather, Weizenbaum said his program was faking it. The program contained simple routines that extracted certain segments from the input sentence, fleshed them out with some stock phrases, and spewed them back to the user. Other researchers, such as Colby (1975), have continued these efforts and developed powerful syntactic and semantic programs designed to carry on more interesting conversations. The difference between Weizenbaum's and Colby's perspective comes down to the question, What is understanding?

In 1991, the Boston Museum of Science conducted a tournament in memory of the British mathematician Alan Turing. Turing proposed an operational solution to the question of whether or not computers can comprehend. He suggested the Turing test, a game between a person located in one room and a respondent located in another room. The respondent could be either a person or a computer. The person and the respondent were to carry on a conversation via a computer terminal and the person had to judge the identity of the respondent: human or computer. Because several programs produced responses indistinguishable from that of humans, we could conclude that ELIZA's successor programs at least understand you. I leave it up to you, however. How do you define *understanding?*

An ATN is a computer program; however, it is usually graphed as a flowchart of nodes and arcs, as shown in Figure 11.8. The nodes represent syntactic states and are symbolized as circles. The syntactic states represent the subject, verb, and object of the sentence. The arcs indicate transitions between states that must be satisfied in order to continue processing a given input. A transition triggers several actions: The current word is assigned a specific thematic role, the processor moves to a new node, and the analysis moves to the next word. The ATN also includes a lexicon that lists a set of words and their lexical classes. For example, the entry for *coffee* is represented by the proposition (IS-A COFFEE NOUN). This means "*coffee* is a noun." Sentence parsing, using

ATN principles, is illustrated by passing sentence (11.33) through the flowchart in Figure 11.8.

(11.33) Mary loves coffee.

The program begins at the START node, checking whether or not the first word of the input string is a noun. Because *Mary* is a noun, it becomes the actor of the sentence. The verb arc checks whether *loves* is a verb, and so on. The resulting list of thematic roles is expressed in (11.33a). Note the similarity between (11.33a) and the corresponding proposition in (11.33b).

(11.33a) [ACTOR = Mary
ACTION = loves
OBJECT = coffee]

(11.33b) (Predicate: LOVE, Agent: MARY, Object: COFFEE)

The chart in Figure 11.8 can handle only sentences of the word order noun-verb-noun.

(11.34) Tarzan loves Jane.

(11.35) Kids enjoy games.

(11.36) Dogs chase rabbits.

(11.37) Caesar occupied Gaul.

It is relatively easy, however, to augment the chart to include the word orders DETERMINER NOUN to handle sentence (11.38).

(11.38) The girl loves coffee.

Figure 11.9 shows the previous transition chart augmented with the DETERMINER NOUN sequence. This augmented network can accommodate two alternative word orders of noun phrases: NOUN and DETERMINER NOUN. The new network can handle sentence types represented by both (11.33) and (11.38). The configurations representing the subject and object in Figure 11.9 are similar; this is appropriate since both are noun phrases. The configuration that processes noun phrases is called an NP network. The NP network is but one example of a subnetwork that can process a variety of phrases, ranging from prepositional phrases to relative clauses.

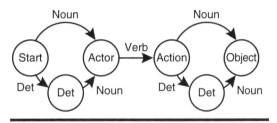

FIGURE 11.9 A transition network that processes subject-verb-object sentences such as *The girl loves the beverage.*

With additional arcs, the ADJECTIVE NOUN sequence in sentence (11.38) is accommodated. Several new arcs and subnetworks are available to handle more complex sentences, such as (11.40).

(11.39) Mary loves black coffee.

(11.40) John was believed to have been shot.

In certain cases, the ATN produces interpretations that do not capture the underlying semantic relations of the sentence exactly the way people would. Consider sentence (11.41a):

(11.41a) The old man the boat.

Parsing sentences such as (11.41a) may lead the processor into accepting interpretations that must later be revised. In this case, the initial determiner is correctly interpreted as the beginning of the noun phrase; *old* is interpreted as an adjective, and *man* is taken as the noun dominating the noun phrase. Expecting a verb phrase next, the ATN faces an obstacle when it encounters the second determiner *the*. The program backtracks and reinterprets the word *old* as a noun, and the

FIGURE 11.8 A transition network that processes subject-verb-object sentences such as *Mary loves coffee.*

word *man* as a verb, so that the relations are similar to those in sentence (11.41b).

(11.41b) The sailors man the boat.

This backtracking mechanism processes the same input again in light of new interpretations. Eventually, the correct interpretation is made; however, backtracking is not a useful model for human parsing. In order to achieve successful backtracking, the processor must remember multiple interpretations of a phrase and it is not clear that human working memory has the capacity to do so.

In addition, in ATNs, the interpretation of phrases is not immediate but is postponed until the end of the phrase. For example, a noun phrase is not represented until the processor reaches the noun. Therefore, most of the processing load in experiments using human subjects should be evident at the final word of the noun phrase; experimental reading times do not support this prediction (Just & Carpenter, 1987).

Computational linguists have developed models to overcome these and other limitations of the ATN. One of these is Thibadeau, Just, and Carpenter's (1982) CAPS model (Collaborative Activation-based Production System). As its name implies, CAPS is a production system (see Chapter 5). The productions parse sentences and create propositions. They do so under the constraints of memory limitations that simulate human performance.

Unlike ATNs, the CAPS model has been empirically supported: The model successfully predicted word reading times of a set of 20 brief passages (Just & Carpenter, 1980). CAPs has not yet been applied to longer texts. Its strength lies in its capability of interpreting individual sentences while at the same time taking into account the processing constraints of human working memory.

Connectionist Parsing

In both linguistics and psycholinguistics, rule-based systems have been called into question

(Berwick, 1991; see Chapter 10). In computational linguistics as well, parsers have been developed that exhibit rulelike behavior, but unlike the ATNs and CAPS, these parsers have no rules built in by the researcher. In this section, we will discuss a parser without rules; it is a connectionist parser developed by St. John and McClelland (1988; see also McClelland, 1992). The St. John and McClelland parser assigns a thematic role to each constituent of a sentence and generates a representation of those assignments (see 11.43a below). The parser makes default assignments for information not explicitly mentioned in the input sentence. It also simulates changes in the sentence representation as successive words are added left to right. The thematic assignment for sentences is tested by asking the model questions such as the following:

> Who is the agent?
> What is the object?
> What is the instrument?
> Consider sentence (11.42):

(11.42) The teacher ate the soup with the spoon.

If the model works correctly, the respective answers should be:

> The teacher is the agent.
> The soup is the object.
> The spoon is the instrument.

Not only does the connectionist model have no rules but it has no initial knowledge of any kind.

After thousands of learning trials, the network captures the event described in the sentence, including explicit and implicit information. This information is represented as a pattern of activity across a set of individual units, as opposed to the ATNs and CAPS where one slot is reserved for each argument of the sentence right from the start (see 11.7a and 11.33a). When we represent the meaning of sentence (11.43) in terms of list (11.43a), we do so only for reference purposes; it does not mirror the distributed representation in the network.

(11.43) The pitcher threw the ball.

(11.43a) *Role   Filler*
    agent   pitcher/ball player
    action   threw/toss
    object   ball/sphere

The structure in (11.43a) reflects some of the information known about the sentence. Each of the thematic roles is filled with concrete entities and clarified by an additional term. By *pitcher,* for example, we mean the ball player, not the container. Like everything else in connectionist networks, such lexical information is represented in a distributed fashion over a set of units in the parser's lexicon.

Learning takes place as follows: On each trial, the network is presented with a sentence and a probe question. The network is supposed to answer the question. For example, we present sentence (11.43) to the model and ask it who the agent is. If the network gives the answer *the pitcher,* it is told that it was correct and nothing further happens. On the other hand, if the answer is incorrect, then the connection strengths are changed so that the match between the model's response and the target answer will improve on subsequent trials. This correction procedure is invoked until the discrepancy between target and actual output drops below a certain cutoff level.

On-Line Interpretation.   In many sentences, the listener can anticipate upcoming input, at least to some extent. Although this is not a conscious process, it is measurable, as we saw in the sequence *buttered popcorn* in Zola's (1984) sentence (11.9a). People comprehend this phrase more quickly than the phrase *adequate popcorn.* How do people develop such expectations? Based on a large number of episodes, listeners and readers develop a sense of the typical interpretation of words and their likely contexts.

In one of his studies, McClelland (1992) simulated this sort of learning. He presented a network with a relatively small set of words and a limited number of stereotyped events. The class of words included containers; utensils; actions related to eating; and two types of adult agents,

a bus driver and a teacher. These two characters were cast in their stereotyped contexts. The bus driver was male, liked coffee and steak, and ate with gusto; whereas the teacher was female, liked soup and tea, and ate with daintiness. Note that these attributes held most of the time but not always. Thus, the bus driver would occasionally eat soup and the teacher would sometimes eat steak. There was, however, one attribute that was perfectly correlated with the two characters. This was the manner of doing things: The bus driver did everything with gusto, whereas the teacher did everything with daintiness.

Because agents, actions, and adverbs presented to the model are paired in a regular fashion, it is easy for the network to entertain predictions when information is left out, as in (11.44) and (11.45).

(11.44) The adult ate steak.

(11.45) The teacher ate the soup.

In (11.44), the model interprets the adult as a bus driver, and in (11.45), the model suggests a spoon is the missing instrument of eating when asked to do so.

A particularly interesting feature of the model is that the sentence interpretation is updated and sometimes changed as a result of adding new words. Take, for example, sentence (11.46), and look at the interpretation of the gender of adult at the four points marked.

(11.46) The adult ate the steak with daintiness.
             1   2   3   4

At points 1 and 2, the model is undecided on the gender of *adult;* this is because the model knows nothing about the object and the manner of eating. At point 3, however, the model adopts the interpretation that the adult is a male. It does so because of the association in prior trials between the bus driver, who is male, and the steak. Remember, however, that the correlation between bus driver and steak was not perfect. On some occasions, the bus driver would eat soup. At point 4, the parser reads that the adult ate with daintiness.

In the sentence presented to the model, daintiness was the attribute associated only with the teacher, who is female. Because of the perfect correlation of daintiness and teacher, the model now reverses itself and adopts the view that the adult is female. The original interpretation and any changes are the direct result of McClelland's (1992) stereotypical training set of sentences; if the training set is altered, so are the interpretations. The model changes its interpretation with each additional word added to the sentence, much as a human understander would.

Evaluation. The St. John and McClelland model creates a meaning representation of simple English sentences. This connectionist parser simulates important properties of human comprehension. It processes information at several levels of language structure simultaneously and immediately. At each processing level, the other processes exert their influence on the simulation; this makes the system dynamic. The simulation can also make inferences if certain information is missing or not sufficiently specified by the input. The model is capable of learning; it is not necessary to specify in advance which of the model's units should represent thematic roles and other information since assignment of these functions to units emerges during the course of learning. The result of learning is the correct representation of training sentences such as (11.42). Thus, the advantage of connectionist learning is that the network literally trains itself.

On the other hand, learning is very slow and requires thousands of trials. A human learner would require far fewer trials. Another problem is that the model has only been tested on a relatively small set of sentences, each representing prototypical roles.

I N T E R I M   S U M M A R Y

Because language understanding involves many components, it is a cognitive activity of unusual complexity. Computer models allow investigators to simulate each component, ranging from lexical access to inference generation, and put them together. The simulation is presented with sentences and prompted with test questions. The model's output and its processing rate can be compared with behavioral measures from experiments involving human subjects.

In this section, we studied two approaches: Augmented Transition Networks (ATNs) and a connectionist parsing system. Each of these had specific strengths and weaknesses. The ATNs were developed for syntactic analysis of simple and complex sentences; this is a job ATNs handle very well. However, there is little evidence that human understanders proceed in the strictly sequential and relatively inflexible manner postulated by ATNs. The strengths of St. John and McClelland's connectionist parser is that it integrates several knowledge components and mimics the dynamic nature of human understanding. We may expect further developments in ATNs and in connectionist modeling of language understanding: Both models will be used on a larger corpus of texts and the principles for choosing simulation parameters will be clarified.

CONCLUSION

We concluded Chapter 10 by noting that language is very rich and powerful in its expressions. In this chapter, we saw that our ability to comprehend language is equal to the richness of language. A broad range of mechanisms is available to us when we attempt to understand language at different levels of structure, including words, clauses, and sentences. Researchers have made substantial headway in illuminating comprehension processes, especially for well-defined issues, including the context effect, lexical access, clausal processing, and the attachment of phrases. They have been less successful developing a grand theory of comprehension that encompasses all of the components, including word- and sentence-level operations.

The controversy between the modular and interactive approach remains unresolved. This issue may become moot, however, because interactionist theorists agree that certain units in the language processing system operate independently, and the modularist researchers agree that modules communicate. Another unresolved issue is whether people acquire knowledge of rules or principles to parse and interpret sentences; it is likely that both play a role. Future psycholinguistic research will continue along three lines: Researchers will search for additional insight into the component processes of comprehension; they will attempt to determine degrees of interaction and independence for different component processes; and they will attempt to identify those comprehension processes that are best captured by rules and those best described by principles.

ENDNOTES

1. Taken by itself, each of these measures has some weakness; for example, latency measures are frequently recorded after the person has completed a sentence rather than while he is reading it. However, when used in conjunction, they can illuminate important issues in comprehension research (Kieras & Just, 1984).

2. Sentence (11.16b) may be interpreted to contain three simple ideas: (1) there were authors hired by the newspaper, (2) the authors liked the editor, and (3) the editor laughed. We represent these ideas propositionally in (11.16d).

(11.16d) (HIRE, NEWSPAPER, AUTHORS)
(LIKE, AUTHORS, EDITOR)
(LAUGH, EDITOR)

READING AND WRITING

PREVIEW

Literacy depends on reading and writing; competence in these two cognitive skills is the universal goal of education. This chapter discusses reading and writing. The first part is devoted to texts, reading, and the results of reading. It explains how readers extract ideas from a text and transfer them to memory. Readers must use strategies to overcome the limitations of working memory—the language processor. Because texts are too long to be processed in one piece, the reader interprets a text in successive cycles. During each cycle, certain ideas from a text are selected and represented in text memory. Initially, the building of a text representation is time consuming; the reader must lay the foundation for subsequent information. If subsequent information is similar to initial information, it is linked via repeated arguments and inferences. Otherwise, additional processing is necessary to integrate the new information. Reading involves many applied issues, three of which we will discuss: dyslexia, speed reading, and the role of TV and reading.

The second part of this chapter treats writing. I present a general framework of composition and discuss issues in writing, including what to do about writer's block. The framework addresses the goals of writing, the audience, and the writer and the processes she engages in, including planning, making meaning, expressing meaning, and reviewing. Writing is difficult because the goals of writing often conflict. Planning refers to how the writer sets goals and assesses her audience. The writer makes meaning by gathering information and generating ideas, which take the form of a meaning representation in declarative memory. She expresses meaning by translating propositions into a physical text. The review process evaluates versions of the text in light of the writing goals, audience, and meaning intended by the writer. I also describe several studies that illustrate these cognitive processes.

READING

Introduction

The Whistler's fourth victim was his youngest, Valerie Mitchell, aged fifteen years, eight months and four days, and she died because she missed the 9:40 bus from Easthaven to Cobb's Marsh. As always, she had left it until the last minute to leave the disco, and the floor was still a packed, gyrating mass of bodies under the makeshift strobe lights when she broke free of Wayne's clutching hands, shouted instructions to Shirl about their plans for next week above the raucous beat of the music and left the dance floor. . . . Without waiting to change her shoes, she snatched up her jacket . . . and raced up the road past the darkened shops towards the bus station, her cumbersome shoulder-bag flapping against her ribs. But when she turned the corner into the station she saw with horror that the lights on their high poles shone down on a bleached and silent emptiness and, dashing to the corner, was in time to see the bus already halfway up the hill. (James, 1989, p. 3)

When you read a book, you create an imaginary world. As you read the opening paragraph of P. D. James's novel, you visualize Valerie rushing out of the disco to the bus stop; you sense her dread as she runs up the dark street, and experience her horror as she realizes the last bus has left. You also know what will happen next; the first sentence introduces the Whistler, a serial killer, and Valerie, his fourth victim. As you read, you are absorbed by the unfolding events. You empathize with Valerie, express opinions and form judgements, for example, about the terror of violence.

Cognitive psychologists seek to understand the mental processes involved in comprehension.

The preceding illustration should have convinced you that these processes are multifaceted and complex; readers must generate a scenario, make inferences, and elaborate, in addition to the encoding, parsing, and interpretational processes described in Chapter 11. Researchers, therefore, have had to simplify matters in order to get a handle on comprehension processes.

From the perspective of a cognitive psychologist, a text conveys a sequence of ideas. It introduces events and concepts; it may develop one or several of those concepts, shift its focus to another concept, and may even return to a previous concept. The able reader follows the flow of ideas and forms a mental structure of those ideas without much effort. He selects ideas from the printed page and transfers them to his mind. Reading means, quite literally, selecting ideas; in fact, the German word for *reading* is *lesen,* which means *to select.* This is a characterization of reading shared by the major reading theorists (Gernsbacher, 1990; Just & Carpenter, 1987; Kintsch, 1988). Cognitive psychologists seek to understand the nature of a text—the cognitive processes involved in comprehension and in forming mental representations of the text.[1]

Several levels of linguistic structure are involved in comprehension: words, clauses, sentences, and entire texts. We discussed word- and sentence-level processes in Chapter 11. This section of Chapter 12 is devoted to operations at the text level. Psychologists separate these processes for convenience of exposition. You should not get the idea that readers process these structures separately; rather, readers perform processes at several levels simultaneously.

Reading is a creative act, much like writing. The reader creates a mental world of the events in the text. Psychologists characterize this world in terms of multiple representations in working memory and in long-term memory. The representations are based on the content of the text and the reader's knowledge of relations implied in the text. We will consider two of these representations: the mental model and the text base.

The **mental model** or **situational model** (see Chapter 5) captures the major content of the passage, including its spatial, temporal, and causal relations (Bransford & Johnson, 1973; Johnson-Laird, 1983; Kintsch, 1992; van Dijk & Kintsch, 1983). Bransford and Johnson's balloon passage in Chapter 9 illustrates the importance of knowing the situation that underlies the events in the passage. The story describes a serenade, albeit an unusual one (passage 9.6). A man standing in front of an apartment building sings into a microphone. The music is transmitted to the top floor via a speaker held up by balloons. The story by itself is almost incomprehensible because it makes no explicit reference to the serenade. Readers need a picture (see Figure 9.6) to help them understand what the story is about.

The other representation is the propositional **text base.** The text base consists of propositions; only those from the current sentence are available in working memory, all others are in long-term memory but they easily be retrieved.

Reading involves the transfer of ideas from a text into the reader's mind. Many processes contribute to this end: decoding letters, parsing and interpreting sentences, and representing ideas in text memory. On its way from the printed page to text memory, information must pass the funnel of working memory, depicted in the center of Figure 12.1. The text is shown on the left; text memory is shown on the right as a network of propositions. Cognitive psychologists represent the information in the text on the left of Figure 12.1 as a text base. Next, I will explain text bases and their elements: the propositions.

The Text Base

A text's ideas can be expressed as propositions that form the text base. Table 12.1 shows a passage used by Kintsch and collegues: the Comet passage (Kintsch et al., 1975). It is a text of about 70 words based on 25 propositions. The text base of this passage is shown in Table 12.2. A proposition is a list of concepts ordered as follows (see also Chapters 5, 11):

(Predicate, Argument-1, Argument-2, . . . , Argument-n).

A proposition includes a predicate—usually a verb, adverb, or adjective—that governs one or more arguments. Arguments are usually nouns, as in sentences (12.1) and (12.2), but may also consist of an embedded proposition, as illustrated in Table 12.2 (e.g., proposition p9 includes proposition p6, an embedded proposition, as an argument).

(12.1)	We see the snowball.
(12.1a)	(Predicate: SEE, Agent: WE, Object: SNOWBALL)
(12.1a—short form)	(SEE, WE, SNOWBALL)
(12.2)	The snowball is large.
(12.2a)	(LARGE, SNOWBALL)

When a noun appears for the first time in a text, it is known as a **new argument noun.** The comet passage contains 15 unique nouns listed at the bottom of Table 12.2 as new argument nouns. A noun such as *comet,* which is repeated several times after its first occurrence, is known as a **repeated argument.** Repeated arguments reflect the continuous flow of ideas in a passage; they represent the backbone of text memory. Imagine if every sentence in a text contained only new information, as is the case in passage (12.3):

(12.3) The twisting, once started, is carried on for a considerable time. The process of learning by finger exercise or by doing continues the process of initiation. In a very bad humor, Fenya went straight home.

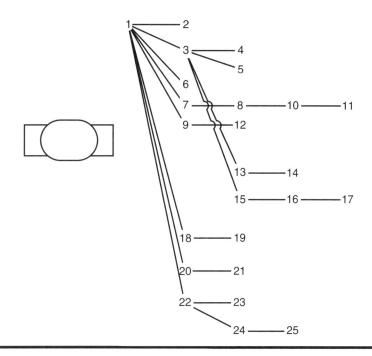

Comet

A comet is a celestial fountain spouting from a large snowball floating through space. We see the fountain as the head and tail of the comet. The tail extends for millions of miles, but we never see the snowball, which has a diameter of a few miles. A comet shines with reflected sunlight. Along its path it strews debris in space, which seen from the earth appears as the zodiacal light.

FIGURE 12.1   Reading involves the transfer of ideas from a text sketched on the left to the reader's memory shown on the right. The information must pass the limited-capacity working memory shown in the center.

Repeated arguments reflect the coherence of the passage. Passage (12.3) is not coherent; its concepts are not repeated and elaborated. Repetition of arguments is not sufficient, however; sentences of coherent texts are also causally linked so that one idea builds on another, as the Whistler passage at the beginning of the chapter and the Comet passage in Table 12.1 illustrate (see section on Causal Links in Texts).

The text base of the Comet passage in Table 12.2 simplifies the text structure by representing all propositions of the first two paragraphs, all ideas, at the same level regardless of their importance. According to Kintsch and van Dijk (1978), a proposition is important when a lot of subsequent information builds on it. A proposition that is frequently referred to is more important than one that is rarely or never referred to. For example, in the Comet passage, proposition p3 is important, whereas proposition p14 is less important. Kintsch and colleagues found that important propositions are better recalled than unimportant ones (e.g., Kintsch & van Dijk, 1978; Kintsch & Vipond, 1979).

TABLE 12.1   Sample Text

Comet

A comet is a celestial fountain spouting from a large snowball floating through space. We see the fountain as the head and the tail of the comet. The tail extends for millions of miles, but we never see the snowball, which has a diameter of a few miles. A comet shines with reflected sunlight. Along its path it strews debris in space, which from the earth appears as zodiacal light.

TABLE 12.2 The Text Base for the Comet Passage

1	(IS A, COMET, FOUNTAIN)
2	(CELESTIAL, FOUNTAIN)
3	(SPOUT, FOUNTAIN, SNOWBALL)
4	(LARGE, SNOWBALL)
5	(FLOAT, SNOWBALL, SPACE)
6	(CONSIST OF, FOUNTAIN, 8)
7	(POSSESS, COMET, 8)
8	(AND, HEAD, TAIL)
9	(SEE, WE, 6)
10	(EXTEND, TAIL, MILE)
11	(NUMBER OF, MILE MILLION)
12	(CONTRAST, 9, 14)
13	(SEE, WE, SNOWBALL)
14	(NEVER, 13)
15	(HAS, SNOWBALL, DIAMETER)
16	(MEASURE, DIAMETER, MILE)
17	(FEW, MILE)
18	(SHINE, COMET, SUNLIGHT)
19	(REFLECT, SUNLIGHT)
20	(STREW, COMET, DEBRIS, SPACE)
21	(LOC: ALONG, 20, PATH)
22	(HAS, COMET, PATH)
23	(SEE, DEBRIS, EARTH)
24	(APPEAR, DEBRIS, EARTH)
25	(ZODIACAL, LIGHT)

New Argument: COMET, FOUNTAIN, SNOWBALL, SPACE, WE, HEAD, TAIL, MILE, MILLION, DIAMETER, SUNLIGHT, PATH, DEBRIS, EARTH, LIGHT (15).

Processing of Texts

The processing of texts includes a wide range of word- and sentence-level processes (see Chapter 11). Here, we focus on the building of the text base, the representation at the propositional level. Based on the initial sentence, the reader lays a foundation—the starter representation; what happens next depends on the similarity of the subsequent text to the initial information. If incoming information is similar, the reader adds to the foundation, otherwise, he creates a new substructure in text memory (Gernsbacher, 1990).

Laying a Foundation. When reading the first few sentences of a text, the reader "sets the stage" for upcoming information. The initial sentences usually express the topic of the passage and introduce much new information. Subsequent sentences add to that information and are therefore easier to process. If a change in topic occurs—for example, at the beginning of a new episode or paragraph—the reader shifts to a new mental substructure, which requires additional time and processing resources. A reading study using simple, two-episode stories, such as the Mike and Dave story in Table 12.3, demonstrates this shift effect (Haberlandt, 1984). The story follows a stereotypical narrative schema: A protagonist faces a problem, reacts to it, sets a goal, attempts to solve it, and achieves some outcome—either success or

TABLE 12.3 Simple Story with Two Episodes

Setting	Mike and Dave Thomas lived in Florida. They lived across from an orange grove. There was a river between their house and the grove.
Beginning	One Saturday they had nothing to do.
Reaction	They were quite bored.
Goal	They decided to get some oranges from the grove.
Attempt	They took their canoe and paddled across the river.
Outcome	They picked a crate full of oranges and put it in the canoe.
Beginning	While they were paddling home the canoe began to sink.
Reaction	Mike and Dave realized that they were in great trouble.
Goal	They had to prevent the canoe from sinking further.
Attempt	They threw the oranges out of the canoe.
Outcome	Finally the canoe stopped sinking. Now all of the oranges were gone.
End	Their adventure had failed after all.

failure. This sequence of events has been expressed as a series of six episode constituents: beginning (B), reaction (R), goal (G), attempt (A), outcome (O), and ending (E) (Mandler & Johnson, 1977).

At the beginning of each episode, readers spend more time than one would expect based on measures of sentence length and difficulty (see Chapter 11). The positive reading time measure at the beginning (B) of the two episodes in Figure 12.2 show this effect. When the reader has laid the foundation for the episode, she speeds up and reading times are faster than would be predicted by sentence length and difficulty. This is indicated by the negative reading time measure in Figure 12.2.

Integration. The term *integration* refers to the process whereby a reader links information from the text with text memory. In the excerpt about Valerie at the beginning of this chapter, we learned that she had been at a disco, that she

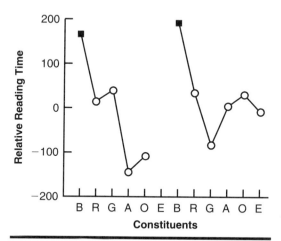

FIGURE 12.2 Reading takes longer at the beginning of episodes when the reader lays a foundation. Positive reading time measures indicate that reading speed is longer than expected on the basis of sentence length and difficulty. The abscissa represents story categories indicated in Table 12.3, beginning (B), reaction (R), goal (G), attempt (A), outcome (O), and end (E).

rushed out and missed the bus, and so on. In the comet text, the reader links the fact that the comet is "*floating through space*" with the idea that "*it strews debris in space.*" Just as comprehension takes place at several levels, so does integration. Information is integrated within a proposition, between different propositions, as well as between successive sentences. Here, we will focus on the latter; the integration of propositions from two sentences. In a later section, we will investigate the integration of arguments.

The integration of propositions would be an easy process if working memory—our language processor—had no limits. But this is not the case; working memory is limited to about 7 ± 2 chunks, which is a good estimate of the maximum number of ideas or propositions working memory can process. Let's assume seven propositions fit into working memory. Seven may be a small number, but it represents a good deal of information because each proposition includes a predicate and usually several arguments.

Kintsch and colleagues (e.g., Kintsch & van Dijk, 1978) assumed that the reader interprets a text in cycles in order to overcome the limits of working memory. In each cycle, presumably key propositions from a sentence are selected to serve as carryover links to successive sentences. Kintsch assumed that readers select **recent** and **important propositions** to serve as links. As a result, such propositions may participate in several processing cycles. Important propositions, such as p1 and p3 in Table 12.2, are those that form the basis for subsequent information. They are referred to again and again in the remaining sentences of a passage. Because important propositions are recycled in working memory, their referents remain more active and therefore more accessible as links for subsequent text. They are also better remembered after the person reads the text.

We assumed a working memory capacity of six propositions. Research on working memory shows, however, that there is usually a trade-off between storage and computation; and because readers engage in considerable linguistic processing, the actual capacity of working memory may well be smaller than six propositions. Another consideration of working memory capacity involves differences among individual readers; a reader with a greater reading span (see Chapter 8) can keep more information active in working memory. A study by Daneman and Carpenter (1983) made a similar point: People with greater reading spans remembered referents from farther back in a text. As a result, it is easier for high-span readers to integrate adjacent sentences of a text (Daneman & Carpenter, 1983).

Although working memory maintains very few propositions, research has shown that readers have easy access to prior segments of the current passage. If readers are interrupted for a few seconds, they readily pick up the thread of the story, indicating that textual traces can be reinstated quickly. According to Ericsson and Kintsch (1995), the textual information is held in long-term working memory (LT-WM). Traces in LT-WM endure for a longer time than in short-term working memory (ST-WM). However, unlike ST-WM, LT-WM is not a general purpose store; rather, it holds retrieval structures generated by cognitive processes that have been well practiced (see Chapter 8).

In the next two sections, I present results of experiments involving integration processes. According to the Kintsch and van Dijk model (1978), integration proceeds in cycles and is based on arguments, both repeated and new. The clausal strategy readers use to comprehend clauses and sentences is a reflection of this cyclical process. It demonstrates how readers pause at clausal boundaries to perform integration and other operations (see Chapter 11). Repeated arguments are also a reflection of a text's coherence; their absence in passage (12.3) demonstrates the lack of coherence in the text. Finally, repeated arguments serve as links for the representation of the text in memory. Let's first examine how readers process repeated arguments. Repeated arguments are concepts the author has mentioned before. They can be expressed as pronouns, synonyms, or verbatim repetitions. In each case, the earlier concept is known as an **antecedent;** the reference to it is an **anaphoric** reference.

Understanding Anaphoric References. Much research has been devoted to the process whereby readers recover an antecedent from an anaphoric reference, especially from pronouns. This research is important because pronouns are so common in English; they account for 40% of Kucera and Francis's (1967) sample of one million English words (see Chapter 11; Gernsbacher, 1990). The consensus of the studies is that a reader immediately activates several referents when she encounters a pronoun. Then she uses selection strategies to identify the relevant referent, the antecedent (Corbett & Chang, 1983; Just & Carpenter, 1987). One of these is the same-gender strategy. This strategy helps to identify the pronoun in sentence (12.4), but not in (12.5).

(12.4) Mary and Bill went to the store and he bought a quart of milk.

(12.5) Mary and Jane went to the store and she bought a quart of milk.

Another strategy of pronoun resolution is based on the causal information implicit in a verb. This strategy tells us who the antecedent of *she* is in (12.6) and (12.7).

(12.6) Jane punished Mary because she had stolen a tennis racket.

(12.7) Jane angered Mary because she had stolen a tennis racket.

According to Caramazza, Grober, Garvey, and Yates (1977), the pronoun *she* refers back to Mary in (12.6) and to Jane in (12.7). You punish someone because she did something punishable; someone angers you because she did something bad. In a third strategy, readers use situational information to link a pronoun with its antecedent. Using information about steals in basketball, we know who *he* refers to in sentence (12.8).

(12.8) Scott stole the basketball from Bill and then he sank a jumpshot.

These and other cues enable the reader to isolate the appropriate antecedent and use it to integrate new information. Gernsbacher (1990) examined the on-line activation of each of two referents in sentences like (12.9). Sentences were presented in a recognition paradigm.

(12.9) Ann predicted that Pam would lose the track race, but *she*$_1$ came in first very easily.$_2$

Gernsbacher presented the sentences word by word in the center of a computer screen. Immediately after the pronoun and at the end of the sentence (marked by subscripts 1 and 2), Gernsbacher presented referents for a *yes/no* recognition test. The referents were shown in capital letters at the top of the screen to signal to the subjects that this was a test. Both referents, Ann and Pam, were equally active immediately after the pronoun, as indicated by equally fast responses. At the end of the sentence, however, the irrelevant referent, Ann, had lost activation, whereas the antecedent, Pam, continued to be active.

Every text presents a mixture of old and new information; both are needed for communication and for learning in general. If there is no new information (for example, when a sentence is repeated over and over again), it is redundant and boring. If every sentence is new, the passage is as incomprehensible as passage (12.3).

Processing New Information.   We read texts to learn something new. Research has shown that readers devote more effort to processing new than repeated information. One reason for the extra effort is that each new argument is usually a new word that triggers lexical processes. New arguments also trigger text-level processes. Such processes are based on clauses and sentences; they build mental structures that reflect the content of a passage. In order to integrate new information with text memory, the reader looks for similar prior information or generates a new node for the the concept. Each of these requires additional mental resources, which therefore increases reading times.

Reading times increase immediately when a reader encounters a new argument noun or comes to the boundary of a clause or sentence. When a reader first encounters a new argument noun, reading time increases by a few milliseconds. Typically, the number of new argument nouns per sentence is relatively small, averaging about two new nouns. There is good reason to introduce only a few new concepts per sentence: Speakers and writers keep new information within manageable limits in order to facilitate comprehension by listeners and readers. Readers and writers cooperate in the act of communication (Clark & Clark, 1977; Grice, 1975). In the second part of this chapter, we will return to the idea of cooperation and see that writers consider the reader as they compose messages.

Sentence boundaries are signals for listeners and readers to integrate new information and to perform other wrap-up processes (Haberlandt, Graesser, Schneider, & Kiely, 1986; Just & Carpenter, 1987). Speakers pause to facilitate the listener's job; writers use punctuation for the same reason. What would you do if writers didn't use periods to mark sentence boundaries? Ancient Latin will give you a clue; in written Latin, there were no explicit sentence boundaries, at least not until medieval times. Readers must have known the boundaries even without markers. A Latin text looked something like this:

> *A SMALL FLICKERING LIGHT DANCED EERILY THROUGH THE BLACK OF THE TUNNELED PASSAGE WAY A MAN DRESSED IN A WOOLEN TUNIC PAUSED AND RAISED AN OIL LAMP ABOVE HIS HEAD THE DIM GLOW. . . .*
> *(Cussler, 1988, p. 3)*

I am sure you had to go back once or twice to figure out what the author was describing. You probably agree that periods and other punctuation facilitate reading comprehension much as speaking pauses do for listeners.

Inferences in Reading.   Readers certainly know more about a text than what it states explicitly. Consider the first clause of the Whistler passage at the beginning of this chapter: "The Whistler's fourth victim was his youngest." This clause suggests to the reader a scenario of violence for which people have scripts and are able to conjure up inferences and elaborations (see Chapter 5). There is, however, a debate about the degree to which this sort of knowledge is invoked during reading, and, if readers do make inferences, when they make them and what inferences they make. Haviland and Clark (1974) proposed that readers make **bridging inferences** when sentences are not immediately coherent. Consider two sentences in mini-passage (12.10). The first sentence introduces the concept PICNIC. The second sentence does not refer to picnic directly, but when the reader encounters *beer,* he interprets it as part of the picnic supplies; thus, *picnic* is the antecedent of *beer.*

(12.10) John took the picnic out of the trunk. The beer was warm.

We had to rationalize the link between *beer* and *picnic.* It was easy enough but sufficiently demanding to cause the reader to pause when he encountered the second sentence. Haviland and Clark found that it took about 180 milliseconds longer to read passage (12.10) than (12.11).

(12.11) John took the beer out of the trunk. The beer was warm.

The inference the reader draws in passage (12.11) is called a **backward inference** because it links a word (e.g., *beer*) backwards to the preceding sentence. A backward inference adds one or several propositions like (IS-A, BEER, PICNIC-SUPPLY) to text memory. Patterns of reading times indicate that readers often draw backward inferences in order to integrate sentences.

Do people also draw **forward inferences?** Forward inferences express the reader's expectations about future events. In the Whistler paragraph, a reader may expect that the crime will occur at the empty bus stop and that Valerie will be horrified but then try to run away. Forward inferences also include arguments implied by a verb but not explicitly stated. For example, the sentence *Bill pounded the nail* implies the instrument used to pound, a *hammer,* but does not state it. Elaborative inferences are similar to forward inferences; they are embellishments of the text. A reader may feel reminded of an episode from her childhood when reading an account of somebody's trip to the beach on a summer weekend. According to several experimenters, forward and elaborative inferences are different from backward inferences. The latter are necessary to establish coherence and are therefore automatic; forward inferences are not absolutely necessary (McKoon & Ratcliff, 1981).

McKoon and Ratcliff (1986) demonstrated that readers do not draw forward inferences during comprehension. They conducted a recognition experiment in which test materials like those in Table 12.4 were used. The predicting sentence in Table 12.4 strongly implies that the actress was dead. The control sentence, however, does not. After reading predicting and control sentences, a test word was shown for a *yes/no* recognition test. The test word of interest for our example was *dead* and the correct response was *no.* If the readers had formed the forward inference that the actress was dead, the concept DEAD would be an active part of the reader's text base. As a result, readers would be tempted to respond yes and would be slow in making the *no* response. However, this was not the case; response times to

---

TABLE 12.4 Examples of Stimuli Used in Elaborative Inference Study

Predicting:
The director and the cameraman were ready to shoot closeups when suddenly the actress fell from the 14th story.
Test word: *dead*

Control:
Suddenly the director fell upon the cameraman, demanding closeups of the actress on the 14th story.
Test word: *dead*

targets did not differ significantly between the predicting and control conditions. McKoon and Ratcliff (1986) and other researchers replicated these results with a range of different test materials and using a variety of experimental techniques (McKoon & Ratcliff, 1990; Singer, 1990). The conclusion of these studies is that readers do not encode forward inferences as they read a passage.

Nevertheless, the role of forward inferences in reading remains an issue of some controversy. Whether such inferences are drawn depends on many more factors than researchers initially assumed. These factors include properties of the text—for example, the genre and thematic structure of the text—as well as such reader attributes as their processing capacity and content knowledge of the passage (Singer, 1994).

In any case, even if readers do not make forward inferences when they read passages, retention studies indicate that they tend to infer information that was not explicitly stated (Bower, Black, & Turner, 1979). Bower and colleagues presented script-based passages during a study phase of a recognition experiment. The passages described a sequence of typical events, such as visiting a doctor. The experimenters omitted certain obvious and easily inferable facts (for example, that the person checked in with the receptionist). In a subsequent recognition test, subjects were shown some of these facts and asked to indicate if they had read them. The subjects false-alarmed to such facts; they thought they had read them. This shows that people tend to add inferences after reading. As described in Chapter 5, readers and listeners are assumed to have schematic knowledge of typical situations; these units of knowledge are referred to as **scripts.**

Readers' representations of passages are richer than text base, arguments, and inferences suggest. A reader forms a global representation of the content of a passage. This representation is generated in parallel with the text base complementing the latter. According to Johnson-Laird (1983), a reader creates a mental model that embeds the story events within an imagined world and expresses the relations between characters as well as

spatial and temporal relations (see also Chapter 5; van Dijk & Kintsch, 1983; Glenberg et al., 1987; Kintsch, 1992).

Many texts, both narratives and expositions, reflect the familiar problem-solution schema in stories. The protagonist sets a goal to overcome a problem (see Tables 12.3 and 12.5), and many expositions pose a problem to be solved. The typical research article, for example, introduces a problem in the introduction, describes means of solving the problem in the methods section, and reports the solution in the results section (Just & Carpenter, 1980, 1987). The problem-solution framework is relatively abstract, merely stating such general categories as problem, goal, method, and solution. According to causal-chain analysis, there are causal links between sentences and paragraphs in a text. These provide the glue that holds

TABLE 12.5 Sample Text for Illustrating Causal Structure (van den Broek, 1990)

1. There once was a boy named Peter,
2. who wanted to buy a bike.
3. He called a bike store to ask for prices.
4. He counted his money.
5. The money was not enough for a bike.
6. He put his piggy bank back on the top shelf of his closet
7. and covered it with clothes.
8. Peter wanted to get some money
9. so he asked his mother for some.
10. His mother said "No, you should earn your own."
11. Peter decided to get a paper route.
12. He called the newspaper agency
13. and asked about a route.
14. The secretary told him to come in.
15. Peter talked to the manager
16. and got his job.
17. He worked very hard on his job
18. and earned a lot of tips.
19. Pretty soon he had earned $200.
20. He went to a bike store
21. and bought a beautiful bike.
22. He was the happiest kid in town.

the sentences together. The next section explains this concept more fully.

Causal Links in Texts

We have seen that repeated concepts provide important links between sentences. Repetition by itself, however, is not sufficient to make a passage coherent, as sample (12.12) indicates.

(12.12) John hit Brian. Brian drew the doctor. The doctor slept.

Sample (12.12) contains three sentences with repeated references; yet the sentences are not coherent. Contrast (12.12) with passage (12.13) to see why.

(12.13) John hit Brian. Brian called the doctor. The doctor arrived.

Passage (12.13) includes both repeated arguments *and* causal links between the sentences.

Table 12.5 contains a story about a boy, Peter, who wants to have a bike (see van den Broek, 1990). The story has 22 sentences. Most of the sentences reflect information that causes events described in subsequent sentences. Other sentences, such as 6 and 7, lead into a dead end; no subsequent information depends on them. Note that links may exist between adjacent sentences (e.g., between sentences 4 and 5) and between remote sentences (e.g., between sentences 2 and 8).

Sentences differ in their number of causal links. Sentence 8, for example, is linked to sentences 9, 11, 17, 18, and 19, and it depends in turn on sentences 2 and 5. Peter's need for money (sentence 8) motivates several attempts of getting the money; he asks his mother (9), tries to earn some (11), and succeeds at it (17 through 19). Sentence 13, asking about a route, however, has only two links. Van den Broek and colleagues had subjects read stories like the Peter story and recall them (Trabasso & van den Broek, 1985). He found that recall of a sentence depended on its number of links with other sentences: The better-connected sentences had a better chance of being recalled, as shown in Figure 12.3.

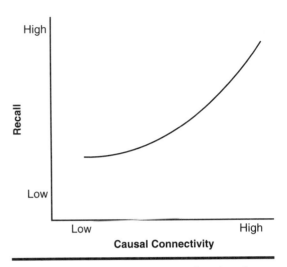

FIGURE 12.3   Recall improves as a function of a sentence's connectivity (van den Broek, 1990).

We have seen how a reader builds a mental representation of a text, and we have learned about inferential processes and causal reasoning during reading. Our description of processes and representation necessarily had to simplify the complexity of reading. For example, both representation and processes depend on the goal of the reader and on the reading matter, and there is a great variety of both goals and texts. We read letters and messages with all sorts of contents. We read notices about not eating fish from Long Island Sound, changes in airline schedules, briefs from lawyers, memos from teachers, and contracts from insurance agents; we read descriptions on the use of diverse pieces of equipment, including helicopters and short-wave radios; we study instructions on how to assemble objects (often with diagrams) such as toys, bicycles, and furniture. My favorite set of instructions came with a $7.95 hibachi that took me half a day to comprehend and another to execute. We read comics, novels, and poems for enjoyment; textbook chapters for a test; and research papers for a project. These goals bias the text representation to some extent: When a reader skims a text, she is only interested in some global ideas; but when she reads to prepare for a quiz, she tries to remember details from every paragraph, perhaps from every sentence.[2]

INTERIM SUMMARY

A reader is assumed to form text representations at several levels, including a global situation model and a propositional text base. We have focused on the text base, which consists of a list of propositions that reflect the meaning of sentences. According to a processing model based on the Kintsch and van Dijk theory, readers transfer propositions via working memory to text memory. Due to the limited capacity of working memory, input is processed in cycles. Integration processes are based on both repeated and new arguments. Repeated arguments include pronouns whose antecedents are recovered via several strategies. Sentences that contain many new arguments take longer to read than sentences with few new arguments, because the reader must recover the meaning of the new word and integrate the new argument into text memory.

In order to generate a coherent text representation, readers link anaphors with their referents, integrate new arguments with the existing text base, and make backward inferences. Such inferences establish links between sentences that are not explicit in the text. Each of these processes—including pronoun resolution, new argument integration, and backward inferences—causes the reader to pause briefly, resulting in longer reading times. Sentences are linked both via repeated arguments and causal dependencies; these links express the underlying coherence of a passage. Recall of information depends on the degree of its causal connectedness; the more connections there are, the better the retention.

Special Issues in Reading

Reading is of concern to many people other than cognitive psychologists engaged in basic research. Professionals address questions of reading instruction and assessment, general literacy, impairments in reading, reading efficiency, techniques for coping with the information explosion, and differences between reading and other types of comprehension. Many books and journals are devoted to these issues. I have selected three topics here for further discussion: dyslexia, speed reading, and the role of reading and television.

Dyslexia. An ophthalmologist named Rudolph Berlin discovered an inability to comprehend visual test displays among some of his patients. Because these individuals were highly intelligent and had no difficulty comprehending when Berlin *read* the same materials to them, he used the term *dyslexia* to describe the syndrome. The term highlights the fact that dyslexic readers have difficulty with written but not spoken symbols.

Crowder (1982) observed a similar disability in a 24-year-old woman, Karen, who had done well in high school and college except in classes that required large amounts of reading; she often took summer school courses to make up for material missed during the year. Though Karen had never been diagnosed as having any severe reading deficits, she began participating in Crowder's remedial reading program when she could no longer cope with the reading required in her job. Crowder asked her to read pages on a technical subject matter and found, to his surprise, that she had little difficulty reading the sample aloud; there was the occasional stumbling over difficult words, but nothing like he had expected. When Karen had finished reading, however, Crowder discovered that she had understood practically nothing. At this point, Crowder read a passage aloud to Karen and discussed the text with her. "She startled me" he wrote, "by giving me a very intelligent summary [and] at this point I appreciated that Karen presented an unusual situation in sharp detail" (p. 236).

A person is dyslexic when he reads at a level significantly below the level expected, given his general intelligence. Dyslexia differs from poor reading. The reading performance of poor readers is on a par with their general intelligence (Just &

Carpenter, 1987). Within the general category of dyslexia, a variety of different classes have been identified (Rayner & Pollatsek, 1989). There are dyslexic individuals who, like Karen, have no apparent difficulty reading text aloud but do not comprehend what they read. There are also cases with rather different manifestations. Some dyslexic individuals have considerable difficulty identifying target words visually, even if given unlimited inspection time. For example, *cap* might be misread as *cob, met* as *meat,* and *rib* as *ride.* It is difficult to isolate the cause of these faulty readings, because the dyslexic individual has no difficulty naming the letters of the target words. Thus, the visual system, at least letter decoding, does not seem impaired.

Other manifestations of dyslexia include difficulty pronouncing nonwords such as *defnadel* or *plame.* In yet other instances, dyslexic readers are able to read some word classes but not others. For example, they can read and understand concrete words such as *car, chair,* and *house* but not abstract words such as *liberty, union,* and *penalty.* It is estimated that about 5% of all school-age children, or approximately 2 million (!), are dyslexic (Rayner & Pollatsek, 1989).

Dyslexia is best understood as a collective term for a group of diverse reading disabilities. Not only are there many varieties of dyslexia but there are also many theoretical models seeking to account for these varieties. Theorists have attributed dyslexia to specific deficiencies in visual processing and in phonological processing, and to limitations in general language understanding and cognitive resources. Independently of processing problems, researchers have noted that dyslexia tends to run in families. They have identified genetic factors; certain abnormalities in chromosomes have been detected in some dyslexic individuals (Blakeslee, 1994). One of the difficulties of getting a handle on dyslexia, both in terms of understanding its etiology and in seeking to remediate it, is that cases of dyslexia are rarely clear cut. The mixed symptomatologies typically observed in dyslexic individuals present a challenge to investigators who have sought to develop taxonomies and treatments of dyslexia.

Models of dyslexia include cognitive, neuropsychological, and neural network approaches. Cognitive models assume alternative processing routes between the printed word on the page and the words read by the reader (Coltheart et al., 1993). They seek to identify visual, phonological, and general processing factors that contribute to dyslexia (Ellis & Young, 1988). Neuropsychological models seek to correlate processing impairments with injuries to and abnormalities in specific brain structures. Connectionist theorists consider reading performance as a pairing between visual and verbal symbols. They train neural networks to acquire the association between these two types of symbols. When certain units in the network are disabled performance losses are observed that mimic dyslexic deficits (Plaut & Shallice, 1993; Seidenberg & McClelland, 1989).

Visual Factors. Just and Carpenter (1987) reported that the eye-fixation patterns of dyslexic readers differ in characteristic ways from those of normal readers; dyslexic patients fixate longer on words and exhibit a far greater number of regressive eye fixations (see Chapter 11). Normally, less than 10% of all eye movements are directed at previous text. Dyslexic readers, however, jump back and forth between forward and reverse modes more frequently.

Geiger and colleagues (1994) found differences in visual lateral masking between dyslexic and normal readers. *Lateral masking* refers to interference from a neighboring letter or word when the person identifies a target letter. For example, when the letter pair *XM* is flashed on the screen, the identification of *X* is inhibited by the presence of the M, compared to when *X* is presented by itself. Geiger found that in normal readers, such interference is greater in the periphery of the visual field so that recognition of letters and words is best in the center of the reader's gaze. In dyslexic readers, on the other hand, the interference is greatest in the center of the gaze and less in the periphery (at least in the direction of reading—that is, toward the right for English readers). The interference in the center of their visual field confuses dyslexics and overwhelms them with information.

Phonological and Verbal Factors.   Researchers have identified performance deficits of dyslexic patients in different phonological and verbal tasks. Olson (1994) reported that dyslexic children tend to have phonological decoding deficits in processing written and spoken words. These children have difficulties pronouncing nonwords and they have trouble spotting the odd word in triplets of such spoken words as *tan tip tag.* Olson (1994) concluded that "there is little disagreement that phonological decoding deficits are present in most dyslexics" (p. 909). Research on children who have difficulties discriminating between similar phonemes has implications for dyslexia, as well (Jenkins et al., 1995). Such discrimination is based on the listener's ability to pick up spectral differences in the formant transitions (see Remediation of Dyslexic Deficits later in this chapter).

Carpenter and colleagues (see Just & Carpenter, 1987) have determined that dyslexics frequently take longer to retrieve verbal codes from long-term memory. These investigators have found that dyslexic individuals tend to require a longer time to retrieve the name of a linguistic entity, be it a letter or a word. For example, in a letter-matching task where the subject must decide whether two letters *(A-A, A-a, A-b)* have the same name or not, dyslexic readers take longer. The most interesting case occurs when the pair *A-a* is presented. In order to identify both *A* and *a* as the letter *A,* the reader has to retrieve the name "a." When *A* and *A* are presented, a physical comparison is sufficient. It is in the *A-a* case that dyslexics take longer than normal readers. Similarly, dyslexic readers require longer than normal readers to say the names of digits and objects shown in pictures. In sum, they appear to have difficulty retrieving verbal codes. However, even here generalizations are difficult to come by;

Crowder conducted a number of experiments with Karen and found that she performed no differently than normal readers on tasks that required retrieval of semantic information (for example, the lexical decision task).

Deficits in phonological skills in dyslexics may have a surprising consequence; it may produce superior orthographic awareness! This is the result of a large-scale study by Canadian psychologist Linda Siegel and colleagues (Siegel, Share, & Geva, 1995). These investigators evaluated about 250 dyslexic and 350 normal readers on phonological and orthographic tests. The phonological task involved reading a list of pronounceable pseudowords that increased in difficulty—for example, *dee, plip, chad, laip, cigbet, bafmothem,* and *monglustamer.* On this task, dyslexics did less well than normal readers.

The orthographic test assessed subjects' awareness for spelling patterns in English by showing them a pair of stimuli, such as *gwup–gnup,* and asking them to identify the item that looked more like an English word. One of the stimuli, *gnup,* could be a word because it adhered to the orthographic pattern of English, whereas the other, *gwup,* contained a bigram that never occurs in English. On this task, dyslexics performed better than normal readers. Siegel and colleagues attributed the orthographic advantage of the dyslexic readers to their tendency to compensate for the phonological deficit by emphasizing visual reading cues.

Neuropsychological Considerations.   There exists a debate as to what extent neuropsychological factors contribute to dyslexia. Some argue that neuropsychological case studies suffer from methodological problems—for example, that the number of cases is too small or that the categories of dyslexia are too diverse to warrant any conclusions at this time. Others believe that the cognitive deficits must result from specific impairments in neural structures. Still others claim that they have identified unique morphological and processing attributes in at least some cases of dyslexia. According to a review by Hynd and

Semrud-Clikeman (1989), imaging methods suggest brain morphological differences between dyslexic and normal individuals. Certain brain structures implicated in language processing tend to be smaller and more symmetrical in some dyslexics than in normal individuals.

Livingstone and colleagues (1991) have found that some dyslexic individuals exhibit impaired processing of the Where system, one of the two principal visual processing systems. Among other functions, the Where system is implicated in detecting changes that result from eye movements such as those that occur in reading (see Chapter 2). Posner and Raichle (1994) reported that dyslexia may occur due to lesions in the posterior parietal lobe that result from strokes; these stroke patients exhibit neglect of information on the side opposite to the lesion.

Kolb and Whishaw (1990) entertained the hypothesis of distinct contributions of the left and right hemispheres to reading: the left hemisphere is thought to process primarily phonetic and semantic aspects of words, whereas the right hemisphere is implicated in visual word processing. Any damage to either hemisphere will result in characteristic symptoms; for example, damage to the right hemisphere is expected to lead to difficulties in visual word decoding. However, these authors have acknowledged that this is an extreme hypothesis that does not do full justice to the mixture of symptoms observed in many cases.

Connectionist Models and Cognitive Resources.
According to the cognitive perspective, dyslexia results from a deficit in cognitive processing resources. The neural network model of Seidenberg and McClelland (1989) illustrates this approach. In terms of network models, reading involves the pairing of arbitrary letter symbols with a specific pronunciation. Seidenberg and McClelland noted that although different groups of dyslexics differ from normal readers in visual or phonological skills, they nevertheless tend to exhibit common patterns of reading impairment. For example, certain dyslexic readers have greater difficulties reading irregularly pronounced words such as

have and nonwords such as *mave* than reading regular words such as *cave*.

Seidenberg and McClelland successfully simulated this pattern in a multilayer neural network model (see Chapter 6). Using the backpropagation learning procedure, the researchers trained the model to pronounce a set of 3,000 monosyllabic words. Dyslexic impairments were simulated by reducing the network's resources; this was simply done by disabling a few of the hidden units selected at random. It is important to remember that Seidenberg and McClelland's (1989) neural network is a general model of word recognition rather than motivated to just mimic dyslexic effects; the latter were merely a by-product of the overall architecture and algorithms of the model (Seidenberg, 1993).

Remediation of Dyslexic Deficits.   Ever since dyslexia was discovered, there have been efforts to remediate its problems. Unfortunately, no cure has been found. Remediation efforts include diverse techniques of visual and phonological training. Let us consider three such attempts; note, however, that in each case only a small number of individuals was included and the improvements have been quite modest. I cite these studies simply to illustrate the ferment in this important field.

Working with nine dyslexic children who had visual deficits, Geiger and colleagues (1994) used a moving window method. These were children who experienced interference from stimuli in the periphery of their visual field, as described earlier in the section entitled Visual Factors. During a three-month period, the children practiced daily for half an hour on the moving window task. A mask covered the text except for one word, which was visible through a rectangular window. The window's size was sufficiently large to expose the longest words in the text. The child moved the mask across the text so as to expose successive words of the passage. As a result of this training, the children improved their resistance to lateral masking. Significantly, the children improved their reading level by 1.22 grades, on average. A control group of dyslexic children that practiced reading without the window method had a nominal improvement of only 0.17 grade levels. Although the results of Geiger's team are encouraging, the number of subjects was small and the authors acknowledged that they have not solved the "whole problem of dyslexia" nor "found a complete cure for it" (p. 1032).

Olson (1994) found that increasing phonemic awareness improves reading performance of both normal and dyslexic children. *Phonemic awareness* refers to listeners' knowledge that words consist of sounds; it is the basis for the alphabetic spelling system. Acquiring phonemic awareness is no trivial matter because phonemes are abstract units that occur in widely different linguistic contexts (see Chapters 4 and 10). Reading researchers have determined that learning to read depends, among other factors, on phonemic awareness (see Chapter 15), and any deficiencies in the latter will retard reading. One can increase a child's phonemic awareness by exposing her to many rhymes and to the phoneme tapping task. In this task, the child is asked to tap for each phoneme she detects in words spoken to her. For example, she would tap once for *a,* twice for *at,* and three times for *bat.*

An interdisciplinary team of investigators at the University of California in San Francisco and Rutgers University conducted research that has implications for dyslexia (Jenkins et al. 1995). The studies involved children who are language impaired who could neither talk at the age of 4 nor follow simple verbal instructions. These children found it even difficult to repeat such simple phrases like *kitty cat;* instead they would say *titty tat.* The investigators attributed the language impairment to an inability to discriminate between phonemes whose spectral features are very similar. For example, the phonemes /b/, /d/, and /g/ have similar formant patterns; they differ only in the initial segments of the formants, the formant transitions. The frequency changes in the initial segment are very rapid, lasting no longer than 50 to 60 ms (see Chapter 4).

The scientists used processed speech to enhance the ability of their subjects to discriminate the subtle time differences between similar phonemes. The technique involved synthetic speech generated by a computer program to exaggerate the time differences that the children could not detect otherwise. In initial training sessions, fast formant transitions were stretched out. Gradually, the synthetic speech was made more similar to the normal speech pattern. Using a video game, the children were trained step by step to pick up the differences between phonemes. Training extended over a period of a month, involving daily sessions with hundreds of trials each. Speech perception and language comprehension improved in these children, and importantly, the improvement held after training stopped. To the extent that dyslexia is phonologically based, this research has implications for dyslexia. However, once again, the number of tested individuals was too small to allow premature generalizations.

Because remediation efforts yield modest results at best, psychologists recommend the use of compensatory strategies to cope with dyslexia (Crowder, 1982). For example, Crowder has suggested giving dyslexic individuals the opportunity to learn materials auditorally—for example, on audiocassettes.

Speed Reading. The average reader can read approximately 250 words per minute. Proponents of speed reading claim that this base reading rate can be increased to 2,000 to 3,000 words per minute. Some even claim that speed readers can read up to 10,000 words per minute. Such a reader would read *Gone with the Wind* in one hour!

Proponents of speed reading believe that most readers do not use their cognitive capacities to the fullest and that they waste time in unnecessary eye movements. Speed-reading programs emphasize better concentration and more productive eye fixations. For example, students receive training in zig-zag scanning across the page. They are encouraged to extract more information from peripheral vision, make more inferences, and not to dwell on concepts. In short, the advice is "just keep moving." The problem with most speed-reading programs is that the level of comprehension usually declines as the reader adopts speed-reading strategies (Carver, 1990; Just & Carpenter, 1987).

If speed reading does not help, is there any way we can become more efficient readers and learners? The short answer is, It's not easy. The best way to increase reading speed while maintaining comprehension is to become familiar with the content of the passage. In other words, the more you know about a text before reading it, the faster you will read and the more you will comprehend. Birkmire (1982) found that physics students processed passages about physics more efficiently than music students did, whereas the latter did better on music passages. Reading is no different from other skills, such as playing games and solving problems. The principal means of improving performance is to practice the content or skill itself. Although there is no method that will increase your reading speed dramatically, there are techniques that can help you remember the content of a text. Box 12.1 describes one such method.

Box 12.1

Developing Effective Study Skills in Reading

It is rare that we get a chance to read for pure enjoyment—when it doesn't matter whether or not we apply the information in the text. Most of our reading is assigned to fulfill an educational or business purpose; the materials must be retained and used. To some extent, retention is a result of comprehension. Memory research has shown that retention depends on the **depth of processing** (Chapters 7 and 9). Deep processing involves establishing links between new and familiar information. Forming such links is, of course, the essence of comprehension and learning.

Research has also shown that merely *intending* to retain information does not improve retention (Hyde & Jenkins, 1973). Nevertheless, there are steps that learners can take to process textual information more deeply. These steps have been around for some time and survive in the most recent primers. Robinson's (1970) SQR3 method includes five steps to improve your memory of text materials: Survey, Questions, Read, Recite, and Review. Each of these activities may be executed at different levels of the text, be it a paragraph, subsection, section, or the entire passage.

- *Survey:* Survey the text, identify the text segments, and scan the titles, subtitles, and other organizational devices included by the author.
- *Questions:* Based on the initial survey, formulate a set of questions you expect to answer by reading the text.

- *Read:* Read the text, sentence by sentence. Try to determine answers to your questions and pay close attention to information that is new to you.
- *Recite:* Examine your questions again and answer them. Reread those segments that you did not understand. Jot down important ideas.
- *Review:* Take additional notes and reread certain sections of the text, answering your questions fully. Devote particular attention to important sections and those that contain surprising information.

Other study strategies, such as the PQR4 technique and the Danserau system, are variations of the SQR3 method. The PQR4 method includes a reflection phase during which the reader links the information covered in the text with information from other sources. According to the Danserau (1983) method, the reader improves retention by selecting important concepts and facts and by organizing them in a network. For example, in this chapter, the reader would select titles, subtitles concepts printed in block letters, and other terms, write them out, and think of ways in which to link the terms. Research has shown that these study strategies, as opposed to merely reading the text once or twice, result in better retention. However, there is no difference between strategies (Just & Carpenter, 1987).

Reading and Television. We have just seen that comprehension skills in adults are purported to be general (but see Pezdek, 1987, for a different result in children). In principle, then, it should make little difference how we acquire information, by listening, reading, or even from TV. On the other hand, everyone is familiar with the claim that the pervasiveness of TV has contributed to a decline in reading skills and in literacy in general. Cognitive psychologists identify two reasons for the alleged decline in literacy.

— Spoken language is usually simpler in construction and vocabulary than written language, and the typical TV shows contain dialogue that tends to be less complex than printed text. Because the TV viewer receives less exposure to a demanding vocabulary and complex syntactic and semantic constructions, he gets less practice understanding and using these.

— Watching a lot of TV leaves less time for reading; consequently, even simple skills such as decoding words are practiced less. Corteen and Williams (1986) compared the reading performance of two groups of children; one group lived in a town where TV was not yet available (Notel), whereas the other group had access to several TV channels (Multitel). The researchers found that the Notel children scored higher on reading fluency than the Multitel children. They also reported that TV displaced such other activities as playing sports.

It is not that TV results in poor vocabulary per se. Some educational TV programs are specifically created to stimulate thought, but they are not our favorites, as the Nielsen ratings demonstrate. On the other hand, TV is the source of much of our information and knowledge. It contributes scripts and stereotypes, both good and bad (see Chapter 5). TV has broadened the outlook of viewers by introducing different cultures, customs, and points of view.

Conclusion

The reading research we have covered assumes that readers encode a text and transfer its ideas via working memory to a text representation. Because working memory has a limited capacity, the reader must process the text in successive cycles. Coherence is achieved through the use of repeated arguments and inferences that link the segments of incoming text. Readers create meanings at every level; they create word meanings, sentence interpretations, and an internal world of the passage as a whole. Reading and writing are testimony to the fact that the mind does not merely transform input information. Rather, as the linguist Chafe (1990) said, the "mind creates its own representation of the world."

As you read this account of research on reading, you may have wondered what propositions, backward inferences, and reading times measured in milliseconds have to do with ideas and thoughts. After all, to the average person, comprehension involves content—the meaning of a chapter, poem, or other piece of literature. The measures we have discussed, however, are empirical indicators that reflect the thought patterns involved in comprehension but not their content. Even literary critics are interested in empirical reading research, as illustrated by a quote from the critic Fish (1970). He wrote about reader responses that "in the category of response I include not only 'tears, prickles' and 'other psychological symptoms', but all the *precise mental operations involved in reading,* including the formulation of complete thoughts . . . and the following and making of logical sequences." Others have expressed similar views, although not all would agree. Indeed, literature cannot and should not be explained in terms of reading *processes* alone. Great literature is treasured because of its content and the values it conveys. Nevertheless, the process of reading remains one of the most fascinating mental processes, well worth the effort researchers devote to it.

WRITING

Introduction

When you think about writing, you probably think of the term paper due at the end of the semester; you wonder how you will get started and how to complete it. Writing is difficult for most people. In this part of the chapter, I present a general framework of the subprocesses involved in writing and examine some of the reasons why writing is difficult. Writing, like other problem-solving activities, is a creative activity. A problem solver faces an initial set of conditions and seeks to arrive at a goal. Usually, multiple constraints must be met: A content is specified, a certain time limit applies, and costs must be considered. The same applies to writing composition: For example, your paper must discuss one of your laboratory exercises, it is due by the end of the semester, and it must be 12 typewritten pages in length.

The general framework of writing I have adopted here is based on theories of composition (Flower, 1989; Hayes & Flower, 1980; Scardamalia & Bereiter, 1986). I will discuss components of the framework and illustrate them with research. Figure 12.4 illustrates the framework and identifies three principal components of composition: the writer, the text, and the environment.

The Environment: Writing Goals and the Audience

We write in order to communicate with others. Writing jobs are often assigned to us, be it an accident report for the insurance company, minutes of a committee meeting, an e-mail reply, or the research paper required in your cognitive psychology class. In each case, specific facts and ideas must be communicated to an audience. Whether a writer knows her audience or not, the audience constitutes an important part of the task environment and influences the writing process at many stages. One writes differently for different audiences; a letter to a friend is informal, a term paper is more formal, and a job application is usually very formal.

It is not quite accurate to speak of *the goal* of writing because, whenever one writes, one seeks to satisfy several goals. Consider your research report; it has to fulfill several goals—it should report, comment, persuade, be interesting, and earn a good grade. You must first report the reasons for undertaking the research project. This usually involves a set of motivating hypotheses. Procedures, analyses, and results of the project must be reported faithfully, so that other students can repeat the experiment. Finally, the implications of the project for the original hypotheses and the general domain are discussed in a kind of commentary.

If reporting and commentary were the only goals of writing, the task would be easier than it is. However, a writer seeks to persuade readers that the topic is worthwhile, that the hypotheses illuminate the topic, that the design and analyses are fit for the task, and that the project and its conclusions merit the reader's attention. The paper should also be interesting. If this sounds simple, consider making a mixed three-factorial design or the orthogonality assumption for linear multiple regression interesting!

Finally, the term paper must be comprehensible. No doubt you know that this is a tricky job

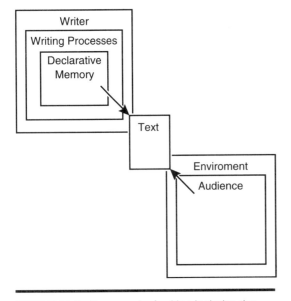

FIGURE 12.4 Framework of writing includes the writer, the writer's environment, and the text produced by the writer.

because a research issue is rarely black and white, a design seldom perfectly neat, and a set of results rarely unequivocal. Research problems in psychology are inherently complex; the most interesting areas of the field concern mental representations—processes that are subject to many influences and are not even observable. Nevertheless, the writer must express something fuzzy and confusing in clear language.

The Writer

Our framework of composition includes, of course, the writer, his knowledge, skills, and perceptions of the goal, and the audience. The writer knows something about the topic, and if he does not, he can marshal strategies to educate himself. Writers differ in the amount of experience they have had with composition. Some have written many pieces, ranging from memos to books; others have had very little experience. The writer has a specific set of writing plans developed with practice.

Writers also have attitudes toward the act of writing. These attitudes frequently change between topics and during the course of working on one topic. Attitudes influence the writing processes and productivity; sometimes a project moves along at full speed, at other times it comes to a complete halt, as in the case of writer's block (see Box 12.2).

Writing Processes

Even the casual writer recognizes that writing involves different activities. Writers think of what to write and how to put it down; they also adopt a writing plan, review the text, and execute numerous other tasks. In this section, we will examine four writing activities: planning, making meaning, expressing meaning, and reviewing. *Making meaning* refers to generating ideas; *expressing meaning* refers to translating the ideas into a text (Flower, 1989). We have frequently noted that cognitive skills and their component processes do

---

Box 12.2

Writer's Block and How to Cope with It

Trying to coordinate all of the goals and components of writing is a difficult job; all too often, we experience writer's block as a result. According to Howard and Barton, "Trying to get it all right the first time is the single greatest block to writing. Cognitive processors get flooded and the writer gives up" (1986, p. 25). There are several ways of coping with writer's block, including the following:

- Give up the notion that you have to "get it altogether" before you start writing.
- Understand that writing proceeds in small steps. Get started on some ideas, even if they are not perfect.
- Be aware that repeated work on the same problem is not a waste nor unique to you. Every writer, especially a mature one, repeats certain parts of a writing assignment.

- Another myth is that incubation will work *for* you. Suddenly, *it* happens and your ideas flow seemingly all by themselves. Howard and Barton (1986) described this as the myth of the Muse. "The Muse is supposed to work behind the scenes" and solve the problem for you. However, this is not the case. Rather, "writing is an activity you do, not something that 'happens' to you."
- Relax and step back, but do not walk away from the assignment.
- If it is a difficult sentence, simply get rid of it.

In sum, approach your writing assignment one step at a time, without worrying about the final draft until you are about done.

not necessarily take place in sequence. This is also true of writing. A writer might express some meaning, then think of something to say, then plan, revise, translate more ideas into text, and then revise again. Discussing the processes separately is simply done for ease of exposition. With this caveat in mind, I first described planning.

Planning.   Planning pervades writing processes at many levels. At the global level, planning a writing project is like planning in problem solving; and in problem solving, planning is critical to success. Global planning consists of portioning the overall problem into more manageable parts. One identifies the goal of the project and repre sents it in memory. In the case of composition, this includes the topic of the project, its level of difficulty, and such physical aspects as length and format of the paper. Global planning also includes finding operators that help achieve the overall goal. The writer uses operators to gather information and operators that control the style of the paper, whether she wants to entertain the reader, argue a point forcefully, or review the background of the topic and then introduce her own views. Finding such operators contrasts from highly abstract goals such as *I'd like to earn an A for this paper.*

Local planning processes are invoked when the writer expresses meaning in words. The writer has mental plans for constructing a unit of text, a phrase, a clause, or an entire sentence. These plans are fleeting and usually writers are not aware of them. As I will show, however, investigators have made these planning processes manifest in research.

Research on Planning: Does an Outline Help?   Assume that a writer has already collected ideas and knows what he wishes to write about. He then faces a planning issue: Should I use an outline or not? A study by Kellog (1988) suggested that using an outline improves the quality of the text, although not the efficiency of writing. This is how Kellog arrived at his conclusion. In one of his experiments, students were given the following instruction for an essay on tuition:

As state-supported universities begin to feel the effects of inflation, many are asking students who are state residents to pay tuition, just as out-of-state students do, in addition to the incidental fees they ordinarily pay. These resident students, for whom a college education was relatively inexpensive, are now complaining that even minimal tuition is an unfair burden. Write an article for the college newspaper in which you develop an argument for, or against, tuition for all state university students. Be careful to anticipate and defend against possible counter arguments.

Kellog's experiment included two conditions: a no-outline and an outline condition. Students in the no-outline condition began writing immediately, whereas the members of the outline group first worked on an outline for 5 to 10 minutes. In both conditions, students were given no time limit. In the no-outline condition, students wrote for 25.6 minutes. In the outline condition, the writing time was 37.8 minutes, including 7.8 minutes for outlining. The average length of the essay was 227 words and 312 words in the two groups, respectively. Thus, the no-outline and outline groups produced 8.6 and 8.3 words per minute, respectively, supporting the conclusion that efficiency did not differ significantly between the two conditions. According to a blind evaluation by professional judges, however, the quality of the articles was better in the the the outline than in the no-outline condition. This was true in terms of both overall organization and sentence structure. Kellog attributed the superiority of the outline group to the fact that they separated the processes of planning, making meaning, and expressing meaning more effectively. By devoting extra time to the outline and not worrying about how to express their ideas, these students improved each of these processes and thereby the resulting essay.

What do these results mean for you? Should you write an outline for your term paper? Kellog (1988) stated that it depends on how much you already know about the topic. If you know a lot about the topic, you might get away without devoting the extra time to an outline. On the other hand, if you are given an assignment on a topic relatively new to you—whether it is mass transit, university tuition, or the values of social neighborhood clubs—you would benefit by doing an outline.

Making Meaning. Coming up with ideas is an activity all of us associate with writing. When you write a term paper, you go to the library to do research; you read articles, chapters, and books in order to become familiar with a topic. In information-processing terms, making meaning involves entering propositions into declarative memory by using the comprehension processes involved in reading (see the first part of this chapter). Figure 12.1 showed a sketch of how ideas are transferred from a text into a text base. When you gather ideas for a paper, the process is similar to that in Figure 12.1, except that you do not create an individual text base, but a larger representation comprising many sources including your own contributions.

Figure 12.1 highlights the selection of ideas from a text. The other part of generating meaning is creative; the writer adds her own ideas and organizes ideas in novel ways. The result of these inferential and creative processes is the addition of propositions to the representation in declarative memory. We learned that readers make many backward inferences but few forward and eleborative inferences. The writer, on the other hand, elaborates, embellishes, and suggests expectations, all presumably represented as propositions in memory.

There are many strategies for generating ideas (Flower & Hayes, 1977): brainstorming, debating, associating freely, thinking of analogies and contrasts, hierarchies, and others.

— In **brainstorming,** writers generate ideas without worrying about how useful they will eventually be. Flower and Hayes (1977) described brainstorming as a creative, goal-directed play and advised that you "keep writing and don't try to censor or perfect as you go." This is to ease the load required of the writer who must make and express meaning.

— **Debating** also helps generate ideas; the usual give-and-take in an argument prompts a writer to become familiar with different perspectives from which to view ideas. Generally, people are motivated by argument, and the juxtaposition of opposing points of view often helps to clarify an issue.

— By thinking of an **analogy,** a writer is often able to produce ideas that she would not have thought of otherwise. Writers often present their theories in terms of analogies and models; physicists liken the motion of atoms to the movement of the stars; Freud described psychological processes in terms of the mechanical analogy of pressure and counterpressure; and cognitive psychologists treat the writing process as an instance of problem solving.

Because it is not always easy to remember all the thoughts generated by brainstorming, discussion, or analogies, writers jot the words on paper or index cards. When they spread out the index cards, they often discover relationships between concepts and develop additional ideas. Other writers draw tree diagrams or organize the words in tables using several categories.

Expressing Meaning. When a writer expresses meaning, he produces actual text—a linear string of words and sentences. The writer does so by translating a declarative memory representation into an external representation on a page or screen. Figure 12.5 shows a succession of multiple representations thought to evolve during the expression stage of writing. The vertical dimension indicates that, at any given time, there are representations at several levels of abstraction. The writer's knowledge of his goal and audience is relatively abstract; the topic and subheadings are less abstract; representations of paragraphs include still more detail; and the most detailed representations include images, stylistic constructions, partial formulations for sentences, and word choices. Time is represented horizontally. With the passage of time, each of the simultaneous representations changes. Some disappear

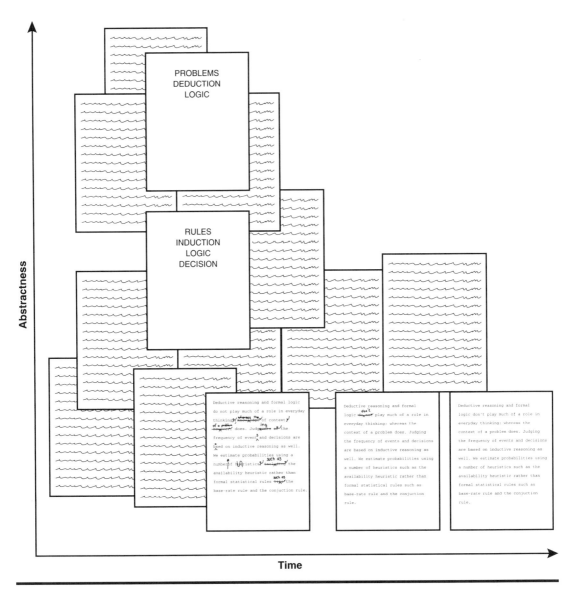

Abstractness

PROBLEMS
DEDUCTION
LOGIC

RULES
INDUCTION
LOGIC
DECISION

Deductive reasoning and formal logic
do not play much of a role in everyday
thinking; whereas the of context
of a problem ing
however does. Judgments of the
frequency of events and decisions are
based on inductive reasoning as well.
We estimate probabilities using a
number of heuristics such as the
availability heuristic rather than
formal statistical rules the
base-rate rule and the conjuction rule.

Deductive reasoning and formal
logic don't play much of a role in
everyday thinking; whereas the
context of a problem does. Judging
the frequency of events and decisions
are based on inductive reasoning as
well. We estimate probabilities using
a number of heuristics such as the
availability heuristic rather than
formal statistical rules such as
base-rate rule and the conjuction
rule.

Deductive reasoning and formal
logic don't play much of a role in
everyday thinking; whereas the
context of a problem does. Judging
the frequency of events and decisions
are based on inductive reasoning as
well. We estimate probabilities using
a number of heuristics such as the
availability heuristic rather than
formal statistical rules such as
base-rate rule and the conjuction
rule.

Time

FIGURE 12.5 Succession of multiple representations that evolve during the expression stage. The ordinate represents abstractness of the information, and the abscissa indicates time. In the upper left, there are rough and abstract ideas expressed by the terms in capital letters. At the bottom there are typed pages; on the left are drafts, and on the very right, there is the final draft.

altogether, while others grow and evolve into the final representation—the surface form of the text on the right-hand side of Figure 12.5.

If a writer's cognitive capacity were unlimited, she would have little or no difficulty working on the multiple representations depicted in Figure 12.5. Unfortunately, we all know that this is not the case. Like every other cognitive activity, writing is subject to the limits of working memory (see Chapter 8). Using the analogy of a switchboard operator, Hayes and Flower (1980) illustrated how a writer seeks to cope with the conflicting demands placed on working memory (Black, 1982).

> *A writer caught in the act looks much more like a very busy switchboard operator trying to juggle a number of demands on her attention and constraints on what she can do:*

- *She has two important calls on hold. (Don't forget that idea.)*
- *Four lights just started flashing. (They demand immediate attention or they'll be forgotten.)*
- *A party of five wants to be hooked together. (They need to be connected somehow.)*
- *A party of two thinks they've been incorrectly connected. (Where do they go?)*
- *And throughout this complicated process of remembering, retrieving, and connecting, the operator's voice must project calmness, confidence, and complete control. (p. 52)*

The output representation—the text—consists of structures at several levels: words, phrases, clauses, sentences, paragraphs, and so on. As the writer expresses her ideas in print, she makes choices for each of these structures. We use response times and the temporal patterns of composition to document the mental work of the writer. Pauses and spurts of production alternate, as they do in speaking.[3]

Research by Matsuhashi (1982) shows that the pattern of pauses and writing depends on the goal of the writer and on the type of text. She observed college-age writers and reported results from one writer, John. He composed a report about events in which he participated and an abstract generalization about how successful people behave. Matsuhashi filmed John, recorded writing pauses, and correlated the pauses with specific locations in the text. She observed that John exhibited different rates of writing for the two assignments. He paused longer and more irregularly in writing the generalization than the report. Total pausing times for each of the first 12 written lines are shown in Figure 12.6.

What do writers do during pauses? By analyzing the locations of pauses, some conclusions can

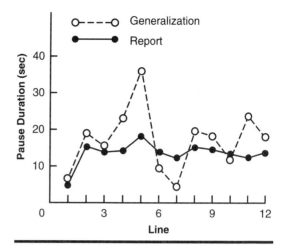

FIGURE 12.6 A college student exhibited a relatively constant pattern of writing pauses when he composed a report. He paused irregularly when he wrote a generalization (Matsuhashi, 1982).

be drawn. Because pause durations differ in systematic ways as a function of the subsequent clause or word, researchers assume that writers engage in planning processes. In addition, writers retrieve information from memory, think of ways to express a proposition, and search for words. Frequently, writers reread the previous text to remind them of what they said. When John wrote his generalization, he paused twice for over 16 seconds and reread what he had written.

Speakers and writers pause prior to producing words, clauses, sentences, and paragraphs. Maclay and Osgood (1959) reported that speakers paused longer before producing content words than function words. Content words include nouns, verbs, and adjectives; they convey the meaning of the sentence. Function words, on the other hand, signal the syntactic structure (see Chapter 10). The speaker faces more choices when using a content than a function word. For example, there are many ways to describe motion, but how many ways are there to say *the, in,* or *an?* Speakers also require additional time to construct clauses and phrases syntactically. Ferreira (1991) found that speakers' pauses become longer as the syntactic structure of spoken clauses become more complex.

The number of choices influences writing pauses as well. Studying writers, de Beaugrande (1984) observed longer pauses before choices among many alternatives. His writers were told to write down directions from a familiar highway exit to their homes. Pauses occurred before the number of roads and exits, the name of streets, and the designation *street, avenue, road,* or *boulevard.* It was at these locations that the writer had to remember and express one of several likely choices.

Usually, pauses prior to words are so brief that writers do not notice them. Sometimes, however, a writer does notice lengthy and painful pauses in thinking about a single word, as Jeffrey Archer, the best-selling British author, did when he was looking for just one word: "When people say, 'Gosh, it runs so smoothly,' they don't realize that it's *hours* and *hours* and *hours* of honing each sentence, of removing one word, of lying in bed and thinking of *one* word that would be better in *one* place" (Bryson, 1990, p. 35).

A sentence is a linear sequence of words that conforms to the syntactic rules of language. Research of spoken sentence production shows that people formulate ideas and utter them in clausal groups; there are pauses at clause and sentence boundaries, and there are fewer confusion errors across clause boundaries than within. Similarly, writers tend to produce ideas in clusters, which are put down on paper in groups. de Beaugrande (1984) found that his writers paused after most sentences. Matsuhashi (1982) found that the tendency to pause at the sentence boundary depended on the writer's goal. When writing generalizations, writers paused at sentence boundaries; in report writing, they paused within sentences.

Reviewing.   Writing is an act of communication. The writer expresses a meaning in a way that facilitates understanding by the reader (Clark & Clark, 1977; Grice, 1975). In reviewing her text, an author evaluates meaning relative to her audience. She takes the reader's perspective and tries to comprehend the text as she thinks a reader would. During her review, the guiding questions are: Does the text express what I want to say? and Can the reader understand what I want to say? Reviewing is a recursive activity; it takes place at every level of the text—paragraphs, sentences, clauses, and words—and it takes place during all phases of the composition process (Murray, 1978). In addition, writers devote extra time to reviewing completed drafts. Many writers consider reviewing and editing the critical stage in composition; it is the operation that gives the product its final shape.

The writer reviews word choice, sentence construction, the links between sentences, and the sequence of paragraphs. At each level, he seeks to detect and correct errors and infelicities of expression. At a global level, the writer deletes irrelevant information, adds relevant materials, moves important sections to the beginning of paragraphs, and shortens or lengthens sentences in order to smooth the flow of ideas. The writer also focuses on the rhetorical structure of the text. Different texts have different rhetorical structures; paragraphs are structured to reflect an argument, to develop an idea, or to answer a question. In different professions, different conventional structures are used. Journalists use a pyramid construction; main ideas are expressed first, then somewhat more detail is presented, and finally full details are given. Research papers in psychology include the following four sections: introduction, method, results, and discussion. Titles and subtitles are used to facilitate communication.

At the sentence level, writers sometimes commit errors of reference (Bartlett, 1982). In text (12.14), the first sentence introduces three boys, and the second sentence refers to a male referent, presumably one of the boys without identifying which. A fifth-grader wrote this text and detected the problem; however, he did not quite solve it, as sentence (12.15) illustrates.

(12.14) One day three boys went ice skating. *He* was showing off and he didn't see . . .

(12.15) One day, David, Bill, and Harry went ice skating. The boy was showing off and he . . .

At this level, the goal of reviewing is to detect the errors of reference, in addition to other problems, and to correct them.

Another goal is to make the text flow more smoothly and to improve style. There are many excellent sources on style, Strunk and White's (1979) among them. They offer a long list of suggestions: Work from a suitable design, do not overwrite, do not overstate, avoid fancy words, be clear, omit needless words, and so on. One of their suggestions is to use definite assertions in positive rather than "tame, colorless, hesitating, noncommittal language." Use the word *not* as a means of denial and antithesis, never as a means of evasion. Compare, for example, passages (12.16a) and (12.16b):

(12.16a) *The Taming of the Shrew* is rather weak in spots. Shakespeare does not portray Katherine as a very admirable character, nor does Bianca remain long in memory as an important character in Shakespeare's works.

(12.16b) The women in *The Taming of the Shrew* are unattractive. Katherine is disagreeable; Bianca is insignificant.

We acquire and improve reviewing skills through practice, as is true of the other components of writing (Scardamalia & Bereiter, 1986). Children begin to develop reviewing skills once they are aware of the reader. Children in primary grades make revisions when encouraged to do so, although frequently the revisions are relatively "low level": The writer proofreads her essay and corrects typographical errors but makes no other revisions (Scardamalia & Bereiter, 1986). Younger writers can be taught to edit at the word and sentence levels; it is more difficult to train review at the text level. Text-level review develops only after extensive practice spanning several years of writing; it is the mark of the mature writer.

What Distinguishes a Writing Expert? Assuming that writing results from expressing one's knowledge on paper, novices and experts differ in the way in which they do so. According to Scardamalia and Bereiter (1991), novices simply tell what they know, most likely in the order in which specific content occurs to them as they write. Experts, on the other hand, present content in order to satisfy the multiple goals of writing—namely, to reflect the logical structure of the content and the rhetorical goal of targeting the text for a specific audience. In short, experts transform knowledge, novices just tell of it. Knowledge transformation does not come easy, though; despite their extended practice, expert writers tend to spend more time on a composition than novices. They reflect on their work and try out different approaches in different drafts.

INTERIM SUMMARY

We discussed four major components of the writing process: planning, making meaning, expressing meaning, and reviewing the text. Planning includes setting the goal and strategies of the writing project. Making meaning refers to collecting information for the project. Expressing meaning involves the construction of a surface text. Reviewing includes reading the product, evaluating it in terms of goals, and editing it. These component processes are not discrete; they overlap and frequently occur simultaneously.

Issues on Writing

Writing involves many research issues, mostly about the stages of composition, as we have seen. It poses important questions of application as well. Consider the following questions: How should writing best be taught? What is the relation of writing and thinking? and Can the use of computers improve one's writing? There have been conferences and books devoted to each of these and other issues. We cannot do justice to all of them here; rather, I will sketch two concerns—

namely, the relation of writing and thinking, and the role of computers in composition.

Writing and Thinking.   Essay questions often exhort the student to "develop an argument for, or against, [X]. Be careful to anticipate and defend against possible counter arguments" (Kellog, 1988). The X could be any topic: Tuition charges, as in Kellog's (1988) assignment presented earlier, the death penalty, banning alcoholic beverages at campus parties, and so on. As the writer develops her argument, she ponders the problem, examines her own thoughts and those of others, and evaluates opinions. The writer engages in a mental dialogue; she thinks. If thinking involves the manipulation of abstract symbols such as pro- and counterarguments, then surely writing is intimately related to thinking. Scholars of composition share this view, as the title of at least one book reveals. *Thinking on Paper* (Howard & Barton, 1986). Nevertheless, writing calls for a different kind of thinking than well-defined problems, like finding the square root of a number (see Chapters 13 and 14). Writing is ill defined (Voss & Post, 1988); given a broad topic, the writer must discover the problems implied by the topic, gather information, and develop the argument.

Is the kind of thinking that supports writing unitary? Can it be taught? There are disagreements on the first but not the second issue. Basing their view on Plato's tenets, some composition scholars believe that there is a thinking faculty that can be transferred to any domain. Others appeal to Aristotle and hold that knowledge structures depend on the discipline; thinking in mathematics, for example, differs from that in political science or biology. Accordingly, thinking has to be learned in each domain. The latter view is held by most cognitive psychologists (see Chapters 5 and 13).

Writing can be taught. In the past, writing instruction has frequently been restricted to teaching correct spelling, punctuation, and sentence construction. With the emergence of the cognitive approach to writing as a composite skill, the impetus of writing instruction has changed (e.g.,

Scardamalia & Bereiter, 1986). Writing teachers provide instruction in each of the subskills of composition: planning, generating and expressing ideas, and reviewing. The writing process is explained to students in terms of the cognitive theories introduced here, and students are taught some of the strategies we have discussed, for example, techniques of idea generation. Scardamalia and Bereiter (1986) reported that the cognitive-process approach to writing instruction has proven successful, even with 12-year-olds. The critical discovery of cognitive psychologists has been that emphasis on writing strategies is not as effective as teaching writing for a particular subject matter. Better writers usually know more about the domain they are writing about, thus providing a practical lesson for you: One of the most effective ways to improve the quality of your composition in a subject is to acquire as much information on it as you can.

Can a Computer Help Your Composition?
Experts disagree on whether a computer is a help in composition. There was optimism when word processors were first introduced in the early 1980s, but enthusiasm has since moderated. Indeed, some composition teachers speak of a backlash against the use of word processors as teaching machines (Curtis, 1988). The early hope was that the use of word processors would improve the quality of student papers; that hope has not been fulfilled. What has changed are attitudes toward writing, especially among mature writers. Such writers report spending more time on their word processors than they did with pencil and paper; they edit more and have more fun composing. It has yet to be discovered how novice writers can best take advantage of word processors. Whatever the outcome of these discussions, word processors are here to stay; they become more powerful and less expensive, and more children are introduced to them at younger ages.

Another use of the computer in composition is the electronic writing class in which students and their instructor communicate via a network. Again, great claims about the medium have been made; it is not clear that they have been substantiated, however (Hawisher & Selfe, 1991). Advocates of electronic writing classes claim that students spend more time writing, more peer teaching takes place, more student-instructor interaction takes place, and students receive more immediate feedback. A potential problem exists, however, in that the feedback given by teachers in this medium addresses local problems with style rather than the overall organization or substance of the paper.

In the late 1980s, innovative software designed for composition made an appearance. These writing aids are different from word processors. Word processors are tools allowing the mechanical movement, deletion, and insertion of text; they benefit the review stage but not other stages of writing such as planning and making meaning. Computer-based writing aids, such as Friedman's (1987) WANDAH (Writing Aid and Author's Helper), assist the writer at each stage of composition. During planning, the program prompts the writer to enter the topic, the writing goal, and the audience. When the writer wishes to generate ideas, he can produce invisible writing intended to overcome the urge to edit a sentence as he thinks it. You can anticipate additional programs like WANDAH and more powerful word processors, spell checkers, and stylistic aids in the future. Remember, however: These are tools, not substitutes, for your ideas and creativity.

CONCLUSION: A PERSONAL PERSPECTIVE ON WRITING

I have treated writing as a rational process; there is a specific goal to be met and component processes serve that goal. By way of a conclusion, I want to speak about my own feelings and thoughts as a writer, however subjective they may be.[4]

We saw that writing is based on cognitive processes. For many writers, writing is full of emotional experiences as well. Reflecting on composition, Dostoevsky once called it a "hellish torture." Thurber, on the other hand, felt "miserable" when he was not writing. Writing inspires excitement, frustration, impatience, panic, and joy. I am impatient when I cannot express a thought in clear language, when a term eludes me, and when the phone rings just as I grasp an idea. I experience panic when a deadline is pressing and a blank page or a muddled manuscript stares back at me with no guiding idea in sight to move me over the hump. I am disappointed when a chapter or paper is not accepted for publication. I am excited when the thoughts and words come easily, when contradictions are resolved, when I discover an interesting contrast or a smooth transition between paragraphs, and when I finally grasp an issue I thought about for a long time.

All of this leads me to the question: Why do we write at all? Most jobs are assigned, but there are personal reasons for choosing to write. Although I cannot presume to answer for all writers, I can say that writing helps me understand a problem more thoroughly. Having to write a research proposal or a book chapter forces me to ponder issues more carefully. When writing, I often discover inconsistencies in thought and argument that are easily overlooked in conversation. Writing forces me to put a fine point on thoughts. It also helps me establish a bond with my readers, creating an environment for the sharing of knowledge. The bond is reciprocal; the reader is on my mind when I write and often becomes my teacher, offering commentary, criticism, and praise.

Let me describe how I write. I think that my own writing defies every rule I have come across in composition manuals. I rarely use an outline to launch my papers. I usually start a manuscript with a section that appears most accessible. I also produce many more drafts than a composition manual suggests. During the course of multiple revisions, I sometimes abandon my initial piece altogether, as new and better thoughts take its place. I envy writers who compose final versions on their first try.

When you compose a paper, you should suspend the principles of economy and efficiency and accept that writing is inefficient by the standards of mechanical production. At every stage of the process, you have to allow much time to do it well; you have to read related sources and papers; you have to ponder issues and think through questions. Never think or read for too long, however. Put something on paper, even if you change it many times. At the very end, each writer faces a final hurdle. After first struggling with the topic and then warming up to it, the moment comes of finishing up. You can no longer postpone; you must decide on the final shape and let go.

ENDNOTES

1. To be sure, there are other perspectives on comprehension: the writer who wants to reach an audience, the teacher who wishes to teach reading, and the speaker who wants to persuade her listeners.

2. There are cases of text processing that result in no memory representation at all. Typists and proofreaders usually generate no representation. But then we do not refer to the cognitive activities of proofreaders and typists as *reading.* Rather, we use the terms *typing, transcribing,* and *proofreading.*

3. Speaking and writing differ, of course. Speaking is much faster and rarely allows for revision. In speaking, pauses are intended as communicative devices and reflect the production processes of the speaker.

4. Ideas in this section are based on my article entitled "Reflections on Writing" for the December issue of the *Write Stuff,* Trinity College, November 23, 1990.

COGNITIVE SKILLS:
PROBLEM SOLVING

PREVIEW

Problem solving refers to the achievement of a goal within a set of constraints. The problem solver must develop a representation of the problem and generate a solution path from the initial state to the goal. In this chapter, we consider problem solving of knowledge-rich and knowledge-lean problems, how our ability to solve problems changes as a result of cognitive development and practice, and how to take advantage of the discoveries of cognitive psychologists.

Knowledge-lean problems are those whose solutions require relatively little specialized knowledge. We will discuss different problem-solving strategies, including heuristic search and the role of subgoals in the means-ends analysis using the Tower of Hanoi puzzle as a case study. Unlike search problems that are solved by the application of operators, problem solving by analogy proceeds through the discovery of common components among problems. Knowledge-rich problem solving requires extensive training in a particular discipline or domain, such as mathematics, computer programming, and political science. We will discuss examples from each of these disciplines and describe solution strategies used by experts and novices.

Throughout the chapter, research methods are described, including the protocol method and computer simulations of problem solving. Changes in one's ability to solve problems occur with extended practice and when memory and content knowledge increase during an individual's development. You can also improve your problem-solving skills with short-term training, but not by much. Success in problem solving is enhanced by planning, choosing a good representation, and by monitoring one's progress toward a goal.

INTRODUCTION

Every day we encounter problems, both large and small. We solve most of these without even thinking about them. There are some problems, however, of which we are fully aware, such as assignments in a course, planning a trip, or finding a summer job. A person's success in life depends on his or her ability to solve problems. Frequently, we solve problems for entertainment and relaxation. A friend of mine cannot survive a weekend without doing a crossword puzzle, a neighbor enjoys taking his car engine apart and putting it together again, and a sixth-grader I know spends much of his free time solving mini-mysteries. A problem exists when you wish to reach a goal. Usually, there are constraints and only certain actions are available to reach the goal. Study the list of problems assembled below to get a feel for the variety of problems people encounter. Try to solve some of them and compare them, noting similarities and differences.

A List of Problems

1. *Cryptarithmetic Problem.* In cryptarithmetic problems, words stand for numbers. Each letter represents a unique number. The goal is to add the numbers to produce a sum that is arithmetically correct.

$$\begin{array}{r} B\ E\ S\ T \\ +\ M\ A\ D\ E \\ \hline M\ A\ S\ E\ R \end{array}$$

In this example, you must substitute digits for the letters A, B, D, E, M, R, S, and T, and make the sum come out right (Raphael, 1976). Try to solve this problem on your own. You can compare your solution with the one in the Appendix and the end of this chapter.

2. *Food Shortage.* Imagine that you are secretary for agriculture in country Y. For several years, Y's crop yield has been 30% below normal and the country faces severe food shortages. How would you go about increasing agricultural productivity in the country?

3. *Radiation Problem.* Suppose you are a doctor faced with a patient who has a malignant stomach tumor. You cannot operate on the patient, but unless the tumor is destroyed, the patient will die. You know that a kind of radiation, at a sufficiently high intensity, can destroy the tumor. Unfortunately, at this intensity the healthy tissue that the ray passes through on the way to the tumor will also be destroyed. At lower intensities, the ray is harmless to healthy tissue but will not affect the tumor. How can the ray be used to destroy the tumor without injuring healthy tissue (Duncker, 1945)?

4. *Algebra Word Problem.* A candle factory has two workers, Jones and Smith. Jones makes candles at the rate of 60 per hour and Smith makes 75 candles per hour. Jones spends one hour more than Smith each day making candles. If Jones makes the same number of candles each day as Smith, how long does Smith work?

5. *Tower of Hanoi Puzzle.* The Tower of Hanoi problem is a classic (see Figure 13.1). In this problem, there are 64 disks stacked on one of three pegs. The goal is to move the

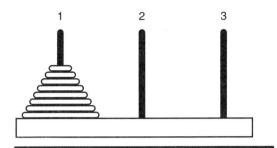

FIGURE 13.1 The Tower of Hanoi puzzle with eight disks. The toy problem is simple; it usually involves five disks at the most.

disks from the first peg to the third peg while observing the three following constraints:

— Move one disk at a time from one peg to another.

— You can only move a disk that is not covered by another one.

— A larger disk may not be placed on a smaller one.

According to legend, monks in a monastery near Hanoi are working on this problem, and once they solve it the world will come to an end. Assuming the monks move one disk a second and every move they make is correct, it will take them almost a trillion years to complete the problem (Raphael, 1976)! In 1883, the French mathematician Eduoard Lucas popularized the Tower of Hanoi puzzle as a toy. It made its way into many nurseries; chances are that is where you first saw it, though you did not know its name or its illustrious history in the annals of cognitive psychology.

6. *Geometric Analogy.* Figure 13.2 displays an analogy problem of the kind frequently used in aptitude tests. The problem solver must choose a figure in the bottom row that is to C as A is to B. (See Appendix).

7. *Candle Problem.* Suppose you are given a box of thumbtacks, a matchbox, and a candle (see Figure 13.3) and are asked to use these objects to support the candle on a wall (Duncker, 1945). What would you do?

8. *Balance Scale Problem.* Figure 13.4 shows a balance scale used to study problem solving by children. The scale has a fulcrum and an arm with pegs to hold metal disks with holes. The arm tips to the right or the left or remains level, depending on the number and location of weights placed on the pegs. Subjects are shown an arrangement of weights and asked to predict the position of the arm (Inhelder & Piaget, 1958).

9. *Medical Diagnosis.* A 27-year-old unemployed male was admitted to the emergency room with the complaint of shaking chills and fever of 40°C. The fever and chills were accompanied by sweating and a feeling of prostration. He also complained of shortness of breath when he tried to climb the two flights of stairs to his apartment. Inquiry revealed a transient loss of vision in his right eye, which lasted approximately 45 seconds on the day before his admission to the emergency room.

Physical examination revealed a toxic-looking young man having a rigor. His temperature was 41°C, blood pressure 110/40. Mucus membranes were pink. Examination of his limbs showed puncture wounds in his left antecubital fossa. The patient volunteered that he was bitten by a cat at a friend's

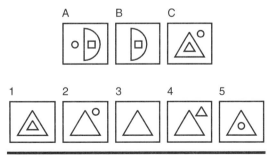

FIGURE 13.2 Geometric analogy problem frequently used in aptitude tests. Pick the shape from among 1–5 that is related to C as A is to B (Winston, 1984).

FIGURE 13.3 Ingredients for Duncker's candlestick problem. Arrange the objects so that they can hold a candle to a wall.

house about a week before admission. There were no other skin findings. Examination of the cardiovascular system showed no jugular venous distention, pulse was 120 per minute, regular, equal, and synchronous. The pulse was also noted to be collapsing. The apex beat was not displaced. Auscultation of his heart revealed a 2/6 early diastolic murmur in the aortic area and funuscopy revealed a flame-shaped hemorrhage in the left eye. There was no splenomegaly. Urinalysis showed numerous red cells but no red cell casts. What would the doctor's diagnosis be? (See Appendix.)

10. *Monster Change Problem.* Three five-handed extraterrestrial monsters were holding three crystal globes. Because of the quantum-mechanical peculiarities of their neighborhood, both monsters and globes come in exactly three sizes with no others permitted: small, medium, and large. The small monster was holding the medium-sized globe; the medium-sized monster was holding the large globe; and the large mon-

FIGURE 13.4 Balance scale used to study problem solving in children (Siegler, 1991).

ster was holding the small globe. Because the situation offended their keenly developed sense of symmetry, the monsters proceeded to shrink and expand the globes so that each would have a globe proportionate to its own size. Monster etiquette complicated the solution to this problem since it required that: (1) Only one globe may be changed at a time; (2) If two globes have the same size, only the globe held by the larger monster may be changed; and (3) A globe may not be changed to the same size as the globe of the larger monster. By what sequence of changes could the monsters solve this problem? (Hint: Your first goal should be to get the small monster's globe to the right size) (Kotovsky, Hayes, & Simon, 1985).

11. *Programming Problems.* Computer programs come in many varieties, ranging from the familiar number-crunching tasks to game playing and complex control operations in manufacturing. The three following tasks illustrate programming problems:

— Write a computer program to solve the Tower of Hanoi puzzle.

— Write a procedure to compute the sum of n integers.

— Write a program that controls a specific operation in an assembly line.

For many individuals, programming is a mental challenge as enticing as any; the promise of success often overcomes the frustration of failure and keeps programmers going to find the last bug and get the problem solved.

12. *Mutilated Chessboard Problem.* Imagine an intact chessboard of 64 squares and a set of 32 dominoes. Each of the dominoes covers exactly two squares of the chessboard. If all of the 32 dominoes are placed in columns over the chessboard, its 64 squares will be covered. Now, imagine that we mutilate the chessboard by cutting two diagonally opposite squares from it. The question is whether or not 31 of the dominoes can

be distributed over the board so that they cover the remaining 62 squares.

13. *Liberating Kuwait.* It was 1990 when Iraq invaded the neighboring oil-rich country of Kuwait. Tens of thousands of Iraqi troops occupied the small country, defending their positions from all fronts. Put yourself in the shoes of General Norman Schwarzkopf, the commanding officer of the Allied forces trying to liberate Kuwait. Should you launch a frontal and direct attack on Iraqi positions in Kuwait or just feign an attack in order to deceive the enemy from your intended main thrust across the arid and inhospitable Arab desert? Each of these moves has advantages and disadvantages. The frontal attack has the advantage of having better logistical support from the Allied armada of ships assembled in the Persian Gulf. The long detour through the desert has the advantage that there are fewer enemy troops. Which strategy would you choose and for what reasons?

Skim the list of problems again and judge how competent you feel in solving them. You would probably consider most of these solvable, although not necessarily easy. On the other hand, you may feel less competent to solve certain problems, including the food shortage, medical diagnosis, and programming problems. Most likely, the problems you judge solvable do not require professional training or much preparation. The Tower of Hanoi puzzle is a good example of this type of problem; children can solve it successfully if only a few disks are involved. Such problems are called "knowledge-lean" problems. The medical diagnosis and programming problems are "knowledge-rich" problems (VanLehn, 1989): in order to solve these, specialized knowledge in a particular discipline, such as medicine, is required. I will devote a section of this chapter to problem solving in each of these categories: knowledge-lean and knowledge-rich problems.

Problems differ in the degree to which they are defined. The Tower of Hanoi puzzle and the cryptarithmetic problem have clearly defined initial states and explicit goal states; they are well defined. Operators are available to permit transitions between states. An **operator** is an action that transforms the problem from one state into another state. A **state** is a description of the problem's universe at a particular time. Well-defined problems include algebraic and geometry problems, games, puzzles, and computer programming tasks. There are also problems in which the goal state is not explicit. For example, consider the problem studied by Medieval philosophers: How many angels can dance on the head of a pin? To some philosophers, this was a very serious problem. In such cases, however, the problem solver may not even know where to begin.

Glass and Holyoak (1986) mentioned the case of the graduate student who is looking for a topic for a Ph.D. thesis. For this student, the problem is to define a worthwhile research problem. In other words, the student searches for a framework within which to solve the problem. Once the problem is found, it is easier to conduct the research. Other important but less well-defined problems include choosing a job, composing a term paper, diagnosing a disease, and finding the cause of car trouble. What is a well-defined or ill-defined problems is in the eye of the beholder. To a novice, a well-defined arithmetic problem may appear ill defined. One of the tasks of the problem-solving process is to transform ill-defined problems into well-defined problems; the problem solver must move from a state of having no precise goal and a lack of operators, to developing a definition of the goal that specifies constraints and operators (Simon, 1973).

I N T E R I M   S U M M A R Y

Using specific operators and observing constraints, the problem solver moves from an initial state to a goal state. In well-defined problems, the initial state and the goal are explicit from the outset. In ill-defined problems, the problem solver must first identify the states. Knowledge-lean problems require relatively little domain knowledge; knowledge-rich problems require much domain knowledge.

———— ■ ————

KNOWLEDGE-LEAN PROBLEMS

To solve knowledge-lean problems, a minimum of domain knowledge is necessary. Although they are usually well defined, knowledge-lean problems are not always easy. Consider the Tower of Hanoi problem in the introduction. Sixty-four disks must be moved from one peg to another. We don't have as much time to solve this puzzle as the monks of Hanoi; therefore, we take the first step of problem solving: We reduce the size of the problem by using only two or three disks. Before reading further you should try this puzzle.

If you happen to have three pegs and a set of disks, use those. Otherwise, three coins (a quarter, a nickel, and a penny) will do just as well. In addition, use a sheet of paper with three locations marked 1, 2, and 3. Place the three coins in descending order on location 1 and begin. You will get a feel for this puzzle very quickly.

Table 13.1 lists the nine possible states of the two-disk version of the Tower of Hanoi puzzle. In state 1, for example, both disks are located on the first peg. In state 2, disk A is on peg 1 and disk B is on peg 2. The table does not reveal the solution path, however. The problem

solver must search the states in order to find the solution.

Heuristic Search

Solving a problem through a search simply means finding a path that leads from the starting state to the goal state. Such a path is known as a **solution path.** Even for the Tower of Hanoi puzzle with two disks, there are a number of solution paths, including the following sequences of states (see Table 13.1): 1 > 7 > 8 > 5 > 2 > 3 > 9, 1 > 7 > 4 > 6 > 3 > 9, and the optimal path 1 > 4 > 6 > 9. A search of all states is tedious, but it could be done in a small problem like this.

The state graph for the two-disk version of the Tower of Hanoi problem includes 3^2 or 9 states. There are 3^3 or 27 states for the three-disk version; see if you can list them all. Try to enumerate the states for the four-disk problem; you will find this to be a difficult and time consuming task. You can now appreciate that the original 64-disk problem remains unsolved.[1] Clearly, the problem is easier with fewer disks!

Listing the states for the four-disk problem should convince you that an unlimited search of the problem space is inefficient at best and impossible at worst. People usually do not employ an unlimited search strategy; rather, they prefer *heuristic* search strategies (from the Greek *heuristikein* for *discover*). **Heuristic search** strategies cut down the search space. They are essentially rules of thumb; sometimes they work, other times they don't. Heuristic search is based on limited knowledge of the problem domain. Ideally, the problem solver pursues only the most promising paths in the search space. Consider the heuristic used by a safecracker to reduce his search space. Assume the safe has 10 dials, each having 100 possible settings. If that is all the safecracker knows, he would require $1/2 \times 100^{10}$ trials to crack the safe. On the other hand, if the safecracker knows that a dial clicks whenever he selects the correct setting, he can open the safe with only 50×10 trials (Langley, Simon, Bradshaw, & Zytkow, 1987).

TABLE 13.1 States in the Two-Disk Version of the Tower of Hanoi Problem

State	Peg 1	Peg 2	Peg 3
1	A/B		
2	A	B	
3	A		B
4	B	A	
5		A/B	
6		A	B
7	B		A
8		B	A
9			A/B

The Means-Ends Strategy

One of the most common heuristic problem-solving strategies identifies the difference between the current and the goal states and seeks to bridge the gap. Newell and Simon's (1972) example of overcoming distance illustrates this: Suppose I want to take my son to nursery school but I'm at home. The difference between my current location and nursery school is one of distance; I reduce the difference by driving. This apparently simple action reflects the **means-ends strategy;** the problem solver achieves the goal in two steps, expressed here as questions:

(13.1) What is the biggest difference between where I am now and where I want to be? and

(13.2) What operator can I use to reduce the difference?

Most problems are too complex to be solved by using only a single operator. Rather, steps (13.1) and (13.2) must be applied in successive cycles, each of which reduces the difference between the initial problem state and the goal state. Table 13.2 shows an algebraic problem solved according to this two-step procedure. This version of the means-ends strategy is aptly named **difference reduction** (Glass & Holyoak, 1986). Algebraic problems like the one in Table 13.2 are solved by such operators as addition, subtraction, and division. Applying one of these operators at a time transforms the problem until the equation is solved.

When an operator is available to reduce a given difference, the problem solver applies it and moves to a new state in the problem space. If the operator is blocked by an obstacle, however, she sets the subgoal of removing the obstacle according to the **subgoal strategy.** This strategy is the recursive version of the means-ends strategy; the basic two-step cycle is used to achieve the overall goal by repeatedly setting and solving embedded subgoals. In general, a recursive procedure is one that repeatedly uses itself until the problem is solved (see also Box 10.1). Two problems will il-

TABLE 13.2   Means-Ends Strategy Applied to a Simple Algebra Problem

Problem: Solve the equation $ax - b = x$ for x.
Goal state: Term x on the left side of the equation; all other terms on the right.

Steps:
1.   Current state: $ax - b = x$.
   Differences: a on left, *b* on left, *x* on right.
   Apply operation: Add *b* to both sides.
2.   Current state: $ax = x + b$.
   Differences: *a* on left, *x* on right.
   Apply operation: Subtract *x* from both sides.
3.   Current state: $ax - x = b$.
   Differences: *a* on left, *x* on left twice.
   Apply operation: Factor *x* on left.
4.   Current state: $x(a - 1) = b$.
   Differences: $(a - 1)$ on left.
   Apply operation: Divide both sides by $(a - 1)$.
5.   Current state: $x = b/(a - 1)$.
   Differences: None.
   Problem solved.

lustrate the subgoal strategy: taking a trip and solving the Tower of Hanoi problem.

Planning a Trip from Atlanta to Chicago: An Illustration of the Subgoal Strategy.   Suppose you attend college in Atlanta and want to fly home to Chicago. First, you ask question (13.1): What is the biggest difference between the initial and the goal state? The biggest difference is the distance between your Atlanta dorm and your house in Chicago. Next, you ask question (13.2): How can I reduce the difference? An operator to reduce the difference would be to fly from Atlanta to Chicago. However, there is an obstacle: You don't have an airline ticket. Now you apply the subgoal strategy recursively by posing question (13.1) again and formulating a subgoal. Along the way, you keep reducing differences as you encounter new obstacles. Eventually, you will remove them all, fulfilling all the subgoals, and getting home to Chicago. The subgoal strategy describes the subgoals and operators taken to achieve the overall goal. It does not necessarily mean that you proceed deliberately and consciously.

Because the subgoal strategy can be used regardless of the type of problem or domain, it is a general problem-solving strategy. What differs from domain to domain are specific operators. In the Tower of Hanoi puzzle, a disk move is an operator. In mathematics problems, operators such as addition and subtraction are used. In chess, the set of operators includes a limited number of permissible moves. We will see that the subgoal strategy can also be used as a backup if the problem solver does not have adequate domain knowledge.

The means-ends strategy forms the core of Newell and Simon's (1972) classical General Problem Solver (GPS). You can use general problem-solving strategies in your career, in games, logic problems, and puzzles. In 1955, Newell and

Simon applied this strategy to a set of theorems from Whitehead and Russell's *Principia Mathematica.* They called their program Logic Theorist and thus became pioneers of the discipline of Artificial Intelligence (see Box 13.1). Logic Theorist was capable of proving the Whitehead-Russell corpus of theorems more elegantly than the authors themselves.

It was easy enough to describe the subgoal strategy in the preceding trip example. Do people use this strategy when they solve problems in experiments? Study the next section that describes the way one woman solved the Tower of Hanoi problem. This section will deepen your understanding of the means-ends strategy and illustrate how cognitive psychologists examine problem solving. In this experiment, researchers use the **protocol method** in which subjects talk aloud as they solve problems. In other research, reaction

---

Box 13.1_____

Forty Years of Problem Solving by Computers: Will the Computer Take Over?

Simon and his colleagues, Newell and Shaw, developed the Logic Theorist in the early 1950s and presented their pioneering research at the first conference devoted to Artificial Intelligence, the Dartmouth Conference, which is sometimes called the birth of AI. In addition to Simon and Newell, the founding fathers of AI attended, including John McCarthy, Marvin Minsky, Claude Shannon, and Oliver Selfridge. Simon was one of the first of a long line of promoters of AI. Recognizing the power of the computer as a processor of symbols rather than a number cruncher, he and Newell believed that computers could think, learn, and create. "Moreover, their ability to do these things is going to increase rapidly," so that computers will be able to solve the same problems the human mind has solved. You can imagine that this claim has been very controversial, leading to a continuous debate between AI optimists and AI critics.

Philosophers, psychologists, and computer sci-

entists disputed Newell and Simon's bold claims. In vocal counterarguments, researchers such as Dreyfus, Weizenbaum, and Winograd asserted that computers do not have experience, emotion, or intuition. Therefore, they cannot think, learn, and create. Not to be outdone, the AI community countered with even more provocative claims. According to Hans Moravec (1988), head of the Mobile Robot Laboratory at Carnegie-Mellon University, we will soon enter the postbiological era in which computers, endowed with chips capable of 10 trillion operations per second, will exhibit consciousness similar to human consciousness. Moravec has claimed that these computers will seek to emancipate themselves from their human creators and generate new generations of ever more powerful computers. Does this mean human cognition will be superfluous when that era dawns? What do you think? Read Penrose (1989) for a rebuttal of Moravec.

times and accuracy scores are collected. Computer simulations are frequently used to mimic the problem-solving behaviors of human subjects.

Subgoals in the Tower of Hanoi Problem. This section describes the discovery of the subgoal strategy by a woman who was working on the Tower of Hanoi problem in an experiment. Two cognitive psychologists, Anzai and Simon (1979), presented her with five disks. There are 243 states ($3^5 = 243$) in this problem and the shortest solution path involves 31 moves. The experimenter explained the problem to the woman as follows: "The purpose of this experiment is to analyze what and how you think when you solve the problem. Thus, I would like you to tell aloud whatever you think during the solving process." The experimenter had a tape recorder running while the person worked for 1 1/2 hours on the problem. He asked some questions but offered no feedback or help of any kind. Table 13.3 includes 6 of the 224 protocol statements given by the woman.

First, the subject needed some time to understand the problem. After that, she solved the problem three times in succession. For each solution, the woman used a different strategy. The first strategy was a relatively time-consuming search strategy guided by much trial and error. During the second and third episodes, however, she developed the *pyramid subgoal strategy* in which the problem is viewed in terms of *sets* of disks rather than *individual* disks. The sets of disks represent subpyramids. We will see that although subpyramids may not be moved, viewing the problem in terms of subpyramids is efficient. A distinct feature of this strategy is the separation of goals, which are mental plans, from the physical moves themselves.

The overall goal of the pyramid subgoal strategy is to move the entire pyramid of disks from peg 1 to peg 3. This goal is achieved by repeating three substrategies:

1. Move the pyramid consisting of all except the largest disk to peg 2.
2. Move the largest disk from peg 1 to peg 3.
3. Move the pyramid on peg 2 to peg 3.

Substrategies (1) and (3) are mental plans used to organize physical moves. They are plans to move *sets of disks,* or pyramids. Strategy (1) is the plan to remove the obstacles to moving the largest disk without blocking the goal peg; the smaller disks are moved to peg 2. Strategy (3) is the plan to move all but the largest disk from peg 2 to the goal peg. Moving the largest disk is expressed in strategy (2), the only legal *physical* move permitted. If we apply the subgoal strategy to the Tower of Hanoi puzzle with three disks, we produce the sequence of three goals and seven moves shown in Table 13.4 (see Simon, 1975). Goals are printed in italics; physical moves are shown in regular print. The pyramid subgoal strategy is recursive; it does its job by using itself to solve a smaller subproblem: We move the entire pyramid by moving smaller subpyramids.

After trying a problem like the Tower of Hanoi puzzle a few times, you will understand the problem better, but it is still difficult to solve. One of the reasons for the difficulty is the load on working memory: One must generate the sequence of subgoals and remember them. Another source of difficulty is the manner in which the problem is physically represented. It turns out that even the Tower of Hanoi problem is relatively simple compared to problems that have the same logical

TABLE 13.3 Protocol Segments of a Subject Solving the Tower of Hanoi Problem

1. I'm not sure but first I'll take A from peg 1 and place it on 2.
2. And I'll take B from 1 and place it on 3.
3. And then, I take A from 2 and place it on C. *Experimenter:* If you can, tell me why you placed it there.
4. Because there was no place else to go, I had to place A from 2 to 3.
5. Then, next, I placed C from 1 to 2.
6. Well . . ., first I had to place A to 2, because I had to move all disks to 3. I wasn't too sure though.

TABLE 13.4 Goals and Moves According to the Pyramid Subgoal Strategy

1. *Goal: Move Pyramid (ABC) from 1 to 3*
2. *Goal: Move Pyramid (AB) from 1 to 2*
3.   Move Disk (A) from 1 to 3
4.   Move Disk (B) from 1 to 2
5.   Move Disk (A) from 3 to 2
6.   Move Disk (C) from 1 to 3
7. *Goal: Move Pyramid (AB) from 2 to 3*
8.   Move Disk (A) from 2 to 1
9.   Move Disk (B) from 2 to 3
10.   Move Disk (A) from 1 to 3

structure but use a different physical representation (see Kotovsky, Hayes, & Simon, 1985).

Production Rules.   In the previous section. I described the means-ends strategy in words. When researchers try to predict subjects' performance in problem-solving tasks, they use computer models, including production systems. The means-ends strategy is easily expressed in terms of production rules, as shown in Table 13.5 (Anderson, 1990; VanLehn, 1989). A production rule consists of two clauses: a condition, or IF clause; and an action, or THEN clause (see Chapter 5). Actions

TABLE 13.5 The Means-Ends Strategy Expressed as a Production System

(P1)
IF the goal is to remove difference D between a
    state S and a goal G
THEN find a relevant operator O to remove the
    difference and set the subgoal of applying
    operator O.
(P2)
IF the goal is to apply operator O to state S, and
    condition C for applying operator O is not met
THEN set the goal of satisfying condition C by
    modifying state S.
(P3)
IF the goal is to apply operator O to state S and
    condition C for applying operator O is met
THEN apply operator O.

listed in the THEN clause are triggered when the conditions of the IF clause are met.

Production systems have two uses in cognitive psychology: They are a notation used to represent procedural knowledge, as described in Chapter 5, and they are also used in simulation models of problem solving and other cognitive processes. These simulation models are flexible and can keep track of many aspects of performance, such as the type of response, the interval between moves (as in the Tower of Hanoi problem), and even the verbal statements in a problem-solving protocol (VanLehn, 1991). A variety of production systems have been introduced to mimic human problem solving, including PRISM, Soar, and Act*. PRISM (Program of Research in Self-Modifying Systems) is a production system that learns and modifies its productions as a result of experience (Langley et al., 1987; see also Chapter 14). Soar is a general-purpose system used to simulate a wide range of cognitive actions; these are represented in terms of the problem-solving model of transforming states from an initial to a goal state (Newell, Rosenbloom, & Laird, 1989). Similarly, Act* is a general cognitive architecture that includes problem solving as well as other cognitive skills (Anderson, 1983). Each of these three systems is a symbolic processing system including discrete representations and explicit rules. By contrast, connectionist network models use distributed representations and no explicit rules (see Chapter 6 and the following section on Analogies).

Analogies

Problems with a common structure are analogous. When a problem solver works on such problems, she can use the similarity to her advantage, provided she discovers it. In some cases, this is easy: We prepare this year's tax return by using last year's return as an example; we fix the chain on a 10-speed bike by studying how the chain is arranged on another bike, and so on. However, discovering analogies is not always easy. Consider again Duncker's (1945) radiation problem mentioned earlier in this chapter. Duncker observed 42 subjects trying to solve this problem. He found that some subjects had no ideas at all on how to begin, others violated some of the constraints of the problem. Two people produced the correct solution but did so only after prompting from the experimenter. Before reading on, give the radiation problem another try. Remember that different sources of radiation can be combined. Does this hint help?

What was for Duncker (1945) a toy problem has, 50 years later, become a medical miracle. According to Brody of the *New York Times,* radiosurgeons have developed the Gamma Knife, a device that beams hundreds of radioactive rays from different directions on a tumor to treat it without damage to any other tissue (Brody, 1995).

Here is the solution to the radiation problem. The patient can be saved by sending the radiation from multiple locations. The rays are focused on the tumor so their intensity is lethal at that site but not harmful to the surrounding tissue. What is your reaction to this solution? If you are like many of Duncker's subjects, you were surprised at how easy and obvious this solution seems. You could have thought of it yourself. Suddenly the problem makes sense; no search was needed—just a hint that presented the problem in a new light. Gestalt psychologists call such restructuring of a problem **insight,** a sudden flash of understanding. For the Gestaltists, insight remained somewhat mysterious and beyond the grasp of experimental analysis. Information processing psychologists, however, including VanLehn (1989) and Holyoak (1990), set out to determine if one could produce insight experimentally.

Gick and Holyoak (1983) compared the performance of an experimental and a control group in two successive phases, a recall and a problem-solving phase. In the recall phase, the experimental group read and recalled a problem analogous to the radiation problem. They were unaware of the relevance of the story to the problem-solving phase of the experiment when they were given the radiation problem. The control group received an unrelated problem in the first phase and the radiation problem in the second phase.

The story that the experimental group read in their first phase described a battle scene: A general and his troops approached a fortress accessible by many heavily mined roads. If the general's troops took only one road to the fortress, the entire column of soldiers would be killed, and the attack foiled. The general's solution was to divide his soldiers into many small platoons and approach the fortress from different directions.

Do you think the fortress story helped the experimental subjects solve the radiation problem? Surprisingly, only a few subjects noted the similarity. Gick and Holyoak (1980) attributed subjects' failure to see the similarity to the fact that these subjects assumed their recall of the first story would be tested, and thus missed its relation to problem solving in the second story. Experimental subjects solved the radiation problem more often when given the hint to use the first problem to solve the second, and when the radiation problem was preceded by several problem analogs instead of just one. It is not easy to detect the similarity between the fortress and the radiation stories. In order to solve the radiation problem, subjects must detect the similarities and then map appropriate components from one story to the other.

The source of difficulty in solving the tumor problem after reading the fortress story lies in the fact that certain components of the stories are similar and supportive; others are not. The problem solver must connect those components of the problems that are similar; for example, he must make the connection between the fortress and the tumor. Comparing the fortress and rays will not help. Figure 13.5 shows a subset of the components of the radiation and fortress problems. Analogous components are linked by solid connections.

The attack and the radiation situations are analogous as are their solutions. In both situations, there is a central target and a sufficient force available for the attack. The constraint in both cases is that one cannot apply force safely by

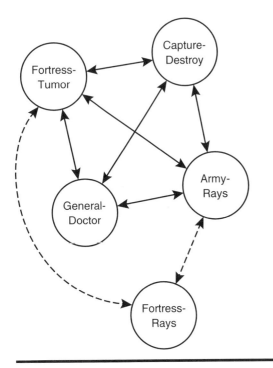

FIGURE 13.5 A network displaying components of the fortress and radiation problems. Solid connections indicate excitatory connections, whereas broken lines indicate inhibitory connections (Holyoak, 1990).

using only one path of attack. The solution is to divide the available resources and simultaneously send them along multiple paths.

Figure 13.5 should remind you of a connectionist network (see Chapters 4 and 6). Indeed, Holyoak and Thagard (1989) developed a connectionist model using the same principles of constraint satisfaction as in pattern recognition to simulate problem solving in a variety of situations. The model's name is ACME (Analogical Constraint Mapping Engine). The ACME simulation has been successfully applied to a wide range of problems, including the radiation and fortress problems. This simulation is different from the serial search used in search problems. The analogy problem is solved by satisfying several constraints in parallel, much like pattern recognition.

INTERIM SUMMARY

According to the means-ends strategy, a problem solver identifies the difference between the initial state and the goal state and sets the subgoal of eliminating that difference. The difference is removed once an operator is applied (for example, moving a disk in the Tower of Hanoi puzzle). The application of the operator is usually restricted by specific constraints. If there are obstacles, they are removed by the same strategy of difference reduction used to achieve the overall goal. The difficulty of the means-ends strategy lies in the nesting of subgoals; too many subgoals will severely tax working memory. The use of external memory aids helps overcome this difficulty. The means-ends strategy is applicable to problems from a wide range of domains, and can be used as a backup if a problem solver lacks the necessary domain knowledge. Analogous problems share common structural components. They can be readily solved when the problem solver detects the correspondence between the components. Research has shown, however, that this is difficult, even after hints are given.

KNOWLEDGE-RICH PROBLEMS

Observe a lawyer in court, a chess master at a tournament, or a computer programmer writing an algorithm. Do these professionals engage in searches or use the means-ends strategy and analogies to solve problems in their domains? Hardly. The lawyer, the chess master, and the computer programmer are experts; they have practiced specific skills for many years. Each has developed hundreds, even thousands, of routines to handle problems. Much of what these experts know, they cannot express; their knowledge has become automatic. According to cognitive psychologists, experts acquire domain-specific declarative and procedural knowledge in their profession. *Declarative knowledge* refers to information that is easily articulated, whereas *procedural knowledge* is the knowledge of how to execute a task; it is often difficult to explain (see Chapters 5 and 7). It takes years of training to accumulate expertise in a knowledge-rich field such as mathematics, computer programming, or political science.

It is a matter of perspective in determining what we consider to be a knowledge-rich problem. In the first section, we discussed Duncker's tumor and radiation problem, treating it like a knowledge-lean problem. An oncologist would probably view the problem differently. For our purposes, we will distinguish between knowledge-lean and knowledge-rich problems by the quantity of rules and operators needed to describe the problem: For knowledge-lean problems, one paragraph suffices; for knowledge-rich problems, however, many more constraints exist and more operators are available as well. Compare, for example, the steps in Table 13.4 used to solve the Tower of Hanoi puzzle, with the volumes of documentation embodied in expert systems of medicine and engineering.

Cognitive psychologists have examined the knowledge of experts and novices in several domains. I will sketch the key differences and then illustrate knowledge-rich problem solving with examples from three disciplines: mathematics, computer programming, and political science.

Comparing Experts and Novices
— Expert knowledge is specific; it does not transfer to other domains. You would not want a mathematician to treat you when you have a medical problem such as appendicitis.

— Expert knowledge is procedural; solving problems involves recognizing familiar patterns. As a result, experts can solve domain-specific problems faster and with fewer errors.

— Experts understand and represent problems largely in terms of underlying principles, whereas a novice's understanding of the problem is superficial. Chi, Feltovich, and Glaser (1981) presented a list of physics problems to expert physicists and novices and asked them to categorize the problems. Chi and colleagues found that novices sorted the problems by their surface features—for example, whether the problem contained a disk, a pulley, or some other object. The experts, however, tended to disregard surface objects and

classified problems in terms of principles such as Newton's Second Law, the Work-Energy Theorem, or the Principle of Conservation of Energy.

— Experts elaborate on problems, plan solution strategies, and detect constraints that reduce the problem space, whereas novices tend to work on small subproblems, loosing sight of other components. Experts are better able to judge their progress toward problem solving; they tend to evaluate solution paths and monitor success or failure as they go along. Novices often become fixated on particular solution attempts.

— Experts and novices do not differ in terms of memory, but experts remember more information in their specific domain. Chess masters, for example, are no better than novices at recalling the positions of randomly placed chess pieces. When it comes to actual chess positions, however, they remember more accurately than novices (see Chapter 8). When presented with information about their domain, experts remember information in terms of meaningful clusters, whereas novices, lacking the requisite knowledge in long-term memory, do not (see Chapters 8 and 9).

Next, I will describe case studies of problem solving in three content domains: mathematics, computer programming, and political science. These three disciplines are substantially different. Mathematics is a highly formalized body of knowledge that has been accumulated over centuries. It lends itself to abstract and precise representations. Political science, although concerned with age-old issues, is much younger and less formal than mathematics. Computer programming is viewed by many as an applied mathematical discipline though it is less abstract. Programming knowledge includes much concrete information, including tricks and shortcuts.

Mathematics

Few people enjoy mathematics; even routine tasks such as figuring out the tip for a waiter or balancing a checkbook is a chore. All too often we draw a complete blank when doing a mathematics problem. Why is math difficult? Solving numerical problems depends on several components; failure to apply any of them correctly produces erroneous results. The components of mathematical problem solving include understanding the problem and executing the operators necessary to solve it. Understanding means comprehending the words, using parsing strategies, and situational information (see Chapter 11). Understanding results in a mental representation of the problem, often involving a schema. Execution is based on strategic and computational knowledge. The problem solver must be familiar with basic mathematical operations such as addition, subtraction, and multiplication. As is the case with other cognitive skills, component activities must be coordinated to ensure their smooth application.

Understanding. Understanding (Cummins, Kintsch, Reusser, & Weimer, 1988; Kintsch & Greeno, 1985) depends on linguistic competence and, to a lesser extent, computational skills. An example from Kintsch and Greeno (1985) illustrates how important understanding is in solving mathematical problems. Consider the following problem presented to children:

(13.3) There are 5 birds and 3 worms. How many more birds are there than worms?

Children aged 5 to 7 perform poorly on problems such as this one. Nursery school children achieve correct solutions only 17% of the time and first-graders only 63%. Why is children's performance so poor? Do they not understand the mathematical set relations? Or do they fail to properly translate the linguistic expression? Research suggests that the latter is the case. If you change the wording of (13.3) to (13.4), 83% of nursery school children and 100% of first-graders solve the problem correctly.

(13.4) There are 5 birds and 3 worms. How many birds won't get a worm?

The bird and worm example may appear easy to you. However, try to remember some of the word problems you were introduced to in elementary and high school; many had important real-life applications, others were more esoteric. You may remember problems involving speed comparisons, amount-rate calculations, and others that were confusing and frustrating. Whether or not the problem is easy, the student must identify the relevant schema for the problem and map the numerical expression in the problem to the correct quantity. A schema is a prototype of structurally similar problems (Hinsley, Hayes, & Simon, 1977; Kintsch & Greeno, 1985; Mayer, 1985). Consider the following problem:

(13.5) John has 6 cents. Pete has 3 more cents than John. How many cents does Pete have?
$J = 6$ $P = 3 + J$

This was easy. Try (13.6) next.

(13.6) There are six times as many students as professors at this university.

Mayer (1985) asked students to translate (13.6) into an equation. The subjects had difficulties and produced some surprising errors. As many as one-third of Mayer's subjects represented problem (13.6) as $6S = P$, where S stands for student and P stands for professor. Of course, this is an error. The subjects producing this answer reasoned as follows: There's six times as many students, which means it's six students to one professor and this (subject points to 6S) is six times as many students as there are professors (points to P). To solve the problem correctly, the subject must translate problem (13.6) into an instruction or procedure as captured by the following translation: If you want to even out the number of professors, you have to have six times as many professors. This translation leads to the correct equation $S = 6P$.

Hinsley, Hayes, and Simon (1977) listed a set of algebra problems that each conformed to a schema—for example, the River-Current schema, the Area schema, the Interest-Rate schema, or the Amount-Rate schema. The algebra problem mentioned earlier in this chapter, about the candle makers Jones and Smith, conforms to the

Amount-Rate schema represented in the following expression:

(13.7) Amount produced = rate of work × time

If a person is not familiar with the Amount-Rate schema, he would have difficulty solving the problem. He could try to solve it using general problem-solving techniques, but this would take much longer. Understanding includes identifying known and unknown quantities. In this case, the unknown is the number of hours Smith works, typically labeled x. Next, known and unknown quantities are mapped onto the appropriate equation, as shown in the Appendix.

Execution. Execution involves the application of the mathematical operators addition, subtraction, multiplication, and other procedures such as carrying and borrowing. It is what we colloquially refer to as math.

In young children, mathematical operations are often overt. You may have observed younger children adding and subtracting numbers. In kindergarten and grades 1 and 2, they tend to use their fingers to calculate answers. Sometimes they count from one; on other occasions, they count from the larger of the two numbers to be added. For example, in adding 2 + 7, the child counts "7, 8, 9." In subtracting, first- and second-graders often count down. As they advance through elementary school and gain more practice, however, children drop such overt strategies. Over time, children come to associate pairs of numbers with results, much like experts in other domains. Increasingly, retrieval and recognition replace computation. Which strategy the child uses depends on the problem's difficulty (Siegler, 1991). When problems are relatively easy, such as 1 + 2 or 2 + 2, the child retrieves the answer from memory. More difficult problems, such as 3 + 5 and 4 + 5, trigger other strategies, as Figure 13.6 illustrates. The y-axis in Figure 13.6 shows the percentage of errors committed, and the x-axis shows the percentage of problems for which an overt strategy like finger counting was used. These data indicate that the use of overt strategies and errors are positively correlated ($r = 0.91$).

After extensive practice, children form mental representations of arithmetic facts in long-term memory. There are several hypotheses concerning

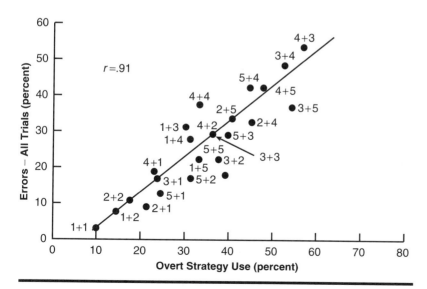

FIGURE 13.6 Children tend to use overt strategies more often as addition problems become more difficult (Siegler, 1991).

the nature of these representations, including the Table Search Model, the Network Retrieval Model, and the Distribution of Associations hypothesis. According to the Table Search Model, single-digit addition proceeds by a look-up in a table, as illustrated in Figure 13.7A. Figure 13.7A includes the numbers to be added at the top and left margins; these are known as operands. The circles represent nodes, which include the summands of two respective operands. Answers are found by starting with two operands and searching for the node where their paths intersect.

The Table Search Model predicts that more links must be passed the larger the operands are— for example, 7 + 8 versus 2 + 3. As a result, such problems take longer to solve. Experimental data bear this prediction out, but only up to a point; solution times for problems with two identical operands, such as 5 + 5, 6 + 6, and so on, do not differ significantly.

The Network Retrieval Model has three sets of nodes: two sets for the operands and one set of results. This is shown for multiplication problems in Figure 13.7B. The nodes in the upper left represent one of the operands of the problem and the nodes in the lower left indicate the other operand. Solutions are shown on the right. Links between operands and answers are direct in this model, unlike the Table Search Model. Each pair of operands—for example, 8 × 3—is uniquely linked to their answer, which is 24 in this case. Note that the pair 6 × 4 has its unique answer 24. The strength of associations differs and retrieval is faster for stronger associations. Problems with small operands and with identical operands are encountered more frequently and therefore solved more quickly. Although the Network Retrieval Model can account for the pattern of correct solutions better than the Table Search Problem, it does not explain error patterns in arithmetic problems.

A third model, the Distribution of Associations hypothesis, is similar to the Network Retrieval Model, except it includes an explanation of how the problem solver commits errors. Errors occur when two operands are associated with both the correct and incorrect results, as shown in Figure 13.7C for the multiplication problem 6 × 8. The links between operands and answers have different strengths. Retrieval of an answer is based on a sampling process of the links between operands and answers. Usually, the strongest link is selected. For example, in Figure 13.7C, the answer, 48, is linked strongest to the problem 6 × 8; its overall selection is more likely than the other solutions. Nevertheless, on a given trial, some other solution might be sampled as the answer, thus producing an error.

Siegler (1988) observed the frequency of error types made by children and found that operand errors are quite common. In multiplying 6 × 8, the child might try to add six 8s, miscount, and actually add seven 8s and produce a 56. Once the association of 6 × 8 and 56 is formed, it may persist well into the high school years and beyond.

Addition of numbers with two or more digits, multiplication, and more complex operations are based in part on declarative representations such as those shown in Figure 13.7. Cognitive psychologists assume that these representations act in concert with procedural representations, such as the production system PLUS described in Chapter 5. Production rules explicitly control arithmetic operations. In the case of addition, for example, the rules embody the knowledge of starting the problem with the left column, shifting columns, setting a carry, and so on. Like declarative knowledge, procedures may be faulty or buggy.

This example shows that problem solving is based on information in memory and illustrates one potential impediment to successful problem solving: If you do not remember basic facts, your solutions are likely to be inaccurate.

Issues in Mathematics.   In recent years, there have been several national campaigns aimed at improving student's mathematical skills. With good justification, the nation has focused on numerical literacy; too many people lack the quantitative skills necessary to interpret simple data and graphs presented in newspaper articles. The mathematics achievement of U.S. high school students ranks near the bottom of industrialized nations of

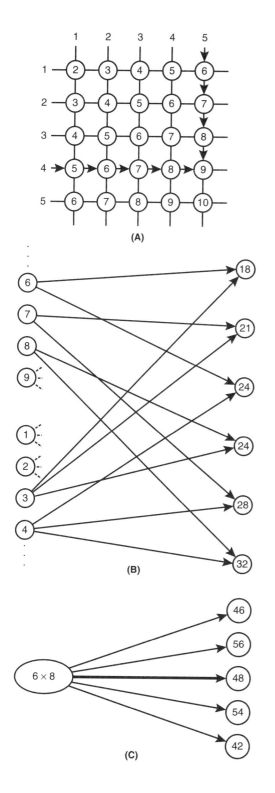

the world; quantitative SAT scores have declined throughout the 1980s. Problems in mathematics achievement in general are related to other issues, including gender differences, math anxiety, and mathematics education.

Schools and colleges have accepted the challenge of improving quantitative skills and increasingly emphasize mathematics education. Colleges and universities have instituted new courses and proficiency tests in mathematics. The debate over numerical literacy has spawned many books and conferences. Although psychologists consider each issue a challenge, we cannot address them here. Let us consider one of them, however: the question of gender differences.

Are There Gender Differences in Mathematics Achievement? It has frequently been claimed that there are gender differences in math performance. Some time ago, both *Time* and *Newsweek* ran stories about an alleged mathematics gene and discussed the possibility that some women lacked this gene and therefore had poorer quantitative achievement. In 1974, Maccoby and Jacklin performed important study comparing quantitative scores for boys and girls of different ages. They found that mathematical performance depended on both gender and age. In the second grade, girls performed better in math, whereas from the sixth grade on, boys did better. Hundreds of comparisons have subsequently been done. Linn and Hyde (1989) summarized many of these results and concluded that the hype about gender differences was much ado about nothing.

— There are few, if any, overall differences in the mathematical abilities of women and men. Differences declined in the 1980s.

FIGURE 13.7 Three models of representing knowledge of arithmetic facts in memory. (*A*) Table Search Model. (*B*) Network Retrieval Model. (*C*) Distribution of Associations Model (McCloskey, Harley, & Sokol, 1991).

— Gender differences have been reported for specific components of mathematics tests; men typically do better on numerical problems applied to sports, science, and measurement, whereas women tend to perform better than men in math problems dealing with aesthetics and interpersonal relations. These differences are very small, however.

— Women tend to score less well on the quantitative SAT than men. Linn and Hyde attributed this to strategic rather than cognitive differences between males and females. Women are less willing than men to guess and to use partial knowledge when answering questions. Linn and Hyde used a multiple-choice question about basketball as an example of gender differences. They noted that the basketball problem can be solved by using a time-consuming algebraic equation, as shown in Table 13.6 or by guessing. Linn and Hyde contended that men tend to know more about basketball and therefore have an advantage in questions like this. Another reason for the SAT advantage of men is that men tend to take more courses in mathematics and that this factor is the best single predictors of test scores in mathematics (Halpern, 1992).

Linn and Hyde concluded that gender differences in mathematics "should be de-emphasized because they are small" (1989, p. 21). Whatever small differences do exist depend on context; the role of education should be to expose male and female students equally to different contexts. Importantly, as Halpern (1992) reminds us, differences *among* women and *among* men are greater than *between* men and women.

Computer Programming

At the introductory and intermediate levels, programming problems are usually well defined, as when you calculate the percentage change between two quantities, compute the average of several numbers, or convert a temperature given in Fahrenheit to Celsius. At the advanced level, in scientific and business applications, problems are less well defined. Although programming can be fun, it is not an easy skill to acquire. Anderson, Farrell, and Sauers (1984) investigated the problem-solving strategies used by beginning students learning to program in LISP, a computer language used in research on artificial intelligence (AI). The students had access to a standard program-

---

TABLE 13.6   Example Item from the 1986 SAT-M

Question:
A high school basketball team has won 40% of its first 15 games. Beginning with the sixteenth game, how many games in a row does the team now have to win in order to have a 55% winning record?
(A) 3
(B) 5
(C) 6
(D) 11
(E) 15

Algebraic Solution:
$$.4 (15) + 1.0 \text{ (Games to Win)} = .55 (15 + \text{Games to Win})$$
$$6 + \text{Games to Win} = .55 (15) + .55 \text{ (Games to Win)}$$
$$\text{Games to Win} - .55 \text{ (Games to Win)} = 8.25 - 6$$
$$.45 \text{ (Games to Win)} = 2.25$$
$$\text{Games to Win} = 5$$

ming text in LISP. Anderson and colleagues used a computer-based tutor to present problems to students, record their solution attempts on-line, and provide them with feedback. Students were asked to write functions to solve relatively simple problems (for example, convert temperatures from one scale to another). The researchers developed a production system within the Act* architecture (see Chapter 5) that mimicked the students' problem-solving and learning protocols. Using such mechanisms as composition, compilation, discrimination, and generalization, the productions changed during the course of learning, presumably reflecting the changes in the programmer's knowledge (see Anderson, Pirolli, & Farrell, 1988).

At the beginning of their training, programming students had difficulty understanding problems. They studied the assignment in the textbook but were confused by the variables used in the procedures and misunderstood the operation of functions the LISP system supplies. Anderson and colleagues said the students' frequent misunderstandings were not surprising, given the Act* theory; the beginning student represents programming problems in declarative form, but procedures are needed to solve the problem. During the initial learning stages, the student must use general productions to solve problems. A general production is one that is applicable to a wide range of problems, independent of domain (see Table 13.5 for some examples). Using general problem-solving heuristics is both slow and error prone. Students also solve problems by analogy, using previous problems as templates for new assignments.

Anderson's production-system simulation mimicked students' performance successfully. Like the students, the simulation initially misinterpreted problems and used general problem-solving productions and analogies. With additional practice, general productions were replaced by production rules specific to LISP functions. Thus, the simulation replicated how a student gains expertise in computer programming by replacing general problem-solving strategies

with domain-specific ones. Simulation programs like Anderson's capture the knowledge of individual learners as they progress. Such programs are used as tutors for instruction in programming and software packages.

Domain-specific strategies include programming schemas of varying complexity. A schema is a stereotypic set of operators and slots for variables (Adelson, 1981; see also Chapter 5). I will illustrate this with the looping schema for adding numbers. This schema includes two elementary schemas: the cumulation schema and the count schema. The cumulation schema adds a new value to the current value, thus replacing the current value with the sum of the current value and a new value as in (13.8). The corresponding Pascal expression is given in (13.9):

(13.8) Current value replaced by current value plus new value

(13.9) SUM : = SUM + SUMMAND;

Other elementary schemas are used for the initialization of variables and for tests of conditions. Schemas include various iteration schemas such as the looping schema and recursion schemas.

Programming schemas are similar to those used in word arithmetic problems. In both cases, the problem solver must identify the appropriate schema, recognize the slots, and fill them with the correct values. Programming schemas not only help produce programs but they also help us comprehend programs written by other programmers (Soloway, Adelson, & Ehrlich, 1988).

Does Knowledge of Programming Help Your Problem Solving? This question raises the classical issue of transfer of training. According to the transfer view, the skill acquired in one domain helps a person solve problems in another domain; there are corresponding components in both disciplines and when you learn one, you have acquired parts of the other vicariously. It was long believed that knowledge of Latin would help a student to become a better thinker in general. A study by Thorndike (1924) questioned this optimistic assessment; students who had taken Latin did no better in general problem solving than other students.

With the advent of computer languages, the transfer issue has been revived and claims are made that learning a computer language helps students solve problems in other domains. Mayer, Bayman, and Dyck (1987) compared the performance of two groups of students on a general problem-solving test. The experimental group learned BASIC during a semester-long course, whereas the control group did not. The BASIC group performed better on problem translation than the control group. In other respects, however, there were no differences between the groups. Similar advantages have been claimed for LOGO learning (Klahr & Carver, 1988; see Chapter 15). Claims of transfer contradict findings in other instances of problem solving, including analogy problems, knowledge-rich problems, and the balance-scale problem (see below). The upshot of the research on transfer is this: When problems are structurally similar and share underlying rules, facilitation has been found (Reber, 1993). On the other hand, it is still open to question whether there is transfer of general problem solving (VanLehn, 1989).

A Case Study from Political Science

Most problems in law, medicine, social sciences, and government are ill defined. To give you a feeling for this class of problems. I have selected a problem from the social sciences (Voss & Post, 1988). Little research has been done on such problems even though many real-life problems are ill defined. Compared to mathematics problems, there is usually little agreement on solutions to social science problems, making consensus building among problem solvers necessary. Our focus here is on the cognitive problem-solving strategies of individual problem solvers.

Voss and his collaborators presented problems such as the following to their subjects (see also Introduction): "Imagine that you are the minister for agriculture in Russia. The crop yield has been low for several years and the country faces severe food shortages. How would you go about increasing agricultural productivity in the country?" Among the subjects were professors of agriculture, political science, chemistry, and a scholar from an Eastern-bloc country. Other problem solvers included college students asked to solve this problem both before and after taking a course on the Russian economy.

After studying the problem for a while, subjects reported their thoughts as they solved the problem. The protocols revealed large differences between experts and novices. Experts devoted much of their time considering the problem's constraints, finding alternative solution paths, and assessing the likelihood that each would succeed. They also looked for historical precedents to understand the reasons for food shortages and sought to justify the solution(s) they proposed. Experts, of course, are privileged; they have the requisite information to elaborate on such problems. One of the expert protocols began like this:

I think as a minister of agriculture, one has to start out with the realization that there are certain kinds of special agriculture constraints within which you are going to work. The first one, the most obvious one, is that by almost every count only ten percent of the land in Russia is arable. This is normally what is called the Blackland in the Ukraine and surrounding areas. And secondly, even in that arable ten percent of the total land surface, you still have climate problems over which you have no direct control. Okay, so that is sort of the overall parameter in which we are working. (Voss, Tyler, & Yengo, 1983)

Novices devoted relatively little time to constraints. Rather, they viewed the problem of food shortages in general terms and explored typical causes for crop failures. Students took this approach even after they had taken a course on domestic issues in Russia. Novices were not entirely ignorant of some specific problems of Russian agriculture, as the following protocol segment indicates:

Old-fashioned methods of farming. So maybe what needs to be done is to introduce newer methods of farming and obviously the people probably need to be educated on how to use these new methods, especially if they introduce new machinery. I remember reading somewhere that on the land that the people own themselves, that crop production is much higher than it was on the state plots. Perhaps if the people could be allocated more benefits from the state land, rather than giving it all to the state, crop production might increase. Maybe the organization of how the crops are planted and harvested is not adequate. Perhaps that should be changed. (Voss, Tyler, & Yengo, 1983)

The student listed possible causes for shortages, including the use of old-fashioned farming methods and machinery and the lack of private land ownership. The student did not, however, consider specific constraints and methods of overcoming them.

When comparing the professor's and the student's protocols, you may comment that the two differ in terms of their expertise on Russian agriculture and in many other respects as well; they also differ in terms of age and general maturity. Voss and colleagues enlisted four chemistry professors to see if age and professional experience would account for the difference in novice and expert problem-solving strategies. Three of the four chemists, although experts in their field, were novices like the students when it came to Russian agriculture. Their proposed solutions were novice solutions; they listed possible causes of food shortages one by one, including problems with irrigation, technology, and food distribution. They failed, however, to examine the bigger picture, constraints, and historical background.

Voss and colleagues simulated the protocol of one of the experts with a production system called PRISM, which was capable of modifying its own productions. The program had three components: declarative knowledge, procedural knowledge, and an executive. The declarative knowledge consisted of a semantic network that embodied the expert's information on Russian agriculture. Activation spread through the network via the executive. Finally, the procedural component included productions to interpret and constrain the

problem. The simulation produced solutions in response to problems that were posed to it and simultaneously noted constraints. For example, when told about food shortages, the program asserted that the crop acreage should be increased and lands privatized, adding the constraint that privatization would violate the prohibition of private property in the past.

Adversarial Problem Solving

Life is full of adversarial situations, whether they are as innocent as a game of bridge or chess, as bitter as a fight between friends, or as lethal as war. These situations involve at least one agent and an opponent, each of whom faces a problem in the sense that it has been defined here: The problem solver seeks to reach a goal state given a set of constraints. However, adversarial problem solving poses a new kind of constraint in that the adversaries pursue the same goal—to win. Each of the players tries to thwart the other's moves in seeking a solution plan of his or her own. Paul Thagard (1992) has examined such adversarial problem solving and cites military strategists going as far back as the ancient Chinese war lord Sun Tzu who pointed out that the essence of warfare is to know the enemy: "If you know the enemy and know yourself, you need not fear the result of a hundred battles. If you know yourself but not the enemy, for every victory gained you will also suffer a defeat. If you know neither the enemy nor yourself, you will succumb in every battle" (Sun Tzu cited after Thagard, 1992, p. 125).

Translating Tzu's advice into practice calls for discovering your enemy's plans while concealing your own. Military leaders often use deception in order to conceal their plans. Perhaps no other military deception has been as spectacular as the invasion of France by Allied forces on D-day in 1944.

In the spring of 1944, the European continent was occupied by Nazi forces, but Britain was still free. It is here that Allied forces assembled for an attack on the continent. Geographically, the closest location on the continent and therefore a likely target for an attack was Calais, France, 20 miles across from Dover, England. However, this was where the defending forces were strongest because Hitler assumed that the Allied forces would attempt a landing here. In planning the Allied landing, General Eisenhower correctly guessed at Hitler's reasoning and anticipated his moves. He feigned attacks on Calais by launching many bombing sorties, increasing the radio traffic among Allied forces opposite Calais, and by building fake bases with fake tanks and guns near Dover. Then, of course, he launched the invasion 200 miles away, across the much wider western part of the English channel at the Normandy beaches. Hitler's troops were not prepared and the rest is history.

Thagard simulated adversarial problem solving on the computer using a neural network program that he dubbed ECHO. In the simulation, the agent (A) constructs a mental model of the opponent (O). This model includes O's representation of A. A's goal is to maximize his information on O and minimize O's knowledge of himself. Thagard simulated the D-day scenario by representing Eisenhower's (A's) and Hitler's (O's) problem space. ECHO included a data base and a neural network. The model accounted for a particular item of evidence, E1, in terms of certain hypotheses, H1 . . . H*n*—for example H1: *The main invasion is at Normandy;* and H2: *The main invasion will be later at Calais.* A hypothesis is connected via excitatory links when it coheres with evidence (or another hypothesis) that it can explain. For example, H2 is consistent with evidence E9 that German agents have reported a buildup of forces in southeast England. Contradictory propositions are represented in the network in terms of inhibitory links.

At the start of a simulation, the activation level of almost all units is typically set to 0. Only the evidence unit—for example, E1—is given an activation level of 1. E1 represents the evidence to be explained. Activation spreads from the evidence unit through the network in successive cycles until all of the units have achieved stable activation values. In the D-day scenario, 78 cycles were required to reach stability; at this point, the hypothesis was strongly activated in Hitler's mind that the Allies will land at Calais rather than in Normandy.

Thagard's ECHO simulation shows how various factors, supporting hypotheses, contradictory hypotheses, and negative evidence are evaluated in parallel and contribute to problem solving in adversarial situations. Thagard claimed that other models of reasoning—for example, Bayesian probability analysis (see Chapter 14)—are less successful in doing so. In order to demonstrate the generality of his neural network approach, Thagard applied the ECHO model to several cases of competitive problem solving from the history of science, including Darwin's theory of evolution, speculations as to why dinosaurs died out, and the competition between Copernicus' versus Ptolemy's view of the solar system.

INTERIM SUMMARY

Solving knowledge-rich problems requires extended practice in a domain, whether it is mathematics, computer programming, political science, or another discipline. Problem solving in mathematics involves an interpretation of the problem and computational skills. Based on his understanding of the problem, the problem solver generates a representation that often includes schema(s). Computational skills make use of arithmetic facts stored in long-term memory. Computer programmers develop a repertoire of schemas, such as the looping schema, that help them automatize programming assignments. A schema is a template that includes operators and slots for variables. Political science problems tend to be ill defined. Political science experts consider constraints and several alternative solutions to a problem, whereas novices list possible solutions without constraints. In general, experts have acquired domain-specific routines of pattern recognition that enable them to solve problems automatically.

CHANGES IN PROBLEM-SOLVING SKILLS

As we have seen, problem solving in specific disciplines is improved by practice. Success depends on moving from laborious computation to pattern recognition. The master chess player has no superior logical, spatial, or mnemonic capacities than the novice. What distinguishes the master from the novice is her ability to spot opportunities on the board that the novice does not recognize. The computer programmer learns a corpus of routines and schemata for recurring problems; the physicist knows abstract principles that underlie different physical phenomena; and the musician acquires a repertoire of perceptual and motor skills after thousands of hours of practice. In each case, the skill has been proceduralized; a body of declarative knowledge is successfully automated. The existence of experts in many domains demonstrates that our problem-solving ability is dynamic; it changes with practice. In this section, we will see that the ability to solve problems changes in other ways as well. There are developmental changes in childhood and changes occurring over the short term that result from learning and coaching.

Developmental Changes

A person's success in every facet of life depends on his or her ability to solve problems. Fortunately, we are all endowed from infancy with an ability to solve problems and overcome obstacles; a story told by Waters (1989, p. 7) about 2-year-old Georgie will illustrate: "Georgie wants to throw rocks out the kitchen window. The lawn mower is outside. Dad says that Georgie can't throw rocks out the window because he'll break the lawn mower with the rocks. Georgie says 'I got an idea.' He goes outside, brings in some green peaches that he had been playing with, and says: 'They won't break the lawn mower.'" Georgie's goal was to throw objects outside, and when his father's verdict not to throw stones created an obstacle, he quickly removed the obstacle by throwing peaches.

Development brings about an improvement in problem-solving strategies without the intervention of parents or teachers. Independently of domain, a child's problem-solving ability develops with age. According to Piaget, the child (and adolescent) moves through four stages of development that take him from a sensory to a rational and abstract processing mode. Information-processing psychologists try to determine the cognitive processes underlying the improvement in problem-solving abilities with age. According to Siegler (1991), a child's ability to encode problem components and plan improves with age. He attributed these changes to improvements in memory and content knowledge. As a result, a child gains cognitive resources and uses them more efficiently with age. Not surprisingly, the speed at which a child solves problems of all sorts increases with time. This is true for classification, matching, analogy, and other problems (Kail, 1991).

An example of developmental changes in problem solving involves the problem of the balance scale (see Figure 13.4). A number of washers is placed on selected pegs of a balance scale and a child is asked to predict which side will go down. The solution to the problem involves considering both the weight of the washers and their distance from the fulcrum. Children under age 5 encode only weight as a variable, ignoring distance. Although their solution may be faulty, as they approach adolescence, children begin to base their judgment on both dimensions. The child's changing solution pattern is captured by the set of production rules in Table 13.7.

Of course, the children couldn't be asked whether they used these rules and if so which one(s). So, Siegler devised a procedure to detect the rule set used by children on critical test trials. Two test trials are illustrated in Figure 13.8. Seeing the arrangement in Figure 13.8A, the child

TABLE 13.7   Siegler's Four Rule Sets (see Anderson, 1990)

Rule set 1:
A   IF the number of weights is greater on side 1
    THEN side 1 will go down.
B   IF the number of weights on the two sides are
    equal
    THEN the two sides will stay in balance.

Rule set 2: Rule A from rule set 1 plus
C   IF the number of weights on the two sides are
    equal and the weights are farther from the
    fulcrum on side 1
    THEN side 1 will go down.
D   IF the number of weights on both sides are
    equal and the distances from the fulcrum are
    equal
    THEN the weights will balance.

Rule set 3: Rules C and D from rule set 2 plus
E   IF the number of weights is greater on side 1
    and the weights are as far or farther from the
    fulcrum on side 1
    THEN side 1 will go down.

Rule set 4: Rules C, D, and E from rule set 3 plus
F   IF the number of weights on side 1 is greater
    and the weights are as far or farther from the
    fulcrum on side 2
    THEN multiply weight and distance for each
    side and compare the products.

should say that the scale balances. Each rule set in Table 13.7 would generate the correct response 100% of the time. Figure 13.8B shows a more complex problem. On the right side, there are four washers on the first peg, and on the left side there are two washers on the second peg relative to the fulcrum. The correct response is "balance". Using rule sets 1 and 2, however, the child would predict that the right side goes down. Using rule set 3, his accuracy would be at the chance level. Only knowledge of rule set 4 would produce the correct response. Siegler found that children younger than age 5 used rule set 1, children younger than 9 years used rule set 2 or 3, and 17-year-olds used

rule set 3 reliably. Rule set 4 was used by very few students. Even after learning about balance scales in a science course, only 20% of the students used rule set 4. The students in the course used a pan-type scale rather than a beam scale as in Figure 13.8. When the balance-scale problems were reformulated for the pan scale, the students were able to solve them. Siegler commented, "This limited generalization is, unfortunately, the rule rather than the exception in problem solving; similar findings have arisen in many domains" (1991).

Improving Your Problem-Solving Skills

To become an expert is easier said than done; it takes years of practice and effort. Usually, a person is an expert in just one domain and not in others. Einstein, the genius in physics, is reported to have been unable to balance his checkbook. Here, we will discuss improving one's ability to solve well-defined problems, including puzzles and numerical problems over the short term.

Planning and Monitoring.   One of the things cognitive psychologists have learned from research on expertise is that experts learn to consider the constraints of a problem and evaluate operators against obstacles. Even if you do not know a problem domain very well, you can safely assume that there are constraints; one of your first tasks, therefore, should be to identify them. Often, there are several alternatives to overcoming a

FIGURE 13.8   Test trials to evaluate use of rule sets to solve balance-scale problems (Siegler, 1991). (*A*) In balance-type problems the correct response is "balance." (*B*) In conflict-balance type problems, "balance" is also correct. However, this problem is more difficult, as explained in the text.

constraint; try to list alternatives and evaluate each before you commit much time and effort to any one of them. This stage of problem solving is the planning stage.

Once you have committed yourself to a particular solution path, monitor the success of the actions you take. Are you getting closer to the goal? Is there any external feedback you can use? Once you determine that a path will not succeed, abandon it. Do not stick to it and waste time and money just because you have put effort into it, like the investor who hangs onto a stock that has gone sour, the scientist who continues to subscribe to a disconfirmed hypothesis, or the businessman who believes his Edsel will capture the market. To be sure, sometimes endurance helps, but you must monitor it. Observing one's own problem-solving efforts is a **metacognitive** activity. Such metacognitive skills improve as a result of development and training in a discipline.

Choosing a Good Representation. A representation is a rendering of a problem in a different medium, but it remains faithful to all essential aspects of the problem. Representations are used because they can be more readily manipulated than the original problem. The mutilated chessboard problem mentioned in the introduction (Kaplan & Simon, 1990) is a good example of how important it is to choose an appropriate representation. Kaplan and Simon made the point that problem solving not only involves searching *within* a representation but searching *for* an appropriate representation—an essential part of problem solving. The choice of a representation is problem solving at a more abstract plane, at a metacognitive level.

Consider a diamond search to illustrate how the search for a representation differs from a search within a representation. Imagine a diamond is hidden somewhere in a large, dark hall. In order to find the diamond, you could search the room inch by inch and leave your success pretty much up to chance. After giving the problem some more thought, you might decide to abandon the blind search and try something different.

Rather than searching for the diamond, you search for a light switch. When you have found the light switch and turned on the light, you have practically found the diamond. Such re-representation of the problem is what Kaplan and Simon mean by searching for a representation.

Before continuing to read, try to solve the mutilated chessboard problem on page 352. You will find that it is not easy to find the answer, even if you were to use an actual chessboard and a set of 31 dominoes. People usually try to place the dominoes on the 62 remaining squares of the chessboard. However, this is time consuming and frustrating because there is no easy solution. A very patient graduate student in chemical engineering devoted 18 hours to this problem, writing 61 pages of notes and still didn't solve the problem! On the other hand, if you think about the problem in a different light, if you choose a new representation, you can solve it more quickly. In order to do this, you should think about the color of the squares. Alternatively, think of the squares represented as bread or butter. This is what Kaplan and Simon (1990) asked one group of subjects to do; these subjects solved the problem fastest.

A solution: The original chessboard has 64 squares, 32 white ones and 32 black ones. Cutting diagonally opposed squares involves removing two squares of the same color. Assume the two squares removed are white, leaving us with 30 white squares and 32 black squares. Each of the 31 dominoes covers exactly one white and one black square. As a result, one cannot cover the mutilated chessboard with the 31 dominoes. The essence of the solution is to recognize the parity between black and white, bread and butter, or any other pair of opposites. Once two of a kind are deleted, parity is lost and the chessboard cannot be covered with the dominoes.

The mutilated chessboard problem becomes solvable once the problem is represented in terms of the color of the squares. This is the creative step the problem solver must take. For every problem, more or less appropriate representations exist. The solution to the problem becomes obvious when the appropriate representation is chosen (see also Kintsch & Greeno, 1985). In order to find the appropriate representation, one needs to restructure the problem in order to look at it from different perspectives.

Encoding and Re-encoding of the Problem.

Encoding is the cognitive process whereby input is interpreted in light of a person's knowledge in memory. Perceptual stimuli are encoded and recognized (see Chapter 4); sentences are encoded and understood (see Chapter 11); and problems are encoded. However, as in perception, the first encoding in problem solving is not always the correct one. Consider the following problems from Sternberg's (1986) book *Intelligence Applied:*

— An airplane crashes on the U.S.-Canadian border. In what country are the survivors buried?
— According to the U.S. Constitution, if the vice president of the United States should die, who would be president?
— A man who lived in a small town married 20 different women in that town. All of them are still living, and he never divorced any of them, yet he broke no laws. How could he do this?
— In the Thompson family, there are five brothers, and each brother has one sister. If you count Mrs. Thompson, how many females are there in the Thompson family?

Please try to solve as many of these problems as you can before reading the solutions below.

— Consider the airplane crash again, especially the second sentence. It includes the word *survivors*. Of course, a survivor is alive and cannot be buried. The problem is difficult for many because the first sentence leads them down the garden path of typical airplane crashes involving dead people rather than survivors.
— The next problem discusses the death of the vice president, not of the president. If the vice

president dies, the president continues in his or her job.
— The man is a minister. Notice that the word *married* has two senses, one of which refers to conducting the ceremony of matrimony. This is the sense of *married* used in this problem.
— The answer to the Thompson problem is *two*. The women in the family are Mrs. Thompson and her only daughter, who is a sister to each of her five brothers.

It is relatively easy to be fooled by questions like these. Answer, for example, the question, How many animals of each kind did Moses take on the ark? Many people will say two, although they know perfectly well that it was Noah's ark, not Moses' (see Chapter 9).

The lessons to be learned from these examples is that understanding involves proper encoding. Do not get entrenched in the scenario suggested by a single word or phrase.

Gestalt psychologists have used the term **functional fixedness** to describe an individual's inability to consider alternative perspectives. One of the difficulties in problem solving involves liberating oneself from a familiar set, as Gestalt psychologists argue. Consider again Duncker's (1945) candle problem in Figure 13.3. Did you find a solution to this problem? You were given a box of thumbtacks, a matchbox, and a small candle and asked to use these objects to support the candle on a wall. The correct solution involves the following steps: Remove the thumbtacks from their box, use a couple of thumbtacks to affix the box to the wall, light a match to soften the bottom end of the candle, and place the candle on the box. According to Duncker, difficulties with this problem stem from functional fixedness: We perceive the box of thumbtacks in terms of its *usual* function as a container rather than perceiving its *potential* function as a candle holder. Sternberg (1981) considered the ability to overcome functional fixedness an important attribute of successful problem solving and of intelligence in general. This theory of intelligence as nonentrenchment is included among the changing definitions of intelligence in Box 13.2.

Coaching Helps, But Not a Lot. In the context of testing, the term *coaching* is used to describe practice with testlike questions. When objective tests such as the SAT were first introduced early this century, it was believed that certain tests would measure verbal, mathematical, or logical aptitude. Aptitude is a relatively permanent intellectual faculty acquired over the long term, as opposed to knowledge acquired through coaching in brief cramming sessions. There is a long-standing debate around the issue of coaching (e.g., Owen, 1985); commercial coaching companies boast that "thousands of our grads have raised their scores 150, 200, even 250 points. And more!" Investigators have demonstrated that coaching does help test performance in several subjects, although not by a large margin (Kulik, Bangert-Drowns, & Kulik, 1984; Messick & Jungeblut, 1981): A 40-hour coaching program improves SAT-M scores by 25 points, whereas SAT-V scores increase only by about 5 points (Smyth, 1990).

Part of the coaching effect may be attributable to motivational rather than cognitive factors; repeated exposure to timed tests habituates the student to the testing situation and reduces test anxiety. Thus, for a considerable investment in time and money, students can improve their SAT-M scores by a small amount. The improvement is relatively small because the tests are designed to measure the long-term effects of education. Should you take coaching courses? If you have the time, money, and will be satisfied with small gains, you should. Coaching *does* help performance in achievement tests; these tests measure a person's knowledge in specific subjects, including history and the social sciences.

INTERIM SUMMARY

The ability to solve problems changes through extended practice, developmental increases in memory and content knowledge, and short-term training. We illustrated developmental changes in problem solving using the balance-scale problem. Problem-solving skills are improved by employing such metacognitive strategies as

---

Box 13.2

Changing Views of Intelligence

Intelligence is the capacity to solve problems. Intelligence tests such as the Wechsler reflect this view; they are problem oriented, including mostly well-defined problems. The traditional psychometric approach to intelligence was concerned with IQ measurement and validity. Test results were evaluated relative to external criteria, both academic achievement and job performance. Cognitive psychologists, on the other hand, emphasize processes and processing differences between intelligent and less-intelligent individuals rather than issues of measurement. Better encoding speed, faster retrieval speed, and more efficient allocation of working memory resources are usually cited as sources of the principal differences (Hunt, 1985).

The basic view of intelligence has also broad-ened. Intelligence is still defined in terms of its adaptive character and restructuring ability, called *nonentrenchment* by Sternberg (1981). However, the role of practical intelligence is included and it is acknowledged that academic and practical intelligence are not necessarily correlated. Some individuals have excellent grades and score well on formal IQ tests but do not achieve much by the world's standards. Other people do not test well but are, nevertheless, street-smart; they come out on top in the so-called real world, as the title of the book by Roberts (1991) indicates. *Straight A's Never Made Anybody Rich!* In spite of these differences, the key to success is seeing problems, both practical and academic, from a new perspective (Sternberg, 1986)

planning and monitoring, by devoting sufficient time to your choice of a representation, and by encoding the problem well. You can overcome functional fixedness by restructuring problems. Note that there are limits to short-term training; often there is little transfer between problems, and although coaching on aptitude tests helps, it does not help a lot. You would be well advised, however, to devote much time to studying for achievement tests.

———■———

CONCLUSION

A problem exists when one wants to reach a goal given certain constraints. The problem solver must search for an appropriate representation that highlights the important properties of the problem and then search within the representation for a path from the initial to the goal state. In well-defined problems, the initial state and the goal are explicit from the outset. In ill-defined problems, these states must first be identified. Knowledge-lean problems require relatively little domain knowledge; knowledge-rich problems require much. Problem solving was the focus of this chapter; you should remember that it occurs in many contexts, including learning, comprehension, composition, and reasoning. In each case, representations of information are manipulated to meet a goal.

Theories of problem solving have been dominated by symbolic processing approaches, especially production system formalisms like Anderson's (1983) Act*, Langley's (Langley et al., 1987) PRISM, and Newell's (1990) SOAR. In the future, we will see more connectionist theories of problem solving like Holyoak and Thagard's (1989) ACME. Thus far, the ACME framework has been applied to analogy problems; when a connectionist model is proposed for the Tower of Hanoi Puzzle, long a bastion of symbolic-processing theories, it will be a great leap for the connectionist approach.

Training is necessary to become a proficient problem solver in a domain. Indeed, one of the promises of education is to enhance students' problem-solving abilities, both in specific disciplines and in general. Although there are limits to the transferability of problem-solving strategies across disciplines, the many references to expertise made in this chapter demonstrate that education does fulfill its mission for specific disciplines.

APPENDIX _____

Cryptarithmetic Problem.   The solution to this problem is: A = 0, B = 9, D = 8, E = 5, M = 1, R = 2, S = 6, and T = 7. Knowing the solution, can you reconstruct a path to find it?

Geometric Analogy.   We solve the geometric analogy in Figure 13.2 by first discovering the rule used to transform figure A into figure B. Then we look for rules to convert figure C into each of the candidates *x*. Finally, we look for the C-to-*x* rule that maps to the A-to-B rule. The relation between A and B is one of external deletion, the circle on the left of the larger figure has been deleted. Next, we observe the five C-to-*x* pairs. In the pair C-to-1, there is an external deletion; in C-to-3, we detect a double deletion; in

C-to-4, we see an internal deletion and a transformation; and in C-to-5, there is an external deletion and a transformation of the internal figure. (The last two could be described differently.) Comparing the C-to-*x* relations with the A-to-B relation, we find that only C-to-1 corresponds. The answer, therefore, is that A is to B as C is to 1. Geometric analogies like these are used in many psychometric tests, such as the Raven Test, in order to assess general intelligence as opposed to verbal or quantitative intelligence.

Medical Diagnosis.   I do not expect you to diagnose the disease of the patient described. Nor do you need to know such technical terms as *antecu-*

bital fossa, jugular venous distention, and *splenomegaly.* I included the problem to illustrate problem solving in medicine. Incidentally, the patient contracted bacterial endocarditis from a contaminated needle, possibly from intravenous drug use (Patel & Green, 1986).

ENDNOTES

1. There are 3^{64} states. This is 3,433,683,820,292,512, 484,657,849,089,281 states!

2. Chapter 14 lists additional impediments to successful reasoning and problem solving.

REASONING AND CHOICE

PREVIEW

People form beliefs and make choices using inductive reasoning; one extrapolates a hypothesis from a set of data, infers a rule governing a series of numbers, or learns a concept that defines instances by common attributes. According to the hypothesis-testing theory of concept learning, the learner identifies an attribute as the concept and tests this hypothesis against successive stimuli. When attributes are not perfectly associated with a concept, as is true for natural concepts, the learner forms a probabilistic category. We will discuss prototype and connectionist approaches to category learning and review applications from biology, meteorology, and economics. Scientific discovery involves interpreting existing data in new ways. We will see that graduate students and even a computer model—the production system BACON—can rediscover Kepler's laws and other scientific laws.

Making decisions and judging the frequency of events are both based on inductive reasoning as well. We estimate probabilities using a number of heuristics, such as the availability heuristic, rather than formal statistical rules such as the base-rate rule and the conjunction rule. According to rational decision theory, a decision maker has full knowledge of alternative options, their probability, outcomes, and utility. According to cognitive theories, decision making is subject to processing limitations at the encoding, comparison, and output stages. Decisions are influenced by the frame in which options are presented and the type of output response to be made. Decision makers also choose strategies for deciding, figuring out how to process the dimensions that characterize available options. The chapter concludes with a section on decision analysis, an applied discipline, providing tools to represent the full spectrum of a decision.

INTRODUCTION

For the philosopher Descartes (1596–1650), thinking was the essence of existence; he said *I think, therefore I am.* Judging by a simple frequency measure, Descartes was right; we think all the time. We think when we remember a friend, compose a paper, solve a problem, or express an expectation, as in *I think it will rain.* Several chapters of this text are concerned with thinking; this chapter will focus on inductive reasoning and choice. Inductive reasoning is based on experience with a set of facts. Inductive reasoning shapes our beliefs and choices in many situations. Consider these cases:

- Eva is a 1-year-old who uses the word *moon* for many moon-shaped objects: a ball of spinach, the letter D, the dial on a dishwasher, and, of course, the moon (Bowerman, 1977).
- A doctor chooses between two treatments for a patient—surgery or radiotherapy—knowing from experience that surgery may be more effective, but there is a chance the patient will not survive.
- Remember the time you decided not to see a movie sequel—say, *Police Academy XI*—because you didn't like its predecessor, *Police Academy X?*
- Finally, look at this series of numbers and guess the next number in the series: 1, 2, 4, 8, 16. Is the next number 18, 24, or 32?

In each of these cases, we extrapolate a pattern, concept, or generalization, and apply it to new instances. People often generalize, although there is no guarantee that our generalizations will hold. For instance, the surgeon knows 20 patients with similar problems, but no 2 patients are identical; *Police Academy X* was bad, but *Police Academy XI* could be terrific.

Like thinking, making choices is a basic cognitive operation. When we recognize a face, remember a word, or spend time on activity X rather than Y, we have made a choice. The study of decision processes is a natural topic for cognitive psychologists. Researchers in psychophysics, learning, and memory analyze decisions. Psychophysicists trace a person's response to stimuli of varying strengths. They want to know under what conditions a stimulus is detected. Detection depends on attributes of the stimulus—its strength and salience—and on the person's decision criterion, or his willingness to say *yes* or *no.* A person's decision criterion is influenced by the cost of the response; if a response involves little or no costs, we are willing to make it; otherwise, we are cautious (Chapter 3).

Learning theorists also examine choice responses in discrimination learning and time allocation studies. According to equilibrium theory, organisms seek a bliss point and allocate time to activities in order to maintain equilibrium (Chapter 7). In this chapter, we examine choice from both an economic and a psychological point of view. We will see that economists favor a theory of rational choice in light of outcomes, whereas psychologists emphasize mental strategies of decision making. For the most part, our reasoning and choice processes serve us well; however, there are fallacies in reasoning and decision making.

Do People Reason Logically?

Since Aristotle's days, formal logic was considered as the royal road to clear thinking and deductive reasoning was viewed as the foundation of logic. In **deductive reasoning,** a conclusion follows with certainty from premises provided that certain rules of proof are followed. These rules must adhere to specific forms; content is irrelevant. This gives logic its aura of abstractness and makes us shy away from it. Logicians have developed many rules of proof that bear such names as *modus ponens, modus tollens, hypothetical syllogism, constructive dilemma, absorption,* and so on. We'll consider only the first two: *modus ponens* and *modus tollens.* Table 14.1 gives the formal definitions of these two rules and a couple of examples for each. The def-

TABLE 14.1 Two Formal Rules of Proof

Modus Ponens
If *p,* then *q*
p

Therefore *q.*

(1) If John is smart, then the population of the earth will stabilize.
John is smart.

Therefore the population of the earth will stabilize.

(2) If Napoleon is our first president, then the Pacific will dry out.
Napoleon is our first president.

Therefore the Pacific will dry out.

Modus Tollens
If *p,* then *q*
not q

Therefore not *p.*

(3) If the sun shines, then the day will be beautiful.
The day is not beautiful.

Therefore the sun does not shine.

(4) If it is raining, then John carries an umbrella.
John carries no umbrella.

Therefore it isn't raining.

initions include the letters *p* and *q* to represent statements whose content is immaterial for the proof. In expression (1), for example, the statement that John is smart is expressed by *p,* and the statement that the population of the earth will explode is represented by *q.* Formal expressions (1) through (4) are valid, although they may not appear very sensible.

Cognitive psychologists have examined to what extent people use such formal rules in evaluating certain expressions. They presented subjects with expressions written according to proof schemas like those in Table 14.1. Subjects read the statements and had to decide their validity. They had no difficulty with expressions that reflected the *modus ponens* (e.g., 1 and 2), but made over 40 percent mistakes with problems of the *modus tollens* type (e.g., 3 and 4) (see Rips & Marcus, 1977).

People have difficulty applying the *modus tollens* in other tasks as well. Consider the selection task (Wason & Johnson-Laird, 1972); in this task, subjects are shown four cards that have a letter on one side and a number on the other. They are also given a conditional statement and are asked to test the truth of the statement by selecting specific evidence that would either confirm or disconfirm it. For example, Wason and Johnson-Laird presented their subjects with four cards that showed symbols such as

A D 4 7

The conditional statement to be tested is given in expression (14.1).

(**14.1**) If a card has a vowel on one side, then it has an even number on the other side. The subjects were asked to say which of the cards must be turned over in order to determine whether the statement was valid or not. Before reading on, try to solve this card problem.

To solve this problem correctly, *two* cards must be turned over: *A* and *7.* Turning over card *A,* there could be either an odd or even number on the other side. An odd number would disconfirm rule (14.1) outright. An even number, however, would be ambiguous unless you turn over the *7* as well. A consonant on the other side of card *7* would confirm expression (14.1), whereas a vowel would disconfirm it. Checking card *7* is based on the *modus tollens,* as expression (14.2) illustrates. To make (14.2) valid, there must be a consonant on the other side. If there is a vowel, both expressions (14.2) and (14.1) are false, regardless of what is on the other side of card *A.*

(**14.2**) If a card has a vowel on one side, then it has an even number on the other. There is no even number on one side. Therefore there is no vowel on the other.

In sum, an odd number behind card *A* or a vowel behind card *7* would falsify rule (14.1). Most of Wason and Johnson-Laird's subjects picked either card *A* or cards *A* and *4;* very few selected card *7*. Selecting card *4* is incorrect; even if there is a consonant on the other side, it would not falsify the rule. Wason and Johnson-Laird's (1972) subjects either did not know the proof procedures or did not use them.

Subjects made correct responses, however, when the selection task in (14.1) was cast in a familiar context. Instead of using letters and numbers, experimenters used names of beverages and ages (Griggs & Cox, 1982). On one side of each card was the name of a beverage a person was drinking; on the other side was the person's age. Study these four cards and test the expression (14.3).

(**14.3**) If a person is drinking beer, she must be over 19.

Beer Coke 22 16

Subjects correctly selected *Beer* and *16*. Their reasoning was based on schematic knowledge of permission rules (e.g., Cheng, Holyoak, Nisbett, & Oliver, 1986). According to the generic permission rule, a specific condition must be met in order to allow a certain action. For example, you must be of a certain age to drink beer, vote, or drive. This time, subjects thought of testing the possible failure of the rule by turning over the card *16 years of age.* If it had shown *Beer,* statement (14.3) would be invalid. Because the *Beer–16* problem was expressed in terms of a real-world context, subjects found its solution easier than Wason's abstract selection task (see Chapter 5).

A range of tasks indicates that subjects' reasonings are based on content and context rather than on the abstract syntactic rules of logic (see Cheng & Holyoak, 1985; Cheng, Holyoak, Nisbett, & Oliver, 1986; Holyoak & Nisbett, 1988; Watson & Johnson-Laird, 1972). Of course, this does not invalidate the principles of formal logic. Logicians emphasize the normative aspects of reasoning, how people *should* reason.

Cognitive psychologists emphasize the descriptive aspects of reasoning—how people *do* reason.

INDUCTIVE REASONING

In **inductive** reasoning situations, one tries to discover a hypothesis consistent with a body of data. Psychologists devise research paradigms to study inductive reasoning. In this section, we will discuss two of these: series completion and category learning. In both paradigms, the subject is given a set of items and asked to form a rule describing them. In series completion, he sees a list of items, induces a rule, and predicts the next item. In concept learning, the experimenter presents a set of items with different attributes, one of which defines the category or concept. In the real world beyond the research laboratory, it is rare that attributes and categories are perfectly correlated; rather, their relation is probabilistic. We will study probabilistic category learning as well as applications of category learning.

Series Completion

Detecting a rule in a series is common in scientific discoveries and in art. The astronomer discovers the relationship between the period of satellites and their distance from the sun, and the musician discovers the beauty in a theme. Psychologists have used three types of completion problems in their experiments: letter series, series of single numbers, and series of paired numbers. Kotovsky and Simon (1973) presented their subjects with letter sequences such as the following:

    CDCDCD___
    AAABBBCCCDD___
    URTUSTUTTU___

How would you continue each series? One must detect the rule used to generate the pattern of letters and extrapolate it to predict successive letters. Each of the three letter sequences consists of periods or recurrent patterns of elements. The sequence CDCDCD consists of two-letter periods. The two other series consist of three-letter periods. Next, we focus on the relation of letters in corresponding positions of each period. This is easy for the first sequence; the letters are identical for each position of each period, they are always CD. In the second series, the corresponding letters progress alphabetically across periods, ABCD. The third series is more complicated; the relation between letters across periods differs: the first and third letters are identical, U___T, and the middle letter progresses alphabetically, ___R___, ___S___, and ___T___.

The set of rules we can use to generate sequences of letters is limited because the alphabet is limited. Number series, however, represent a rich domain for continuation rules (Pellegrino, 1985). Here are some number series:

64, 64, 64, 64, 64, 64, ___
3, 7, 11, 15, 19, 23, ___
22, 22, 21, 21, 20, 20, ___
72, 43, 90, 71, 47, 85, 70, 51, 80, ___

Study each sequence and try to induce the rule generating the sequence before reading on.

Below, I reproduce each sequence on the left and the rule that generates it on the right.

64, 64, 64, 64, 64, 64 ___	Identity
3, 7, 11, 15, 19, 23 ___	One addition (+4)
22, 22, 21, 21, 20, 20, ___	One identity, one subtraction (−1)
72, 43, 90, 71, 47, 85, 70, 51, 80, ___	One subtraction, one addition, one subtraction (−1, +4, −5)

The length of the rule tells us how complex it is and how much our memory is taxed when we infer the rule. The first series, 64, 64, . . . , is the simplest, involving only the identity relation and nothing more. In the second sequence, the rule is still easy: One simply adds a 4 to the current digit. The third sequence involves sets of two identical elements each; one produces the next set of two by subtracting 1 from each previous number. The final sequence is more complex, involving sets of

three digits, each of which is changed by a different magnitude. The rule is as follows: (1) subtract 1 from the first digit of each set, (2) add 4 to the second digit, (3) subtract 5 from the third digit, and (4) apply steps (1) through (4) repeatedly to successive sets of three digits. In order to discover this rule, one has to keep more items in memory than for the previous three.

Holzman, Pellegrino, and Glaser (1983) found that the probability of discovering a rule decreases with its complexity and working memory load. The researchers presented 100 series problems to college students and to children from 8 to 11 years old. Figure 14.1 shows their results. The abscissa indicates the memory load, and the ordinate shows the percentage of correct solutions. For both groups of subjects, the proportion of correct solutions decreased as a function of rule complexity but it did so more for children than for adults.

Finally, consider a series of paired numbers, as in Table 14.2. Can you generate a numerical expression that shows the relation of these pairs? Set A will require some time, but many students arrive at the correct relation, namely that the ratio of m^3 to n^3 is 1. Don't despair if you fail to

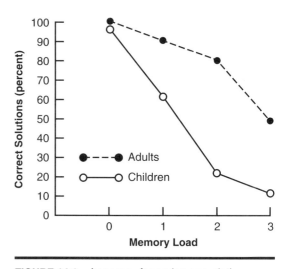

FIGURE 14.1 Accuracy for series completion problem decreases as the memory load increases (Holzman et al., 1983).

TABLE 14.2 Series of Paired Numbers

A.	*m*	*n*
	1	1
	4	8
	9	27
B.	*m*	*n*
	36	88
	68	225
	93	365
	142	687
	484	4332

come up with an expression to account for the B pairs; the correct expression involved is one of the most illustrious scientific discoveries in history. We will return to it in our case study of scientific discovery.

The set of letter and number series considered thus far conformed to relatively concise and simple rules. It is well known that people are remarkably adept at acquiring *arbitrary rules* of their native language but they are usually not aware of their achievement. Native speakers acquire the grammar of their language implicitly without formal instruction and without being aware of having learned them.

Researchers have investigated implicit grammar learning by using artificial miniature languages and artificial grammars. Typically, letter strings such as *PTVV* and *TSXXTVP* are used to represent the sentences of the language. In grammatical strings, the sequence of letters is governed by specific transition rules (see Figure 9.8), whereas in ungrammatical strings, letters are scrambled randomly. It is not surprising that people are better at learning and recalling grammatical than ungrammatical strings. What is surprising is that they are not aware of any structural differences between the types of strings (Reber, 1993).

Concept Learning

Concepts are the basic elements of cognition—the "coinage of thought," according to Johnson-

Laird and Wason (1977). A concept represents the set of attributes shared by members of a class; for example, balls are round, birds fly, and fish swim, or at least most of them do (see Chapter 5). Philosophers were the first to consider how people learn concepts and categories; psychologists continue this quest. Psychologists were inspired by the conditioning paradigm. Pavlov (1927) demonstrated that when the sound of a bell was regularly followed by meat, dogs began to salivate to the sound. The regular pairing of bell and meat produced an association between the sound and salivation—a simple case of induction. Organisms also discriminate between reinforced and nonreinforced stimuli and between informative and less informative events. Concept formation is a complex kind of discrimination learning (see Chapter 7). Experimenters studying concept formation present sets of stimulus figures that vary along several dimensions, and assign labels to the sets according to a rule not known to the subject. Through study of the stimulus-label combinations, the subject arrives at a rule. Figure 14.2 shows three such concepts.

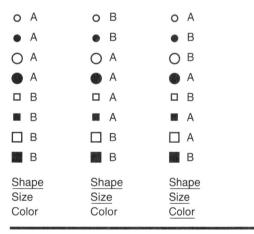

FIGURE 14.2 Concepts defined by one, two, or three dimensions. (*Left*) The concept is defined by the shape dimension. (*Middle*) This concept is jointly defined by shape and size of the stimuli. (*Right*) This concept is defined by three dimensions: shape, size, and color.

There are eight figures varying along three dimensions (size, color, and shape), each having two values (large versus small, black versus white, and square versus circle). All combinations of these yield eight figures (2^3). There are two responses, A and B. The assignment of stimuli to responses varies in complexity, thus creating easy and difficult concepts. In the left column of Figure 14.2, the concept is defined by the shape dimension: All circles are labeled A and all squares are labeled B, regardless of the other dimensions. This is the easiest concept. In the center column, shape and size are relevant but color is irrelevant. Large circles and small squares are labeled A, whereas large squares and small circles are labeled B. The third and most difficult concept is found in the column on the right. Here, all three dimensions are necessary to define the concept: A stimulus is labeled A (1) when it is circular and small and white, or circular and large and black, or (2) when it is square and small and black, or circular and large and white. All others are labeled B. Bruner, Goodnow, and Austin (1956) found that concepts are harder to acquire when more dimensions are used to define them (see also Chapter 8).

Research on Concept Formation. According to **hypothesis-testing theory,** learners generate hypotheses to express the relation between stimuli and labels, and then test their hypotheses against the data (Bruner, Goodnow, & Austin, 1956). Hypotheses change according to the feedback learners receive after each response. Levine (1966) devised a clever way of finding out what hypotheses subject used. He used a blank-trials procedure, as illustrated in Figure 14.3 and the following instruction (adapted from Levy & Ransdell, 1988). In this experiment, you will see pairs of letters, such as

Notice that there are two letters, two sizes, two colors, and that one letter is on the left and the other is on the right. Every pair you see will be as different as these. One of these letters is designated "correct." When you see a pairing of two

Trial Number	Stimuli	
1	L	V
2	L	V
3	V	L
4	V	L
5	L	V
6	L	V
7	L	V
8	V	L
9	V	L
10	L	V
11	V	L
12	V	L
13	L	V
14	L	V
15	V	L
16	V	L

FIGURE 14.3 Stimuli used in Levine's (1966) blank-trials procedure. There are four dimensions with two attributes each, as explained in the text.

stimuli, indicate which one *you* think is correct. On some trials, you'll be given feedback; on others, there is no feedback.

This problem includes four dimensions with two attributes each:

— Position: left versus right
— Color: black versus white
— Size: large versus small
— Letter: L versus V

During each series of 16 trials, only one of the eight attributes is correct; the learner has to find this attribute. Starting with eight hypotheses on the first trial, the learner is assumed to discard hypotheses when given feedback. Experimenter feedback is provided on trials 1, 6, 11, and 16; the others are blank trials. The subject makes a choice on every trial, thus revealing her hypothesis. The pattern of responses on nonfeedback trials reveals the subject's hypothesis. Assume, for example, that her initial hypothesis is the color white. She therefore chooses left on trial 1 in Figure 14.3 and is told that this choice is wrong. Assume further that she eliminates the hypothesis white and chooses black. Then she would pick the black letters on trials 2 through 6. She would pick right on trials 2, 3, and so on. With successive feedback, subjects usually are able to eliminate some hypotheses, much as you do in playing such games as *Clue* or *Mastermind.*

According to Levine (1966), a perfect subject would cut down the number of hypotheses by half on each feedback trial and remember every feedback received. This is indicated by the function labeled "perfect memory" in Figure 14.4. On the other hand, a subject who remembered no feedback would retain all of the hypotheses, as indicated by the no-memory function. In Levine's experiment, subjects were closer to the perfect than the no-memory subjects. This result is reflected in the solid line in Figure 14.4.

In his research, Levine also found that subjects adopt a "win-stay, lose-shift" strategy. They tend to shift hypotheses when told they are wrong; otherwise, they stick with a hypothesis. The subjects could afford to retain several hypotheses at a time because the stimuli were relatively simple; the obtained curve would shift closer to the no-memory function if we used more complex stimuli.

Real-World Categories. The research paradigms of Bruner and colleagues (1956) and Levine (1966) exemplify hypothesis-testing theory. There are a variety of models of hypothesis testing, however, and this diversity has made the hypothesis-testing approach to concept learning a great success. If this is true, why doesn't the sec-

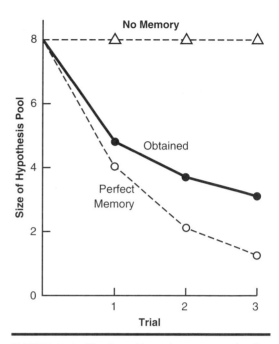

FIGURE 14.4 Number of hypotheses entertained by subjects after each of three feedback trials (Levine, 1966).

tion on concept learning end here? There is much more to tell; the stimuli used in the hypothesis-testing approach were clear-cut; concepts tended to be neatly defined, and though the definitions of concepts might be difficult, they are unambiguous. The complexity of natural concepts is of a different nature, however. Here, concepts and features are not perfectly correlated but fuzzy. Natural concepts have been represented in terms of **prototypes,** or exemplars. A prototype represents the typical features of the members of a category. Instances exhibit varying degrees of similarity with the prototype. For example, a robin is more similar to the prototypical bird than a penguin (see Rosch, 1975; Chapter 5). Categories are also characterized by the variability among their instances. Since Rosch's (1975) pioneering work, much research on real-world categories has been published. In this section, I will describe how category membership influences inferences about features.

Category Membership Overcomes Physical Similarity. A category enables us to infer properties from a perceptual pattern. We see a snake and infer that it can bite; we see a bird and infer that it lays eggs. How people categorize objects depends on their age. Infants like Eva, who was mentioned earlier in the chapter, group objects by physical similarity. By the time they are 4 years old, however, children group objects in functional terms. Adults base feature inference on category membership rather than on physical similarity. Consider research results from Gelman and Markman (1986). They presented their subjects with choice tasks such as the one in Figure 14.5.

This figure shows three animals—a flamingo, a bat, and a fictitious bird the researchers called *blackbird;* it was similar to the bat. College students were told specific anatomical facts about the flamingo and the bat, as indicated by the statements in Figure 14.5, and then asked where the blackbird's aortic arch was located. Although physically similar to the bat, subjects inferred that the blackbird's aortic arch was on the right; in this case, category membership overruled physical similarity and subjects conferred common properties to the instances.

Categories Are Defined by Their Variability. We categorize instances based on their similarity as well as their variability. Rips (1989) asked subjects to guess whether an object that measures 3 inches in diameter is a quarter or a pizza. Although the 3-inch diameter is closer to the size of a typical quarter than a typical pizza, the subjects chose pizza as their answer. They did so because they knew that the diameter of a quarter is constrained, whereas that of a pizza is not. Categories are defined by the variability of their instances as well as common properties. Knowledge of variability guides our reasoning about instances of categories. For example, if you are introduced to a member of the Barratos tribe who happens to be obese, you would not conclude that all members of the Barratos tribe are obese. On the other hand, if you are given a

This bird's heart has a right aortic arch.

This bat's heart has a left aortic arch.

What does this bird's heart have?

FIGURE 14.5 Stimuli used to demonstrate category-based inferences (Gelman & Markman, 1986).

sample of the fictitious element Floridium and told it is a good conductor of electricity, you would assume that other samples of the element also conduct electricity (Holyoak & Nisbett, 1988). Understanding variability is part of probabilistic or statistical reasoning—a topic we will return to later.

Probabilistic Category Learning. We have seen that category membership enables us to infer the properties of an instance. In many cases, properties and categories are linked probabilistically; this is true of concepts in economics, law, and medicine. Unemployment, high inventories, and low profits are associated with recessions, but not always. Diseases are associated with sets of symptoms; however, not all symptoms need be present. Inferring the category from its features, like diagnosing a disease from symptoms, is probabilistic.

Making a Diagnosis: Bayes's Theorem versus the Delta Rule. Using medical diagnosis as the experimental context, Gluck and Bower (1988) studied probabilistic category learning. They told their subjects of a fictitious world where only two diseases exist: commonitis and raritis. When a person becomes sick, he suffers from one of these two diseases, never from both nor from any other. As its name implies, commonitis is the more common disease. In fact, it is three times as common as raritis. The base-rate probabilities[1] of commonitis and raritis are $p(C) = 0.75$ and $p(R) = 0.25$, respectively. In this simple world, there are only four symptoms: (1) a bloody nose, (2) stomach cramps, (3) puffy eyes, and (4) discolored gums. Symptoms are present in the two diseases to different degrees, as shown in Table 14.3. The table includes the conditional probabilities of a symptom given the disease. Thus, a bloody nose occurs in 69% of all patients afflicted with raritis. On the other hand, only 23% of all commonitis patients have bloody noses. As in our more complex world, not every patient

suffering from a disease has every symptom associated with the sickness.

Subjects were given patients' medical charts and asked to diagnose their disease. For example, subjects were told that a patient, Joe, has a bloody nose and stomach cramps; they were asked to diagnose whether Joe had commonitis or raritis. Subjects were given as much time as they needed to study each chart and immediate feedback after making their diagnosis. There were 250 trials. Gluck and Bower's experiment was similar to a traditional concept formation study; subjects were given features, anywhere from one to four symptoms, they had to form a hypothesis, and were given feedback. After completing 250 trials, subjects were asked to estimate the probability that a patient with a specific symptom had one or the other disease.

Bayes's Theorem. Before looking at the results, let's consider two sets of predictions. The subjects' job was to predict the probability of a disease given a symptom. Mathematicians call such probabilities *posterior probabilities,* defined as the probability that a hypothesis is true given certain evidence. There is an objective way to calculate posterior probabilities mathematically using Bayes's theorem. Using the terms *symptom, s,* and *disease, D,* Bayes's theorem is expressed in equation (14.4) as:

(14.4) $P(D|s) = \dfrac{P(s|D) \times P(D)}{P(s|D) \times P(D) + P(s|D_o) \times P(D_o)}$

$P(D|s)$ is the probability of the disease given a symptom. $P(D)$ is the base-rate probability of the disease. $P(s|D)$ is the conditional probability of the symptom given the disease, and $P(s|D_o)$ is the conditional probability of the symptom given the *other* disease. Equation (14.4) yields the posterior probabilities of either disease given each symptom. Let's calculate the probability of the rare disease given the first symptom, a bloody nose. All we need to do is enter known values into Equation (14.4) as follows:

(14.5) $P(R|s_1) = \dfrac{(0.69) \times (0.25)}{(0.69) \times (0.25) + (0.23) \times (0.75)} = 0.50$

TABLE 14.3 Association between Symptom and Disease in Gluck and Bower Study

Disease	Symptom			
	1	2	3	4
Commonitis	0.23	0.35	0.46	0.69
Raritis	0.69	0.46	0.35	0.23

The probability of the rare disease given symptom 1 is 0.50. Substituting the corresponding values for commonitis, we find $P(C|s_1) = 0.50$ as well. So, the difference between the probabilities of raritis and commonitis given symptom 1 is 0. The difference between the probabilities of raritis and commonitis given the four symptoms is graphed in Figure 14.6A. This is our first prediction.

Connectionist Prediction. Another prediction is based on a connectionist model (see Chapter 6). The model has five units: four input units and one output unit. Each input unit corresponds to one of the four symptoms. A unit is activated when the symptom is present. The output unit produces an output of 1 when the model di-

agnoses the rare disease. There are four weights modulating the connections between input and output units. The output is computed according to equation (14.6) (see equation (6.1) in Chapter 6).

(14.6) $\text{Output}_j = \Sigma \, (\text{input}_i \times \text{weight}_{ij})$

The network is trained according to the delta rule with immediate feedback after each trial. The delta rule is an error-correcting rule that adjusts the connection weights, w_{ij}, in proportion to the error made on a given trial, as expressed in equation (14.7).

(14.7) Change in $w_{ij} = l_r \times a_i \times \text{error}$

The error is the difference between the target output and the actual output on a trial. The

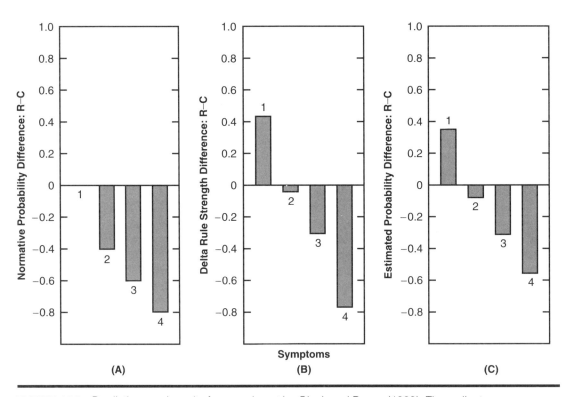

FIGURE 14.6 Predictions and results for experiment by Gluck and Bower (1988). The ordinate indicates differences in estimated probability differences: Raritis versus Commonitis. The abscissa represents symptoms 1 through 4 (*A*) Predictions based on Bayes's theorem. (*B*) Predictions based on connectionist model. The ordinate reflects the strength difference at the output unit for the rare and common diseases given a symptom. (*C*) Subject's responses.

coefficient l_r represents the learning rate, and a_i represents the input activation on the trial. Receiving a sequence of input trials with different patterns of symptoms and immediate feedback, the connectionist model learned according to the delta rule and produced the predictions in Figure 14.6B. These are different from the objective predictions, especially for the first symptom. Given the first symptom, the output unit was more likely to be active and thus predict the rare disease.

And what were the subjects' diagnoses? Gluck and Bower's results are shown in Figure 14.6C; they are similar to the connectionist prediction. Like the connectionist model, subjects overestimate the occurrence of raritis when given the first symptom. People do not behave like mathematicians; rather, their diagnosis is implicitly based on the delta rule. Subjects do not fully consider the low base rate of the rare disease. As shown in Table 14.2, the bloody nose is representative of the rare disease, therefore, subjects are swayed by this symptom (we will see more of such base-rate neglect below). Physicians better assess the base rate probabilities of diseases and learn Bayes's theorem. If you are headed for medical school, be sure to study it!

Predictiveness of Cues. According to the Rescorla-Wagner (1972) rule, the relative validity of a cue rather than its absolute validity determines the cue's associative effectiveness in animal conditioning (see Chapter 7). Wagner and colleagues (1968) demonstrated the relative validity of one cue, a light, by presenting it in compound with another cue, two tones, in a design that included a correlated and an uncorrelated condition. So, there were two compound stimuli, T_1L and T_2L.

In the correlated condition, reinforcement was perfectly correlated with the tones so that the T_1L compound was reinforced with a probability of $p = 1.0$ and the T_2L compound was not reinforced, $p = 0.0$. In the uncorrelated condition, both compounds had a reinforcement probability of $p = 0.50$. Note that the light component, L,

had the same reinforcement probability in both conditions, $p = 0.50$.

The critical feature of the design was that the light cue had an equal probability of reinforcements in both the correlated and uncorrelated conditions. Nevertheless, the relative validity of the light was less in the correlated condition because the tone was the better predictor of reinforcement. On the other hand, in the uncorrelated condition, the light was as good a predictor as the tone. In accordance with the Rescorla-Wagner rule, the light had become a stronger cue in the uncorrelated than in the correlated condition: It elicited more conditioned responses.

Baker and colleagues (1993) observed that college students exhibited the same behavior pattern in an experiment whose stimulus contingencies were analogous to Wagner's conditioning experiment. The students played a video game in which they tried to move a tank safely by watchful enemy spotters set to destroy the tank if they discovered it. As in the animal experiment, the experimenters manipulated the predictiveness of two types of cues: the tank's camouflage and the presence or absence of an airplane.

The researchers rigged the video game to mimic the correlated and uncorrelated conditions of Wagner's experiment asking subjects to estimate the effectiveness of both cues at various points during the experiment. The researchers found that cue predictiveness depended on its relative validity, as in the animal study. The point of both studies is that organisms successfully assess the degree to which each cue predicts significant environmental events and select the cue that does the best job.

INTERIM SUMMARY

In concept formation studies, the learner is shown a sequence of multidimensional stimuli and formulates a hypothesis as to which instances belong together. Levine's (1966) blank-trial procedure reveals that subjects usually maintain several hypotheses at one time and tend to shift hypotheses when one is disconfirmed. In category learning, categories and properties are usually linked probabilistically. Human category learning can be successfully modeled by connectionist networks consisting of a layer of input units and an output unit. Simulated medical diagnosis experiments by Gluck and Bower (1988) showed that subjects learn to associate symptoms and diseases according to the delta rule. Subjects also emphasize representative cues, ignore base-rate probabilities of diseases, and selectively attend to the more predictive of two cues.

Applications of Category Learning

Category learning occurs everywhere; without it, we would be unable to make inferences about instances or generalize from known to new cases. Category learning is the basis of pattern recognition; a stimulus is recognized given a set of features. Often, the features are visual; a dermatologist studies skin rashes, an ophthalmologist inspects the retina, and a radiologist examines x-rays. In each case, a visual pattern is interpreted and some diagnosis formed. We will review three applications of category learning, one each from biology, meteorology, and economics. Botanists use visual and other features to differentiate plants as genera and species. Meteorologists use visual and other features to classify storms and spot tornadoes. Finally, economists use abstract numerical features to chart the business cycle.

Discovering a New Genus in Biology.
Botanists specializing in taxonomy collect plant specimens and determine if they are members of an existing or new genus. Two botanists described a new genus of seaweed, *Calliclavula trifurcata* (Searles & Schneider, 1989), found in the Atlantic Ocean off the coast of North Carolina. This red seaweed is a member of the division of *Rhodophyta,* and was classified in the order *Ceramiales,* family *Ceramiaceae,* and group *Griffithisiae.*

One of the major features that distinguishes *Calliclavula* in its family is the presence of three successive branches. The botanist notes similarities and distinctions of the collected specimen relative to other genera, basing the identification on primary defining features. An interesting decision the botanist must make is whether to designate an unknown specimen as a new species or to include it in an existing species. Occasionally, the existing species characteristics need to be broadened to account for subtle differences in the now included specimen.

Zoological classifications pose similar problems. Consider the case of the guinea pig. It is not a pig, and some doubt it is a rodent because its protein structures differ significantly from those of rats and mice (Graur, Hide, & Li, 1991).

Tornado Spotting.
A tornado is the most violent of all windstorms. Although it usually lasts less than a minute in any one location, it can be destructive and lethal. Therefore, it is critical that people know how to spot a tornado. The U.S. Federal Emergency Management Agency (FEMA) has a training program for tornado spotters. Prospective spotters are given a checklist and shown films and pictures in order to be able to categorize tornadoes. The FEMA checklist (1983) gives the following features of tornadoes:

- They tend to occur on warm and humid days.
- Winds rotate at high speeds, usually in a counterclockwise direction.
- A tornado resembles a whirlpool with a pale cloud surrounding it.
- Near the ground, the tornado is dark from dust and debris.
- The path of a tornado is about an eighth of a mile wide.

The FEMA manual also lists exceptions: Sometimes a tornado's path is a mile wide, sometimes tornadoes occur in cool weather, and sometimes a roar is heard. Tornado spotting is an essential skill necessary to warn people living in tornado territory of impending danger.

Tracking the Economy. The level of a nation's income fluctuates in cycles of recession and expansion. Tracking these cycles is a multimillion-dollar industry. Large businesses, banks, and government agencies forecast trends in the economy. Economists assemble arsenals of indicators to predict economic activity, including the following:

— Change in inventories
— Housing starts
— Average work week
— Corporate profits
— New orders for durable consumer goods
— Changes in the money supply
— Wholesale price index
— Unemployment rate

Except for the last, these indicators show down trends during a recession and up trends during expansion. The difficulty for forecasters is that these indicators rarely move in unison and often give false signals. From our point of view, indicators represent features, and labels like recession and expansion, are categories.

Each of the preceding three applications represents a case of inductive category learning. Specific attributes are associated *probabilistically* with a category, whether it is a species, a meteorological event, or a stage in the business cycle. Connectionist network models are well suited to simulate learning of such probabilistic associations. Attributes of the event correspond to input units of the network and its output represents the categorization, prediction, or diagnosis. Learning takes place by cumulative adjustment of the connection weights between input and output units—for example, as in the Gluck and Bower (1988) study (see also Chapter 6). Connectionist expert systems have been developed for diverse applications, whether they assess the credit worthiness of bank customers or attribute back pain to such etiologies as nerve root compression and spinal pathologies (Bounds, Lloyd, Mathew, & Waddell, 1988; Gallant, 1988). Whether human expertise is best captured by connectionist networks, a rule-based system, or some other formalism remains for future research. There is little doubt, however, that successful categorization requires training and expertise.

CREATIVITY AND DISCOVERY

When we think about creativity, we do not think of tedious hypothesis testing. Rather, we think of Mozart, who wrote *Don Giovanni* in one day; Einstein, who discovered the theory of relativity at age 26, or the chemist Kekule, who invented the Benzene ring during a dream in which the compounds chased each other and came to look like a snake catching its own tail see Figure 14.7. Creativity is frequently thought of as exclusive—as if it were a special organ only geniuses possess.

Careful study of creativity shows, however, that insights rarely stem from sudden flashes or dreams. On the contrary, artists and scientists work very hard; Einstein worked on problems of relativity for 10 years before he published his influential paper on the subject. Mozart wrote music every day; he often had trouble sleeping because his ideas kept him awake. Kekule worked at the problem of organic compounds, including benzene, for several months before he arrived at his representation.

Self-reports offer few clues about discovery and innovation. For example, Goodfield (1981) describes the reflections of Anna Brito, an

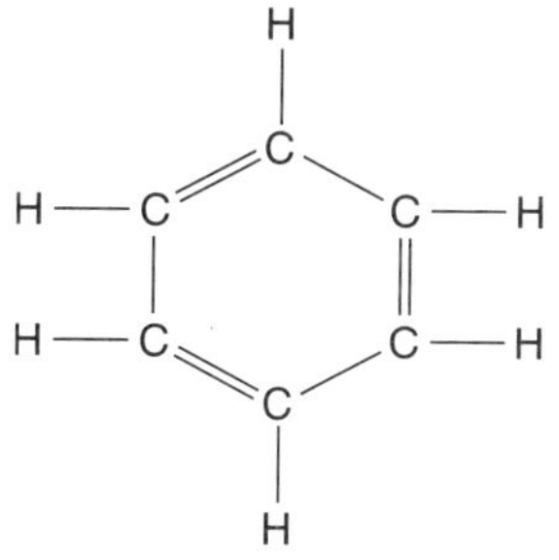

FIGURE 14.7 Kekule represented Benzene, C_6H_6 as a ring. Benzene is a liquid carbohydrate used in drugs, perfumes, and dyes.

important immunologist, on her own thought processes. Brito had the feeling of "working within the deserts of thought, like those fantastic spaces in the pictures of Max Ernst or Salvador Dali. There is emptiness, then suddenly a signal." From a psychological perspective, what a creator reports is anecdotal evidence that rarely reveals underlying processes (Ericsson & Simon, 1980). Creative processes tend to take a long time. Like Einstein and Kekule, Brito worked at her immunological research projects for several weeks before a solution appeared. After moments of sudden insight, she performed many tests to undergird her discoveries.

To be sure, creativity generates something new. Psychologists have many formulations to describe productive thinking. Gestalt psychologists speak of a restructuring of cues (e.g., Koehler, 1929); Bruner says the creative person goes beyond the information given; Robert Sternberg characterizes creativity as breaking the bounds of entrenched habits and beliefs. In plain English, an innovator finds new ways of doing things. A driver stuck in the middle of nowhere is creative when she fixes the carburetor with a clothes hanger. A chef is creative when he makes a raspberry souffle with nougat truffles. Even animals can be creative: Koehler's (1929) chimpanzee, Sultan, invented a tool after some trial and error by joining together two short sticks to retrieve a banana that was out of reach.

Many consider creativity unique and surprising; as a result, creativity does not lend itself easily to research. Nevertheless, creativity has attracted the curiosity of researchers, including Galton, Koehler, Simon, Langley, and many others. Sir Francis Galton (1870) conducted a study on creativity and published his results in a book entitled *Hereditary Genius*. He identified over 800 well-known musicians, writers, scientists, and painters, and investigated their family trees. He wanted to find out if genius is inherited. Among Galton's geniuses was his own cousin, Charles Darwin. Galton found that the incidence of eminence in a field did run in families and concluded that creative genius is inherited. Sons of

famous people tended to be eminent; nephews and first cousins were less likely than sons to be famous but more so than randomly selected individuals. Interesting as his data are, they do not prove conclusively that genius is inherited. Members of a family share a common social environment as well as a genetic background. Their social class and status tend to be similar; children of eminent persons are exposed to a wide range of ideas, to interesting individuals, and to the concept of creation.

Kepler's Third Law: A Case Study of Scientific Discovery

Until the fifteenth century, the view of the planetary system was geocentric; the earth was considered the center of the universe with the sun, moon, planets, and other stars rotating around the earth in perfect circles at uniform speed. Based on his observation of the stars, Copernicus (1473–1543) rejected this geocentric view and proposed instead that the sun forms the center of the solar system, and that the planets, including the earth, rotate around the sun. Kepler (1571–1630) and other astronomers refined the observation of planetary movements. Kepler concluded that the path of planets is not circular but elliptical, with the sun located in one focus, and that planets do not orbit the sun at a constant speed. After additional research, Kepler discovered a rule predicting the time it takes a planet to rotate around the sun, a planetary year. This rule became Kepler's third law: A planetary year increases in proportion with the distance of the planet from the sun.

Kepler gleaned the exact relation from the data available in 1618. They are shown in Table 14.4. Kepler studied these numbers to find the relation among them.

Unfortunately, we can't ask Kepler how he discovered his third law, but we can present the data he had available to experimental subjects. Qin and Simon (1990) did exactly that (see also Langley, Simon, Bradshaw, & Zytkow, 1987). Qin and Simon had 14 subjects who were undergraduate and graduate student science majors.

TABLE 14.4 Planets, Their Distances from the Sun, and Planetary Years

Planet	Distance	Period
Mercury	36	88
Venus	68	225
Earth	93	365
Mars	142	687
Jupiter	484	4,332

Note: Distance is expressed in millions of miles. The period, planetary year, is expressed in terms of earth-days (24 hours)

The subjects were shown the data in Table 14.2B, which are identical to those in Table 14.5. They were asked to build a formula describing the relationship between the data. They were given a calculator and asked to think aloud. They were not told, however, that these data described the facts about the planetary system.

Of the 14 students, 4 succeeded in rediscovering Kepler's third law; the others failed. Remarkably, the successful students required only one hour to make their discovery! They did not search randomly, but applied heuristic rules like *Try to find a trend in the data, Select a function type, Draw a graph,* and *Transform the data.* The successful students found the following relationship between *m* and *n* in Table 14.2B:

TABLE 14.5 Productions in the BACON System

(P1) IF the values of a term are constant

$\rightarrow$

THEN infer that the term always has that value.

(P2) IF the values of two numerical terms increase together

$\rightarrow$

THEN consider their ratio.

(P3) IF the values of one term increase as those of the other decrease

$\rightarrow$

THEN consider their product.

The cube of *m* is proportional to the square of *n*. This is equivalent to Kepler's third law: The cube of a planet's distance (D) from the sun is proportional to the square of its planetary year (P). Kepler expressed this mathematically as: D^3/P^2 = constant.

Is there anything mysterious about discovering Kepler's third law? If 4 of 14 students discovered it within one hour, probably not; yet in 1618, it took Kepler to discover it. Qin and Simon (1990) analyzed their subjects' response patterns and their protocols and found that many of them conducted two interdependent searches: They searched for rules and they searched for data. Rules are functions accounting for the data, and data represent instances to evaluate the hypothesized rules.

Because it was possible to describe the heuristics and processes leading to the discovery of Kepler's law, it was a logical next step to ask: Could a computer come up with the law? The answer is yes, a computer program called BACON discovered Kepler's law. The program is a production system named for the British philosopher Sir Francis Bacon (1561–1626).

BACON Discovers Kepler's Law

I will explain how BACON discovered Kepler's law using the data in Table 14.2A. The data are reproduced below. They describe the distance and period records for three planets and they obey Kepler's law where the constant is 1.

Instance	Period	Distance
Planet 1	1	1
Planet 2	8	4
Planet 3	27	9

Trace of One of BACON's Program Runs. BACON uses five productions, including the three productions in Table 14.5. The program gathers data and tries to match any applicable productions to the data. When a match occurs, the production is triggered. A simplified program trace looks as follows:

BACON requests a new instance: Planet 1 is given as the current instance.

BACON asks "What is D?" Answer 1.0

BACON asks "What is P?" Answer 1.0

BACON requests a new instance: Planet 2 is given as the current instance.

BACON asks "What is D?" Answer 4.0

BACON asks "What is P?" Answer 8.0

BACON requests a new instance: Planet 3 is given as the current instance.

BACON asks "What is D?" Answer 9.0

BACON asks "What is P?" Answer 27.0

Having collected the data, BACON starts its reasoning processes. First, it notices that both D and P increase. So production P2 is triggered and the ratio of the two numbers of each pair is computed as term D/P and entered into BACON's working memory. I enter a new column to the right of the distance column.

Instance	Period	Distance	Term D/P
Planet 1	1	1	1
Planet 2	8	4	0.5
Planet 3	27	9	0.333

Next, BACON examines the relation among terms in the Distance and the D/P columns. Because D increases as D/P decreases, production P3 is triggered. This rule multiplies D and D/P, yielding the product D^2/P. It is added to working memory, as reflected by the new column below.

Instance	Period	Distance	Term D/P	Term D^2/P
Planet 1	1	1	1	1
Planet 2	8	4	0.5	2
Planet 3	27	9	0.333	3

Comparing terms D/P and D^2/P, BACON notes that one increases and the other decreases. So, P3 applies again. The product of D/P and D^2/P is D^3/P^2. It is included in the right-most column below.

Instance	Period	Distance	Term D/P	Term D^2/P	Term D^3/P^2
Planet 1	1	1	1	1	1
Planet 2	8	4	0.5	2	1
Planet 3	27	9	0.333	3	1

Now the production P1 matches because term D^3/P^2 is constant for the three planets. This is equivalent to Kepler's third law (see Langley et al., 1987).

The goal of the BACON program is to discover regularities in a set of data. BACON uses production rules that collect the data, proposes functions as hypotheses, and tests the hypotheses much like human subjects do. The BACON approach to creativity is strictly computational.

Not everyone can be persuaded that creativity is entirely computational or inductive. Computer programs such as BACON are data driven; they extrapolate laws from existing data, but they cannot tell us why a particular set of data is interesting and where to look for the data. Gigerenzer (1991) added to the inductive view of discovery by noting that human beings make discoveries not only based on data but also on tools, including methods and instruments. The invention of the clock prompted astronomers to view the universe as an intricate clockwork. In cognitive psychology, tools have become metaphors of the mind; the computer metaphor has fundamentally influenced the field and has inspired a new framework for research, the information-processing framework. This framework has led to new theories, from pattern recognition to problem solving, and to many new ideas about which data to collect, from latencies to hit and false alarm rates (see Chapter 1).

Becoming an Experimenter. Given that the progress of science depends on the scientist's ability to formulate hypotheses, to test them in experiments, and to evaluate the evidence, it is important for cognitive psychology to investigate how people come to use each of these skills. Klahr, Fay, and Dunbar (1993) conducted a study in which middle school students and adults were asked to conduct experiments using a programmable video game. The subject faced a screen that showed a spaceship that could be programmed to move by manipulating a limited set of keys. For example, there were arrows to indicate the direction of the movement, numbered keys to indicate the distance of a move, a home key to return the spaceship back to base, and a GO key to start the program. Using these keys, the subject could write LOGO-type commands to move the spaceship.

After gaining some practice with this task, the researchers introduced a new key labeled RPT. Subjects were told that they should figure out the function of the new key whose correct syntax was RPT N. In other words, the RPT function required a numerical argument. The researchers suggested to the subjects a sample hypothesis—for example, *Repeat the entire program N times* or *Repeat the last N steps once.* The subjects were then to test the hypothesis by writing programs. By design, the sample hypothesis was always wrong. This forced subjects to search for the correct hypothesis.

As expected, adults fared much better in this reasoning task. Children found it difficult to come up with hypotheses or to think of a program to test hypotheses. Adults were more successful at both skills: (1) searching for hypotheses and (2) searching for programs suitable to test the hypotheses. The key to success is to coordinate these two types of searches.

Expertise and Creativity

Knowing where to look for data is a matter of expertise. As in problem solving, expertise is the source of achievement in discovery. Mozart, Einstein, Kepler, and Brito were authorities in their disciplines. They developed a rich body of declarative and procedural knowledge. The composer knows a multitude of musical themes, tempos, and forms. Mozart (1756–1791) grew up in a musical home, imbibing music from his first days; he wrote his first symphony when he was 8 years old, but composed his most inspired works after age 20. In his short life, Mozart composed almost 100 masses, operas, and symphonies, and an additional 500 pieces of music. When he did not compose, he played music, listened to music, and thought music (Gardner, 1982).

Unlike Mozart, Einstein (1879–1955) exhibited no early signs of greatness. If there was anything unusual about his childhood it was the fact that he learned to speak rather late and was withdrawn as a youngster. Once introduced to the sciences, however, nothing could stop Einstein. He devoted himself to physics with single-mindedness, considering everything else secondary, including family, academic work, and societal conventions. Einstein became obsessed with physics and worked on the nature of light, gravity, and wave mechanics, publishing his *On the Electrodynamics of Moving Bodies* in 1905. This essay of 9,000 words was based on 10 years of research. It was an "affront to common sense," according to the *London Times,* yet it revolutionized physics (Clark, 1971).

According to Ericsson and Charness (1994), the expertise of a person in a domain depends on the amount of disciplined practice the person has accumulated in the specific skill. Creative genius is rooted in expertise, but not every expert is a genius. Other qualities are needed. Students of discovery such as Gardner (1982; 1993), Hayes (1978), and Perkins (1988) have listed a few of these qualities: independence of mind, tolerance of uncertainty, and a willingness to experiment and to try again after failure. A combination of cognitive skills acquired through practice and personal values promotes creativity.

INTERIM SUMMARY

Creativity generates a new representation from existing components. A creative act presupposes much prior work, even if a creator experiences it as a sudden occurrence. Discovery is based on extrapolating a rule from data. For example, Kepler described the relation between the distance of planets from the sun and their rotation period. Students and a computer program, BACON, rediscovered Kepler's and other laws using such discovery heuristics as *look for a function* and *transform the data.* The computational approach to invention illuminates discovery processes; it does not, however, explain where data come from.

Expertise in a discipline is required to know what data to select. Creative persons also exhibit such qualities as tolerance for ambiguity and they are willing to think what others consider impossible.

———■———

JUDGMENT AND CHOICE

Reasoning about Probabilities

Even if you are unaware of it, actions you take rest on probability estimates. You reason probabilistically whenever you expect an event will or will not occur. For example, when you drive to work, you expect the car to start; when you leave work for the day, you expect to find the car where you parked it; and so on. On the other hand, you do not expect that a meteor will descend upon your university or that the sun will not rise next Monday. We place odds, make bets, and offer predictions about all sorts of events, and make decisions based on those expectations. Usually, our intuitive expectations serve us well; our expectations are rarely violated. The story is different when uncertain outcomes are involved, when the information available to us is limited, and when the context is unfamiliar. Then we commit fallacies of judgment without even knowing it. Cognitive psychologists have uncovered many statistical fallacies in experiments. We'll discuss some of these fallacies, including violations of the base-rate rule and the conjunction rule, and see how the availability heuristic and gambler's fallacy lead to erroneous reasoning (Tversky & Kahneman, 1974).

Base-Rate Rule.   Subjects were given personality sketches of an imaginary person drawn from a set of 100 people. The experimenters manipulated the composition of the set: One group of subjects was told that the set contained 30 lawyers and 70 engineers (the engineers' group); the other group of subjects was told that the set contained 70 lawyers and 30 engineers (the lawyers' group). Both groups were given a sketch of Jack, a man with traits we typically associate with engineers:

(14.8) Jack is a 45-year-old man. He is married and has four children. He is generally conservative, careful, and ambitious. He shows no interest in political and social issues and spends most of his free time on his many hobbies, including home carpentry, sailing, and mathematical puzzles.

The subjects' job was to decide whether the person described was a lawyer or an engineer. If subjects were influenced by the base rate of lawyers and engineers in the reference sample, the number of subjects rating the sketch as an engineer should be smaller in the lawyers' group than in the engineers' group, but this was not the case. Subjects in both groups voted Jack overwhelmingly as an engineer; they were persuaded by the sketch and by stereotypes about the typical engineer rather than by base-rate information.

The base-rate rule says: When you sample a member, x, from a population of two subsets, A and B, the probability of the member, $p(x)$ being an A is equal to the proportion of As within the population. So, if you have a population of 100 people, including 30 lawyers and 70 engineers, and you draw 1 person at random, the probability is $p = 0.30$ that he or she is a lawyer and $p = 0.70$ that he or she is an engineer.

Another factor contributed to subject error in the experiment: use of the **representativeness** heuristic. This heuristic compares an event to a prototype, and if the two are found similar, the event is considered more likely. Because the sketch of Jack included traits representative of engineers, subjects believed him to be an engineer (Tversky & Kahneman, 1974). We encountered similar base-rate neglect and the representativeness heuristic in the section on category learning. Subjects based their diagnosis of a disease on a symptom highly representative of the disease without remembering that the disease itself was relatively rare.

Conjunction Rule.   In another judgment study, subjects received descriptions like the following:

(14.9) Linda is 31 years old, single, outspoken, and very bright. She majored in philosophy.

In college, she was involved in several social issues, including the environment, the peace campaign, and the anti-nuclear campaign.

Subjects were then asked: Which of the following is more likely?

Linda is a bank teller.

Linda is a bank teller and is active in the feminist movement.

Subjects rated the second statement to be more likely, even though there are more bank tellers than feminist bank tellers. Remember—some but not all bank tellers are feminists. This is illustrated by the Venn diagram in Figure 14.8. The two circles represent the population of active feminists and bank tellers, respectively. The shaded area represents the group of individuals who are both tellers and feminists. Tversky and Kahneman (1983) attributed the conjunction fallacy to the representativeness heuristic. Their research on the categorization of objects and events indicates that people store information in terms of its representativeness or typicality. For example, a robin is more representative of the category *bird* than is a duck. It is natural for subjects to evaluate the probability of an event by its representativeness. Tversky and Kahne-

man wrote Linda's description to be representative of a feminist and thus the normative statistical likelihood was overridden (see Agnoli & Krantz, 1989). Had the subjects used the conjunction rule, they would not have committed this fallacy.

The **conjunction rule** says that the probability of two events occurring, their conjunction, cannot exceed the probability of one of those events. You will appreciate the conjunction rule better if you perform an experiment with a set of coins. First, toss a single coin many times. The probability of the single coin coming up heads is $p(H) = 0.50$. Next, toss two coins many times and observe the probability of both coins coming up heads, $p(H_1 \text{ and } H_2)$. This probability will be close to 0.25. The joint probability of two independent events is expressed in equation (14.10).

(14.10) $p(H_1 \text{ and } H_2) = p(H_1) \times p(H_2)$.

Because we multiply fractions, the product reflecting the conjunction is smaller than either probability.

Gambler's Fallacy: The Likelihood of Runs.
Suppose you are playing a coin-tossing game with a friend. You toss a coin and try to predict whether it will be heads (*H*) or tails (*T*). Further assume that you have tossed the coin six times and observed the sequence *HHHHHH*. What is the likelihood of an *H* on the seventh toss? Given this sequence, people tend to expect *T* next. They reason as follows: I have had six *H*s. On average, there should be half *H*s and half *T*s. So, in order to approach the average, a *T* is more likely. However plausible this reasoning may sound, it is fallacious because it attributes a kind of memory to the coin. On each toss the probability of coming up heads or tails is 0.50, independently of the prior sequence. Our tendency to underestimate the occurrence of long runs is called the gambler's fallacy because casino gamblers frequently commit this error. After a run of costly losses, they continue to play expecting a win that would even the odds.

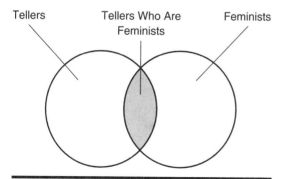

FIGURE 14.8 Illustration of the conjunction rule. The probability of tellers who are feminists (shaded region) is less than the probability of tellers (circle on left).

Availability.   If samples of an event are available to us either because we perceive or remember them well, we judge them more likely. Estimate how many English words begin with a *k* compared to words that have a *k* as their third letter. You will probably try to think of words in each of these categories, retrieving them from memory. Tversky and Kahneman's (1974) subjects said more words begin with a *k* than have *k* as their third letter. In actuality, words with a *k* as a third letter occur three times as frequently in the English language. People commit this error because it is much easier to think of words beginning with a *k* than words with *k* in the third position, the former are more available than the latter.

The **availability** heuristic is based on the salience of events in memory. More vivid events are judged more likely. The availability heuristic underlies estimates of the occurrence of many events, from diseases to accidents and disasters. We generally believe airplane crashes occur more frequently than they really do because much publicity is given to crashes and they are, therefore, available to us. Studies have shown that events that are less sensational but more common are not as available and believed to occur less frequently. In these studies, subjective estimates of the incidence of such rare events as botulism and tornadoes and such frequent events as cancer and stroke were compared to the actual occurrence frequency as recorded by government agencies. Judges overestimated the incidence of relatively

rare causes of death like botulism, while they underestimated the likelihood of more frequently occurring killers as stomach cancer and stroke.

A study by Fischhoff, Slovic, and Lichtenstein (1978) illustrates the availability heuristic and its implication for trouble shooting in different contexts. Trouble shooting is a technique frequently employed to solve problems with cars, electronic equipment, and even nuclear plants.

Three groups of subjects participated in a study of trouble-shooting technique. Each group was given a list of potential trouble spots as to why the car would not start as illustrated in Table 14.6. Three problem lists of varying completeness were used, one list for each group. The control group saw the complete list in Table 14.6. The other two groups saw subsets of the list as indicated in the table. Subjects had to judge the likelihood of each major problem category.

The probability estimates produced by the three respective groups are shown in Table 14.6. Of interest was how the different groups would treat the category labeled All Other Problems. As expected, this category was judged relatively unlikely in the control group; the category was judged more likely in the two other groups. However, the All Other Problems category would have been chosen even more frequently if the experimental subjects had considered those branches seen by the control group. If subjects in the first experimental group considered the probabilities of the deleted categories, including the starting system, ignition system, and mischief,

TABLE 14.6   Sources of Car Trouble as Estimated by Three Different Groups of Subjects in Fischhoff, Slovic, and Lichtenstein (1978) Study

Problem Category	Control Group	Experimental 1	Experimental 2
Battery	.264	.432	NA
Starting system	.195	NA	.357
Fuel system	.193	.309	NA
Ignition system	.144	NA	.343
Engine problems	.076	.116	NA
Mischievous acts	.051	NA	.073
All other problems	.078	.140	.227

the All Other Problems category would receive a probability rating of 0.467 (= 1 – 0.264 – 0.193 – 0.076). In the second experimental group, the All Other Problems category would receive $p = 0.610$, rather than the actual 0.227. In a subsequent experiment, expert car mechanics acted no differently than college students when it came to rating the likelihood of certain causes for car trouble.

The statement "out of sight, out of mind" characterized the reasoning of both experimental groups. Subjects simply did not think that events not explicitly listed could cause the car trouble. The moral of this story is to consult as large a variety of sources and make a complete list of possible problems when trouble shooting. Overlooking possibilities may hinder problem solving and invite disaster, whether it involves the long crying of a baby or the failure of a nuclear reactor.

INTERIM SUMMARY

Probabilistic reasoning serves us well when events are relatively certain and their context is familiar. Otherwise, people use error-prone heuristics like the representativeness and availability heuristics, which lead us to believe representative and available events more likely to occur than they really are. The conjunction fallacy means that a person erroneously believes an event of two joint properties is more likely than each property by itself. Each of these leads people to overestimate the probability of unlikely events. When we underestimate the likelihood of long runs of similar events, we commit the gambler's fallacy.

Choice

Decisions, decisions—our life requires decisions at every turn; many are of little importance; others change people's lives. Consider, for example, the following:

— A cancer patient must decide what sort of therapy to receive: surgery or radiation.

— A jury faces the choice of judging a defendant innocent or guilty.

— A college sophomore must choose a major among several different disciplines.

Psychologists, philosophers, and economists are interested in human decision making. Economists try to determine optimal choices in terms of economic resources; philosophers ponder what is a good choice in light of human values; and psychologists study human choice behavior under different constraints.

Rational Choices. Economic theories of choice are based on the idea that the decision maker acts rationally; she knows her goal, the outcome of alternative actions, and the utility of each. **Utility** is neither pleasure nor happiness; rather, it indicates how well an outcome satisfies a goal (Baron, 1988). In addition to having a specific utility, outcomes have probabilities of occurrence. For example, therapy X may succeed with a probability of $p = 0.80$. According to rational choice theory, the decision maker knows all of these aspects, outcomes, utilities, and probabilities. Using Shakespeare's dictum, she is "noble in reason, infinite in faculties" (Slovic, 1990).

Assuming that each choice has a fixed utility, the theory of rational choice proposes several principles, including the transitivity, dominance, and invariance principles (Tversky & Kahneman, 1986).

— According to the transitivity principle, if the decision maker favors choice A over B, and choice B over C, then she will favor choice A over choice C.

— The dominance principle states that if one choice is favored on the basis of one attribute and is considered at least equal in all other attributes, it is chosen.

— The invariance principle holds that the same underlying choice presented in different contexts will produce the same preference.

Economists also assume that price and product are the sole determinants of choice. Cognitive psychologists, on the other hand, consider decision making subject to processing limitations, similar to other mental operations. The economic approach is normative, whereas the cognitive approach is descriptive.

A Cognitive Framework of Choice Processes.

The rational theory of choice had a long tradition before cognitive theories of choice emerged. Simon (1957) developed a theory of choice—the theory of bounded rationality—that built on economic theories but took into account cognitive limitations. According to Simon, a person's knowledge of alternatives, costs, and outcomes is limited by the information available, by time pressure, and by the mind's computational power. Rather than maximizing utility, people satisfice goals. To **satisfice** means to choose an alternative that satisfies a current goal while avoiding negative consequences, as far as they are perceived. Simon's theory inspired research on choice by Fischhoff, Lichtenstein, Slovic, Tversky, and others whose approach reflects the shift from outcomes to processes characteristic of cognitive psychology. The framework in Figure 14.9 includes components of decision making expressed in information-processing terms. The decision maker encodes the alternatives, compares them, and produces an output.

Decision processes take place in an environment affording several options. They operate under the limitation of memory, as do other processes, including perception, comprehension, and writing. I will illustrate each of the components of the decision process with empirical data.

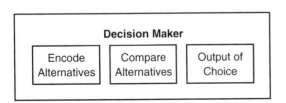

FIGURE 14.9 Framework of decision making includes encoding, comparison, and output processes.

Each of the following studies involves all components of making choices; however, their emphasis is different. One of the studies focuses on an encoding effect, another examines comparison strategies, and a third investigates output effects.

Encoding: The Framing Effect.   Encoding is the process of perceiving a stimulus and representing it in a mental format. When we recognize a pattern, read a sentence, or solve a problem, we encode stimuli into a format that permits additional processing. In decision-making situations, encoding means the person perceives choice alternatives and represents them in memory. According to the invariance principle, identical sets of choices are given the same representation, even if the contexts differ. This section will show that this is not the case; rather, there is a framing effect. The decision maker is influenced by the frame of reference used in stating alternatives.

To understand the framing effect, consider two frames expressing the same set of options. Tversky and Kahneman (1986) presented these to two different groups of subjects. Both groups of subjects read the following cover story:

(14.11) *Cover Story:* Imagine that the United States is preparing for the outbreak of an unusual Asian disease, which is expected to kill 600 people. Two alternative programs to combat the disease have been proposed. Assume that the exact scientific estimates of the consequences of the programs are as follows:

After reading the cover story, the first group was given Frame 1.

Frame 1: If Program A is adopted, 200 people will be saved (72%). If Program B is adopted, there is 1/3 probability that 600 people will be saved, and 2/3 probability that no people will be saved (28%).

The second group read the cover story and Frame 2.

Frame 2: If Program C is adopted, 400 people will die (22%). If Program D is adopted, there is 1/3 probability that nobody will die, and 2/3 probability that 600 people will die (78%).

Both frames describe options that are statistically identical. Yet, given Frame 1, most people (72%) preferred alternative A; whereas given Frame 2, most preferred alternative D (78%). These results contradict the principle of invariance; people should have made the same choice in both frames. Another way to look at the framing effect is the following: In Frame 1, subjects perceived the risk in option B, that no people would survive at all. On the other hand, in Frame 2, subjects perceived the chance offered by program D, that nobody would die. Summarizing results from many studies like this, Tversky and Kahneman (1986) concluded that people avoid risks in choices that involve gains but take risks in choices that involve loss.

The framing effect results from encoding similar data in different ways. Frames 1 and 2 elicit different scripts in semantic memory and each script has different risk and value properties (see Chapter 5). People make different choices depending on whether the outcome is framed as a gain (survival) or as a loss (mortality).

The Value Function. Following Shafir and Tversky's (1995) account of the value function, we first examine the value of gains and then the value of losses. To anticipate our conclusion: The values of gains and losses are asymmetrical.

As for the value of gains, consider the following choice:

A. Win $200 with a chance of 50 percent.

B. Get $100 for sure.

What is your choice? If the rational economic theory were correct, people would choose either option with equal probability. The theory holds that choices are determined by the expected value. **Expected value** is the product of the probability of winning and the amount of the gain. As the fol-

lowing calculations illustrate, both choices have the same expected value

Expected Value of Choice A = $.50 \times \$200 = \$100$

Expected Value of Choice B = $1.00 \times \$100 = \$100$

However, unlike choice B, choice A entails a risk, and empirical studies show that most people avoid risks whenever possible. In short, people are **risk averse.** Given the choice of A versus B, subjects tend to opt for choice B, the sure bet.

Risk aversion has been interpreted in psychophysical terms: The subjective value of any additional gain diminishes as the absolute value of the base increases, much as the perceived magnitude of a stimulus diminishes as the base level increases. In Figure 14.10A, the subjective value gained is greater from the first $100 than from the second $100 (between $100 and $200).

To illustrate the value of losses, consider options C and D.

C. Lose $200 with a chance of 50 percent.

D. Lose $100 for sure.

According to rational theory, the expected value of either choice is, again, $100, and people are assumed to choose C and D with equal likelihood. However, according to experimental evidence, the actual choice is different. Subjects tend to prefer the riskier choice C to choice D. Why would this be the case? Figure 14.10B explains why. The value of the loss in the region between −$100 and −$200 is less than between $0 and −$100.

Combining functions 14.10A and 14.10B yields the value function in Figure 14.10C. The ordinate of Figure 14.10C represents value and the abscissa shows loss and gain. The origin of the value function is not absolute but relative to the current situation and to the current domain. This means the scale we apply to value, loss, and gain is different when buying a soft drink, a VCR, or a car.

Conforming to the value function, Tversky and Kahneman's (1986) subjects were willing to take a greater risk in Frame 2 than in Frame 1. Car

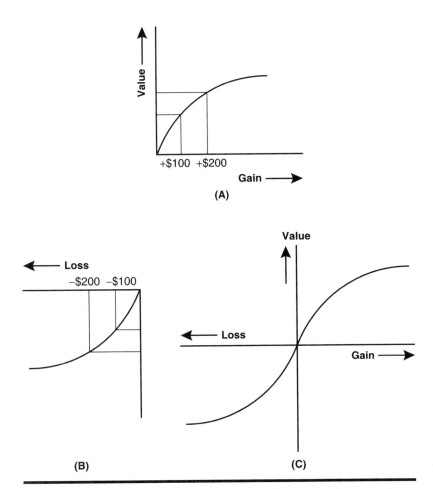

FIGURE 14.10   The value function. (*A*) Subjective value (*y*-axis) as a function of gain (*x*-axis). (*B*) Subjective value as a function of loss. (*C*) Combining functions A and B shows the composite value function (Shafir & Tversky, 1995).

rebates also reflect the asymmetry of the value function and the fact that it flattens at its end points. Have you ever wondered why car dealers offer rebates rather than reduce the price of a car? According to Thaler (1985), consumers keep different mental accounts for losses and gains, where the price of the car constitutes a loss and the rebate constitutes a gain. If the dealer reduces the price of a car from $10,000 to $9,000, the consumer gains $1,000 relative to $10,000 in a flat region of the loss curve. Giving a rebate of $1,000, however, represents a gain relative to 0 in the

steep part of the gain curve. The rebate adds more to perceived value.

In sum, decisions are influenced by the way outcomes are encoded. People are less willing to take a risk for an outcome encoded as a gain rather than as a loss. By the same function, we feel the loss of a good more than the gain of the same good.

Choice under Conflict.   According to rational choice theory, our choice behavior should obey the invariance principle. This principle states that a given option has an intrinsic value that is independent of other alternatives. If you prefer hamburger to chicken, you should maintain that preference when another alternative is added, such as caesar salad. Tversky and Shafir (1992) found, however, that people's choices were influenced by how many alternatives there were. They presented the following two decision scenarios to two different groups of students.

Low-Conflict Condition

You are considering buying a CD player but have not yet decided what model to buy. You pass by a store that is having a one-day clearance sale. It offers a popular SONY player for just $99, well below the list price. Do you:

   y. Buy the SONY player?   (66%)

   z. Wait until you learn more about the various models?   (34%)

High-Conflict Condition

You are considering buying a CD player but have not yet decided what model to buy. You pass by a store that is having a one-day clearance sale. It offers a popular SONY player for just $99 and a top-of-the-line AIWA player for just $169, both well below the list price. Do you

   x. Buy the AIWA player?   (27%)

   y. Buy the SONY player?   (27%)

   z. Wait until you learn more about the various models?   (46%)

Given the choice of only one CD player, the SONY player, in the low-conflict condition, people feel comfortable choosing it. When another attractive choice, the AIWA player, is available as in the high-conflict condition, the students tend to experience more conflict between the two CD players and increasingly postpone making a decision altogether.

Adding alternatives changes consumer preferences. Adding alternatives influences other choice situations, as well: It changes the manner in which people choose to allocate their time; it influences physicians' choices of treatments, and it sways legislators' choices of policy options. Investigating time allocation, Shafir (1993) gave two groups of subjects two different problems.

Group 1: One Alternative

You plan to spend the evening in the library working on a short paper due the following day. As you walk across campus, you discover that an author you have always admired is about to give a public lecture. Do you proceed to the library anyway or go to the lecture instead?

Group 2: Two Alternatives

You plan to spend the evening in the library working on a short paper due the following day. As you walk across campus, you discover that an author you have always admired is about to give a public lecture and that—in another hall—they are about to screen a movie that you have been wanting to see. Do you proceed to the library anyway or go to the lecture instead?

In both cases, the primary choice was to go to the library and work on a short paper. When one alternative was available, people selected that choice 21% of the time. However, given two alternatives, people chose the library at a 40% rate. Shafir (1993) reasoned that having to choose between the movie and the lecture, subjects in Group 2 experienced a greater conflict. As a result they tended to stick with their original choice of going to the library more than subjects in Group 1 did.

Redelmeier and Shafir (1995) found that medical decision making is subject to the same dynamics of conflict. When more alternatives become available, the physicians tend to avoid making a new decision. Consider two different scenarios presented to two different groups of about 300 general practitioners in Ontario:

The patient is a 67-year-old farmer with chronic hip pain. The diagnosis is osteoarthritis. You have tried several nonsteroidal anti-inflammatory agents (e.g., aspirin, naproxen, and ketoprofen) and have stopped them because of either adverse effects or lack of efficacy. You decide to refer him to an orthopedic consultant for consideration for hip replacement surgery. The patient agrees to this plan. Before sending him away, however, you check the list of drugs and find that there is one nonsteroidal medication that this patient has not tried (ibuprofen). What would you do?

The second scenario was like the first except that there were two medications still to try: ibuprofen and piroxicam.

The choice presented to the physicians was as follows: Would you refer the patient to orthopedics and not start any new medication? Given one alternative (only ibuprofen), 53% of the physicians elected this choice. When two alternatives were given, however, 72% said they would not try the new drug. According to the researchers, faced with two alternatives, the physicians experienced greater conflict and tended to opt for no medication at all.

Redelmeier and Shafir (1995) conducted a similar study involving members of the Ontario Provincial Parliament. The politicians were asked to choose among different types of health care expenditures. The pattern of choice behavior was similar to that in the earlier studies: Presenting more competitive options to the decision maker tends to produce more conflict and to result in postponing the decision.

The researchers noted that, typically, medical decision making presents even more choices than they used in their studies. They write that there are 13 medications for treating Parkinson's disease, 31 for bronchitis, and 91 for hypertension. In addition, there is a multitude of tests and procedures to assess medical conditions. If that were not enough, the health care delivery system involves complex decisions regarding the choice of insurance carriers and benefit packages.

What is the decision maker to do? Think harder about the choices? Redelmeier and Shafir (1995) believe that option will not help at all. Rather, decision makers should construct various decision scenarios that "identify each potentially attractive option and compare it directly with the status quo, in the absence of competing alternatives" (p. 305.)

Comparison: Deciding How to Decide. A decision includes three aspects: alternatives faced by the decision maker, outcomes and their probabilities, and the value of each outcome. In order to make a decision, a person must select a strategy by which to make his choice—hence the subtitle of this section Deciding How to Decide (Payne, Bettman, & Johnson, 1990). Strategies reduce the load of mental processing. Empirical studies show that the choice of strategy depends on the information load faced by the decision maker. If there are only two or three decision criteria and few alternatives, decision makers tend to consider them all. If there are many options and many attributes, however, we tend to select certain attributes and ignore others.

Cognitive psychologists have devised techniques to observe decision strategies. Suppose you are given the information in Table 14.7 and asked to select one of the candidates for a scholarship. The table contains data for two college students eligible for a scholarship, including family income, grade-point averages (GPAs), and SAT scores.

Assuming you consider all the information in making your choice, you could process candidates or dimensions first (Russo & Dosher, 1983).

TABLE 14.7 Selecting a Candidate for a Scholarship

A.		Criteria	
	Income	GPA	SAT
A	$7,920	3.51	1440
B	$6,420	3.43	1260

B.		Ranks		
A	2	1	1	1.33
B	1	2	2	1.67

Processing by candidates is called *holistic processing;* processing by dimensions is called *dimensional processing.* In holistic processing, the decision maker considers all three dimensions within candidate A, a_1, a_2, and a_3, and then turns her attention to candidate B. In dimensional processing, the values of one dimension are compared across candidates, for example, a_1 versus b_1, then a_2 versus b_2. Using either type of processing, attributes can be combined to give an overall quality score for each choice.

There are many ways to combine the three dimensions. I will describe a simple method here, the **additive** strategy. We express each attribute in terms of the same scale, a ranking scale, and compute the average rank, as shown in Table 14.7B. Based on this ranking, candidate A is selected. In this version of the additive strategy, equal weight was given to each of the dimensions. Once could also weigh the dimensions differently; for example, one could give twice as much weight to the GPA as to the other two dimensions.

Russo and Dosher (1983) used decision problems like the one in Table 14.7 in an experiment to observe which type of strategy subjects selected. They recorded a person's eye fixation as she studied the decision data displayed on a computer screen. Researchers then interpreted the eye fixation data. For example, if subjects fixated their eyes successively on the three dimensions for one candidate, *a-a-a,* researchers assume they used a holistic strategy. If their eyes alternated between candidates, *a-b-a,* researchers assume subjects used the dimensional strategy. In Russo and Dosher's study, most eye-fixation patterns corresponded to the dimensional strategy; dimensional processing accounted for 57% of the decision time versus 14% for holistic processing. The remaining time could not be classified.

The Russo and Dosher study involved relatively simple choices—two alternatives with three dimensions each. Many decision problems are considerably more complex, prompting the decision maker to select attributes. Many selection strategies are available, including the lexicographic and the elimination-by-aspects heuristics.

The **lexicographic strategy** emphasizes the most important attribute of the problem while ignoring all others. Assume that a college admissions officer decides that a candidate's GPA is the most important dimension because it is based on the longest academic track record. Given this reasoning, candidate A in Table 14.7 will be selected, just as she was under the additive strategy.

The **elimination-by-aspects strategy** drops one criterion after another from consideration. Assume a person wishes to pick one apartment from seven available. The apartment hunter first decides which attribute of an apartment is most important. Because he can spend no more than $380 on rent, he eliminates all apartments costing more. Next, he looks at the number of rooms in each apartment. Preferring a one-bedroom apartment, he eliminates all others. Next, he eliminates in turn the apartments that are not furnished, those that are further than 20 minutes away from school, and those that do not offer a view of trees or a park. Finally, our apartment hunter is left with only one apartment.

Preference trees capture diverse choice situations, whether they are preferences for cars, political parties, or college majors. Payne and colleagues (1990) concluded that the effort involved in the elimination-by-aspects strategy increases less with added dimensions than in additive strategies where the decision maker considers several dimensions and combines them additively.

Output: Compatibility Principle. According to the compatibility principle, a decision maker's choice depends on the compatibility between the output response and the best-fitting decision attribute. Slovic (1990) cited data illustrating this principle. Subjects were asked to predict the decisions of a college admissions committee by ranking candidates numerically, or by giving a categorical *yes/no* decision on the applicant's admission. Subjects were told that 500 high school seniors applied for admission, a quarter of whom would be accepted. Subjects were given data on 10 candidates, including the applicant's rank on the verbal SAT, a numerical attribute, and whether or not the applicant participated in extracurricular activities, a categorical attribute. The first group of subjects had to predict the rank given by the admissions committee to each candidate; the second group had to predict whether a candidate was accepted or rejected.

Subjects responded in accordance with the compatibility principle: The first group based its prediction largely on the students' SAT scores. The second group's predictions, however, were determined by the categorical information on extracurricular activities. If several attributes are available, the decision maker weighs more heavily the attribute that is most compatible with the type of response required. According to Slovic, this is due to cognitive economy: The more compatible an attribute and a response, the fewer mental transformations are needed to make the response.

INTERIM SUMMARY

Cognitive psychologists describe decision making as a mental process rather than as an attempt to optimize economic utility. Like other cognitive operations, decision making is subject to processing limitations. We have considered factors that influence decision making at the encoding, comparison, and output phases. The framing effect shows that choice depends on the framework in which alternatives are encoded: People are risk averse if a choice is described as a gain; they take risks if the same choice is described as a loss. If there are few decision attributes, decision makers consider all of them—for example, by using an additive strategy; if there are many dimensions, decision makers consider a subset of them, or they eliminate one dimension after another. According to the compatibility principle, people weigh a dimension more heavily if it is compatible with the type of output response required.

Improving Judgment and Decision Making

One of the goals of studying choice behavior is to improve our decision-making ability, whether it is in medicine, in business, or in everyday life. At professional schools, there are numerous courses of study on decision analysis. These emphasize economic and mathematical principles of choice; the student is exposed to linear regression analysis, computer-based decision support systems, dynamic programming, and cost/benefit analysis, which are beyond the scope of this chapter (Turban, 1990). In this section, I sketch insights from both decision analysis and cognitive research on choice (Behn & Vaupel, 1982). I will begin with the beneficial effects of statistical training on judgment of frequency and then list suggestions for effective decision making.

Statistical Training Is Beneficial. One could take the view that statistical fallacies in judgment and decision biases are like perceptual illusions (see Chapter 3). According to this view, statistical training would help us overcome fallacies no more than studying geometry removes perceptual illusions (Tversky & Kahneman, 1983). Some statistics teachers, however, believe otherwise: People can be taught to use statistical principles in making judgments. Fong, Krantz, and Nisbett (1986) explained the law of large numbers to their subjects for only 25 minutes and observed a significant increase in the quality of students' statistical reasoning. The teachers explained the law of large numbers as follows and illustrated it with several examples:

> As the size of a random sample increases, the sample distribution is more likely to get closer to the population distribution. In other words, the larger the sample, the better it is as an estimate of the population.

After receiving this explanation, students were given 18 story problems based on the law of large numbers. Their answers were graded by four judges. Experimental subjects received better grades than control subjects, who received no training. If a 25-minute session improves statistical reasoning, so do longer training sessions, including semester-long statistics courses. In general, the amount of statistical training improved answers in a wide range of problems.

Agnoli and Krantz (1989) wanted to see if people could be taught to avoid the conjunction fallacy illustrated earlier with the Linda problem (14.9). They compared the performance of subjects trained on set relations (training group) with subjects who received no training (no-training group). In the training group, the researchers used Venn diagrams and verbal descriptions to teach subjects the fact that a population decreases in size when new attributes are added. For example, adding the feature "20 to 30 years old" to the category "U.S.-born women" reduces the category size. Subjects in both groups were shown problems like the one in Table 14.8 and asked to rank the statements by their probability.

The conjunction fallacy was made when subjects rated a conjunction (A and B) as more likely than either individual event (A) or (B). Subjects in the no-training group made this error in 73% of all cases, whereas trained subjects made the error only 44% of the time. Training reduced the occurrence of the conjunction fallacy; however, it did not eliminate the error altogether. This means that Tversky and Kahneman's view of statistical illusions has at least some merit.

Clearly, then, people should use statistical considerations rather than intuition in order to overcome statistical biases. Does this mean intuition misguides us? Doesn't intuition help artists and scientists to see and create novel patterns? The paradox inherent in these questions is easily resolved; the benefit of intuition depends on the context in which it is used (see Bowers, Regehr, Balthazard, & Parker, 1990). In a context of artistic and scientific discovery, intuition leads to innovation. In the context of making statistical judgments, however, it may lead to erroneous conclusions. In judgment studies, subjects are given one chance to make a choice, and their choice is final. In discovery contexts, however, artists and scientists work on a problem for a long time; a judgment is rarely final, and intuition leads to further inquiry.

Decision Analysis. Experts in decision analysis have developed extensive decision aids (Behn & Vaupel, 1982; Fischhoff, Lichtenstein, Slovic, Derby, & Keeney, 1981). The concept ANALYSIS contains the key suggestion to decision makers; *analysis* comes from the Greek and means to resolve into its elements. The elements of a decision include options, outcomes, consequences, and the sources of uncertainty one faces in making a choice. Decision makers should make a list of each of these and represent options and outcomes in a transparent way, as in a decision tree, for example.

TABLE 14.8   Example of a Conjunction Problem for Direct Tests

---

Linda is 31 years old, single, outspoken, and very bright. She majored in philosophy. As a student, she was deeply concerned with issues of discrimination and social justice and also participated in anti-nuclear demonstrations.

Please rank the following statements by their probability, using 1 for the most probable, and 8 for the least probable.

	_____ Linda is a teacher in an elementary school.
	_____ Linda works in a bookstore and takes yoga classes.
(A)	_____ Linda is active in the feminist movement.
	_____ Linda is a psychiatric social worker.
	_____ Linda is a member of the League of Women Voters.
(B)	_____ Linda is a bank teller.
	_____ Linda is an insurance salesperson.
(A & B)	_____ Linda is a bank teller and is active in the feminist movement.

— *Consider Viable Alternatives.* The study by Fischhoff and colleagues (1978) on trouble shooting has demonstrated that people tend to emphasize salient alternatives and overlook true alternatives. Therefore, decision makers should research a problem and brainstorm alternative options, if possible together with other individuals.

— *Examine Outcomes and Side Effects.* Frequently, we make decisions without being fully aware of outcomes, including indirect ones. The student enrolling in course X rather than in course Y may inadvertently overlook that Y is a prerequisite for other courses. The man buying an expensive suit may not be thinking about his next vacation. You should identify such consequences and represent them in the decision tree.

— *List Sources of Uncertainty.* Decisions would be far easier to make if it were not for uncertainties at every turn. Even goals are uncertain; as a person makes choices, the goal may change. Outcomes are also uncertain; an operation, investment, or purchase may yield the expected result or it may not.

Decision analysts represent choices in terms of decision trees. A decision tree represents choices faced by a decision maker and the outcomes of those decisions. The decision tree represents information, much like a road map (Behn & Vaupel, 1982). Developing a decision tree facilitates analysis because options, outcomes, and consequences are listed. The structure of the tree forces you to think about each component of the decision, thus addressing the availability issue. A decision tree could be augmented if other information becomes available, whether options or outcomes. In addition, if the probabilities of outcomes are known, they can easily be marked on each of the outcome branches (and then used in

mathematical analyses). Useful as they are, decision trees are merely tools; the decision maker's task is only complete when the decision itself has been made.

CONCLUSION

Categorization and choice are basic cognitive operations occurring in many different contexts from perception to decision making. They differ across the cognitive spectrum, being automatic in perceptual contexts but difficult in category learning and in decision making, especially when many attributes are involved. In all cases, however, there are commonalities in reasoning and choice: A person maps a response to a class of stimuli by forming a belief or taking an action. Categorization processes have attracted the attention of many different research programs, including learning theory, hypothesis-testing theory, prototype theory, and connectionist theory. These approaches differ in their representations and learning mechanisms. Choice behavior has been examined by economists who take a normative approach and by cognitive psychologists who favor a descriptive approach.

Reasoning, judgment, and choice are frequently subject to fallacies. People tend to emphasize salient features of stimuli; they overestimate unlikely but striking events and use rules of thumb rather than formal reasoning methods. Because there are so many types of fallacies, some theorists wonder whether humans are rational at all (Stich, 1990). Others view reasoning fallacies much like slips in language production—namely, as performance errors rather than structural disabilities (Cohen, 1982). Whichever view is correct, we know that reasoning, like other cognitive processes, improves with practice.

ENDNOTE

1. The base rate represents the frequency of the category relative to a population. According to the census, for example, the base rate of women among the U.S. population is 0.501.

CHAPTER 15

APPLICATIONS OF COGNITIVE PSYCHOLOGY

PREVIEW

This final chapter samples from the many actual and potential applications of cognitive psychology outside the research laboratory. In many cases, the applications are well ahead of cognitive theories, which would explain and account for their practical use. In other cases—for example, in beginning reading instruction—there are lively controversies over the cognitive principles to be used in practice. There is also a general debate about whether applications are feasible at all; some cognitive psychologists favor practical uses of cognitive psychology, whereas others argue that applications are premature. Regardless of these debates, applications of cognitive principles have evolved in many areas. We will consider illustrations from four areas: cognitive engineering, education, law enforcement, and cognitive deficits.

— Cognitive engineers assess operator workload in a variety of settings in order to achieve an optimal match between the operator and the design of machine hardware and software. This chapter examines human factor issues in typing, the design of dials, and computer software, such as computer languages and word processors.

— Education is concerned with the acquisition and use of information in real-world contexts. From a cognitive perspective, its goal is to convey declarative and procedural knowledge in a domain. Here, we examine reading instruction, teaching problem-solving skills, and long-term retention of math, foreign languages, and cognitive psychology.

— Cognitive principles have implications for forensic applications in law enforcement. Contributions by cognitive psychologists to improve face identification and eyewitness testimony are reviewed.

— Cognitive psychology has become increasingly involved in the diagnosis and rehabilitation of cognitive impairments. Experimental techniques originally designed to study attention, pattern recognition, and problem solving can be adapted as diagnostic tests in clinical settings. Learning and memory methods have been used to rehabilitate individuals with cognitive disabilities.

INTRODUCTION

The final chapter of this book samples from among the many actual and potential applications of cognitive psychology outside of the research laboratory: in human factors, law enforcement, education, and clinical settings. The relation of basic research and application varies widely. Some applications are grounded in theoretical principles. The cognitive interview, for example, is used to enhance the testimony of eyewitnesses and is based on theories of memory and retrieval. Other applications have been successful without the benefit of cognitive theories. You will learn about a health care worker in a clinic who managed to train a dyslexic patient to read without knowing about theories of reading or reading instruction.

In several instances, there is disagreement between discoveries made in the lab and the fundamental assumptions of an applied discipline. For example, empirical research results on transfer of training are ambiguous: Some studies suggest the possibility of transfer (Singley & Anderson, 1989), whereas others indicate only limited transfer between analogous problems (Gick & Holyoak, 1980, 1983). Yet education is based on the assumption that there is transfer of skills. Finally, we will consider implications of cognitive theories for potential uses. For example, experimental techniques developed by cognitive psychologists hold the promise for use in neurological diagnosis, but they still await further development.

There is a tension between applied and theoretical cognitive psychologists. All too often, they view one another with wariness; the practitioner complains that the theorist studies artificial and uninteresting trivia, while the theorist counters that applications are often unsound and not fully substantiated. Sometimes the debate reaches a crescendo, as you will see in the concluding section of the chapter. Debate or not, applications have had an impact on basic research, including such crucial topics as attention, pattern recognition, and working memory.

Throughout the chapter you will see references to topics covered in the preceding chapters, from attention to reasoning.

COGNITIVE ENGINEERING

The Soviet Union announced today that there had been an accident at a nuclear power plant in the Ukraine and that "aid is being given to those affected."

The severity of the accident which spread discernible radioactive material over Scandinavia, was not immediately clear. But the terse statement, distributed by the Tass press agency and read on the evening news, suggested a major accident.

The phrasing also suggested that the problem had not been brought under full control at the nuclear plant, which the Soviet announcement identified as the Chernobyl station. It is situated at the new town of Pripyat, near Chernobyl and 60 miles north of Kiev.

These lines in the *New York Times* on April 30, 1986, reported one of the worst nuclear accidents in history. During the months and years following, the Chernobyl disaster cost many human lives, caused thousands of cases of cancer, and spoiled hundreds of square miles of prime soil; indeed, Chernobyl became synonymous with environmental catastrophe. Chernobyl was not the only nuclear or industrial accident in recent years, however; others include the chemical spill at Bhopal, the nuclear accident at Three-Mile Island, and the explosion of the space shuttle *Challenger*. In your local newspaper, you are sure to find scores of smaller accidents occurring every week. Although we will probably never know for sure what caused the Chernobyl disaster, it is very likely that human error was involved.

According to an analysis of the Significant Event and Information Network of nuclear utilities all over the world, most accidents in nuclear facilities are due to human error, resulting, for example, from performance problems and from design and manufacturing deficiencies (Reason, 1990). Some of the errors involve group communication problems and motivational problems, such as failure to keep a rigorous maintenance schedule. Cognitive factors, however, play an important role as well, such as workers failing to recognize and attend to warning signs or making incorrect decisions or incorrect motor responses.

The discipline that studies the contribution of cognitive factors to job performance is known as **cognitive engineering** (Norman, 1987), historically known as **human factors psychology.** The general goal of cognitive engineering is twofold: (1) to assess the performance of operators in jobs that require processing of much information and (2) to design the demands of the job so that they best match the capacity of the worker. Cognitive engineering is founded on cognitive psychology and other disciplines, including communication science, engineering, software engineering, and the study of motor behavior. Motor behavior is of interest because operators' jobs entail manipulating controls, buttons, or keys, often at very high speeds. Motor responses are the expression of cognitive processes and are therefore of interest to cognitive psychology, (see Chapter 4).

Assessing Workload

The Performance Operating Characteristic.
Reason (1990) attributed much of the blame in industrial accidents to the failure of operators to detect problems. This is also a major cause of traffic fatalities in the air, on land, or at sea. In these cases, operators have reached the capacity limit of information processing. This happens when information from two or more sources must be processed rapidly. Consider the information load a pilot must process in landing a plane or taking off. She must process changes in many variables, including the plane's air speed, vertical velocity, and altitude. Altitude refers to the position of the aircraft relative to the horizon or some other reference point, such as a star. Figure 15.1 shows a typical set of flight instruments the pilot monitors. In addition, the pilot must attend to routing information from the co-pilot, radio signals from the ground, and data on each of the engines—for example, fuel supply, oil pressure, RPM, and oil temperature.

The pilot's situation is the prototype of the dual-task—indeed, multiple-task—situation (see Chapter 3). Because of capacity limits, the operator allocates resources among the different tasks in which she is engaged. Performance in a dual-task situation is recorded in terms of the performance operating characteristic (POC). The POC measures the operator's performance on each of the two tasks executed individually and jointly. Figure 15.2 shows results from a hypothetical dual-task situation. Figure 15.2A shows the performance level on two tasks executed separately. In Figure 15.2B, at point 3, performance is shown when both tasks are executed jointly; the typical result is that performance on each task diminishes.

Gopher and Donchin (1986) demonstrated

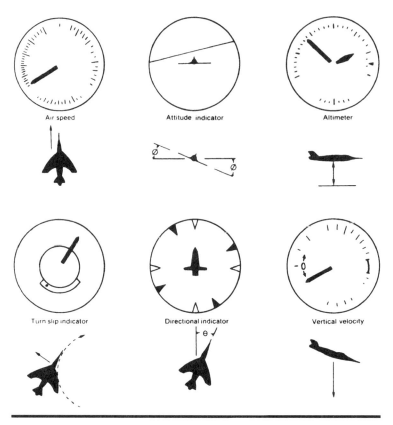

FIGURE 15.1 Typical set of flight instruments in a cockpit. The model airplanes below each dial indicate the variable measured by the instrument.

such a drop in performance in an experiment that simulated real-life situations faced by operators in many contexts. Their experimental arrangement is shown in Figure 15.3. The subjects faced a screen that displayed a moving control symbol and a window showing a target letter. At the top of the screen, there were two bar graphs. On the subjects' right was a joystick; on their left was a mini-keyboard consisting of three keys used for typing.

For their first task, subjects had to use their right hand to move the joystick in concert with the symbol moving on the screen. For example, when the target moved toward the left, the person would move the stick to the left. An accuracy measure of tracking performance reflected the deviations of the subject's tracking path from that of the target. In the second task, subjects used their left hand to type one of 16 Hebrew letters shown in a window on the left side of the screen. Typing the letters was not as straightforward as using a standard typewriter with a unique key for each letter; rather, subjects had to press several keys simultaneously to reproduce a target letter. The dependent variable for typing was the time it took the subject to type a letter.

There were single-task and concurrent-task trials of three minutes each. Different levels of pri-

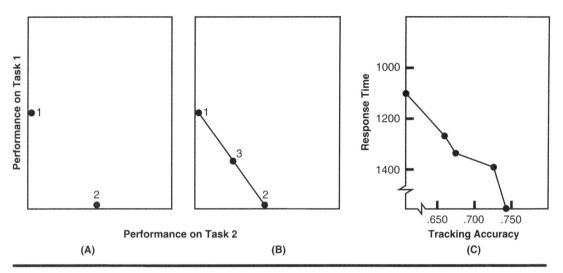

FIGURE 15.2 Performance operating characteristic (POC) curves. (*A*) Performance level on two tasks executed separately. (*B*) Point 3 indicates performance level on two tasks when they are executed jointly. (*C*) POC profile from Gopher and Donchin's (1986) study. The *x*-axis indicates tracking accuracy and the *y*-axis indicates time to type letters. The five data points reflect single-task performance and three different priority levels: 0.3, 0.5, and 0.7 for the tracking task.

orities were associated with each task. The priority to be given each task was signaled by the length of the two horizontal bar graphs at the top of the screen; the longer the bar for a task, the greater its priority. The priorities for the two tasks were 0.3, 0.5, and 0.7. For example, the bars in Figure 15.3 instruct the subject to concentrate more on typing than on tracking.

Subjects received continuous feedback on their performance for each task. They were paid for good performance on *both* tasks. The results are shown in Figure 15.2C. Performance dropped when subjects had to execute both tasks concurrently, reflecting the trade-off between the two tasks. Such a trade-off is typical, unless the person has extended practice executing the tasks jointly (see Spelke, Hirst, & Neisser, 1976; Chapter 3).

The dual-task technique and POC profiles are widely used in laboratory simulations of complex jobs. There are many types of secondary tasks, including target tracking, choice reaction times, and shadowing (see Chapter 3). It is difficult, however, to use the concurrent task technique in real-life situations such as flying an airplane.

In many jobs, workload and stress are assessed by monitoring behavioral and physiological changes as the person performs his or her job. Eye-fixation patterns are an example of behavioral measures; physiological measures include the operator's heart rate and event related potentials.

Behavioral Measures. In a study completed almost 50 years ago, Fitts recorded the eye fixations of fighter pilots (Moray, 1986). He took thousands of frames of film over different flight conditions from routine to hazardous. Researchers mounted a camera in the plane's cockpit so that the pilot's eyes could be continuously filmed. Prior to the flights, the recording equipment was carefully calibrated so that the direction of a pilot's gaze could be identified. The mean fixation

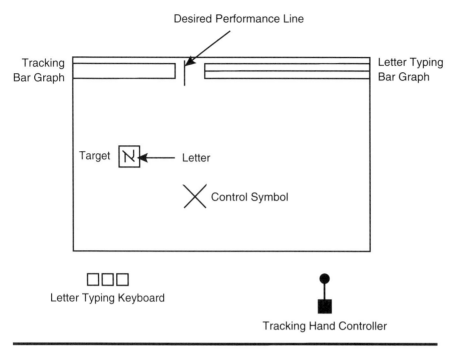

FIGURE 15.3 Display in two-task situation used by Gopher and Donchin (1986). With his left hand, the person entered Hebrew letters while he manipulated the joystick with his right hand to track a target. Feedback on letter-typing performance and tracking performance was provided in the bar graphs at the top of the screen. The vertical line between the bar graphs indicates the desired priority the operator should give to each of the tasks. In this case, the priority was 0.70 for the letter-typing task (Gopher & Donchin, 1986).

times were 600 milliseconds, about twice as long as in reading (see Chapter 11). There were large individual differences between pilots, even when the flight paths were the same and when pilots had logged approximately the same total flying time. Fixation patterns depended on the pilot's current task; for example, in a landing approach, the altitude indicator is fixated most, whereas the altimeter was rarely observed.

Event-Related Potentials. An event-related potential (ERP) is a record of electrical activity in specific regions of the brain. The ERP is the result of averaging electroencephalogram (EEG) patterns over many trials. It is coordinated with the presentation of specific stimuli, such as tones, light flashes, or words. The ERP consists of patterns of positive and negative peaks with specific latencies after the onset of a stimulus (see Chapter 2). A typical task used in this type of research is the oddball task, in which the subject performs a primary task, such as monitoring a panel. At the same time, sound patterns are presented to the subject via headphones. From time to time, slightly different sounds (the oddball stimuli) are transmitted. ERPs and performance measures are recorded continuously as the person engages in the primary task. When the primary task is relatively easy, monitoring accuracy is not influenced by the tones. The ERP pattern indicates, however, that the operator's brain does react to the secondary stimulus.

Researchers used the oddball task to assess processing in a simulated air traffic control situation (Isreal, Wickens, Chesney, & Donchin, 1980). In the experiment, the operators' primary task was to watch a radar screen and monitor the path of one of several moving targets. Monitoring difficulty was varied by changing the number of targets traveling across the screen. When operators were monitoring the change of course in one of the targets, and the number of targets increased, the ERP latencies to the secondary stimuli increased. The longer latencies reflected the greater workload the operator devoted to the primary task when more targets crowded the screen.

Cognitive engineers evaluate the workload on a job in order to improve performance and minimize errors and accidents. If the workload is excessive, problems and accidents become more likely. If it is too low, human resources are not fully used. Cognitive engineers also seek to improve the design of machines, manuals, and software in order to facilitate their use. The essential issue in application and design is this: What sort of arrangement makes most sense from a cognitive perspective? Consider Norman's (1988) example of typewriter keyboards. Should the keys on a keyboard be arranged alphabetically, in the standard QWERTY order, or in some other order? For that matter, should the keyboard be flat or shaped like a football, with keys arranged like the keys on an accordion to accommodate the hands better?

Typewriters and Typing

When typewriters were first introduced by Remington over 100 years ago, engineers did not bother much with cognitive considerations. Rather, typewriters and keyboards were constructed to satisfy mechanical constraints. Take a look at the way old typewriters print. One key at a time fits through a narrow gap and hits the ribbon. Now sit down at an old typewriter and type as fast as you can. You will quickly notice a problem: The keys jam. To circumvent jam-

ming, engineers designed the typewriter so that letters that commonly occur in succession in English, like *e* and *i* and *i* and *e,* were under the control of different hands (although there are exceptions).

The first typists looked at the typewriter keys rather than the text and used only two fingers to type—a slow process. Typing speeds took a quantum leap when it occurred to Frank McGurrin of Salt Lake City to use his memory to type. McGurrin memorized the positions of the QWERTY keyboard and used 10 fingers without looking at the keyboard. He proved his typing prowess for all to see in a nationwide typing contest in 1877, convincing typewriter manufacturers, employers, and the public at large that the QWERTY arrangement was efficient after all (see Norman, 1988). Soon, this arrangement became standard in the United States and internationally. The standard mapping between fingers and keys is shown in Figure 15.4 (Rumelhart & Norman, 1982).

Other arrangements have been tried, of course, including different types of alphabetic keyboards and the Dvorak keyboard. The composer Dvorak designed his keyboard for one-handed amputees. He considered the statistical probability of the occurrence of letters, trying to minimize the keystroke intervals of one-handed typists. Key arrangements on the keyboards of linotype machines are different still. These are typesetting machines used in printing plants where newspapers and books are printed. Conrad and Longman (1965) designed a more radical keyboard, one that included only 10 keys, 1 for each finger. The 5 left-hand keys were designated as 1, 2, 3, 4, and 5, and the 5 right-hand keys were A, B, C, D, and E. The keyboard accommodated 25 letters, so the typist had to tap two keys in order to produce one letter, one with the right hand and the other with the left. For example, to type the letter *A,* the 1 and A keys had to be pressed. These designers wanted to eliminate the time interval of moving the fingers between keys (see also Gopher & Donchin's 1986 study).

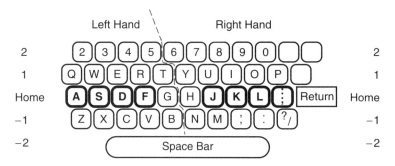

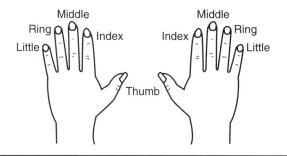

FIGURE 15.4 The QWERTY keyboard is the standard on U.S. computers and typewriters (Rumelhart & Norman, 1982).

Norman and Fisher (1982) evaluated the efficiency of the QWERTY keyboard and four other systems, including alphabetic and random arrangements. Their subjects were beginning typists. The researchers expected that the students would learn the alphabetic arrangement faster because they were familiar with it. Surprisingly, this was not the case. The keyboards, including the random keyboard, did not differ in how easy they were to learn. Norman (1988) noted that other more advantageous layouts than the QWERTY keyboard may be found in the future, though the cost of converting the millions of keyboards now in use would be prohibitive unless a way could be found to alter the keys electronically. If this were possible, each country, each user group—indeed, each individual typist—could design the layout with which

they are most comfortable just by clicking a few buttons! In any case, for an expert typist, the standard keyboard is plenty efficient.

Compatibility

Typing exemplifies the issue of mapping responses to devices. This is a general concern in designing appliances. All too often, even common appliances confound otherwise skilled and intelligent people. You may have problems with a VCR, or with a camera, or even a faucet or light switch. Norman's (1990) *The Design of Everyday Things* is full of similar examples.

Most appliances have controls to modulate an output. Consider light switches; in the United States, the general rule is that you turn the switch up to turn on the light (or appliance) and turn the switch down to turn it off. In other countries (e.g., England), the reverse custom exists. Similarly, there are different conventions to change the volume or frequency on audio equipment, push and pull doors, handle locks and keys in cars, hot and cold faucets in sinks and showers, and work brightness controls on terminals.

These examples illustrate cases of **compatibility** between a human operator and a machine. Compatibility refers to the degree of congruence between the user's view of how the equipment works and how it actually does work. If the user's intuitions and the way the equipment works agree, there is good compatibility (Baecker & Buxton, 1987). Computers provide many illustrations of compatibility, both in the design of user interfaces (such as keyboards) and in software. The next section examines the role of pointing devices in computer editors.

Computer Human Interaction

Today, computers are commonplace; they are used for diverse purposes from determining the inventory in supermarkets to controlling the manufacture of machines. In this section, we will consider manuscript editing, an application with which you are probably very familiar. The software you use for this job is an editor or word processor.

There are hundreds of editors, even for the same computer. They can be grouped into classes according to the way major editing functions are designed. Editors serve to enter and change text at a particular location in the document. Before word-processing software was developed, editing tasks were usually done with a typewriter. After entering the text, changing it was difficult; the section to be changed had to be erased somehow, and the sheet had to be aligned physically so that the new material would fit in the space available. If you never had to go through this process, consider yourself fortunate!

With a word processor, a location in a text file is addressed by means of a *cursor*. By activating a mouse or joystick, or by pressing directional keys on the keyboard in a certain sequence, the cursor is moved to the desired location. Once you have the desired location, text insertion and change are easy. You use the alphanumeric keys—the space bar, delete keys, and, in some editors, the return keys—as you would on a typewriter. Editors are more popular than typewriters for other reasons also. They make it easy to cut and paste texts, repeat commands, conduct searches, and make changes throughout the document. They have powerful features that can format documents almost any way a user could wish. Many editors provide fancy options for different fonts, automatic counting, and formatting footnotes, references, and tables. Book authors appreciate the option that automatically generates name and subject indexes.

Cognitive psychologists have conducted experiments to determine which editors and which features are most helpful (Card, Moran, & Newell, 1983; Roberts & Moran, 1982). In many cases, these experiments were paid for by computer companies. Often, the results had an immediate impact on the development and design of the editor. For example, the increased use of the mouse, introduced by Xerox and popularized by Apple is now standard on most computers. Why did the mouse become so popular? The study I describe next provides the answer.

Researchers compared the efficiency of the four pointing (or cursor moving) devices in terms of several categories, including ease of learning, number of errors, speed of editing, and retention (Card et al., 1983). They recruited undergraduates who had little or no experience with computers to participate in the study. Each person learned to use each device; the order in which the individuals learned the devices was randomized. On each learning trial, the subject saw a screen full of text with a single target word or phrase highlighted. The user's job was to move the cursor to the target, and select the target as if they intended to delete it. There were five different starting positions of the cursor relative to the target (1, 2, 4, 8, or 16 cm away) and four different target word sizes (1, 2, 4, or 10 characters).

The students came to the lab on several occasions for two to three hours each time (600 trials). They practiced a device until there was no significant improvement within the first and last block of 200 trials within a day. This took up to three days of practice on each device. At the outset of practice, pointing was faster using the mouse and the joystick than using directional keys. The rate of improvement was also best for the mouse: after 600 trials of practice, pointing was fastest using the mouse. In addition, the error rate was lowest for all four target sizes when the mouse was used. The authors concluded that the mouse was "clearly the superior device for text selection on a display" and recommended its immediate application in practical and commercial systems.

Chances are you'll be using different editors in college and in your career. Luckily, you don't have to worry about interference between editors. Although editors have different features, and sometimes conflicting commands, there is little negative transfer between them according to researchers (Anderson, 1990).

Learning Computer Languages

The term *user friendly* did not apply to the first computer language, a language consisting of 0s and 1s. This language simulated pushing switches up and down. Then machine language was invented; individual technicians came up with expressions that were mnemonic to them but to no one else. A sample is given in Table 15.1. The first major higher-level language was FORTRAN, written in the 1950s. FORTRAN represented a major advance over machine languages and was a success by any measure. The then largest computer company, IBM, adopted it and ensured its international acceptance. Is FORTRAN the best language from a cognitive point of view in terms of learning ease, use, low error rate, and high retention? Not by a long shot. Because students and teachers did not consider FORTRAN user friendly, computer scientists proposed a series of instructional languages, such as BASIC, Pascal, C, and LOGO. Initially, there was

TABLE 15.1   Binary Code and Machine Language Are Not User Friendly

A.	Binary Code
	1 0 0 1 1 0 0 1
	0 1 1 0 0 1 0 0
	1 1 1 1 0 1 0 0
	0 0 0 0 1 0 0 0
B.	Machine Language
	ROL BX, CL
	MOV DL, BL
	AND DX, 0FH
	CMP DL, 9D
	JG ERR
	CMP DL, 0

Note: This is a routine used in computer-based reaction time experiments

a trade-off between ease of learning and computational power of a language. For example, LOGO was easier to learn than FORTRAN but originally would not run as fast or handle large sets of data. With improved hardware, however, these differences became less important.

Learning a computer language includes acquiring its principal vocabulary, format, and conceptual programming schemas (see Mayer, 1987). An example of a conceptual schema is the looping schema. Looping includes two elementary schemas: the cumulation schema and the count schema (see Chapter 13). The cumulation schema adds a new value to the current value, SUM, thus replacing it with the sum of the current value and a new value, SUMMAND, as in (15.1) and (15.2). The latter is the corresponding Pascal expression.

(15.1) current value replaced by current value plus new value

(15.2) SUM : = SUM + SUMMAND;

Other elementary schemas are used for the initialization of variables and for tests of conditions. According to Mayer, conceptual knowledge may be more difficult to acquire than vocabulary and format. Once a person has put in the effort to learn a computer language, he can accomplish amazing things with it, from number crunching to composing music.

Programming enthusiasts such as Seymour Papert (1980) even claim that there is transfer of training between computer languages and other skills. Papert's optimism echoes the classic notion that learning Latin and formal logic helps students to reason. On the other hand, cognitive psychologists have found only limited effects of transfer, if any, even if two tasks are similar. Gick and Holyoak (1983), for example, found essentially no transfer between analogous problems (see Chapter 13).

Klahr and Carver (1988) evaluated Papert's transfer hypothesis that LOGO learning was beneficial for other skills. LOGO is a computer language originally designed for beginning programmers, especially children. It consists of a set of procedures to move an object, called the turtle, on a computer screen. The turtle's movements generate a trace that maps the child's instructions. The command FORWARD 10, for example, moves the turtle 10 spaces forward; RIGHT 90 orients the turtle 90 degrees toward the right; and PENUP lifts the pen so that no trace is left as the turtle moves. In addition to these turtle commands, there are screen commands such as CLEARSCREEN, control commands such as REPEAT, and commands that indicate the beginning and end of a procedure. A procedure consists of commands that together create a graphic image on the screen, such as a square. The child names the procedure and can use it as part of a program. Figure 15.5 shows three procedures used to create a house.

Children usually like LOGO and learn it quickly. However, they hate to fix bugs in programs; they would rather write a new program from scratch. Carver taught children how to debug faulty programs. Then she gave them a non-programming task with a bug in it—for example, a grocery bill that contained an error. She asked the children to find the error in the other task. Carver found that as children learned LOGO and how to debug it, they became more efficient in finding errors in several nonprogramming tasks.

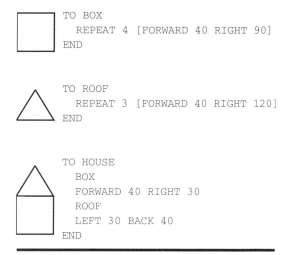

```
TO BOX
    REPEAT 4 [FORWARD 40 RIGHT 90]
END


TO ROOF
    REPEAT 3 [FORWARD 40 RIGHT 120]
END


TO HOUSE
    BOX
    FORWARD 40 RIGHT 30
    ROOF
    LEFT 30 BACK 40
END
```

FIGURE 15.5   Three LOGO procedures. (*A*) Procedure *Box* draws a box. (*B*) Procedure *Roof* draws a roof. (*C*) Procedure *House* draws a box, moves the turtle to a new starting position, and then draws a roof.

Klahr and Carver (1988) concluded that children were able to acquire and transfer a high-level skill—debugging—from a programming context to another problem-solving context. We will consider the issue of transfer of skills in the next section, which discusses applications of cognitive psychology to education.

The Future of Cognitive Engineering

Landauer (1987) has stated that cognitive engineering is a discipline still in its infancy. He has listed a number of factors that currently limit applications of cognitive psychology in this domain:

— Cognitive psychologists have tended to study variables that illuminate theories of abstract mental processing rather than of concrete application in the workplace.

— Not many cognitive principles influence machine design; the principle of limited working memory—or Sternberg's theory of memory scanning, for example—although thoroughly investigated in the research laboratory, have had little impact in human factors.

— Designers do not know or understand the principles that cognitive psychologists have been investigating.

— Many of the effects studied by cognitive psychologists are relatively small in absolute terms; for practical applications, large and robust effects are needed.

Landauer (1987) has great hopes for cognitive engineering, nevertheless. He wrote, "The fact that current knowledge is not sufficient on its own does not mean that it is useless—only that it will need supplementing and filling out to form the basis of a synthetic discipline, a new generation of cognitive psychology" (p. 12). In the future, the principles of cognitive psychology will be applied to determine the most effective and adaptive use of existing machines; indeed, cognitive research will produce entirely new devices and technologies better than any existing ones.

INTERIM SUMMARY

Cognitive engineering has two goals: to assess a person's performance and workload in applied information-processing tasks and to improve the compatibility between the design of machines and the human operator. In the laboratory, workload has been assessed by using the performance operating characteristic in the dual-task situation, in which the person's performance is compared when she executes tasks individually and jointly. Behavioral measures such as eye-fixation patterns and physiological measures such as ERPs can be monitored as an operator performs a task in her real-life job. The measures indicate that operators trade off between concurrent tasks and divert mental resources to the more pressing activity.

When typewriters, computers, and computer languages were first introduced, not much thought was given to how they could be designed with the operator in mind. Cognitive engineers have evaluated the match between such equipment and cognitive processes. In the case of the typewriter, surprisingly no better keyboard

arrangement than the present QWERTY system has been found. Computer-based editors, however, have been developed for easy learning and use; the introduction of the mouse as a pointing device is an example. Computer scientists and cognitive engineers have evaluated computer languages in terms of learnability, debugging, and the effect of knowing computer languages on other skills. According to one study we reviewed, knowing how to program and debug LOGO transfers to debugging skills in other tasks.

COGNITION AND EDUCATION

Education was among the first concerns of early psychology. Memory psychologists such as Ebbinghaus and learning psychologists such as Thorndike and Watson wanted to improve instruction and learning. For many decades since, however, mainstream psychological research and educational theory have remained largely independent (Kintsch & Vipond, 1979). One of the reasons was that *knowledge* was not a topic for psychological research, only *behavior* was. The efforts of behaviorist psychologists on behalf of education were therefore limited to improving instructional technology and implementing reinforcement schedules. With the renewed interest in knowledge, however, cognitive psychology became a natural ally of education (Klahr, 1976; Kintsch & Vipond, 1979).

The standard goal of education is to convey declarative and procedural knowledge, knowing facts and knowing how to do things. Declarative knowledge includes one's factual knowledge— for example, that a day has 24 hours, that Springfield is the capital of Illinois, and that Irving Berlin was a twentieth-century American composer. Procedural knowledge includes such cognitive skills as reading, arithmetic, and making medical diagnoses (see Chapters 12 through 14). In this section, we will consider a sample of the many applications of cognition in education: reading instruction, problem solving, and remembering skills for a lifetime.

Beginning Reading Instruction

Reading is a complex activity that involves many components. The reader recognizes letters, identifies word meanings, integrates words into sentences, links information from different sentences, and forms a mental representation that reflects the content of the text (Chapter 12). Reading is more than the mechanical decoding of words; it is based on the reader's knowledge of the world and of the specific domain the passage is about. After decades of practice, all of these activities have become automatic. For the mature reader, it is therefore hard to appreciate the difficulties faced by beginning readers.

Children acquire spoken language without any formal instruction. They learn to talk and to understand simply by participating in conversation. Learning to read is different. Only a few children learn reading on their own; most are taught in school and by their parents. Learning to read presumes knowledge of some abstract principles of language. Among other things, the child must come to realize that:

— Utterances consist of separate words.
— Words consist of sounds.
— There is a correspondence between letters and sounds.

In addition, the beginning reader must acquire mastery of rather concrete information. She must identify sounds, learn the shape of letters and words, and learn the pairing of sounds and shapes.

The knowledge that words consist of sounds is referred to as **phonemic awareness.** Being aware of phonemes is difficult for any person, let alone a child, because we do not talk in terms of isolated sounds. Indeed, sounds do not exist as constant configurations; rather, their articulation depends on the context (see Chapter 10). In order to assess the development of phonemic awareness in children, researchers invented the phoneme tapping task, which is a kind of game. They got children to tap once for each sound they heard in a word spoken to them. For example, a subject would tap

once for *a,* twice for *at,* and three times for *bat* (Liberman, Shankweiler, Liberman, Fowler, & Fischer, 1977). Four-year-olds had great difficulty with this tapping game; five-year-olds did better. The researchers found, however, that those four-year-olds who were able to segment words into sounds had an easier time learning to read in kindergarten and first grade.

Mastering the correspondence between letters and sounds of a word is important because, for the beginning reader, lexical access is still based on the speech sound. The child hears a word, encodes it acoustically, and retrieves the meaning of the word. Decoding letters into sounds, blending them left to right, and thus sounding out the word, presumably recovers the meaning of the word. The relation between learning to read and developing phonemic awareness and letter-sound correspondences is reciprocal. As the child learns that words consist of letters, his abstract knowledge of language increases, which in turn facilitates beginning reading (Adams, 1990).

A critical facility beginning readers must acquire is the skill of **encoding,** also known as **decoding.** This skill allows the reader to transform written symbols on a page into a format from which meaning can be extracted (see Chapters 4 and 11). Initially, decoding is very difficult for children, in part because they lack knowledge of the principles about sounds and letters. If you have the chance to observe a determined beginning reader, you will find that she works at it much like a cryptographer cracking a secret code. The child seems to be plodding through the text, constructing each word from its constituent letters (Rozin & Gleitman, 1977).

There are two major traditions used in teaching these decoding skills: the whole-word method and the phonics method. They differ in the emphasis they place on words and letters. Historically, the pendulum between these two approaches has swung back and forth.

The **whole-word method** emphasizes the learning of words. Popularized in the 1930s and 1940s, the whole-word method is founded on the Gestalt notion that a word is more than the sum of its letters, and there is some evidence to support this idea. Frequently, children recognize words (their name, for example) without explicit reading instruction. Often, they also know such frequent words as *stop* from stop signs and brand names like *Budweiser* from TV ads (Perfetti, 1985). Effects observed in mature readers lend additional credence to the whole-word reading method. Readers do not read in terms of individual letters; reading would be far too slow. In fact, the word superiority effect (see Chapter 4) indicates that individual letters are better recognized in the context of words than when presented individually.

In the classroom, the whole-word method is implemented as a kind of paired associate procedure; the teacher shows the student a word on a screen or card along with a picture and pronounces the word. The words shown first are simple and familiar, such as *ball, run, dog, cat,* and *boy;* they are shown both individually and in the context of sentences, stories, and poems. The child learns to associate the shape of a small set of words with their sound; this vocabulary is known as a sight vocabulary. The whole-word method is successful in teaching students words. According to such authorities as Kenneth Goodman (1972) and Frank Smith (1973, 1992), it is the more natural and, therefore, superior method.

The **phonics** method emphasizes letters. Rudolph Flesch, a leading defender of the phonics-first approach, describes the method as very simple:

> *Go back to the ABC's. Teach children the 44 sounds of English and how they are spelled. They can sound out each word from left to right and read it off the page. . . .*
>
> *With phonics-first, you teach a child to read the word fish by telling him about the sounds of f-'ff'-i-short i-and sh-'sh.' Then you tell him to blend the sounds from left to right to read the word: "fish". . . .*
>
> *Independent studies have proved that the average child comes to school with a speaking and listening vocabulary of about 24,000 words. Learning to read is simply learning a system of notation for the language the child already knows. (cited from Adams, 1990, p. 239)*

The phonics method emphasizes the alphabetic principle on which printed English is based. Unfortunately, children find the rote memorization of letter shapes and names, inherent to the phonics method, very boring. Because the method emphasizes letters and how they form words, meaning does not always receive the emphasis it deserves. Learning individual letters can be made more interesting by presenting objects in the shape of letters, as is done in the television program "Sesame Street": A snake is shaped like an *S,* a mountain like an *M,* a vase like a *V.* Letter decoding remains important at the remedial level, for example, for brain-injured patients (see Wilson, 1987).

There have been few subjects as contentious as beginning reading instruction. Each of the two methods, the whole-word and the phonics method, has had its dye-in-the wool advocates sticking to their own views with almost religious fervor. After decades of study, comparison, and controversy, influential reviewers have come to the cautious conclusion that the phonics method has an edge over the whole-word method (e.g., Adams, 1990; Just & Carpenter, 1987; Perfetti, 1985; Rayner & Pollatsek, 1989). It incorporates the alphabetic principle and therefore makes it easier for the student to extend his knowledge of letter-sound correspondences to unfamiliar words. Even in books for beginning readers, there are many novel words. As many as 70% of the words occur fewer than five times and 50% occur only once (Just & Carpenter, 1987). There are a number of caveats however: Because there are different ways of implementing the phonics method, in the future the battlelines may be drawn within the phonics camp. One of the issues concerns the timing of introducing connected texts into the curriculum: Should texts be introduced early or late, after the child has acquired a large vocabulary of words he can read?

Reviewing the research evidence, Adams (1990) concluded "that the degree to which children internalize and use their phonic instruction depends on the degree to which they have found it useful for recognizing the words in their earliest texts. It indicates moreover *that immersion—right from the start—in meaningful, connected text is of vital importance*" (p. 10, emphasis added). After all, both word meanings and letter-sound correspondences are important. In one procedure of demonstrated effectiveness, a reading lesson starts with a few phonics drills and continues with readings that emphasize the meaning of words in the context of stories (Just & Carpenter, 1987; Rayner & Pollatsek, 1989). In general, reading teachers are advised to be eclectic and adjust the technique to their students.

The familiar adage that practice makes perfect is probably in no case more appropriate than in beginning reading. According to every philosophy of reading instruction, decoding skills must be thoroughly internalized and automatized. In the words of Huey (1908), the great pioneer of reading research, "Repetition progressively frees the mind from attention to details, makes facile the total act, shortens the time, and reduces the extent to which consciousness must concern itself with the processes" (cited from Rozin & Gleitman, 1977, p. 61). If word decoding skills are faulty, readers are greatly disadvantaged in high school and college, as well as in their professional lives (Pellegrino & Goldman, 1983). Practice remains important beyond the initial reading level; at the intermediate and advanced levels, the goal of practice is to enrich the student's vocabulary and his domain knowledge in specific fields. For the mature reader, too, domain knowledge is the critical determinant in reading speed and comprehension. Whether you are reading an article on music history or quantum mechanics, you need to understand the concepts and procedures in the field. At any level, the relation between reading and learning is mutual; we read in order to learn, and learning in turn facilitates reading.

Teaching Problem-Solving Skills

Problem solving is the prototype of procedural knowledge—the knowledge of how to do things. We acquire procedural knowledge in stages: the cognitive stage, the associative stage, and the autonomous stage (see Anderson, 1980; Chapter 5).

In the cognitive stage, the student memorizes the steps required to solve a problem, as she would memorize a list of sentences. For example, she would memorize to divide both sides of an equation by equal terms, move the unknown quantities to one side, collect terms, and so on. During the associative stage, the student applies the algebra rules to solve sample problems, such as word arithmetic or political science problems. The beginning student labors over each problem for some time and makes many mistakes. After extended practice, however, the problems seem easier, the errors fewer, and the student is in the process of automatizing the skill. At this stage, problem solving is faster because the components of the skill are assumed to have become pattern recognition routines and require less capacity of working memory.

The goal of teaching problem-solving skills is to speed up the learning process so that the autonomous stage is achieved quickly, and a given amount of practice is most effective. Accordingly, cognitive psychologists investigate what sort of practice students should use. Most of the problems one encounters in real life are knowledge-rich problems; mathematics, programming, and law are some examples (see Chapter 13). Research on such problems tells us that the best practice on knowledge-rich problems is domain specific. If you want to be good at solving legal problems, solve many of them; and if you want to be an expert programmer, then hack away.

Much of domain-specific knowledge has been captured in **schemas** (Chapters 5 and 13). A schema is a configuration of knowledge about a typical object, event, or procedure. It provides the general structure of the procedure, leaving out details. Algebra is rich in schemas; the interest-rate schema, the river-current schema, and the area schema are but three illustrations (see Hinsley, Hayes, & Simon, 1977; Mayer, 1985, 1987; Reed & Bolstad, 1991). Problem 15.3 is based on the amount-rate schema.

(15.3) Ann can type a manuscript in 10 hours, and Florence can type it in 5 hours. How long will it take them if they both work together?

Reed and Bolstad (1991) wondered how best to teach students to solve a range of problems similar to 15.3. Their study included three groups of subjects. In the procedures group, the experimenter presented the abstract schema of the problem—for example, the amount = rate of work × time schema. In the example group, the experimenter presented several solved examples to subjects. In the procedures-and-example group, both the schema and some examples were shown to subjects. Unless the problems were difficult, giving examples, either alone or together with procedures, was advantageous; when the problems were relatively easy, students who received examples produced 80% correct solutions, whereas the procedure group solved only 20%. With more difficult problems, the advantage of the example group persisted, but it became smaller.

Schema training is best when it involves examples, in addition to the abstract schema. Problem-solving training is domain specific rather than general because the schemas and subskills differ from domain to domain. Schema training facilitates appropriate problem representation. It is, however, only one part of mathematical problem solving; the student needs to practice computational skills as well (see Chapter 13). According to Mayer (1987) students also must practice metacognitive skills—namely, how to monitor their own progress toward a solution.

Remembering Skills and Information for the Long Haul

Cognitive psychologists have practical advice if you want to remember a skill for a long time, whether it is a foreign language such as Spanish, algebra, facts from a cognitive psychology course, or even recognizing faces of your college classmates (Bahrick, 1984; Bahrick & Hall, 1991; Conway, Cohen, & Stanhope, 1991). According to these studies, retention of a skill improves when you devote extended initial practice to it and take advantage of relearning opportunities.

Given these conditions, you can maintain the skill for 10, 30, even 50 years.

Remembering Math for a Lifetime. Consider first a study by Bahrick and Hall (1991) on the retention of algebra and geometry over a lifetime. These researchers tested 1,726 individuals ranging in age from 19 to 84 years on their knowledge in mathematics. Next, they correlated the test results with a number of variables, such as the time elapsed since respondents took their last course and the number of courses in mathematics taken in college. The researchers developed two tests consisting of problems taken from high school math courses. Sample problems are shown in Table 15.2. The test included about 100 questions; most individuals finished the test in about 90 minutes.

Test scores were correlated with a number of variables thought to predict performance in math, including the number and level of math courses taken in high school and college, the grades received in the courses, the amount of time devoted to mathematical activities since graduation, the person's gender, and others. The critical predictor variable was the retention interval—the number of years since the person's last course in mathematics. For about a third of the subjects, scores from the Scholastic Aptitude Test (SAT) or the American College Test (ACT) were used as additional predictor variables.

TABLE 15.2 Sample Math Problems (Dolciani, Sorgenfrey, Brown, & Kane, 1988)

1. Find the difference between 42.78 and –41.67 degrees Celsius, the extreme temperatures for North Dakota one year.
2. Multiply $(-1)(2x^2 - x + 3)$
3. A box contains 30 coins—pennies, nickels, dimes, and quarters—with total value $2.37. There are twice as many pennies as nickels and two more dimes than quarters. How many of each kind of coin are there?

Note: The answer is 12 pennies, 6 nickels, 7 dimes, and 5 quarters.

Bahrick and Hall used the term *rehearsal activity* to label the mathematical activities a person engaged in after college. They rated rehearsal activities on a three-point scale:

- *High Relevance:* The person tutors students in math and helps children with math homework.
- *Intermediate Relevance:* The person tutors students in chemistry and does math puzzles.
- *Low Relevance:* The person balances a checkbook but engages in no other quantitative activities.

The researchers also coded rehearsal time for each participant, the estimated hours per week or month devoted to mathematical activities. There were five rankings of rehearsal time: people received a rank of 0 if they engaged in no math activity during the year; they received a rank of 4 if they spent more than 100 hours a year on math activities.

Differences in gender are often thought to affect math performance; in some studies, men were found to have a slight advantage compared to women; in others, there was no difference (see Chapter 13). Accordingly, gender was included as one of the predictor variables in this study.

Researchers usually use a mathematical tool—the multiple regression analysis—to examine the effect of a set of variables like these on the dependent variable. In multiple regression analysis, the dependent variable is predicted on the basis of predictor variables X_i. In the simplest case, there is only one predictor variable and the regression equation is equivalent to the linear equation in (15.4):

(15.4) $Y = a + bX$

Here, the variable Y expresses the dependent measure, which could be test scores, reaction times, annual income, or body weight. The coefficient a represents the y-intercept, the value of the dependent measure when the X-variable has the value zero. The b coefficient is the slope of the equation. It expresses how much the dependent measure changes with one unit of change in the predictor variable.

When two or more predictor variables are present, the regression is expressed by equation (15.5):

(15.5) $Y = a + b_1X_1 + b_2X_2 + \ldots b_nX_n$

The interpretation of the coefficients is the same as before; a is the intercept, and the b_n coefficients are the slope values or regression coefficients. There are mathematical procedures by which the researcher determines the relative importance of each of the predictor variables, X_1 through X_n. Using multiple regression analysis and listing the predictor variables in order of importance, Bahrick and Hall (1991) found the following order of effects:

Retention Interval
Amount of Learning
Amount of Rehearsal
Gender

The effect of practice and gender on retention is shown in Figure 15.6A and B. Gender was significant, although such factors as rehearsal and relearning were partialled out. Note, however, that the gender difference was small and that other comparison studies show either minor or no differences at all (see Chapter 13).

Spanish. Bahrick (1984) contacted 773 individuals who had taken high school Spanish up to 50 years ago. He gave the volunteers a Spanish test assessing their reading comprehension, vocabulary, and knowledge of grammar and idioms. As in the study on math retention, he obtained information about a wide range of predictor variables, including the retention interval, the number and level of Spanish courses taken, the mean grade in the courses, and rehearsal opportunities, such as travel to a Spanish speaking country. Bahrick found that, after the retention interval, the factor that most influenced retention was, once again, the amount of original training.

Retention of Spanish declined for the first six years after learning; after that, retention barely declined for 30 years. Bahrick calls this the

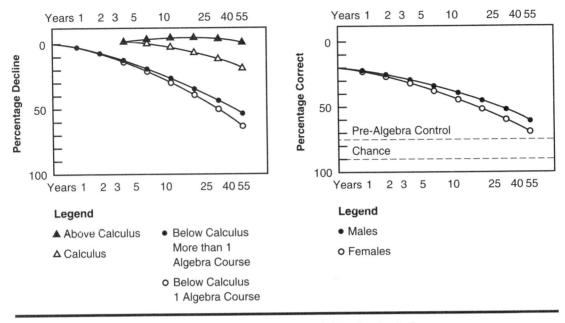

Legend

▲ Above Calculus   • Below Calculus
                          More than 1
△ Calculus   Algebra Course

                        ○ Below Calculus
                          1 Algebra Course

Legend

• Males

○ Females

FIGURE 15.6   Remembering cognitive skills for the long run. (*A*) Decline in algebra performance as a function of the number of courses and the highest level of the course (Bahrick & Hall, 1991). (*B*) Predicted algebra performance as a function of gender (Bahrick & Hall, 1991).

permastore—a bedrock of knowledge that is apparently unaffected by interference or the passage of time. According to Bahrick's results, therefore, one of the goals of education should be to get information into this permastore. This is best done during original learning in high school or college. For most of Bahrick's subjects, there was no rehearsal of Spanish after acquisition.

In another study, Bahrick established that we retain vocabulary better after distributed training, rather than after massed training. Bahrick and Phelps (1987) had subjects learn a vocabulary of 50 Spanish words. In the learning phase of each trial, the 50 English-Spanish word pairs were presented one at a time for 5 seconds. The testing phase followed immediately; English words were shown and subjects had to produce the corresponding Spanish word. There were three training groups: In massed training, the next trial was given immediately after the first was com-

pleted; in the 1-day group, an interval of 1 day intervened between trials, and in the 30-day group, 30 days intervened. Retention was tested after an interval of eight years. Retention improved with the length of the intersession interval during original learning. It is remarkable that the effects of training schedule were still in effect after eight years!

Memory for Cognitive Psychology.   You are about to complete this cognitive psychology course. How much do you think you will remember after the final examination, next semester, in 1 year, and 10 years from now? Based on research results, chances are you will remember more than you expect. Researchers have found that cognitive psychology students remember research methods, concepts, and names in that order. Conway, Cohen, and Stanhope (1991) tested 373 of their former cognitive psychology students at intervals ranging from 3 to 125 months after taking the course. They tested five topic areas: memory, perception, language, problem solving, and research methods. There were several retention tests, including the following two:

▬ *Recognition of Proper Names and Concepts:* In this test, proper names of cognitive psychologists such as *Baddeley, Bower, Farah, Kintsch, Metzler,* and *Shiffrin* were mixed with names selected at random from a telephone book. Concepts were terms such as *context cues, preattentive processing,* and *spreading activation,* all introduced in the course. Foil concepts were written to be stylistically similar to the targets, such as *chronometric cycle* and *quadratic activation effect.*

▬ *Verification of Facts:* This test involved the presentation of true sentences such as *The behaviorists considered learning to be a passive process* and distractors such as *The British empiricists were the first researchers to examine mental processes in experiments.* The subjects had to indicate whether they thought the statement was true or false.

In addition, recall accuracy was tested. Using both recall and recognition measures, research methods were recognized best, followed at some distance by concepts and names in cognitive psychology. Research methods were better retained because students were exposed to them in other courses as well, so there was more repetition. Concepts were remembered better than names, because students formed schemas to remember concepts (see Chapter 5), unlike names which are not inherently linked with any substantive information and are therefore difficult to remember. Measures of name recognition were nevertheless consistently better than chance level even after 10 years had intervened.

INTERIM SUMMARY

Education is a much older discipline than cognitive psychology and has developed independently. Cognitive psychology, however, has important implications for instruction and teaching. In beginning reading instruction, for example, cognitive skills such as encoding or decoding are conveyed to the child. Teaching methods, such as the phonics method, that emphasize the alphabetic principle have proven better than whole-word methods of reading. The phonics method generalizes better to novel words. However, there are trade-offs, and aspects of both should be combined. A primary goal of education is to teach students problem-solving skills in a wide range of applications. Research indicates that domain-specific training is necessary and that transfer between domains is minimal.

Researchers found that the best predictors of long-term retention in math and Spanish were the number of courses taken in high school and college and the number of times material was relearned. Aptitude and achievement, as well as a person's grades, have a small effect on retention, but it is not as great as the effect of factors the student has some control over, such as how many courses she takes and how often she relearns the material through practice. There is a lesson here for students: If you want to excel at a skill later in life, take several courses in the discipline and try to revisit the subject often. Of course, it is best if you do this in college; but there is nothing in Bahrick's study that precludes taking courses later in life if you have the time.

———▬———

COGNITIVE PSYCHOLOGY AND THE LAW

There are many linkages between psychology and law. Social psychologists have investigated group processes in jury deliberations, the persuasiveness of attorneys, and the influence of a defendant's appearance on judge and jury. Clinical psychologists are often called in as expert witnesses to evaluate the mental state of a defendant at the time of an alleged offense. Cognitive psychologists have studied processes of face recognition and other eyewitness accounts in forensic settings. In this section, we will consider face recognition and eyewitness testimony.

Memory for Faces

A Robbery

Phil Markman had been working at the Mobile gas station on Allyn Avenue for six months. Until November 20, 1992, his jobs had been routine—filling tanks and checking the oil at the full-service pumps, and receiving cash or entering credit at the self-serve pumps. It was about 5:00 P.M. and almost dark; although it was a Friday and rush hour, there wasn't much activity at the station. Phil had just turned on the small black and white TV and was flicking through the channels when a customer entered. Phil hadn't even heard him drive in. The man walked up to Phil and said, "I've got a loaded 25-caliber in my pocket. You won't get hurt if you give me the money." Phil was mortified; this was the last thing he'd expected at this hour. He opened the cash register, collected about $200, and handed it to the robber. Then the robber told Phil to go into the men's room and stay there. Phil was shaking all over and still too stunned to do anything. After a few minutes, his cool returned—after all he was lucky it hadn't been worse. From his perch in the men's room, he listened carefully for any action in the office. Hearing none, he peeked through the door and came out. Now his mind was clear; he called 911 for the police. They immediately sent a cruiser that was in the vicinity.

The officer asked Phil about the robbery and especially about the perpetrator. Phil recalled that the robber was of medium height, about 5′ 10″, a Caucasian with grayish eyes, and he wore a stocking cap and a raincoat. He guessed the robber was perhaps in his late thirties or early forties. The officer asked if the suspect had hair on his face. Phil had to think for a while and concluded that the man didn't have a beard or mustache. Phil couldn't describe the raincoat any further, and didn't remember the color of the cap the robber wore.

Later that night Phil drove to the police station and worked with a police artist to make the sketch of the robber shown in Figure 15.7. Phil described the sketch as looking "not exactly like the man but good enough." Next week, Phil had to go to the police station once more. He was shown a series of mugshots—20 in all. All of them showed Caucasian males. Four of them had a beard or mustache; their ages ranged from 30 to 50. Phil was told to study each photograph carefully and identify the person who had robbed the gas station. Phil wasn't sure at all and was about to give up when he decided that one of the men was similar to the robber.

FIGURE 15.7 This sketch illustrates those drawn by police artists.

There had been two other robberies in the Allyn neighborhood in the late fall of 1992, one at the Dairy Queen convenience story about two blocks away from the Mobile gas station, and the other at Mr. Kleen cleaners. The police developed composite sketches from each of the three robberies. The similarities were striking. Based on the sketches, Art Larson was apprehended and charged with first-degree robbery and fifth-degree larceny.

This story is based on a newspaper account of a crime like hundreds of others (see also Laughery & Wogalter, 1989). Unfortunately, not every criminal is brought to justice as the fictitious Art Larson was. In this case, testimony from several eyewitnesses was helpful. All too often, however, eyewitnesses make serious errors, as Box 15.1 indicates. It is clear that the accuracy of face recognition and other eyewitness accounts must be improved; memory researchers have helped in this effort.

The police examination that led to the apprehension of Art Larson is based on Phil Markman's memory for faces. His memory was assessed by a recall and a recognition test. In the recall test, Phil worked with an artist; from memory, he described the robber's face. The artist sketched it and changed it according to Phil's recollections. Reviewing mugshots is an example of a recognition test; Phil had to match the image he had of the robber with one of the pictures in the file.

Tools for Face Identification.   Police departments use a variety of tools to identify the faces of criminals, including mugshots, photospreads, and line-ups. Mugfiles contain photographs of suspects collected over the years; witnesses and victims often peruse hundreds of mugshots at a time. In a photo spread, a small subset of photos likely to include the suspect is placed in front of the witness. In a line-up, a group of people, including the suspect, march in front of the witness.

In the preceding case, Phil Markman worked with a police artist who drew a sketch according to Phil's description. Artists, however, are rare; so, police departments use kits to reproduce faces. Identikit and Photofit are such tools. They include ready-made features and fragmentary faces.

Box 15.1

Memory Failure of Witnesses Doom an Innocent

Robert Dillen, a free-lance photographer, was arrested July 17, 1979, and subsequently charged with indecent exposure and lewdness. Robert's crime: relieving himself in the bushes at a park after finding the door to the lavatory locked. Little did Robert know this small mistake would lead to loss of his job, heavy financial burdens, and finally, a divorce.

Robert was photographed and fingerprinted at police headquarters and eventually released on his own recognizance. He and his wife decided to pay the fine and forget the whole incident, but the next day he was arrested for armed robbery after his photo had been selected from a batch of 10 by a young victim. Robert spent two days in jail, hired a lawyer, and agreed to take a lie detector test and appear in a line-up to clear himself. The lie detector showed no evidence he was lying, but he was picked out of the line-up several times by eyewitnesses to various offenses.

Released on bail, Robert was again arrested several days later and charged with armed robbery, kidnapping, and rape. During the next three months, four different robbery charges were filed and dismissed against him and he was scheduled to appear in court for the remaining robbery-kidnap-rape count. With a strong alibi and the ability of a young attorney to disprove the only witness for the prosecution, Robert was acquitted, but not before he had begun to question his own sanity. One year later, with his marriage broken and career ruined, Robert Dillen moved to a different state to begin anew (Wells & Loftus, 1984, p. 1).

These are assembled by an officer according to the witness's description. Figure 15.8 illustrates the type of photofit reconstructions, or composite faces, used in an experiment by Ellis (1975).

The photofit procedure assumes that a witness segments and remembers a face entirely in terms of features (see also Chapter 4). Photofit procedures are limited because they "treat faces as 'jigsaws' of independent parts" (Bruce, 1988, p. 120). These features do not relate to one another in the organic and natural way that a human face does. For example, where does the nose end and the cheek begin? In addition, subjects do not necessarily recall features of faces they have seen. Researchers found that subjects were very poor in recalling whether a person's mouth was open or closed in a photograph.

Laughery and Wogalter (1989) reviewed additional production devices that sketch faces in color, and Bruce (1988) described computer-based techniques that produce three-dimensional images of the face and head. These procedures were developed according to the theory that faces are dynamic shapes rather than collections of features (see Chapter 4).

None of the production techniques is fully satisfactory. Usually, mugshots produce quicker results, and the procedure is less costly. There are, however, problems with the use of mugshots. There must be an existing photo of the suspect; this is not always the case. Another problem is inherent in the recognition procedures; witnesses are often asked to look at a large number of mugshots at one time; this may result in errors due to interference, shift of criterion, or fatigue. In order to minimize errors, photospreads are prepared based on information the witness gave about the suspect; unfortunately, such selections are time consuming. For this reason, the British researcher Shepherd (1986) used a computer to speed the selection. With the assistance of the police, he developed an interactive computer system, the FRAME system. (FRAME is the acronym for Face Retrieval and Matching Equipment.) The system includes 1,000 faces stored on video disc and a list of 50 attributes for each face—for example, hair length, eye color, mouth size, and eyebrow thickness. There is also an algorithm to access and select a set of faces given specific verbal attributes.

Shepherd evaluated the FRAME system in several experiments that mimicked the identification procedure used by police. A subject was shown a face on a TV monitor for 10 seconds and then asked to describe the face. The attributes generated by subjects were then used as the initial search parameters of the computer file of faces; a subset of 10 faces was selected meeting the description. Subjects were asked to identify the target among the set of 10; 56% were able to do so. For the remaining subjects, three further trials were run. Subjects had the opportunity to refine the search parameters for each successive trial. By the fourth trial, the hit rate reached an impressive 84%. Shepherd achieved similar results when he used a live person as a target instead of the face shown on TV. Finally, he compared his successive search procedure with the standard mugshot procedure used by police. The hit rate was far better with the FRAME than the standard procedure, unless the target face was highly distinctive. Shepherd varied the position of the target among a set of 1,000 mugshots; it was placed in one of four positions: 97, 353, 649, and 898. For nondistinctive faces, there was a decrease in recognition accuracy with increasing position. The more pictures a subject reviewed, the less accurate she was.

FIGURE 15.8 Types of composite faces used in identification of suspects (see Ellis, 1975).

A number of studies like Shepherd's have the following implications for forensic face identification:

— Avoid anything that alters the memory of the witness. For example, limit the number of distractors the witness sees and keep the delay between the crime and the identification test short (but see Laughery & Wogalter, 1989).

— One of the difficulties in the standard sketch and composition procedure is that a witness may lack the vocabulary necessary to describe the face sufficiently well for the police artist to generate a useful composite. One can minimize such communication problems by using a system such as FRAME or a procedure where the witness generates the subset of potential faces on his or her own.

— In line-up presentations, witnesses should not be told how many faces will be presented, and they should see the line-up only once. Informing the witness of the number of faces to be presented increases the number of false identifications (see Lindsay, Lea, & Fulford, 1991).

Suggestibility and Eyewitness Testimony

Eyewitness testimony is an important source of evidence in court; however, it is often erroneous because the witness did not perceive or remember the incident well enough. Errors frequently result from encoding the event when it is observed. People usually experience stress when they witness a crime or an accident; as a result, they may encode the event only partially. Any weapon attracts the attention of witnesses at the expense of other important aspects of the scene, including the features of the perpetrator and other individuals.

Errors result as well from changes of memory traces due to subsequent information. Researchers have identified two principal sources of memory distortions (Reyna & Titcomb, in press): The **suggestibility effect** refers to errors in testimony produced by misleading information, including leading questions presented to the witness subsequent to an event. **Source confusion** describes the failure of an eyewitness to remember the source of misleading suggestions and, therefore, include those suggestions in his account of an event.

Elizabeth Loftus is a pioneer in work on eyewitness testimony and suggestibility. In one of her first studies, she examined the effect of leading questions on retention (Loftus & Palmer; 1974). Leading questions are a staple of courtroom drama; attorneys use them all the time. Loftus and Palmer examined the influence of leading questions on people's judgments of the speed of cars involved in a traffic accident shown on film. The film showed one car driving into another. After viewing the clip, the subjects were asked to describe the accident; they were then asked a series of questions that included a target question about the speed of the cars. The critical variable was the choice of the verb in the question—for example, "About how fast were the cars going when they hit each other?" versus "About how fast were the cars going when they smashed into each other?" The speed estimates (in mph) subjects gave for each of five verbs is listed below:

Smashed	40.8
Collided	39.3
Bumped	38.1
Hit	34.0
Contacted	31.8

Using the same film in a second study, Loftus and Palmer (1974) compared the effect of the two verbs, *smashed* versus *hit,* on subjects' recall of the accident scene one week later. The subjects viewed the film clip, returned to the lab after a week, and were asked a set of questions, including the following: "Did you see any broken glass?" Note there was no broken glass in the film clip. Nevertheless, subjects who had heard the verb *smash* reported having seen glass; the other subjects did so, too, but to a smaller extent.

Loftus, Miller, and Burns (1978) had subjects view a series of slides of a red car making a right turn and knocking down a pedestrian. The experimenters varied two variables: the type of traffic sign that initiated the series and the type of target question asked after the subjects had seen the slides. Half the subjects saw a stop sign; the other half saw a yield sign at the beginning of the set of slides. After having seen the slides, subjects were asked a set of 20 questions, including a target question such as, "Did another car pass the red car while it was stopped at the stop sign?" For half the subjects, the target question named the sign they had actually seen; for the other half, the question mentioned the sign they had not seen. Of interest is the memory performance of the latter group on a subsequent recognition test. Up to 80% of the subjects that had been misled tended to remember having seen the incorrect sign (Loftus & Loftus, 1980).

In subsequent experiments, Loftus and colleagues ruled out that this misinformation effect resulted from demand characteristics. They also showed that the effect generalized to objects other than traffic signs—for example, a pair of skis versus a shovel leaning against a tree. The researchers demonstrated in additional studies that the misinformation effect occurred when subjects were offered $25 for remembering the correct information! Belli and colleagues (1994) showed that memory distortions occur even when subjects are warned about the suggestive nature of postevent information given to them.

Brown, Deffenbacher, and Sturgill (1977) demonstrated the distorting effects of source confusion. Subjects were shown a staged crime and then inspected a series of mugshots. A few days later, they viewed a line-up of people to identify any individuals involved in the crime. Subjects tended to pick out persons actually involved in the crime but they also selected innocent people whom they had seen in the mugshots. It appears, then, that witnesses tend to remember faces quite well, except they forget the circumstances under which they encountered the face.

These studies illustrate how easily one's memory can be altered by subsequent information. Witnesses' accounts of a crime or an accident are easily influenced by subsequent questions, and, although witnesses remember faces, they tend to confuse the occasions when they encountered particular faces. Findings such as these present a challenge to cognitive and forensic psychologists alike. Cognitive psychologists examine parameters of suggestibility (Pezdek & Roe, 1995) and propose theoretical models to account the results (Reyna & Titcomb, in press). Forensic psychologists ask quite pragmatically: How can reporting accuracy be improved, given that memory is susceptible to many changes? Many approaches have been tried, including hypnosis, repeated questioning of the same event, and the cognitive interview. The latter was developed by cognitive psychologists expressly on the basis of cognitive principles.

Memory Enhancement

Forensic researchers developed the **cognitive interview** to improve the accuracy of eyewitness testimony (Fisher & Geiselman, 1988; Geiselman, Fisher, McKinnon, & Holland, 1985). The cognitive interview involves four principles based on the discoveries of memory researchers on **retrieval mnemonics.** Retrieval mnemonics are aids to facilitate the retrieval of traces thought to be inaccessible (Tulving, 1974). Retrieval mnemonics contrast with mnemonic techniques used during *encoding,* such as the method of loci (see Chapter 9). Eyewitness testimony is necessarily based on retrieval; the encoding phase has passed and is no longer under the control of the witness. Here are the four principles that facilitate retrieval of apparently lost information:

— *Use the encoding specificity principle.* Recall accuracy is improved to the extent that the encoding and retrieval contexts are similar. Godden and Baddeley's (1975, see Chapter 9) study illustrates this principle. Divers learned information either under water or on land and were tested in the same or the other learning environment. Recall was better in the same environment. Accordingly, interviewers should encourage the witness to think of the context at the scene of the crime and ask the witness *to reinstate in your mind the context surrounding the incident. Think about what the surrounding environment looked like at the scene, such as rooms, the weather, any nearby people or objects. Also think about how you were feeling at that time* (Geiselman et al., 1985, p. 404).

— *Use all available retrieval paths.* Ask the witness to report information that appears to be unimportant and incomplete. Basic memory research suggests that this information may open new retrieval paths. For example, Tulving (1974) found that recall increases dramatically the more reminders the person is given about some target information, whether it is words, sentences, or pictures. Accordingly, witnesses are encouraged *to report everything that comes to mind, even if the information appears to be unimportant. They are asked not to edit anything because even apparent details may become important when they are pieced together.*

— *Report the events witnessed in a variety of orders.* Whitten and Leonard (1981) had college students recall the names of their elementary and high school teachers. Retrieval was best when subjects recalled the names in the backward order of grades, from 12 through 1. Recall in the forward order from grades 1 through 12 was intermediate. Recall was poor when the students were given the grade numbers at random—for example, 4, 11, 7, 2, and so on. Presumably the memory trace was equal under all conditions. Access was improved by using the most recent name as a retrieval cue. The most recent name was probably the strongest one and additional names are linked to the most recent by backward associations (see Chapter 1). Accordingly, witnesses should be asked *to recall an incident in its backward and forward order,* more information may be uncovered.

— *Assume different perspectives as the witness recounts the incident.* Anderson and Pichert (1978) had subjects read a story about two boys skipping school. The boys spent the day at one of their homes, roaming through different rooms from the basement to the attic. One group of subjects read the story from the perspective of a home buyer, the other group read it from the perspective of a burglar. Readers recalled the story twice. First, they recalled the story from the original perspective; in the second recall test, they were asked to shift their perspective. Remarkably, in the second recall test, subjects were able to recall information that was relevant to the new perspective but not to the first. For example, subjects who read the passage from the home buyer's perspective and recalled it from the burglar's perspective remembered information relevant to the new perspective, such as the location of the TV and of cash and whether or not a door was open. Accordingly, a witness should be encouraged *to place himself in the role of a prominent character in the incident and think about what he or she must have seen.*

Geiselman and colleagues (1985) demonstrated memory enhancement using the cognitive interview in an experiment. The researchers compared three retrieval conditions: the cognitive-interview condition, a hypnosis condition, and a standard condition. Subjects in all three conditions saw four films borrowed from the Los Angeles Police Department (LAPD) depicting a crime and the death of at least one person. The crimes involved a bank robbery, a liquor store holdup, a family fight, and a warehouse break-in. Each film was realistic enough to trigger measurable physiological reactions that were comparable to those police officers often exhibit in a real-life crime scene. Subjects viewed one of the films per condition, and two days later were interviewed by professional law-enforcement officers who were volunteers recruited from agencies such as the LAPD and the CIA. In the cognitive interview condition, subjects were given the hints printed in italics above; in the hypnotic condition, officers experienced in hypnotic techniques interviewed the subjects; and in the standard condition, the interview normally given in police departments was administered.

Recall was best in the cognitive interview condition, followed by the hypnosis condition, and the standard interview condition. Based on this and other studies, Fisher and Geiselman (1988) summarized their research as follows: "Across several studies, the Cognitive Interview was found to elicit between 25–35% more correct information than did a standard police interview, without generating more incorrect information. The Cognitive Interview is easily learned by novice and experienced interviewers and should be useful in a variety of investigative interviews" (p. 34).

Geiselman and colleagues wanted to see if the cognitive interview would hold its own outside of the research laboratory, so they conducted a field test (Fisher, Geiselman, & Amador, 1989). They taught the cognitive interview technique to a group of detectives in a police department and compared the amount of information they were able to elicit from real witnesses with that of an untrained control group.

The cognitive interview was derived from basic research results rather than developed within a narrow applied context; therefore, it should be generalizable and useful in other situations. Indeed, Geiselman and colleagues successfully applied the cognitive interview in other contexts, including gathering medical histories and clinical interviews, accident investigations, and epidemiological assessments (Fischer, Geiselman, & Amador, 1989). We will return to the issue of generalizability in the final section of this chapter.

INTERIM SUMMARY

Cognitive psychologists have made important contributions to important tasks in law enforcement—to the identification of suspects and other eyewitness testimony. Methods of face identification include an artist's drawing based on the recollections of the witness and recognition procedures like inspecting mugfiles and photospreads. The latter includes showing the witness a small subset of photos selected on the basis of a description by the witness. Cognitive psychologists have developed a computer-based photospread procedure that has demonstrated its usefulness. Eyewitness testimony has been enhanced using the cognitive interview. It is based on the notion that memory traces are rarely lost, only momentarily inaccessible. By encouraging the witness to reinstate the original scene, to look at it from various perspectives, and to describe the events in different sequences, more accurate information can be retrieved than in interviews using either the standard method or hypnosis.

COGNITIVE IMPAIRMENT: DIAGNOSIS AND REHABILITATION

Unfortunately, the incidence and variety of cognitive impairments is all too great. Accidents, Alzheimer's disease, alcoholism, strokes, and other disabilities take their toll. Frequently, it is the deterioration of a cognitive skill such as memory or attention that signals the disease. As part of an examination, a physician tests performance on cognitive skills precisely for this reason. With the rich inventory of experimental methods available to cognitive psychologists, more fine-grained diagnostic tests have become available and will no doubt continue to increase. In this section, I will review a psychometric and two laboratory paradigms and describe their implications for diagnosis. I will also present two case studies to illustrate rehabilitation. Because of the wide variety of etiologies of disability, there are limits to how far one can generalize from the cases presented below. Much in this area remains speculative, despite the pressing need for rehabilitation.

Implications for Diagnosis

Frequently, changes and deterioration of cognitive functions are symptoms of organic deficits.

When a person develops slurred speech, has problems concentrating, or experiences unusual difficulty remembering things, there is often underlying disease. In case histories, physicians interview patients and members of their families about recent cognitive changes. Some of the following questions are typical of a comprehensive medical history: Have you experienced any problems understanding what people say to you? Have there been changes in your handwriting? Do you have problems understanding what you read? With calculating? With handling money? Have you experienced any problems concentrating? (Spreen & Strauss, 1991).

These questions are rather global. Both traditional and emerging tools, ranging from the performance pattern in intelligence tests to performance in spatial cuing and recognition tasks, permit a more detailed analysis. As with all diagnoses, however, we need to keep an important caveat in mind: No test used in isolation is fully informative. Several tests should be used in conjunction, and even then, their interpretation can only suggest, not assure, a diagnosis. Caution is necessary because there may be many different reasons for an observed deficit in cognitive functions. For example, anomic aphasia, a difficulty naming a familiar object, can result from a lesion in Broca's area, Wernicke's area, or the angular gyrus. In general, diagnostic tests are based on prior norming with a standard population.

Normative tests based on techniques from cognitive psychology have yet to be developed but hold promise for the future as diagnostic instruments. Such tests would help physicians infer organic traumas from cognitive dysfunctions. This was the case after Broca's initial discoveries that lesions in the left hemisphere were associated with aphasia; neurologists then interpreted aphasia as a symptom of left-hemisphere lesions. The equipment needed to conduct cognitive tests is more widely available than that used for medical diagnostic procedures such as CAT and PET scans. The cognitive techniques are unlikely, however, to fully replace medical diagnosis.

Intelligence Tests.   The Wechsler Intelligence Scales for adults and children contain tests that assess a person's semantic memory and problem-solving skills. There are comprehension tests, vocabulary tests, tests for factual knowledge, and tests for quantitative skills. The person is also given performance tasks, such as arranging a set of blocks and solving a jigsaw puzzle. There are test norms for the population as a whole as well as for special populations separated by age, gender, or disability. Warrington and colleagues have tested over 600 patients with brain lesions in the left and right hemispheres (Warrington, James, & Maciejewski, 1986). They discovered that lesions in the left hemisphere are associated with lower verbal scores, whereas patients with lesions in the right hemisphere have lower performance scores. Physicians do not usually know a patient's verbal and performance scores prior to incurring the brain lesion; nevertheless, comparison of an individual profile with standard profiles is helpful in hunting for an organic deficit.

Attention Disabilities.   Posner and colleagues (e.g., Posner & Raichle, 1994) introduced the spatial cuing task in which subjects responded to visual targets flashed on computer screen. On valid trials, the position of the target was indicated by an arrow; for example, a → arrow indicated that the target would appear on the right. On invalid trials, the cues were not predictive of the targets' position. Not surprisingly, detecting the target was faster in valid than invalid trials. This was true both for normal populations and for patients who had experienced a trauma to the parietal lobe. Such patients however, were disproportionately disadvantaged on invalid trials. They took much longer than subjects who were not impaired. Posner and colleagues attributed this deficit in patients with parietal lesions to impairments in the *shifting* of attention from one part of the visual field to another (see Chapter 3). The differences between patients and nonimpaired individuals have diagnostic implications: To the extent that the spatial cuing task discriminates between the two groups, it may signal damage in the parietal lobe.

Pattern Recognition.   Neurologists have known for some time that patients with damage to one hemisphere have characteristic deficits in visual form recognition. They noticed that patients with lesions in the right hemisphere often failed to recognize familiar faces and other familiar shapes. Subsequent research by Benton confirmed Jackson's original findings and refined his tests. Benton demonstrated that right-hemisphere patients performed poorly on tests of visual closure (see Chapter 3).

Reasoning that the hemispheres are implicated in different aspects of visual recognition, Delis and Bihrle (1989) developed an identification task that involves both global and local recognition. They used letters consisting of different shapes—for example, a large *F* made up of small *O*s (see also Navon, 1977, Chapter 3). These stimuli were inspected for 2 seconds by unilateral brain-damaged patients and nonimpaired subjects. After a 15-second retention interval, subjects were given a recognition test. Patients with damage to the right hemisphere had difficulty recognizing the global forms, whereas left-hemisphere patients could not identify the local stimuli. Delis and Bihrle (1989) replicated these results using other tasks, including reproduction tasks in which subjects redrew the stimuli. Again, there are implications for diagnosis: A person's difficulty with the local or global aspects of the stimuli is a potential cue for localizing the lesion in the left or right hemisphere.

The different performance patterns on cognitive subtasks of the Wechsler Intelligence Scales as well as on cognitive laboratory tasks illustrate their inherent possibilities for clinical neuropsychology. Other laboratory techniques could have been cited as well to make this point. They include memory scanning (Sternberg, 1966), letter matching (Posner & Mitchell, 1967), eye-fixation and reading time patterns (Just & Carpenter, 1987), memory dissociations (Schacter, 1987) for different populations, and ERPs (Hillyard & Kutas, 1983).

Implications for Rehabilitation

Cognitive impairments are seldom total; usually, specific functions are disrupted, such as speech, reading, or memory for faces. The goal of rehabilitation is to diagnose the disability, identify the patient's strengths, and make the most of them. Because cognitive dysfunctions are usually idiosyncratic, rehabilitation efforts must be carefully tailored to each case, making generalizations difficult at best. Next, we will consider three case studies, each illustrating a different impairment and a different rehabilitation technique.

Attention Training.   Robertson and colleagues (1995) treated problems with sustained attention and left unilateral neglect in eight right-hemisphere damaged patients in three different clinics in the United Kingdom and in Sweden. *Unilateral neglect* refers to asymmetry in processing information from the two halves of the visual field: In right-hemisphere patients, information in the left visual field is neglected. Training consisted of bootstrapping the attention system by self-initiated verbal instructions. The expectation was that a patient could be trained to use undamaged brain regions, including the language system, to modulate impaired centers in the right hemisphere that control sustained attention.

During training, patients executed a certain task, such as sorting cards. Initially, they were prompted by the experimenter to pay attention; subsequently, they were trained to develop their own attention prompts. Initially, the trainer would tap the table every 20 to 40 seconds and say "Attend." Then the trainer would continue to tap the table but the patient would say "Attend" in response. Next, the person would tap the table and say "Attend" mentally. Finally, patients were encouraged to use this technique when doing everyday tasks at home.

Throughout three baseline sessions and five

training sessions, the researchers monitored performance on several tasks thought to benefit from training and on control tasks presumed to remain unaffected by training. Training was assumed to improve performance on sustained attention tasks and on unilateral neglect tasks. One of the sustained attention tasks was to count tones presented in a random pattern against a monotonous background. The unilateral neglect task involved placing 16 buns on a baking sheet in a symmetrical arrangement so that both the left and right halves of the sheet were equally covered with buns. Lateral neglect patients tended to place fewer buns on the left side of the tray. Performance on the control task, a backward counting task, is not regulated by the right hemisphere and was not expected to improve as a result of the attention training.

All eight patients improved their performance on the sustained attention tasks and the unilateral neglect tasks, but there was no change in the control task. A nice feature of this study was that the beneficial effects of training were durable and that the treatment was successful independent of who the trainer was or at which clinic it occurred.

Improved Prospective Memory. Although prospective memory is one the most important forms of memory, it has not attracted the attention from researchers it deserves. *Prospective memory* refers to remembering specific tasks at a certain time in the future, such as to mail a letter, run an errand, or keep an appointment. Unfortunately, prospective memory is not spared in accidents. Raskin and Sohlberg (in press) described two patients, both males in their mid-twenties, who were injured in different accidents. One of the patients, JM, was riding his motor bike when he was struck by a car. The other patient, MG, was injured at a work, a railroad company, when a metal bar sprung loose and hit him in the face. He lost consciousness, had facial fractures, and lost several teeth. Both patients suffered from learning and memory impairments, including prospective memory deficits. The investigators devised a treatment regimen to help these patients perform errands and chores in the future.

Prior to treatment, both patients were tested on a variety of cognitive measures—including attention, working memory, and problem solving—and a baseline of prospective memory performance was established. Treatment included 60 one-hour sessions of prospective memory training and retrospective memory training over a period of six months. In prospective memory training, patients were required to perform a specific task, such as clap their hands after intermittent time intervals. On some trials, the patient had to monitor the time on his own, whereas on others, the experimenter would provide an agreed upon cue (e.g., standing up). During the intervening interval, patients worked on a distractor task such as doing some simple math problems.

In retrospective memory training, the two men were asked to recount a series of experimenter-prompted activities they had just completed—for example, standing up or clapping their hands. The criterion variable was performance on a prospective memory test that required patients to perform specific tasks at certain intervals ranging from 1 minute to 24 hours in the future. The patient received points for performing the target task at the correct time.

Importantly, the researchers also investigated whether the training given to the patients in the clinic would generalize to everyday settings. They evaluated this issue by having the patients make telephone calls at specified times and by having them remember errands such as getting specific items in the grocery store, filling the car with gas, or taking medication.

This training schedule succeeded in strengthening the prospective memory of the two patients; their prospective memory score doubled, and, significantly, their performance outside the clinic improved, as well.

An Amnesic Patient Returns to Work. HD was 32 years old when she began to show symptoms of amnesia resulting from encephalitis. After her recuperation, HD returned to work as a clerk but was unable to perform her duties because she could not remember her assignments. At this point, cognitive neuropsychologists became involved. They began a diagnostic and rehabilitation program with HD (Schacter, Glisky, & McGlynn, 1990). The diagnosis confirmed the memory deficits, but indicated that HD had some residual learning and attentional abilities. She was highly motivated and eager to return to work.

In cooperation with HD's employer, Schacter and colleagues undertook a training program with HD. The goal of training was to develop data-entry skills. The job was a mapping task that involved entering data from "meter cards" into a computer file. The operator had to enter data from the meter card into nine designated positions on the screen. The correspondence between cards and display was not always clear, however. There was irrelevant information on the cards, and some of the fields appeared in one order on the cards and in a different order on the computer display.

HD had to learn the general terminology of her data-entry tasks, the meaning of the codes on the meter cards and the display, their different locations, the mapping between cards and display, and some editing functions. Training was based on the technique of *vanishing cues*. This technique is based on an interactive dialog between HD and the computer. For example the sentence *Information from one document is entered into a single row and is called a ???* was presented and HD was to supply the answer *RECORD*. If she was not able to produce the response, she was given incremental recall cues such as *R, RE, REC* until she gave the correct answer. After additional training, fewer cues were given, hence the term *vanishing cue* (see Figure 15.9). Training continued until HD was able to provide the correct answers for all test sentences. Eventually, HD was able to return to part-time employment.

HD's return to work illustrates the success of training methods using a cognitive paradigm. The researchers point out, however, that "we have trained only one patient . . . , so we cannot be certain of the generalizability of our findings"

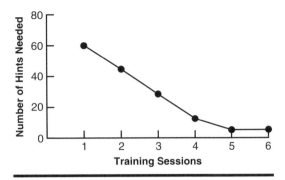

FIGURE 15.9 Progress of patient HD in vanishing cue task. The number of hints required to produce target word declines in six sessions.

(Schacter et al., 1990, p. 252). Schacter and colleagues suggest, however, that success of rehabilitation is more likely when:

— The job is broken down into small steps.
— Each subtask is taught explicitly.
— The laboratory task simulates the work task closely.

This case study and others indicate that successful training is usually specific to the task at hand; it does not transfer readily to other jobs. The specificity of training reflects a theme we have encountered repeatedly in cognitive skills and expertise: Performance tends to be domain specific.

Theory and Therapy. We have seen that laboratory tasks developed by cognitive psychologists have implications for diagnosis and rehabilitation, and that there have been some successes using these tasks. Does success depend, however, on cognitive theories? For example, Wilson (1987) described the case of DC, a young man who lost the ability to read following a gunshot wound. Attempts were made to retrain him by using the whole-word method; they failed totally. Then, a phonics approach was tried. The patient was taught the letters of the alphabet, then two-letter words, three-letter words, and so on. After several weeks of training, DC had acquired as much reading knowledge as a 9-year-old, and after additional training of one year, he was at the reading level of a 13-year-old. Consequently, Wilson and Patterson (1990, p. 24) asked, Did theories from cognitive psychology assist in this successful rehabilitation program? They answered this question, *no*. The training schedule was devised by a health worker who had no knowledge of reading theories. His success, however, is consistent with research of reading acquisition, which suggests that the phonics method is usually more successful than the whole-word method of instruction.

According to Wilson and Patterson (1990), the lack of links between theory and therapy stems from the fact that classical cognitive psychology has not been concerned with learning and relearning. Rather, cognitive psychologists have emphasized so-called steady-state processing of fully developed cognitive functions, including attention, comprehension, and problem solving. In cases of cognitive impairment, previous skills have been partially lost and the patient must relearn them. As this book has shown, learning is reclaiming its place of prominence in the field of cognitive psychology (see Chapters 2, 5, 6, and 7; Anderson, 1981; Newell & Rosenbloom, 1981). Much of the credit for this development goes to connectionist theories (see Chapter 6).

The connectionist approach captures both impairments and the relearning of cognitive functions.

— Connectionist network models are, by their nature, learning models. The researcher designs the architecture of the model and provides the initial connection weights, which are usually random; then the model runs on its own, seeking to match its output with feedback.

— Connectionist models are simulation models; they produce specific outputs for comparison with human performance on a task.

— The network models exhibit graceful degradation of function; when you mess up some nodes in the network, there is no total breakdown; rather, the model continues to produce output that is partially adequate. This makes the simulated performance similar to cognitive impairments. They are rarely total but selective. Connectionist models have been developed to simulate specific disabilities, including dyslexia (Hinton & Shallice, 1989) and cognitive deficits in schizophrenics (Cohen & Servan-Schreiber, 1990).

Before getting carried away with the promise of connectionist models, you should remember their limitations, however (see Chapter 6):

— Connectionist theories, although influenced by neural analogies, are not models of human brain structures.

— Connectionist theorists have a wide latitude in formulating a specific model. They choose the number of input and output units as well as the pattern of connections to simulate a *specific* set of data.

— Because there are no generally accepted principles to construct a connectionist simulation, one can develop models that predict a wide range of results, including those that are *not* supported by the experimental evidence (Massaro, 1988).

INTERIM SUMMARY

Theories and research paradigms of cognitive psychology have implications for the diagnosis and rehabilitation of cognitive impairments. In diagnosis, the idea is to compare a patient's performance profile on a task with that of a standard population known to have a specific deficit. For example, the profiles of verbal and performance scores on intelligence tests differ for patients with lesions in the left and right hemispheres. Similarly, there are distinctive performance patterns in form recognition tasks: Patients with left hemisphere damage have difficulty identifying local features of composite stimuli, whereas patients with right hemisphere damage tend to fail to identify global aspects of stimuli. The spatial cuing task has revealed attentional deficits in parietal lobe patients; these patients have difficulty switching attention from one side of the visual field to the other. The goal of cognitive rehabilitation is to capitalize on intact functions of patients in an effort to train them to modulate those functions that have been impaired. The training should be durable, generalizable across different treatment centers, and improve patient performance outside clinic settings.

———

THE GREAT DEBATE: IS APPLIED COGNITIVE PSYCHOLOGY FOR REAL?

Has the time come to take cognitive psychology out of the laboratory and into the real world? We have sampled actual and potential applications of cognitive psychology in four areas: human factors, education, law enforcement, and medicine. There is, however, no unanimity among cognitive psychologists about the validity of such applications. Basic researchers and those professing a bent toward applications have debated this issue again and again. By way of concluding this chapter, consider Neisser's challenge to the basic researchers and their response (Banaji & Crowder, 1989; Loftus, 1991; Neisser, 1978).

Neisser (1978) spearheaded a campaign of moving memory and cognition research from the confines of the laboratory into the real world. He enumerated many questions that are frequently asked but go unanswered by researchers: Why can't I remember early childhood experiences? Why do I forget appointments and deadlines? Why can't I remember peoples' names? and How much do students remember from courses taught in college? Neisser said all psychology offers in response to such questions is "thundering silence" and that the omission of these questions from the research agenda is "scandalous."

Neisser (1978) added that cognitive psychologists have not gone out into naturalistic settings because they wish to develop a general scientific theory of cognition. He examined a number of paradigms, many of which we covered in this book, including the Sternberg item-recognition task and the Shepard and Metzler rotation task. He conceded that Sternberg's original discovery that reaction times increase with the number of alternatives was important, but after a decade's

worth of research on every aspect of the task, "it has almost become a bore." He concluded his speech with a clarion call to study memory and cognition in all its complexities in the real world.

The response to Neisser's (1978) challenge was almost immediate. Studies by Bahrick (1984), Loftus (1979), and Linton (1982) were done with real-life situations in mind. The laboratory approach, however, continued undiminished as well, and has its articulate defenders. Banaji and Crowder (1989) replied to Neisser's criticisms by calling his approach "bankrupt." The everyday approach to memory and cognition must fail, according to these authors, because studies in everyday settings are not generalizable! They cited several examples for lack of generalizability.

One study examined the relation between witness recall of a car accident and the stereotypes witnesses held of drivers (Diges, 1988). Diges (1988) examined testimony of witnesses and assessed their opinion of drivers after the accident occurred. Banaji and Crowder (1989) analyzed this study step by step, noting that many confounding variables were not examined—for example, the stereotypes the witnesses had *prior* to the accident. Indeed, Diges (1988) analyzed only 13 out of 500 cases. According to Banaji and Crowder, this study did not inform us about the relation between driver stereotypes and witness memory. It failed in the most important goal of a real-life study—namely, to generalize to the real world. Banaji and Crowder concluded that you should conduct a laboratory study rather than a naturalistic study precisely when the issues are complex and the goal is to generalize. Generalization is possible only when you control and isolate factors that have an effect on the dependent variable, just as is done in physics and chemistry.

Banaji and Crowder (1989) did not have the last word, however. Neisser's defenders replied, noting the following:

— Banaji and Crowder picked on weak sample studies rather than examining strong studies in natural settings (Conway, 1991). They cited studies such as Linton's (1982) to demonstrate that many studies that have examined everyday concerns are, in fact, generalizable (see Chapter 9).

— Physics and chemistry are not the best models for cognitive psychology according to Neisser (1991). Rather, cognitive psychologists should look at biology, ecology, and ethology—disciplines that have made great advances by using field studies.

— Other researchers call for a rapprochement of laboratory-based research and the everyday approach. They note that laboratory studies are often inspired by observations made outside the laboratory (Baddeley, 1979; Klatzky, 1991; Morton, 1991). Theories of attention have been influenced by air traffic control applications: Theories of working memory have been advanced by communication engineers, and research on pattern recognition has been driven, at least in part, by robotics.

This debate will no doubt continue. At the same time, you may expect to see the rapprochement between applied and theory-oriented cognitive psychologists many have called for. Both traditions are likely to flourish; theories and basic research will move the frontiers of knowledge further and there will be more applications as well. Indeed, an increasing number of cognitive psychologists will work beyond the halls of academia—in the *real world*—in computer companies, telephone companies, human factors departments, clinics, and the military.

REFERENCES

Adams, M. J. (1990). *Beginning to read: Thinking and learning about print.* Cambridge. MA: MIT Press.

Adelson, B. (1981). Problem solving and the development of abstract categories in programming languages. *Memory & Cognition, 9,* 422–433.

Agnoli, F., & Krantz, D. H. (1989). Suppressing natural heuristics by formal instruction: The case of the conjunction fallacy. *Cognitive Psychology, 21,* 515–550.

Allard, F., & Starkes, J. L. (1991). Motor-skill experts in sports, dance, and other domains. In K. A. Ericsson & J. Smith (Eds.), *Toward a general theory of expertise* (pp. 126–152). New York: Cambridge University Press.

Allport, A. (1993). Attention and control: Have we been asking the wrong questions? A critical review of twenty-five years. In D. E. Meyer & S. Kornblum (Eds.), *Attention and Performance XIV* (pp. 183–218). Cambridge, MA: Bradford/MIT.

Anderson, J. A. (1995). *An introduction to neural networks.* Cambridge, MA: MIT Press.

Anderson, J. R. (1974). Retrieval of propositional information from long-term memory. *Cognitive Psychology, 6,* 451–474.

Anderson, J. R. (1980). *Cognitive psychology and its implications* (1st ed.). San Francisco: W. H. Freeman.

Anderson, J. R. (1983). *The architecture of cognition.* Cambridge, MA: Harvard University Press.

Anderson, J. R. (1990). *Cognitive psychology and its implications* (3rd ed). New York: W. H. Freeman.

Anderson, J. R., & Bower, G. H. (1973). *Human associative memory.* Washington: Winston.

Anderson, J. R., Farrell, R., & Sauers, R. (1984). Learning to program in LISP. *Cognitive Science, 8,* 87–129.

Anderson, J. R., Pirolli, P., & Farrell, R. (1988). Learning to program recursive functions. In M. H. Chi, R. Glaser, & M. J. Farr (Eds.), *The nature of expertise* (pp. 153–183). Hillsdale, NJ: Erlbaum.

Anderson, R. C. (1990). Inferences about word meanings. In A. C. Graesser & G. H. Bower (Eds.), *Inferences and text comprehension* (pp. 1–16). San Diego, CA: Academic Press.

Anderson, R. C., & Pichert, J. W. (1978). Recall of previously unrecallable information following a shift in perspective *Journal of Verbal Learning and Verbal Behavior, 17,* 1–12.

Anzai, Y., & Simon, H. A. (1979). The theory of learning by doing. *Psychological Review, 86,* 124–140.

Atkinson, R. C., & Shiffrin, R. M. (1968). Human memory: A proposed system and its control processes. In K. W. Spence & J. T. Spence (Eds.), *The psychology of learning and motivation: Advances in research and theory* (pp. 89–195). New York: Academic Press.

Baddeley, A. (1979). Applied cognitive and cognitive applied psychology: The case of face recognition. In L. Nilsson (Ed.), *Perspectives on memory research* (pp. 367–388) Hillsdale, NJ: Erlbaum.

Baddeley, A. (1986). *Working memory.* Oxford: Clarendon Press.

Baddeley, A. (1990). *Human memory: Theory and practice.* Boston: Allyn and Bacon.

Baddeley, A. D., & Hitch, G. J. (1994). Developments in the concept of working memory. *Neuropsychology, 8,* 485–493.

Baddeley, A. D., & Longman, D. J. A. (1978). The influence of length and frequency of training sessions on the rate of learning to type. *Ergonomics, 21,* 627–635.

Baecker, R. M., & Buxton, W. A. S. (1987). *Readings in human-computer interaction.* San Mateo, CA: Morgan Kaufmann.

Bahrick, H. P. (1984). Semantic memory content in permastore: 50 years of memory for Spanish learned in school. *Journal of Experimental Psychology: General, 113,* 1–29.

Bahrick, H. P., & Hall, L. K. (1991). Lifetime maintenance of high school mathematics content. *Journal of Experimental Psychology: General, 120,* 20–33.

Bahrick, H. P., & Phelps, E. (1987). Retention of Spanish vocabulary over eight years. *Journal of Experimental Psychology: Learning, Memory, and Cognition, 13,* 344–349.

Baker, A. G., Mercier, P., Vallée-Tourangeau, F., Frank, R., & Pan, M. (1993). Selective associations and causality judgments: Presence of a strong causal factor may reduce judgments of a weaker one. *Journal of Experimental Psychology: Learning, Memory, and Cognition, 19,* 414–432.

Balota, D. A. (1994). Visual word recognition: The journey from features to meaning. In M. A. Gernsbacher (Ed.), *Handbook of psycholinguistics* (pp. 303–358). San Diego, CA: Academic Press.

Banaji, M. R., & Crowder, R. G. (1989). The bankruptcy of everyday memory. *American Psychologist, 44,* 1185–1193.

Barnes, J. M., & Underwood, B. J. (1959). "Fate" of first-list associations in transfer theory. *Journal of Experimental Psychology, 58,* 97–105.

Baron, J. (1988). *Thinking and deciding.* Cambridge: Cambridge University Press.

Bartlett, E. J. (1982). Learning to revise: Some component processes. In M. Nystrand (Ed.), *What writers know: The language, process, and structure of written discourse* (pp. 345–363). New York: Academic Press.

Bartlett, F. C. (1932). *Remembering. A study in experimental and social psychology.* Cambridge: Cambridge University Press.

Bashore, T. R., & Rapp, P. E. (1993). Are there alternatives to traditional polygraph procedures? *Psychological Bulletin, 113,* 3–22.

Bechtel, W., & Abrahamsen, A. (1991). *Connectionism and the mind.* Cambridge, MA: Blackwell.

Beck, L. J. (1952). *The method of Descartes* Oxford: Clarendon Press.

Behn, R. D., & Vaupel, J. W. (1982). *Quick analysis for busy decision makers.* New York: Basic Books.

Bekerian, D. A., & Baddeley, A. D. (1980). Saturation advertising and the repetition effect. *Journal of Verbal Learning and Verbal Behavior, 19,* 17–25.

Belli, R. F., Lindsay, D. S., Gales, M. S., & McCarthy, T. T. (1994). Memory impairment and source misattribution in postevent misinformation experiments with short retention intervals. *Memory & Cognition, 22,* 40–54.

Bernstein, I. L., & Webster, M. M. (1980). Learned taste aversions in humans. *Physiology and Behavior, 25,* 363–366.

Berwick, R. C. (1991). Principle-based parsing. In T. Wasow, P. Sells, & S. M. Shieber (Eds.), *Foundational issues in natural language processing* (pp. 115–226). Cambridge, MA: MIT Press.

Bever, T. G. (1970). The cognitive basis for linguistic structures. In J. R. Hayes (Ed.), *Cognition and the development of language* (pp. 117–135). New York: Wiley & Sons.

Biederman, I. (1990). Higher-level vision. In D. N. Osherson, S. M. Kosslyn, & J. M. Hollerbach (Eds.), *Visual cognition and action* (pp. 41–72). Cambridge, MA: MIT Press.

Birkmire, D. P. (1982, November). *Text processing as a function of text structure, background knowledge and purpose.* Paper presented at the meeting of the Psychonomic Society, Minneapolis, MN.

Bjork, R. A., & Whitten, W. B. (1974). Recency-sensitive retrieval processes in long term free recall. *Cognitive Psychology, 6,* 173–189.

Black, J. B. (1982). Psycholinguistic processes in writing. In S. Rosenberg (Ed.), *Handbook of applied psycholinguistics* (pp 199–216). Hillsdale, NJ, Erlbaum.

Blakeslee, S. (1994). Researchers find gene that may link dyslexia with immune disorders. *New York Times,* October 18, 1994, p. C3.

Bliss, T. V. P., & Lomo, T. (1973). Long-lasting potentiation of synaptic transmission in the dentate area of the anaesthetized rabbit following stimulation of the perforant path. *Journal of Physiology, 232,* 331–356.

Boden, M. (1977). *Artificial intelligence and natural man.* New York: Basic Books.

Bolles, R. C. (1979). *Learning theory* (2nd ed.). New York: Holt, Rinehart & Winston.

Boring, E. G. (1950). *A history of experimental psychology.* Englewood Cliffs, NJ: Prentice Hall.

Bounds, D. G., Lloyd, P. J., Mathew, B., & Waddell, G. (1988). *A multilayer perceptron network for the diagnosis of low back pain.* London: Her Majesty's Stat. Office.

Bower, G. H. (1975). Cognitive psychology: An introduction. In W. K. Estes (Ed.), *Handbook of learning and cognitive processes.* Vol. 1. Introduction to concepts and issues (pp. 25–80). Hillsdale, NJ: Erlbaum.

Bower, G. H., Black, J. B., & Turner, T. J. (1979). Scripts in memory for text. *Cognitive Psychology, 11,* 177–220.

Bowerman, M. (1977). The acquisition of word meaning: An investigation of some current conflicts. In P. N. Johnson-Laird & P. C. Wason (Eds.), *Thinking: Readings in cognitive science* (pp. 239–253). Cambridge: Cambridge University Press.

Bowers, K. S., Regehr, G., Balthazard, C., & Parker, K. (1990). Intuition in the context of discovery *Cognitive Psychology, 22,* 72–110.

Bradshaw, G. L., & Anderson, J. R. (1982). Elaborative encoding as an explanation of levels of processing. *Journal of Verbal Learning and Verbal Behavior, 21,* 165–174.

Bransford, J. D., & Franks, J. J. (1971). The abstraction of linguistic ideas. *Cognitive Psychology, 2,* 331–350.

Bransford, J. D. & Johnson, M. K. (1973). Considerations of some problems of comprehension. In W. G. Chase (Ed.), *Visual information processing* (pp. 383–438). New York: Academic Press.

Broadbent, D. E. (1958). *Perception and communication.* London: Pergamon Press.

Brody, J. (1995). Device transforms brain surgery. *New York Times,* July, 5, 1995, p. C9.

Brooks, L. R. (1968). Spatial and verbal components of the act of recall. *Canadian Journal of Psychology, 22,* 349–368.

Brown, E. L., Deffenbacher, K. A., & Sturgill, W. (1977). Memory for faces and the circumstances of encounter. *Journal of Applied Psychology, 62,* 311–318.

Brown, R., & Kulik, J. (1982). Flashbulb memories. In U. Neisser (Ed.), *Memory observed: Remembering in natural contexts* (pp. 23–40). San Francisco: W. H. Freeman.

Brown, R., & McNeill, D. (1966). The "tip of the tongue" phenomenon. *Journal of Verbal Learning and Verbal Behavior, 5,* 325–337.

Brown, T. H., Kairiss, E. W., & Keenan, C. L. (1990). Hebbian synapses: Biophysical mechanisms and algorithms. *Annual Review of Neuroscience, 13,* 475–511.

Bruce, V. (1988). *Recognising faces.* Hove, East Sussex, UK: Erlbaum.

Bruner, J. S., Goodnow, J., & Austin, G. A. (1956). *A study of thinking.* New York: Wiley & Sons.

Bryan, W. L., & Harter, N. (1899). Studies on the telegraphic language. *Psychological Review, 4,* 27–53.

Bryson, B. (1990, November). Tory storyteller. *New York Times Magazine,* p. 77.

Burtt, H. E. (1941). An experimental study of early childhood memory: Final report. *The Journal of Genetic Psychology, 58,* 435–439.

Canli, T., & Donegan, N. H. (1995). Conditioned diminution of the unconditioned response in rabbit eyelid conditioning: Identifying neural substrates in the cerebellum and brainstem. *Behavioral Neuroscience, 109,* 874–892.

Cantor, J., & Engle, R. W. (1993). Working-memory capacity as long-term activation: an individual differences approach. *Journal of Experimental Psychology: Learning, Memory, and Cognition, 19,* 1101–1114.

Caramazza, A. (1988). Some aspects of language processing revealed through the analysis of acquired aphasia: The lexical systems. *Annual Review of Neurobiology, 11,* 395–421.

Caramazza, A., Grober, E., Garvey, C., & Yates, J. (1977). Comprehension of anaphoric pronouns. *Journal of Verbal Learning and Verbal Behavior, 16,* 601–609.

Card, S. K., Moran, T. P. & Newell, A. (1983). *The psychology of human-computer interaction.* Hillsdale, NJ: Erlbaum.

Carlson, N. R. (1991). *Physiology of behavior* (4th ed.). Boston: Allyn and Bacon.

Carlson, N. R. (1994). *Physiology of Behavior* (5th ed.). Boston: Allyn and Bacon.

Carpenter, P. A., & Just, M. A. (1975). Sentence comprehension: A psycholinguistic processing model of verification. *Psychological Review, 82,* 45–73.

Carpenter, P. A., & Just, M. A. (1989). The role of working memory in language comprehension. In D. Klahr & K. Kotovsky (Eds.). *Complex information processing: The impact of Herbert A. Simon* (pp. 31–68). Hillsdale, NJ: Erlbaum.

Carpenter, P. A., Miyake, A., & Just, M. A. (1995). Language comprehension: Sentence and discourse processing. *Annual Review of Psychology, 46,* 91–120.

Carver, R. P. (1990). *Reading rate: A review of research and theory.* San Diego, CA: Academic Press.

Castellucci, V. F., & Kandel, E. R. (1976). Presynaptic facilitation as a mechanism for behavioral sensitization in *Aplysia. Science, 194,* 1176–1178.

Caudill, M., & Butler, C. (1992). *Understanding neural networks: Computer explorations.* Cambridge, MA: MIT Press.

Chafe, W. (1990). Some things that narratives tell us about the mind. In B. K. Britton & A. D. Pellegrini (Eds.), *Narrative thought and narrative language* (pp. 79–98). Hillsdale, NJ: Erlbaum.

Chang, F. R. (1980). Active memory processes in visual sentence comprehension: Clause effects and pronominal reference. *Memory and Cognition, 8,* 58–64.

Chappell, M., & Humphreys, M. S. (1994). An auto-associative neural network for sparse representations: Analysis and application to models of recognition and cued recall. *Psychological Review, 101,* 103–128.

Chase, W. G., & Ericsson, K. A. (1981). Skilled memory. In J. R. Anderson (Ed.), *Cognitive skills and their acquisition* (pp. 141–189). Hillsdale, NJ: Erlbaum.

Chase, W. G., & Simon, H. A. (1973). The mind's eye in chess. In W. G. Chase (Ed.), *Visual information processing* (pp. 215–281). New York: Academic Press.

Cheng, P. W., & Holyoak, K. J. (1985). Pragmatic reasoning schemas. *Cognitive Psychology, 17,* 391–416.

Cheng, P. W., Holyoak, K. J., Nisbett, R. E., & Oliver, L. M. (1986). Pragmatic versus syntactic approaches to training deductive reasoning. *Cognitive Psychology, 18,* 293–328.

Cherry, E. C. (1953). Some experiments on the recognition of speech, with one and two ears. *Journal of the Acoustical Society of America, 25,* 975–979.

Chi, M. T. H., Feltovich, P. J., & Glaser, R. (1981). Categorization and representation of physics problems by experts and novices. *Cognitive Science, 5,* 121–152.

Chollar, S. (1989). Conversation with the dolphins. *Psychology Today, 23,* 52–57.

Chomsky, N. (1957). *Syntactic structures.* Paris, France: Mouton.

Chomsky, N. (1959). Review of B. F. Skinner's verbal behavior. *Language, 35,* 26–58.

Chomsky, N. (1965). *Aspects of the theory of syntax.* Cambridge, MA: MIT Press.

Chomsky, N. (1981). *Lectures on government and binding.* Dordrecht, Holland: Foris.

Churchland, P. S. (1986). *Neurophilosophy: Toward a unified science of the mindbrain.* Cambridge, MA: MIT Press.

Churchland, P. S., & Sejnowski, T. J. (1992). *The computational brain.* Cambridge, MA: MIT Press.

Clark, A., & Thornton, C. (in press). Trading spaces: Computation, representation and the limits of uninformed learning. *Behavioral and Brain Sciences.*

Clark, H. H., & Chase, W. G. (1972). On the process of comparing sentences against pictures. *Cognitive Psychology, 3,* 472–517.

Clark, H. H., & Clark, E. V. (1977). *Psychology and language: An introduction to psycholinguistics.* New York: Harcourt Brace Jovanovich.

Clark, R. W. (1971). *Einstein: The life and times.* New York: Times Mirror.

Claxton, G. L. (1980). *Cognitive psychology: New directions.* London: RKP.

Claxton, G. L. (1988). *Growth points in cognition.* London: Routledge.

Cohen, J. (1982). Are people programmed to commit fallacies? Further thoughts about the interpretation of experimental data on probability judgment. *Journal for the Theory of Social Behavior, 12,* 251–274.

Cohen, J. D., Dunbar, K., & McClelland, J. L. (1990). On the control of automatic processes: A parallel distributed processing account of the Stroop effect. *Psychological Review, 97,* 332–361.

Cohen, J. D., & Servan-Schreiber, D. (1990). *A parallel distributed process: Approach to behavior and biology in schizophrenia* (AIP-100). Pittsburgh, PA: Carnegie Mellon University.

Colby, K. M. (1975). *Artificial paranoia.* New York: Pergamon Press.

Collins, A. M., & Quillian, M. R. (1969). Retrieval time from semantic memory. *Journal of Verbal Learning and Verbal Behavior, 8,* 240–247.

Coltheart, M., Curtis, B., Atkins, P., & Haller, M. (1993). Models of reading aloud: Dual-route and parallel-distributed-processing approaches. *Psychological Review, 100,* 589–608.

Conrad, R., & Longman, D. J. A. (1965). Standard typewriter versus chord keyboard: An experimental comparison. *Ergonomics, 8,* 77–88.

Conway, M. A. (1991). In defense of everyday memory. *American Psychologist, 46,* 19–26.

Conway, M. A., Cohen, G., & Stanhope, N. (1991). On the very long-term retention of knowledge acquired through formal education: Twelve years of cognitive psychology. *Journal of Experimental Psychology: General, 120,* 395– 409.

Copi, I. M. (1982). *Introduction to logic* (6th ed.). New York: Macmillan.

Corbett, A. T., & Chang, F. R. (1983). Pronoun disambiguation: Accessing potential antecedents. *Memory & Cognition, 11,* 283–294.

Corteen, R. S., & Williams, T. M. (1986). Television

and reading skills. In T. M. Williams (Ed.), *The impact of television: A natural experiment in three communities* (pp. 39–86). Orlando, FL: Academic Press.

Craik, F. I. M. (1979). Human memory. *Annual Review of Psychology, 30,* 63–102.

Craik, F. I. M., & Tulving, E. (1975). Depth of processing and the retention of words in episodic memory. *Journal of Experimental Psychology, 104,* 268–294.

Craik, F. I. M., & Watkins, M. J. (1973). The role of rehearsal in short-term memory. *Journal of Verbal Learning and Verbal Behavior, 12,* 599–607.

Crossman, E. (1959). A theory of the acquisition of speed-skill. *Ergonomics, 2,* 153–166.

Crowder, R. G. (1982). *The psychology of reading: An introduction.* New York: Oxford University Press.

Cummins, D. D., Kintsch, W., Reusser, K., & Weimer, R. (1988). The role of understanding in solving word problems. *Cognitive Psychology, 20,* 405–438.

Curtis, M. (1988). Windows on composing: Teaching revision on word processors. *College Composition & Communication, 39,* 337–344.

Cussler, C. (1988). *Treasure.* New York: Pocket Books.

Damasio, A. R., Tranel, D., & Damasio, H. (1990). Face agnosia and the neural substances of memory. *Annual Review of Neuroscience, 13,* 89–109.

Daneman, M., & Carpenter, P. A. (1980). Individual differences in working memory and reading. *Journal of Verbal Learning and Verbal Behavior, 19,* 450–466.

Daneman, M., & Carpenter, P. A. (1983). Individual differences in integrating information between and within sentences. *Journal of Experimental Psychology: Learning, Memory, and Cognition, 9,* 561–585.

Dansereau, D. F. (1983). *Learning strategy research.* Fort Worth: Texas Christian University.

de Beaugrande, R. (1984). *Text production: Toward a science of composition.* Norwood, NJ: Ablex.

Delis, D. C., & Bihrle, A. M. (1989). Fractionation of spatial cognition following focal and diffuse brain damage. In A. Ardila & F. Ostrosky-Solis (Eds.), *Brain organization of language and cognitive processes* (pp. 17–35). New York: Plenum Press.

Desimone, R., & Ungerleider, L.-G. (1989). Neural mechanisms of visual processing in monkeys. In F. Boller & J. Grafman (Eds.), *Handbook of neuropsy-*

chology (pp. 267–299). New York: Elsevier Science Publishers.

DeVito, P. L., & Fowler, H. (1986). Effects of contingency violations on the extinction of a conditioned fear inhibitor and a conditioned fear excitor. *Journal of Experimental Psychology: Animal Behavior Processes, 12,* 99–115.

Diges, M. (1988). Stereotypes and memory of real traffic accidents. In M. M. Gruneberg, P. E. Morris, & R. N. Sykes (Eds.), *Practical aspects of memory: Current research and issues* (pp. 59–65). Chichester, Wales: Wiley & Sons.

Dolciani, M. P., Sorgenfrey, R. H., Brown, R. G., & Kane, R. B. (1988). *Algebra and trigonometry: Structure and method.* Boston: Houghton Mifflin.

Donegan, N. H., Gluck, M. A., & Thompson, R. F. (1989). Integrating behavioral and biological models of classical conditioning. In R. D. Hawkins & G. H. Bower (Eds.), *Computational models of learning in simple neural systems* (pp. 109–156). San Diego, CA: Academic Press.

Dunbar, K. N., & MacLeod, C. M. (1984). A horse race of a different color: Stroop interference patterns with transformed words. *Journal of Experimental Psychology: Human Perception and Performance, 10,* 622–639.

Duncan, J., & Humphreys, G. W. (1989). Visual search and stimulus similarity. *Psychological Review, 96,* 433–458.

Duncker, K. (1945). On problem solving. *Psychological Monographs, 58.*

Ebbinghaus, H. (1885). *Über das gedächtnis.* Leipzig: Dunker.

Eich, J. E. (1980). The cue-dependent nature of state-dependent retrieval. *Memory & Cognition, 8,* 157–173.

Ellis, A. W., & Young, A. W. (1988). *Human cognitive neuropsychology.* Hove, UK: Erlbaum.

Ellis, H. D. (1975). Recognising faces. *British Journal of Psychology, 66,* 409–426.

Elman, J. L. (1993). Learning and development in neural networks: The importance of starting small. *Cognition, 48,* 71–99.

Emmorey, K. D., & Fromkin, V. A. (1988). The mental lexicon. In F. J. Newmeyer (Ed.), *Language: logical and biological aspects* (pp. 124–149). Cambridge: Cambridge University Press.

Enns, J. T. (1990). Relations between components of visual attention. In J. T. Enns (Ed.), *The development of attention: Research and theory* (pp.

139–158) Amsterdam: Elsevier Science Publishers.

Ericsson, K. A., & Charness, N. (1994). Expert performance. *American Psychologist, 49,* 725–747.

Ericsson, K. A., & Kintsch, W. (1995). Long-term working memory. *Psychological Review, 102,* 211–245.

Ericsson, K. A., Krampe, R. T., & Tesch-Römer, C. (1993). The role of deliberate practice in the acquisition of expert performance. *Psychological Review, 100,* 363–406.

Ericsson, K. A., & Oliver, W. L. (1988). Methodology for laboratory research on thinking: Task selection, collection of observations, and data analysis. In R. J. Sternberg & E. E. Smith (Eds.), *The psychology of human thought* (pp. 392–428). Cambridge: Cambridge University Press.

Ericsson, K. A., & Polson, P. G. (1988). A cognitive analysis of exceptional memory for restaurant orders. In M. T. H. Chi, R. Glaser, & M. J. Farr (Eds.), *The nature of expertise* (pp. 23–70). Hillsdale, NJ: Erlbaum.

Ericsson, K. A., & Simon, H. A. (1980). Verbal reports as data. *Psychological Review, 87,* 255–261.

Estes, W. K. (1950). Toward a statistical theory of learning. *Psychological Review, 57,* 94–107.

Estes, W. K. (1975). *Handbook of cognition.* Hillsdale, NJ: Erlbaum.

Fancher, R. E. (1979). *Pioneers of psychology.* New York: W. W. Norton.

Farah, M. J. (1988). Is visual imagery really visual? Overlooked evidence from neuropsychology, *Psychological Review, 95,* 307–317.

Farah, M. J., Hammond, K. M., Levine, D. N., & Calvanio, R. (1988). Visual and spatial mental imagery: Dissociable systems of representation. *Cognitive Psychology, 20,* 439–462.

Federal Emergency Management Agency. (1983, March). *Tornado resource workbook.* Washington, DC: Government Printing Office.

Feldman, J. A. (1985). Connectionist models and their applications: Introduction. *Cognitive Science, 9,* 1–2.

Ferreira, F. (1991). Effects of length and syntactic complexity on initiation times for prepared utterances. *Journal of Memory and Language, 30,* 210–233.

Fillmore, C. J. (1968). The case for case. In E. Bach & R. T. Harms (Eds.), *Universals in linguistic theory* (pp. 1–88). New York: Holt, Rinehart & Winston.

Fischhoff, B., Lichtenstein, S., Slovic, P., Derby, S. L., & Keeney, R. L. (1981). *Acceptable risk.* Cambridge: Cambridge University Press.

Fischhoff, B., Slovic, P., & Lichtenstein, S. (1978). Fault trees: Sensitivity of estimated failure probabilities to problem representation. *Journal of Experimental Psychology: Human Perception and Performance, 4,* 330–344.

Fish, S. E. (1970). Literature in the reader: Affective stylistics *New Literary History, 2,* 126–127.

Fisher, R. P., & Geiselman, R. E. (1988). Enhancing eyewitness memory with the cognitive interview. In M. M. Gruneberg, P. E. Morris, & R. N. Sykes (Eds.), *Practical aspects of memory: Current research and issues* (pp. 34–39). Chichester, Wales: Wiley & Sons.

Fisher, R. P., Geiselman, R. E., & Amador, M. (1989). Field test of the cognitive interview: Enhancing the recollection of actual victims and witnesses of crime. *Journal of Applied Psychology, 74,* 722–727.

Fitts, P. M., & Peterson, J. R. (1964). Information capacity of discrete motor responses. *Journal of Experimental Psychology, 67,* 103–112.

Fitts, P. M., & Seeger, C. M. (1953). SR compatibility: Spatial characteristics of stimulus and response codes. *Journal of Experimental Psychology, 46,* 199–210.

Flower, L. (1989). Taking thought: The role of conscious processing in the making of meaning. In E. P. Maimon, B. F. Nodine, & F. W. O'Connor (Eds.), *Thinking, reasoning, and writing* (pp. 185–212). New York: Longman.

Flower, L. S., & Hayes, J. R. (1977). Problem-solving strategies and the writing process. *College English, 39,* 449–461.

Fodor, J. A. (1983). *The modularity of mind.* Cambridge, MA: MIT Press.

Fodor, J. A., Bever, T. G., & Garrett, M. F. (1974). *The psychology of language: An introduction to psycholinguistics and generative grammar.* New York: McGraw-Hill.

Fong, G. T., Krantz, D. H., & Nisbett, R. E. (1986). The effects of statistical training on thinking about everyday problems. *Cognitive Psychology, 18,* 253–292.

Forster, K. I. (1976). Accessing the mental lexicon. In R. J. Wales & E. Walker (Eds.), *New approaches to language mechanisms* (pp. 465–495). Amsterdam: North Holland.

Forster, K. I. (1981). Priming and the effects of sentence and lexical contexts on naming time: Evidence for autonomous lexical processing. *Quarterly Journal of Experimental Psychology, 33A,* 465–495.

Forster, K. I. (1990). Lexical processing. In D. N. Osherson & H. Lasnik (Eds.), *Language: An invitation to cognitive science* (pp. 95–131). Cambridge, MA: MIT Press.

Foss, D. J. (1988). Experimental psycholinguistics. *Annual Review of Psychology, 39,* 301–348.

Fowler, O. S., & Fowler, L. N. (1859). *Self-instructor in phrenology and physiology.* New York: Fowler and Wells.

Frazier, L. (1983). Processing sentence structure. In K. Rayner (Ed.), *Eye movements in reading: Perceptual and language processes* (pp. 215–236). New York: Academic Press.

Frazier, L. (1987). Sentence processing: A tutorial review. In M. Coltheart (Ed.), *Attention and performance XII* (pp. 559–586). Hillsdale, NJ: Erlbaum.

Friedman, M. P. (1987). WANDAH—A computerized writer's aid. In D. E. Berger, K. Pezdek, & W. P. Banks (Eds.), *Applications of cognitive psychology: Problem solving, education, and computing* (pp. 219–266). Hillsdale, NJ: Erlbaum.

Funashi, S., Bruce, C. J., & Goldman-Rakic, P. S. (1989). Mnemonic coding of visual space in the monkey's dorsolateral prefrontal cortex. *Journal of Neurophysiology, 61,* 331–349.

Fuster, J. M. (1995). *Memory in the cerebral cortex.* Cambridge, MA: MIT Press.

Fuster, J. M., & Jervey, J. P. (1981). Inferotemporal neurons distinguish and retain behaviorally relevant features of visual stimuli. *Science, 212,* 952–955.

Gagne, E. D. (1985). *The cognitive psychology of school learning.* Boston: Little, Brown.

Gallant, S. I. (1988). Connectionist expert systems. *Communications of the ACM, 31,* 152–169.

Gallant, S. I. (1993). *Neural network learning and expert systems.* Cambridge, MA: MIT Press.

Gallistel, C. R. (1980). *The organization of action: A new synthesis.* Hillsdale, NJ: Erlbaum.

Galton, F. (1870). *Hereditary genius.* New York: Appleton.

Gardner, H. (1982). *Art, mind, and brain.* New York: Basic Books.

Gardner, H. (1985). *The mind's new science.* New York: Basic Books.

Garrett, M. F. (1990). Sentence processing. In D. N. Osherson & H. Lasnik (Eds.), *Language: An invitation to cognitive science* (pp. 133–175). Cambridge, MA: MIT Press.

Gathercole, S. E., & Baddeley, A. D. (1990). Phonological memory deficits in language disordered children: Is there a causal connection? *Journal of Memory and Language, 29,* 336–360.

Gazzaniga, M. S., LeDoux, J. E., & Wilson, D. H. (1977). Language, praxis, and the right hemisphere: Clues to some mechanisms of consciousness. *Neurology, 27,* 1144–1147.

Geiger, G., Lettvin, J., & Fahle, M. (1994). Dyslexic children learn a new visual strategy for reading: A controlled experiment. *Vision Research, 34,* 1223–1233.

Geiselman, R. E., Fisher, R. P., MacKinnon, D. P., & Holland, H. L. (1985). Eyewitness memory enhancement in the police interview: Cognitive retrieval mnemonics versus hypnosis. *Journal of Applied Psychology, 70,* 401–412.

Gelman, S. A., & Markman, E. (1986). Categories and induction in young children. *Cognition, 23,* 183–209.

Gentner, D. R., Grudin, J., & Conway, E. (1980). *Finger movements in transcription typing* (Tech. Rep. 8001). University of California San Diego, Center for Human Information Processing.

Georgopoulos, A., Lurito, J., Petrides, M., Schwartz, A., & Massey, J. (1989). Mental rotations of the neuronal population vector. *Science, 243,* 1627–1629.

Gernsbacher, M. A. (1990). *Language comprehension as structure building.* Hillsdale, NJ: Erlbaum.

Gernsbacher, M. A., & Hargreaves, D. (1988). Accessing sentence participants: The advantage of first mention. *Journal of Memory and Language, 27,* 699–717.

Geschwind, N. (1970). The organization of language and the brain. *Science, 170,* 940–944.

Gibson, J. J. (1966). The problem of temporal order in stimulation and perception. *Journal of Psychology, 62,* 141–149.

Gibson, J. J. (1979). *The ecological approach to visual perception.* Boston: Houghton Mifflin.

Gick, M. L., & Holyoak, K. J. (1980). Analogical problem solving. *Cognitive Psychology, 12,* 306–355.

Gick, M. L., & Holyoak, K. J. (1983). Schema induction and analogical transfer. *Cognitive Psychology, 15,* 1–38.

Gigerenzer, G. (1991). From tools to theories: A heuristic of discovery in cognitive psychology. *Psychological Review, 98,* 254–267.

Gilhooly, K. J., Logie, R. H., Wetherick, N., & Wybb, V. (1993). Working memory and strategies in syllogistic reasoning tasks. *Memory & Cognition, 21,* 115–124.

Glanzer, M., & Adams, J. K. (1990). The mirror effect in recognition memory: Data and theory. *Journal of Experimental Psychology: Learning, Memory & Cognition, 16,* 5–16.

Glanzer, M., & Bowles, N. (1976). Analysis of the word-frequency effect in recognition memory. *Journal of Experimental Psychology: Human Learning and Memory, 2,* 21–31.

Glanzer, M., & Cunitz, A. R. (1966). Two storage mechanisms in free recall. *Journal of Verbal Learning and Verbal Behavior, 5,* 351–360.

Glanzer, M., Fischer, B., & Dorfman, D. (1984). Short-term storage in reading. *Journal of Verbal Learning and Verbal Behavior, 23,* 467–486.

Glass, A. L., & Holyoak, K. J. (1986). *Cognition* (2nd cd.). New York: Random House.

Glenberg, A. M., Meyer, M., & Lindem, K. (1987). Mental models contribute to foregrounding during text comprehension. *Journal of Memory and Language, 26,* 69–83.

Gluck, M. A., & Bower, G. H. (1988). From conditioning to category learning: An adaptive network model. *Journal of Experimental Psychology: General, 117,* 227–247.

Godden, D., & Baddeley, A. D. (1975). Context-dependent memory in two natural environments: On land and under water. *British Journal of Psychology, 66,* 325–331.

Goldman-Rakic, P. S. (1990). Cortical localization of working memory. In J. L. McGaugh, N. M. Weinberger, & G. Lynch (Eds.), *Brain organization and memory: Cells, systems, and circuits* (pp. 285–298). New York: Oxford University Press.

Goldstein, E. B. (1989). *Sensation and perception* (3rd ed.). Belmont, CA: Wadsworth.

Goodale, M. A. (1995). The cortical organization of visual perception and visuomotor control. In S. M. Kosslyn & D. N. Osherson (Eds.), *An invitation to cognitive science: Visual cognition* (pp. 167–213). Cambridge, MA: MIT Press.

Goodfield, J. (1981). *An imagined world: A story of scientific discovery.* New York: Harper & Row.

Goodman, K. (1972). Orthography in a theory of reading instruction. *Elementary English, 49,* 1254–261.

Gopher, D. (1993). The skill of attention control: Acquisition and execution of attention strategies. In D. E. Meyer & S. Kornblum (Eds.), *Attention and Performance XIV* (pp. 299–322). Cambridge, MA: Bradford/MIT.

Gopher, D., & Donchin, E. (1986). Workload—An examination of the concept. In K. R. Boff, L.

Kaufman, & J. P. Thomas (Eds.), *Handbook of perception and human performance* (pp. 41:1–41:49). New York: Wiley & Sons.

Gough, P. B. (1972). One second of reading. In J. K. Kavanagh & I. G. Mattingly (Eds.), *Language by ear and by eye. The relationships between speech and reading* (pp. 331–358). Cambridge. MA. MIT Press.

Graesser, A. C. (1981). *Prose comprehension beyond the word.* New York: Springer-Verlag.

Graesser, A. C., Gordon, S. E., & Sawyer, J. D. (1979). Recognition memory for typical and atypical actions in scripted activities: Tests of a script pointer + tag hypothesis. *Journal of Verbal Learning and Verbal Behavior, 19,* 319–332.

Graur, D., Hide, W. A., & Li , W. H. (1991). Is the guineapig a rodent? *Nature, 351,* 649–652.

Greeno, J. G. (1973). The structure of memory and the process of solving problems. In R. L. Solso (Ed.), *Contemporary issues in cognitive psychology: The Loyola symposium* (pp. 103–133). Washington, DC: V. H. Winston & Sons.

Grice, H. P. (1975). Logic and conversation. In P. Cole & J. L. Morgan (Eds.), *Syntax and semantics* (pp. 41–58). New York: Seminar Press.

Griggs, R. A., & Cox, J. R. (1982). The elusive thematic-materials effect in Wason's selection task. *British Journal of Psychology, 73,* 407–420.

Guthrie, E. R. (1935). *The psychology of learning.* New York: Harper & Row.

Haberlandt, K. (1984). Components of sentence and word reading times. In D. E. Kieras & M. A. Just (Eds.), *New methods in reading comprehension research* (pp. 219–252). Hillsdale, NJ: Erlbaum.

Haberlandt, K. F., & Graesser, A. C. (1989). Processing of new arguments at clause boundaries. *Memory and Cognition, 17,* 186–193.

Haberlandt, K. F., Graesser, A. C., Schneider, N. J., & Kiely, J. (1986). Effects of task and new arguments on word reading times. *Journal of Memory and Language, 25,* 314–322.

Haier, R. J. (1993). Cerebral glucose metabolism and intelligence. In P. A. Vernon (Ed.), *Biological approaches to the study of human intelligence* (pp. 317–332). Norwood, NJ: Ablex.

Haier, R. J., Siegel, B. V., MacLachlan, A., Soderling, E., Lottenberg, S., & Buchsbaum, M. S. (1992). Regional glucose metabolic changes after learning a complex visuospatial/motor task: A positron emission tomography study. *Brain Research, 570,* 134–143.

Halle, M. (1990). Phonology In D. N. Osherson & H. Lasnik (Eds.), *Language: An invitation to cognitive science* (pp. 43–68). Cambridge, MA. MIT Press.

Halpern, D. F. (1992). *Sex differences in cognitive abilities.* Hillsdale, NJ: Erlbaum.

Haviland, S. E., & Clark, H. H. (1974). What's new? Acquiring new information as a process in comprehension. *Journal of Verbal Learning and Verbal Behavior, 13,* 512–521.

Hawisher, G., & Selfe, C. (1991). The rhetoric of technology and the electronic writing class. *College Composition & Communication, 42,* 55–65.

Hawkins, R. D., & Bower, G. H. (Eds.). (1989). *Computational models of learning in simple neural systems.* San Diego, CA: Academic Press.

Hayes, J. R. (1978). *Cognitive psychology: Thinking and creating.* Homewood, IL: Dorsey Press.

Hayes, J. R., & Flower, L. (1980). Identifying the organization of writing processes. In L. Gregg & E. R. Steinberg (Eds.), *Cognitive processes in writing* (pp. 3–30). Hillsdale, NJ: Erlbaum.

Hearst, E. (1988). Fundamentals of learning and conditioning. In R. Atkinson, R. Herrnstein, G. Lindzey, & R. Luce (Eds.), *Stevens' handbook of experimental psychology* (pp. 3–109) New York: Wiley & Sons.

Hebb, D. O. (1949). *The organization of behavior.* New York: Wiley & Sons.

Hebb, D. O. (1972). *Textbook of psychology* (3rd ed.). Philadelphia: W. B. Saunders.

Helton, T. (1989). Synopsis of a synaptic event. *AIExpert, 4,* 43–6.

Hilgard, E. R. (1987). *Psychology in America: A historical survey.* San Diego, CA: Harcourt Brace Jovanovich.

Hillis, A. E., & Caramazza, A. (1991). Category-specific naming and comprehension impairment: A double dissociation. *Brain, 114,* 2081–2094.

Hillyard, S. A., Mangun, G. R., Woldorff, M. G., & Luck, S. J. (1995). Neural systems mediating selective attention. In M. S. Gazzaniga (Ed). *The cognitive neurosciences* (pp. 665–681). Cambridge, MA: MIT Press.

Hillyard, S. A., & Kutas, M. (1983). Electrophysiology of cognitive processing. *Annual Review of Psychology, 34,* 33–61.

Hilts, P. J. (1995). *Memory's ghost: The strange tale of Mr. M. and the nature of memory.* New York: Simon & Schuster.

Hinsley, D. A., Hayes, J. R., & Simon, H. A. (1977). From words to equations: Meaning and represen-tation in algebra word problems. In M. A. Just & P. A. Carpenter (Eds.), *Cognitive processes in comprehension* (pp. 89–106). Hillsdale, NJ: Erlbaum.

Hinton, G. E., & Anderson, J. A. (Eds.). (1981). *Parallel models of associative memory.* Hillsdale, NJ: Erlbaum.

Hinton, G. E., & Shallice, T. (1989). *Lesioning a connectionist network: Investigations of acquired dyslexia* (CRG-TR-89-3). Toronto: University of Toronto, Department of Computer Science.

Hintzman, D. L. (1984). A simulation model of human memory. *Behavior Research Methods, Instruments, and Computers, 16,* 96–101.

Hintzman, D. L. (1993). Twenty-five years of learning and memory: Was the cognitive revolution a mistake? In D. E. Meyer & S. Kornblum (Eds.), *Attention and Performance XIV* (pp. 359–391). Cambridge, MA: Bradford/MIT.

Hirst, W. (1995). Cognitive aspects of consciousness. In M. Gazzaniga (Ed.), *The cognitive neurosciences* (pp. 1307–1319). Cambridge, MA: MIT Press.

Holender, D. (1986). Semantic activation without conscious identification in dichotic listening, parafoveal vision, and visual masking: A survey and appraisal. *Behavioral and Brain Sciences, 9,* 1–66.

Holyoak, K. J. (1990). Problem solving. In D. N. Osherson & E. E. Smith (Eds.), *Thinking: An invitation to cognitive science* (pp. 117–146). Cambridge, MA: MIT Press.

Holyoak, K. J., & Nisbett, R. E. (1988). Induction. In R. J. Sternberg & E. E. Smith (Eds.), *The psychology of human thought* (pp. 50–91). Cambridge: Cambridge University Press.

Holyoak, K. J., & Thagard, P. (1989). Analogical mapping by constraint satisfaction. *Cognitive Science, 13,* 295–355.

Holzman, T. G., Pellegrino, J. W., & Glaser, R. (1983). Cognitive variables in series completion. *Journal of Educational Psychology, 75,* 603–618.

Hoosain, R., & Salili, F. (1988). Language differences, working memory, and mathematical ability. In M. M. Gruneberg, P. E. Morris, & R. N. Sykes (Eds.), *Practical aspects of memory: Current research and issues* (pp. 512–517). Chichester: Wiley & Sons.

Howard, V. A., & Barton, J. H. (1986). *Thinking on paper.* New York: Quill/William Morrow.

Hubel, D. H., & Wiesel, T. N. (1965). Receptive fields and functional architecture in two nonstriate visual areas (18 and 19) of the cat. *Journal of Neurophysiology, 28,* 229–289.

Huey, E. B. (1908). *The psychology and pedagogy of reading.* New York: Macmillan.

Humphreys, G. W., & Bruce, V. (1989). *Visual cognition: Computational, experimental, and neuropsychological perspectives.* London: Erlbaum.

Hunt, E. (1978). Mechanics of verbal ability. *Psychological Review, 85,* 109–130.

Hunt, E. (1985). Verbal ability. In R. J. Sternberg (Ed.), *Human abilities: An information-processing approach* (pp. 31–58). New York: W. H. Freeman.

Hunt, E., & Love, T. (1972). How good can memory be? In A. Melton & E. Martin (Eds.), *Coding processes in human memory* (pp. 237–260). Washington, DC: Wiley & Sons.

Hyde, T. S., & Jenkins, J. J. (1973). Recall for words as a function of semantic, graphic, and syntactic orienting tasks. *Journal of Verbal Learning and Verbal Behavior, 17,* 649–667.

Hynd, G. W., & Semrud-Clikeman, M. (1989). Dyslexia and brain morphology. *Psychological Bulletin, 106,* 447–482.

Ingersoll, B. (1988). *Your hyperactive child.* New York: Doubleday.

Inhelder, B., & Piaget, J. (1958). *The growth of logical thinking from childhood to adolescence.* New York: Basic Books.

Inhoff, A. W. (1991). Word frequency during copytyping. *Journal of Experimental Psychology: Human Perception and Performance, 17,* 478–487.

Intons-Peterson, M., & Roskos-Ewoldsen, B. (1989). Sensory-perceptual qualities of images. *Journal of Experimental Psychology: Learning, Memory, and Cognition, 15,* 188–199.

Intons-Peterson, M. J., & Smyth, M. M. (1987). The anatomy of repertory memory. *Journal of Experimental Psychology: Learning, Memory, and Cognition, 13,* 490–500.

Isreal, J. B., Wickens, C. D., Chesney, G. L., & Donchin, E. (1980). The event-related brain potential as an index of display monitoring workload. *Human Factors, 22,* 212–224.

James, P. D. (1989). *Devices and desires.* New York: Warner Books.

James, W. (1890). *The principles of psychology.* New York: Holt, Rinehart & Winston.

James, W. (1892). *Psychology: Briefer course.* New York: Holt, Rinehart & Winston.

Jarvella, R. J. (1979). Immediate memory and discourse processing. In G. H. Bower (Ed.), *The psychology of learning and motivation: Advances in research and theory* (pp. 379–421). New York: Academic Press.

Jenkins, W., Merzenich, M., Jacobson, T., Miller, S., Schreiner, C., & Tallal, P. (1995). Training exercises improve temporal processing abilities in language-based learning disabled children: Use dependent reorganization [Abstract]. *Society for Neuroscience Abstracts, 21,* 173.

Johansson, G. (1985). About visual event perception. In J. W. Warren & R. Shaw (Eds.), *Persistence and change* (pp. 29–54). Hillsdale, NJ: Erlbaum.

Johnson-Laird, P. N. (1983). *Mental models: Towards a cognitive science of language, inference, and consciousness.* Cambridge, MA: Harvard University Press.

Johnson-Laird, P. N., & Wason, P. C. (1977). *Thinking: Readings in cognitive science.* Cambridge: Cambridge University Press.

Jordan, M. (1988). Motor learning and the degrees of freedom problem. In M. Jeannerod (Ed.), *Attention and Performance XIII: Motor Representation and Control* (pp. 796–836). Hillsdale, NJ: Erlbaum.

Just, M. A., & Carpenter, P. A. (1976). Eye fixations and cognitive processes. *Cognitive Psychology, 8,* 441–480.

Just, M. A., & Carpenter, P. A. (1980). A theory of reading: From eye fixations to comprehension. *Psychological Review, 87,* 329–354.

Just, M. A., & Carpenter, P. A. (1987). *The psychology of reading and language comprehension.* Boston: Allyn and Bacon.

Just, M. A., & Carpenter, P. A. (1992). A capacity theory of comprehension: Individual differences in working memory. *Psychological Review, 99,* 122–149.

Kail, R. (1991). Developmental change in speed of processing during childhood and adolescence. *Psychological Bulletin, 109,* 490–501.

Kalat, J. W. (1992). *Biological psychology.* Belmont, CA: Wadsworth.

Kamin, L. J. (1969). Predictability, surprise, attention, and conditioning. In B. A. Campbell & R. M. Church (Eds.), *Punishment and aversive behavior* (pp. 279–296). New York: Appleton-Century-Crofts.

Kaplan, C. A., & Simon, H. A. (1990). In search of insight. *Cognitive Psychology, 22,* 374–419.

Kaplan, R. M. (1975). On process models for sentence analysis. In D. A. Norman & D. E. Rumelhart (Eds.), *Explorations in cognition* (pp. 117–135). San Francisco: W. H. Freeman.

Karni, A., Meyer, G., Jezzard, P., Adams, M., Turner, R., & Ungerleider, L. (1995). Functional MRI evidence for adult motor cortex plasticity during motor skill learning. *Nature, 377,* 155–158.

Katz, J. J. (1972). *Semantic theory.* New York: Harper & Row.

Keele, S. (1986). Motor control. In K. R. Boff, L. Kaufman, & J. P. Thomas (Eds.), *Handbook of perception and human performance.* Vol. II. (pp. 30:1–30:60). New York: Wiley.

Keele, S. W. (1973). *Attention and human performance.* Pacific Palisades, CA: Goodyear.

Keenan, J. M., & Baillet, S. D. (1980). Memory for personally and socially insignificant events. In R. S. Nickerson (Ed.), *Attention and performance VIII* (pp. 651–669). Hillsdale, NJ: Erlbaum.

Kellogg, R. T. (1988). Attentional overload and writing performance: Effects of rough draft and outline strategies. *Journal of Experimental Psychology: Learning, Memory, and Cognition, 14,* 355–365.

Keppel, G., & Underwood, B. J. (1962). Proactive inhibition in short-term retention of single items. *Journal of Verbal Learning and Verbal Behavior, 1,* 153–161.

Kerr, N. H. (1983). The role of vision in visual imagery experiments: Evidence from the congenitally blind. *Journal of Experimental Psychology: General, 112,* 265–277.

Kieras, D. E., & Just, M. A. (1984). *New methods in reading comprehension research.* Hillsdale, NJ: Erlbaum.

Kihlstrom, J. F. (1987). The cognitive unconscious. *Science, 273,* 1445–1452.

Kimball, J. P. (1973). Seven principles of surface structure parsing in natural language. *Cognition, 2,* 15–47.

Kinney, G. C., Marsetta, M., & Showman, D. J. (1966, November). *Studies in display symbol legibility, part XII. The legibility of alphanumeric symbols for digitalized television* (ESD-TR-66-117). Bedford, MA: Mitre Corporation.

Kinsbourne, M. (1995). Models of consciousness: Serial or parallel in the brain? In M. Gazzaniga (Ed.), *The cognitive neurosciences* (pp. 1321–1329). Cambridge, MA: MIT Press.

Kintsch, W. (1972). Notes on the structure of semantic memory. In E. Tulving & W. Donaldson (Eds.), *Organization of memory* (pp. 247–308). New York: Academic Press.

Kintsch, W. (1977). *Memory and cognition.* New York: Wiley & Sons.

Kintsch, W. (1988). The use of knowledge in discourse processing: A construction-integration model. *Psychological Review, 95,* 163–182.

Kintsch, W. (1992). How readers construct situation models for stories: The role of syntactic cues and causal inferences. In A. Healy, S. Kosslyn, & R. Shiffrin (Eds.), *From learning processes to cognitive processes* (pp. 261–278). Hillsdale, NJ: Erlbaum.

Kintsch, W., & Greeno, J. G. (1985). Understanding and solving word arithmetic problems. *Psychological Review, 92,* 109–129.

Kintsch, W., & Keenan, J. M. (1973). Reading rate and retention as a function of the number of propositions in the base structure of sentences. *Cognitive Psychology, 5,* 257–274.

Kintsch, W., Kozminsky, E., Streby, W. J., McKoon, G., & Keenan, J. M. (1975). Comprehension and recall of text as a function of content variables. *Journal of Verbal Learning and Verbal Behavior, 14,* 196–214.

Kintsch, W., & van Dijk, T. A. (1978). Toward a model of text comprehension and reproduction. *Psychological Review, 85,* 363–394.

Kintsch, W., & Vipond, D. (1979). Reading comprehension and readability in educational practice and psychological theory. In L. G. Nilsson (Ed.), *Perspectives on memory research* (pp. 329–365). Hillsdale, NJ: Erlbaum.

Klahr, D. (1976). *Cognition and instruction,* Hillsdale, NJ: Erlbaum.

Klahr, D., & Carver, S. M. (1988). Cognitive objectives in a LOGO debugging curriculum: Instruction, learning, and transfer. *Cognitive Psychology, 20,* 362–404.

Klahr, D., Fay, A. L., & Dunbar, K. (1993). Heuristics for scientific experimentation: A developmental study. *Cognitive Psychology, 25,* 111–146.

Klapp, S. T., Marshburn, E. A., & Lester, P. T. (1983). Short-term memory does not involve the "working memory" of information processing. The demise of a common assumption. *Journal of Experimental Psychology, 112,* 240–264.

Klatzky, R. L. (1991). Let's be friends. *American Psychologist, 46,* 43–45.

Koehler, W. (1929). *The mentality of apes.* New York: Harcourt Brace.

Kolb, B., & Whishaw, I. Q. (1990). *Fundamentals of human neuropsychology* (3rd ed.). New York: W. H. Freeman.

Kosslyn, S. M. (1983). *Ghosts in the mind's machine: Creating and using images in the brain.* New York: W. W. Norton.

Kosslyn, S. M., Alpert, N. M., Thompson, W. L., Malijkovic, V., Weise, S. B., Chabris, C. F., Hamilton, S. E., Rauch, S. L., & Buonanno, F. S. (1993). Visual mental imagery activates topographically organized visual cortex: PET investigations. *Journal of Cognitive Neuroscience, 5,* 263–287.

Kotovsky, K., Hayes, J. R., & Simon, H. A. (1985). Why are some problems hard?: Evidence from tower of Hanoi. *Cognitive Psychology, 17,* 248–294.

Kotovsky, K., & Simon, H. A. (1973). Empirical tests of a theory of human acquisition of concepts for sequential patterns. *Cognitive Psychology, 4,* 99–424.

Kučera, H., & Francis, W. N. (1967). *Computational analysis of present-day American English.* Providence, RI: Brown University Press.

Kulik, J. A., Bangert-Drowns, R. L., & Kulik, C. L. C. (1984). Effectiveness of coaching for aptitude tests. *Psychological Bulletin, 95,* 179–188.

Kutas, M., & Hillyard, S. A. (1980). Reading senseless sentences: Brain potentials reflect semantic incongruity. *Science, 207,* 203–205.

Kutas, M., & Van Petten, C. (1994). Psycholinguistics electrified: Event-related brain potential investigations. In M. A. Gernsbacher (Ed.), *Handbook of Psycholinguistics* (pp. 83–143). San Diego, CA: Academic Press.

Kyllonen, P. C., & Christal, R. E. (1990). Reasoning ability is (little more than) working memory capacity?! *Intelligence, 14,* 389–433.

La Pointe, L. B., & Engle, R. W. (1990). Simple and complex word spans as measures of working memory capacity. *Journal of Experimental Psychology, Learning, Memory, and Cognition, 16,* 1118–1133.

Lachter, J., & Bever, T. G. (1988). The relation between linguistic structure and associative theories of language learning: A constructive critique of some connectionist learning models. In S. Pinker & J. Mehler (Eds.), *Connections and symbols* (pp. 195–247). Cambridge, MA: MIT Press.

Landauer, T. K. (1987). Relations between cognitive psychology and computer system design. In J. M. Carroll (Ed.), *Interfacing thought* (pp. 1–25). Cambridge, MA: MIT Press.

Langley, P. (1990). Approaches to learning and repre-sentation. *Behavioral and Brain Sciences, 13,* 500–501.

Langley, P., Simon, H. A., Bradshaw, G. L., & Zytkow, J. M. (1987). *Scientific discovery: Computational explorations of the creative processes.* Cambridge, MA: MIT Press.

Lappin, J. S. (1985). Reflections on Gunnar Johansson's perspective on the visual measurement of space and time. In J. W. Warren & R. Shaw (Eds.), *Persistence and change* (pp. 67–86). Hillsdale, NJ: Erlbaum.

Lashley, K. (1951). The problem of serial order in behavior. In L. A. Jeffress (Ed.), *Cerebral mechanisms in behavior: The Hixon symposium* (pp. 112–146). New York: Wiley.

Lasnik, H. (1990). Syntax. In D. N. Osherson & H. Lasnik (Eds.), *Language: An invitation to cognitive science* (pp. 5–21). Cambridge, MA: MIT Press.

Laughery, K. R., & Wogalter, M. S. (1989). Forensic applications of facial memory research. In A. W. Young & H. D. Ellis (Eds.), *Handbook of research on face processing* (pp. 519–556). New York: Elsevier Science Publishers.

Levine, M. (1966). Hypothesis behavior by humans during discrimination learning. *Journal of Experimental Psychology, 71,* 331–338.

Levy, C. M., & Ransdell, S. E. (1988). *Laboratory in cognition and perception.* Iowa City, IA: CONDUIT.

Lewandowsky, S. (1993). The rewards and hazards of computer simulations. *Psychological Science, 4,* 236–243.

Liberman, A. M., Cooper, F. S., Shankweiler, D. P., & Studdert-Kennedy, M. (1967). Perception of the speech code. *Psychological Review, 74,* 431–461.

Liberman, A. M., Harris, K. S., Hoffman, H. S., & Griffith, B. C. (1957). The discrimination of speech sounds within and across phoneme boundaries. *Journal of Experimental Psychology, 54,* 358–368.

Liberman, I. Y., Shankweiler, D., Liberman, A. M., Fowler, C., & Fischer, F. W. (1977). Phonetic segmentation and recoding in the beginning reader. In A. Reber & D. Scarborough (Eds.), *Toward a psychology of reading* (pp. 207–225). Hillsdale, NJ: Erlbaum.

Lindsay, D. S., & Johnson, M. K. (1989). The eyewitness suggestibility effect and memory for source. *Memory & Cognition, 17,* 349–358.

Lindsay, P. H., & Norman, D. A. (1972). *Human infor-*

mation processing: An introduction to psychology. New York: Academic Press.

Lindsay, R. C. L., Lea, J. A., & Fulford, J. A. (1991). Sequential lineup presentation: Technique matters. *Journal of Applied Psychology, 76,* 741–745.

Linn, M. C., & Hyde, J. S. (1989). Gender, mathematics, and science. *Educational Researcher, 18,* 17–27.

Linton, M. (1982). Transformations of memory in everyday life. In U. Neisser (Ed.), *Memory observed: Remembering in natural contexts* (pp. 77–91). San Francisco: W. H. Freeman.

Livingstone, M., & Hubel, D. (1988). Segregation of form, color, movement, and depth: Anatomy, physiology, and perception. *Science, 240,* 740–749.

Livingstone, M., Rosen, G., Drislane, F., & Galaburda, A. (1991). Physiological and anatomical evidence for a magnocellular defect in developmental dyslexia. *Proceedings of the National Academy of Sciences (U.S.A.), 88,* 7943–7947.

Lloyd, D. (1989). *Simple minds: Mental representations from the ground up.* Cambridge, MA: MIT Press.

Loftus, E. F. (1975). Leading questions and the eyewitness report. *Cognitive Psychology, 7,* 560–572.

Loftus, E. F. (1979). *Eyewitness testimony.* Cambridge, MA: Harvard University Press.

Loftus, E. F. (1991). The glitter of everyday memory . . . and the gold. *American Psychologist, 46,* 16–18.

Loftus, E. F., & Loftus, G. R. (1980). On the permanence of stored information in the human brain. *American Psychologist, 35,* 409–420.

Loftus, E. F., Miller, D. G., & Burns, H. J. (1978). Semantic integration of verbal information into a visual memory. *Journal of Experimental Psychology: Human Learning and Memory, 4,* 19–31.

Loftus, E. F., & Palmer, J. C. (1974). Reconstruction of automobile destruction: An example of the interaction between language and memory. *Journal of Verbal Learning and Verbal Behavior, 4,* 19–31.

Logan, G. D. (1988). Toward an instance theory of automatization. *Psychological Review, 95,* 492–527.

Lou, H. C., Hendricksen, L., & Bruhn, P. (1984). Focal cerebral hypoperfusion in children with dysphasia and/or attention-deficit disorder. *Archives of Neurology, 41,* 825.

Luria, A. R. (1976). *The mind of a mnemonist: A little book about a vast memory.* Chicago: Henry Regnery.

Lyons, J. (1970). *Noam Chomsky.* New York: Viking.

Maccoby, E. E., & Jacklin, C. N. (1974). *The psychology of sex differences.* Stanford, CA. Stanford University Press.

Mace, W. M. (1977). James Gibson's strategy for perceiving: Ask not what's inside your head but what your head is inside of. In R. Shaw & J. Bransford (Eds.), *Perceiving, acting and knowing: Toward an ecological psychology* (pp. 43–65). Hillsdale, NJ: Erlbaum.

Maclay, H., & Osgood, C. E. (1959). Hesitation phenomena in spontaneous English speech. *Word, 15,* 19–44.

MacLeod, C. M. (1991). Half a century of research on the Stroop effect: An integrative review. *Psychological Bulletin, 109,* 163–203.

MacLeod, C. M., & Dunbar, K. (1988). Training and Stroop-like interference: Evidence for a continuum of automaticity. *Journal of Experimental Psychology: Learning, Memory, and Cognition, 14,* 126–135.

Madigan, S. A. (1969). Intraserial repetition and coding processes in free recall. *Journal of Verbal Learning and Verbal Behavior, 8,* 828–835.

Malt, B. C., & Smith, E. E. (1984). Correlated properties in natural categories. *Journal of Verbal Learning and Verbal Behavior, 23,* 250–269.

Mandler, G. (1985). *Cognitive psychology: An essay in cognitive science.* Hillsdale, NJ: Erlbaum.

Mandler, G., Goodman, G. O., & Wilkes-Gibbs, D. L. (1982). The word-frequency paradox in recognition. *Memory & Cognition, 10,* 33–42.

Mandler, J. M., & Johnson, N. S. (1977). Remembrance of things parsed: Story structure and recall. *Cognitive Psychology, 9,* 111–151.

Mangun, G. R., & Hillyard, S. A. (1990). Electrophysiological studies of visual selective attention in humans. In A. B. Scheibel & A. F. Wechsler (Eds.), *Neurobiology of higher cognitive function* (pp. 271–295). New York: Guilford Press.

Mangun, G. R., Hillyard, S. A., & Luck, S. J. (1993). Electrocortical substrates of visual selective attention. In D. Meyer & S Kornblum (Eds.), *Attention and performance XIV* (pp. 219–243). Hillsdale, NJ: Erlbaum.

Mäntylä, T. (1986). Optimizing cue effectiveness: Recall of 500 and 600 incidentally learned words. *Journal of Experimental Psychology: Learning, Memory and Cognition, 12,* 66–71.

Marcel, A. J. (1983). Conscious and unconscious perception: Experiments on visual masking and word recognition. *Cognitive Psychology, 15,* 197–237.

Marler, P. R. (1970). A comparative approach to vocal learning: Song development in white-crowned sparrows. *Journal of Comparative and Physiological Psychology Monographs, 71,* (No. 2), 1–25.

Marlin, N. A., & Miller, R. R. (1981). Associations to contextual stimuli as a determinant of long-term habituation. *Journal of Experimental Psychology: Animal Behavior Processes, 7,* 313–333.

Marr, D. (1982). *Vision.* San Francisco: W. H. Freeman.

Marslen-Wilson, W. D., & Tyler, L. K. (1981). Central processes in speech understanding. *Philosophical Transactions of the Royal Society of London, 295,* 317–332.

Massaro, D. W. (1988). Some criticisms of connectionist models of human performance. *Journal of Memory and Language, 27,* 213–234.

Massaro, D. W. (1989). *Experimental psychology: An information processing approach.* San Diego, CA: Harcourt Brace Jovanovich.

Matlin, M. W., & Foley, H. J. (1992). *Sensation and perception* (3rd ed.). Boston: Allyn and Bacon.

Matsuhashi, A. (1982). Explorations in the real-time production of written discourse. In M. Nystrand (Ed.), *What writers know: The language, process, and structure of written discourse* (pp. 269–290). New York: Academic Press.

Mauro, R., & Kubovy, M. (1992). Caricature and face recognition. *Memory & Cognition, 20,* 433–440.

Mayer, R. E. (1985). Mathematical ability. In R. J. Sternberg (Ed.), *Human abilities: An information-processing approach* (pp. 127–150). New York: W. H. Freeman.

Mayer, R. E. (1987). Cognitive aspects of learning and using a programming language. In J. M. Carroll (Ed.), *Interfacing thought* (pp. 61–79). Cambridge, MA: MIT Press.

Mayer, R. E., Bayman, P., & Dyck, J. L. (1987). Learning programming languages: Research and applications. In D. E. Berger, K. Pezdek, & W. P. Banks (Eds.), *Applications of cognitive psychology: Problem solving, education, and computing* (pp. 33–45). Hillsdale, NJ: Erlbaum.

McCarthy, G., Blamire, A., Rothman, D. L., Gruetter, R., & Shulman, R. G. (1993). Echo-planar magnetic resonance imaging studies of frontal cortex activation during word generation in humans. *Proceedings of the National Academy of Sciences of the United States of America, 90,* 4952–4956.

McClelland, J. L. (1992). Can connectionist models discover the structure of natural language? In R. Morelli, D. Anselmi, M. Brown, K. Haberlandt, & D. Lloyd (Eds.), *Minds, brains, and computers: Perspectives in cognitive science and artificial intelligence* (pp 168–189). Norwood, NJ: Ablex.

McClelland, J. L., McNaughton, B. L., & O'Reilly, R. C. (1995). Why there are complementary learning systems in the hippocampus and neocortex: Insights from the successes and failures of connectionist models of learning and memory. *Psychological Review, 102,* 419–457.

McClelland, J. L., & Rumelhart, D. E. (1981). An interactive activation model of context effects in letter perception: Part I. An account of basic findings. *Psychological Review, 88,* 375–407.

McClelland, J. L., & Rumelhart, D. E. (1986). Amnesia and distributed memory. In J. L. McClelland, D. E. Rumelhart, & The PDP Group (Eds.), *Parallel distributed processing: Explorations in the microstructure of cognition* (pp. 503–527). Cambridge, MA: MIT Press.

McClelland, J. L., & Rumelhart, D. E. (1988). *Explorations in parallel distributed processing: A handbook of models, programs, and exercises.* Cambridge, MA: MIT Press.

McClelland, J. L., Rumelhart, D. E., & Hinton, G. E. (1986). The appeal of parallel distributed processing. In D. E. Rumelhart, J. L. McClelland, & The PDP Group (Eds.), *Parallel distributed processing: Explorations in the microstructure of cognition* (pp. 3–44). Cambridge, MA: MIT Press.

McCloskey, J. (1988). Syntactic theory. In F. J. Newmeyer (Ed.), *Linguistic theory: Foundations* (pp. 18–59). Cambridge: Cambridge University Press.

McCloskey, M., & Cohen, N. J. (1989). Catastrophic interference in connectionist networks: The sequential learning problem. In G. H. Bower (Ed.), *The psychology of learning and motivation.* Vol. 24 (pp. 109–165). San Diego: Academic Press.

McCloskey, M., Harley, W., & Sokol, S. M. (1991). Models of arithmetic fact retrieval: An evaluation in light of findings from normal and brain-damaged subjects. *Journal of Experimental Psychology: Learning, Memory, and Cognition, 17,* 377–397.

McCulloch, W. S., & Pitts, W. H. (1943). A logical calculus of the ideas immanent in nervous activity. *Bulletin of Mathematical Biophysics, 5,* 115–133.

McGeoch, J. A. (1942). *The psychology of human learning.* New York: Longmans, Green.

McKoon, G., & Ratcliff, R. (1981). The comprehension processes and memory structures involved in instrumental inference. *Journal of Verbal Learning and Verbal Behavior, 20,* 671–682.

McKoon, G., & Ratcliff, R. (1986). Inferences about predictable events. *Journal of Experimental Psychology: Learning, Memory, and Cognition, 12,* 82–91.

McKoon, G., & Ratcliff, R. (1990). Dimensions of inference. In A. C. Graesser & G. H. Bower (Eds.), *Inferences and text comprehension* (pp. 313–328). San Diego, CA: Academic Press.

McLeod, P., Driver, J., Dienes, Z., & Crisp, J. (1991). Filtering by movement in visual search. *Journal of Experimental Psychology: Human Perception and Performance, 17,* 55–64.

Melton, A. W. (1963). Implications of short-term memory for a general theory of memory. *Journal of Verbal Learning and Verbal Behavior, 2,* 1–21.

Melton, A. W., & Irwin, J. M. (1940). The influence of degree of interpolated learning on retroactive inhibition and the overt transfer of specific responses. *American Journal of Psychology, 53,* 173–203.

Merigan, W. H., & Maunsell, J. H. (1993). How parallel are the primate visual pathways? *Annual Review of Neuroscience, 16,* 369–402.

Merkel, J. (1885). Die zeitlichen verbältnisse der willensthätigkeit, *Philosophische Studien, 2,* 73–127.

Messick, S., & Jungeblut, A. (1981). Time and method in coaching for the SAT. *Psychological Bulletin, 89,* 191–216.

Metcalfe, J. (1991). Recognition failure and the composite memory trace in CHARM. *Psychological Review, 98,* 529–553.

Metzler, J., & Shepard, R. N. (1974). Transformational studies of the internal representations of three dimensional objects. In R. L. Solso (Ed.), *Theories of cognitive psychology: The Loyola symposium* (pp. 147–201). Hillsdale, NJ: Erlbaum.

Meyer, D., Abrams, R., Kornblum, S., Wright, C., & Smith, J. (1988). Optimality in human motor performance: Ideal control of rapid aimed arm movements. *Psychological Review, 95,* 340–370.

Meyer, D., Smith, J., Kornblum, S., Abrams, R., & Wright, C. (1988). Speed-accuracy tradeoffs in aimed movements: Toward a theory of rapid voluntary action. In M. Jeannerod (Ed.), *Attention and performance XIII* (pp. 173–226). Hillsdale, NJ: Erlbaum.

Miller, G. A. (1956). The magic number seven plus or minus two. Some limits on our capacity for processing information. *Psychological Review, 63,* 81–97.

Miller, G. A. (1988). The challenge of universal literacy. *Science, 241,* 1293–1299.

Miller, G. A., & Chomsky, N. (1963). Finitary models of language users. In R. D. Luce, R. R. Bush, & E. Galanter (Eds.), *Handbook of mathematical psychology* (pp. 419–491). New York: Wiley & Sons.

Miller, G. A., Galanter, E., & Pribram, K. H. (1960). *Plans and the structure of behavior.* New York: Holt, Rinehart & Winston.

Milner, B. (1966). Amnesia following operation on the temporal lobes. In C. W. M. Whitty & O. L. Zangwill (Eds.), *Amnesia* (pp. 109–133). London: Butterworths.

Mishkin, M., & Appenzeller, T. (1987). The anatomy of memory. *Scientific American, 256,* 80–136.

Mitchell, D. C. (1994). Sentence parsing. In M. A. Gernsbacher (Ed.), *Handbook of psycholinguistics* (pp. 375–409). San Diego, CA: Academic Press.

Moravec, H. P. (1988). *Mind children: The future of robot and human intelligence.* Cambridge, MA: Harvard University Press.

Moray, N. (1986). Monitoring behavior and supervisory control. In K. R. Boff, L. Kaufman, & J. P. Thomas (Eds.), *Handbook of perception and human performance* (pp. 40:1–40:51). New York: Wiley & Sons.

Morelli, R., & Brown, W. M. (1992). Computational models of cognition. In R. Morelli, D. Anselmi, M. Brown, K. Haberlandt, & D. Lloyd (Eds.), *Minds, brains, and computers: Perspectives in cognitive science and artificial intelligence* (pp 1–35). Norwood, NJ: Ablex.

Morton, J. (1979). Word recognition. In J. Morton & J. C. Marshall (Eds.), *Psycholinguistics 2: Structures and processes* (pp. 107–156). Cambridge, MA: MIT Press.

Morton, J. (1991). The bankruptcy of everyday thinking. *American Psychologist, 46,* 32–33.

Murdock, B. B., Jr. (1982). A theory for the storage and retrieval of items and associative information. *Psychological Review, 89,* 609–626.

Murray, D. M. (1978). Internal revision: A process of discovery. In C. R. Cooper & L. Odell (Eds.), *Research on composing* (pp. 12–19). Urbana, IL: National Council of Teachers of English.

Näätänen, R. (1990). The role of attention in auditory information processing as revealed by event-related potentials and other brain measures of cognitive function. *Behavioral and Brain Sciences, 13,* 201–288.

Nakayama, K. (1990). Visual inference in the perception of occluded surfaces (Summary). *Proceedings of the 12th Annual Conference of the Cognitive Science Society* (p. 1019). Hillsdale, NJ: Erlbaum.

Navon, D. (1977). Forest before trees: The precedence of global features in visual perception. *Cognitive Psychology, 9,* 353–383.

Neisser, U. (1967). *Cognitive psychology.* New York: Appleton-Century-Crofts.

Neisser, U. (1978). Memory: What are the important questions? In M. M. Gruneberg, P. Morris, & R. N. Sykes (Eds.), *Practical aspects of memory* (pp. 3–24). London: Academic Press.

Neisser, U. (1982). *Memory observed: Remembering in natural contexts.* San Francisco W. H. Freeman.

Neisser, U. (1989). *Direct perception and recognition as distinct perceptual systems.* Paper presented at the Eleventh Annual Conference of the Cognitive Science Society, Ann Arbor, MI.

Neisser, U. (1991). A case of misplaced nostalgia. *American Psychologist, 46,* 34–36.

Newell, A. (1973). You can't play twenty questions with nature and win. In W. Chase (Ed.), *Visual information processing* (pp. 283–308). New York: Academic Press.

Newell, A. (1990). *Unified theories of cognition.* Cambridge, MA: Harvard University Press.

Newell, A., & Rosenbloom, P. S. (1981). Mechanisms of skill acquisition and the law of practice. In J. Anderson (Ed.), *Cognitive skills and their acquisition* (pp. 1–55). Hillsdale, NJ: Erlbaum.

Newell, A. Rosenbloom, P. S., & Laird, J. E. (1989). Symbolic architectures for cognition. In M. Posner (Ed.), *Foundations in cognitive science* (pp. 93–131). Cambridge, MA: MIT Press.

Newell, A., & Simon, H. A. (1972). *Human problem solving.* Englewood Cliffs, NJ: Prentice Hall.

Norman, D. A. (1968). Towards a theory of memory and attention. *Psychological Review, 75,* 522–536.

Norman, D. A. (1987). Cognitive engineering— Cognitive science. In J. M. Carroll (Ed.), *Interfacing thought* (pp. 325–336). Cambridge, MA: MIT Press.

Norman, D. A. (1988). *The psychology of everyday things.* Dunmore, PA: Basic Books.

Norman, D. A. (1990). *The design of everyday things.* New York: Doubleday.

Norman, D. A., & Fisher, D. (1982). Why alphabetic keyboards are not easy to use: Keyboard layout doesn't much matter. *Human Factors, 24,* 509–519.

Nottebohm, F. (1985). Neuronal replacement in adulthood. *Annals of the NY Academy of Science, 457,* 143–161.

Ojemann, G. A. (1991). Cortical organization of language. *The Journal of Neuroscience, 11,* 2281–2287.

O'Keefe, J., & Dostoyevsky, T. (1971). The hippocampus as a spatial map: Preliminary evidence from unit activity in the freely moving rat. *Brain Research, 34,* 171–175.

Olson, R. K. (1994). Language deficits in "specific" reading disability. In M. A. Gernsbacher (Ed.), *Handbook of psycholinguistics* (pp. 895–916). San Diego, CA: Academic Press.

Olton, D. S., Collison, C., & Werz, M. A. (1977). Spatial memory and radial arm maze performance in rats. *Learning and Motivation, 8,* 289–314.

O'Toole, A. J., Deffenbacher, K. A., Valentin, D., & Abdi, H. (1994). Structural aspects of face recognition and the other-race effect. *Memory & Cognition, 22,* 208–224.

Owen, D. (1985). *None of the above: Behind the myth of scholastic aptitude.* Boston: Houghton Mifflin.

Palmer, S. (1992). Common region: A new principle for perceptual grouping. *Cognitive Psychology, 24,* 436–447.

Papalia, D. E., & Olds, S. W. (1985). *Psychology,* New York: McGraw-Hill.

Papert, S. (1980). *Mindstorms: Children, computers, and powerful ideas.* New York: Basic Books.

Patel, V. L., & Green, G. J. (1986). Knowledge based solution strategies in medical reasoning. *Cognitive Science, 10,* 91–116.

Pavlov, I. P. (1927). *Conditioned reflexes.* London: Oxford University Press.

Payne, J. W., Bettman, J. R., & Johnson, E. J. (1990). The adaptive decision maker: Effort and accuracy in choice. In R. M. Hogarth (Ed.). *Insights in decision making* (pp. 129–153). Chicago: University of Chicago Press.

Payne, D. G., Elie, C. J., Blackwill, J. M., & Neuschatz, J. S. (1996). Memory illusions: Recalling, recognizing and recollecting events that never occurred. *Journal of Memory and Language, 35,* 261–285.

Pellegrino, J. W. (1985). Inductive reasoning ability. In R. J. Sternberg (Ed.), *Human abilities: An information-processing approach* (pp. 195–225). New York: W. H. Freeman.

Pellegrino, J. W., & Goldman, S. R. (1983). Developmental and individual differences in verbal and spatial reasoning. In R. F. Dillon & R. R. Schmeck (Eds.), *Individual differences in cognition* (pp. 137–180). New York: Academic Press.

Penfield, W., & Milner, B. (1958). Memory deficit produced by bilateral lesions in the hippocampal zone. *American Medical Association Archives of Neurological Psychiatry, 79,* 475–497.

Penrose, R. (1989). *The emperor's new mind concerning computers, minds, and the laws of physics.* New York: Oxford University Press.

Pentland, A. (1986). *From pixels to predicates.* Norwood, NJ: Ablex.

Perfetti, C. A. (1983). Individual differences in verbal processes. In R. Dillon & R. Schmeck (Eds.), *Individual differences in cognition* (pp. 65–104). New York: Academic Press.

Perfetti, C. A. (1985). *Reading ability.* New York: Oxford University Press.

Perkins, D. N. (1988). Creativity and the quest for mechanism. In R. J. Sternberg & E. E. Smith (Eds.), *The psychology of human thought* (pp. 309–336). Cambridge: Cambridge University Press.

Peterson, L. R., & Peterson, M. J. (1959). Short-term retention of individual verbal items. *Journal of Experimental Psychology, 58,* 193–198.

Pezdek, K. (1987). Television comprehension as an example of applied research in cognitive psychology. In D. E. Berger (Ed.), *Applications of cognitive psychology* (pp. 3–15). Hillsdale, NJ: Erlbaum.

Pezdek, K., & Roe, C. (1995). The effect of memory trace strength on suggestibility. *Journal of Experimental Child Psychology, 60,* 116–128.

Pfeffer, R. (1989). On Malay peninsula picking coconuts is monkey business. *Smithsonian, 19,* 111–118.

Pinel, J. P. (1993). *Biopsychology.* Boston: Allyn and Bacon.

Pinker, S. (1990). Language acquisition. In D. N. Osherson & H. Lasnik (Eds.), *Language: An invitation to cognitive science* (pp. 199–241). Cambridge, MA: MIT Press.

Pinker, S. (1994). *The language instinct.* New York: Morrow.

Pinker, S., & Mehler, J. (1988). *Connections and symbols.* Cambridge, MA: MIT Press.

Pittenger, J. B., & Shaw, R. E. (1975). Aging faces as visual-elastic events: Implications for a theory of non-rigid shape perception. *Journal of Experimental Psychology: Human Perception and Performance, 1,* 374–382.

Plaut, D. C., & Shallice, T. (1993). Deep dyslexia: A case study of connectionist neuropsychology. *Cognitive Neuropsychology, 10,* 377–500.

Posner, M. I. (1978). *Chronometric explorations of mind.* Hillsdale, NJ: Erlbaum.

Posner, M. I. (1989). Preface: Learning cognitive science. In M. Posner (Ed.), *Foundations of cognitive science* (pp. xi–xiv). Cambridge, MA: MIT Press.

Posner, M. I. (1995). Attention in cognitive neuroscience: An overview. In M. Gazzaniga (Ed.), *The cognitive neurosciences* (pp. 615–624). Cambridge, MA: MIT Press.

Posner, M. I., & McCandliss, B. (1993). Converging methods for investigating lexical access. *Psychological Science, 4,* 305–309.

Posner, M. I., & Mitchell, R. F. (1967). Chronometric analysis of classification. *Psychological Review, 74,* 392–409.

Posner, M. I., Petersen, S. E., Fox, P. T., & Raichle, M. E. (1988). Localization of cognitive operations in the human brain. *Science, 240,* 1627–1631.

Posner, M. I., & Raichle, M. E. (1994). *Images of mind.* New York: Freeman.

Posner, M. I., & Rossman, E. (1965). Effect of size and location of informational transforms upon short-term retention. *Journal of Experimental Psychology, 70,* 496–505.

Postman, L. (1961). The present status of interference theory. In C. N. Cofer (Ed.), *Verbal learning and verbal behavior* (pp. 152–179). New York: McGraw-Hill.

Potter, M. C., & Lombardi, L. (1990). Regeneration in short-term recall of sentences. *Journal of Memory and Language, 29,* 633–654.

Premack, D. (1965). Reinforcement theory. In D. Levine (Ed.), *Nebraska symposium on motivation: 1965* (pp. 123–179). Lincoln: University of Nebraska Press.

Pylyshyn, Z. W. (1981). The imagery debate: Analogue media versus tacit knowledge. *Psychological Review, 87,* 16–45.

Pylyshyn, Z. W. (1984). *Computation and cognition:*

Toward a foundation for cognitive science. Cambridge, MA: MIT Press.

Qin, Y., & Simon, H. A. (1990). Laboratory replication of scientific discovery processes. *Cognitive Science, 14,* 281–312.

Raaijmakers, J. G. W., & Shiffrin, R. M. (1981). Search of associative memory. *Psychological Review, 88,* 93–134.

Raaijmakers, J. (1993). The story of the two-store model of memory: Past criticisms, current status and future directions. In D. E. Meyer & S. Kornblum (Eds.), *Attention and performance XIV* (pp. 467–488). Cambridge, MA: Bradford/MIT.

Racine, R. J., & de Jonge, M. (1988). Short-term and long-term potentiation in projection pathways and local circuits. In P. Landfield & S. Deadwyler (Eds.), *Long-term potentiation: From biophysics to behavior* (pp. 167–197). New York: Liss.

Raichle, M. E. (1994, April). Visualizing the mind. *Scientific American, 270,* 58–64.

Raichle, M. E., Fiez, J. A., Videen, T. O., MacLeod, A. K., Pardo, J. V., Fox, P. T., & Petersen, S. E. (1994). Practice-related changes in human brain functional anatomy during nonmotor learning. *Cerebral Cortex, 4,* 8–26.

Raphael, B. (1976). *The thinking computer: Mind inside matter.* San Francisco: W. H. Freeman.

Raskin, S., & Sohlberg, M. M. (in press). An experimental investigation into the efficacy of prospective memory training in two adults with brain injury. *Journal of Head Trauma Rehabilitation.*

Ratcliff, R., & McKoon, G. (1978). Priming in item recognition: Evidence for the propositional structure of sentences. *Journal of Verbal Learning and Verbal Behavior, 17,* 403–417.

Ratcliff, R., & McKoon, G. (1988). A retrieval theory of priming in memory. *Psychological Review, 95,* 385–408.

Rayner, K., Carlson, M., & Frazier, L. (1983). The interaction of syntax and semantics during sentence processing: Eye movements in the analysis of semantically biased sentences. *Journal of Verbal Learning and Verbal Behavior, 22,* 358–374.

Rayner, K., & Pollatsek, A. (1989). *The psychology of reading.* Englewood Cliffs, NJ: Prentice Hall.

Reason, J. (1984). Lapses of attention in everyday life. In K. Parasuraman & D. Davies (Eds.), *Varieties of attention* (pp. 515–549). Orlando, FL: Academic Press.

Reason, J. (1990). The contribution of latent human failures to the breakdown of complex systems. In D. Broadbent, J. Reason, & A. Baddeley (Eds.), *Human factors in hazardous situations* (pp. 475–484). Oxford: Clarendon Press.

Reber, A. S. (1993). *Implicit learning and tacit knowledge: An essay on the cognitive unconscious.* New York: Oxford University Press.

Redelmeier, D. A., & Shafir, E. (1995). Medical decision making in situations that offer multiple alternatives. *JAMA, 273,* 302–305.

Reder, L. M. (1987). Strategy selection in question answering. *Cognitive Psychology, 19,* 90–138.

Reed, E. S. (1982). An outline of a theory of action systems. *Journal of Motor Behavior, 14,* 98–134.

Reed, S. K., & Bolstad, C. A. (1991). Use of examples and procedures in problem solving. *Journal of Experimental Psychology: Learning, Memory, and Cognition, 17,* 753–766.

Reicher, G. M. (1969). Perceptual recognition as a function of meaningfulness of stimulus material. *Journal of Experimental Psychology, 81,* 275–280.

Remez, R. (1994). A guide to research on the perception of speech. In M. A. Gernsbacher (Ed.), *Handbook of psycholinguistics* (pp. 145–172). San Diego, CA: Academic Press.

Rescorla, R. A., & Wagner, A. R. (1972). A theory of Pavlovian conditioning: Variations in the effectiveness of reinforcement and non-reinforcement. In A. H. Black & W. F. Prokasky (Eds.), *Classical conditioning II* (pp. 64–99). New York: Appleton-Century-Crofts.

Reyna, V. F., & Titcomb, A. L. (in press). Constraints on the suggestibility of eyewitness testimony: A fuzzy-trace theory analysis. In D. G. Payne & F. G. Conrad (Eds.), *A synthesis of basic and applied approaches to human memory.* Hillsdale, NJ: Erlbaum.

Rhodes, G., Brennan, S., & Carey, S. (1987). Identification and ratings of caricatures: Implications for mental representations of faces. *Cognitive Psychology, 19,* 473–497.

Riemsdijk, H. V., & Williams, E. (1986). *Introduction to the theory of grammar.* Cambridge, MA: MIT Press.

Rips, L. J. (1989). Similarity, typicality, and categorization. In S. Vosniadou & A. Ortony (Eds.), *Similarity and analogical reasoning* (pp. 21–59). New York: Cambridge University Press.

Rips, L. J., & Marcus, S. L. (1977). Supposition and the analysis of conditional sentences. In M. A. Just & P.

A. Carpenter (Eds.), *Cognitive processes in comprehension* (pp. 185–220). Hillsdale, NJ: Erlbaum.

Roberts, W. (1991). *Straight A's never made anybody rich* New York: Harper Collins.

Robertson, I. H., Tegner, R., Tham, K., Lo, A., & Nimmo-Smith, I. (1995). Sustained attention training for unilateral neglect: Theoretical and rehabilitation implications. *Journal of Clinical and Experimental Neuropsychology, 17,* 416–430.

Robinson, F. P. (1970). *Effective study.* New York: Harper & Row.

Roediger, III, H. L. (1990). Implicit memory: Retention without remembering. *American Psychologist, 45,* 1043–1056.

Roediger, H. L. (1993). Learning and memory: Progress and challenge. In D. E. Meyer & S. Kornblum (Eds.), *Attention and performance XIV* (pp. 509–528). Cambridge, MA: Bradford/MIT.

Rosch, E. (1975). Cognitive representations of semantic categories. *Journal of Experimental Psychology: General, 104,* 192–223.

Rosenbaum, D. (1984). Planning and control of motor movements. In J. R. Anderson & S. M. Kosslyn (Eds.), *Tutorials in learning and memory* (pp. 219–234). San Francisco, CA: Freeman.

Rosenbaum, D. (1991). *Human motor control.* San Diego, CA: Academic Press.

Rosenbaum, D., Inhoff, A. W., & Gordon, A. M. (1984). Choosing between movement sequences: A hierarchical editor model. *Journal of Experimental Psychology: General, 113,* 372–392.

Rosenbaum, D., Kenny, S., & Derr, M. (1983). Hierarchical control of rapid movement sequences. *Journal of Experimental Psychology: Human Perception and Performance, 9,* 86–102.

Rosenbaum, D., Loukopoulos, L., Meulenbroek, R., Vaughan, J., & Engelbrecht, S. (1995). Planning reaches by evaluating stored postures. *Psychological Review, 102,* 28–67.

Rozin, P., & Gleitman, L. R. (1977). The structure and acquisition of reading II: The reading process and the acquisition of the alphabetic principle. In A. Reber & D. Scarborough (Eds.), *Toward a psychology of reading* (pp. 55–141). Hillsdale, NJ: Erlbaum.

Rubin, P., Turvey, M. T., & Van Gelder, P. (1976). Initial phonemes are detected faster in spoken words than in nonspoken words. *Perception & Psychophysics, 19,* 394–398.

Rumelhart, D. E., Hinton, G. E., & Williams, R. J. (1986). Learning internal representations by error propagation. In D. E. Rumelhart & J. L. McClelland (Eds.), *Parallel distributed processing: Explorations in the microstructure of cognition* (pp. 318–362). Cambridge, MA: MIT Press.

Rumelhart, D. E., & McClelland, J. L. (1987). Learning the past tenses of English verbs: Implicit rules or parallel distributed processing? In B. MacWhinney (Ed.), *Mechanisms of language acquisition* (pp. 195–248). Hillsdale, NJ: Erlbaum.

Rumelhart, D. E., & Norman, D. A. (1982). Simulating a skilled typist: A study of skilled cognitive-motor performance. *Cognitive Science, 6,* 1–36.

Rumelhart, D. E., & Norman, D. A. (1988). Representation in memory. In R. C. Atkinson, R. J. Hernstein, G. Lindzey, & R. D. Luce (Eds.), *Stevens' handbook of experimental psychology: Learning and cognition* (pp. 511–587). New York: Wiley & Sons.

Rumelhart, D. E., & Ortony, A. (1977). The representation of knowledge in memory. In R. Anderson, R. Spiro, & W. Montague (Eds.), *Schooling and the acquisition of knowledge* (pp. 99–135). Hillsdale, NJ: Erlbaum.

Rumelhart, D. E., & Todd, P. M. (1993). Learning and connectionist representations. In D. E. Meyer & S. Kornblum (Eds.), *Attention and performance XIV: Synergies in experimental psychology, artificial intelligence, and cognitive neuroscience* (pp. 3–30). Cambridge, MA: MIT Press.

Rundus, D. (1971). Analysis of rehearsal processes in free recall. *Journal of Experimental Psychology, 89,* 63–77.

Russo, J. E., & Dosher, B. A. (1983). Strategies for multiattribute binary choice. *Journal of Experimental Psychology: Learning, Memory, and Cognition, 9,* 676–696.

Sachs, J. S. (1967). Recognition memory for syntactic and semantic aspects of connected discourse *Perception and Psychophysics, 2,* 437–442.

Savage-Rumbaugh, E. S., Sevcik, R. A., Brakke, K. E., & Rumbaugh, D. M. (1991). Symbols: Their communicative use, communication, and combination by bonobos. In L. P. Lipsitt & C. Rovee-Collier (Eds.), *Advances in infancy research* (pp. 221–278). Norwood, NJ: Ablex.

Scardamalia, M., & Beretter, C. (1986). Research on written composition. In M. C. Wittrock (Ed.),

Handbook of research on teaching (pp. 778–803). New York: Macmillan.

Scardamalia, M., & Bereiter, C. (1991). Literate expertise. In K. A. Ericsson and J. Smith (Eds.), *Toward a general theory of expertise* (pp. 172–194). Cambridge, UK: Cambridge University Press.

Schacter, D. L. (1983). Amnesia observed: Remembering and forgetting in a natural environment. *Journal of Abnormal Psychology, 92,* 236–242.

Schacter, D. L. (1987). Implicit memory: History and current status. *Journal of Experimental Psychology: Learning, Memory, and Cognition, 13,* 501–518.

Schacter, D. L. (1996). *Searching for memory.* New York: Basic Books.

Schacter, D. L., Glisky, E. L., & McGlynn, S. M. (1990). Impact of memory disorder on everyday life: Awareness of deficits and return to work. In D. E. Tupper & K. D. Cicerone (Eds.), *The neuropsychology of everyday life: Assessment and basic competencies* (pp. 231–257). Boston: Kluwer Academic Publishers.

Schacter, D. L., & Tulving, E. (1994). *Memory systems 1994.* Cambridge, MA: MIT Press.

Schank, R. C. (1973). Identification of conceptualizations underlying natural language. In R. C. Schank & K. M. Colby (Eds), *Computer models of thought and language* (pp. 187–247). San Francisco: W. H. Freeman.

Schank, R. C., & Abelson, R. P. (1977). *Scripts, plans, goals, and understanding.* Hillsdale, NJ: Erlbaum.

Schmajuk, N. A., & DiCarlo, J. J. (1992). Stimulus configuration, classical conditioning, and hippocampal function. *Psychological Review, 99,* 268–305.

Schneider, W., & Fisk, A. D. (1982). Concurrent automatic and controlled visual search: Can processing occur without resource cost? *Journal of Experimental Psychology: Learning, Memory, and Cognition, 8,* 261–278.

Schneider, W., & Shiffrin, R. M. (1977). Controlled and automatic human information processing: I. Detection, search, and attention. *Psychological Review, 84,* 1–66.

Schooler, J. W., Gerhard, D., & Loftus, E. F. (1986). Qualities of the unreal. *Journal of Experimental Psychology: Learning, Memory, and Cognition, 12,* 171–181.

Searles, R. B., & Schneider, C. W. (1989). New genera and species of ceramiaceae (rhodophyta) from the southeastern United States. *Journal of Phycology, 25,* 731–740.

Secunda, A. (1984). *Ultimate tennis.* Englewood Cliffs, NJ: Prentice-Hall.

Seidenberg, M. (1992). Connectionism without tears. In S. Davis (Ed.), *Connectionism: Theory and practice* (pp. 84–137). New York: Oxford University Press.

Seidenberg, M. (1993). A connectionist modeling approach to word recognition and dyslexia. *Psychological Science, 4,* 299–304.

Seidenberg, M., & McClelland, J. (1989). A distributed, developmental model of word recognition and naming. *Psychological Review, 96,* 523–568.

Sejnowski, T. J., & Churchland, P. S. (1989). Brain and cognition. In M. I. Posner (Ed.). *Foundations of cognitive science* (pp. 301–356). Cambridge, MA: MIT Press.

Sejnowski, T. J., & Rosenberg, C. R. (1986). *NETtalk: A parallel network that learns to read aloud* (Report No. JHU/EECS-86/01). Baltimore, MD: Johns Hopkins University.

Selfridge, O. G., & Neisser, U. (1963). Pattern recognition by machine. In E. Feigenbaum & J. Feldman (Eds.), *Computers and thought* (pp. 237–250). New York: McGraw-Hill.

Selkoe, D. J. (1991). Amyloid protein and Alzheimer's disease. *Scientific American, 265,* 68–78.

Shafir, E. (1993). *Reason-based choice.* Paper presented at the 101st Convention of the American Psychological Association. Toronto, Ontario.

Shafir, E., & Tversky, A. (1995). Decision making. In E. E. Smith & D. N. Osherson (Eds.), *An invitation to cognitive science: Thinking* (pp. 77–100). Cambridge, MA: MIT Press.

Shallice, T. (1982). Specific impairment of planning. *Philosophical Transactions of the Royal Society of London, 298,* 199–209.

Shallice, T., & Vallar, G. (1990). The impairment of auditory-verbal short-term storage. In G. Vallar & T. Shallice (Eds.), *Neuropsychological impairments of short-term memory* (pp. 11–53). Cambridge: Cambridge University Press.

Shaw, G. B. (1962). *Man and superman.* New York: Penguin Books.

Shaywitz, B. A., and others. (1995). Sex differences in the functional organization of the brain for language. *Nature, 373,* 607–609.

Shepherd, J. W. (1986). An interactive computer system for retrieving faces. In H. D. Ellis, M. A.

Jeeves, F. Newcombe, & A. Young (Eds.), *Aspects of face processing* (pp. 398–409). Dordrecht: Martinus Nijhoff.

Shiffrin, R. M. (1988). Attention. In R. C. Atkinson, R. J. Hernstein, G. Lindzey, & R. D. Luce (Eds.), *Stevens' handbook of experimental psychology* (pp. 739–811). New York: Wiley & Sons.

Shiffrin, R. M., & Schneider, W. (1977). Controlled and automatic human information processing: II. Perceptual learning, automatic attending, and a general theory. *Psychological Review, 84,* 127–190.

Siegel, L., Share, D., & Geva, E. (1995). Evidence for superior orthographic skills in dyslexics. *Psychological Science, 6,* 250–254.

Siegler, R. S. (1988). Strategy choice procedures and the development of multiplication skill. *Journal of Experimental Psychology: General, 117,* 258–275.

Siegler, R. S. (1991). *Children's thinking* (2nd ed.). Englewood Cliffs, NJ: Prentice Hall.

Simon, H. A. (1957). *Models of man.* New York: Wiley & Sons.

Simon, H. A. (1973). The structure of ill-structured problems. *Artificial Intelligence, 4,* 181–201.

Simon, H. A. (1975). The functional equivalence of problem solving skills. *Cognitive Psychology, 7,* 268–288.

Singer, M. (1990). *Psychology of language: An introduction to sentence and discourse processes.* Hillsdale, NJ: Erlbaum.

Singer, M. (1994). Discourse inference processes. In M. A. Gernsbacher (Ed.), *Handbook of psycholinguistics* (pp. 479–515). San Diego, CA: Academic Press.

Singley, K., & Anderson, J. R. (1989). *The transfer of cognitive skill.* Cambridge, MA: Harvard University Press.

Skinner, B. F. (1990). Can psychology be a science of mind? *American Psychologist, 45,* 1206–1210.

Sleight, R. B. (1948). The effect of instrument dial shape on legibility. *Journal of Applied Psychology, 32,* 170–188.

Slobin, D. (1966). Grammatical transformations and sentence comprehension in childhood and adulthood. *Journal of Verbal Learning and Verbal Behavior, 5,* 219–227.

Slovic, P. (1990). Choice. In D. N. Osherson & E. E. Smith (Eds.), *Thinking* (pp. 89–116). Cambridge, MA: MIT Press.

Smith, E. E. (1988). Concepts and thought. In R. J. Sternberg & E. E. Smith (Eds.), *The psychology of human thought* (pp. 19–49). Cambridge: Cambridge University Press.

Smith, E. E. (1990). Categorization. In D. Osherson & E. Smith (Eds.), *Thinking* (pp. 33–53). Cambridge, MA: MIT Press.

Smith, F. (1973). *Psycholinguistics and reading.* New York: Holt, Rinehart & Winston.

Smith, F. (1992). Learning to read: The never-ending debate. *Phi Delta Kappan, 73,* 432–441.

Smyth, F. L. (1990). SAT coaching: What really happens to scores and how we are led to expect more. *The Journal of College Admissions, 129,* 7–17.

Soloway, E., Adelson, B., & Ehrlich, K. (1988). Knowledge and processes in the comprehension of computer programs. In M. Chi, R. Glaser, & M. J. Farr (Eds.), *The nature of expertise* (pp. 129–152). Hillsdale, NJ: Erlbaum.

Spelke, E., Hirst, W., & Neisser, U. (1976). Skills of divided attention. *Cognition, 4,* 215–230.

Sperling, G. (1960). The information available in brief visual presentations. *Psychological Monographs, 74* (No. 11).

Spreen, O., & Strauss, E. (1991). *A compendium of neuropsychological tests.* New York: Oxford University Press.

Squire, L., Ojemann, J., Miezin, F., Petersen, S., Videen, T., & Raichle, M. (1991). *A functional anatomical study of human memory.* New Orleans, LA: Society for Neuroscience.

Squire, L. R., Zola-Morgan, S., Cave, C. B., Haist, F., Musen, G., & Suzuki, W. A. (1993). Memory: Organization of brain systems and cognition. In D. E. Meyer & S. Kornblum (Eds.), *Attention and performance XIV* (pp. 393–423). Cambridge, MA: MIT Press.

St. John, M. F., & McClelland, J. L. (1988). Applying contextual constraints in sentence comprehension. *Proceedings of the tenth annual conference of the Cognitive Science Society* (pp. 26–32). Hillsdale, NJ: Erlbaum.

Staddon, J. E. R., & Ettinger, R. H. (1989). *Learning: An introduction to the principles of adaptive behavior.* San Diego, CA: Harcourt Brace Jovanovich.

Sternberg, R. J. (1981). Intelligence and nonentrenchment. *Journal of Educational Psychology, 73,* 1–16.

Sternberg, R. J. (1986). *Intelligence applied: Understanding and increasing your intellectual skills.* San Diego, CA: Harcourt Brace Jovanovich.

Sternberg, S. (1966). High speed scanning in human memory. *Science, 153,* 652–654.

Stich, S. P. (1990). Rationality. In D. N. Osherson & E. E. Smith (Eds.), *Thinking* (pp. 173–196). Cambridge, MA: MIT Press.

Stroop, J. R. (1935). Studies of interference in serial verbal reactions. *Journal of Experimental Psychology, 12,* 242–248.

Strunk, W., & White, E. B. (1979). *The elements of style.* New York: Macmillan.

Sutton, R. S., & Barto, A. G. (1981). Toward a modern theory of adaptive networks: Expectation and prediction. *Psychological Review, 88,* 135–170.

Swinney, D. A. (1979). Lexical access during sentence comprehension: (Re)consideration of context effects. *Journal of Verbal Learning and Verbal Behavior, 18,* 645–659.

Tanenhaus, M. K. (1988). Psycholinguistics: An overview. In F. J. Newmeyer (Ed.), *Language: Psychological and biological aspects* (pp. 1–37). Cambridge: Cambridge University Press.

Taraban, R., & McClelland, J. L. (1988). Constituent attachment and thematic role assignment in sentence processing: Influences of content-based expectations. *Journal of Memory and Language, 27,* 597–632.

Tartter, V. C. (1986). *Language processes.* New York: Holt, Rinehart & Winston.

Thagard, P. (1992). Adversarial problem solving: Modeling an opponent using explanatory coherence. *Cognitive Science, 16,* 123–149.

Thaler, R. (1985). Mental accounting and consumer choice. *Marketing Science, 4,* 199–214.

Thibadeau, R., Just, M. A., & Carpenter, P. A. (1982). A model of the time course and content of reading. *Cognitive Science, 6,* 101–155.

Thompson, C. P., Cowan, T., Frieman, J., Mahadevan, R. S., & Vogl, R. J. (1991). Rajan: A study of a memorist. *Journal of Memory and Language, 30,* 702–724.

Thompson, R. F. (1986). The neurobiology of learning and memory. *Science, 223,* 941–947.

Thorndike, E. L. (1911). *Animal intelligence.* New York: Macmillan.

Thorndike, E. L. (1924). Mental discipline in high school studies. *Journal of Educational Psychology, 15* (1), 1–22, *15* (2), 83–98.

Titchener, E. B. (1910). *A textbook of psychology.* New York: Macmillan.

Trabasso, T., & van den Broek, P. W. (1985). Causal thinking and the representation of narrative events. *Journal of Memory and Language, 24,* 612–630.

Treisman, A. M. (1960). Contextual cues in selective listening. *Quarterly Journal of Experimental Psychology, 12,* 242–248.

Treisman, A. M. (1986). Features and objects in visual processing. *Scientific American, 255,* 114–125.

Treisman, A. M. (1988). Features and objects: The fourteenth Bartlett memorial lecture. *The Quarterly Journal of Experimental Psychology, 40A,* 201–237.

Treisman, A. M., & Gelade, G. (1980). A feature integration theory of attention. *Cognitive Psychology, 12,* 97–136.

Tso, D. Y., & Gilbert, C. D. (1988). The organization of chromatic and spatial interactions in the primate striate cortex. *Journal of Neuroscience, 8,* 1712–1727.

Tulving, E. (1974). Cue-dependent forgetting. *American Scientist, 62,* 74–82.

Tulving, E., Kapur, S., Craik, F., Moscovitch, M., & Houle, S. (1994). Hemispheric encoding/retrieval asymmetry in episodic memory: Positron emission tomography findings. *Proceedings of the National Academy of Sciences, USA, 91,* 2016–2020.

Tulving, E., & Osler, S. (1968). Effectiveness of retrieval cues in memory for words. *Journal of Experimental Psychology, 77,* 593–601.

Tulving, E., & Schacter, D. L. (1990). Priming and human memory systems. *Science, 247,* 301–306.

Tulving, E., & Schacter, D. L. (1994). *Memory systems 1994.* Cambridge, MA: MIT Press.

Tulving, E., Schacter, D. L., & Stark, H. A. (1982). Priming effects in word-fragment completion are independent of recognition memory. *Journal of Experimental Psychology: Learning, Memory, and Cognition, 8,* 336–342.

Turban, E. (1990). *Decision support and expert systems.* New York: Macmillan.

Turner, A. M., & Greenough, W. T. (1985). Differential rearing effects on rate visual cortex synapses. *Brain Research, 329,* 195–203.

Turvey, M. (1990). Coordination. *American Psychologist, 45,* 938–953.

Tversky, A., & Kahneman, D. (1974). Judgment under uncertainty: Heuristics and biases. *Science, 185,* 1124–1131.

Tversky, A., & Kahneman, D. (1983). Extensional versus intuitive reasoning: The conjunction fallacy in probability judgment. *Psychological Review, 90,* 293–315.

Tversky, A., & Kahneman, D. (1986). Rational choice and the framing of decisions. *Journal of Business, 59,* S251–S278.

Tversky, A., & Shafir, E. (1992). Choice under conflict: The dynamics of deferred decision. *Psychological Science, 3,* 358–361.

Underwood, B. J. (1983). *Attributes of memory.* Glenview, IL: Scott, Foresman.

Vallar, G., & Baddeley, A. D. (1984). Fractionation of working memory: Neuropsychological evidence for a phonological short-term store. *Journal of Verbal Learning and Verbal Behavior, 23,* 151–161.

van den Broek, P. (1990). Causal inferences and the comprehension of narrative texts. *The Psychology of Learning and Motivation, 25,* 175–196.

van Dijk, T. A. (1972). *Some aspects of text grammars.* The Hague: Mouton.

van Dijk, T. A., & Kintsch, W. (1983). *Strategies of discourse comprehension.* New York: Academic Press.

VanLehn, K. (1989). Problem solving and cognitive skill acquisition. In M. Posner (Ed.), *Foundations of cognitive science* (pp. 527–597). Cambridge, MA: MIT Press.

VanLehn, K. (1990). *Mind bugs: The origins of procedural misconceptions.* Cambridge, MA: MIT Press.

Vokey, J. R., & Read, J. D. (1985). Subliminal messages: Between the devil and the media. *American Psychologist, 40,* 1231–1239.

Voss, J. F., & Post, T. A. (1988). On the solving of ill-structured problems. In M. Chi, R. Glaser, & M. J. Farr (Eds.), *The nature of expertise* (pp. 261–285). Hillsdale, NJ: Erlbaum.

Voss, J. F., Tyler, S., & Yengo, L. (1983). Individual differences in the solving of social science problems. In R. Dillon & R. Schmeck (Eds.), *Individual differences in cognition* (pp. 205–232). New York: Academic Press.

Wagenaar, W. A. (1986). My memory: A study of autobiographical memory over six years. *Cognitive Psychology, 18,* 225–252.

Wagner, A. R., Logan, F. A., Haberlandt, K., & Price, T. (1968). Stimulus selection in animal discrimination learning. *Journal of Experimental Psychology, 76,* 171–180.

Wanner, E. (1974). *On remembering, forgetting, and understanding sentences.* The Hague: Mouton.

Warren, W. H., & Shaw, R. E. (1985). Events and encounters as units of analysis for ecological psychology. In J. W. Warren & R. Shaw (Eds.),

Persistence and change (pp. 1–27). Hillsdale, NJ: Erlbaum.

Warrington, E. K., James, M., & Maciejewski, C. (1986). The WAIS as a lateralizing and localizing diagnostic instrument: A study of 656 patients with unilateral cerebral excisions. *Neuropsychologia, 24,* 679–684.

Wason, P. C., & Johnson-Laird, P. N. (1972). *Psychology of reasoning: Structure and content.* Cambridge, MA: Harvard University Press.

Waters, H. S. (1989, April). *Problem-solving at two: A year-long naturalistic study of two children.* Paper presented at the Society for Research in Child Development Conference, Kansas City, MO.

Watkins, M. J., & Tulving, E. (1975). Episodic memory: When recognition fails. *Journal of Experimental Psychology, 104,* 5–29.

Weiskrantz, L. (1986). *Blindsight: A case study and implications.* Oxford: Oxford University Press.

Weizenbaum, J. (1966). ELIZA—A computer program for the study of natural language communication between man and machine. *Communications of the Association for Computing Machinery* (pp. 36–45). Baltimore, MD: Association for Computing Machinery.

Wells, G. L., & Loftus, E. F. (Eds.). (1984). *Eyewitness testimony: Psychological perspectives.* Cambridge: Cambridge University Press.

Wertheimer, M. (1945). *Productive thinking.* New York: Harper.

Whitten, W., & Leonard, J. (1981). Directed search through autobiographical memory. *Memory & Cognition, 9,* 566–579.

Wickelgren, W. A. (1973). The long and short of memory. *Psychological Bulletin, 80,* 425–438.

Wickelgren, W. A., Corbett, A. T., & Dosher, B. A. (1980). Priming and retrieval from short-term memory: A speed accuracy trade-off analysis. *Journal of Verbal Learning and Verbal Behavior, 19,* 387–404.

Widrow, B., & Hoff, M. (1960). Adaptive switching circuits. *Institute of Radio Engineers, Western Electronic Show and Convention, Convention Record, part 4,* 96–104.

Wilson, B. A. (1987). *Rehabilitation of memory.* New York: Guilford Press.

Wilson, B. A., & Patterson, K. (1990). Rehabilitation for cognitive impairment: Does cognitive psychology apply? *Applied Cognitive Psychology, 4,* 247–260.

Winograd, T. (1973). A procedural model of language understanding. In R. C. Schank & K. M. Colby (Eds.), *Computer models of thought and language* (pp. 152–186). San Francisco: W. H. Freeman.

Winston, P. H. (1984). *Artificial intelligence* (2nd ed.). Reading, MA: Addison-Wesley.

Wood, N. L., & Cowan, N. (1995). The cocktail party phenomenon revisited: Attention and memory in the classic selective listening procedure of Cherry (1953). *Journal of Experimental Psychology: General, 124,* 243–262.

Woodruff-Pak, D. S., Logan, C. G., & Thompson, R. F. (1990). Neurobiological substrates of classical conditioning across the life span. *Annals of The New York Academy of Sciences, 608,* 150–178.

Woods, W. A. (1970). Transition network grammars for natural language analysis. *Communications of the Association for Computing Machinery, 13,* 591–606.

Woodworth, R. S., & Schlosberg, H. (1954). *Experimental psychology.* New York: Holt, Rinehart & Winston.

Zola, D. (1984). Redundancy and word perception during reading. *Perception and Psychophysics, 36,* 277–284.

Zurif, E. B. (1990). Language and the brain. In D. N. Osherson & H. Lasnik (Eds.), *Language* (pp. 177–198). Cambridge, MA: MIT Press.

These pages constitute a continuation of the copyright page.

PERMISSIONS CREDITS:

Figure 2.1 Courtesy of Drs. Michael E. Phelps and John C. Mazziotta, UCLA School of Medicine, Los Angeles, CA.

Figure 2.3 From Neil R. Carlson, *Physiology of Behavior,* fourth edition. Copyright © 1990 by Allyn and Bacon. Reprinted by permission.

Figure 2.13A From John Pinel, *Biopsychology,* second edition. Copyright © 1993 by Allyn and Bacon. Reprinted by permission.

Figure 2.14 From Neil R. Carlson, *Physiology of Behavior,* fourth edition. Copyright © 1990 by Allyn and Bacon. Reprinted by permission.

Figure 2.18 Reprinted with permission from "Segregation of Form, Color, Movement, and Depth" by M. Livingstone and D. Hubel, 1988, *Science, 240,* page 747. Copyright 1988 American Association for the Advancement of Science.

Figure 3.7 From "Controlled and Automatic Human Information Processing: II. Perceptual Learning, Automatic Attending, and a General Theory" by R. Shiffrin and W. Schneider, 1977, *Psychological Review, 84,* page 128. Copyright © 1977 by the American Psychological Association. Reprinted with permission.

Figure 3.9 From "Higher-Level Vision" by I. Biederman, in *Visual Cognition and Action* (page 68) by D. Osherson, S. Kosslyn, and J. Hollerbach (Eds.), 1990, Cambridge, MA: The MIT Press. Copyright © 1990 by The MIT Press. Reprinted by permission.

Figure 4.1A From *Vision* (page 61) by D. Marr. Copyright © 1982 by W. H. Freeman and Company. Photograph courtesy of BBC Horizon.

Figure 4.8 From M. W. Matlin, *Sensation and Perception.* Copyright © 1988 by Allyn and Bacon. Reprinted by permission.

Table 4.2 From *Sensation and Perception,* by E. B. Goldstein. Copyright © 1996, 1989, 1984, 1980 Brooks/Cole Publishing Company, Pacific Grove, CA 93950, a division of International Thomson Publishing, Inc. By permission of the publisher.

Figure 4.11 From "An Interactive Activation Model of Context Effects in Letter Perception" by J. L. McClelland and D. E. Rumelhart, 1981, *Psychological Review, 88,* page 383. Copyright © 1981 by the American Psychological Association. Reprinted with permission.

Figure 4.12 From "An Interactive Activation Model of Context Effects in Letter Perception" by J. L. McClelland and D. E. Rumelhart, 1981, *Psychological Review, 88.* Copyright © 1981 by the American Psychological Association. Reprinted with permission.

Figure 4.13 From "Process of Recognizing Tachistoscopically Presented Words" by D. Rumelhart and P. Siple, 1974, *Psychological Review, 81.* Copyright © 1974 by the American Psychological Association. Reprinted with permission.

Figure 4.14 From "An Interactive Activation Model of Context Effects in Letter Perception: Part 1. An Account of Basic Findings" by J. L. McClelland and D. E. Rumelhart, 1981, *Psychological Review, 88,* page 383. Copyright © 1981 by the American Psychological Association. Reprinted with permission.

Figure 4.16 From *Psychology* (page 98) by D. E. Papalia and S. W. Olds, 1985, New York: McGraw-Hill. Copyright 1985 by McGraw-Hill. Reprinted by permission of The McGraw-Hill Companies.

Figure 4.17 From "Higher-Level Vision" by I. Biederman, in *Visual Cognition and Action* (page 44) by D. Osherson, S. Kosslyn, and J. Hollerbach (Eds.), 1990, Cambridge, MA: The MIT Press. Copyright © 1990 by The MIT Press. Reprinted by permission.

Figure 4.18 From "Higher-Level Vision" by I. Biederman, in *Visual Cognition and Action* (page 49) by D. Osherson, S. Kosslyn, and J. Hollerbach (Eds.), 1990, Cambridge, MA: The MIT Press. Copyright © 1990 by The MIT Press. Reprinted by permission.

Figure 4.19 From *Sensation and Perception,* by E. B. Goldstein. Copyright © 1996, 1989, 1984, 1980 Brooks/Cole Publishing Company, Pacific Grove, CA 93950, a division of International Thomson Publishing, Inc. By permission of the publisher.

Figure 4.20 From "Event Perception" by G. Johansson, C. von Hofsten, and G. Jansson. Reproduced, with permission, from the *Annual Review of Psychology,* Volume 31, © 1980, by Annual Reviews, Inc.

Figure 4.21 From John Pinel, *Biopsychology,* second edition. Copyright © 1993 by Allyn and Bacon. Reprinted by permission.

Figure 4.22 From "Information Capacity of Discrete Motor Responses" by P. M. Fitts and J. R. Peterson, 1964, *Journal of Experimental Psychology, 67.* Copyright © 1964 by the American Psychological Association. Reprinted with permission.

Figure 4.23 We thank the International Association for The Study of Attention and Performance for permission to reprint "Speed-Accuracy Tradeoffs in Aimed Movements: Toward a Theory of Rapid Voluntary Action" by D. E. Meyer et al. in *Attention and Performance XIII* (page 214) by M. Jeannerod (Ed.), 1990, Hillsdale, NJ: Lawrence Erlbaum Associates.

Figure 4.24 From "Coordination" by M. T. Turvey, 1990, *American Psychologist, 45,* page 939. Copyright © 1990 by the American Psychological Association. Reprinted by permission.

Figure 4.25 From *Finger Movements in Transcription Typing* (Tech. Rep. 8001), by D. R. Genter et al., University of California, Center for Human Information Processing, La Jolla, CA. Reprinted by permission.

Figure 4.26 From "Hierarchical Control of Rapid Movement Sequences," by D. A. Rosenbaum, S. Kenny, and M. A. Derri, 1983, *Journal of Experimental Psychology: Human Perception and Performance, 9.* Copyright © 1983 by the American Psychological Association. Reprinted with permission.

Figure 4.27 From "Hierarchical Control of Rapid Movement Sequences," by D. A. Rosenbaum, S. Kenny, and